AMNESTY INTERNATIONAL REPORT 2008
FOREWORD

A hand-painted sign wards off those who threaten this inner-city community in Kingston, Jamaica, October 2007. The majority of victims of violence live in inner-city areas, perpetuating their poverty and exclusion.

Irene Khan, Secretary General of Amnesty International, visits a grassroots project to empower women in Bangladesh.

BROKEN PROMISES

AMNESTY
INTERNATIONA
REPORT 2008

World leaders owe an apology for failing to deliver on the promise of justice and equality in the Universal Declaration of Human Rights (UDHR), adopted 60 years ago. In the past six decades, many governments have shown more interest in the abuse of power or in the pursuit of political self-interest, than in respecting the rights of those they lead.

This is not to deny the progress that has been made in developing human rights standards, systems and institutions internationally, regionally and nationally. Much has improved in many parts of the world based on these standards and principles. More countries today provide constitutional and legal protection for human rights than ever before. Only a handful of states would openly deny the right of the international community to scrutinize their human rights records. 2007 saw the first full year of operation of the UN Human Rights Council, through which all UN member states have agreed to a public debate on their human rights performance.

But for all the good, the fact remains that injustice, inequality and impunity are still the hallmarks of our world today.

In 1948, in an act of extraordinary leadership, world leaders came together to adopt the UDHR. Member states of the fledgling UN showed great foresight and courage by putting their faith in global values. They were acutely aware of the horrors of World War II, and conscious of the grim realities of an emerging Cold War. Their vision was not circumscribed by what was happening only in Europe. 1948 was also the year in which Burma gained independence, Mahatma Gandhi was assassinated, and apartheid laws were first introduced in South Africa. Large parts of the world were still under the yoke of colonization.

Budhist monks accompanied by civilians march through Yangon.

The drafters of the UDHR acted out of the conviction that only a multilateral system of global values, based on equality, justice and the rule of law, could stand up to the challenges ahead. In a genuine exercise of leadership, they resisted the pressure from competing political camps. They rejected any hierarchy between the right to free speech and the right to education, the right to be free from torture and the right to social security. They recognized that the universality of human rights – every person is born free and equal – and their indivisibility – all rights, whether economic, social, civil, political or cultural, must be fulfilled with equal commitment – is the basis for our collective security as well as our common humanity.

In the years that followed, visionary leadership gave way to narrow political interests. Human rights became a divisive game as the two 'superpowers' engaged in an ideological and geopolitical struggle to establish their supremacy. One side denied civil and political rights, while the other demoted economic and social rights. Human rights were used as a tool to further strategic ends, rather than to promote people's dignity and welfare. Newly independent countries, caught in the superpower competition, struggled in the pursuit of democracy and the rule of law or abandoned them altogether for various forms of authoritarianism.

Hopes for human rights rose with the end of the Cold War but were dashed by the explosion of ethnic conflicts and implosion of states that unleashed a spate of humanitarian emergencies, marked by massive and vicious human rights abuses. Meanwhile, corruption, poor governance, and widespread impunity for human rights violations reigned supreme in many parts of the world.

As we entered the 21st century, the terrorist attacks of 11 September 2001 transformed the human rights debate yet again into a divisive and destructive one between "western" and "non-western", restricting liberties, fuelling suspicion, fear, discrimination and prejudice among governments and peoples alike.

The forces of economic globalization brought new promises, but also challenges. Though world leaders claimed to commit themselves to eradicating poverty, for the most part they ignored the human rights abuses that drive and deepen poverty. The UDHR remained a paper promise.

Looking back today, what seems most surprising is the unity of purpose shown by the UN member states at the time in adopting the UDHR without a dissenting vote. Now, in the face of numerous, pressing human rights crises, there is no shared vision among world leaders to address contemporary challenges of human rights in a world that is increasingly endangered, unsafe and unequal.

The political landscape today is very different from that of 60 years ago. There are many more states today than in 1948. Some former colonies are now emerging as global players alongside their former colonial masters. Can we expect the old and new powers to come together, as their predecessors did in 1948, and recommit themselves to human rights? The record for 2007 was not encouraging. Will new leadership and pressure from civil society make a difference in this anniversary year?

Can we expect the old and new powers to come together, as their predecessors did in 1948, and recommit themselves to human rights?

A dismal record

As the world's most powerful state, the USA sets the standard for government behaviour globally. With breathtaking legal obfuscation, the US administration has continued its efforts to weaken the absolute prohibition against torture and other ill-treatment. Senior officials refused to denounce the notorious practice of "water-boarding". The US President authorized the CIA to continue secret detention and interrogation, although they amount to the international crime of enforced disappearance. Hundreds of prisoners in Guantánamo and Bagram, and thousands in Iraq, continued to be detained without charge or trial, many for more than six years. The US government has failed to ensure full accountability for abuses by its forces in Iraq. An Order issued by the CPA (Coalition Provisional Authority) in June 2004 granting immunity from prosecution in Iraqi courts to foreign private military and security firms operating in Iraq, presents further obstacles to accountability. There was wide concern about the killings of at least 17 Iraqi civilians by guards employed by the private security company, Blackwater, in September 2007. These actions have done nothing to further the fight against terrorism and a great deal to damage the USA's prestige and influence abroad.

The hollowness of the US administration's call for democracy and freedom abroad was displayed in its continued support of

People protest against police during a major police operation in Complexo do Alemão, Rio de Janeiro, Brazil, when at least 19 people were shot dead by police.

President Musharraf as he arrested thousands of lawyers, journalists, human rights defenders and political activists for demanding democracy, the rule of law and an independent judiciary in Pakistan. As President Musharraf unlawfully imposed a state of emergency, dismissed the Chief Justice and packed the higher courts with more compliant judges, the US administration justified its support for him as an "indispensable" ally in the "war on terror". The growing insecurity in the cities and border regions of Pakistan, however, indicates that, far from arresting extremist violence, President Musharraf's repressive policies, including enforced disappearances and arbitrary detention, have fed grievances, helped to spur anti-western sentiment and laid the seeds for greater instability in the sub-region. The Pakistani people have shown their strong repudiation of President Musharraf's policies, even as the USA continues to embrace him.

The world needs a USA genuinely engaged and committed to the cause of human rights, at home and abroad. In November 2008, the US people will elect a new President. For the USA to have moral authority as a human rights champion, the next administration must close Guantánamo and either try the detainees in ordinary federal courts or release them. It must repeal the Military Commissions Act and ensure respect for international humanitarian law and human rights in all military and security operations. It must ban evidence obtained through coercion and denounce all forms of torture and other ill-treatment no matter to what end. The new administration must establish a viable strategy for international peace and security. It must ditch support for authoritarian leaders and invest instead in the institutions of democracy, rule of law and human rights that will provide long-term stability. And it must be ready to end US isolation in the international human rights system and engage constructively with the UN Human Rights Council.

If the US administration has distinguished itself in recent years through its defiance of international law, European governments have shown a proclivity for double standards. The European Union (EU) professes to be "a union of values, united by respect for the rule of law, shaped by common standards and consensus, committed to tolerance, democracy, and human rights". Yet, in 2007 fresh evidence came to light that a number of EU member states had looked the other way or colluded with the CIA to abduct, secretly detain and illegally transfer prisoners to countries where they were tortured and otherwise ill-treated. Despite repeated calls by the Council of Europe, no government has fully investigated the wrongdoings, come clean and/or put in place adequate measures to prevent future use of European territory for rendition and secret detention.

On the contrary, some European governments sought to water down the 1996 ruling from the European Court of Human Rights prohibiting the return of suspects to countries where they could face torture. The Court pronounced itself in one of two cases pending before it in 2007, reaffirming the absolute prohibition of torture and other ill-treatment.

While many grumble about the regulatory excesses of the EU, there is little outrage at the lack of EU regulation of human rights at home. The truth of the matter is that the EU is unable to hold its member states accountable on human rights matters which fall outside EU law. The Fundamental Rights Agency, created in 2007, has been given such a limited mandate that it cannot demand any real accountability. While the EU sets a high bar on human rights for candidate countries seeking accession (and rightly so), once they are allowed in, they are able to breach the standards with little or no accountability to the EU.

The EU is unable to hold its member states accountable on human rights matters which fall outside EU law

Can the EU or its member states call for respect for human rights by China or by Russia when they themselves are complicit in torture? Can the EU ask other – much poorer – countries to keep their borders open, when its own member states are restricting the rights of refugees and asylum-seekers? Can it preach tolerance abroad when it has failed to tackle discrimination against Roma, Muslim and other minorities living within its borders?

As for the USA, so too for the EU, the year ahead will bring important political transitions. The Lisbon treaty signed by EU governments in December 2007 demands new institutional commitments to be forged among the member states. In some key member states elections and other developments have brought about or will lead to new political leadership. They provide opportunities for action on human rights within the EU and globally.

As the USA and the EU stumble on their human rights record, their ability to influence others declines. The most glaring example of

Gay rights activists attend a protest in Moscow, Russian Federation, 27 May 2007. Russian police detained gay rights protesters calling for the right to hold a Gay Pride parade in central Moscow.

Hrant Dink, a Turkish journalist and human rights defender, was shot dead in January 2007.

their neutering on human rights was the case of Myanmar in 2007. The military junta violently cracked down on peaceful demonstrations led by monks, raided and closed monasteries, confiscated and destroyed property, shot, beat and detained protesters, harassed or held friends and family members as hostages. The USA and the EU condemned the actions in the strongest terms and tightened their trade and arms embargoes, but to little or no effect on the human rights situation on the ground. Thousands of people continued to be detained in Myanmar, among them at least 700 prisoners of conscience, the most prominent being the Nobel Laureate Aung San Suu Kyi, who has spent 12 of the last 18 years under house arrest.

As in Myanmar, so too in Darfur, western governments failed to make much of a dent in the human rights situation. International outrage and widepsread public mobilization etched the name of Darfur on world conscience but brought little change to the suffering of its people. Murder, rape and violence continue unabated, and if anything, the conflict has become more complex, a political settlement more remote. Despite a string of UN Security Council resolutions, the full deployment of hybrid African Union/UN forces is yet to take place.

Emerging powers

Whether in relation to Myanmar or Darfur, the world looked not to the USA but to China as the country with the necessary economic and political clout to move things forward – and not without good cause. China is the largest trading partner of Sudan and the second largest of Myanmar. Amnesty International's research has shown that Chinese arms have been transferred to Darfur in defiance of the UN arms embargo. China has long justified its support for abusive governments, such as those of Sudan, Myanmar and Zimbabwe, by defining human rights as an internal matter for sovereign states, and not as an issue for its foreign policy - as it suited China's political and commercial interests.

Yet China's position is neither immutable nor intractable. In 2007, it voted in favour of the deployment of the hybrid peacekeeping force in Darfur, pressured Myanmar to accept the visit of the UN Special Envoy and reduced its overt support for President Mugabe of Zimbabwe. The same factors that drove China in the past to open relations with repressive regimes may well be motivating the changes in its policy towards them today: the need for reliable sources of energy and other natural resources. Amnesty International and other human rights organizations have long argued that countries with poor human rights records do not create good business environments – business needs political stability and human rights provide that. It is possible that China too is beginning to recognize that supporting unstable regimes with poor human rights records does not make good business sense, that if it is to protect its assets and citizens abroad, it must support global values that create long-term political stability.

Notwithstanding its diplomatic shifts, China has a long way to go. It remains the largest arms supplier to Sudan since 2004. It vetoed a UN Security Council resolution condemning Myanmar's human rights practices in January 2007 and has yet to live up to the promises it made on human rights in the run up to the Beijing Olympics. Some reforms in the application of the death penalty and relaxation of rules for foreign media in 2007 were outweighed by the clampdown on human rights activists in China, on domestic media and expanding the scope of "re-education through labour", a form of detention without charge or trial, as part of the "clean-up" of Beijing prior to the Games.

A global player, if it is to be credible, cannot ignore the values and principles which form the collective identity of the international community

The run up to the Beijing Olympics has provided less room for improvement and more for confrontation on human rights in China. As the dust settles on the Olympics, the international community will need to develop an effective strategy for shifting the human right debate with China to a more productive and progressive plane. The Chinese government for its part must recognize that global leadership brings responsibilities and expectations, and that a global player, if it is to be credible, cannot ignore the values and principles which form the collective identity of the international community.

And how does Russia score on human rights leadership? A self-confident Russia, flush with oil revenues, has repressed political dissent, pressurized independent journalists and introduced legislative controls to rein in NGOs. In 2007 peaceful public demonstrations were dispersed with force, and lawyers, human rights defenders and journalists were threatened and attacked. The judicial system remained vulnerable to executive pressure. Pervasive corruption undermined the rule of law and

71 Amnesty International activists protest against the death sentences on 71 child offenders awaiting execution in Iran.

people's trust in the legal system. Impunity was rampant in Chechnya, driving some victims to seek justice in the European Court of Human Rights in Strasbourg.

Will the new Russian President Dmtry Medvedev take a different approach to human rights in 2008? He would do well to look around the world and draw the lesson that long-term political stability and economic prosperity can be built only in societies hat are open and states that are accountable.

If the permanent members of the UN Security Council have done little to promote human rights and much to undermine them, what leadership can we expect from emerging powers such as India, South Africa or Brazil?

As a well-established liberal democracy with a strong legal tradition of human rights and an independent judiciary, India has the makings of a powerful role model. India has played a positive role in the UN Human Rights Council. It is credited with helping to bring together the mainstream parties and Maoist insurgents in Nepal and end a long-standing armed conflict that had generated massive human rights abuses. But it needs to be more forceful in its domestic implementation and more forthright in its international leadership of human rights. In Myanmar, even as the junta struck out violently at the peaceful protests by monks and others, the Indian government continued to engage in oil extraction negotiations. In Nandigram, West Bengal, rural communities were attacked, injured and killed with police complicity when they protested at the setting up of a Special Economic Zone for industry.

South Africa's role in NEPAD (New Partnership for Africa's Development) – which emphasizes good governance – gave hope that African leaders would take responsibility for solving African problems, including on human rights. But the South African government has been reluctant to speak out against the human rights abuses in Zimbabwe. Human rights are universally applicable to all – and no country knows that better than South Africa. Few countries can have a greater moral responsibility to promote those universal values, wherever they are being violated, than South Africa.

Countries such as Brazil and Mexico have been strong on promoting human rights internationally and in supporting the UN human rights machinery. But unless the gap between their policies internationally and their performance at home is closed their credibility as human rights champions will be challenged.

Human rights are not western values – indeed, western governments have shown as much disdain for them as any other. They are global values and, as such, the likelihood of their success is entwined with the leadership of the UN. Although the UN Security Council continued to be hamstrung on human rights by the divergent interests of its permanent members, in 2007 the UN General Assembly showed its potential for leadership by adopting a resolution calling for a universal moratorium on the death penalty. It showed exactly the sort of direction the world needs from the UN: states inspiring each other to better performance, rather than running each other down to the lowest common denominator. This was the UN at its best. Will the UN Human Rights Council show similar leadership in 2008 as it embarks on the Universal Peer Review system?

In a striking example of bold leadership, in the face of opposition from extremely powerful states, 143 of the UN General Assembly's member states voted to adopt the Declaration on the Rights of Indigenous Peoples in September 2007, ending two decades of debate. Two months after Australia voted against the Declaration, the newly elected government of Prime Minister Kevin Rudd offered a formal apology for the laws and policies of successive governments that "inflicted profound grief, suffering and loss" on he Indigenous Aboriginal population.

In a striking example of bold leadership, 143 of the UN General Assembly's member states votes to adopt the Declaration on the Rights of Indigenous Peoples, in September 2007

Forging a new unity of purpose

As the geopolitical order undergoes tectonic shifts, old powers are reneging on human rights and new leaders are yet to emerge or are ambivalent about human rights. So, what future for human rights?

The road ahead is rocky. Entrenched conflicts – highly visible in the Middle East, Iraq and Afghanistan, forgotten in places such as Sri Lanka and Somalia, to name but two – take a heavy human toll. World leaders flounder in their efforts to find a way forward as in Iraq and Afghanistan, or lack the political will to find solutions, as in Israel and the Occupied Palestinian Territories – a longstanding

Women activists at the launch of an Amnesty International report on sexual violence in Sierra Leone.

conflict that has been particularly marked by the failure of collective international leadership (in the form of the Quartet of the USA, the EU, Russia and the UN) to address impunity and injustice.

As the global financial markets wobble and the rich use their position and undue influence to mitigate their losses, the interests of the poor and the vulnerable risk being forgotten. With the tacit support of governments that refuse to scrutinize or regulate them effectively, far too many companies continue to evade accountability for their involvement in human rights abuses and violations.

There is much rhetoric about eradicating poverty but not enough political will for action. At least two billion of our human community continue to live in poverty, struggling for clean water, food and housing. Climate change will affect all of us, but the poorest amongst us will be the worst off as they lose their lands, food and livelihoods. July 2007 marked the half-way point in the timetable set by the UN to achieve the Millennium Development goals. Though far from perfect the achievement of these goals would go some way to improving health, living conditions and education for many in the developing world by 2015. The world is not on track to meet most of these minimum goals and, unfortunately, human rights are not being properly taken into account in that process. A change of effort and emphasis is clearly needed.

And where is the leadership to eradicate gender violence? Women and girls suffer from high levels of sexual violence in almost every region of the world. In war-torn Darfur rape with impunity persists. In the USA, many rape survivors in poor and marginalized Indigenous communities fail to find justice or effective protection from the Federal and tribal authorities. Leaders must give more attention to making rights real for women and girls.

These are global challenges with a human dimension. They require a global response. Internationally recognized human rights provide the best framework for that response because human rights represent a global consensus regarding the acceptable limits and unacceptable shortcomings of government policy and practice.

The UDHR is as relevant a blueprint for enlightened leadership today as it was in 1948. Governments must recommit themselves to human rights.

Restless, angry and disillusioned, people will not remain silent if the gap continues to widen between their demand for equality and freedom and their governments' denial. Popular discontent in Bangladesh at the steep rise of rice prices, disturbances in Egypt over the price of bread, post-electoral violence in Kenya and public demonstrations in China on evictions and environmental issues are not just examples of popular concern about economic and social issues. They are signs of a seething cauldron of grassroots protest at the betrayal of their governments' promise to deliver justice and equality.

To a degree almost unimaginable in 1948, today there is a global citizens' movement that is demanding their leaders recommit themselves to upholding and promoting human rights. Black-suited lawyers in Pakistan, saffron-robed monks in Myanmar, 43.7 million individuals standing up on 17 October 2007 to demand action against poverty, all were vibrant reminders last year of a global citizenry determined to stand up for human rights and hold their leaders to account.

In a village in northern Bangladesh, a group of women sit on bamboo mats in the dusty village enclosure. They are part of a legal literacy program. Most of them can barely read or write. They listen attentively as their teacher, using posters with graphic designs, explain the law prohibiting child marriage and requiring the informed consent of a woman to marriage. The women have just received loans through a micro-credit scheme operated by the Bangladesh Rural Advancement Committee, a large NGO. One woman has bought a cow and hopes to make some extra income by selling milk. Another woman plans to buy a sewing machine and set up a small tailoring business for herself. What does she hope to get out of this class? "I want to know more about my rights," she says. "I don't want my daughters to suffer the way I have, and so I need to learn how to protect my rights and theirs." In her eyes shine the hope and determination of millions like her around the world.

People's power to generate hope and bring about change is very much alive in the 60th anniversary year of the UDHR. A consciousness on human rights is sweeping the globe.

World leaders ignore it at their peril.

> Restless, angry and disillusioned, people will not remain silent if the gap continues to widen between their demand for equality and their governments' denial

After a fire at the Kalma refugee camp for internally displaced persons in Nyala, South Darfur, March 2007. Kalma is home to thousands of people who have fled their homes in Darfur following violent attacks by government-backed militants.

First published in 2008 by
Amnesty International USA
5 Penn Plaza
New York, NY 10001
USA

© Copyright
Amnesty International
Publications 2008
AI Index: POL 10/001/2008

ISBN: 978-1-887204-48-4
ISSN: 0309-068X

Original language: English

Photographs:
All photographs appear with
full credits and captions
elsewhere in the report.

Printed on 100% recycled
post-consumer waste paper by
Pureprint Group
East Sussex
United Kingdom

Pureprint is a CarbonNeutral®
company, and uses only
vegetable-oil-based inks.

www.amnestyusa.org

AMNESTY INTERNATIONAL REPORT 2008
THE STATE OF THE WORLD'S HUMAN RIGHTS

This report covers the period January to December 2007.

Amnesty International Nepal holds a rally in Kathmandu on 1 October 2007 in solidarity with all those being repressed in Myanmar.

PREFACE

'FREEDOM FROM FEAR AND WANT HAS BEEN PROCLAIMED AS THE HIGHEST ASPIRATION OF THE COMMON PEOPLE'

Universal Declaration of Human Rights, 1948

Published in the 60th anniversary year of the Universal Declaration of Human Rights, the *Amnesty International Report 2008* documents human rights issues in 150 countries and territories around the world.

It covers the period January-December 2007, and reveals a world riven by inequality, scarred by discrimination and distorted by political repression.

However, it also captures the persistent spirit of the Declaration, and how over the intervening decades it has inspired the growth of a vibrant worldwide human rights movement, of which Amnesty International is proud to be part.

The book opens with five regional overviews, looking back at human rights developments since the Declaration was adopted, analyzing whether reality has matched rhetoric, and determining how much impact human rights initiatives have had on people's lives. They also highlight the key events and trends that illustrate 2007 for each region.

The heart of the book is a country-by-country survey of human rights, from Afghanistan to Zimbabwe. Each entry begins with a summary of the human rights situation in the country.

Amnesty International's concerns on various issues are then set out, highlighting individual cases where appropriate.

The entries indicate when Amnesty International has visited the country and list some of our relevant documents produced during the year.

This report reveals how far the world has to go before people truly are free from "fear and want". Our vision is for every person to enjoy all of the human rights enshrined in the Universal Declaration of Human Rights, laid out 60 years ago, and in the other international human rights standards and instruments that have evolved since.

Amnesty International is a global movement of 2.2 million people in more than 150 countries and territories. Our members and supporters around the world campaign for internationally recognized human rights to be respected and protected.

Our mission is to conduct research and take action to prevent and end grave abuses of all human rights – civil, political, social, cultural and economic. From freedom of expression and association, to physical and mental integrity, from protection from discrimination, to the right to shelter – these rights are indivisible.

■This report reflects an approach to tackling human rights abuses which is informed by both the challenges and opportunities for change in a given country or region. As a result, Amnesty International addresses particular issues in specific countries. The omission of an issue or country should not be taken as a statement by Amnesty International that abuses within this category or country did not occur.

AMNESTY INTERNATIONAL

Amnesty International is a worldwide movement of people who campaign for internationally recognized human rights to be respected and protected. Its vision is for every person to enjoy all of the human rights enshrined in the Universal Declaration of Human Rights and other international human rights standards.

Amnesty International's mission is to conduct research and take action to prevent and end grave abuses of all human rights — civil, political, social, cultural and economic. From freedom of expression and association to physical and mental integrity, from protection from discrimination to the right to shelter — these rights are indivisible.

Amnesty International is funded mainly by its membership and public donations. No funds are sought or accepted from governments for investigating and campaigning against human rights abuses. Amnesty International is independent of any government, political ideology, economic interest or religion.

Amnesty International is a democratic movement whose major policy decisions are taken by representatives from all national sections at International Council meetings held every two years. The members of the International Executive Committee, elected by the Council to carry out its decisions are: Soledad García Muñoz (Argentina), Deborah Smith (Canada - Eng), Pietro Antonioli (Italy), Lilian Gonçalves-Ho Kang You (Netherlands), Vanushi Rajanayagam (New Zealand), Christine Pamp (Sweden), Levent Korkut (Turkey), Peter Pack (UK - chair) and David Stamps (USA). Amnesty International's Secretary General is Irene Khan (Bangladesh).

A detainee at Guantánamo Bay, US Naval Base, Cuba, 9 October 2007. At the end of the year there were still about 275 people held there.

COUNTRY DATA

The facts at the top of each individual country entry in this report have been drawn from the following sources:

All life expectancy and adult literacy figures are from the UN Development Programme's Human Development Index, found at http://hdr.undp.org/en/media/hdr_20072008_en_indicator_tables.pdf

The latest figures available were life expectancy at birth (2005) and adult literacy rate (percentage aged 15 and above, 1995-2005).

Data refer to national literacy estimates from censuses or surveys conducted between 1995 and 2005, unless otherwise specified. For more information see the UNDP website or www.uis.unesco.org

Some countries that fall into the UNDP's 'high human development' bracket have been assumed by the UNDP to have a literacy rate of 99% for purposes of calculating the Human Development Index. Where this is the case, and the UN has chosen to omit the figure from its tables, we have also done so.

All Population and Under-5 mortality figures are for 2007 and are drawn from the UN Fund for Population Activities' Demographic, Social and Economic Indicators, found at http://www.unfpa.org/swp/2007/english/notes/indicators/e_indicator2.pdf.

Population figures are there solely to indicate the number of people affected by the issues we describe. Amnesty International acknowledges the limitations of such figures, and takes no position on questions such as disputed territory or the inclusion or exclusion of certain population groups.

Some country entries in this report have no reference to some or all of the above categories. Such omissions are for a number of reasons, including the absence of the information in the UN lists cited above.

These are the latest available figures at the time of going to print, and are for context purposes only. Due to differences in methodology and timeliness of underlying data, comparisons across countries should be made with caution.

THE FOLLOWING ABBREVIATIONS ARE USED IN THIS REPORT:

AU	African Union
CoE	Council of Europe
ECOWAS	Economic Community of West African States
European Committee for the Prevention of Torture	European Committee for the Prevention of Torture and Inhuman or Degrading Treatment or Punishment
European Convention on Human Rights	(European) Convention for the Protection of Human Rights and Fundamental Freedoms
EU	European Union
ICRC	International Committee of the Red Cross
ILO	International Labour Organization
NATO	North Atlantic Treaty Organization
NGO	non-governmental organization
OAS	Organization of American States
OSCE	Organization for Security and Co-operation in Europe
UN	United Nations
UN Children's Convention	Convention on the Rights of the Child
UN Convention against Racism	International Convention on the Elimination of All Forms of Racial Discrimination
UN Convention against Torture	Convention against Torture and Other Cruel, Inhuman or Degrading Treatment or Punishment
UNHCR, the UN refugee agency	UN High Commissioner for Refugees
UNICEF	UN Children's Fund
UN Migrant Workers Convention	International Convention on the Protection of the Rights of All Migrant Workers and Members of Their Families
UN Refugee Convention	Convention relating to the Status of Refugees
UN Women's Convention	Convention on the Elimination of All Forms of Discrimination against Women
WHO	World Health Organization

住宿

天津市高級...
駁回再審申...

特別

你窓

A mother trying to find out how her daughter died stands outside a Supreme Court petitions office in Beijing, China, 1 March 2007.

AMNESTY INTERNATIONAL REPORT 2008
PART ONE: REGIONAL OVERVIEWS

Government soldiers go on patrol, Burundi, 22 October 2007. During the years of armed conflict, sexual violence was endemic. Today, despite clashes mainly being confined to the west, women and young girls continue to suffer rape and other forms of sexual violence throughout the country - not just from opposing armed forces, but also increasingly in the home and community.

AFRICA

Universal Declaration of Human Rights: 60 years on

In the 60 years since the Universal Declaration of Human Rights in 1948, Africa has undergone dramatic changes. The decolonization process, and the end of apartheid in South Africa (an era which also started in 1948), have been accompanied by institution-building on a national level and increased respect for the rule of law. Many sub-Saharan African countries now have active civil societies and diverse independent news media. However, despite significant progress, the human rights promised in the Universal Declaration are far from being a reality for all the people of Africa.

A number of protracted armed conflicts have been resolved, such as those in Angola, Southern Sudan, Sierra Leone and Liberia. But their human rights consequences endure, affecting both economic and social development and the political arena. The violent struggle for power, even in states which do not descend into armed conflict, still remains an important component of political life in Africa, in spite of moves towards democratization in many countries.

Durable and lasting solutions to Africa's conflicts have frequently proved elusive, despite the contribution of the Organization of African Unity and subsequently the African Union (AU) to conflict prevention and resolution. There has been a deplorable lack of political will to address the human rights violations that generally lie at the roots of political tensions and hostilities. The AU Peace and Security Council has failed to fulfil its mandate to address the human rights dimension of armed conflicts in Africa.

Over the decades, the human rights framework in Africa has developed through various regional human rights treaties and institutions. In 1986 the African Charter on Human and Peoples' Rights entered into force and the 20th anniversary of the African Commission on Human and Peoples' Rights (African Commission) was celebrated in 2007. However, despite significant developments in African human rights institutions, notably the launch of the African Court on Human and Peoples' Rights, the African Commission has faced continuing financial and political obstacles. Inadequate support from the AU has forced the African Commission to rely on external support for most of its staffing requirements, while many member states show little interest in hosting its meetings.

> The human rights framework in Africa has developed through various regional human rights treaties and institutions. But the human rights promised in the UDHR are far from being a reality for the people of Africa

In recent years many African states have proved reluctant to engage constructively with global human rights institutions, such as the recently established UN Human Rights Council. Many have aligned their positions with a handful of states determined to weaken the work of these institutions. There are, however, notable exceptions, and some African states have played a constructive and at times courageous role in the UN, standing up for victims of grave human rights violations.

2007 under review

The rights of many people in Africa continued to be violated in 2007. Economic and social rights remained illusory for millions of people. The internal armed conflicts that continued to ravage several states were accompanied by gross human rights abuses including unlawful killings and torture, including rape. In some countries all forms of dissent were suppressed, and in many freedom of expression was restricted and human rights defenders suffered intimidation and harassment. Women endured widespread discrimination and systematic human rights abuse. Throughout the continent, those responsible for human rights violations escaped being held to account.

Economic, social and cultural rights

Despite increased economic growth in recent years in many African states, millions of people continued to live without access to the basic requirements of a dignified life, such as adequate housing, education or health care. Political instability, armed conflict, corruption, under-development and under-investment in basic social services all contributed to the failure to make economic, social and cultural rights a reality for men, women and children across the region.

Southern Africa continued to have the highest rates of HIV/AIDS in the world. In South Africa poverty operated as a barrier to access to treatment and care for the rural poor, in particular women, and Amnesty International documented how women's right to health was undermined by the physical inaccessibility of health services, costs of transport, shortage of health personnel, lack of daily access to adequate food and gender-based inequalities.

Families were forcibly evicted from their homes in a number of countries in order to make way for development or urbanization projects. Often, governments did not provide any compensation or alternative housing for those forcibly evicted, violating the right to shelter and adequate housing of hundreds of thousands of people.

■ **From July onwards, hundreds of families were forcibly evicted and had their homes demolished by the Jardim do Éden (Garden of Eden) construction company in the neighbourhood of Iraque in Luanda, Angola ... The forced evictions were carried out to make way for a luxury housing complex. No alternative accommodation or compensation was provided. In November, two journalists reporting on the evictions, António Cascais, a freelancer for the German radio station Deutsche Welle, and Alexandre Neto of the Angolan Radio Despertar, were assaulted by members of a private security company and detained for over three hours by the military police.**

Armed conflicts

The continuing armed conflicts had devastating consequences for civilian populations, with gross human rights violations including unlawful killings, sexual violence and the recruitment of child soldiers. Forced displacement and conflict-related deaths from hunger and disease continued on a large scale.

The conflicts in Somalia and in the eastern Democratic Republic of the Congo (DRC) escalated during 2007. In January the AU authorized the deployment of a peacekeeping force to Somalia (AMISOM), but without an explicit mandate to protect civilians. Less than one fifth of the projected 8,000 troops had been deployed by the end of the year.

Darfur (Sudan), eastern Chad and the northern part of the Central African Republic (CAR) continued to face conflict and widespread insecurity. In Darfur the armed groups involved in the conflict fragmented and proliferated, further complicating the prospects of a political solution. In July the UN Security Council authorized a 26,000 UN-AU hybrid peacekeeping force for Darfur. However, the deployment was delayed as the government of Sudan raised obstacles and UN member states did not provide the necessary military equipment to allow the deployment of an effective force. In September the UN Security Council authorized a multidimensional presence in Chad and the CAR, alongside a European military operation. However, by the end of the year these forces had not yet been deployed.

In northern Niger fighting erupted between government forces and a Tuareg-led armed opposition group, accompanied by human rights violations.

There were some steps towards conflict resolution: in March a peace agreement was signed in Côte d'Ivoire, and negotiations to end the conflict in northern Uganda continued.

The proliferation of small arms remained a major problem. Frequently, arms embargoes imposed by the UN Security Council were not respected or adequately monitored.

Impunity

Police and other law enforcement officers were rarely held accountable for serious human rights violations, including arbitrary arrests and detention, torture and other ill-treatment. Such impunity prevailed in many countries including Angola, Burundi, Equatorial Guinea, Eritrea, Mozambique and Zimbabwe. Law enforcement officers frequently used excessive force in countries including Benin, the Republic of Guinea, Kenya, Mauritania, Nigeria, Sudan and Zimbabwe. Incidents of excessive use of force were often not investigated, even when people were killed.

REGIONAL OVERVIEWS
AFRICA

The African Union authorized the deployment of a peacekeeping force to Somalia, but without an explicit mandate to protect civilians

Amnesty laws or regulations were considered in Burundi and adopted in Côte d'Ivoire for crimes committed during their internal armed conflicts, although government leaders gave reassurances that no amnesty would be granted to those responsible for crimes under international law. However, no progress was made in either country to investigate and prosecute those responsible for serious human rights violations during the conflicts. In Liberia too, the Truth and Reconciliation Commission made little progress.

International justice mechanisms contributed to ensuring accountability for crimes under international law in some cases.

In April the International Criminal Court (ICC) issued arrest warrants against two individuals involved in the conflict in Darfur: Ali Kushayb, a Janjawid militia leader, and Ahmad Muhammad Harun, the Sudanese Minister for Humanitarian Affairs. Both were accused of war crimes and crimes against humanity. However, the Sudanese government refused to surrender the accused to the ICC.

In May the Prosecutor of the ICC announced that an investigation would be opened in the CAR. War crimes and crimes against humanity allegedly committed in Ituri district, DRC, in 2003, led the ICC to issue an arrest warrant for Germain Katanga in July. The DRC government surrendered him to the ICC. However, the leaders of the Lord's Resistance Army (LRA), including Joseph Kony – indicted by the ICC in relation to the situation in Uganda – remained at large.

Trials continued before the International Criminal Tribunal for Rwanda (ICTR) at the same time as the ICTR began its exit strategy by proposing to transfer cases to national jurisdictions, including to Rwanda.

The Special Court for Sierra Leone convicted three members of the Armed Forces Revolutionary Council (AFRC) in July for war crimes and crimes against humanity. Two members of the Civil Defence Forces (CDF) were also convicted of war crimes and crimes against humanity. The trial of Charles Taylor, former President of Liberia, was postponed and was expected to start in 2008.

There was little progress in the case of Hissène Habré, former President of Chad, following the request by the AU in 2006 that he be tried in Senegal, under universal jurisdiction, for crimes under international law.

Death penalty

There were a number of positive developments on the death penalty in 2007, confirming that African states are increasingly becoming abolitionist in practice or by law. Even though the death penalty continued to be applied in various countries, the number of people executed was not large.

> International justice mechanisms contributed to ensuring accountability for crimes under international law in some cases

Rwanda abolished the death penalty in July and the government of Gabon announced in September that it would abolish the death penalty, subject to approval by parliament. In October the government of Mali presented a draft abolitionist bill to parliament. In various countries death sentences were commuted to life imprisonment, such as in the Republic of Congo, Ghana and Zambia.

At the vote on the moratorium on the use of the death penalty at the UN General Assembly in December, 17 African states voted in favour of a moratorium and 20 African states abstained.

However, executions took place in Equatorial Guinea, Ethiopia, Somalia and Sudan, and in Uganda military courts ordered the execution of soldiers. Research by Amnesty International in 2007 indicated that at least seven executions had taken place the previous year in Nigeria, even though government representatives officially declared that no capital punishment had been carried out in Nigeria in recent years.

Violence against women and girls

Violence against women remained largely unaddressed although some countries strengthened their legal framework. Ghana and Sierra Leone passed domestic violence bills, but a children's rights bill in Sierra Leone was only passed into law after the provisions criminalizing female genital mutilation were dropped.

In Kenya, which passed the Sexual Offences Act in 2006, Liberia, which introduced a new law on rape in 2006, and South Africa, where the Criminal Law (Sexual Offences and Related Matters) Amendment Act was signed into law in December, women and girls continued to face widespread violence, including rape. In Nigeria a bill to implement the UN Convention on the Elimination of All Forms of Discrimination against Women (CEDAW) failed to pass in the National Assembly, 22 years after Nigeria ratified CEDAW. Furthermore, a bill addressing domestic violence failed to become law at federal level even though individual states within Nigeria, such as Lagos state, passed similar legislation.

Sexual violence remained widespread in various conflicts, with life-long consequences for women and girls, many of whom had no access to adequate medical and psychological care or to any justice mechanisms. Perpetrators of violence against women, including rape, were rarely held accountable. The lack of reparations for women and girls subjected to sexual violence during and after armed conflict was extensively documented in Burundi, Côte d'Ivoire, Sierra Leone, and Uganda. Often such women and girls are stigmatized by society and further marginalized.

REGIONAL OVERVIEWS AFRICA

■ On 20 September, a soldier from the Uganda Peoples' Defence Forces (UPDF), Corporal Geoffrey Apamuko, was sentenced to death by hanging for murder. Military courts in Uganda continued to hand down death sentences and order executions of soldiers in the UPDF. The exact number of soldiers put to death under military law remained unclear.

In July UN peacekeepers in Côte d'Ivoire were accused of widespread sexual abuse against women and girls. The allegations were investigated by the UN and Morocco, as troops from Morocco were involved, but the results of these inquiries had not been made public by the end of 2007.

In eastern Chad women and girls displaced as a result of the conflict were at risk of rape and other forms of sexual violence when they ventured outside camps for the displaced. A similar pattern prevailed in Darfur, where women and girls were at risk of sexual violence when collecting firewood and water outside camps, or when going to the market. Often the sexual violence remained unreported as women feared repercussions.

In the DRC rape and other forms of sexual violence also remained widespread, particularly in the east. The perpetrators included soldiers and police officers as well as members of the various armed groups. Some of the armed groups abducted women and girls and subjected them to sexual slavery. Numerous reports of rape also emerged from the conflict in Somalia, committed by Ethiopian troops, Transitional Federal Government forces and gunmen.

In Malawi boys and girls, some as young as 10, were employed to work on farms. Mauritania adopted a law to make slavery a criminal offence, 26 years after slavery had been officially abolished, as there were indications that slavery was still being practised.

■ A 14-year-old girl living in the Aradip camp for internally displaced people (IDPs) in the Dar Sila region of Chad was caught and raped by several armed men when she left the camp to collect firewood early in the morning of 30 April.

Refugees, asylum-seekers and migrants

Hundreds of thousands of people in Africa were on the move across borders in search of protection or an adequate standard of living, often at great risk to their lives.

Thousands of people tried to escape the armed conflict in Somalia by fleeing to Kenya, but Kenyan authorities closed the border in January in violation of international refugee law. In addition Kenya forcibly returned hundreds of asylum-seekers to Somalia. As a result of the armed conflict and violence in Darfur and in the CAR, tens of thousands of people fled to neighbouring countries, in particular Chad. Many did not receive adequate humanitarian assistance.

Tanzania continued in 2007 to forcibly return refugees from Rwanda, Burundi and the DRC, labelling them illegal immigrants even though many had or were seeking refugee status. The Ugandan authorities claimed that the return of 3,000 Rwandese refugees and asylum-seekers was voluntary, but many complained of being forcibly returned to Rwanda. Asylum-seekers and refugees were also forcibly returned to Eritrea from Sudan and the United Kingdom, contrary to the guidelines of the UN High Commissioner for Refugees.

The Angolan authorities violently expelled thousands of Congolese migrants from northern Angola to the DRC. Many women were reported to have been raped by Angolan soldiers during the expulsion.

'War on terror'

The impact of the US-led "war on terror" was increasingly apparent in the Horn of Africa and other parts of Africa. In January, at least 140 people fleeing from Somalia to Kenya were detained by the Kenyan authorities. More than 80 of these detainees, who were detained incommunicado without charge or trial on suspicion of links with the Council of Somali Islamic Courts, or in some cases with al-Qa'ida, were unlawfully transferred to Somalia and then onwards to Ethiopia. More than 40 were still detained incommunicado and in secret in Ethiopia at the end of 2007.

A number of individuals, including foreign nationals, were arrested in Mauritania for suspected involvement with a cell linked to al-Qa'ida. In June and July, 14 people were tried in Mauritania, accused of belonging to the Algerian Groupe Salafiste pour la Prédiction et le Combat.

The UN Special Rapporteur on human rights and counter-terrorism expressed concern, following his visit to South Africa, at the administrative detention of immigrants for 30 days or more without mandatory judicial review, and at the failure of the authorities to respect the principle of *non-refoulement* in suspected "terrorism" cases as well as in other immigration cases.

Human rights defenders and repression of dissent

In many African countries it continued to be dangerous to express critical or independent views. Political opposition groups, human rights defenders, independent journalists and wider civil society, all faced state repression.

The space for human rights defenders remained restricted in many countries including Angola, Eritrea, Gambia and Rwanda. In some countries human rights defenders were personally at risk. In many, they were intimidated and harassed, including through arrests or surveillance.

Numerous women human rights activists were arrested in Zimbabwe during peaceful protests. Many were ill-treated by the police while in detention. In the DRC a woman human rights defender was raped by a security official during a work visit to a detention facility. The daughters of another were violently sexually assaulted by soldiers.

In Sudan human rights defenders were arrested and some were reportedly tortured by the national intelligence and security forces. In Ethiopia two prominent human rights defenders were unfairly

The impact of the US-led 'war on terror' was increasingly apparent in the Horn of Africa and other parts of Africa convicted in December and were sentenced to two years' eight months' imprisonment. A prominent human rights defender was murdered in Somalia, while in the DRC human rights defenders continued to be exposed to attacks and death threats, primarily by government agents.

The space for lesbian, gay, bisexual and transgender (LGBT) activists was particularly restricted. In Cameroon, Nigeria, South Africa and Uganda, LGBT activists came under attack from various groups within society in reaction to efforts to defend and promote their human rights.

Political prisoners and prisoners of conscience were detained in countries including the Republic of Congo, Eritrea, Ethiopia, Equatorial Guinea, Niger and the self-declared Republic of Somaliland.

■ In February, the presidential guards in the Republic of Guinea arrested two people working for the radio station FM Liberty and looted the broadcasting centre. The soldiers accused the radio station of carrying out interviews which were critical of President Lansana Conté. One of the employees, David Camara, was arrested by members of the security forces who threatened to kill him and stubbed a cigarette out on his neck. He was unconditionally released after two days.

The work of independent media was severely impeded in a wide range of countries and the right to freedom of expression violated, including through legislation to restrict media activities and arbitrary arrests of journalists. In Somalia and the DRC journalists were killed because of their work.

At the beginning of 2007, security forces in the Republic of Guinea violently repressed demonstrations organized by trade unions – hundreds of people were killed or injured. The government declared a state of siege, granting powers that normally lie with the civilian authorities to the military. In Zimbabwe hundreds of human rights defenders and members of the opposition were violently repressed while exercising their right to freedom of expression, association and peaceful assembly.

In Nigeria elections in April were severely affected by irregularities and violence. Voters, candidates and supporters were threatened and attacked by opponents or armed groups sponsored by political leaders. Police officers in Kenya killed dozens of protesters during demonstrations following elections in December.

AMERICAS

Universal Declaration of Human Rights: 60 years on

If human rights are today at the heart of the UN project, it is in large part thanks to the efforts of Latin American countries. Human rights ranked low in the list of priorities for the major post-war powers involved in drafting the UN Charter, including the USA. However, in 1945, just before the San Francisco UN founding meeting, the Inter-American Conference met in Mexico City and decided to seek the inclusion of a transnational declaration of rights in the UN Charter which eventually led to the adoption of the Universal Declaration of Human Rights. In May 1948, several months before the adoption of the UDHR, the Inter-American Conference adopted the American Declaration of the Rights and Duties of Man, the world's first general human rights instrument.

This crucial contribution to international human rights has been overshadowed in the intervening years by the military rule which dominated much of the region. From the 1960s to the mid-1980s many Latin American countries endured years of military government characterized by widespread and systematic human rights violations. Some violations, such as enforced disappearances, became emblematic of both the regimes and of Amnesty International's campaigning focus in the region during those years.

The end of military rule and the return to civilian, constitutionally elected governments have seen an end to the pattern of widespread and systematic enforced disappearances, extrajudicial executions and torture of political opponents. However, the hopes that a new era of respect for human rights had arrived have in many cases proved unfounded.

Most constitutions guarantee fundamental rights and most countries in the region have ratified key international human rights treaties. A notable exception to the latter is the USA, one of only two countries in the world not to have ratified the UN Convention on the Rights of the Child and one of only a handful of countries not to have ratified the UN Women's Convention. The US government has also informed the UN of its intention not to ratify the Rome Statute of the International Criminal Court.

The legacy of the authoritarian regimes of the past lives on in the

In May 1948, several months before the adoption of the Declaration, the Inter-American Conference adopted the world's first general human rights instrument institutional weaknesses which continue to bedevil many Latin American countries, particularly in Central America, and in the Caribbean. Corruption, the absence of judicial independence; impunity for state officials, and weak governments have undermined confidence in state institutions. Equal protection may exist in law, but it is often denied in practice, particularly for those in disadvantaged communities.

The gulf that remains between law and practice in many countries in the region has its origins in the historical abuse of law enforcement which successive governments have failed to address. Police and security forces and justice systems have long been used to repress dissent and to sustain corruption and entrenched economic and political interests. This abuse of power persists. The vast majority of those punished or imprisoned by justice systems are powerless and underprivileged. Those responsible for abuses of power and human rights frequently remain unpunished.

Although abusive practices have remained largely unchanged, the rationale for them has shifted. The techniques previously used to repress political dissent, have now been turned on those challenging social injustice and discrimination - such as human rights defenders - and those they seek to support.

A whole range of rights is being championed by these rights defenders in the context of vibrant and increasingly self-confident social movements across the region. A wide variety of organizations, far from the thoughts and experiences of those who adopted the UDHR 60 years ago, are taking forward the continuing struggle to ensure the rights it guaranteed become a reality.

2007 under review
'War on terror'

Six years into the so-called "war on terror", the USA continued to hold hundreds of people in indefinite military detention without charge or trial in Afghanistan and Guantánamo Bay, in addition to the thousands held in Iraq.

In July, President George W. Bush gave the green light for the CIA's programme of secret detention and interrogation to continue. One in a long list of unlawful policies adopted by the administration as part of the "war on terror", the President's re-authorization of this programme was a clear rejection of the principles underlying the UDHR. Indeed, President Bush issued his executive order a year after two UN treaty-monitoring bodies told the US government in no uncertain terms that secret detention violates the USA's international obligations.

■ **Ali al-Marri, a Qatari national resident in the USA who was designated an "enemy combatant" in June 2003 by President Bush, remained in indefinite military detention on the US mainland at the end of 2007. In June, a three-judge panel of the Court of Appeals for the Fourth Circuit ruled that the Military Commission Act did not apply to Ali al-Marri's case and ruled that his military detention "must cease". However, the US government successfully sought a rehearing in front of the full Fourth Circuit court; a ruling was pending at the end of the year.**

For those seeking justice for the detainees in Guantánamo, attention during 2007 focused on the US Supreme Court in what was seen as a crucial moment for human rights. In February, the Court of Appeals for the District of Columbia Circuit ruled that provisions of the Military Commissions Act stripping the courts of the jurisdiction to consider habeas corpus petitions applied to all detainees held in Guantánamo. An appeal against this ruling was initially dismissed by the Supreme Court. However, in June the Supreme Court took the historically unusual step of vacating its earlier order. On 5 December it heard oral arguments with the government arguing that, even if the detainees did have the right to habeas corpus (which it claims they do not), the limited judicial review to which they have access was an "adequate substitute".

Habeas corpus – the right to have a judge rule on the lawfulness of one's detention – is a fundamental principle of the rule of law. Detainees in US custody who have been denied recourse to this procedure have been subjected to enforced disappearance, secret detention and transfer, torture and other cruel, inhuman or degrading treatment or punishment, and unfair trial procedures. Sixty years after the UDHR, such policies and practices are an affront to the world it envisaged. The Supreme Court is due to rule on the habeas corpus issue by mid-2008.

REGIONAL OVERVIEWS
AMERICAS

All parties to the conflict in Colombia continued to commit serious human rights abuses

Conflict

Civilians continued to bear the brunt of Colombia's long-running internal armed conflict. Although the number of those killed or kidnapped continued to fall, all parties to the conflict – the security forces, paramilitaries and guerrilla groups – continued to commit serious human rights abuses. Hundreds of thousands of people were again displaced by confrontations between the warring parties.

Death penalty

For many years, US policy on the death penalty has run counter to the abolitionist trend in the rest of the region. While 2007 saw death sentences imposed in the Bahamas, Trinidad and Tobago, and the USA, the USA was the only country to carry out executions. However, even in the USA, there are signs that support for the death penalty is softening.

On 17 December, New Jersey became the first US state since 1965 to abolish capital punishment. The following day, the UN General Assembly passed its landmark resolution calling for a global moratorium on executions. Sixty years after the right to life and the prohibition of cruel, inhuman or degrading punishment were written into the UDHR, and three decades after executions resumed in the USA, advocates of the death penalty are increasingly on the defensive across the world.

In the USA, the abolitionist cause looks far less bleak than it was even a decade ago. A number of factors have contributed to this trend, including the release of more than 100 people from death row since 1977 on grounds of innocence – three of them in 2007. The number of death sentences passed each year continues to decline from its peak in the mid-1990s. Just over 100 death sentences were believed to have been handed down in the USA during 2007. Yet from 1995 to 1999, on average 304 people were sent to US death rows annually.

The 42 executions in the USA during 2007 – while 42 too many – represented the lowest annual judicial death toll in the country since 1994. This was at least in part due to the moratorium on lethal injections since late September 2007 when the US Supreme Court agreed to consider a challenge to the constitutionality of that method of execution.

In Canada, there was widespread concern about a government decision in October to reverse a long-established policy of seeking clemency for all Canadian citizens sentenced to death abroad. Under the new policy, clemency will no longer be sought from "democratic countries that adhere to the rule of law".

Violence against women

Latin America continued to take important and innovative steps to stamp out violence against women and make gender equality a reality. Mexico and Venezuela, for example, passed new laws to combat violence against women. These laws broaden the definition of violence against women and provide a more comprehensive framework of protection mechanisms. Some initiatives to tackle violence against women – for example the pioneering women's police stations in Brazil – continued to be hampered by a lack of adequate resources and continuing misconceptions about the nature and extent of the problem. In the USA, following concerted campaigning by a wide coalition of groups, Congress recommended increased funding to implement the Violence Against Women Act, a federal law providing a range of measures at state and local level.

Most of those responsible for violence against women were not held to account, reflecting a continuing lack of political will to address the problem. Many of the difficulties faced by women seeking justice were replicated from country to country. Amnesty International's research consistently revealed a lack of shelters providing appropriate protection; poor training of law enforcement officials in appropriate

> Latin America continued to take important and innovative steps to stamp out violence against women and make gender equality a reality

investigation techniques, including forensic examinations; and prosecution processes that did not address the needs of women for protection and ensure women's rights and dignity were promoted. Those women who did manage to get their cases as far as prosecution often faced discriminatory attitudes from the criminal justice system and further intimidation from their abusers.

Gender discrimination was often compounded by other forms of discrimination. If a woman is black, Indigenous, lesbian or poor, she will often face even greater barriers in getting justice. And if abusers know that they can beat, rape and kill women with impunity, then these abuses become both more widespread and more entrenched. For example, Native American and Alaska Native women in the USA who experience sexual violence are regularly met with inaction or indifference. They also experience disproportionately high levels of rape and sexual violence; US Justice Department figures have indicated that American Indian and Alaska Native women are some 2.5 times more likely to be raped or sexually assaulted than women in the USA in general. In Canada, government statistics demonstrate that Indigenous women are five times more likely than other women to die from violence, highlighting the desperate need for a comprehensive national action plan to address the violence and protect Indigenous women from discrimination.

Justice and impunity

In April, a federal court of appeals in Buenos Aires, Argentina, ruled that pardons granted to former military ruler Jorge Videla and former Admiral Emilio Massera in 1989 for crimes under international law were unconstitutional and therefore null and void.

In September, the Chilean Supreme Court of Justice delivered a historic decision when it approved the extradition of former Peruvian President Alberto Fujimori to face charges of corruption and human rights abuses in Peru.

However, in November the Chilean Supreme Court acquitted a retired colonel of the enforced disappearance of three people in 1973 on the basis that the statute of limitations had expired. This judgment flouted international human rights standards and was a setback for all those seeking justice and redress for crimes committed under the military government of former President Augusto Pinochet. The Supreme Court of Panama also ruled that enforced disappearances committed in the late 1960s and early 1970s by state agents were covered by the statute of limitations.

Amnesty laws remained in place in Chile and Uruguay for crimes committed during the military governments of the 1970s and 1980s.

In Canada, government statistics demonstrate that Indigenous women are five times more likely than other women to die from violence

However, in Uruguay the appeals court confirmed in September the trial and detention of former President Juan Maria Bordaberry (1971-1976) as co-author of 10 homicides. In December, former President General Gregorio Alvarez (1981-1985) was arrested and charged as co-author of the enforced disappearances of more than 30 people.

In Mexico a federal judge concluded in July that the massacre of students in Tlatelolco square in 1968 constituted a crime of genocide, but that there was insufficient evidence against former President Luis Echeverría to continue the prosecution.

Human rights violations committed by agents of the state continued to be poorly investigated in most countries. In Brazil, El Salvador, Guatemala, Haiti and Jamaica, for example, human rights violations committed by law enforcement officials were rarely, if ever, prosecuted.

Corruption, inefficiency and lack of clear political will to bring those responsible for human rights violations to account characterized justice systems in many parts of the region. In addition the use of military and police courts to try personnel who commit human rights violations remained a serious concern. In Colombia, for example, many of the more than 200 killings by the security forces reported in 2007 were referred to the military justice system where the military's assertion that the victims were killed in combat was usually accepted and the cases closed without further scrutiny. In Mexico, the National Human Rights Commission found that military personnel were responsible for committing serious abuses against a number of civilians while participating in policing operations. Despite the consistent failure of military courts to ensure justice in human rights cases, the Commission failed to recommend that such cases be tried in civilian courts.

In the context of US conduct in the "war on terror", a lack of accountability for human rights violations remains a serious problem, particularly at higher levels in the chain of command.

Universal jurisdiction

In Argentina and Panama new legislation was introduced providing for universal jurisdiction. In December, President Bush signed into law the US Genocide Accountability Act of 2007, which permits the investigation and prosecution of genocide if the alleged offender is brought into, or found in, the USA, even if the crime occurred outside the country.

There was no substantial progress in the cases against former President General José Efraín Ríos Montt and other high-ranking former officers in the Guatemalan military. A ruling by the Constitutional Court, preventing the implementation of warrants for

■ In March, Rufina Amaya, the last remaining survivor of the El Mozote massacre in El Salvador, died of natural causes. The El Salvadorian Armed Forces reportedly killed 767 people in El Mozote and surrounding areas in an operation carried out in December 1980. To date, nobody has been brought to justice for that massacre or others that occurred during the internal armed conflict.

General Ríos Montt's arrest and a request for his extradition issued by a Spanish judge in 2006, was widely criticized for failing to recognize the principle of universal jurisdiction.

In December, an Italian judge issued arrest warrants for 146 former military and political officials from Argentina, Bolivia, Brazil, Chile, Paraguay, Peru and Uruguay. The arrests related to the killing and enforced disappearance of South American citizens of Italian origin during Operation Condor, a joint plan agreed between at least six military governments in the 1970s and 1980s to eliminate political opponents.

Economic and social discrimination

Pressure mounted on new Latin American and Caribbean governments to fulfil their promises to address deep-rooted economic and social inequalities. Some poverty reduction programmes were recognized as having a positive impact, but others were criticized for their emphasis on charity rather than on the realization of human rights and the promotion of equality.

The persistent political exclusion of large sections of the population, particularly Afro-descendants and Indigenous Peoples, was linked to discrimination and barriers to accessing a whole range of services essential for the realization of human rights. This was coupled with a continuing tendency to treat large sectors of the population as peripheral or to exclude them when defining economic development. A lack of transparency and accountability frequently served to protect vested economic interests and remained a major obstacle to overcoming poverty and discrimination.

However, communities continued to organize to campaign for the realization of their rights, often in the face of threats and intimidation. In Mexico, for example, large numbers of members of Indigenous and peasant communities opposed projects such as the construction of a dam at La Parota. In several South Andean countries, communities organized to oppose mineral extraction activities which threatened to encroach on protected lands or to cause serious environmental damage.

Several states, including Nicaragua and Paraguay, continued to fail to implement decisions of the Inter-American Court of Human Rights regarding the land rights of Indigenous Peoples.

Hundreds of activists and community leaders across the region were subject to spurious criminal charges for attempting to protect the lands of poor rural communities from illegal encroachment, often by national and multinational companies. Some were wrongfully convicted and imprisoned.

> Despite a tendency to treat large sectors of the population as peripheral when defining economic development, communities continued to organize to campaign for the realization of their rights, often in the face of threats and intimidation

In countries such as the Dominican Republic, Peru and Guatemala, social exclusion was reinforced by the failure of the authorities to provide sectors of the population with proper birth certificates. Those without documents risked being denied access to a range of services, including education and health. They were also effectively denied the right to vote, to participate in public affairs, the right to security of tenure for housing and land, and regular employment.

In the USA, racial discrimination was characterized by disparities in law enforcement and the criminal justice system, and the treatment of non-US nationals held by the US military in the context of the "war on terror".

Discriminatory laws criminalizing same-sex relationships remained in force in the Caribbean and Central America. However, in Nicaragua a new Penal Code removed provisions criminalizing gay and lesbian relationships.

HIV/AIDS continued to affect women more than men, with the highest incidence among women in the Caribbean (especially in Haiti and the Dominican Republic); Cuba remained the exception with low reported infection rates. Disproportionate rates of both HIV infection and maternal mortality among Indigenous Peoples across the region also reflected the impact of discrimination in access to health services.

Four countries in the region continue to criminalize abortion in all circumstances: Chile, El Salvador, Honduras and Nicaragua. By October, a year after Nicaragua criminalized abortions in all circumstances, women's rights groups were reporting that women were paying with their lives for this backward step in maternal protection. Their research showed an increase in maternal deaths which could have been prevented if abortion was decriminalized. By contrast, in Mexico City deaths due to unsafe abortions fell after a law decriminalizing abortion was passed in April.

Exposing abuses remained a dangerous activity in many countries. Journalists, reporting on corruption, and environmentalists, reporting on the damage caused by pollution to natural resources on which millions of people depended for their livelihoods, were threatened and attacked.

The UDHR promises freedom from fear and freedom from want, but freedom from want remains illusory for many in the region, both north and south. Despite the astonishing growth in wealth in the past 60 years, entrenched social injustice continues to exclude entire communities from the potential benefits. Millions of people continue to face social exclusion and discrimination. Diverse, multi-faceted and dynamic movements are rising to this challenge, in all parts of the region, and developing a whole new form of activism and empowerment. They are demanding that all the rights set out in the UDHR be made a reality, for all.

Diverse, multi-faceted and dynamic movements are rising to this challenge, developing a new form of activism and empowerment. They are demanding that all the rights set out in the Declaration be made a reality, for all

ASIA-PACIFIC

Universal Declaration of Human Rights: 60 years on

Many of the Asia-Pacific states that adopted the Universal Declaration of Human Rights in 1948, including India and Burma (Myanmar), had recently achieved independence from colonial rule. For them, a global commitment to a world where all are "free and equal in dignity and rights" held special significance.

"Freedom from fear and want" were equally powerful aspirations for the citizens of the many Asia-Pacific nations that joined the UN thereafter, from Laos to Indonesia, Cambodia to Fiji.

On the face of it, "freedom from want" appeared to find some vindication in Asia's subsequent, explosive emergence as a powerful economic force. Despite disparities between individual economies in the region, on the whole, Asia has seen its wealth increase faster than any other region in the world since 1960. Asia is home to the two most populous countries in the world – China with 1.3 billion people and India with 1.1 billion. These two states' economies are also among the fastest-growing globally. Not all citizens have benefited, however. The growth has been accompanied by a widening gap between rich and poor, exacerbating entrenched patterns of discrimination.

The challenge to match unbridled economic expansion with an increase in economic, social and cultural rights for the region's poor remains unmet.

Ongoing conflicts and the growing violence perpetrated by armed groups have continued to generate grave abuses across the region, undermining the security of millions. In addition to refugee populations denied a durable solution, hundreds of thousands remain internally displaced by conflict. Meanwhile in many countries security forces have enjoyed impunity for decades for human rights violations, including extrajudicial executions, enforced disappearances, torture and other ill-treatment perpetrated in the name of "national security". Political instability and the reassertion of military authority – often via the imposition of states of emergency – have undermined institutions crucial for the protection of human rights, or stalled their reform, in several countries.

In this anniversary year of the UDHR, the prospect of an effective remedy for victims of human rights violations in many countries remains illusory.

> Despite disparities between individual economies in the region, on the whole, Asia has seen its wealth increase faster than any other region in the world since 1960

Even where legal systems are well established, and fundamental rights enshrined in constitutions, protection and enforcement are often undermined for political expediency. Asia-Pacific countries that have ratified the core UN human rights treaties, have been reluctant to adopt optional protocols providing international mechanisms for individual complaints. National human rights institutions have now been established in 13 countries, but their independence and efficacy in many countries has been sorely challenged in recent years.

Asia remains the only region in the world that does not have an overarching human rights instrument. However, in a major development in November 2007, the leaders of the Association of Southeast Asian Nations (ASEAN) 10 member countries – Brunei, Cambodia, Indonesia, Laos, Malaysia, Myanmar the Philippines, Singapore, Thailand and Vietnam – marked ASEAN's 40th anniversary by signing their first formal charter which included a commitment to establish a human rights body for the sub-region. The Pacific Islands Forum began examining similar mechanisms within initiatives to promote Pacific integration and co-operation.

2007 also saw the finalizing of the new UN human rights body, the Human Rights Council, of which Bangladesh, China, India, Indonesia, Japan, Malaysia, Pakistan, the Philippines, South Korea and Sri Lanka are current members. Each member state has committed to respecting human rights, co-operating with UN human rights mechanisms, creating and maintaining strong national human rights frameworks and ratifying and upholding international standards. Time will tell whether new Council mechanisms, notably the Universal Periodic Review, will facilitate robust international scrutiny and response when members fail to honour such commitments, and make a real difference to the day-to-day lives of the people of the Asia-Pacific region.

2007 under review
Economic growth, globalization and poverty
The defining feature of 2007 in the Asia-Pacific region was runaway economic growth. While statistically convincing, rampant growth remained suspect in human rights terms. Figures across the region showed a growing gap between rich and poor. Uneven processes of wealth generation continued to disproportionately favour the educated, skilled and urban.

China's economy expanded by 11.4%, the highest growth rate since 1994. But growth was accompanied by social tensions and increasing impoverishment among some rural populations, and

> Figures across the region showed a growing gap between rich and poor. Uneven processes of wealth generation continued to disproportionately favour the educated, skilled and urban

environmental degradation. Vocal protests by farmers did little to prevent forced evictions by the authorities to make way for developments, including those supporting the 2008 Beijing Olympics. In India, the economic boom was accompanied by further marginalization of the 300 million already poor and vulnerable people. Business interests, in many cases multinational, outweighed the needs of the poor as the exploitation of natural resources left tens of thousands homeless with no hope of return or reparations. In Cambodia, thousands were forcibly evicted from their homes following rapacious land grabs by the authorities.

Migration, internal and across borders, was a key contributor to the buoyancy of the region's economy. Yet in country after country, it was seen as an unwanted and unsightly development. In particular, irregular migrants (those without documented legal permission to remain in a host country) were subjected to discriminatory treatment, violence and abuse.

In Malaysia, more than 20,000 migrants were detained by Rela, the People's Volunteer Corps, a body used by the government to tackle the "problem" of "illegal" immigration. Rela routinely raided places where migrant workers, refugees and asylum-seekers lived. In many cases, people were severely beaten and arbitrarily detained. Some were sent to immigration detention camps from which they risked being forcibly returned to countries where they might be tortured or otherwise ill-treated.

Not only did migrants live under the constant threat of detention from the authorities, but they were also subjected to physical and mental abuse by their employers, and were frequently denied equal access to benefits and protections guaranteed to local workers.

In 2007, there were some 500,000 migrants living in South Korea, about half of whom were irregular migrant workers. Many faced severe restrictions on job mobility and had little or no redress against discriminatory treatment or other abuses in the workplace.

REGIONAL
OVERVIEWS
ASIA-PACIFIC

■ Ten migrants detained pending deportation were killed and 17 others were injured during a fire at the Yeosu detention facility in South Korea in February. The relatives of those killed in the fire were given compensation. The other detainees were promptly deported back to the countries of origin, many without any compensation or recourse to unpaid wages.

Armed conflict and political repression

The region remained one of the frontlines in the US-led global "war on terror", which continued to influence domestic and regional armed conflicts, rivalries, and power struggles. Protracted fighting between government forces and armed groups in Afghanistan and Pakistan continued to cause high levels of civilian casualties and a deterioration in the enjoyment of basic human rights. These conflicts are having significant geo-political influence as international forces and the NATO alliance support the Afghan state, and the US-led international coalition continues to pressure Pakistan to address the "war on terror" agenda more rigorously.

In Afghanistan, the ongoing conflict between insurgent groups and the internationally backed Afghan government intensified. At least 6,500 people lost their lives in the violence – civilians accounted for up to two thirds of that number. All parties to the conflict committed human rights abuses. Armed groups, including the Taleban, deliberately targeted civilians, killing those perceived to be sympathetic to the Afghan government or international forces. At the same time, international forces killed hundreds of civilians in offensive operations and aerial bombardments. Afghan national security forces were also involved in the deaths of large numbers of civilians.

Keen to present itself as an ally in the "war on terror", an already fragile Pakistan was plunged into political chaos in November when General Pervez Musharraf declared a state of emergency and suspended Pakistan's Constitution. His actions followed challenges by the Supreme Court to his presidential candidacy while being the Army Chief of Staff. Around 50 judges were removed from the higher judiciary. The subsequent crackdown led to severe curbs on freedom of expression and movement, with the arbitrary detention of thousands of lawyers, journalists and human rights activists. Elections were set for January 2008 and former Prime Ministers Benazir Bhutto and Nawaz Sharif returned from exile at the end of the year to put themselves forward as candidates. From the beginning, the process was marred by violence, culminating in the assassination of Benazir Bhutto in December.

Increasing violence, insecurity and political repression, including restrictions on freedom of expression, were widespread elsewhere in the region. Human rights defenders and others attempting to peacefully safeguard their rights were vulnerable to a wide range of abuses. Abductions and enforced disappearances, arbitrary detentions, torture and other ill-treatment plagued the region and, in many cases, were carried out with impunity.

In August, large-scale protests began in Myanmar against the government's economic and political policies. At least 31 people, and likely more than 100, were killed in the subsequent crackdown by the authorities, and a similar number were thought to be the victims of enforced disappearance. Although the initial response from the international community was robust, by the end of the year, it had waned. Political prisoners continued to be arrested and sentenced at year end, despite government assurances to the UN and their claims of a return to "normalcy".

Enforced disappearances, unlawful killings, arbitrary arrests and torture continued to be a feature of the ongoing and escalating conflict between Sri Lankan government forces and the armed opposition

■ **Zakia Zaki, who ran the private Peace Radio, was killed by gunmen in her home in the central province of Parwan, Afghanistan, on 5 June. The Journalists Independent Union of Afghanistan registered 53 cases of violence against journalists in 2007 by the Afghan government and Taleban insurgents. In six of the cases a journalist was killed.**

group, the Liberation Tigers of Tamil Eelam (LTTE). Armed attacks on civilians were perpetrated by both sides. The LTTE engaged in indiscriminate attacks on civilians.Enforced disappearances appeared to remain part of the government's counter-insurgency strategy and were often reportedly carried out by security forces or by armed groups acting with their complicity. Hundreds of thousands of civilians were displaced from their homelands, particularly in the north, as conflict continued. As hostilities intensified the space for dissent was increasingly restricted, and journalists, particularly those associated with the Tamil media, were attacked, abducted and killed. Despite compelling evidence, the authorities failed to effectively investigate or prosecute those responsible for unlawful killings.

In Bangladesh, a prolonged state of emergency severely restricted the space for freedom of expression and assembly, and due process of law. Hundreds of thousands of people were reportedly arrested as emergency regulations granted sweeping powers of arrest to law enforcement agencies.Human rights defenders and journalists were threatened, intimidated, and implicated in fabricated cases. Law enforcement agencies were implicated in the deaths of more than 100 people in custody, but no one was held to account for the deaths.

Death penalty

Against a global backdrop of growing repudiation, the death penalty remained widespread in the region. In Afghanistan, 15 people were shot, the first executions to take place in three years. Between 70 and 110 people remained on death row. Pakistan continued to extend the scope of the death penalty, bringing more offences within its ambit, and in 2007 more than 100 people were executed.

Secrecy around the death penalty is still a major concern in many countries in the Asia-Pacific region. Death penalty statistics in China continued to be regarded as a state secret, and despite the welcome decision of the Supreme People's Court to reinstate their final review of all cases, the death penalty continued to be used extensively. At least 470 people were executed during 2007 – although the true figure could be much higher.

The death penalty continues to be widely used in the region not just for murder, but for non-violent crimes such as drug-related offences, corruption and other economic crimes. In North Korea, those executed, by hanging or firing-squad, included political prisoners and people charged with economic crimes.

The Anti-Death Penalty Asia Network (ADPAN) expressed concern that more people in the region were sentenced to death for drug offences

Secrecy around the death penalty is still a major concern in many countries in the Asia-Pacific region. Statistics in China, for example, continue to be regarded as a state secret than for any other crime. In February, a group of Indonesian lawyers representing five people who had been sentenced to death for drug-related offences, tried to appeal the convictions by arguing that the Indonesian narcotics law contravened the "right to life" enshrined in the Indonesian Constitution. The appeal was rejected in October. In Viet Nam, at least 83 people were sentenced to death for drug trafficking offences.

Violence against women

Gender-based violence, including sexual violence, remained an everyday threat for women and girls, as alleged perpetrators, including policemen and others in powerful positions, escaped justice. In many countries, women reporting rape faced serious obstacles. In Papua New Guinea, violence against women was seen as a key reason for the HIV/AIDS epidemic, which, in turn, fuelled further abuses against women.

Domestic violence and physical and psychological abuse in the workplace also continued. In China, cases of domestic violence increased 120 per cent in the first three months of the year – a surge attributed to a greater willingness to report abuses.

In Pakistan, the state failed to prevent and prosecute violence in the home and community, including mutilation, rape and "honour" killings. From January to October in the province of Sindh alone, 183 women were murdered for supposedly harming family "honour". The practice of "*swara*", the handing over of a girl or woman for marriage to opponents to settle a dispute, was made punishable by law in 2005 but continued to be practised with impunity.

In March, the Human Trafficking Criminal Actions Eradication Act became law in Indonesia and was welcomed by local NGOs for including a definition of sexual exploitation and immunity for victims. However, trafficking in women and girls remained widespread in the region.

Also in March, the Taiwanese legislature passed several amendments to the Domestic Violence Prevention Law to include cohabiting same-sex and unmarried couples.

Parliaments around the world adopted resolutions calling for justice for the survivors of Japan's World War II system of military sexual slavery. However, the thousands of "comfort" women who were forced to deliver sexual services to Japanese soldiers continued to be denied a full apology or compensation from the Japanese government. In March, Japan's Prime Minister, Abe Shinzo, stated that there was no evidence that the "comfort" women were coerced into becoming sexual slaves.

The thousands of 'comfort' women who were forced to deliver sexual services to Japanese soldiers continued to be denied a full apology or compensation from the Japanese government

Moving human rights forward

Activists, civil society and social movements across the region were increasingly organized in mobilizing protests and actions challenging human rights issues, such as the widespread impunity concerning enforced disappearances, extrajudicial killings, torture and the rights of marginalized peoples.

In Papua New Guinea, the Coalition to Stop Gun Violence was formed in response to government inaction to combat the proliferation and use of illegal firearms. Women human rights defenders were increasingly vocal, organizing a high-profile silent protest addressing violence against women in October.

In Myanmar, fuel price increases, on top of an economy already in decline, sparked peaceful protests. Monks began leading nationwide protests against the government's economic policies, and formed a new group, the All Burma Monks Alliance.

Laos ratified the International Covenant on Economic, Social and Cultural Rights in February. Thailand's accession in October to the UN Convention against Torture brought to fruition many years of activism by Thai civil society and others, and followed hot on the heels of the Thai government signing the statute of the International Criminal Court in August.

In India, there has been a vigorous debate led by NGOs and civil society around the costs of globalization, and what this process means for the poor. The challenge for Asia-Pacific states is how to ensure the growing economic prosperity enjoyed by a lucky few in a handful of countries filters down the social scale and across borders.

This will only be achieved when human rights are enshrined at the centre of the region's laws, and rhetoric is translated into action.

REGIONAL
OVERVIEWS
ASIA-PACIFIC

■ **Venerable U Thilavantha, Deputy Abbot of a monastery in Myitkyina, Myanmar, was beaten to death in detention on 26 September, having also been beaten the night before when his monastery was raided.**
An unconfirmed number of prisoners died in detention after the crackdown in September, due to their treatment during interrogation.

EUROPE AND CENTRAL ASIA

Universal Declaration of Human Rights: 60 years on

In 1948, Europe lay devastated by the Second World War. Soon it was to be further divided by the Cold War. Over the next 60 years, these experiences had a deep influence on collective and individual responses to the need for common ground, as the region sought to build prosperity, ensure security and embed the rule of law.

In fact, within a decade western Europe had laid the foundations of what would become a pan-European regional institutional architecture – set to create a human rights system unrivalled elsewhere in the world, and transform what began as a localized coal and steel community into a union with global economic and political power.

In that time, the Council of Europe drew up the first international legal instrument to protect human rights, created the European Court of Human Rights to enforce it, and established a Parliamentary Assembly. Now comprising 47 member states, the Council's system has been augmented by a Commissioner for Human Rights and various monitoring bodies. The vision for human rights, pluralist democracy and the rule of law remains.

> Within a decade western Europe had laid the foundations of what would become a pan-European regional institutional architecture – set to create a human rights system unrivalled elsewhere in the world

The economic communities established in the 1950s have evolved today into the European Union. The EU has expanded in range – to embrace new member states from the former Communist bloc – and in vision – to a "union of values", aspiring to place human rights at the centre of its internal and external policies.

The post-war political configuration of Europe was also behind the formation of the Organization for Security and Co-operation in Europe (OSCE). This is the world's largest regional security organization, with 56 participating states, including those of Central Asia. It traces its origins to the détente phase of the early 1970s, when it served as a multilateral forum for dialogue and negotiation between East and West. One of the key results of the OSCE was the "Helsinki Process", which in turn inspired the creation of a range of NGOs to monitor the key human rights commitments states had made to their citizens.

The path to this point has not been smooth, however. The intervening 60 years have seen military dictatorships in Greece, Portugal, Spain, Turkey, and repressive states of the Soviet bloc. Armed groups have sought to advance the cause of a particular minority or ideology by force. Savage conflicts have convulsed parts of the former Soviet Union and Yugoslavia as they fell apart. New states emerged, but so did entities with unresolved status still unrecognized by the international community.

Major challenges remain. Much of the region is stable, but impunity endures for crimes committed in recent conflicts, with hundreds of thousands of people still displaced and with little prospect of imminent return. Much of the region has grown in prosperity, but not for those excluded from fundamental economic and social rights, either through racism or other forms of discrimination.

Europe remains a magnet for those seeking to escape persecution, violence or poverty, but still fails them with repressive approaches to irregular migration. Security is a paramount concern of states across the region, yet it is consistently undermined by those who privilege it over human rights in the name of counter-terrorism, or blatantly abuse it to stifle dissent or resist a challenge to the status quo.

The region is still unsafe territory for the countless victims of domestic violence.

It is also sadly true that this region, which regards itself as a beacon of human rights, still embraces a yawning gap between rhetoric and reality, standards and application, principles and performance.

States that entered voluntarily into the various commitments of the regional institutions, have equally voluntarily evaded their obligations – attacking and eroding human rights, and failing to find the political will needed to address key abuses.

It is also sadly true that this region, which regards itself as a beacon of human rights, still embraces a yawning gap between rhetoric and reality, standards and application, principles and performance

2007 under review

Security and human rights

One of the most striking cases in point is that of renditions. Evidence emerged during 2007 that finally placed the complicity of European states in the US-led programme of secret and unlawful detentions beyond dispute. It also proved governments had been complicit in transfering people to foreign countries outside the rule of law, in enforced disappearances, and in the torture and other ill-treatment of those subjected to these renditions and secret detentions.

The gaps in legislation which facilitated foreign and European national intelligences' unlawful conduct, and shielded them from accountability, have also been clearly identified – but the signature response of states has continued to be silence and inaction.

In many other areas, security was privileged over fundamental human rights; to the detriment of both. Kazakstan, Russia and Uzbekistan continued to co-operate, between themselves and with China, in the name of regional security and the "war on terror", in ways that breached obligations under international human rights and refugee law – including forcibly returning people despite them being at risk of torture and other severe violations.

The UK government continued to undermine the universal ban on torture by deporting people it deemed a threat to national security to states where they would face a real risk of grave human rights abuses on the strength of unenforceable "diplomatic assurances". It also attempted to persuade other European states, and indeed the European Court of Human Rights, that such assurances were legitimate.

In Turkey and Tajikistan there were concerns over the lack of fair trials in cases prosecuted under anti-terror laws.

Refugees, asylum-seekers and migrants

Foreign nationals, including those seeking international protection, continued to face a consistent pattern of human rights violations. Men, women and children were blocked from easy access to asylum procedures; some were unlawfully detained, others were denied the necessary guidance and legal support. Many were unlawfully expelled before their claims could be heard, and some were sent to countries where they were at risk of human rights violations. In some places rejected asylum-seekers were forced into destitution.

New legislation in countries such as Belgium, France and Switzerland further restricted the rights of asylum-seekers and migrants.

Racism and discrimination

Across the region identity-based discrimination remained rife against Roma, who continued to be largely excluded from public life and unable to enjoy full access to housing, employment and health services. In some countries, the authorities failed to ensure Romani children's access to education without discrimination. They tolerated, and often promoted, the creation of special classes or schools, including those where a reduced curriculum was taught. Roma were also among those subjected to hate crimes, as were Jews and Muslims. In Russia, violent racist attacks occurred with alarming regularity.

Many people faced discrimination on account of their legal status, including those displaced by conflicts in the former Yugoslavia and

■ In July, the European Court of Human Rights delivered its judgment in the 1996 racial killing of Angel Dimitrov Iliev, a Romani man, by a group of six teenagers in the town of Shumen, Bulgaria. The Court noted that the authorities recognized the heinous nature of the crime yet failed to conduct a prompt and effective investigation into the incident.

Soviet Union, whose access to a range of rights was restricted or outright denied, linked with issues of their registration and residency.

Authorities in Lithuania, Moldova, Poland and Russia continued to foster a climate of intolerance against lesbian, gay, bisexual and Transgender (LGBT) communities. Some highly placed politicians used openly homophobic language, for example, and public events were obstructed. In Latvia, however, unlike in two previous years, an LGBT march was permitted and adequately protected by the police against counter-demonstrators.

Impunity and accountability

Although some progress was made in tackling impunity for crimes committed in the territory of the former Yugoslavia during the 1990s, many perpetrators of war crimes and crimes against humanity continued to evade justice. This was due to a lack of co-operation with the International Criminal Tribunal for the former Yugoslavia, as well as insufficient efforts by domestic courts.

Torture and other ill-treatment continued to be used across the region, frequently as a means to extract confessions, and often in a race-related context. Obstacles to tackling impunity for such violations included police circumvention of safeguards, lack of prompt access to a lawyer, victims' fear of reprisals, lack of a properly resourced and independent system for monitoring complaints, and corruption in law enforcement and the judiciary. In places such as Bosnia and Herzegovina, Moldova, Spain, Russia, Turkey, Turkmenistan, Ukraine and Uzbekistan, a failure to conduct prompt, thorough and impartial investigations perpetuated the culture of impunity.

Death penalty

Significant progress continued towards abolition of the death penalty throughout the region. In May Kazakstan reduced the number of capital crimes to one terrorism-related offence and maintained its moratorium on executions, as did Tajikistan. In June Kyrgyzstan and Uzbekistan signed into law amendments which replaced the death penalty with life or long-term imprisonment. However, Uzbekistan refused to impose a moratorium on executions pending the entry into force of the changes, from the beginning of 2008.

Bucking the trend, Belarus remained steadfast in its role as Europe's last actual executioner. There, as in all the other countries, secrecy remained an issue. Relatives were not given the body of the executed person or told the burial site; no statistics on the use of the death penalty were made public.

■ In November, 10 police officers were found not guilty of the torture of two women in police custody in Istanbul, Turkey, in 2002. The two women, "Y" and "C", reportedly suffered torture including beatings, being stripped naked and then sprayed with cold water from a high pressure hose, and attempted rape. The verdicts followed a new medical report requested by the defendants that did not show "definite evidence that the crime of torture had been committed".

Violence against women

Violence against women and girls in the home remained pervasive across the region for all ages and social groups. It was manifested through a range of verbal and psychological abuse, sexual and other violence, economic control and murder. Commonly, only a small proportion of women reported this abuse, deterred among other things by fear of reprisals from abusive partners; fear of prosecution for other offences; self-blame; fear of bringing "shame" on their family; financial insecurity; insecure immigration status; or lack of shelters or other effective measures such as restraining orders to ensure protection for them and their children. But above all, by the widespread impunity enjoyed by perpetrators.

Women also frequently lacked confidence that the relevant authorities would regard the abuse as a crime, rather than a private matter, and deal with it effectively as such. Failure to bridge that confidence gap in reporting not only hampered justice in individual cases but also impeded efforts to tackle such abuses across society by hiding the full extent and nature of the problem.

While there were some positive moves on legislative protection in this area, other crucial gaps remained. Some countries had no laws specifically criminalizing domestic violence, and some failed to collect comprehensive statistical data; thus hampering the provision of appropriate services or the prevention of abuse, and failing women further.

Since the 2006 new law in Georgia on domestic violence, police and the courts have issued or approved protection and restraint orders in many cases. However, some key provisions of the law were not implemented swiftly or fully and the number of shelters for victims of domestic violence remained insufficient. In Spain, positive measures introduced included a protocol for health workers dealing with victims of domestic violence. However, migrant women remained particularly vulnerable to violence as they continued to suffer discrimination in law and practice when trying to access justice and essential resources such as financial assistance, psychological treatment and access to shelters.

Trafficking

Within and across Europe, women, men and children continued to be trafficked for exploitation in informal sectors such as domestic work, farming, manufacturing, construction, hospitality and forced sexual exploitation. Such trafficking was widespread, and thrived on poverty, corruption, lack of education and social breakdown.

Rather than being treated as victims of heinous crimes, as was their right, when trafficked people came to the attention of the

■ In January the Serious Crimes Court in Albania sentenced Fatos Kapllani and Arben Osmani to 16 and 15 years' imprisonment respectively for trafficking children to Greece and forcing them to work as prostitutes or beggars. Witness protection remained problematic in Albania. Employees at the Department for the Protection of Witnesses at the Ministry of the Interior received training on witness protection and in April the government approved standards for the treatment of victims. Nonetheless, in November, police reportedly initiated proceedings against a 17-year-old girl for "failing to report a crime" after she refused to identify the people who had trafficked her to Italy for forced prostitution at the age of 14.

authorities they were typically treated as criminals, unlawful aliens, or merely as a useful tool in the criminal justice system. Assistance, when offered to trafficked people to recover from their ordeal, was frequently made conditional on their agreement to co-operate in prosecutions against their traffickers. Such co-operation frequently placed trafficked persons and members of their families in further danger.

Access to justice including redress, compensation, restitution and rehabilitation for the abuses was rare. Non-nationals without rights to residence in the country in which they were found were frequently deported without consideration of the risks that they may face on return, be they re-trafficking, retribution or other violence.

Many states failed to ensure that their focus in this area be on respect for and protection of the rights of trafficked persons. In Greece the vast majority of trafficked women remained unidentified as such by the authorities and therefore unable to exercise their rights to protection and assistance. In Switzerland survivors of human trafficking could be given a temporary residence permit for the duration of any criminal procedure in which they testified, but they lost the right to remain when the procedure ended.

However, in a positive development, in 2007 the number of countries ratifying the Council of Europe's Convention on Action against Trafficking in Human Beings reached 10, meaning that it will come into force for those countries as of February 2008. In Portugal, survivors of trafficking were no longer classed as irregular migrants.

Repression of dissent

In many areas across the region, the space for independent voices and civil society shrunk, as freedom of expression and association remained under attack. In Turkey laws that muzzled peaceful dissenting opinion remained in force, with lawyers, journalists and human rights defenders among the victims of harassment, threats, unjust prosecutions and violent attacks. An atmosphere of intolerance prevailed following the shooting in January of Turkish-Armenian journalist Hrant Dink.

In Uzbekistan freedom of expression and assembly continued to deteriorate and pressure on human rights defenders, activists, and independent journalists showed no sign of abating. The clampdown on civil society continued in Belarus, where any form of public activity not sanctioned by the state, including religious worship, was liable to prosecution and rights to freedom of expression, association and assembly were disregarded. Although the new President in Turkmenistan reversed some of his predecessors' policies, there was no fundamental improvement in the realization of human rights.

The number of countries ratifying the Council of Europe's Convention on Action against Trafficking in Human Beings reached 10, meaning it will come into force

■ **76-year-old Sumaia Abzueva was allegedly beaten up on the way to the market in Argun, Chechnya, on 9 January by a group of young men. She had been seeking an investigation into the killing of her son in 2005. She said she had been threatened more than once by the men who had detained and taken her son away from the family home, and who were suspected to be members of Chechen security forces.**

Dissidents, independent journalists, civil society activists and members of religious minorities were among those reportedly harassed, detained or imprisoned. In Azerbaijan independent and opposition journalists faced imprisonment on libel charges, harassment by law enforcement officials and in some cases, physical assault by unknown assailants. Two widely read opposition newspapers were shut down, and editions of opposition newspapers carrying politically sensitive reporting were confiscated or banned from sale by local government bodies.

The Russian authorities were increasingly intolerant of dissent or criticism, branding it "unpatriotic". A crackdown on civil and political rights was evident throughout the year and particularly in the run-up to parliamentary elections in December. NGOs continued to be weighed down by burdensome reporting requirements imposed by changes to legislation. In Chechnya and the wider North Caucasus region, people seeking justice faced intimidation and reprisals.

In spite of threats, intimidation and detention, however, human rights defenders across Europe held onto the vision of 1948. They remained resolute in their work, and in inspiring others to join them in their quest for lasting change and respect for the human rights of all.

MIDDLE EAST AND NORTH AFRICA

Universal Declaration of Human Rights: 60 years on

Sixty years ago, representatives of several Middle Eastern governments participated in the negotiations to adopt the Universal Declaration of Human Rights. Egypt, Iran, Iraq, Lebanon and Syria were among the 48 states with the vision to adopt the Declaration. Saudi Arabia, along with the Soviet Union and South Africa's apartheid government, was among the eight who abstained.

Six decades on, it might have been expected that with such initial support the UDHR would have had greater impact on the lives of those in the Middle East and North Africa region. Yet, the region has lagged behind Africa, the Americas and Europe in developing effective legal frameworks and enforcement systems for the promotion and protection of people's human rights. Indeed, certain states, such as Saudi Arabia and some of the Gulf states, are yet to become party to the two key International Covenants spawned directly from the UDHR, those concerning Civil and Political Rights, and Economic, Social and Cultural Rights – both of which most other states ratified many years ago. Similarly, Iran is one of very few states that thus far has failed to become party to the UN Convention on the Elimination of All Forms of Discrimination against Women (CEDAW).

Indeed, it is only now, in the 60th anniversary year of the UDHR, that an Arab Charter on Human Rights is about to take effect. This Charter has positive features which enlarge on the rights enshrined in international human rights treaties, but it also has severely negative aspects – such as failing to outlaw the executing of children – that states could seek to use to undermine their obligations under binding global standards.

The international human rights system has been slow to develop in the Middle East and North Africa region for many and complex reasons. To an extent the UDHR was depicted by many leaders as representing an attempt to impose "western" values in the aftermath of the Second World War. The UDHR's references to non-discrimination, for example, jarred with legal and customary systems in countries in the region, views on freedom of religion, and the different roles and positions of women and men.

> With such initial support, it might have been expected that the Declaration would have had greater impact on the lives of those in the region

Such concerns, however, might have been overcome were it not for other key developments in 1948, namely the creation of the state of Israel and the resulting dispossession of the Palestinian population. This building of a Jewish state in the midst of the Arab Muslim world had a cataclysmic effect, setting off effectively a continuing state of war between Israel and its Arab neighbours. The dispossession of the Palestinians and the creation of a Palestinian refugee population in exile created a challenging situation that remains unresolved and which has been punctuated by recurrent bursts of fighting between Israel and its neighbours – most recently, the 34-day war between Israel and Hizbullah in 2006.

Popular sentiments are often exploited for political expediency. Thus, it is largely the "threat" posed by Israel that the Syrian, and to an extent the Egyptian, governments have used to justify their decades-long states of emergency, while it is the "threat" posed to Israel by its Arab neighbours that is used to justify Israel's militaristic policies and to secure its continuing Western support. The international community's failure to end Israel's military occupation of the Palestinian Territories, and to ensure a durable solution which recognizes and guarantees the fundamental rights of both Israelis and Palestinians, throws a dark shadow over the wider region, and remains a potential source of regional or global confrontation.

Governments in the region continue to focus on "state security" and "public safety" to the detriment of human rights, and the lives of their citizens. This has been exacerbated since the onset of the "war on terror". Grievous human rights abuses continue to be both widespread and firmly entrenched in many Middle Eastern and North African states. Despite talk of greater democracy, good governance and accountability, most power remains firmly in the grasp of small elites – the clerical oligarchy in Iran; civilians with close links to the military in Algeria, Egypt and Tunisia; religious minorities in the Gulf states; secularist Ba'athists in Syria. All are largely unaccountable to those they govern.

> **Governments in the region continue to focus on 'state security' and 'public safety', to the detriment of human rights and the lives of their citizens**

Throughout the region, state power is maintained, and dissenting voices or debate repressed, by all-powerful security and intelligence services. Those who speak up risk arbitrary arrest and detention without trial, torture and other ill-treatment by security police whose political masters allow them to abuse human rights with impunity. Such victims all too often have no means of remedy or redress. Courts lack independence and are subservient to the executive powers of the state.

Western governments used at least to speak out about such abuses and advocate a process of change, even if they were unprepared to risk their economic interests and, indeed, had themselves pursued grossly repressive policies in the colonial period.

Since 11 September 2001, however, even their criticism has become muted. In pursuit of the "war on terror", the USA and other Western states have made allies among the security and intelligence services of some of the most repressive regimes in the region. They have secretly "rendered" suspects to states such as Egypt, Jordan and Syria, so they can be detained, interrogated and tortured, or they have deported them to Algeria or Tunisia despite such risk. In doing so, they have not only breached international law, but helped entrench the abusive methods of the region's security apparatus.

Today, hope for reform lies primarily with the growing generation of young people in the region, who increasingly ask why they cannot access or enjoy their inalienable human rights. The growing reach of satellite broadcasting and rising internet usage, means the space for debate cannot now so readily be closed down.

The assumptions of the region's ruling elites are being called into question. There is a pressure to adapt, and to become more accountable to the populations they represent. Slowly a transformation is beginning. The signs are all around – the "One Million Signatures" and "Stop Stoning Forever" campaigns of human rights activists in Iran; protests by judges demanding greater judicial independence in Egypt; the emancipation of women in Kuwait; efforts in Morocco to confront the abuses of the past and to abolish the death penalty; the strength of purpose shown by the jailed signatories of the Damascus Declaration in Syria; and the community bridge-building efforts of Israeli and Palestinian organizations working for human rights.

2007 under review

Conflict

Almost five years after the US-led invasion that toppled Saddam Hussein, 2007 saw little easing of the conflict in Iraq. Early in the year US President George W. Bush committed an additional 26,000 troops to a major "surge" intended to improve security, but human rights abuses remained widespread and involved a variety of perpetrators – Shi'a and Sunni armed groups and militias, Iraqi government forces and the US-led Multinational Force (MNF). Sectarian violence caused thousands of deaths, and gross mutilation and torture. Many Iraqis were forced to flee their homes – some 2 million refugees and a further 2.2 million internally displaced. Towards the end of the year, US and Iraqi government sources suggested the "surge" had proved effective, contributing to a fall in the number of civilian killings and the return of some refugees, but attacks remained frequent and conditions for most Iraqis were dire. More than 60,000 people were being detained without

■ **In August in Iraq, Mostafa Ahmad, a taxi driver and Palestinian refugee, was abducted by armed men apparently from the Mahdi Army. Two days later his abductors used his mobile phone to tell his family to collect his body from the morgue; he had been tortured with a drill, his teeth had been ripped out, and he had been shot six times.**

trial by the US-led Multinational Force and the Iraqi authorities; torture was common and used by Iraqi security forces with impunity; and those accused of attacks and killings were hauled before courts where they failed to get a fair trial, yet, increasingly, were sentenced to death.

As 2007 closed, Turkish troops were massing along the border with Iraq to launch attacks against Turkish Kurdish separatists based there. The increasingly strident war of words between the US and Iranian governments threatened the entire Gulf.

The situation was no better in the Israel-occupied Palestinian Territories. Palestinian armed groups continued to fire home-made "qassam" rockets indiscriminately against southern Israel, causing civilian casualties, while Israel used its military might to hit back, killing and injuring Palestinian civilians. At the same time, the Israeli authorities continued to expand illegal settlements in the occupied West Bank, maintain strict controls on Palestinians' movements and build a "protective" wall/fence for which they expropriated increasing amounts of Palestinian lands. In the West Bank and Gaza, the impact of these measures was exacerbated by deepening divisions within the Palestinian community. Clashes in the first half of the year between rival Palestinian security forces and armed groups loyal to Fatah and Hamas climaxed in June when Hamas seized control of the Gaza Strip, leaving the Fatah-led Palestinian Authority to administer no more than the West Bank. Immediately, the international community cut aid to Gaza and the Israeli authorities mounted a blockade – enforcing collective punishment on the Gaza Strip's 1.5 million population. The impact was heaviest on the most vulnerable – children, the elderly and the sick. Those suffering life-threatening illnesses were prevented from leaving the territory to seek medical help.

■ The families of Abdallah Hsein Bisharat and Ahmad Abdallah Bani Odeh, totalling some 40 people, most of them children, were made homeless in August, when Israeli forces destroyed several homes and animal pens in Humsa, a small village in the Jordan Valley area of the West Bank. The army also confiscated the villagers' water tanks and tractor. The villagers had been forced to move from nearby Hadidiya to Humsa after the Israeli army threatened to destroy their homes. The army considers the site a "closed military area" to be used by Israeli forces for shooting practice.

'War on terror'

The impact of the "war on terror" remained profound across the region and was exacerbated by attacks such as those carried out by an armed group in Algeria which claimed the lives of some 130 people, including many civilians. These deplorable attacks were condemned absolutely by Amnesty International, but they did not justify the widespread human rights violations that continued to be committed in the name of the "war on terror" and which targeted many people not involved in either terrorism or other violence.

At the end of the year, Yemenis comprised the largest single group held at the US prison at Guantánamo Bay, Cuba. Some nationals of other states, such as Bahrain, Kuwait, Libya, Saudi Arabia and Tunisia, were returned to their home countries. Usually detained on arrival, a number were soon released, although others were tried and sentenced to prison terms. In Saudi Arabia, returnees were subject to a "reform" programme, details of which were scarce, including whether it was voluntary or coerced. In some cases – such as those of two men returned to Libya and then apparently detained without trial – their fate was uncertain at the end of the year.

In Saudi Arabia, as in other countries, the "war on terror" was also used by authorities to justify repressive measures that long predated the emergence of al-Qa'ida. Extreme powers of arbitrary arrest, secret and incommunicado detention, and search and seizure were deployed not only against suspected terrorists but also more broadly to stifle dissent. In Egypt, leading members of the Muslim Brotherhood were charged and, although civilians, sent before a military court by presidential order after a civilian court dismissed all charges against some of them. In Morocco, more than 100 people were detained as suspected Islamist militants.

Detention without trial, torture and other ill-treatment

Thousands of people across the region were detained without trial for political reasons. The Egyptian authorities were reported to hold some 18,000 administrative detainees, including some arrested years previously, although the Interior Ministry contended that those held numbered no more than 1,500. The Saudi Arabian government disclosed that 9,000 people had been detained since 2003, more than 3,000 of whom continued to be held in July 2007. The Israeli government held more than 800 Palestinians as administrative detainees. They, like the more than 8,000 other Palestinians, including children, who the Israeli authorities held on remand or who were serving sentences, were mostly held in Israel, in breach of international law and effectively preventing family visits.

Detainees – both political prisoners and criminal suspects – were commonly subject to torture and other ill-treatment by security police whose modus operandi was to beat "confessions" out of those they suspected, with impunity. In political cases, they were assisted in several countries by courts whose judges repeatedly ignored pre-trial torture, denying defence lawyers' requests that defendants be medically examined and delivering guilty verdicts based solely on "evidence" obtained through torture. Syria's Supreme State Security Court was but one example. Ominously, the Libyan authorities established a State Security Court, reviving memories of the unfair, discredited People's Court they abandoned only in 2005.

Cruel and inhuman punishments such as flogging and amputation were used in several countries, including Qatar, Saudi Arabia and the United Arab Emirates (UAE).

REGIONAL OVERVIEWS
MIDDLE EAST AND NORTH AFRICA

■ A video clip released in April showed images of prisoners being tortured in al-Hair Prison, Riyadh, Saudi Arabia. The government said it would investigate the incident and the prison authorities later said that one soldier had been disciplined for the torture and suspended for a month and another had been suspended for 20 days for failing to intervene and stop the assaults on prisoners. It was not known whether any independent investigation was carried out or whether the perpetrators had been brought to justice.

Restriction of freedom of expression and dissent

Most governments maintained close controls on freedom of expression and targeted journalists and others whose statements and writings, or blogs, they deemed too critical or subversive. State authorities brought criminal defamation charges against journalists and bloggers in Algeria, Egypt, Morocco, Tunisia, UAE and Yemen. In Iran, journalists were jailed for expressing opinions; in Iraq, they were murdered by shadowy armed groups. In many countries, those who expressed dissent and political and human rights activists faced arrest and imprisonment, harassment and intimidation at the hands of state authorities.

Conversely, and despite government blocks on access, the rising use of the internet and mobile phones provided greater public access to information and, on occasion, exposed and mobilized a new pressure on authorities. In Egypt, a few moments of mobile phone film footage taken by police and circulated in the victim's neighbourhood caused outrage and highlighted the endemic torture by police, and their sense of invulnerability. Countless words over many years had failed to achieve such impact. It threw the authorities onto the defensive, obliging them to prosecute the police responsible.

Death penalty

The death penalty continued to be used extensively in Iran, Saudi Arabia, Iraq and Yemen, whose governments remained among the world's foremost executioners. The Iraqi authorities maintained they were responding to the desperate security situation and would prefer not to resort to such extremes. By contrast, the Maghreb states maintained their long-standing moratorium on executions, despite civilians being killed in terrorist attacks.

In December, Algeria's representatives voted in support of the worldwide moratorium on executions agreed by the UN General Assembly

The Iranian authorities used executions to intimidate opponents – carrying out public hangings. The Saudi Arabian government talked of legal reform but presided over a rapid increase in executions after unfair trials. Many defendants were foreign nationals, typically poor African or Asian migrant workers, who were sentenced after trials conducted in a language they did not comprehend. Some learned that they were to be executed only shortly before their deaths. Both Iran and Saudi Arabia executed child offenders, in gross breach of international law. In Iran, those executed included people convicted of morality crimes; at least one was stoned to death. In Yemen and Syria too, there were executions, often after unfair trials. In Yemen, one convicted child offender, Hafez Ibrahim, was saved only hours before he was due to be executed by shooting – after an urgent call made to Amnesty International, and President 'Ali Abdullah Saleh intervened following international appeals.

In December, Algeria's representative voted in support of the worldwide moratorium on executions agreed by the UN General Assembly. The Moroccan, Lebanese and UAE representatives abstained and the Tunisian representative failed to vote. There had been concern the Arab states might vote against the moratorium as a bloc; their refusal to do so was an encouraging development.

Violence against women

In countries such as Algeria, Iraq, Israel, Kuwait, Tunisia and Yemen, women held cabinet posts in government or seats in the national parliament or occupied leading roles in a widening range of professions.

Nevertheless, women remained subordinate in status to men under family laws and other legislation in most of the region. Violence against women remained widespread and deep-seated, often a product of prevailing social and cultural norms, facilitated and exacerbated by the failure of state authorities to address abuses. In Egypt, almost 250 women were reported to have been killed in the first half of 2007 by violent husbands or other family members; on average two women were raped every hour and genital mutilation of girls was widely practised despite now being totally illegal. "Honour killings" continued to be perpetrated in Jordan, Syria and elsewhere. In southern Iraq women were killed by Shi'a militants for breaking strict dress and morality codes.

Perhaps the most emblematic case, however, occurred in Saudi Arabia, where a male-headed court sentenced a young woman to flogging and imprisonment although it accepted that she had been the victim of a gang-rape. Her offence? She had been in the company of a male friend when the two of them were attacked by the rapists. Following wide publicity, the case against her was withdrawn after the King issued a pardon in December.

In this regard too, however, there were encouraging developments. In particular, two leading Muslim clerics – Syria's Grand Mufti Ahmad Badreddin Hassoun and Lebanon's most senior Shi'a cleric, Ayatollah Mohammed Hussein Fadlallah – both spoke out firmly against "honour crimes" and other violence against women, denouncing such abuses as un-Islamic.

Refugees and migrants

Continuing conflict and human rights abuses led thousands more Iraqis to flee their homes. More than two million were internally displaced; another two million were refugees. Within Iraq, some governorates reportedly closed their borders to the displaced while Syria and Jordan, in particular, felt the strain of the refugee crisis. The international response to UNHCR's appeal for

■ In June the Criminal Court in Jordan sentenced a man to a reduced six-month sentence for murdering his unmarried sister, because it accepted that he had killed her "in a fit of fury" after she said she was pregnant.

humanitarian assistance was inadequate, although some states established resettlement schemes to take a small number of those most vulnerable.

Several hundred thousand Palestinian refugees remained marooned in impoverished camps in Lebanon, where their families had fled at the time of Israel's creation in 1948. They continued to face discrimination and were denied access to health, education and work opportunities, despite many having lived all their lives in Lebanon. In May their plight was thrown into the spotlight when fighting broke out at Nahr al-Bared, one of the largest refugee camps near Tripoli, between members of an Islamist armed group that had taken up positions there and the Lebanese army. Some 30,000 Palestinian residents were forced to flee the camp.

Migrants, refugees and asylum-seekers from sub-Saharan African countries also faced serious difficulties in Morocco, Algeria and Libya, particularly when they sought to cross those countries and gain entry to southern Europe. In Morocco, recognized refugees were among those arbitrarily detained and dumped without adequate food or water at the country's inhospitable border with Algeria. The Libyan authorities carried out mass arrests and deportations without considering whether the individuals were refugees genuinely fleeing persecution and in need of protection or economic migrants whose human rights they also had an obligation to respect; and amid allegations of torture and other ill-treatment. In Egypt, security forces killed at least six refugees or migrants who were attempting to cross the border into Israel.

In the Gulf states, migrant workers carrying out essential but low-paid jobs in the construction or service industries, and especially women employed in domestic service, were subject to abuses by employers and others, including rape and other sexual violence. They were denied adequate protection under the law and governing authorities showed little commitment to upholding their human rights.

Human rights defenders

Defenders – the vanguard in the struggle for human rights – faced many challenges and risks across the region. They were frequently the target of repression. In countries such as Libya and Saudi Arabia, they could hardly surface at all due to the threat from the state. In others, such as Tunisia and Egypt, they were hemmed in by official requirements that they register their NGOs in order to operate legally but had no recourse when the authorities then blocked such registration. In Syria, leading advocates of reform who had the temerity to put their names to the Damascus Declaration, were locked up, sentenced to prison terms after grossly unfair trials and subjected to rough treatment in prison. Yet, despite such vicissitudes, all across the region human rights defenders carried the torch for all those who identify with the standards set down so persuasively 60 years ago.

All across the region, human rights defenders carried the torch for all those who identify with the standards set down so persuasively 60 years ago

A member of the Campaign for Equality protests at the continuing detention of human rights defenders Maryam Hosseinkah and Jelveh Javaheri on 13 December 2007. Both women were eventually released on bail in January 2008.

AMNESTY INTERNATIONAL REPORT 2008
PART TWO: COUNTRY ENTRIES

08

A man walks past his home – a former school residence hall - in Tirana, Albania, April 2007. In violation of domestic law, the state has failed to provide many adult orphans with adequate housing.

AFGHANISTAN

AFGHANISTAN

Head of state and government:	Hamid Karzai
Death penalty:	retentionist
Population:	32.3 million
Life expectancy:	42.9 years
Under-5 mortality (m/f):	234/240 per 1,000
Adult literacy:	28 per cent

Increasing conflict and insecurity affected large parts of Afghanistan and, aggravated by drought and floods, led to large-scale displacement of people throughout the year. At least 6,500 people were estimated to have been killed in the context of the conflict. Violations of international humanitarian and human rights law were committed with impunity by all parties, including Afghan and international security forces and insurgent groups. All sides carried out indiscriminate attacks, which included aerial bombardments by the International Security Assistance Force (ISAF) and US-led Operation Enduring Freedom (OEF) forces, as well as suicide attacks by armed groups. According to the Afghanistan NGO Security Office, there were around 2,000 non-combatant civilian deaths, with international forces causing over a quarter of casualties and insurgent groups just under half. Rights associated with education, health and freedom of expression were violated, particularly for women. Human rights defenders and journalists, many of them women, were threatened, physically intimidated, detained or killed. Reforms of key government institutions, including the police and intelligence service, made limited progress. Government officials and local power-holders were not held accountable for reported abuses and there was little or no access to justice in many areas.

Background

The Afghan government continued with the implementation of the Afghanistan Compact, agreed in 2006 with its international partners, relating to development, security and governance. The number of international military forces, including both OEF and ISAF troops, increased to at least 49,000.

Levels of insurgency intensified, with the Taleban and other armed groups gaining temporary control of a number of districts, particularly in the south, and clashing repeatedly with Afghan and international military forces.

Taleban demands for the withdrawal of international forces were rejected by the Afghan government. There were increasing attempts to facilitate dialogue between parties to the conflict. In addition, efforts to encourage a regional resolution to the conflict led to a peace *jirga* (informal tribal council) being held in August 2007 with participants from both Afghanistan and Pakistan.

Abuses by the Afghan government
Justice system

In June an international conference highlighted serious and systematic flaws in Afghanistan's administration of justice, including the Ministry of Justice, courts, prisons, the police, the army and the Afghan intelligence service, the National Directorate of Security (NDS), despite several years of international support to reform these institutions.

The NDS mandate continued to be opaque as the presidential decree that outlines its powers remained classified. In practice, the NDS appeared to continue to exercise extensive powers including detaining, interrogating, investigating, prosecuting and sentencing people alleged to have committed crimes against national security. The lack of separation of these functions violated the right of suspects to a fair trial, contributed to impunity for perpetrators of human rights violations and undermined the rule of law. There were consistent reports of torture and other ill-treatment of detainees held by the NDS.

Other serious failings that continued to undermine the effective administration of justice included: a judiciary hampered by some unqualified judicial personnel; a poorly trained and paid police force; the threat to judicial independence through pressure from armed groups; and unfair trial procedures, including violations of the right to call and examine witnesses, and the denial of defendants' rights to legal defence and access to information. The lack of confidence in or access to the formal justice system resulted in reliance on informal justice systems, especially in rural areas where up to 80 per cent of cases were reportedly resolved using informal justice mechanisms.

Impunity

A culture of impunity continued, boosted in February by the introduction of the Amnesty Bill, which absolves the government of responsibility for bringing to justice suspected perpetrators of past human rights violations and crimes under international law, including war crimes and crimes against humanity. In December, President Karzai stated that his administration did not yet have the capacity to arrest and prosecute many of those responsible for past and continuing human rights abuses. Those accused of such abuses included members of parliament as well as provincial government officials.

There was no progress on the implementation of the Action Plan on Peace, Justice and Reconciliation in Afghanistan launched in February 2006.

Death penalty

Fifteen people were executed in October, the first executions for three years. One person sentenced to death allegedly bribed his way out of the execution; the 15 were gunned down as they attempted to flee the execution. The execution was immediately followed by a 10-day hunger strike by some prisoners in Pul-e Charkhi prison. The prisoners said that the executions were not based on fair and transparent trials, and that some were politically motivated.

Between 70 and 110 people were believed to remain on death row.

Abuses by international forces

Killings of civilians

International military forces reportedly caused the deaths of several hundred civilians. Some may have been victims of indiscriminate attacks in aerial bombardments and other operations that may have violated international humanitarian law. After several high-profile incidents in mid-2007 involving civilian deaths caused by international military forces, ISAF forces instituted new rules of engagement. It remained unclear what impact this had, although there were regular reports of disproportionate civilian casualties as a result of international military operations.

■ On 4 March, following a suicide attack on a US convoy on the Jalalabad highway in Nangarhar province, US troops opened fire indiscriminately along a 12km stretch of road killing at least 12 civilians and injuring 35 people. Investigations by the Afghanistan Independent Human Rights Commission (AIHRC) found that US forces had used indiscriminate and excessive force. The US military referred the case to its Naval Criminal Investigative Service citing the need for further investigation.

Torture and other ill-treatment

ISAF forces continued to transfer detainees to the NDS, despite allegations of torture and other ill-treatment by the NDS. Attempts by international forces to monitor transferred detainees were inconsistently applied.

In addition, forces involved in the US-led OEF continued to transfer people to the NDS and to US-run detention facilities, including at Bagram airbase near Kabul. US authorities transferred more than 100 detainees from Bagram and Guantánamo to the newly refurbished D-Block of the high security Pul-i Charkhi prison outside Kabul. It was not clear who had oversight of the D-Block. About 600 detainees were believed to remain in Bagram at the end of the year.

Abuses by armed groups

Abductions and killings

Armed groups, including the Taleban, Hizb-e Islami and al-Qa'ida, deliberately targeted civilians as part of their ongoing struggle with the Afghan government and international military forces. This included killing people perceived to be working or co-operating with the Afghan government or international military forces. Mullah Dadullah, a Taleban commander, commented that kidnapping was a "good tactic"and encouraged Taleban fighters to use it more. There was a sharp rise in kidnappings across southern and south-eastern Afghanistan.

■ Four Afghan provincial court employees were abducted by the Taleban while travelling in Andar district, Ghazni, on 24 July. Their bodies were found later by Afghan authorities.

■ Taleban forces abducted 23 Korean nationals on 19 July while they were travelling through Ghazni. Two of the hostages were killed; the rest were released after six weeks' captivity.

■ Taleban forces abducted five Afghan and two German nationals on 18 July in Wardak province.One of the Afghans escaped and one of the Germans died in captivity. The remaining hostages were released in October.

Suicide attacks

Armed groups carried out some 140 suicide attacks against military and civilian targets, killing around 300 civilians.

■ Up to 80 people were killed during a suicide bomb attack on 6 November at a ceremony in Baghlan province. Scores of people were injured. Some of the deaths and injuries may have been caused by guards of members of parliament present at the ceremony who apparently opened fire after the initial bomb attack.

■ On 17 June, 24 people were killed and 35 injured by a suicide bomber aboard a bus transporting Afghan police trainees.

Killings following quasi-judicial processes

The Taleban and other groups unlawfully killed people following quasi-judicial processes.

■ On 30 September, Taleban fighters seized Zainullah, a 15-year-old key maker, from the bazaar where he worked in Sangin district, Helmand province in southern Afghanistan. They accused him of being a spy and hanged him from an electricity pole with a note warning that others caught spying would suffer the same fate.

Freedom of expression

Severe restrictions on freedom of expression remained in place. Several journalists were arrested or intimidated and killed. Members of the AIHRC and representatives of national human rights organizations also faced threats.

The Journalists' Independent Union of Afghanistan registered 53 cases of violence against journalists in 2007 by the Afghan government and Taleban insurgents. In six of the cases a journalist was killed.

■ Zakia Zaki, who ran the private Peace Radio, was killed by gunmen in her home in the central province of Parwan on 5 June.

■ Kamran Mir Hazar, a journalist for Radio Salaam Watandar and editor of the internet news service Kabul Press, was arrested twice, apparently for criticizing the government, and subsequently released without charge.

Violence against women and girls

Women's rights continued to be eroded in many areas. Women working for the government faced threats and several survived attempted assassinations.

■ Massoma Anwary, head of the Department of Women's Affairs in Ghor province, survived an assassination attempt in November.

A decrease in the number of attacks against schools allowed some schools in insecure areas to reopen and there was an overall rise in the number of children attending school. However, fears about safety meant many girls could not go to school. According to the

AIHRC's second report on economic and social rights, published in August, 36.1 per cent of school-aged girls were not attending schools due to issues of accessibility, including security.

Amnesty International reports

▤ Afghanistan: Detainees transferred to torture – ISAF complicity? (ASA 11/011/2007)

▤ Amnesty International dismayed by execution of 15 in Afghanistan (ASA 11/014/2007)

▤ Afghanistan: Amnesty International condemns the unlawful killing of 15-year-old boy by Taleban (ASA 11/013/2007)

▤ Afghanistan: Amnesty International demands immediate release of all hostages (ASA 11/010/2007)

▤ Afghanistan: Justice and rule of law key to Afghanistan's future prosperity (ASA 11/007/2007)

▤ Afghanistan: Mounting civilian death toll – all sides must do more to protect civilians (ASA 11/006/2007)

▤ Afghanistan: Taleban attacks against civilians increasing and systematic (ASA 11/002/2007)

▤ Afghanistan: All who are not friends, are enemies – Taleban abuses against civilians (ASA 11/001/2007)

ALBANIA

REPUBLIC OF ALBANIA

Head of State:	Bamir Topi (replaced Alfred Moisiu in July)
Head of government:	Sali Berisha
Death penalty:	abolitionist for all crimes
Population:	3.2 million
Life expectancy:	76.2 years
Under-5 mortality (m/f):	32/28 per 1,000
Adult literacy:	98.7 per cent

Public confidence in the judicial system remained low. The Prosecutor General was dismissed in November, on questionable legal grounds. Conditions of many remand and convicted prisoners continued to be harsh, as a result of overcrowding and poor hygiene and medical care. There were reports that a number of detainees had been ill-treated by police while in custody or in remand detention. The trafficking of women and children for forced prostitution or other forms of exploitation continued, though was reportedly declining.

Background

Despite economic progress, poverty and unemployment levels remained high. This, together with poor health and educational services in rural areas, led to continued urban migration, resulting in homelessness and unlawful settlements.

Legal, constitutional or institutional developments

In April, Parliament adopted amendments to the Military Criminal Code revoking all provisions allowing for the death penalty, which was abolished for ordinary crimes in 2000.

In September, Albania ratified the International Convention for the Protection of All Persons from Enforced Disappearance. In November it ratified the Optional Protocols to the UN Children's Convention on the sale of children, child prostitution and child pornography; and on children in armed conflicts.

Violence against women

Domestic violence

A government study published in November found that up to a third of women had experienced domestic violence, with occurrences apparently on the increase. Domestic violence was not specifically prohibited in the Criminal Code, and few cases reached the courts, unless they resulted in death or serious injury.

In June a civil law, On Measures against Violence in Family Relations, entered into force, which aims to prevent such violence and provide victims with effective protection. In July a Tirana court issued the first emergency protection order under the new provisions. In November a special unit dealing with domestic violence and the protection of minors was established within the Tirana police force.

Trafficking

In February, Albania ratified the Council of Europe's Convention on Action against Trafficking in Human Beings. According to police sources, the trafficking of women and children decreased sharply in 2007, with 13 reported cases in which the victims were women and seven cases involving children. However, NGOs apparently suspected that considerably more cases went unreported. Eight men were convicted of trafficking women and two other men were convicted of trafficking children.

■ In January the Serious Crimes Court sentenced Fatos Kapllani and Arben Osmani to 16 and 15 years' imprisonment respectively for trafficking children to Greece and forcing them to work as prostitutes or beggars.

■ In June, two men from Lushnja were arrested and charged with trafficking a 16-year-old girl to Greece where she was forced to work as a prostitute.

Witness protection remained problematic and victims were often reluctant to report their traffickers to the police for fear of reprisals. Employees at the Department for the Protection of Witnesses at the Ministry of the Interior received training on witness protection and in April the government approved standards for the treatment of victims. Nonetheless, in November, police reportedly initiated proceedings against a 17-year-old girl for "failing to report a crime" after she refused to identify the people who had trafficked her to Italy for forced prostitution at the age of 14.

Prison conditions

In September the European Committee for the Prevention of Torture (CPT) published its report on its March 2006 visit to Albania. Remand facilities in Durrës and Fier police stations and cells at two police stations in Tirana were visited. The report criticized "deplorable conditions" in Durrës, Fier and the holding cells at one Tirana police station, and inadequate health care.

The transfer of responsibility for remand prisoners from the Ministry of the Interior to the Ministry of Justice was completed in June and those held at police stations were moved to prisons. Although conditions were better, the accommodation of remand prisoners placed further strains on already overcrowded facilities. The building of two new prisons and a remand centre was not completed during 2007.

The total prisoner population stood at 4,638 in October, 1,172 above capacity. As a result, a number of remand prisoners were returned to, or remained in, police stations, in breach of the law.

In September, 16 detainees were reportedly being held at Tirana police headquarters in four cells designed to hold only one person each. Prisoners with mental illnesses were often held with other prisoners because of lack of space in Tirana prison hospital. Work on the construction of a hospital for mentally ill prisoners in Durrës began in August.

■ In November the Albanian Helsinki Committee criticized conditions at Vlora remand prison, where

92 detainees were being held in cells with a capacity of only 46. They included five minors aged between 14 and 17 years, who were held in cells with adults, in breach of the law.

Torture and other ill-treatment

Amendments to Article 86 of the Criminal Code concerning Torture and other degrading or inhuman treatment were introduced in February. These adopted the definition of torture set out in the UN Convention against Torture. However, the failure to fully revise the Criminal and Criminal Procedure Codes meant that police officers, if prosecuted for ill-treatment or torture, were more likely to be charged with lesser offences. No police officers were known to have been convicted of torture or ill-treatment in 2007.

The CPT reported that in March 2006 it received a number of allegations from detainees claiming they had been subjected to "deliberate physical ill-treatment whilst in police custody, in particular, during police questioning." Additionally, a number of remand prisoners at Durrës police station alleged that members of the facility's special intervention force had handcuffed them, placed helmets on their heads and beaten them about the head with hard objects.

■ In August a journalist reported witnessing several police officers brutally punch and kick an acquaintance of his, Ilir Nastimi, at a police station in Tirana Student City.

■ While commissioners from the Ombudsperson's office were inspecting conditions at Vlora remand prison in November, they heard that a detainee, Ilirian Malaj, had the same day been beaten by prison guards after protesting about a cell search. Ilirian Malaj had visible injuries, later documented by a medical forensic examination; his account was supported by other detainees. The Ombudsperson called for an investigation on charges of torture against four named guards.

Housing

Over 45,000 families were registered as homeless; among the most vulnerable groups affected were some 340 people who had been orphaned as children. In violation of domestic law, the state had failed to provide them with adequate housing when they reached adulthood and completed secondary school. Many of them were living in dilapidated school residence halls, sharing a single room with several others, without security of tenure.

Amnesty International visits/report

🚗 Amnesty International delegates visited Albania in April and November.

📄 Albania: "No place to call home" – Adult orphans and the right to housing (EUR 11/005/2007)

ALGERIA

PEOPLE'S DEMOCRATIC REPUBLIC OF ALGERIA

Head of state:	Abdelaziz Bouteflika
Head of government:	Abdelaziz Belkhadem
Death penalty:	abolitionist in practice
Population:	33.9 million
Life expectancy:	71.7 years
Under-5 mortality (m/f):	35/31 per 1,000
Adult literacy:	69.9 per cent

Continuing political violence across the country left at least 491 people dead, an increase over 2006. Many were killed in bomb attacks for which a group calling itself al-Qa'ida Organization in the Islamic Maghreb claimed responsibility. People suspected of links with terrorism were held incommunicado and in secret and were at risk of torture and other ill-treatment. Several terrorism suspects returned to Algeria by other states were sentenced to jail terms after proceedings which did not conform to international standards. Human rights defenders and journalists were harassed. The government took encouraging steps towards addressing violence against women and abolishing the death penalty, but did nothing to break the shield of impunity protecting members of armed groups and government security forces who committed gross human rights abuses during the internal conflict of the 1990s.

Background

A low turnout in the May parliamentary elections apparently reflected a lack of public confidence in the effectiveness of state authorities in addressing security, unemployment, lack of housing, water shortages and other problems. Concern about corruption fuelled discontent as it appeared that profits from rising oil and gas exports were not benefiting the wider population, and there was a continuing flow of migrants to Europe.

In November, the UN Human Rights Committee (HRC) recommended that the government address the continuing problems of impunity, secret detention and torture, discrimination against women and restrictions on freedom of expression.

Political killings

Al-Qa'ida Organization in the Islamic Maghreb, formerly known as the Salafist Group for Preaching and Combat, the main active Islamist armed group in Algeria, attacked both civilian and military targets. The group claimed responsibility for bomb attacks in Algiers in April and December and in Batna and Dellys in September, which killed at least 130 people, many of them civilians, and injured hundreds of others. In September, the authorities announced that Hassan Hattab, the Salafist Group's first leader, had turned himself in.

Government forces killed dozens of alleged members of armed groups during search operations and in clashes. Few details were available but there was concern that some of the victims may have been extrajudicially executed.

Violations in the context of counter-terrorism
Secret detention

The Department for Information and Security (Département du renseignement et de la sécurité, DRS), the military intelligence agency, continued to detain alleged terrorism suspects incommunicado and in secret locations, often military barracks, where they were at risk of torture and other ill-treatment. Those detained included several Algerian nationals returned from other states.

■ Mohamed Rahmouni was arrested by security officials in plain clothes on 18 July near his home in Bourouba, Algiers. His family inquired as to his whereabouts and a month after his arrest his mother was called to the judicial police office in Bourouba and told that her son was being detained and well-treated by the DRS. At the end of the year, however, it remained unclear where he was being held and whether he was facing charges, and relatives were still denied access to him.

■ A man known as "K" because of legal restrictions and Reda Dendani were detained by the DRS when they were deported to Algiers on 20 and 24 January respectively by the UK authorities, who considered them a threat to national security. "K" was released uncharged on 4 February after being held for longer

than the legal limit of 12 days without charge or access to legal counsel; Reda Dendani was held by the DRS until 5 February and then transferred to prison to await trial (see below). Both were held secretly, probably in military barracks in Algiers, and without access to their relatives.

Unfair judicial proceedings

Terrorism suspects faced unfair judicial proceedings. Detainees were not always assisted by legal counsel when they were first brought before a judge and some said that they had not reported torture or other ill-treatment by the DRS for fear of reprisals. In any event, detainees' allegations of torture and other ill-treatment were not investigated by judicial authorities even when "confessions" allegedly extracted under torture or other duress were used as evidence against them in court.

■ A man known as "H" returned to Algeria by the UK authorities was sentenced to three years' imprisonment on 10 November for "belonging to a terrorist network abroad". At trial, he alleged that he had been tortured by the DRS and made to sign a statement whose contents were not disclosed to him before he was brought before the judicial authorities. The court accepted this statement as evidence against him without investigating his allegations. It also dismissed his claim that the Algerian embassy in London had assured him that he would benefit from the amnesty measures adopted in 2006 in Algeria if he was returned there from the UK.

■ Reda Dendani was sentenced to eight years' imprisonment in November for "belonging to a terrorist network abroad". At trial, he alleged that DRS officers had beaten him when he asked to see a statement they had prepared and required him to sign, and that he had not reported this when first brought before a judge because of DRS threats. The court did not investigate his allegations.

Impunity

The government took no steps to address the gross and widespread human rights abuses committed by armed groups and state security forces during the internal conflict of the 1990s in which as many as 200,000 people were killed.

In November, the HRC called for the government to amend Articles 45 and 46 of the 2006 Decree implementing the Charter for Peace and National Reconciliation (Law 06-01), which give impunity to the security forces and criminalize public criticism of their conduct.

Enforced disappearances

Algeria signed the new International Convention for the Protection of All Persons from Enforced Disappearance on 6 February but failed to take any steps to investigate the fate of thousands of victims of enforced disappearances and continued to implement Law 06-01. Under this, relatives can seek compensation if they obtain a death certificate from the authorities for the person who disappeared. Some families complained that they were pressurized to seek such certificates, while others refused to do so out of concern that this would close the door to any investigation. The authorities told the HRC that they had selected 6,233 requests for compensation and had categorized some 17,000 cases as "killed terrorists", but provided no details of the disappeared to whom these referred. Some families received death certificates stating that relatives who had disappeared had been killed while active in armed groups. It was not known how many families received compensation.

■ No progress was made in resolving the disappearance of Salah Saker, a teacher arrested by state agents in 1994, even though the HRC had called in 2006 for an immediate investigation into his case.

■ In July, the HRC ruled on the cases of Mohamed Grioua and Mourad Kimouche, who disappeared after arrest by state agents in 1996. The HRC found that the state had failed to protect their rights and lives, and called for full investigations and for the perpetrators to be prosecuted.

Freedom of expression

Human rights defenders and journalists were harassed by the authorities. A number of them were prosecuted and threatened with imprisonment on criminal defamation charges, apparently to punish or deter criticism of government policies and officials. The HRC recommended that the law be changed to decriminalize defamation, but the law remained in place.

■ Human rights lawyer Amine Sidhoum was charged with defamation in relation to comments attributed to him in a 2004 newspaper article. The journalist who wrote the article was also charged in late October. Their trial, set for November, was adjourned until January 2008. In March, Amine Sidhoum and another human rights lawyer, Hassiba Boumerdessi, were acquitted of passing prohibited items to prisoners who were their clients.

■ Mohamed Smain, President of the Relizane branch of the Algerian League for the Defence of Human Rights, was convicted on 27 October of "denouncing imaginary crimes". He had alleged that the bodies of some 20 people who had disappeared after they were seized by local state-armed militia had been buried in a mass grave in Sidi Mohamed Benaouda. He was sentenced to two months' imprisonment and ordered to pay a fine and damages. The court had first convicted him in 2002 but had been ordered to retry him following a ruling by the Supreme Court. Mohamed Smain lodged a new appeal and remained at liberty.

■ Hafnaoui Ghoul, a journalist and human rights activist with the Djelfa branch of the Algerian League for the Defence of Human Rights, was notified in September that the head of the Djelfa gendarmerie had charged him with defamation and ordered him to report to the gendarmerie weekly. He had been imprisoned for six months in 2004 after being convicted of defaming local officials.

Refugees and migrants

Refugees, asylum-seekers and irregular migrants were at risk of detention, collective expulsion and ill-treatment. Although details were sparse, thousands were believed to have been deported to countries in sub-Saharan Africa without being able to apply for asylum or appeal against their deportation.

■ In August, 28 people from countries in sub-Saharan Africa, who were recognized as refugees by UNHCR, were deported to Mali after they were tried without legal counsel or the assistance of interpreters on charges of entering Algeria illegally. They were dumped near the desert town of Tinzaouatene, where a Malian armed group was active, without food, water or medical aid. The refugees were stuck there for days because of insecurity, before being able to reach the Malian capital.

Violence and discrimination against women

In February, the UN Special Rapporteur on violence against women visited Algeria. She welcomed important amendments made in 2005 to reduce discrimination against women, but drew attention to aspects of the Family Code which allow discrimination against women in matters of housing and inheritance. She also expressed concern as to whether victims of rape and sexual enslavement during the internal conflict were being compensated.

The HRC recommended that Algerian law be amended to ensure equality between men and women in terms of marriage, divorce and housing and to criminalize marital rape.

Death penalty

The authorities maintained a de facto moratorium on executions although death sentences continued to be passed. Dozens of members of armed groups were sentenced to death on terrorism charges, mostly in their absence. In November, Algeria co-sponsored a resolution at the UN General Assembly calling for a global moratorium on executions.

Amnesty International report

📄 Algeria: Briefing to the Human Rights Committee (MDE 28/017/2007)

ANGOLA

REPUBLIC OF ANGOLA
Head of state: **José Eduardo dos Santos**
Head of government: **Fernando da Piedade Dias dos Santos**
Death penalty: **abolitionist for all crimes**
Population: **16.9 million**
Life expectancy: **41.7 years**
Under-5 mortality (m/f): **245/215 per 1,000**
Adult literacy: **67.4 per cent**

Human rights defenders and organizations faced increasing intimidation and threats in a climate of restricted freedom of expression, which also saw a journalist imprisoned for several months. Cases of forced evictions and human rights violations by police were reported, but on a smaller scale than in previous years. A prison rebellion in Luanda Central Prison led to deaths and injuries, but the number of casualties was contested.

Background

In May, Angola was elected to the UN Human Rights Council. In November it ratified the Protocol to the African Charter on Human and Peoples' Rights on the Rights of Women in Africa and acceded to the UN Optional Protocol on the Elimination of All Forms of Discrimination against Women.

The agreement reached in 2006 to end the armed conflict in the province of Cabinda continued to be implemented. Ex-combatants from the Front for the Liberation of the Cabinda Enclave (Frente de Libertação do Enclave de Cabinda, FLEC) were incorporated into the Angolan Armed Forces in January. More than 60 military personnel held in Landana Military Prison for crimes committed during the conflict were released in January in accordance with the 2006 Amnesty Law. In August FLEC changed its name to the Front for the Liberation of the Cabinda State (Frente de Libertação do Estado de Cabinda).

Legislative and presidential elections postponed to late 2007 were further postponed to 2008 and 2009 respectively. Voter registration, initially planned to end on 15 June, was extended to 15 September because of heavy rains and impassable roads which made it difficult to reach millions of people. More than eight million people registered to vote.

The cholera epidemic that broke out in 2006 continued and by the end of August had killed more than 400 people. The situation was aggravated by torrential rains in January and February in Luanda, which killed more than 110 people and destroyed about 10,000 houses, leaving an estimated 28,000 families homeless. A mystery disease, which caused sleepiness, vomiting and diarrhoea, appeared in Cacuaco District, Luanda in October, hospitalizing at least 400 and killing two people. In late November the World Health Organization said it was possibly caused by bromide poisoning.

In September the former director of Angola's External Security Services, General Fernando Garcia Miala, was sentenced to four years' imprisonment by a military court for insubordination. He had failed to appear at a ceremony to demote him after he was dismissed from his post in 2006. Three others – Ferraz António, Miguel André and Maria Domingos – were convicted of insubordination for the same reason and sentenced to two and a half years' imprisonment. They lodged an appeal against the sentence.

Housing – forced evictions

Although fewer people were forcibly evicted than in previous years, the risk of forced evictions continued. Some of those forcibly evicted in 2007 were rehoused. However, the government made little or no attempt to rehouse or compensate hundreds of families repeatedly evicted from their homes in the

Cambamba I, Cambamba II and Cidadania neighbourhoods since 2005. They continued to live without shelter in the ruins of their homes, at risk of further forced evictions.

About 200 families were left homeless after forced evictions in the neighbourhoods of Comandante Jika and Camama, in the municipalities of Maianga and Kilamba Kiaxi, Luanda, in July. In Comandante Jika a number of residents alleged that some of the alternative accommodation provided had been allocated to people from outside the area, resulting in some families being left with nowhere to go. They received no other compensation.

From July onwards, hundreds of families were forcibly evicted and had their homes demolished by the Jardim do Éden (Garden of Eden) construction company in the neighbourhood of Iraque in Luanda. Most were reportedly evicted by employees of the construction company, protected by private security guards and the national police. The forced evictions were carried out to make way for a luxury housing complex. No alternative accommodation or compensation was provided. In November, two journalists reporting on the evictions, António Cascais, a freelancer for the German radio station Deutsche Welle, and Alexandre Neto of the Angolan Radio Despertar, were assaulted by members of a private security company and detained for over three hours by the military police.

In Lubango, capital of Huíla province, between four and 20 families were reported to have been forcibly evicted in July to make room for a luxury hotel complex. Attempts were made to rehouse those affected, but the alternative housing was mostly in areas far from their workplaces and schools, and transport links and amenities were inadequate. They were not offered other forms of compensation.

Police and security forces

Human rights violations by police included arbitrary arrests and detentions, as well as torture and ill-treatment leading to deaths in custody. Police officers responsible for these violations, and for violations committed in 2006, were not brought to justice.

■ In February police officers arrested Francisco Levi da Costa and two other men after a shop owner accused them of attempting to steal three boxes of fish. The police took the men to the Eighth Police Station in Luanda, where they beat the men for four consecutive

days. Allegedly, Francisco Levi da Costa was beaten on his head and lost consciousness, but police accused him of faking in order to be released. He died four days later in the police cell. No one was arrested in connection with his death. Police authorities informed Amnesty International that investigations were continuing.

■ In March, police officers reportedly shot at Isaias Samakuva, president of the National Union for the Total Independence of Angola (União Nacional para a Independência Total de Angola, UNITA), during a meeting at the party's office in Ndalatando, Kwanza North province. A bullet reportedly hit the foot of a 14-year-old boy sitting on a wall outside the house. Isaias Samakuva was unharmed. The Kwanza North police commander stated that an investigation into the incident was being carried out. However, the results were not released by the year's end.

Prison conditions

The UN Working Group on Arbitrary Detentions visited Angola in September and reported that prisoners were held in harsh and alarmingly overcrowded conditions.

In early October, prisoners at the Luanda Central Prison rebelled. The authorities claimed that two prisoners died and six were injured, but others said the number of casualties was much higher. One message sent from the prison reportedly said 80 prisoners had been killed in cell 11. Prison authorities denied this, stating that some of the prisoners had been transferred to Viana Central Prison. The Rapid Intervention Police (Polícia da Intervenção Rapida, PIR) was called in to control the prisoners and the crowds outside. Relatives of the prisoners demanded the list of prisoners transferred to Viana, as well as the names of those killed and injured. They attempted to march to the Presidential Palace but were prevented by police. Two days after the rebellion, the vice-Minister of the Interior promised that prison conditions would be improved.

Human rights defenders

Human rights defenders faced increasing intimidation and threats. In April the Director General of the Technical Unit for the Coordination of Humanitarian Assistance, a government department, announced that the government would soon stop the activities of non-governmental organizations (NGOs) "without a social impact". In July he accused several NGOs of inciting violence and threatened to ban them: the Association for Justice, Peace and Democracy (Associação de Justiça, Paz e Democracia, AJPD); Mãos Livres; the Open Society Foundation (Fundação Open Society); and SOS-Habitat.

Raul Danda, a journalist and leader of a banned human rights organization, was informed in January that charges imposed on him after his arrest in Cabinda in September 2006 had been dropped, in accordance with the 2006 Amnesty Law. He had been charged with instigating, inciting and condoning crimes against the security of the state.

Freedom of expression

There were restrictions on freedom of expression. One journalist (see below) was sentenced to several months' imprisonment and two journalists were briefly detained when reporting on forced evictions in the neighbourhood of Iraque (see above).

■ In July, officers of the Provincial Criminal Investigation Police (Direcção Provincial de Investigação Criminal, DPIC) in Cabinda arrested four men during a mass celebrating the visit of the Vatican's special envoy. They were carrying placards protesting at the appointment in 2005 of a non-Cabindan as the province's Bishop. They were held in the DPIC headquarters for three days, then charged with injury to a public authority and inciting violence against a religious authority. They were released 10 days later, after a summary judgment at Cabinda Provincial Court. Pedro Maria António was acquitted, André and Domingos Conde were each sentenced to two months' imprisonment, and Paulo Mavungo was sentenced to six months' imprisonment. The prison sentences were converted to fines and all sentences were suspended for two years.

■ In October the Provincial Court of Luanda sentenced Felisberto da Graça Campos, director of the weekly newspaper, *Semanário Angolense*, to eight months' imprisonment for defamation and injury to a former Minister of Justice (now the Justice Ombudsman). The charges arose from articles published in April 2001 and March 2004 accusing the then Minister of Justice of appropriating ministry funds. Felisberto da Graça Campos was detained in Viana Central Prison and was conditionally released in November pending the outcome of an appeal.

Violence against women

The Angolan authorities violently expelled thousands of Congolese migrants from diamond-mining areas in northern Angola to the Democratic Republic of the Congo. Many of the migrant women expelled were reported to have been raped by the Angolan military during the expulsion.

Amnesty International visit/reports

🚌 Amnesty International delegates visited Angola in February.

📄 Angola: Lives in ruins – forced evictions continue (AFR 12/001/2007)

📄 Above the Law: Police accountability in Angola (AFR 12/005/2007)

ARGENTINA

ARGENTINE REPUBLIC

Head of state and government:	Cristina Fernández (replaced Néstor Kirchner in December)
Death penalty:	abolitionist for ordinary crimes
Population:	39.5 million
Life expectancy:	74.8 years
Under-5 mortality (m/f):	17/14 per 1,000
Adult literacy:	97.2 per cent

Several people were injured and one person was killed during demonstrations by public sector workers calling for higher pay and improved conditions. There were reports that police ill-treated peasants and members of Indigenous communities.

Background

In October Cristina Fernández was elected President at the head of the Front for Victory, a coalition including the governing Justicialist Party. A law implementing the Rome Statute of the International Criminal Court, making genocide, crimes against humanity and war crimes offences in national law, came into force in January. A bill incorporating the crime of enforced disappearance into the Penal Code was awaiting approval by the Senate at the end of the year.

Impunity – justice for past violations

Several people charged with committing human rights violations during the period of military government (1976-1983) were sentenced during the year.

- Christian von Wernich, former chaplain of the Buenos Aires police, was sentenced to life imprisonment in October for his involvement in 42 abductions, seven murders and 31 cases of torture.
- In July the Supreme Court ruled that the presidential pardon granted by former President Carlos Menem to former general Santiago Riveros for past human rights violations was unconstitutional. In its ruling the Court stated that international legislation prohibits impunity for crimes against humanity.

Police and security forces

Municipal workers held strikes and demonstrations in support of their pay demands in the Province of Santa Cruz in May and August. Some demonstrations ended in violent confrontations with police. Twelve demonstrators were injured by rubber bullets fired by provincial police. Five police officers were also injured.

In April, a protester was killed by a tear gas canister during a demonstration by teachers demanding better working conditions in Neuquén, Neuquén Province. An investigation into the death was initiated.

Land disputes

Violent raids by police and armed guards on peasant and Indigenous communities were reported in the context of land disputes, particularly in Santiago del Estero Province. Organizations working on behalf of peasants were harassed.

Discrimination – Indigenous rights

In September the national Ombudsman submitted a preventive writ before the Supreme Court on behalf of Indigenous, mainly Tobas, communities in Chaco Province. The writ highlighted extreme levels of poverty and lack of food, access to drinking water, shelter and medical care in these communities. In October the Supreme Court ruled that the federal and provincial authorities must provide food, drinking water and health and education programmes and allocate specific resources to address the emergency in the communities.

Prison conditions

In November, more than 30 detainees died during a fire in Santiago del Estero prison. The fire had reportedly been started by prisoners protesting against ill-treatment, abuse of authority, degrading body

searches and the failure to investigate their complaints. The Rapporteur on the Rights of Persons Deprived of Liberty of the Inter-American Commission on Human Rights expressed concern and urged the authorities to take steps to protect those held in the prison system and to investigate the allegations.

Amnesty International report

Argentina: Elecciones 2007 – Llamamiento para creación de un Plan Nacional de Derechos Humanos (AMR13/004/2007)

ARMENIA

REPUBLIC OF ARMENIA

Head of state:	Robert Kocharian
Head of government:	Serge Sarkisian (replaced Andranik Markarian 4 April 2007)
Death penalty:	abolitionist for all crimes
Population:	3 million
Life expectancy:	71.7 years
Under-5 mortality (m/f):	36/31 per 1,000
Adult literacy:	99.4 per cent

Freedoms of assembly and expression were restricted. One person died in custody in disputed circumstances. Physical assaults on Jehovah's Witnesses were reportedly not investigated. The authorities failed to introduce a genuinely civilian alternative to military service and conscientious objectors continued to be imprisoned.

Freedom of expression threatened

There were widespread and credible reports of restrictions on the right to freedom of assembly. Opposition parties reported abuses of administrative bureaucracy during the May parliamentary election campaign to obstruct legal demonstrations. In May and October police used force to disperse peaceful demonstrations by opposition parties.

- In June Gagik Shamshian, a freelance journalist with two opposition newspapers, received a suspended sentence of two and a half years for fraud, reduced on appeal to one year. He was charged after he reported being attacked by people linked to the mayor of Nubarashen suburb, Yerevan, in July 2006.

Proceedings against his alleged attackers were closed in February.

■ In October, newspaper editors Nikol Pashinian and Shogher Matevosian were arrested after participating in a march in central Yerevan with supporters of the former President Levon Ter-Petrosian, a vocal critic of the government.

■ On 13 December there was an explosion at the offices of the opposition newspaper *Chorrord Ishkhanutyun* (Fourth Power). Also in December, the Gyumri-based television channel Gala TV faced harassment from the authorities following its broadcasting of Levon Ter-Petrosian's campaigning activities, allegedly in spite of official warnings not to do so.

Death in custody

■ In May Levon Gulyan, a Yerevan restaurant owner, died in custody at the Ministry of Internal Affairs, after two days of questioning as a possible witness to a fatal shooting outside his restaurant. The authorities claimed he died as a result of falling from a window while attempting either escape or suicide. Levon Gulyan's relatives rejected these explanations. Following his initial detention Levon Gulyan was permitted to return home briefly, during which time relatives alleged they had seen bruises on his body. The official forensic examination carried out by the Prosecutor's Office supported the Ministry's claims. Autopsies carried out by international experts were inconclusive.

Impunity

Representatives of the Jehovah's Witnesses in Yerevan reported that physical assaults against their members were not adequately investigated by police.

■ In February Jehovah's Witnesses Ruben Khachaturian and Narine Gevorkian were allegedly beaten and threatened by neighbours in the Shengavit suburb of Yerevan. They said that the police failed to initiate a prompt investigation.

Prisoners of conscience

The Armenian authorities failed to introduce a civilian alternative to compulsory military service, an obligation undertaken on joining the Council of Europe.

Imprisonment of conscientious objectors, all Jehovah's Witnesses, continued. In September there were reportedly 82 Jehovah's Witnesses in detention,

a record number. Numbers of conscientious objectors imprisoned increased due to successful prosecution appeals for maximum sentences and greater reluctance to grant parole.

Jehovah's Witnesses reported further problems on release due to the authorities' refusal to grant them certification of fulfilment of service, without which important documents such as passports and internal residence permits were harder to obtain.

Amnesty International visit/report

🚗 Amnesty International representatives visited Armenia in March.

📖 Europe and Central Asia: Summary of Amnesty International's concerns in the region, July-December 2006 (EUR 01/001/2007)

AUSTRALIA

Head of state:	Queen Elizabeth II, represented by Michael Jeffery
Head of government:	Kevin Rudd (replaced John Howard in December)
Death penalty:	abolitionist for all crimes
Population:	20.6 million
Life expectancy:	80.9 years
Under-5 mortality (m/f):	6/5 per 1,000

Large-scale government intervention to address disadvantaged Indigenous communities in the Northern Territory was developed without adequate consultation and resulted in a reduction of Indigenous control over their land. Counter-terrorism laws continue to cause concern. Asylum-seekers experienced long-term detention offshore under the "Pacific Solution".

Discrimination

Indicators of Indigenous disadvantage remained unacceptably high. The life expectancy of Indigenous Australians is 17 years lower than that of the rest of the population and Indigenous people are 13 times more likely to be imprisoned than non-Indigenous people.

Legislation for unprecedented intervention in the Northern Territory was passed in response to a damning report on child sexual abuse. The intervention, developed without adequate consultation, committed significant resources to address disadvantage in Indigenous communities but overrode Indigenous controls on access to their land. The legislation attempted to by-pass Australia's Racial Discrimination Act and the International Convention on the Elimination of all forms of Racial Discrimination.

Australia voted against the UN Declaration on the Rights of Indigenous Peoples when it was passed by the UN General Assembly in September.

'War on terror'

■ Indian national Dr Mohammed Haneef was detained without charge for 12 days before terrorism charges were dropped, highlighting flaws in Australia's counter-terrorism laws. Subsequently, his visa to work in Australia was revoked, a decision overturned in the Federal Court.

■ In May, Guantánamo Bay detainee David Hicks was repatriated to jail in Australia after entering a plea bargain before a US Military Commission. He was released in December. Under the terms of Hicks' plea bargain, he is not allowed to talk about his experience for twelve months and was required to sign a statement that he was not tortured or otherwise ill-treated while in US custody. On his release he was placed under a control order restricting his movement, association and communication – the second such order to be issued in Australia. The first, on terrorism suspect Joseph "Jack" Thomas, was lifted in August and restrictions were included in his bail conditions. The High Court earlier determined that Thomas' control order did not breach the Constitution.

Refugees and asylum-seekers

Under Australia's "Pacific Solution" offshore detention policy, 82 Sri Lankans continued to be detained on Nauru, 72 of whom had already been deemed by the Australian Immigration Minister to be refugees. The previous Australian government attempted to pressurize seven Burmese Rohingya asylum-seekers to return to Malaysia to avoid its obligations under the Refugee Convention. They remained on Nauru for over 12 months, but were resettled in December following the change in government.

■ Iraqi refugee Mohammed Faisal was resettled in Australia after being detained on Nauru for over five years. Following a review of his security status, which was initially found to be problematic, he was accepted by Australia where he received medical treatment after becoming suicidal.

In October, Australia announced a moratorium on resettling refugees from Africa, citing difficulties regarding their ability to integrate. This raised concerns about discrimination in Australia's resettlement policy.

Continued use of Temporary Protection Visas obliges refugees to re-apply for protection after three years, denying them security to remain in Australia.

Violence against women

In December, a District Court described the gang rape of a 10-year-old Indigenous girl as "childish experimentation" and brought the issue of consent inappropriately into the trial. The nine men found guilty were not given custodial sentences.

AUSTRIA

REPUBLIC OF AUSTRIA

Head of state:	Heinz Fischer
Head of government:	Alfred Gusenbauer
	(replaced Wolfgang Schüssel in January)
Death penalty:	abolitionist for all crimes
Population:	8.2 million
Life expectancy:	79.4 years
Under-5 mortality (m/f):	6/5 per 1,000

Asylum-seekers suffered routine detention and migrants were deported without due consideration of their family ties and private life. The system for monitoring places of detention was neither independent nor comprehensive. Those in police custody throughout the country received little redress in cases of death and ill-treatment.

Refugees and asylum-seekers

Legislative changes meant asylum-seekers no longer had access to the Administrative Court, significantly decreasing their human rights protection.

The 2005 Aliens Police Act, which is not in line with international standards, allowed authorities to persist in routinely detaining asylum-seekers following their arrival, without taking into account their age, physical condition or family ties – thus violating their right to a private and family life. In many cases, the detention was protracted, disproportionate and unlawful. The poor conditions of detention also amounted to ill-treatment, and asylum-seekers had no prompt or regular access to legal representation.

Among those detained pending deportation were minors, in contravention of the UN Children's Convention, and people suffering from trauma.

■ A disabled Moldovan man, who had fled organized crime in his country of origin, was detained for three months before eventually being granted asylum.

■ A Russian citizen was detained for five months pending deportation, despite being very ill. His symptoms included headaches and chest pains.

Police and security forces

In November, the UN Human Rights Committee expressed concern regarding the Austrian authorities handing out lenient sentences in cases of death and ill-treatment in custody. The Committee recommended that such cases be investigated promptly, impartially and independently by a body outside the Ministry of Interior. The Austrian penal code lacks the crime of torture, as codified in the UN Convention against Torture.

■ On 11 September 2007, the appellate disciplinary authority confirmed that four police officers convicted of crimes amounting to torture remained on duty, and ordered that their fines of between one and five months' salary be reduced. On 7 April 2006, the officers had driven Gambian citizen Bakary J. to an empty storehouse in Vienna, where they severely ill-treated him, including performing a mock execution. They claimed the ensuing injuries had been inflicted by Bakary J. himself while attempting to escape. At the end of the year, Bakary J. had not been awarded any reparation.

Arms trade

Loopholes remained regarding the control of weapons transactions, and there was no monitoring or verification system of the use of arms post delivery. The Law on War Material still lacked sufficient safeguards and transparency. In particular the criteria for the denial of arms transfers leave a worrying margin of discretion, which can result in exports to perpetrators of persistent grave human rights abuses.

AZERBAIJAN

REPUBLIC OF AZERBAIJAN

Head of state:	Ilham Aliyev
Head of government:	Artur Rasizade
Death penalty:	abolitionist for all crimes
Population:	8.5 million
Life expectancy:	67.1 years
Under-5 mortality (m/f):	90/81 per 1,000
Adult literacy:	98.8 per cent

Freedoms of expression and assembly continued to be widely restricted. Independent and opposition journalists faced imprisonment on libel charges, harassment by law enforcement officials and, in some cases, physical assault. Two widely read opposition newspapers were shut down; five journalists were pardoned and released at the end of the year. Three teenagers were imprisoned for 10 years without investigation into allegations that they had confessed under torture. Human rights activists were intimidated. An ethnic Azeri activist was extradited to Iran despite risk of torture or other ill-treatment. Internally displaced people were prevented from fully exercising their social and economic rights.

Freedom of expression – journalists

The right to freedom of expression, particularly for journalists reporting on corruption, other abuses of public office or socio-economic problems, continued to be routinely restricted. One journalist was severely beaten by unknown men; two journalists were reportedly beaten by law enforcement officials. Editions of opposition newspapers carrying politically sensitive reporting were confiscated or banned from sale by local government bodies. No progress was made in investigations into the 2005 murder of newspaper editor Elmar Hüseynov or serious assaults perpetrated against journalists in 2006 by unknown men.

■ A persistent campaign targeting Eynulla Fetullayev, outspoken editor of the popular opposition newspapers *Real Azerbaijan* (*Realny Azerbaydzhan*) and *Azerbaijan Daily* (*Gündelik Azerbaycan*), resulted in two separate trials in April and October respectively. In April, he was sentenced to 30 months' imprisonment for defaming victims and survivors of killings in the village of Xocalı during the 1991-1994 war in Nagorny Karabakh. He denied authorship of the internet postings, of unclear origin, on which the case was based. In May, both newspapers closed after a series of inspections of their premises by state authorities, apparently aimed at shutting the newspapers down. In October, Eynulla Fetullayev was sentenced to eight and a half years' imprisonment on separate charges of terrorism, incitement of ethnic hatred and tax evasion. He denied all charges against him. Amnesty International considered him a prisoner of conscience.

■ Four other opposition or independent journalists and editors, Faramaz Novruzoğlu, Yaşar Agazade, Rovşan Kebirli and Nazim Quliyev, were imprisoned on charges of libel and insult after publishing articles about high-ranking political figures or alleging corruption in public office. Faramaz Novruzoğlu, Yaşar Agazade and Rovşan Kebirli were pardoned and released in December. Nazim Quliyev was also released in December by court order.

■ Journalist Rafiq Tağı and editor Samir Sedeqetoğlu of the Art (Sanat) newspaper were sentenced in May to three and four years' imprisonment respectively for incitement of religious hatred after writing and publishing an article critical of Islam. Amnesty International considered both men prisoners of conscience, having found nothing in the article that could be construed as incitement to hostility, violence or discrimination. Both men were pardoned and released in December.

■ A serious assault on opposition journalist Üzeyir Ceferov by unknown men in April, on the same day as he testified in defence of Eynulla Fetullayev (see above), was unsolved at the end of 2007.

■ In September, reporter Süheyle Qemberova of the Impulse (Impuls) newspaper was reportedly beaten by court officials while researching an article on forced evictions. She was hospitalized after being kicked and punched.

■ In Naxçivan (an Azerbaijani exclave bordered to the south by Iran and to the east by Armenia), Hekimeldostu Mehdiyev, journalist for the opposition New Equality (Yeni Müsavat) newspaper, was seized by police, allegedly beaten and detained for four days in September after reporting on socio-economic problems in the region.

■ Qenimet Zahid, chief editor of the opposition Freedom (Azadlıq) newspaper and brother of imprisoned satirist

Sakit Zahidov, was charged in November with hooliganism and causing bodily harm after an incident with two passers-by he claimed was orchestrated by the authorities. His case was still pending at the end of the year.

Police – excessive use of force

Police reportedly used excessive force to prevent journalists from reporting or filming politically sensitive events such as opposition party rallies. In June, about 200 police officers dispersed an unauthorized rally by some 50 journalists against protesting the curtailment of freedom of speech. Journalists at the rally were kicked and punched, and one had to be hospitalized with stomach injuries. In July, President Ilham Aliyev declared that no police officer would face criminal prosecution for allegedly beating journalists during the 2005 parliamentary elections. Human rights activists condemned the comment as contributing to a climate of impunity for the use of force by police against journalists.

Torture and other ill-treatment

There were persistent reports of the use of torture or other ill-treatment by law enforcement officials. In October, the deputy Minister of Internal Affairs, Vilayet Eyvazov, stated at a press conference that police officers occasionally use torture when interrogating suspects in pre-trial detention.

■ In June, the Court of Grave Crimes sentenced teenagers Dmitri Pavlov, Maksim Genashilkin and Ruslan Bessonov, accused of murdering another teenager, Vüsal Zeynalov, to 10 years' imprisonment after a trial characterized by serious irregularities. The boys' allegations that they had incriminated one another under torture following their arrest in March 2005 had not been investigated. The boys' parents told Amnesty International they believed their sons were targeted on account of their Russian ethnicity, allowing the crime to be construed as ethnically motivated since Vüsal Zeynalov was an ethnic Azeri.

Human rights defenders

Law enforcement agents reportedly intimidated human rights defenders, and in one case, failed to intervene to protect an NGO from intimidation.

■ In April, Javid Aliyev, the son of Akifa Aliyeva , Helsinki Citizens' Assembly coordinator in the city of

A

Ganja, was arrested and sentenced to three days' imprisonment for refusal to co-operate with police after being questioned about hanging a curtain in the rear window of his car. The arrest followed alleged threats from local police that Akifa Aliyeva's human rights activism was putting her children in danger.

■ On 5 July, members of the Modern Equality (Müasir Müsavat) party picketed outside the office of the Institute for Peace and Democracy. They threw eggs and other objects at the office, but police officers present did not intervene.

Deportation and extradition

The authorities continued to extradite people despite risk of torture or other ill-treatment.

■ In April, Hadi Sid Javad Musevi, an Iranian citizen and ethnic Azeri activist of the Southern Azerbaijan National Awakening Movement (SANAM) was extradited to Iran. Hadi Musevi had fled to Azerbaijan in 2006 after reportedly being arrested and tortured in Iran.

■ In May, the UN Committee against Torture ruled that the extradition of Elif Pelit (a Turkish citizen of Kurdish ethnicity) to Turkey in October 2006, breached international obligations against forcible return to states where there is a risk of torture.

In another case, people were deported without being given access to appeal procedures.

■ Six Jehovah's Witnesses, consisting of one Dutch, one British, two Russian and two Georgian citizens, were deported in January on the basis of administrative deportation orders, which do not require any court hearings. According to the authorities they were deported for violating the law against foreigners conducting religious agitation. The deportations followed a raid on a Jehovah's Witnesses meeting in December 2006, at which the authorities claimed to have confiscated technological equipment suitable for espionage activities, an allegation the Jehovah's Witnesses denied. Those deported were reportedly not allowed to appeal.

Internally displaced people

Hundreds of thousands of people internally displaced by the conflict in Nagorny Karabakh in 1991-94 continued to face obstacles preventing them from enjoying their economic and social rights. These included reported restrictions on their freedom of movement, resettlement in economically impoverished and isolated locations, difficulties with registering new family units, and the absence of consultative mechanisms.

In September the State Committee on Refugees and Internally Displaced People offered Amnesty International assurances that all displaced people enjoyed uninhibited freedom of movement in the country, while acknowledging problems with the registration of new family units and stating that continued efforts were required to secure the economic and social rights of vulnerable urban displaced people. .

To this end, the State Committee had prepared a programme addressing the needs of urban displaced people housed in former municipal buildings, schools and barracks. However, people resettled following displacement continued to be denied legal tenure of their new accommodation, which was defined as "temporary". This compromised their capacity to exercise the right to choose between eventual return should a peace settlement be reached, integration or permanent resettlement elsewhere in the country.

Amnesty International visit/reports

🚌 Amnesty International representatives visited Azerbaijan in September.

📄 Azerbaijan: The contracting space for freedom of expression (EUR 55/003/2007)

📄 Azerbaijan: Displaced then discriminated against – the plight of the internally displaced population (EUR 55/010/007)

📄 Europe and Central Asia: Summary of Amnesty International's concerns in the region, July-December 2006 (EUR 01/001/2007)

BAHAMAS

COMMONWEALTH OF THE BAHAMAS

Head of state:	Queen Elizabeth II, represented by Arthur Hanna
Head of government:	Hubert Ingraham (replaced Perry Gladstone Christie in May)
Death penalty:	retentionist
Population:	332,000
Life expectancy:	72.3 years
Under-5 mortality (m/f):	12/10 per 1,000
Adult literacy:	95.8 per cent

People continued to be sentenced to death, but no one was executed. Reports of police abuses continued. The authorities deported several thousand migrants, the majority black Haitians; some were reportedly ill-treated.

Police and security forces – excessive use of force

Beatings and unlawful killings by members of the security forces were reported.

■ Kenneth Russell was shot dead by police during arrest on 3 September on the island of Andros. A coroner's inquest into whether justifiable force had been used had not been completed by the end of the year.

■ At the end of the year, Desmond Key remained in a coma after reportedly being beaten with a baseball bat by two police officers on 17 June in a Nassau police station. The officers were charged in connection with his beating in August. They were on bail awaiting trial at the end of the year.

Asylum-seekers and migrants

The authorities continued to deport migrants, the vast majority Haitians, in large numbers. Some were reportedly ill-treated. During the year, 6,996 migrants were reported to have been deported, of whom 6,004 were Haitian nationals.

■ On 4 May a Haitian migrant was shot in the thigh by a member of the Royal Bahamian Defence Force (RBDF) as a vehicle containing a group of suspected irregular immigrants was intercepted during an operation in the capital, Nassau. A court found that there was no evidence that the man had resisted arrest, as had been claimed, and that the RBDF did not have the legal authority to conduct such an operation without immigration officers present. At the end of the year the RBDF officer remained on duty.

Violence against women

The Bahamas has the highest rate of reported rapes in the world, according to a Joint Report issued in March by the UN Office on Drugs and Crime and the Latin America and the Caribbean Region of the World Bank.

Death penalty

New death sentences were passed during the year. A number of prisoners were awaiting a review of their sentences following a ruling in 2006 by the UK-based Judicial Committee of the Privy Council abolishing mandatory death sentences for murder. In November, the Bahamas voted against the UN resolution calling for a global moratorium on the death penalty. Following the vote, the Prime Minister spoke publicly of his hope for a return to executions in the Bahamas.

BAHRAIN

KINGDOM OF BAHRAIN

Head of state:	King Hamad bin 'Issa Al Khalifa
Head of government:	Shaikh Khalifa bin Salman Al Khalifa
Death penalty:	retentionist
Population:	0.8 million
Life expectancy:	75.2 years
Adult literacy:	86.5 per cent

Isolated incidents of repression of human rights defenders, journalists and internet sites were reported. Courts passed two death sentences, but no one was executed.

Background

In February demonstrations were held after three people were arrested and protesters clashed with security forces. The three arrested – 'Abdul Hadi al-Khawaja, President of the dissolved Bahrain Centre for Human Rights; Hassan Mshaima', a former political prisoner and Head of the radical Shi'a opposition al-Haq Movement; and Shakir Mohammed 'Abdul Hussain – were charged with "inciting hatred and seeking to change the political system by illegal means" and other offences. They were released on bail the day of their arrest. Court proceedings against them were later dropped at the request of King Hamad bin 'Issa Al Khalifa.

In September Bahrain acceded to the International Covenant on Economic, Social and Cultural Rights.

Human rights defenders

■ Nabeel Rajab, Vice-President of the dissolved Bahrain Centre for Human Rights, was reportedly harassed: he was followed and he and his wife received offensive anonymous phone calls, letters and messages. In March, he was summoned to appear before the Criminal Investigation Directorate apparently for distributing documents related to a report issued in September 2006 by Salah al-Bandar, a UK national and former adviser to the Bahraini government. The report alleged that officials had planned to manipulate the outcome of the November 2006 parliamentary elections at the expense of the majority Shi'a Muslim population. In October 2006 the High Criminal Court had banned publication of any information related to Salah al-Bandar's report. No charges were known to have been brought against Nabeel Rajab.

Freedom of expression

In May some 200 Bahraini journalists held protests outside the Council of Representatives (parliament) calling for greater press freedom and an end to prison terms for press-related offences. The same month the Shura (Consultative) Council unanimously passed a new draft law that excluded prison terms for press-related offences. However, the law had not been promulgated by the end of the year.

At least 22 internet sites, including some known for carrying criticism of the government, remained banned.

The local media was reportedly banned from interviewing Ghada Jamsheer, a woman human rights defender.

'War on terror'

The two remaining Bahraini nationals still held by the US authorities at Guantánamo – Juma'a Mohammed al-Dossari, a Saudi Arabia resident, and 'Issa 'Abdullah al-Murbati – were returned to Saudi Arabia and Bahrain in July and August respectively. They were released uncharged by the Saudi Arabian and Bahraini authorities.

Counter-terrorism

At least 11 people were reportedly arrested under Bahrain's 2006 counter-terrorism law. Six people were released but five, detained in August, were still being held at the end of the year. They appeared in court on 23 October charged with "preparing attacks against another country, membership of a banned organization and financing terror attacks".

Arbitrary arrests and detentions

Following demonstrations on 17 December and subsequently, about 45 people were arrested. Many were released within hours or days, but at least 20 continued to be held at the Department of Criminal Investigations and in the Central Prison in al-Manama. They were held in solitary confinement and kept blindfolded for lengthy periods. Some were tortured during interrogation by security officials, including with beatings and electric shocks to various parts of the body. According to reports, three detainees – Mohammad Khalil al-Madoob, Hussain Khalil al-Madoob and Hussain 'Abd al-Nabi – alleged that they were tortured in the days following their arrest and had facial injuries apparently caused by beatings when they were seen by their legal representative.

Death penalty

In January a proposed amendment to the 1976 Penal Code to repeal the death penalty for drug trafficking was defeated in the Shura Council. In November the government voted against a moratorium on executions at the UN General Assembly.

Two people were sentenced to death for murder: an unnamed Bangladeshi man in January; and another Bangladeshi national, Mizan Noor Al-Rahman Ayoub Miyah, in April.

BANGLADESH

PEOPLE'S REPUBLIC OF BANGLADESH

Head of state:	Iajuddin Ahmed
Head of government:	Fakhruddin Ahmed (replaced Iajuddin Ahmed in January)
Death penalty:	retentionist
Population:	144.4 million
Life expectancy:	63.1 years
Under-5 mortality (m/f):	65/64 per 1,000
Adult literacy:	47.5 per cent

Human rights were severely restricted under a state of emergency imposed in the wake of widespread political violence. Hundreds of thousands of people were reportedly arrested on suspicion of criminal activity or breaches of emergency rules. Torture continued to be widespread. Law enforcement agencies were implicated in the deaths of more than 100 people in custody, but no one was held to account for the deaths. At least six men were executed.

Background

Following weeks of violent clashes between the supporters of the main political parties, a state of emergency was declared on 11 January. Elections scheduled for 22 January were postponed until 2008. President Iajuddin Ahmed appointed a new caretaker government headed by Fakhruddin Ahmed as Chief Adviser and supported by the army, and the army was deployed with the police to maintain law and order.

The new government embarked on an anti-corruption programme, and took steps towards judicial and electoral reform, but the pace of reforms was disappointingly slow. There were also widespread concerns both about the role of the army in the country's political life and about economic problems, including a sharp rise in the cost of food and other essential goods.

The government announced that it had initiated the creation of a National Human Rights Commission (NHRC). The authorities were urged by Amnesty International to ensure that the NHRC's mandate, independence and resources would enable it to be an effective mechanism for strengthening human rights protection.

More than 60,000 slum dwellers were forcibly evicted when the government demolished slums in Dhaka, and also in Chittagong and Khulna. They were given no alternative accommodation or compensation.

Cyclone Sidr which hit south-western areas in mid-November caused severe devastation to over a million people's homes and livelihoods and killed more than 3,000 people.

State of emergency restrictions

Emergency rules restricted freedom of association and assembly, withdrew some constitutional safeguards against arbitrary arrest and gave far-reaching powers of arrest to law enforcement agencies. The ban on political meetings was partially lifted in September to allow political parties to prepare for dialogue with the Election Commission on electoral reforms. Members of parties supported by the authorities were allowed to meet with no restrictions throughout the year.

Fair trial safeguards were weakened by the use of Special Courts which imposed tight restrictions on defendants' access to lawyers, and by the denial of bail to defendants charged under emergency regulations.

Police and security forces – torture and deaths in custody

The security forces, including army and paramilitary units deployed under emergency rule with the police, committed human rights violations with impunity, including torture and other ill-treatment and alleged extrajudicial executions. The police force was inadequately trained and equipped and lacked effective accountability and oversight mechanisms. Army personnel accused of human rights violations remained almost entirely outside the purview of civilian judicial accountability mechanisms.

■ Rang Lai Mro, a community leader in the Chittagong Hill Tracts, was arrested on 23 February and allegedly tortured by army personnel. He required hospital treatment for his injuries. He was charged with possession of arms and reportedly sentenced to 10 years' imprisonment. In October he was reportedly taken back into police custody, beaten again, and once more needed hospital treatment. There was no reported investigation into the torture allegations.

■ Sahebullah was reportedly detained on 16 May by Rapid Action Battalion (RAB) personnel and tortured in the office of the director of the Rajshahi Medical College Hospital. Both his legs were reportedly broken. He was

B

arrested after demanding that a doctor attend to his wife, who had not been treated for 12 hours. She died the next day.

Law enforcement agencies were implicated in the deaths of more than 100 people in custody. No action was apparently taken to bring those responsible to justice.

■ Khabirul Islam Dulal, from Char Fashion Municipality in Bohla district, was arrested by navy personnel on 20 February. He was reportedly beaten, thrown in a pond with his hands tied with rope, and beaten again. He died that evening.

■ Garo indigenous leader Cholesh Richil died on 18 May while in the custody of Joint Forces (army and police) personnel. There were strong indications that he died under torture. Three other members of the Garo community – Tohin Hadima, Piren Simsung and Protap Jambila – were arrested at the same time and reportedly tortured. The government set up a judicial inquiry into Cholesh Richil's death, but there was no news about it by the year's end.

Arbitrary detention

According to media reports, officials stated that over 440,000 people were arrested on various grounds during the year. Many detainees were detained arbitrarily, initially held under emergency rules, then served with a detention order under the 1974 Special Powers Act (SPA). Some were then charged with politically motivated criminal offences.

Some people held under emergency rules were accused of "extortion" or other criminal activity. Detainees included over 160 politicians from the main political parties, as well as some wealthy business people. A number of detainees held without trial under emergency regulations or the SPA were reportedly tortured or ill-treated.

■ Shahidul Islam, a human rights activist, was charged with murder on the basis of a "confession" by another detainee, Badrul, in February. This charge blocked the release of Shahidul Islam when his detention order under the SPA expired in late February. Badrul retracted his original statement in court, saying he had been forced to make it by police. However, the charge against Shahidul Islam was not dropped and he was reportedly tortured in detention before being released on bail in late August.

■ Following clashes in August between law enforcement agencies and students in Dhaka and Rajshahi demanding an end to the state of emergency, 10 university lecturers from Dhaka and Rajshahi universities were detained. They were prisoners of conscience. Dozens of students were also arrested, accused of involvement in clashes. The six Rajshahi University lecturers were released in December but the four Dhaka University lecturers remained in detention.

Freedom of expression

Although wide-ranging emergency restrictions on the news media were not strictly enforced, their continued existence intensified self-censorship by journalists and editors. Journalists were threatened with arrest if they criticized intelligence agencies or the army.

■ Arifur Rahman, a cartoonist, was arrested on 17 September over a cartoon that used the name of the prophet Muhammad, following threats by Islamist groups. He was charged with "hurting religious sentiments" and was a prisoner of conscience. A 30-day detention order was issued against him under the SPA and extended for a further three months.

Human rights defenders

As in previous years, human rights defenders were subjected to arbitrary detention and torture. Lawyers were allegedly threatened with arrest on corruption charges if they took up high-profile cases.

■ Prisoner of conscience Tasneem Khalil, a journalist who worked with the *Daily Star* newspaper, CNN and Human Rights Watch, was detained on 11 May and reportedly tortured because he had supplied information on human rights violations.

■ Prisoner of conscience Jahangir Alam Akash, journalist and local head of two human rights organizations, was arrested on 24 October by RAB agents in the north-western city of Rajshahi. He was reportedly given electric shocks, was beaten on the soles of his feet with a stick, and was hung from the ceiling with his hands tied. He was transferred to the Rajshahi Jail hospital with multiple injuries. His detention followed his television news report in May about the shooting of an unarmed man by RAB agents. He was charged with extortion, a charge widely believed to be false and politically motivated, and held in detention for over a month before being released on bail.

B

Justice system

The government took steps to implement the Supreme Court's 1999 ruling requiring separation of the judiciary from the executive, including amendments to relevant laws. On 1 November the new system came into effect. However, reports indicated that executive magistrates would retain some judicial powers.

Past human rights abuses

Demands gathered momentum during the year for the investigation of war crimes, crimes against humanity and other serious violations of human rights and humanitarian law committed in 1971. However, as in the past, no action was taken by the government to implement the 1973 International Crimes (Tribunals) Act and no official commission was ever established to provide a comprehensive account of the events of 1971, to determine responsibilities and to make recommendations for reparation for the victims.

Violence against women

Violence against women continued to be reported, including beatings, acid attacks and dowry deaths.
■ In Kushtia district, in the month of June alone, police and hospital records reportedly revealed that at least 19 women committed suicide and 65 more attempted suicide because of violence by their husbands or family members.

Death penalty

At least 90 men and three women were sentenced to death, and at least six men were executed.

Amnesty International visit/reports

An Amnesty International delegation visited Dhaka, Jessore and Khulna in March to assess the impact of the state of emergency on the human rights situation.
Bangladesh: Death in custody and reports of torture (ASA 13/005/2007)
Bangladesh: Amnesty International calls for thorough unrestricted inquiry into violations by security forces (ASA 13/011/2007)

BELARUS

REPUBLIC OF BELARUS

Head of state:	Alyaksandr Lukashenka
Head of government:	Sergei Sidorskiy
Death penalty:	retentionist
Population:	9.6 million
Life expectancy:	68.7 years
Under-5 mortality (m/f):	20/14 per 1,000
Adult literacy:	99.6 per cent

B

The clampdown on civil society by the government continued. Any form of public activity not sanctioned by the state, including religious worship, was liable to prosecution and rights to freedom of expression, association and assembly were disregarded. Opposition activists were given long prison sentences for the peaceful expression of their views, or activists were harassed and prosecuted under the administrative code for lesser offences and fined or detained for short periods. Human rights and opposition organizations faced considerable difficulties in registering and activists were prosecuted for acting in the name of unregistered organizations. Belarus remained the only country in Europe still executing prisoners.

International scrutiny

In December, the UN General Assembly adopted a resolution condemning human rights violations in Belarus and calling for, among other things, the release of all individuals detained for politically motivated reasons, an end to the prosecution, harassment and intimidation of political opponents and human rights defenders, respect for the rights to freedom of speech, assembly and association, and respect for the right to freedom of religion or belief.

Freedom of expression

Government critics were sentenced to long prison terms or continued to serve long prison sentences for voicing their opposition. Alyaksandr Kozulin, presidential candidate during the March 2006 elections, continued to serve his five-and-a-half-year sentence imposed in 2006 for "hooliganism" and "organizing group activities that breach public order". Alyaksandr Kozulin had protested the conduct of the elections, which the OSCE judged to be unfair.

■ On 25 March, 50 to 60 people were detained throughout the country during peaceful demonstrations to mark Freedom Day, the anniversary of the creation of the Belarusian People's Republic in 1918, celebrated by the opposition but not officially recognized. Most of those detained were subsequently sentenced to up to 15 days' administrative detention. Police reportedly used fists and batons against the demonstrators to stop them gathering on October Square in the centre of the capital city of Minsk. Vintsuk Vyachorka and Vyacheslav Siuchyk, two of the organizers, were detained on March 13. Vintsuk Vyachorka was charged with using obscene language; Vyacheslav Siuchyk was initially detained for his likeness to a known criminal and then charged with urinating on the street. Both politicians denied these charges. At separate trials on 4 April both were found guilty of petty hooliganism, but the judge did not impose a fine or detention because the offences were "insignificant".

Freedom of association

Human rights groups and opposition organizations faced considerable obstacles when they attempted to register with the state, and unduly stringent controls on their activities. There were many convictions under Article 1931 of the Criminal Code. This article was added to the Criminal Code in December 2005 and outlaws any activity on behalf of an organization that has been closed or has not been registered regardless of the nature of the activity. In 2007 the law was used almost exclusively against members of the youth opposition movement, Malady Front (Young Front). Malady Front has applied four times for registration and has been turned down on each occasion.

■ On 29 May, five members of Malady Front, Nasta Palazhanka, Boris Garetskii, Oleg Korban, Zmitser Fedoruk, and Aleksei Yanushevskii, were convicted for "organizing or participating in the activity of an unregistered organization". Four of the accused were fined and the fifth member of the group received an official warning. On 4 September two further members of the organization, Ivan Shilo and Nasta Azarka, were also found guilty of the same offence in two separate trials. Nasta Azarka was fined, but in the case of Ivan Shilo the judge did not impose a penalty. Zmitser Dashkevich, one of the leaders of Malady Front who had been sentenced to 18 months' imprisonment in 2006 under Article 1931, was tried while serving his sentence. He was convicted on 9 November for refusing to give evidence as a witness and fined. The charge referred to the police investigations of Ivan Shilo.

■ On 24 July the UN Human Rights Committee ruled that the dissolution of the human rights organization, Viasna (Spring), in 2003 had been a violation of the right to association and that the organization was entitled to an appropriate remedy, including re-registration and compensation. The members of Viasna applied for re-registration on 23 July, but the application was refused on 28 August for several reasons including the fact that 20 of the 69 founders had convictions for administrative offences. The organization's appeal was rejected on 26 October.

Death penalty

Belarus retained the death penalty for "premeditated, aggravated murder" and 12 other offences. There were no official statistics available for the number of executions carried out in the period under review. Execution is by a gunshot to the back of the head, and relatives are not officially told of the date of the execution or where the body is buried. According to press reports, on 22 May the Supreme Court imposed the death sentence on Alyaksandr Syarheychyk for six murders, and other crimes. He was reportedly executed in November, but the exact date and place of burial are not known. On 9 October Syarhey Marozaw and Ihar Danchanka were sentenced to death for a series of murders carried out in the Gomel region. These were the second death sentences imposed on the two men, who had previously been sentenced to death in December 2006 along with Valery Harbaty. On 16 November, commenting on the UN Resolution on a Global Moratorium on the Death Penalty passed the day before, the Minister of Internal Affairs told journalists that it was too early to introduce a moratorium in Belarus.

Discrimination

Restrictions on religious communities continued. Under the restrictive 2002 Law on Religion, only registered nationwide religious associations have the right to establish monasteries, missions and educational institutions, as well as to invite foreign citizens to preach or conduct other religious activity in Belarus. State permission is required to hold religious services in non-religious buildings, yet entities which do not own their own property, such as Protestant churches, found it increasingly difficult to rent property.

■ Polish national Jaroslaw Lukasik, a Protestant pastor and member of the Union of Evangelical Faith Christians, was detained on 27 May when police raided a church service held in the home of Pastor Antoni Bokun of the John the Baptist Pentecostal Church. He was released the same day after the Polish Consul visited the police station. On 30 May he was sentenced under the Administrative Code for holding an unsanctioned meeting and engaging in "illegal religious activity". He was issued with a deportation order and fined one month's salary. Jaroslaw Lukasik had been resident in Belarus since 1999, and his wife and three children are all Belarusian citizens. Jaroslaw Lukasik was deported on 8 June.

Violence against women

Women from Belarus were trafficked, including for sexual exploitation, to western Europe, the Middle East and Russia. According to the US State Department *Trafficking in Persons Report* published in June, the government made significant efforts to prosecute traffickers, but did not offer adequate protection and assistance to victims, relying almost exclusively on non-governmental organizations to provide such support. No progress was made towards introducing a law against domestic violence.

Amnesty International visit/reports

🚌 An Amnesty International delegate carried out a trial observation from 3 to 5 September.

📄 Commonwealth of Independent States: Belarus – the sole executioner (EUR 04/002/2007)

📄 Belarus: Fear of imminent execution (EUR 49/009/2007)

📄 Elections to the United Nations Human Rights Committee: background information on candidate countries (IOR 41/012/2007)

📄 Europe and Central Asia: Summary of Concerns in the Region, January – June 2007 (EUR 01/007/2007)

BELGIUM

KINGDOM OF BELGIUM

Head of state:	King Albert II
Head of government:	Guy Verhofstadt (Prime Minister of interim government)
Death penalty:	abolitionist for all crimes
Population:	10.5 million
Life expectancy:	78.8 years
Under-5 mortality (m/f):	6/5 per 1,000

B

Allegations of ill-treatment by law enforcement officials continued. The rights of asylum-seekers were further restricted by new legislation. For the first time a court qualified a murder as racially motivated. A retrial was ordered in the case of seven individuals convicted on terrorism-related charges due to the appearance of partiality of the judge. Belgium became the first country to ban depleted uranium weapons.

Background

National elections were held on 10 June, but no new government had been formed by the end of the year. On 23 December parliament approved an interim government headed by Guy Verhofstadt.

Migration, refugees and asylum-seekers

New asylum legislation further limiting the rights of asylum-seekers came into full effect in June. The new procedures rely on written appeals which must be submitted within 15 days of the original decision. As a result, asylum-seekers may have greater need of specialist legal representation which, particularly in the case of those held in detention centres, can be difficult to obtain. The new law also increased the grounds on which asylum-seekers can be held in detention.

Evidence emerged that people with mental health difficulties were routinely held in closed migration detention centres, where they may have inadequate access to appropriate psychiatric facilities and treatment.

■ In June, a family of failed asylum-seekers was allegedly subjected to ill-treatment by police officers during an attempt to forcibly expel them to Albania. The expulsion was abandoned when other passengers on the flight protested at the actions of the police officers. The family was subsequently granted refugee status in

Belgium. A complaint regarding the ill-treatment was submitted to the Permanent Commission for Control of Police Services (Comité P).

■ An Iraqi couple was finally granted asylum in Belgium in September, after repeated detention in and expulsion from both Belgium and Greece. The couple first arrived in Greece in December 2004, but their asylum claim was rejected and they were ordered to leave the country without being able to appeal. They travelled to Belgium to join their son who has legal residence in the country, but were detained upon arrival and sent back to Greece on the grounds that Greece was responsible for their asylum claim under the European Union's so-called Dublin II Regulation. In Greece they were detained again, before being ordered to leave the country. The couple returned to Belgium in February 2007 where they were detained once again before finally receiving refugee status.

Racism

■ On 11 October Hans Van Themsche was convicted of the racially motivated double murder of a pregnant black woman and the white child in her care and of the attempted murder of a woman of Turkish origin in May 2006 in Antwerp. He was sentenced to life imprisonment. The Centre for Equal Opportunities and the League for Human Rights were a civil party to the proceedings. It was the first time a court had qualified a murder as racially motivated.

'War on terror'

■ On 19 April the Supreme Court quashed the convictions in the case of Bahar Kimyongür, Kaya Saz, Musa Asoglu, Sükriye Akar, Fehriye Erdal, Zerin Sari, and Dursun Karatas, on the grounds that the designation of a particular trial judge had given rise to an appearance of partiality in the proceedings. The defendants had all been convicted in February 2006 of belonging to or supporting a terrorist organization as a result of their support for the Turkish opposition group, the Revolutionary People's Liberation Party-Front (Devrimci Halk Kurtuluş Partisi-Cephesi, DHKP-C). A retrial was ordered, which began on 8 November at the Court of Appeal in Antwerp. Judgment was pending at the end of the year.

Lawyers for some of the defendants made complaints in relation to the "special detention regime" applied to some of the detainees. Elements of this regime may have constituted a violation of human rights, including excessively frequent strip-searching, the blindfolding of Sükriye Akar during transfer to court, and intrusive night-time cell checks of Kaya Saz, Musa Asoglu and Sükriye Akar.

Arms trade

Following 2006 legislation banning cluster munitions, on 11 May parliament voted unanimously in favour of a bill to ban the use, storage, sale, purchase and transit of weaponry and ammunition containing depleted uranium and all other industrially manufactured uranium. The law will enter into force in June 2009.

Amnesty International report

📖 Europe and Central Asia: Summary of Amnesty International's concerns in the region: January – June 2007 (EUR 01/010/2007)

BENIN

REPUBLIC OF BENIN

Head of state and government:	Thomas Boni Yayi
Death penalty:	abolitionist in practice
Population:	9 million
Life expectancy:	55.4 years
Under-5 mortality (m/f):	149/145 per 1,000
Adult literacy:	34.7 per cent

Members of the presidential guard fired at a crowd in May killing two people. Chronic overcrowding was a problem in several prisons.

Background

In March, gunmen opened fire on President Thomas Boni Yayi's convoy wounding at least four of his bodyguards. The President, who was unharmed, claimed that this attack was an assassination attempt by assailants opposed to his campaign to stamp out corruption. Other sources said that the people who attacked the presidential convoy were ordinary bandits. Seven people detained in connection with the attack remained in detention without trial at the end of the year.

In March, the President's coalition won parliamentary elections.

Police and security forces – excessive use of force

In May, members of the presidential guard killed two people and injured at least five in Ouidah, 35km west of the main city Cotonou. The guards opened fire on a group of people who were reportedly protesting about a road that had remained blocked after the President's car had passed. The then Public Security Minister, Edgar Alia, announced that an investigation had been opened into the shootings, but at the end of the year the results of this investigation had not been made public.

Prison conditions

Prison conditions were very harsh because of severe overcrowding in several prisons. For example, prisons in Cotonou and Abomey (in the centre of the country) held up to six times the number of people they were designed to hold.

BOLIVIA

REPUBLIC OF BOLIVIA

Head of state and government:	Evo Morales Ayma
Death penalty:	abolitionist for ordinary crimes
Population:	9.5 million
Life expectancy:	64.7 years
Under-5 mortality (m/f):	65/56 per 1,000
Adult literacy:	86.7 per cent

At least five people were killed and hundreds were injured during violent confrontations in several cities between government supporters and opponents. These clashes took place in the context of continuing tensions over the new Constitution and economic and political reforms. Journalists were harassed and attacked.

Constitutional and institutional developments

A new Constitution was approved in December amid continuing civil unrest. The Constituent Assembly, inaugurated in August 2006 to draft the Constitution, was dominated by regional and political tensions on a variety of issues, including the future location of the country's capital. The Assembly's sessions were suspended several times.

The text of a new Constitution was approved in the absence of some members of the opposition. It provides for a degree of decentralization by granting autonomy at Indigenous, municipal and regional level as well as at departmental level. The Constitution affirms Bolivia as a unitary, pluralist and multi-ethnic state with a two-house congress. It provides for state ownership of natural resources, free health care and education, and the right to private property. It establishes Sucre as the historical capital of the country and the seat of the judicial and electoral power and La Paz as the seat of executive and legislative power. The text was due to be put to a referendum.

In February an agreement was signed between the government and the UN High Commissioner for Human Rights to establish a UN field presence in the country. The Office of the High Commissioner for Human Rights began work in July to contribute in the promotion and protection of human rights, including improving the administration of justice and enhancing capacity throughout the country to combat racism and racial discrimination.

Freedom of expression – attacks on journalists

Members of the security forces and others were reported to have attacked and threatened media workers during the year. In November dozens of journalists held a demonstration to highlight abuses against them and journalists' unions protested at criticism of their work by members of the government.

■ More than 10 journalists were reportedly attacked in Sucre in November while they were covering violent confrontations between police and demonstrators protesting about the new Constitution.

Political violence

Violence erupted in several cities, including Santa Cruz and Cochabamba, between government and opposition supporters. The clashes left at least five people dead and hundreds injured.

■ In January Christian Urresti and Juan Ticacolque were killed and more than 100 were injured in Cochabamba, Cochabamba Department, following clashes between groups supporting the governing Movement Towards Socialism (Movimiento al Socialismo, MAS), who were calling for the resignation of the Prefect of Cochabamba, and groups supporting the Prefect and calling for greater regional autonomy. Judicial investigations into the killings were initiated but had not concluded at the end of the year.

■ In November, three people were killed and over 100 were injured in two days of violent confrontations in Sucre, Chuquisaca Department. Members of the police, using tear gas and rubber bullets, battled with thousands of demonstrators carrying rocks and clubs. Some protesters attacked the headquarters of the Transport Police using firecrackers and Molotov cocktails (home-made explosive devices). They destroyed office equipment and set fire to police and public vehicles. Gonzalo Durán Carazani and José Luis Cardozo died of gunshot wounds. Juan Carlos Serrudo Murillo died after being hit by a tear gas canister. Members of the police were also injured during the clashes. Investigations into the incidents have been announced.

Amnesty International visit/reports

🖃 Amnesty International delegates visited the country in February.

📃 Bolivia: The national authorities must maintain order and protect inhabitants (AMR 18/001/2007)

📃 Bolivia: Amnesty International calls for Human Rights Plan, action to prevent further clashes and protection for defenders (AMR 18/003/2007)

BOSNIA AND HERZEGOVINA

BOSNIA AND HERZEGOVINA
Head of state:	rotating presidency – Željko Komšić, Nebojša Radmanović, Haris Silajdžić
Head of government:	Nikola Špirić (replaced Adnan Terzić in February)
Death penalty:	abolitionist for all crimes
Population:	3.9 million
Life expectancy:	74.5 years
Under-5 mortality (m/f):	15/13 per 1,000
Adult literacy:	96.7 per cent

Many perpetrators of war crimes and crimes against humanity committed during the 1992-95 war continued to evade justice, and thousands of enforced disappearances remained unresolved. Although efforts to bring perpetrators to justice remained insufficient, progress was made in co-operation with the International Criminal Tribunal for the former Yugoslavia (Tribunal) and in the domestic prosecution of war crimes, including in proceedings at the War Crimes Chamber in Sarajevo. Minorities faced discrimination, including in employment and in access to education. The return of refugees still displaced by the war remained slow. There were reports of ill-treatment by the police and in prisons.

Background

Bosnia and Herzegovina (BiH) remained divided in two semi-autonomous entities, the Republika Srpska (RS) and the Federation of Bosnia and Herzegovina (FBiH), with a special administrative status granted to the Brčko District. The international community continued to exert significant influence over the political process in BiH, in particular through a High Representative with significant executive powers nominated by the Peace Implementation Council, an intergovernmental body monitoring implementation of the 1995 Dayton Peace Agreement. Preparations to close down the Office of the High Representative (OHR) in 2007 were halted after the Peace Implementation Council decided in February against its closure including as a result of lack of progress in political reform. Troop numbers of the European Union-led peacekeeping force EUFOR were reduced from about 6,000 to 2,500.

In February a new state government took office, headed by Prime Minister Nikola Špirić.

Political paralysis delayed progress by BiH towards EU integration for most of 2007. A Stabilisation and Association Agreement with the EU was finally initialled in December after the BiH Council of Ministers adopted an action plan for police reform, a precondition for the conclusion of the agreement.

International prosecutions for war crimes

The Tribunal continued to try alleged perpetrators of war crimes and crimes against humanity. Under the terms of the "completion strategy" laid down in UN Security Council Resolutions the Tribunal was expected to complete all trials, including appeals, by 2010.

■ In April, Dragan Zelenović, a former member of a Bosnian Serb Army (VRS) military unit in Foča, was found guilty of torture and rape committed against Bosniak (Bosnian Muslim) women and girls in 1992. He was sentenced to 15 years' imprisonment.

■ In June, Tribunal indictee Zdravko Tolimir was transferred to the Tribunal's custody after his arrest at the border between Serbia and BiH, reportedly by the RS police acting after a tip-off by the Serbian police. Zdravko Tolimir, former Assistant Commander for Intelligence and Security of the VRS Main Staff, was accused of genocide, conspiracy to commit genocide, crimes against humanity and war crimes, for his alleged role in the killing of thousands of Bosniak men and boys in Srebrenica in 1995.

■ In December the Tribunal sentenced former VRS commander Dragomir Milošević to 33 years' imprisonment for war crimes and crimes against humanity, including murder and inhuman acts committed during the Sarajevo siege in a campaign of sniping and shelling which resulted in many civilian casualties.

Co-operation between the Tribunal and BiH and RS authorities appeared to improve. In June the Tribunal Prosecutor stated that BiH's level of co-operation with her office had progressed in recent months and was now generally satisfactory.

In February, the International Court of Justice ruled in the case of BiH vs. Serbia and Montenegro, confirming that genocide was committed in Srebrenica in 1995 (see Serbia entry).

Domestic prosecutions for war crimes

War crimes proceedings before domestic courts continued, including at the War Crimes Chamber within the BiH State Court, although efforts to bring perpetrators to justice remained insufficient to provide justice to the victims, given the scale of the crimes committed and the potentially huge number of crimes to be investigated and prosecuted. There were significant gaps in witness protection; vulnerable victims, including survivors of crimes of sexual violence, were not provided with adequate assistance and protection.

■ In February, Gojko Janković, a former leader of a military unit of the Foča Brigade of the VRS, was sentenced to 34 years' imprisonment by the War Crimes Chamber for crimes against humanity including murders, torture, rape, sexual slavery, and forcible transfer of population, committed against the Bosniak population in the Foča municipality in 1992 and 1993.

■ In March, a War Crimes Chamber Appeal Panel increased the prison sentence imposed on Radovan Stanković from 16 to 20 years. He was convicted in 2006 of crimes against humanity, including enslavement and rape, committed against women held in detention by Bosnian Serb forces in 1992 in the Foča municipality. The case of Radovan Stanković was the first which had been transferred from the Tribunal to the War Crimes Chamber. Radovan Stanković escaped from detention in May while he was being escorted to a medical examination outside Foča Prison, where he was serving his sentence. He remained at large at the end of 2007.

■ In July, Niset Ramić, a former member of the Territorial Defence of the Republic of Bosnia and Herzegovina, was sentenced by the War Crimes Chamber to 30 years' imprisonment for war crimes, including murders, committed against Bosnian Serb civilians in the Visoko area in 1992.

■ The War Crimes Chamber sentenced former VRS member Jadranko Palija to 28 years' imprisonment in November for crimes against humanity and war crimes committed against non-Serbs in the Sanski Most area. These crimes include the murder of civilians and the rape of a Bosniak woman, committed in 1992.

Some war crimes trials of low-level perpetrators were also held in local entity courts, which continued to face difficulties in dealing with war crimes cases, including as a result of lack of staff and other resources. In these proceedings, victims and witnesses remained without adequate protection from harassment, intimidation and threats.

■ In October, Branislav Berjan, a former member of the VRS, was sentenced to seven years' imprisonment for war crimes against non-Serbs, following proceedings at the Sarajevo Cantonal Court. He was found guilty inter alia of crimes committed against Vladimir and Radislav Mađura, who were abducted from their home in Ilidža, a suburb of Sarajevo, in 1992. Their fate and whereabouts remained unknown until 2004, when their bodies were exhumed and identified.

■ The third retrial for war crimes of four former members of the Croatian Defence Council, the Bosnian Croat armed forces, continued before the Mostar Cantonal Court. The defendants were suspected of being responsible for the detention and subsequent enforced disappearance of 13 Army of Bosnia and Herzegovina soldiers in 1993. Two previous acquittals were quashed by the FBiH Supreme Court.

Enforced disappearances

According to estimates by the International Commission on Missing Persons (ICMP), over 13,000 persons who went missing during the 1992-1995 war were still unaccounted for. Many of the missing were victims of enforced disappearances. Perpetrators continued to enjoy impunity.

Progress continued to be slow in transferring competencies from the missing persons commissions of the FBiH and the RS to the national Missing Persons Institute (MPI). In November, the BiH Council of Ministers adopted a number of documents, including the MPI's statute, with a view to finally enabling the Institute to begin its activities.

The exhumation of a mass grave in Kamenica uncovered 76 complete and 540 incomplete bodies. The remains are believed to be those of victims of killings in Srebrenica in 1995 by Bosnian Serb forces.

■ In December 2006 a commission tasked with investigating the enforced disappearance of Avdo Palić had been reactivated, but attempts to locate his mortal remains and to investigate his enforced disappearance were unsuccessful. Army of Bosnia and Herzegovina Colonel Avdo Palić had disappeared after reportedly being forcibly taken by VRS soldiers from the UN Protection Force compound in Žepa on 27 July 1995.

Refugees and internally displaced people

Since the end of the war, more than a million refugees and internally displaced people out of an estimated 2.2 million people displaced by the conflict have returned to their homes. Progress in the return of those who remain displaced was limited. The Office of the UN High Commissioner for Refugees in BiH registered approximately 7,600 returns between January and December.

Minority returnees continued to face discrimination in access to economic and social rights. Lack of access to employment was a major obstacle to the sustainable return of refugees and the internally displaced, including as a result of discrimination on ethnic grounds.

'War on terror'

The six men of Algerian origin who in 2002 were unlawfully transferred by the authorities in BiH to US custody and detained in Guantánamo Bay, Cuba, remained in detention. In August the BiH authorities reportedly requested guarantees from the US authorities that the detainees would not be subjected to the death penalty, torture, and ill-treatment.

A BiH State Commission for the Revision of Decisions on Naturalization of Foreign Citizens, which had begun its work in 2006, continued its activities amidst statements to the media by politicians to the effect that those stripped of their citizenship, and in particular those deemed to represent a "threat to BiH's national security" would be deported. Reportedly, the Commission concluded that only three of the six men of Algerian origin detained in Guantánamo were BiH citizens. There were concerns about the possible expulsion of those stripped of their citizenship to countries where they would be at risk of serious human rights abuses. In December a man of Algerian origin was deported to Algeria after having been stripped of BiH citizenship following a review of his status by the Commission.

Torture and other ill-treatment

There were reports of ill-treatment by members of police forces and in prisons. Impunity for those responsible prevailed. However, a trial against three Sarajevo Canton policemen suspected of having ill-treated a young man started in April 2007 before the Sarajevo Municipal Court. Proceedings began following the broadcast on the internet in February of a video allegedly showing one of the policemen beating the victim.

The European Committee for the Prevention of Torture and Inhuman or Degrading Treatment or Punishment (CPT) visited BiH in March 2007. Its preliminary observations highlighted "a considerable number of allegations of physical ill-treatment by the police". The CPT also reported numerous allegations of ill-treatment of prisoners by prison staff in Zenica Prison.

Discrimination – Roma

Members of Romani communities continued to suffer discrimination. Primary school attendance rates for Romani children were low and extreme poverty remained one of the main causes of the exclusion of Roma from education. Insufficient progress was made by the authorities at state, entity and cantonal level, in the implementation of the 2004 Action Plan on the Educational Needs of Roma and Members of Other National Minorities.

The FBiH authorities allocated funds for the purchase and distribution of textbooks to Romani and other vulnerable pupils in the school year 2007/08. However, in some cases cantonal and municipal social welfare authorities reportedly failed to distribute textbooks to Romani pupils. No significant progress was made to include in a systematic way Romani language, culture and traditions in school curriculums.

Violence against women

The incidence of domestic violence remained high. In the first 11 months of 2007, Cantonal Ministries of Internal Affairs in the FBiH recorded 1,011 criminal acts of violence in the family, approximately 58 per cent more than in the corresponding period of 2006. Both in the RS and in the FBiH, shelters for victims of domestic violence were facing financial difficulties and in some cases were dependent on financing from foreign donors.

BiH continued to be a country of origin, transit and destination for women and girls trafficked for the purpose of sexual exploitation. In March the BiH Council of Ministers adopted a 2007 operational plan for combating trafficking in human beings and illegal migration. The document envisaged the ratification of the Council of Europe Convention on Action against Trafficking in Human Beings, a number of legislative measures and the coordination of different institutions involved in combating trafficking.

Amnesty International visit/reports

🚍 Amnesty International delegates visited Bosnia and Herzegovina in June.

📄 Europe and Central Asia: Summary of Amnesty International's concerns in the region, January-June 2007 (EUR 01/010/2007)

📄 Open letter to the authorities in Bosnia and Herzegovina on citizenship review and forcible returns to countries where there is a risk of torture (EUR 63/004/2007)

BRAZIL

FEDERATIVE REPUBLIC OF BRAZIL

Head of state and government:	Luiz Inácio Lula da Silva
Death penalty:	abolitionist for ordinary crimes
Population:	191.3 million
Life expectancy:	71.7 years
Under-5 mortality (m/f):	34/26 per 1,000
Adult literacy:	88.6 per cent

People in marginalized communities continued to live amid high levels of violence from both organized criminal gangs and the police. Policing operations in such communities resulted in thousands of deaths and injuries and often intensified social exclusion. Death squads linked to the police were also responsible for hundreds of killings.

The criminal justice system failed to bring those responsible for abuses to account and inflicted a wide range of human rights violations on those held in its overcrowded and underfunded prisons and juvenile detention centres. Women held in prisons and police cells continued to experience torture and other ill-treatment.

Landless activists and Indigenous Peoples campaigning for access to land were threatened and attacked by police officers and private security guards. Forced labour and exploitative working conditions were reported in many states, including in the rapidly growing sugarcane sector.

The federal government introduced a new plan to combat urban violence, consolidated its human rights defenders programme and created an independent body for the prevention of torture.

Background

President Luiz Inácio Lula da Silva began his second term of office in January 2007, along with new state administrations. The main plank of federal government policy was the Plan for Growth Acceleration (Programa de Aceleração do Crescimento, PAC) to upgrade basic infrastructure such as the highway network, port facilities and sanitation, and finance a variety of social programmes. National NGOs voiced concerns about the impact of some of the proposed schemes, including the paving of roads and building of dams near Indigenous lands. The federal government's

B

redistributive programme, the family grant, contributed to reductions in extreme poverty. In November, Brazil was included for the first time in a list of countries with a high human development index, according to the UN Development Programme's Human Development report.

Corruption scandals dogged both the federal and state governments. Major federal police investigations uncovered schemes involving illegal gambling, bribes and the siphoning off of money from overpriced government contracts. Federal funds for infrastructure and social projects in two of Brazil's poorest states, Maranhão and Piauí, were among those illegally diverted.

The federal government set up an independent body for the prevention of torture, in keeping with the Optional Protocol to the UN Convention against Torture, which Brazil ratified in January. The body has the power to make unannounced visits to prisons and police stations.

In August the Special Commission on Political Deaths and Disappearances published *The Right to Memory and Truth*. The report details 475 cases of torture and disappearance during the military government (1964-85) and marks official recognition that human rights abuses were committed under the regime. However, some military files remained closed and relatives continued to search for the remains of victims disappeared by the state during that period. Brazil remained one of the few countries in the region not to have challenged laws affording impunity to officers of the military regime for grave human rights abuses such as torture.

Police and security services

Poor communities remained trapped between the criminal gangs which dominated the areas in which they lived and the violent and discriminatory methods used by police. As a result, many living in such communities experienced entrenched social and economic deprivation.

The federal and state governments' responses to criminal violence were mixed. The federal government introduced the National Public Security and Citizenship Programme (Programa Nacional de Segurança Pública com Cidadania, PRONASCI) which focuses on crime prevention, social inclusion, rehabilitation of prisoners and improved salaries for police officers. However, despite extensive reports of

human rights violations by police, President Lula and leading members of his administration publicly supported certain high-profile militarized police operations, especially in Rio de Janeiro.

At state level, although some governments promised reform most state police forces continued to adopt violent, discriminatory and corrupt methods when combating and containing crime in poor communities with scant oversight or control. Nowhere was this more apparent than in Rio de Janeiro, where early promises of reform were abandoned and the state governor adopted an increasingly draconian and bellicose public stance on issues of security. The policy of large-scale militarized police operations was intensified at the cost of hundreds of lives. According to official figures, police killed at least 1,260 people in the state in 2007 – the highest total to date. All were officially categorized as "acts of resistance" and underwent little or no serious investigation.

■ Scores of people were killed and many more injured during police operations in the Complexo do Alemão – a cluster of 21 socially excluded communities in Rio de Janeiro's north zone housing over 100,000 people – and in neighbouring Vila da Penha. Thousands more faced the closure of schools and health centres as well as cuts in power and water supplies. During the operations there were reports of extrajudicial executions, beatings, vandalism and theft by police officers. Community members alleged that a police armoured vehicle (*caveirão*) was used as a mobile cell in which police administered beatings and electric shocks.

The crackdown culminated in a "megaoperation" at the end of June involving 1,350 civil, military and members of the federal government's elite national police force. Police killed at least 19 alleged criminal suspects, one of whom was 13 years old; a dozen bystanders were injured. Thirteen weapons were seized along with a quantity of drugs; no one was arrested. The Human Rights Commission of the Rio de Janeiro Bar Association and the Special Secretariat of Human Rights of the federal government announced that independent investigations of official forensic reports pointed to strong evidence of summary executions. The UN Special Rapporteur on extrajudicial, summary or arbitrary executions, who visited Rio de Janeiro in November, criticized the lack of official investigations into the killings and concluded that the operation was politically driven.

■ In October, a civil police operation in the Coréia shanty town in Senador Camará in Rio's west zone left 12 dead: a four-year-old boy allegedly caught in the crossfire, a police officer and 10 "suspects", one aged 14. Film footage broadcast on Brazilian national television showed two men being shot and killed from a helicopter as they tried to flee the scene.

Paramilitary-style militias, involving off-duty policemen and firemen, continued to dominate a large swathe of Rio de Janeiro's shanty towns.
■ In April, Jorge da Silva Siqueira Neto, President of the residents' association in the militia-dominated Kelson community in Penha, was forced out of the neighbourhood after receiving death threats. He accused five military police officers of assuming "dictatorial powers" within the community, and lodged his complaint with the police internal investigations unit, the public security secretary and the public prosecutor. Three of the police officers were briefly detained but were released at the beginning of September. Four days later, Jorge da Silva Siqueira Neto was shot dead. An inquiry was launched, but had not advanced by the end of the year.

The state authorities in São Paulo once again reported reductions in official numbers of killings by police, though their figures were contested. However, human rights violations at the hands of police officers continued.
■ In the town of Bauru 15-year-old Carlos Rodrigues Júnior was reportedly tortured and killed by a number of military police officers, in his own home. According to forensic reports, he was given 30 electro-shocks while being interrogated about a stolen motorcycle. Six police officers were provisionally detained at the end of the year.

Death squads

In the first 10 months of 2007, 92 deaths in multiple homicides linked to death squads were recorded in São Paulo – the majority in the city's north zone. Police officers were under investigation in connection with the deaths of more than 30 people in the cities of Ribeirão Pires and Osasco. Killings by death squads were also reported in other states – notably Rio de Janeiro (particularly in the Baixada Fluminense), Espírito Santo, Bahia, Pernambuco, Rio Grande do Norte and Ceará.
■ In August Aurina Rodrigues Santana, her husband Rodson da Silva Rodrigues and her son Paulo Rodrigo

Rodrigues Santana Braga were shot and killed by a group of hooded men while they slept in their house in the Calabetão district of Salvador in Bahia State. The attack took place after the family reported that the son and his 13-year-old sister had been tortured by four military police officers.

In a positive development, in April, the Federal Police broke up a death squad in Pernambuco State thought to have been responsible for the deaths of more than 1,000 people over a five-year period. Another death squad was broken up in November with the arrest of 34 people, among them policemen, lawyers and small traders.

Prisons – torture and other ill-treatment

Severe overcrowding, poor sanitary conditions, gang violence and riots continued to blight the prison system. Ill-treatment and torture were commonplace.
■ In August, 25 inmates were burned to death in the Ponte Nova in Minas Gerais State after factional fighting.
■ In Espírito Santo State, amid accusations of torture and ill-treatment, the government barred the State Human Rights Council, an officially mandated body which under state law has the power to monitor the prison system, from entering prison cells.
■ More than 20 people died in the Aníbal Bruno prison, Pernambuco State in 2007. The prison, which was chronically understaffed and housed more than three times the number of prisoners it was designed to hold, has long been the subject of allegations of torture and ill-treatment.

Conditions within the juvenile detention system throughout Brazil continued to cause concern. There were further reports of overcrowding, beatings and maltreatment. The director of São Paulo's Fundação Casa (formerly known as the FEBEM), was removed from her post in a ruling which criticized the Tietê facility for poor hygiene and substandard accommodation. Her dismissal was later overruled by the State Supreme Court.

Violence against women

Cases brought under the 2006 "Maria da Penha" law, which criminalizes domestic violence, began going through the courts in 2007. Although the law was a major advance, lack of resources, difficulties in enforcing exclusion orders and poor support services hampered effective implementation.

The absence of state protection in marginalized communities left women at risk of both criminal and police violence. In communities run by drug traffickers, women suffered discrimination, violence and lack of access to basic services. There were reports of women having their heads shaved for infidelity, being expelled from communities because they were HIV positive and being forced to trade sexual favours to pay off debts. Women were often too scared to lodge complaints. Women fighting for justice for relatives in cases of police killings were frequently threatened and intimidated.

Though women make up a small but growing part of the prison population, their needs have been consistently neglected. Torture, beatings and sexual abuse were reported in police stations and prison cells.

■ In November, a 15-year-old girl accused of petty theft was imprisoned in a police station in the town of Abaetetuba, Pará State. She was forced to share a cell with between 20 and 30 men for a month. She was repeatedly raped, reportedly in exchange for food. When this was made public, police officers allegedly threatened her and she was taken into protective care. Her family was also reportedly threatened by the police and was taken into a witness protection programme. The case received wide publicity and several federal bodies opened investigations which revealed numerous reports of women suffering grave human rights violations in detention across the state.

Land disputes

Rural violence continued, often in the context of disputes between large landowners and landless rural workers, Indigenous Peoples or quilombolas (members of communities made up of former runaway slaves). Expanding monocultures, such as eucalyptus and soya plantations, illegal logging and mining, along with development projects such as dams and the proposed São Francisco river diversion scheme were sources of conflict. There were also serious concerns over exploitative working conditions in land clearance, charcoal production and the sugarcane sector.

Forced evictions, often involving threats and intimidation, increased. According to the Catholic Church's Pastoral Land Commission, across Brazil 2,543 families were evicted from January to September in 2007, a marked rise on 2006.

■ In November, rural workers occupying a farm near the town of Santa Teresa do Oeste in Paraná State came under attack from 40 gunmen, reportedly hired by a security company working for the farm's Swiss-based multinational owner. They killed landless leader Valmir Motta de Oliveira, shooting him in the chest. A security guard was also shot dead in unclear circumstances. Eight others were injured in the attack, including Izabel Nascimento, who was beaten unconscious. The killing formed part of a long-standing pattern of violence and intimidation perpetrated by rural militias in Paraná state.

Cases of forced labour were reported throughout the country. In December, the Ministry of Labour updated its list of employers found to be subjecting workers to exploitative conditions. The list included 185 employers from 16 states, involving not only workers employed in forest clearance and ranching on agricultural frontiers of the central savannah (cerrado) and Amazonia, but also labourers in plantation monocultures in the wealthier states of São Paulo, Minas Gerais and Rio Grande do Sul.

Exploitation in the growing sugarcane sector continued. In March, attorneys working for the state Ministry for Labour rescued 288 workers from forced labour at six sugarcane plantations in São Paulo State. In the same month, 409 workers, 150 of whom were Indigenous, were rescued from the ethanol distillery Centro Oeste Iguatemi, in Mato Grosso do Sul. In November inspection teams found a further 831 Indigenous cutters lodged in overcrowded, insanitary and substandard accommodations on a plantation in Brasilândia, also in Mato Grosso do Sul.

■ Over a thousand people working in conditions analogous to slavery were released from a sugar plantation owned by ethanol producer Pagrisa in Ulianópolis, Pará State in June. Following the raid, a senate commission accused the inspectors of exaggerating the workers' poor conditions. As a result, the work of the inspection team was briefly suspended by the Ministry for Labour for fear that the allegations would undermine the credibility of the inspection team's work. Inspections resumed in October.

The government took some steps to improve labour conditions in the sugar sector. In São Paulo State, which accounts for over 60 per cent of Brazil's cane production, the State Prosecutor on Labour was proactive in initiating inspections and prosecutions.

At the federal level, the government promised to introduce a social and environmental accreditation scheme aimed at improving working conditions and reducing the environmental impact.

Indigenous Peoples

The state of Mato Grosso do Sul remained the focal point for violence against Indigenous Peoples.

■ In January, Kuretê Lopes, a 69-year-old Guarani-Kaiowá Indigenous woman, died when she was shot in the chest by a private security guard during an eviction from farmlands that the Guarani-Kaiowá occupied as they claim them as their ancestral lands. In September, four Guarani-Kaiowá leaders involved in the occupation were sentenced by state courts to 17 years in prison for the alleged theft of a tractor, a sentence seen by local NGOs as disproportionate, discriminatory and politically motivated. An appeal was pending at the end of the year.

■ In June, the Indigenous leader Ortiz Lopes was shot dead in his house in Coronel Sapucaia. As the gunman opened fire, he reportedly told Ortiz Lopes that he had been sent by the farmers to settle a score. An active defender of Guarani-Kaiowá land rights, Ortiz Lopes had previously received death threats.

In August, the federal government announced its decision to declare 11,009 hectares in the region of Aracruz, Espírito Santo State, Indigenous land. The ruling followed a long-running dispute between the Tupinikim and Guarani Peoples and a paper pulping company.

Impunity

Violators of human rights enjoyed impunity as a result of failures at every stage of the criminal justice system, except in cases with international ramifications.

■ The authorities took steps to investigate, prosecute and convict those responsible for the murder in February 2005 of the US missionary Sister Dorothy Stang. In May, Vitalmiro Bastos de Moura, a farmer accused of ordering the killing, was sentenced to 30 years in prison. In October, Rayfran das Neves Sales, one of the gunmen involved, was sentenced to 27 years' imprisonment, but the conviction was subsequently overturned on appeal.

The prosecution remains atypical in a state in which impunity is the norm for land-related violence. According to the Pastoral Land

Commission, of the 814 people murdered between 1971 and 2006 in Pará State, 568 cases remain unsolved. Ninety-two criminal cases resulted in just one imprisonment.

■ During the wave of violence initiated in May 2006 by criminal gangs in São Paulo State police killed more than a hundred criminal suspects; in a further 87 cases there were indications that death squads with links to the police may have been involved. According to the state Public Prosecutor, by the end of 2007 no one had been prosecuted.

Human rights defenders

The federal government's human rights defenders programme established a national coordination body. However, lack of resources and coordination continued to hamper implementation of the national human rights defenders plan.

Defenders continued to be threatened and intimidated.

■ Indigenous leader Marcos Ludison de Araújo (Marcos Xucuru) received death threats in July. Because of a long history of intimidation by the federal police, who are constitutionally responsible for providing protection, Marcos Xucuru requested protection by trusted members of the military police instead – a measure allowed for under the rules of the defenders programme. However, he remained at risk for several months while negotiations between the state and federal governments took place.

■ NGO worker Marcia Honorato, who repeatedly denounced death squad activity in the Baixada Fluminese, an extremely violent region on the outskirts of Rio de Janeiro, received a series of death threats, including in one case having a gun pointed at her head.

Amnesty International visit/reports

🚌 Amnesty International delegates visited Brazil in May and June.

📓 Brazil: 'From burning buses to *caveirões*' – the search for human security (AMR 19/010/2007)

📓 Brazil: Submission to the UN Universal Periodic Review – First session of the UPR Working Group, 7-11 April 2008 (AMR 19/023/2007)

BULGARIA

REPUBLIC OF BULGARIA

Head of state:	Georgi Parvanov
Head of government:	Sergey Stanishev
Death penalty:	abolitionist for all crimes
Population:	7.6 million
Life expectancy:	72.7 years
Under-5 mortality (m/f):	16/14 per 1,000
Adult literacy:	98.2 per cent

Discrimination against minorities, particularly Roma, continued against a general backdrop of suspicion towards refugees, asylum-seekers and migrants. People with mental disabilities faced harsh living conditions and inappropriate care and treatment. Investigations into cases of alleged unlawful use of firearms and ill-treatment by law enforcement officials were said to be inadequate.

Background

On 1 January Bulgaria became a member state of the European Union (EU). In its progress report in June, the European Commission urged Bulgaria to adopt tougher measures to fight and investigate corruption and to reform its justice system. The Bulgarian authorities were also instructed to implement a strategy to fight organized crime.

Discrimination

The National Plan for Protection against Discrimination (NPAD) was approved by the government in January, making provision for all areas of discrimination covered by Bulgarian law, including sexual orientation. Despite such initiatives, hate speech and intolerance continued. A leader of the far-right Attack (*Ataka*) party reportedly placed an anti-Turkish poster in the parliament building in the run-up to the election to the European Parliament in May, and party members continued to make declarations against minorities.

Roma minority

Roma encountered obstacles in accessing housing, employment, professional qualifications and education. Between 65 and 70 per cent of Bulgaria's Roma labour force were unemployed, according to a report by a Bulgarian NGO. Some 18 per cent of Roma were illiterate and another 65 per cent had never completed high school, the report found. UNICEF reported that around 50 per cent of Romani homes were not connected to running water and that 20 per cent of Romani children had never been to school.

In September the Committee of Ministers of the Council of Europe confirmed the finding of the European Committee on Social Rights (ECSR) that Bulgaria was in violation of the European Social Charter for its systematic denial of the right to adequate housing with regard to Roma. In response, Bulgaria announced new legislation in support of a variety of measures, including the construction of new social housing.

■ In July, the European Court of Human Rights delivered its judgment in the 1996 racial killing of Angel Dimitrov Iliev, a Romani man, by a group of six teenagers in the town of Shumen. The Court noted that the authorities recognized the heinous nature of the crime yet failed to conduct a prompt and effective investigation into the incident. Charges against four of the attackers were dropped, while the remaining two defendants were not brought to court. The Court judged "completely unacceptable" the authorities' failure to bring the perpetrators to justice, even though they were aware of the racist motives of the attack from the beginning.

In October, the NGO European Roma Rights Centre (ERRC) filed a collective complaint with the ECSR accusing the Bulgarian government of failing to eliminate the disparity regarding health insurance and access to medical assistance between Roma and other vulnerable groups and the majority population. It also accused the government of tolerating policies and practices which undermined the health of Roma and other minorities.

Macedonian minority

In September, the European Commission called on the Bulgarian government to respect the decisions by the European Court of Human Rights that Bulgaria should allow the registration of the OMO Ilinden PIRIN party, which represents the Macedonian minority in Bulgaria. Both the Supreme Court and the Sofia City Court had denied the party's application for registration.

Refugees and asylum-seekers

Asylum-seekers, refugees and migrants continued to be detained for months and even years awaiting expulsion. According to Bulgarian NGOs, detentions of asylum-seekers, refugees and migrants became routine practice, contravening legislation that such a measure should be used only as a last resort.

According to a report in the newspaper *Kapital* in June, at least 36 people had been held for more than six months at the Special Centre for Temporary Accommodation of Foreigners in Busmantsi, near the capital Sofia. They were allegedly not informed why they were being held, and were not brought promptly before a judicial or other authority.

■ Annadurdy Khadzhiev, exiled leader of an opposition group in Turkmenistan, and the husband of Turkmen human rights defender Tadzhigul Begmedova, was held in detention in Bulgaria in February, after Turkmenistan requested his extradition to try him on embezzlement charges. Both Annadurdy Khadzhiev and his wife were granted "humanitarian status" which allowed them to remain in the country. In April, Varna district court ruled against his extradition but following protests by the Prosecutor's office an appeal hearing was heard in May. The appeal court upheld the initial decision and Annadurdy Khadzhiev was finally released.

Police and security forces

The NGO Bulgarian Helsinki Committee (BHC) noted that the use of firearms by law enforcement officers continued to violate international standards and that investigations into their use were not prompt, thorough and impartial. The BHC also reported several cases of ill-treatment by police officers, in particular towards Roma.

In October the Committee of Ministers of the Council of Europe assessed Bulgaria's implementation of judgments by the European Court of Human Rights regarding ill-treatment by police. The Committee found that professional training for members of the police was still inadequate, and issues of detention and guarantees for the independence of investigations had yet to be properly addressed.

Mental health care

Bulgaria signed the UN Convention on the Rights of Persons with Disabilities in September.
■ In August, the Mental Disability Advocacy Centre filed a complaint with the European Court of Human Rights regarding the inadequate investigation into the death of an elderly woman in February 2004 after she

was placed in a social care institution near Sofia. While in the care of the institution, she allegedly suffered broken bones, freezing temperatures, poor hygiene and a lack of nutritious food or general health care. Although administrative inquiries in 2005 into her treatment and the conditions at the institution uncovered serious legal and procedural violations, law enforcement authorities failed to carry out adequate investigations and no one was held accountable.

Amnesty International reports

🗐 Europe and Central Asia: Summary of Amnesty International's concerns in the region: January-June 2007 (EUR 01/010/2007)
🗐 Bulgaria: Torture/legal concern: Annadurdy Khadzhiev (EUR 15/001/2007)
🗐 Bulgaria: Further information on torture/legal concern: Annadurdy Khadzhiev (EUR 15/002/2007)

BURUNDI

REPUBLIC OF BURUNDI

Head of state:	Pierre Nkurunziza
Death penalty:	retentionist
Population:	8.1 million
Life expectancy:	48.5 years
Under-5 mortality (m/f):	185/162 per 1,000
Adult literacy:	59.3 per cent

Political tensions impeded the implementation of human rights protection measures by the government. Peace negotiations between the government and the last remaining armed opposition group stalled. The administration of justice remained poor, and people in detention suffered deplorable conditions. Levels of arbitrary arrests and detentions were high, and torture and ill-treatment were commonplace. Sexual violence against women and girls, notably rape, persisted. The government made slow progress in establishing mechanisms for the investigation and prosecution of serious crimes committed during the 12-year conflict that ended in 2005.

Background

Opposition parties boycotted the National Assembly in 2007 in protest against their under-representation within the government. As a result the National Assembly failed to enact several important pieces of legislation, including a proposed new Criminal Code that would have criminalized acts of torture and other cruel, inhuman or degrading treatment, including violence against women and children, and would have abolished the death penalty.

A ministerial reshuffle on 13 July exacerbated tension between the government and opposition parties. The impasse was only broken on 14 November following another ministerial reorganization which increased the representation of opposition parties in government.

The terms of the September 2006 Comprehensive Ceasefire Agreement between the government and the last remaining armed opposition group, the National Liberation Forces (Forces Nationales de Libération, FNL), were not fully implemented. On 19 February 2007, the Joint Verification Monitoring Mechanism – a platform for both sides to discuss the implementation of the peace process – began its work. The FNL delegation pulled out of the peace monitoring team in July, blaming threats to their security. Negotiations were still at a stalemate at the end of the year. Violent clashes between two factions of the FNL were reported near the capital, Bujumbura, during September and October.

The international community expressed concern that political instability threatened the ongoing peace process and the functioning of national institutions.

International financial institutions also urged the government to address corruption.

Arbitrary arrest and detention

Legal limits on the length of time individuals could be detained without charge were regularly breached by the authorities. Arbitrary arrests and detentions by the intelligence services, police and army were reported throughout 2007 – 112 cases of arbitrary detention were recorded in January alone. Many of those arbitrarily arrested were FNL suspects. In addition, the security forces were involved in extrajudicial executions of civilians.

■ On 29 June, in the commune of Buhinyuza (province of Muyinga), a married man and father of two children was reportedly executed by members of the Burundian army. He was sitting and drinking beer with his neighbours close to his house, when several soldiers arrived. The soldiers, who were patrolling the area, demanded that the man and his neighbours lie on the ground. The man panicked and tried to flee. One of the soldiers killed him immediately. No investigation into the killing was reported.

Torture and other ill-treatment

Torture and other ill-treatment were widespread throughout the country. Cases of torture and ill-treatment by the Burundian National Police, the National Defence Force and the Intelligence Services were regularly reported by local human rights organizations, including ACAT Burundi (Action des Chrétiens pour l'Abolition de la Torture).

■ On 28 February the police chief of Bururi town and another police officer reportedly tortured a man to make him confess to an offence he had not committed. They stripped him naked, beat him and threatened to kill him.

■ An 18-year-old man accused of stealing a bicycle was reportedly tortured on 26 July in police custody in the town of Gitega. His arms were tied behind his back and police officers allegedly beat him with batons and then burned him. Human rights monitors reported scars on his arms and neck.

■ A man from Nyanza-Lac, Makamba, was arrested on 18 January. He was severely beaten in custody by four policemen, including the police chief. He was fined and released from detention the same day. No investigation was carried out and the perpetrators were not brought to justice. He suffered from pain in his ears, his right eye and his feet following the attack.

In February, the UN Committee against Torture recommended that the government should address the climate of impunity, strengthen the capacity of the judiciary and ensure its independence, and establish effective mechanisms to monitor all places of detention.

Human rights abuses by an armed group

In Bujumbura Rural, Cibitoke and Bubanza, FNL fighters subjected civilians to repeated acts of violence. They stole, extorted money, kidnapped people for ransom and raped women and girls. Human rights monitors alleged that FNL fighters also recruited child soldiers.

■ On 3 August, FNL fighters were reported to have entered the home of a man they accused of witchcraft in Kabezi Commune, Bujumbura Rural. They reportedly beat him to death with batons.

■ In January, FNL fighters took five members of one

family hostage, including three children, in Kanyosha, Bujumbura Rural. They demanded as ransom the return of a grenade which the head of household had found and taken to the local police station.

Violence against women

Sexual violence, including rape, remained prevalent throughout Burundi. Military and police personnel were responsible for a number of rapes. The majority of reported rape victims were girls under the age of 18. Perpetrators regularly escaped prosecution and punishment by the state. The rate of successful prosecutions for sexual crimes remained extremely low. Most victims remained silent – often out of fear of social stigmatization. Victims and their families resorted to traditional and informal dispute resolution systems, often negotiating and agreeing to payment from the perpetrator or the family of the perpetrator, as recompense.

■ On 19 January, an elderly woman was raped by an unidentified man dressed in military uniform. The rapist ordered her husband to help him by carrying food supplies. The husband refused and his wife did it instead. The unidentified soldier raped her by the side of the road. The victim received medical treatment the following day but did not report the crime to the authorities.

■ On 17 November, a 12-year-old girl was raped by her neighbour. The perpetrator was married and a father of three. The perpetrator was arrested and charged but released two days later. Local human rights defenders appealed to the police chief who ordered his re-arrest, but the man was still at large at the end of 2007.

Justice system

Burundi's law enforcement and justice system remained weak and in need of urgent reform. The judicial system lacked human, financial and material resources. Law enforcement and judicial staff were poorly trained. Corruption remained a problem. Low levels of confidence in the justice system led to numerous incidents of mob justice, including killings and lynching.

■ On 21 February, six policemen arrived in Nkenga Busoro, Kanyosha. They carried guns but only two wore uniform. After a recent spate of armed robberies, the local population thought the men were robbers and attacked them. Four of the policemen escaped, but two were captured and beaten to death.

■ On 24 November, a policeman was killed by the local population of Nyamurenza, Ngozi. He had reportedly robbed a local trader and assaulted the trader's cousin. He also shot and injured a local man who intervened in the attack.

The government reportedly influenced judicial decisions.

■ The perpetrators of the Muyinga massacre, in which at least 16 people with suspected links to the FNL were alleged to have been extrajudicially executed by military personnel in July and August 2006, remained at large. A judicial commission reported to the prosecutor in the case. Both military and civilian personnel were suspected of involvement in the killings, including high-ranking officials. However, the prosecutor stated that no civilians would be prosecuted and passed the file to the military prosecutor's office.

Detention conditions

Prisons were overcrowded and conditions insanitary. Detainees were not provided with adequate access to medical care and attention, especially those suffering from HIV/AIDs. Prison registers were poorly maintained.

By the end of November, the prison population numbered more than 8,000 people, most of whom were not adequately fed. Between 65 and 70 per cent had not been tried, according to human rights organizations and the prison authorities. More than 400 children aged between 13 and 18 were held, often together with adults.

■ Mpimba Prison in Bujumbura was one of the most overcrowded prisons in Burundi. In November, it held 2,289 detainees, although its capacity was only 800. Of these, 145 were minors who were held in the same cells as adults. Only 19 per cent of these minors had been tried and convicted. Medical care from a trained professional was not available in the prison.

Detainees were also held in overcrowded police detention facilities. A total of 76 people were reportedly held in a cell measuring 13m^2 in police detention facilities in Kayanza. In June, 58 detainees were being held in a cell at Kirundo police station whose capacity was 40. Children also shared cells with adults: one minor was incarcerated with 71 men.

■ During a visit to the Public Prosecutor's office in Kirundo in June, a local human rights organization reported that the toilets in the cells had overflowed.

B

Human waste covered the floor of the cells and the corridor outside, preventing human rights monitors from entering.

Transitional justice

Genocide, war crimes and crimes against humanity committed during the conflict remained unpunished. The proposed establishment of a Truth and Reconciliation Commission and a Special Tribunal to investigate and prosecute such crimes had not been implemented. Initially, both sides could not agree on the issues of amnesty, the links between the Truth and Reconciliation Commission and the Special Tribunal, and the independence of the prosecuting body.

The President confirmed in May that no amnesty would be granted for war crimes, genocide, crimes against humanity and other serious human rights violations. Both sides agreed to undertake national consultations on the establishment of the two mechanisms, and on the establishment of a steering committee, comprised of members of the Burundian government, the UN and civil society. The government signed an official agreement on 2 November marking the start of a six-month consultation period. The consultations were praised as an essential first step in establishing transitional justice in Burundi.

Returning refugees

A total of 38,087 Burundian refugees were repatriated between January and November. Between April 2002 and November 2007, UNHCR repatriated more than 374,700 Burundians from neighbouring Tanzania. Approximately 9,000 Burundian families were expelled from Tanzania.

Freedom of expression

Journalists were repeatedly threatened with arrest for carrying out legitimate professional activities.

■ Serge Nibizi, an editor for Radio Publique Africaine, and Domitile Kiramvu, a journalist for the same radio station, who had been arrested in November 2006 and charged with threatening state security, were acquitted on 4 January 2007. The Public Prosecutor lodged an appeal against the acquittal, and the two journalists were summoned three times in 2007. On each occasion, a new date for court attendance was set.

Incidents of harassment and intimidation of journalists, including physical attacks, were also recorded.

■ Gérard Nzohabona was reportedly attacked by eight policemen in October after intervening in the seemingly wrongful arrest of two girls. The officers reportedly called him a "journalist dog" as they beat him.

Amnesty International visit/reports

Amnesty International delegates visited Burundi in October.

Burundi: No protection from rape in war and peace (AFR 16/002/2007)

Burundi: No protection from rape in war and peace (AFR 16/004/2007)

Burundi: Further information on prisoner of conscience / Fear of torture or ill-treatment / harassment / intimidation: Gabriel Rufyiri (AFR 16/001/2007)

CAMBODIA

KINGDOM OF CAMBODIA

Head of state:	King Norodom Sihamoni
Head of government:	Hun Sen
Death penalty:	abolitionist for all crimes
Population:	14.6 million
Life expectancy:	58 years
Under-5 mortality (m/f):	130/120 per 1,000
Adult literacy:	73.6 per cent

Some 150,000 Cambodians were known to live at risk of losing their homes as land disputes and land grabbing proliferated. Forced evictions of poor communities continued and victims had limited access to legal redress. The ruling Cambodian People's Party (CPP) continued to consolidate power and maintained a grip over the judiciary, where deep-seated shortcomings remained largely unchanged. After considerable delays, the Extraordinary Chambers in the Courts of Cambodia (ECCC, Khmer Rouge Tribunal) became operational; five arrests and the first hearing took place.

Background

The CPP won the commune chief seat in over 98 per cent of communes in local elections in April. The mainly peaceful poll gave the party more than 70 per cent of the total seats and the main opposition Sam Rainsy Party 23.4 per cent. The government's junior coalition partner, FUNCINPEC, plummeted to 2.4 per cent, following an internal split and the sentencing to 18 months' imprisonment for "breach of trust" of exiled former party leader Prince Norodom Ranariddh.

Justice system

On 5 February the Code of Ethics for Judges was adopted by the Supreme Council of Magistracy. The new Criminal Procedure Code was promulgated in August, around a month after the new Civil Procedure Code entered into force. Neither the anti-corruption law, a high priority of the international donor community, nor the new Penal Code had been passed by the end of the year.

The President of the Appeal Court was removed after an investigation by the Ministry of Interior found that she had accepted US$30,000 in exchange for the release of two men convicted of trafficking offences. She was replaced by You Bunleng, the Co-Investigating judge on the ECCC. The process of this appointment was described as unconstitutional by the UN Special Representative of the Secretary-General for human rights in Cambodia and the Special Rapporteur on the independence of judges and lawyers.

The legal system remained biased against the poor and marginalized. Reports of breaches of the presumption of innocence, lack of independence, corruption and serious failures to apply the law emerged from trials. Court monitoring by the Center for Social Development showed that coerced confessions, mostly through beatings or threats, continued to be widespread.

■ Born Samnang and Sok Sam Oeun, convicted in 2004 of murdering union leader Chea Vichea after a grossly unfair trial, had their 20-year prison sentences upheld on appeal in April despite the prosecutor calling for a fresh investigation.

The ECCC became operational in June 2007 when the internal rules were adopted, ending a disagreement between national and international judges, and paving the way for investigations and prosecutions. By the end of the year, five suspects were in ECCC detention, including former head of state Khieu Samphan and so-called Brother Number Two, Nuon Chea. All five were charged with crimes against humanity, and three of them also with war crimes. A first hearing was held by the Pre-Trial Chamber in November and trials were expected to begin in 2008.

Killings

On 24 February Hy Vuthy, a factory president of the Free Trade Union of Workers (FTU), was shot dead, the third FTU official to be killed since 2004.

Forced evictions

During 2007, thousands were forcibly evicted and lost land, homes and livelihoods following development projects and land grabbing. The authorities did not uphold their obligations under international law to guarantee the right to adequate housing and protect the population against forced evictions.

Some 150,000 Cambodians were estimated to live at risk of forced eviction, including over 20,000 residents around Phnom Penh's Boeung Kak lake. In February, the Boeung Kak residents were informed that the land had been leased out for 99 years by the municipality to a developer without any prior consultation with those affected.

Several evicted communities in Phnom Penh were resettled in areas that lacked basic infrastructure, water, electricity and sanitation. The distance from their former homes and to the city meant that many lost access to their livelihoods.

■ In a pre-dawn operation on 2 November, the Chong Chruoy village outside Phnom Penh was demolished by security forces. The 132 families, mostly sustained by fishing, were forcibly resettled some 25 kms inland.

Human rights defenders

Hundreds of people staged protests attempting to protect their land and homes. Several such peaceful gatherings were broken up by law enforcement agencies, including in Phnom Penh, Koh Kong, Ratanakiri and Banteay Meanchey.

A number of land activists were jailed as a result of their activities, including on suspicion of having destroyed private property on disputed land which they believed they legally owned. Others, including legal aid lawyers, were charged with incitement for their activities in defence of human rights.

■ On 20 April, security forces forcibly evicted over 100 families from Mittapheap 4 village in Sihanoukville, setting ablaze 80 homes and demolishing another 20. Thirteen men were arrested and tried in July for their role in the violence. Nine were found guilty and sentenced to short prison terms despite the prosecution's failure to produce any evidence linking them to the crimes of which they were accused.

C

Pending the hearing of a prosecution appeal, the group were not released after completing their terms and remained held at the end of the year in what constituted arbitrary detention.

■ On 21 June a criminal complaint was lodged against a group of 10 human rights lawyers from two prominent legal aid NGOs working with a group of indigenous Jarai to protect their collectively owned land. The complainant allegedly acquired 450 hectares of the Jarai land in breach of the 2001 Land Law and against the will of the community. By year's end, the lawyers were under investigation and the land dispute remained unresolved.

In June the international NGO Global Witness released a report which alleged the involvement of high-ranking individuals within the government and armed forces in serious crimes related to illegal logging. The report was suppressed by the authorities and media outlets were reportedly warned against reporting the story. Threats of violence were made against Global Witness staff and two journalists who had covered the story fled the country.

Refugees and asylum-seekers

Buddhist monk Tim Sakhorn disappeared in June after being defrocked by the Supreme Buddhist Patriarch for harming the relationship between Cambodia and Viet Nam. Tim Sakhorn, an abbot in Takeo province and a member of the Khmer Krom minority in southern Viet Nam, had lived in Cambodia since 1979 with dual citizenship. He had provided food and shelter to Khmer Krom Buddhist monks fleeing from Viet Nam. He was believed to have been abducted and deported by Cambodian authorities in breach of Cambodia's obligations under international law. (See Viet Nam entry.)

Other individuals of Vietnamese nationality were forcibly returned from Cambodia, including Le Tri Tue, a pro-democracy activist seeking asylum. He disappeared in May. Four months later it emerged that he was detained in Viet Nam, facing criminal charges.

Over 200 Vietnamese ethnic minority Montagnards crossed the border from the Vietnamese Central highlands into north-eastern Cambodia to seek asylum. Some hid in the jungle before seeking asylum under UNHCR's mandate, fearful of arrest and being forcibly returned home where they are at risk of persecution.

Amnesty International reports

- Extraordinary Chambers in the Courts of Cambodia: Recommendations to address victims and witnesses issues in the Internal Rules effectively (ASA 23/001/2007)
- Cambodia: Time to restore justice in the Chea Vichea case (ASA 23/004/2007)
- Cambodia: Forced evictions must end (ASA 23/008/2007)

CAMEROON

REPUBLIC OF CAMEROON

Head of state:	Paul Biya
Head of government:	Ephraim Inoni
Death penalty:	retentionist
Population:	16.9 million
Life expectancy:	49.8 years
Under-5 mortality (m/f):	164/148 per 1,000
Adult literacy:	67.9 per cent

Eleven men accused of "practising homosexuality" were detained. Several dozen members of the Southern Cameroons National Council (SCNC) were awaiting trial for secessionist activities. One journalist was detained and another charged and convicted for their professional activities. At least 17 prisoners were killed during a mutiny. Over 26,000 people from the Central African Republic (CAR) were living in refugee camps in eastern Cameroon. Students continued to be targeted by security officers.

Background

Several Cameroonian soldiers based in the Bakassi Peninsula were killed during an armed attack in November. Sources in Cameroon claimed that the attackers were Nigerian soldiers, while the authorities said that the attack was carried out by insurgents. Following the attack, members of the Nigerian Senate launched a petition demanding the return of Bakassi to Nigerian sovereignty.

The ruling Cameroon People's Democratic Rally (Rassemblement démocratique du people camerounais) won the July legislative and local elections, amid claims by opposition political parties that the elections were rigged.

The trial of more than 20 former senior managers of state companies continued during 2007. They included former directors of the Real-Estate Company of Cameroon (Société immobilière du Cameroun, SIC) and of the Special Fund for Communal Equipment and Intervention (Fonds spécial d'équipement et d'intervention communale, FEICOM). Emmanuel Gérard Ondo Ndong, the director general of FEICOM, Gilles-Roger Belinga, director general of SIC, and 20 of their former colleagues were found guilty of corruption and sentenced to between 10 and 50 years' imprisonment. The trial of several former managers of the Autonomous Port of Douala was continuing at the end of the year.

One person was killed and 22 others abducted in June by bandits in the Extreme-North province. A further 10 refugees from the CAR and six Cameroonians were also abducted from Adamaoua province and reportedly taken to the CAR. The abductors reportedly demanded ransoms but it was not clear whether the ransoms had been paid by the end of the year.

Southern Cameroons National Council

About 40 members of the SCNC were arrested on 20 January as the organization's National Vice-Chairman, Nfor Ngala Nfor, was about to address a press conference in Bamenda. Several SCNC members, including Nfor Ngala Nfor, were reportedly injured during the arrests. Although most of those arrested were released within a few hours, Nfor Ngala Nfor and at least 12 others were detained without trial for nearly two months. At the end of the year, nearly 40 members of the SCNC were awaiting trial on charges ranging from wearing SCNC T-shirts to agitating for secession. In December, the case against those arrested on 20 January was dismissed by the court after the prosecution repeatedly failed to produce witnesses.

Discrimination – detentions for 'practising homosexuality'

Six men accused of "practising homosexuality" were arrested in July in Douala. In August, a further two men were arrested in Douala and three others in Yaoundé for the same offence. All 11 men continued to be held awaiting trial at the end of the year.

One man who had reportedly been detained for more than two years without trial on charges of "practising homosexuality" was released in February. The High Court in Yaoundé ruled that the state had failed to produce any evidence relevant to the charge.

Freedom of expression

■ Journalist and human rights defender Philip Njaru was detained for several hours in January by the police in Kumba. Before his release, the police told him that they had arrested him for publishing articles accusing the police of extortion and arbitrary arrests.

In March, the UN Human Rights Committee established that the Cameroonian government had in previous years failed to protect Philip Njaru from ill-treatment and intimidation by the security forces on the basis of his human rights activities. The Committee urged the government to take action against the perpetrators and grant him effective reparation.

■ A court in Kumbo, Northwest province, found journalist Wirkwa Eric Tayu guilty of criminal defamation and sentenced him in August in absentia to a one-year prison term and a fine for publishing articles accusing local government officials of corruption. An appeal against the conviction and sentence was pending at the end of the year.

■ In November, four members of the Cameroonian Public Sector Trade-Union (Centrale Syndicale du Secteur Public) – including the president, Jean Marc Bikoko and the vice-president, Brigitte Tamo – were arrested by gendarmes during a peaceful demonstration demanding a rise in civil servant pay. They were released after 10 hours in custody at the gendarmerie station in Enya, Yaoundé. Brigitte Tamo and two others were beaten by the gendarmes. The demonstration took place in front of parliament in Yaoundé where parliamentarians were discussing the 2008 budget. The authorities are not known to have taken any action against the gendarmes responsible for the ill-treatment.

■ Four motorbike taxi riders, popularly known as *bensikin*, were shot dead by riot police in Bamenda on 15 October. The shootings happened during strike action against police harassment which started on 14 October. The authorities are not known to have taken action against the police.

Police and security forces
Prisons

In July, at least 17 prisoners were killed by members of the security forces during an operation to recapture prisoners who had escaped from Yoko prison. Prisoners had seized weapons and ammunition during their escape.

Following a strike by prison guards in protest at low pay and poor working conditions, which started in December 2006, 125 guards were suspended in January 2007. They and many others had been detained for several weeks.

Students killed

■ On 17 November, 17-year-old Charles Mvogo and 15-year-old Shimpe Poungou Zok were shot dead by a security officer at Abong-Mbang during a demonstration against prolonged lack of electricity power at their school.

■ On 9 November, Ngome Nkwele Herbert was killed during a demonstration against the detention of his colleagues by the Kumba police on 7 November following a demonstration over lack of electricity power at their school in Kumba.

■ No progress was made in bringing to justice those responsible for the killing of Ivo Obia Ngemba and Moma Bennet who were shot by police during a peaceful protest on the campus of the University of Buea in November 2006.

CANADA

CANADA

Head of state:	Queen Elizabeth II, represented by Governor General Michaëlle Jean
Head of government:	Stephen Harper
Death penalty:	abolitionist for all crimes
Population:	32.9 million
Life expectancy:	80.3 years
Under-5 mortality (m/f):	6/6 per 1,000

Deaths following the use of electro-shock weapons by police were reported. Indigenous Peoples continued to face discrimination. There were continuing concerns about anti-terrorism legislation and the treatment of refugees and asylum-seekers.

Discrimination – Indigenous rights

The report of the public inquiry into the 1995 police killing of Dudley George released in May provided a blueprint for strengthened protection of the rights of Indigenous Peoples. Disputes over land and resource rights continued, as did the authorities' failure to

ensure they were resolved promptly and impartially. This was exemplified by the situation at Grassy Narrows in north-western Ontario, and the plight of the Lubicon Cree in northern Alberta.

The government refused to address the disparity in funding for Indigenous child protection agencies. Canada voted against adoption of the UN Declaration on the Rights of Indigenous Peoples in September and subsequently argued that the Declaration did not apply in Canada.

'War on terror'

Maher Arar, a Canadian national who was the victim of an illegal transfer (rendition) from the USA to Syria in 2002, received an official government apology and compensation from the government in January. However, many of the recommendations from the public inquiry into his case were not implemented. An inquiry into the role of Canadian officials in the cases of three Canadian citizens – Abdullah Almalki, Ahmed El-Maati and Muayyed Nureddin – detained and tortured abroad was marred by excessive secrecy.

In February the Supreme Court of Canada ruled that the immigration security certificate system, used by the federal government to detain and deport people born in other countries and suspected of terrorist offences, violated the Charter of Rights because a substantial amount of evidence was withheld, preventing individuals from mounting an effective defence. Draft legislation, which proposed creating a Special Advocate, failed to address this concern.

In February, Parliament voted to allow controversial provisions in the Anti-Terrorism Act to expire. In October the government introduced a bill which would reinstate provisions allowing preventive arrest and investigatory hearings. The bill was pending before Parliament at the end of the year.

In November, the Federal Court rejected an application by the government to dismiss a court action launched by Amnesty International and the British Columbia Civil Liberties Association challenging the practice of transferring battlefield detainees in Afghanistan into Afghan custody, where they faced a serious risk of torture.

The Canadian government refused to intervene on behalf of Omar Khadr, detained by US forces in Afghanistan when he was 15 years old and held for more than five years at Guantánamo Bay.

Violence against women

The authorities failed to institute a national strategy to address violence and discrimination against Indigenous women or to take steps to implement long-standing recommendations regarding women in federal prisons. Restrictions on funding to women's organizations involved in advocacy continued, resulting in closures of some groups and cutbacks.

Refugees and asylum-seekers

In November, the Federal Court ruled that the Safe Third Country agreement between Canada and the USA violated the Charter of Rights and international law. The government appealed against the decision. At the end of the year legislation was before Parliament which would require the government to implement the refugee appeal provisions in the 2001 Immigration and Refugee Protection Act.

Police and security forces

At least four people died following the use of tasers (electro-shock weapons) by police. The death of Polish national Robert Dziekanski at Vancouver International Airport after being tasered at least twice by police in October led to numerous reviews and a provincial public inquiry.

Death penalty

In October, Canada reversed a long-standing policy, stating that clemency would no longer be sought for Canadian citizens sentenced to death in democratic countries that adhere to the rule of law.

Amnesty International reports

- Canada: Human rights for all – No exceptions (AMR 20/001/2007)
- Canada: Inappropriate and excessive use of tasers (AMR 20/002/2007)
- Afghanistan: NATO countries at risk of complicity in torture (ASA 11/015/2007)
- Canada: Amnesty International reiterates call to suspend police use of tasers following airport death (AMR 20/004/2007)

CENTRAL AFRICAN REPUBLIC

CENTRAL AFRICAN REPUBLIC

Head of state:	François Bozizé
Head of government:	Elie Doté
Death penalty:	abolitionist in practice
Population:	4.2 million
Life expectancy:	43.7 years
Under-5 mortality (m/f):	183/151 per 1,000
Adult literacy:	48.6 per cent

Armed groups, government soldiers and criminal gangs killed civilians, destroyed and burned property and houses, pillaged, abducted and raped with impunity. Tens of thousands of civilians from northern Central African Republic (CAR) continued to flee from violence and human rights abuses into southern Chad, Cameroon and other neighbouring countries.

Background

Throughout the year, the CAR government was under pressure to seek a peaceful settlement to the armed conflict between government forces and armed groups that started in mid-2005. In February, with the mediation of Libya, the government signed a peace agreement with the Central African People's Democratic front (Front démocratique pour le peuple centrafricain, FDPC), and on 1 April the government signed an agreement with the Union of Democratic Forces for Unity (Union des forces démocratiques pour le rassemblement, UFDR). Both agreements had not been fully implemented by the end of 2007, although in June the government released 18 alleged members of the UFDR. In December, President Bozizé appointed a National Dialogue consultative body.

Government forces, particularly the Presidential Guard, were accused of killing scores of civilians, while armed groups abducted and killed those who refused to support them.

Armed bandits, known as Zaraguinas, some of whom were demobilized soldiers from CAR and neighbouring countries, robbed travellers – killing and wounding some – and abducted adults and children for ransom.

C

The widespread insecurity in the north caused mass displacement of hundreds of thousands of people who had little or no access to humanitarian assistance.

Unlawful killings by government forces

Following attacks by armed groups against government forces and state installations in northern CAR, the Presidential Guard and other security forces carried out punitive attacks against the local population, killing and wounding inhabitants and burning down houses. Suspected members of armed groups were arrested and often summarily executed. Many residents fled into the bush and hid for weeks or months.

■ Yacoub Ahmat Mahmat fled Paoua after government soldiers had destroyed houses, stolen money, beaten residents and abducted three people and killed one in reprisal for an attack by an armed group on 6 January. On 12 February, in the aftermath of the attacks, 15 Zaraguinas stole 15 of Yacoub Ahmat Mahmat's cattle.

■ In March, Raymond Djasrabaye was one of many villagers in Beboura, Paoua, who were wounded or killed by government forces. His father and mother were killed. Raymond Djasrabaye was shot in the arm, developed gangrene and fled to Chad, where his arm was amputated.

Soldiers of the government's Central African Armed Forces (Forces armées centrafricaines, FACA), particularly members of the Presidential Guard, extrajudicially executed people they suspected of belonging to armed opposition groups.

■ On 5 January, FACA soldiers in Kaga Bandoro market publicly executed two men aged 22 and 27. They reportedly paraded the victims' bodies through the streets and took photographs with them. The government is not known to have taken any action against the soldiers or their commander.

Across northern CAR, FACA responded to attacks on government forces by burning houses. At the start of 2007, more than 2,000 homes were reported to have been burned between Kaga Bandoro and Ouandago, displacing more than 10,000 people. Government soldiers looted the inhabitants' property and burned what they could not carry away.

■ On 27 and 28 January, members of the Presidential Guard based in Bossangoa were reported to have burned down nine villages along the Bozoum – Paoua – Pende axis, to have summarily executed at least seven

unarmed civilians, and to have tied a man to a granary and burned him alive. Members of the Presidential Guard under the same commander were reported to have shot dead two Roman Catholic Church catechists in Bozoy III village. At least another 10 people were reportedly killed by members of the Presidential Guard along the Paoua – Bozoum axis.

Unlawful killings by armed groups

Human rights and humanitarian organizations, as well as refugees in southern Chad, reported that in northern CAR armed groups attacked unarmed civilians. The victims were accused of collaborating with or supporting the government.

■ Members of an armed group beat Djibrilla Adamou as he was walking home from Letele in Bocaranga on 19 March, because he failed to give them money. He was so severely injured that the armed group reportedly left him for dead.

■ On 11 June a female French volunteer working with Médecins sans frontières (MSF) was shot dead by a member of an armed group, the Popular Army for the Restoration of Democracy (Armée populaire pour la restauration de la démocratie, APRD). The APRD was subsequently reported to have declared that the killing was a mistake, carried out by one of its combatants, who was said to have been executed by the APRD without a fair trial.

In January more than 50 alleged Zaraguinas in military camouflage, their faces covered in turbans, were reported to have attacked the residents of Voudou village along the Bozoum-Bossangoa axis, killing four civilians.

Abductions of children and adults

Scores of children and adults were abducted by armed bandits, especially in north-western CAR. Virtually no action was taken by the government to prevent the abductions or arrest the perpetrators.

Most of the victims appeared to be members of the Mbororo ethnic group, targeted because they are pastoralists who can sell their cattle to pay ransoms that peasant farmers could not afford.

Some victims were abducted in revenge for anti-Zaraguina activities by members of their families. The wife of a Mbororo community leader, Souley Garga, was abducted in late 2006 and not released until April 2007 when Souley Garga reportedly paid a ransom of FCFA4 million (US$8,000). Three men abducted at the same time were among others who continued to be held by Zaraguinas who demanded a ransom of FCFA 9 million.

Most of those abducted were Mbororo children. Some were repeatedly abducted until, with no resources left to pay ransoms, their families fled.

■ Zaraguinas abducted two of Weti Bibello's children in 2005, and took one of them again in late 2006. Members of an armed political group and Zaraguinas stole most of his remaining 150 cattle in early 2007. An armed opposition group killed several members of his family in January. Fearing further attacks, Weti Bibello fled with his family to Chad in April.

■ Zaraguinas abducted Mahmoud Damsi, aged 10, and several other children in Paoua at 4am one morning in February. His father, Ibrahim Damsi, paid FCFA 550,000 for his release after selling many of his cows. Zaraguinas beat him severely when he met them to pay the ransom.

■ Ousmane Bi Yunusa's daughter Fatimatou, aged five, was kidnapped in January and her father paid for her ransom by selling the last cow he owned. Fatimatou was released after one month in captivity.

Representatives of humanitarian organizations were targeted by armed bandits. On 19 May two workers of an Italian humanitarian organization, Cooperazione Internazionale, COOPI, were abducted by Zaraguinas on the road between Bozoum and Bocaranga. They were released on 29 May. Several workers of the UN office in CAR, BONUCA, were briefly abducted and their property stolen by Zaraguinas in September.

Refugees and internally displaced people

Over 200,000 internally displaced people abandoned their homes, food reserves and other property, which were often looted or destroyed by government soldiers, armed groups or armed bandits. The internally displaced had limited access to humanitarian assistance, and many succumbed to exposure and lack of medical care when they tried to survive in the wild.

At the end of the year, there were some 50,000 CAR refugees in southern Chad, over 26,000 in Cameroon, and several thousand in Sudan. The refugees in southern Chad had limited access to healthcare and other humanitarian assistance, and had only meagre supplies of food. CAR refugees in Cameroon had no access to humanitarian assistance

and were largely surviving on assistance provided by the local Cameroonian population and by selling the animals they had been able to flee with.

Freedom of expression

Michel Alkhaly Ngady, a newspaper director and president of the assembly of Central African private press editors, was arrested on 12 March after the High Council of Communication accused him of defamation. He was convicted of defamation by a court and imprisoned for 63 days.

Amnesty International visit/reports

🚗 Amnesty International delegates visited southern Chad and the Central African Republic in May.

📄 Central African Republic: Civilians in peril in the wild north (AFR 19/003/2007)

📄 Central African Republic: War against children in the wild north (AFR 19/006/2007)

C

CHAD

REPUBLIC OF CHAD

Head of state:	Idriss Déby Itno
Head of government:	Nouradine Delwa Kassiré Comakye
	(replaced Pascal Yoadimnadji in February)
Death penalty:	retentionist
Population:	10.3 million
Life expectancy:	50.4 years
Under-5 mortality (m/f):	206/183 per 1,000
Adult literacy:	25.7 per cent

Civilians were killed in inter-ethnic and inter-communal fighting, some of which spilled over from neighbouring Sudan. Armed conflict, including inter-communal clashes, continued in eastern Chad, as peace efforts broke down. The UN Security Council agreed in September to deploy a UN force in eastern Chad. Sexual violence against women and girls remained prevalent and little or no action was taken against perpetrators. Children continued to be abducted for ransom, trafficked and recruited as soldiers. Independent journalists and human rights defenders faced intimidation, harassment and illegal arrest.

Background

Fighting continued between government forces and a myriad of armed opposition groups. Since independence from France in 1960, Chad has been racked by civil strife. Constitutional changes in 2005, which enabled President Idriss Déby Itno to run for election for a third term, re-ignited the conflict. One of the main drivers of the conflict centred on the control of state power and oil revenues. In addition, inter-communal tensions were fuelled by competition over natural resources, such as land and water, and years of impunity for human rights abuses. These tensions exacerbated violence between groups which define themselves as "Africans" and as "Arabs".

In December 2006, the government of Chad reached a peace agreement with one of the main armed opposition groups, the United Front for Democratic Change (Front uni pour le changement démocratique, FUC). Following this agreement, the FUC's members joined the national army and its leader, Mahamat Nour, was appointed as Minister of Defence. In October 2007, desertions of former FUC members to Darfur were reported, and in December Mahamat Nour was dismissed.

On 4 October the government of Chad reached another agreement in Syrte, Libya, with four other armed opposition groups, including the Union of Forces for Democracy and Development (UFDD), the Rally of Democratic Forces (Rassemblement des forces démocratiques, RAFD) and the Chadian National Concord (Concorde nationale tchadienne, CNT). This agreement was not fully implemented, however, because of divergences between the government and armed opposition leaders over its content and exact extent. At the end of November, renewed fighting erupted between some of these armed groups and the Chadian national army.

On 25 September, the UN Security Council unanimously authorized for a period of one year a UN operation (MINURCAT), alongside a European military operation (EUFOR), in eastern Chad and the north-east of the Central African Republic (CAR). This force was intended to facilitate the provision of humanitarian assistance and create favourable conditions for reconstruction and development, so as to create the conditions conducive to a voluntary, secure and sustainable return of refugees and displaced people.

Prime Minister Pascal Yoadimnadji died in February

and was replaced by Nouradine Delwa Kassiré Comakye.

In August, about 20 political parties, some of them from the opposition, signed a political accord with the government to take part in the public affairs of the country and to prolong the term of the National Assembly until 2009.

Unlawful killings by armed groups

Unlawful killings of civilians by armed groups continued in 2007. Inter-ethnic and inter-communal fighting accounted for most civilian casualties. Attacks on civilians by "Arab" Janjawid militia from Sudan supported by their local Chadian allies were reported, as were attacks by "African" groups on their "Arab" neighbours.

■ On 30 March, the villages of Tiero and Marena and 30 neighbouring villages, which were inhabited mainly by members of the Dajo ethnic group, were attacked by armed Chadian men, allegedly belonging to Arab groups, and members of the CNT, an armed group with bases in Sudan. The Chadian government claimed that the Sudanese Janjawid militia had also been involved in this raid. A UNHCR team visiting the area the day after the attack spoke of "apocalyptic" scenes. Between 270 and 400 people were reportedly killed.

In the area of Dar Sila, Arab communities were attacked on several occasions by armed men reportedly from the Dajo community or from Sudanese armed opposition groups present in the refugee camps known as the Toro Boro. The attacks may have been motivated by the perception among the Dajo and other African Sudanese groups that these Chadian Arab communities were allied to Sudanese Arab armed groups.

Violence against women

Sexual violence against women and girls remained prevalent in Chad. In eastern Chad, women continued to face rape and other forms of sexual violence at the hands of militias, armed groups and Chadian government soldiers. Displaced women and girls were particularly vulnerable to attack when they ventured outside their camps to collect firewood or other essentials. In almost all cases, the perpetrators of these abuses, whether they were state or non-state actors, went unpunished.

■ A 14-year-old girl living in the Aradip camp for internally displaced people (IDPs) in the Dar Sila region was caught and raped by several armed men when she left the camp to collect firewood early in the morning of 30 April.

Rape and other forms of sexual violence against women were also reported in other provinces of the country, such as Moyen Chari.

■ A 15-year-old girl and her brother were stopped on their way to a church service by relatives of the gendarmerie commander of Moissala, Moyen Chari. They were taken to the commander's house where the girl was raped six times. Both children were beaten. The perpetrators demanded that they pay CFA100 (less than US$1) for their release, but they had no money and were beaten again before being released. The perpetrators were not arrested or prosecuted.

Violations against children

The armed conflict in eastern Chad and widespread insecurity in other parts of the country exacerbated violations of children's rights.

Recruitment of child soldiers

Children were recruited into the Chadian army, as well as into armed opposition movements and local defence groups, notably in the east. The UN also reported that Sudanese children from refugee camps in eastern Chad had been forcibly recruited by Sudanese armed groups.

■ On 30 March, military trucks went to Habile IDP camp in Dar Sila. Chadian soldiers in combat uniform called on the local leaders to convene the population, in particular young men. They then took a number of people away in the trucks, reportedly saying they had to defend their country. Several children, including Ateb Khaled Ahmad, aged 17, and Yasin Yakob Issak, aged 16, were among those taken away.

According to UNICEF, by the end of November, about 500 child soldiers had been demobilized from the national army.

In February, in a statement to the Paris Principles and Commitments Conference, the Chadian Minister of Foreign Affairs, Ahmad Allam-Mi, said that Chad respected its international obligations with regard to rights of children.

Abductions

Scores of children were abducted and held for ransom by armed bandits commonly known as *coupeurs de routes*.

■ On 25 November, in the village of Gondoyilla, Tandjilé Est, seven people, including five children, were kidnapped for a ransom of CFA1,000,000 (US$2,200). They were held for 11 days by armed bandits.

■ In November, six members of a French NGO, Zoe's

Ark, as well as four Chadians were charged by the Chadian authorities with fraud and abduction after their attempt to fly out 103 children, aged between one and 10 years old, from the airport of Abeche in eastern Chad. Representatives of the NGO claimed that the children were orphans from Darfur. According to a UN investigation, however, the majority of these children, who were from villages near the Sudanese border, had been living with their families with at least one adult they considered to be their parent.

Other reported abuses against children included trafficking in children to work as domestic servants, herders and beggars.

Freedom of expression

Independent journalists and human rights defenders were subject to intimidation, harassment and illegal arrest. The government restricted freedom of speech and of the press, in particular when the authorities were criticized.

One mechanism of control and censorship used by the government was the state of emergency. While its official purpose was to curb the fighting between different ethnic groups in eastern Chad, the government also used it to censor and muzzle the independent news media. In June, the government lifted the state of emergency in seven provinces and the capital. It was reimposed in mid-November for about two weeks in some provinces of eastern Chad.

■ In January, human rights defender Marcel Ngargoto was unlawfully detained by the gendarmerie of his home town of Moissala, 500 km south-east of the capital, for about a month and a half. He was not charged with any offence, but he was told by the gendarmes that he had been detained because he had been critical of the gendarmerie in the area, and particularly of the commandant, whom he alleged had extorted money from local residents.

■ On 31 October, armed men broke into the home of Mikael Didama, director of *Le temps* newspaper. They fired a volley of shots into his car before leaving. Mikael Didama was abroad, but his family was in the house.

Enforced disappearance

The fate of more than 14 army officers and civilians, victims of enforced disappearance between April and August 2006, remained unknown. The men were detained by members of the security forces because they were suspected of involvement in an attack on the capital, N'Djamena, by an armed group in April 2006. Despite persistent and repeated calls from the victims' families and human rights organizations, the authorities refused to disclose their whereabouts.

■ On 30 November, at least seven members of the Tama ethnic group were arrested in the eastern town of Guéréda. The authorities subsequently refused to disclose their whereabouts. Some were members of the FUC and were arrested during or soon after a meeting with President Déby to discuss disarmament and the integration of former FUC members into the army.

Hissène Habré

The case of Hissène Habré, the former Chadian president accused of committing grave human rights violations, progressed slowly. (See Senegal entry.)

Refugees and internally displaced people

According to UNHCR, eastern Chad hosted some 240,000 Sudanese refugees in 12 camps who had fled the fighting in Darfur. There were also about 50,000 refugees from the Central African Republic living in refugee camps in southern Chad.

More than 170,000 people still lived in IDP camps in eastern Chad.

Amnesty International visits/reports

🚗 Amnesty International delegates visited Chad in March and visited eastern Chad in April and May.

📄 Chad: Civilians under attack – Darfur conflict spreads to eastern Chad (AFR 20/005/2007)

📄 Chad: No protection from rape and violence for displaced women and girls in eastern Chad (AFR 20/008/2007)

📄 Chad: 'Are we citizens of this country?' – Civilians in Chad unprotected from Janjawid attacks (AFR 20/001/2007)

📄 Chad: Escalating violence means UN must deploy, but be adequately resourced (AFR 20/012/2007)

📄 Chad: Urgent need to protect the people of eastern Chad (AFR 20/003/2007)

📄 Chad: Government must accept UN forces to protect civilians in East (AFR 20/006/2007)

📄 Chad: UN Security Council resolution a step forward in protecting civilians but concerns remain (AFR 20/011/2007)

CHILE

REPUBLIC OF CHILE

Head of state and government:	Michelle Bachelet
Death penalty:	abolitionist for ordinary crimes
Population:	16.6 million
Life expectancy:	78.3 years
Under-5 mortality (m/f):	10/8 per 1,000
Adult literacy:	95.7 per cent

Several of those responsible for human rights violations during the military dictatorship were brought to justice. Indigenous communities continued to experience widespread discrimination and other abuses.

Background

A wave of strikes and demonstrations erupted during 2007. The protests expressed widespread anger over economic inequality and debate over the need for a minimum wage intensified. In Santiago, where thousands took to the streets, there were violent clashes and a number of demonstrators and police officers were injured. Hundreds of protesters were detained for short periods.

Impunity – justice for past violations

A number of military officials and former secret service agents were found guilty of involvement in abductions, torture and killings during the military government of Augusto Pinochet (1973-1990).

■ In October, Manuel Contreras, former head of the secret service, and three former agents were sentenced to between 10 and 15 years in prison for the abduction in 1974 of Jorge D'Orival Briceño of the Revolutionary Left Movement (Movimiento de Izquierda Revolucionaria) who was later killed because of his political affiliation.

However, in November the Supreme Court acquitted retired colonel Claudio Lecaros of the enforced disappearance in 1973 of Vidal Riquelme, Cesario Soto, both peasant leaders, and Rubén Acevedo, a businessman, on the grounds that the statute of limitations on these crimes had expired. The Court had previously ruled that crimes against humanity and war crimes were not subject to the statute of limitations, in accordance with customary international law.

In September, former Peruvian President Alberto Fujimori was extradited to Peru to answer charges of corruption and human rights violations.

Discrimination – Indigenous rights

In March the UN Committee on Human Rights expressed concern about the use of anti-terrorism legislation against members of the Mapuche community who had taken part in activities in support of Indigenous land rights.

In February the UN Committee on the Rights of the Child expressed concern at the high levels of poverty faced by Indigenous children and the discrimination they experience in accessing education and health services. The Committee made several recommendations including the incorporation of Indigenous rights into the Constitution and the ratification of ILO Convention No.169.

■ On 15 September police raided the Temucuicui community, IX Region, and confiscated some livestock. When villagers asked for an explanation, police officers allegedly racially abused them. Reportedly the police were searching for stolen animals. The police later returned the animals but re-entered the community firing their weapons and injuring at least one person.

■ On 18 June, three children from the Mapuche community of Ranquilco were interrogated at school by members of the Section of Police Investigation about land occupations. A petition for a protection order for the three children stated that the questioning was "causing real terror for the children and for many parents, who fear reprisals against their children."

Violence against women

Chilean NGOs recorded at least 60 killings of women during 2007. Weaknesses in the legislation, bureaucratic procedures and inadequate policing continued to make prosecutions for domestic and sexual violence against women difficult.

A new law proposed by President Bachelet which would incorporate the killing of women (femicide) as a specific crime in the Chilean Criminal Code was debated in Parliament.

Amnesty International reports

📄 Chile: Fujimori Case – the Supreme Court of Justice must comply with obligations of international law contracted by Chile (AMR 22/006/2007)

📄 Chile: A fair trial without discrimination for members of the Juan Paillalef Mapuche community (AMR 22/009/2007)

CHINA

PEOPLE'S REPUBLIC OF CHINA

Head of state:	Hu Jintao
Head of government:	Wen Jiabao
Death penalty:	retentionist
Population:	1,331.4 million
Life expectancy:	72.5 years

Growing numbers of human rights activists were imprisoned, put under house arrest or surveillance, or harassed. Repression of minority groups, including Tibetans, Uighurs and Mongolians, continued. Falun Gong practitioners were at particularly high risk of torture and other ill-treatment in detention. Christians were persecuted for practising their religion outside state-sanctioned channels. Despite the reinstatement of Supreme People's Court review of death penalty cases, the death penalty remained shrouded in secrecy and continued to be used extensively. Torture of detainees and prisoners remained prevalent. Millions of people had no access to justice and were forced to seek redress through an ineffective extra-legal petition system. Women and girls continued to suffer violence and discrimination. Preparations for the 2008 Olympic Games in Beijing were marked by repression of human rights activists. Censorship of the internet and other media intensified.

Death penalty

Death penalty statistics continued to be regarded as a state secret, making it difficult to assess official claims that the reinstatement of Supreme Court review had reduced the number of executions. Based on public reports, Amnesty International estimated that at least 470 people were executed and 1,860 people sentenced to death during 2007, although the true figures were believed to be much higher.

In June, the Supreme People's Court stipulated that first-instance death penalty cases must be held in open court and that courts must move towards public trials for appeals in capital cases. However, death penalty trials continued to be held behind closed doors, police often resorted to torture to obtain "confessions", and detainees were denied prompt and regular access to lawyers. Death sentences and executions continued to be imposed for 68 offences, including many non-violent crimes such as corruption and drug-related offences.

Justice system

People who peacefully exercised their rights such as freedom of expression and association remained at high risk of enforced disappearance, illegal and incommunicado detention or house arrest, surveillance, beatings and harassment.

An estimated 500,000 people were subjected to punitive detention without charge or trial through "re-education through labour" and other forms of administrative detention. Progress on legislation to reform "re-education through labour" remained stalled in the National People's Congress. Police extended the use of "re-education through labour" and another form of administrative detention, "enforced drug rehabilitation", to "clean up" Beijing in the run-up to the Olympics.

For an estimated 11-13 million people, the only practical channel for justice remained outside the courts in a system of petitioning to local and higher level authorities, where the vast majority of cases remained unresolved.

Torture and other ill-treatment

Torture in detention remained widespread.
■ Yang Chunlin, a human rights activist from Heilongjiang, was detained on 6 July for "subversion of state power". He had supported the legal action brought by over 40,000 farmers whose land had been confiscated without compensation. Yang Chunlin had helped to gather signatures for a petition entitled "We want human rights, not the Olympics" signed by many of the farmers. Police repeatedly refused him access to his family and lawyer on the grounds that his case "related to the state". Yang Chunlin was tortured, including on numerous occasions by having his arms and legs stretched and chained to the four corners of an iron bed, and being forced to eat, drink and defecate in that position.
■ Shanghai housing rights activist Chen Xiaoming died of a massive haemorrhage shortly after being released from prison on medical parole on 1 July.

Human rights defenders

While space for civil society activities continued to grow, the targeting of human rights defenders who raised issues deemed to be politically sensitive intensified. The authorities criminalized the activities of human rights activists by charging them with offences such as damaging public property, extortion and fraud.

Human rights defenders and their relatives, including children, were increasingly subject to harassment, including surveillance, house arrest and beatings by both government officials and unidentified assailants. Lawyers were particularly targeted, and an increasing number had their licence renewal application rejected.
■ Defence lawyer and human rights activist Gao Zhisheng remained under tight police surveillance throughout the year after his conviction in December 2006 for "inciting subversion". Between 24 June and 4 July and again between 22 September and early November, he was held incommunicado and tortured in unknown locations, before being returned to house arrest in Beijing.
■ Human rights lawyer Li Heping was abducted by unidentified individuals in late September, beaten for several hours and told to stop his human rights work. He was then released.

Several activists died either in detention or shortly after their release.

Freedom of expression

The Chinese authorities maintained efforts to tightly control the flow of information. They decided what topics and news stories could be published, and media outlets were sometimes required to respond within minutes to government directives. The authorities continued to block websites and to filter internet content based on specified words and topics.

Around 30 journalists were known to be in prison and at least 50 individuals were in prison for posting their views on the internet. People were often punished simply for accessing banned websites.

Despite a temporary loosening of regulations applying to foreign journalists in China in the run-up to the Olympics, control over both foreign and Chinese journalists remained tight, and many Chinese journalists were imprisoned for reporting on sensitive subjects. In April, the Ministry of Public Security reportedly ordered the screening of all those attending the Beijing Olympics, with 43 categories of people to be barred, including some based on political or religious beliefs.

Violence and discrimination against women

Women suffered discrimination in employment, education and access to health care. The trafficking of women and girls remained widespread, particularly from North Korea (see below). Domestic violence continued to be prevalent and was said to be a primary cause of suicide among women in rural areas.

It was reported in May that dozens of women in the Guangxi Zhuang Autonomous Region in south-west China were subjected to forced abortions under the supervision of local family planning officials, in some cases in the ninth month of pregnancy.

Repression of spiritual and religious groups

Millions of people were impeded from freely practising their religion. Thousands remained in detention or serving prison sentences, at high risk of torture, for practising their religion outside of state-sanctioned channels. Falun Gong practitioners, Uighur Muslims, Tibetan Buddhists and underground Christian groups were among those most harshly persecuted.

During the year over 100 Falun Gong practitioners were reported to have died in detention or shortly after release as a result of torture, denial of food or medical treatment, and other forms of ill-treatment.

Underground Protestant house church meetings were frequently disrupted by the police, participants often detained and beaten, and the churches sometimes destroyed.

■ Hua Huaiqi, a Beijing-based house church leader, was sentenced in a closed trial in June to six months in prison for obstructing justice. He was reportedly beaten in jail. His 76-year-old mother, who protested against her son's treatment, was herself sentenced to two years in prison for destruction of public and private property after her cane struck the headlight of an oncoming police car.

Members of China's unofficial Catholic church were repressed. An elderly Catholic bishop, Han Dingxiang, died in custody under suspicious circumstances after more than 20 years in jail. He was quickly cremated by local authorities.

Religious adherents of all beliefs had difficulty getting legal counsel, as lawyers willing to take up such sensitive cases were often harassed, detained and imprisoned.

Xinjiang Uighur Autonomous Region

The authorities continued to use the US-led "war on terror" to justify harsh repression of ethnic Uighurs, living primarily in Xinjiang Uighur Autonomous Region (XUAR), resulting in serious human rights violations. Non-violent expressions of Uighur cultural identity were criminalized. Uighur individuals were the only known group in China to be sentenced to death and executed for political crimes, such as "separatist activities".

China increasingly successfully used the Shanghai Cooperation Organization to pressurize neighbouring countries, including Kyrgyzstan, Uzbekistan and Kazakhstan, to co-operate in forced returns of Uighurs to China.

There was an increase in the number of Uighurs detained abroad who were forcibly sent to China, where they faced the death penalty and possible execution, including Uighurs with foreign nationality.

■ Ismail Semed, who was forcibly returned to China from Pakistan in 2003, was executed on charges of "attempting to split the Motherland" and possession of firearms and explosives.

■ Ablikim Abdiriyim, son of Uighur activist Rebiya Kadeer, was tried in secret and sentenced to nine years in prison on charges of "instigating and engaging in secessionist activities". According to official sources, these activities consisted largely of asking Yahoo's "Uighur-language webmaster" to post articles on its website. However, both Yahoo! and Alibaba, the Chinese internet company that operates Yahoo! China's services, have stated they do not provide a Uighur-language web service. Ablikim Abdiriyim was reported to have been tortured and otherwise ill-treated in prison, and was said to have had difficulty recognizing family members during a visit in December. The authorities continued to deny him access to medical treatment.

The authorities pursued a policy of large-scale Han Chinese migration to XUAR to address alleged labour shortages, while large numbers of young Uighur women and girls – reportedly more than 200,000 – were sent to work in factories in eastern China, often coerced by local authorities and under harsh conditions with low pay.

Tibet Autonomous Region and other ethnic Tibetan areas

Freedom of religion, expression and association of Tibetans continued to be severely restricted. The State Administration for Religious Affairs established

C

government control over the identification and training of Tibetan Buddhist teachers throughout China. Peaceful expressions of support for the Dalai Lama continued to be harshly punished. Efforts to pass information abroad about crackdowns against Tibetans were harshly punished.

■ Some 40 Tibetan children were detained by police in Gansu Province for writing pro-Tibetan independence slogans on walls. Eyewitnesses said that four of the boys were bruised and dazed, and that one of them was repeatedly taken away at night, returning in the morning appearing battered and unable to speak.

■ Runggye Adak, a Tibetan nomad who during a cultural festival publicly called for the Dalai Lama's return to Tibet, was sentenced to eight years in prison for "inciting to split the country" and "severely disrupting public order". Three others were jailed for 10, nine and three years on charges of "colluding with foreign separatist forces to split the country and distributing political pamphlets" for their efforts to send information to overseas organizations about Runggye Adak's arrest.

North Korean refugees

Approximately 50,000 North Koreans were reportedly hiding in China, living under constant fear of deportation. Each month hundreds of North Koreans were believed to have been forcibly repatriated to North Korea without being given access to UNHCR offices in China. A majority of the North Koreans in China were women, many of whom had been trafficked into China and whose primary means of avoiding forcible return to North Korea was being sold into marriage to Chinese men. Children born to North Korean refugee women in China are effectively stateless and face difficulties gaining access to education and health care.

■ Kim Yong-ja, an undocumented North Korean woman, reportedly committed suicide in detention because she feared forcible return to North Korea. She was among 40 North Korean refugees arrested in December near Qinhuangdao, Hubei Province.

Hong Kong Special Administrative Region

Tens of thousands of people demonstrated for political and human rights reforms on the 10th anniversary of Hong Kong's return to Chinese sovereignty in July. Hundreds of overseas Falun Gong practitioners were denied entry to Hong Kong in the run-up to the anniversary. In December, the Standing Committee of

the National People's Congress ruled it would consider permitting direct elections for the Chief Executive of the Hong Kong Special Administrative Region in 2017, not 2012.

Violence against women

Cases of domestic violence increased 120 per cent in the first three months of the year – a rise attributed to a greater willingness to report such abuses to the police. Activists urged further amendments to the Domestic Violence Ordinance aimed at criminalizing perpetrators of domestic violence and bringing same-sex couples within its scope.

Discrimination against lesbians and gay men

Lesbian and gay activists criticized a January ruling by the Broadcasting Authority that a television programme portraying same-sex relationships was biased and unsuitable for family viewing. In July, the Court of Final Appeal ruled as discriminatory a law which criminalized same-sex sexual relations in public, but did not criminalize heterosexuals for similar conduct.

Asylum-seekers

Asylum-seekers charged with immigration offences continued to be detained pending the outcome of their asylum case. In May, a local NGO reported that many asylum-seekers held in immigration detention facilities had been stripped in front of other inmates, humiliated by immigration officers and denied adequate medical care.

Twenty-nine asylum-seekers held at Castle Peak immigration detention centre went on a three-day hunger strike in October to protest against their prolonged detention. Support groups said some had been detained for nearly a year, while the authorities claimed most had been there for about a month.

Amnesty International reports

📄 Open Letter to Chairman of the Standing Committee of the National People's Congress on the reform of Re-education through Labour (ASA 17/020/2007)

📄 People's Republic of China: The Olympics countdown – one year left to fulfil human rights promises (ASA 17/024/2007)

📄 China: The Olympics countdown – Repression of activists overshadows death penalty and media reforms (ASA 17/015/2007)

📄 Hong Kong's return to Chinese sovereignty: ten years on (ASA 19/001/2007)

📄 China: Internal Migrants: Discrimination and abuse – the human cost of an economic "miracle" (ASA 17/008/2007)

📄 China: Remember the Gulja massacre? China's crackdown on peaceful protesters (ASA 17/002/2007)

COLOMBIA

REPUBLIC OF COLOMBIA

Head of state and government:	Álvaro Uribe Vélez
Death penalty:	abolitionist for all crimes
Population:	47 million
Life expectancy:	72.3 years
Under-5 mortality (m/f):	30/26 per 1,000
Adult literacy:	92.8 per cent

The continuing conflict between army-backed paramilitaries, guerrilla groups and the security forces resulted in serious human rights abuses, especially in some regions and in rural areas. All parties to the 40-year-old conflict committed violations of international humanitarian law (IHL), including war crimes and crimes against humanity. However, fewer civilians were killed than in recent years. People continued to be kidnapped, with guerrilla groups responsible for most conflict-related cases, but there were fewer reported cases than in previous years. The killing in June of 11 hostages held by the Revolutionary Armed Forces of Colombia (Fuerzas Armadas Revolucionarias de Colombia, FARC) provoked widespread condemnation and renewed calls for the FARC to release all its hostages. Attacks on human rights defenders and civil society activists continued; most were blamed on paramilitary groups.

Fewer people were killed by paramilitary groups than in previous years. However, reports of killings of civilians by the security forces rose. Paramilitary groups remained active in many parts of the country despite the fact that they had supposedly been demobilized. The number of people forced to flee their homes by the conflict also rose. The FARC were blamed for many of the killings of candidates in the run-up to October's local elections.

Some progress was made in several high-profile investigations into human rights abuses, but impunity remained a major concern. Around 40 Members of Congress were implicated in continuing judicial investigations into links between state officials and paramilitary groups. Several "demobilized" paramilitary leaders gave evidence about their role in human rights violations and their links with the security forces before special tribunals in return for reduced prison sentences.

Killings by the security forces

At least 280 people were reported to have been extrajudicially executed by members of the security forces in the 12-month period ending in June 2007. The victims, mostly peasant farmers, were often presented by the military as "guerrillas killed in combat". Most of the killings were referred to the military justice system, which usually closed such cases without any serious attempt to hold those responsible accountable.

■ On 22 April, soldiers of the army's XVI Brigade entered the home of Ernesto Cruz Guevara in Aguazul Municipality, Casanare Department. The soldiers interrogated him about guerrilla activities. Before leaving, they told his wife they were taking her husband to the local Office of the Attorney General. Ernesto Cruz's family later identified his body; the army claimed he was a guerrilla killed in combat.

In June, the Ministry of Defence issued Directive 10, which reiterated that extrajudicial executions were a violation of the right to life.

Paramilitary groups

The government claimed that more than 31,000 combatants had been demobilized and that paramilitaries were no longer active. They attributed the continued violence to drug-trafficking criminal gangs. While some paramilitary groups did evolve into drugs-related criminal gangs, and some violence was linked to disputes between such groups, there was strong evidence that traditional paramilitary groups continued to operate in many parts of the country with new names, including the "Black Eagles" and the "New Generation Organization". There were continued reports of collusion between paramilitaries and the security forces.

According to the Eighth Quarterly Report of the OAS Mission to Support the Peace Process in Colombia (MAPP/OEA), published in February, 22 such groups were identified, comprising some 3,000 combatants, although other sources suggested the figure was far higher. At least 230 killings of civilians were attributed to paramilitaries either acting alone or in conjunction with the security forces in the 12-month period ending in June 2007.

■ On 23 February, Alba Milena Gómez Quintero and her 18-year-old son Miguel Antonio were killed after being taken from the taxi in which they were travelling by two suspected paramilitaries on the San Juan de

C

Arama-Granada highway, Meta Department, in a spot which lay between two army roadblocks. Alba Milena Gómez had reportedly made an official complaint against the army, which she claimed had falsely accused her of being a guerrilla auxiliary.

Failure to reveal the truth about paramilitary abuses

Only some 10 per cent of more than 31,000 demobilized paramilitaries qualified for inclusion in the Justice and Peace Law (JPL) under which those who lay down their arms can benefit from significantly reduced prison sentences in return for confessions about human rights violations and reparations to their victims. But with only some 20 investigative units to handle thousands of cases, the process progressed slowly.

Although paramilitary leaders who confessed revealed some information about those whom they killed, information on their victims' identities and the whereabouts of their bodies remained sketchy. More than 1,100 bodies were exhumed from numerous mass graves between 2006 and the end of 2007, but most of these were discovered as a result of information from rank-and-file paramilitaries outside the JPL process. The vast majority of bodies remained unidentified. Most of the at least 4 million hectares of land estimated to have been stolen by paramilitaries had yet to be identified and very little land had been returned to its rightful owners.

Most paramilitaries escaped effective investigation through Decree 128 and Law 782, which granted de facto amnesties to those not under investigation for human rights abuses and who admitted to being members of paramilitary groups, an offence known as "conspiracy to commit a crime". However, in July the Supreme Court of Justice ruled that membership of paramilitary groups was not a political crime and, as such, amnesties were not applicable. This left some 19,000 paramilitaries in legal limbo.

Several victims and those representing them in the JPL process were killed, allegedly by paramilitaries.

■ Carmen Cecilia Santana Romaña, who represented victims seeking the return of their lands and their right to participate in the JPL hearings, was killed by unidentified gunmen on 7 February in Apartadó Municipality, Antioquia Department.

■ Yolanda Izquierdo, who represented survivors at the JPL hearing of paramilitary leader Salvatore Mancuso, and who was herself a victim, was shot dead in Montería, Córdoba Department, on 31 January, by gunmen suspected of being linked to paramilitaries.

'Para-political' scandal

More than 40 legislators were under investigation by the Supreme Court for their alleged links to paramilitaries; almost half of them were in detention at the end of the year. In December, one of these, Erik Morris, was sentenced to six years in prison. Hundreds of other state officials, including governors, mayors, and members of the security forces, were being investigated by the Offices of the Attorney General and Procurator General. In November, Jorge Noguera, the former director of the civilian security agency, the Department of Administrative Security, was disqualified from public office for 18 years by the Office of the Procurator General for his links to paramilitaries.

Several Supreme Court judges investigating the scandal, and their families, were reportedly threatened.

Impunity

Impunity remained the norm in most cases of human rights abuses. Although there was some progress in a number of high-profile cases, in many there were no advances in identifying chain-of-command responsibility.

■ In November, an army captain was arrested for his role in the killing of eight members of the Peace Community of San José de Apartadó, Municipality of Apartadó, Antioquia Department, in February 2005. The Office of the Attorney General claimed the killings were carried out by the army in collusion with paramilitaries. In February, the Attorney General's Office had announced it was investigating 69 soldiers for the killings. More than 160 members of the community have been killed since 1997.

■ In November, it was made public that a team from the Office of the Attorney General had reopened investigations into 294 of the thousands of killings of members of the left-wing Patriotic Union (Unión Patriótica) party since 1985. Paramilitaries and the security forces were believed to have been responsible for most of these killings.

■ In October, former justice minister and senator Alberto Santofimio was sentenced to 24 years in prison in connection with the killing of presidential candidate Luis Carlos Galán in 1989.

■ In September, three members of the air force were sentenced by a civilian judge to six years' house arrest

C

for what was described in the ruling as the accidental killing of 17 people in Santo Domingo, Tame Municipality, Arauca Department, in 1998. The military justice system had previously acquitted the three men, claiming the deaths occurred after a truck belonging to guerrillas exploded. The September ruling concluded the killings were caused by a cluster bomb released from an air force helicopter.

■ In August, four members of the army and a civilian were sentenced to 40 years in prison for the killing of three trade unionists in Saravena Municipality, Arauca Department, in August 2004. The army had claimed they were guerrillas killed in combat.

■ In July, retired army Colonel Alfonso Plazas Vega was arrested for his part in the enforced disappearance of 11 people during a military assault on the Palace of Justice in Bogotá after M-19 guerrillas took hostage those inside in November 1985. Over 100 people died during the military assault, including 12 Supreme Court judges. In September, Attorney General Mario Iguarán said there was strong evidence that many of those who disappeared were alive when they left the building.

Guerrilla groups

The FARC and the National Liberation Army (Ejército de Liberación Nacional, ELN) continued to commit human rights abuses and serious and repeated violations of international humanitarian law, including killings of civilians and hostage-taking. More than 210 killings of civilians were attributed to guerrilla groups in the 12-month period ending in June 2007.

■ Four people were killed, reportedly by the ELN, in San Joaquín, Mercaderes Municipality, Cauca Department, on 14 March.

■ Four people were killed, allegedly by the FARC, in Yarumal Municipality, Antioquia Department, on 1 January. At least two of the victims were community leaders.

In Arauca Department people fled their homes after the ongoing conflict between the FARC and ELN led to armed skirmishes and to the selective killing of civilians. Among the victims were community and social leaders accused by each side of supporting the other.

The FARC continued to target elected officials and were also allegedly responsible for most of the 29 killings of candidates in the run-up to the local elections held on 28 October.

■ Four mayors and councillors were killed in the departments of Caquetá, Chocó and Valle del Cauca between 7 and 10 July.

The use of anti-personnel mines by guerrilla groups continued to be widespread. In 2007, more than 180 civilians and members of the security forces, who continued to be the main victims of land mines, were killed and 680 injured.

■ Five members of the Awá Indigenous community, including two children, were killed by landmines reportedly laid by the FARC in Ricaurte Municipality, Nariño Department, on 14 and 15 July.

Preliminary peace talks between the government and the ELN were suspended in August following disagreement over the terms of a cease-fire.

Kidnapping and hostage-taking

There was widespread condemnation after 11 of the 12 deputies from the Valle del Cauca Departmental Assembly, kidnapped by the FARC in April 2002, were killed in uncertain circumstances on 18 June. The FARC claimed they were killed in crossfire during combat with an unidentified armed group, but the authorities disputed this.

The international community became increasingly involved in discussions over the exchange of FARC prisoners for hostages held by the guerrilla group after President Uribe authorized the release from prison of the FARC's "diplomatic representative", Rodrigo Granda, in June, and the simultaneous release of more than 100 convicted FARC prisoners. President Uribe authorized Venezuelan President Hugo Chávez to help broker an agreement, and a meeting between President Chávez and FARC leaders took place in Caracas in November. However, later that month President Uribe ended Venezuela's mediation role after President Chávez reportedly contacted the head of the Colombian army, in contravention of an agreement not to talk directly to Colombia's army chiefs about the hostage issue. This led to a deterioration in diplomatic relations between the two countries. The much-anticipated release of three high-profile hostages held by the FARC had failed to materialize by the end of the year.

Although kidnappings continued to fall – from 687 in 2006 to 521 in 2007 – the figures remained high. Guerrilla groups, mainly the FARC and to a much lesser degree the ELN, were responsible for kidnapping around 150 people, the vast majority of conflict-related kidnappings, while criminal gangs were responsible for most of the rest. Some 125 kidnappings could not be attributed.

Violence against women

All parties to the conflict continued to subject women and girls to sexual abuse and other forms of violence. Women guerrilla combatants were forced to have abortions or take contraceptives, in violation of their reproductive rights.

■ On 23 May, army soldiers reportedly raided a house in Toribío Municipality, Cauca Department, where they attempted to sexually abuse an 11-year-old girl.

■ On 26 March, five paramilitaries from the Black Eagles – two women, two minors and a man – reportedly entered the home of two sisters aged 14 and 10 in Bello Municipality, Antioquia Department. Some of the paramilitaries allegedly beat the two girls and sexually abused and killed the older one. A 60-year-old neighbour, José Mendieta, who came to the girls' assistance, was reportedly stabbed to death by the assailants.

Paramilitaries and criminal gangs reportedly forcibly recruited women and girls as sex workers in various parts of the country. In Putumayo Department, at least five women who had been forcibly recruited for sex work were reportedly killed.

Civilians targeted

Civilians continued to bear the brunt of the conflict, especially those belonging to Indigenous, Afro-descendant and peasant farmer communities, many of whom lived on lands of economic interest to the warring parties. At least 1,340 civilians were killed or forcibly disappeared in the 12-month period ending in June 2007. There were also more than 305,000 new cases of displacement in 2007. Between 3 and 4 million people had been displaced since 1985.

■ In September, almost 1,000 Awá Indigenous people, almost half of them children, were displaced from the Inda Sabaleta reserve in Tumaco Municipality, Nariño Department, following fighting between the army and guerrilla groups.

■ In April, more than 6,000 people were forced to flee their homes in Nariño Department following repeated outbreaks of fighting between the army and guerrilla groups.

Paramilitaries and guerrillas continued to recruit children. UNICEF estimated there were between 6,000 and 7,000 child soldiers in Colombia.

There was also a series of bomb attacks in urban areas, some of which the authorities attributed to the FARC.

■ A car bomb exploded outside a police building in Cali, Valle del Cauca Department, on 9 April. One civilian was killed and more than 30 were injured.

■ An explosive device detonated in Buenaventura, Valle del Cauca Department, on 16 March, killed four people and injured seven.

Human rights defenders and other activists

Human rights defenders, trade unionists, social and community activists, and journalists continued to be targeted, principally by paramilitaries.

During the year, the offices of several human rights NGOs were broken into and sensitive information stolen, including Reiniciar, Corporación Jurídica Yira Castro, Fellowship of Reconciliation, and Justapaz.

In February, some 70 NGOs, trade unions, and other social organizations reportedly received email death threats from paramilitaries. In June, eight human rights NGOs in Nariño Department received email and telephone death threats, reportedly from the New Generation paramilitary group. This group had sent similar threats to 13 NGOs in Nariño in March.

■ On 4 November, Yolanda Becerra, President of the Popular Women's Organization, was attacked at her home in Barrancabermeja, Santander Department, by two hooded armed men. They reportedly shoved her against a wall, threatened her with a gun, and gave her 48 hours to leave the city.

■ On 4 April, Judith Vergara, a community activist from Comuna 13 in Medellín, Antioquia department was shot dead while travelling by bus in the city.

At least 39 trade union members were killed in 2007. The Permanent Representation of the International Labour Organization in Colombia, set up to monitor the rights of trade unionists in the country and the work of the special unit created by the Attorney General to investigate killings of trade unionists, began operating in January.

Efforts to secure a free trade agreement between Colombia and the USA were hampered by concerns in the US Congress over the killing of Colombian trade unionists.

President Uribe again made comments which implied that human rights organizations were linked to guerrilla groups. In July, he said "the guerrillas have another strategy: every time there is a casualty in the guerrillas, they immediately mobilize their chorus leaders in the country and abroad to say that it was an extrajudicial execution".

US military aid

In 2007, US aid for Colombia amounted to some US$727 million, some 82 per cent of which was destined for the security forces. The total included some US$595 million from the Foreign Operations funding bill, 25 per cent of which was dependent on progress by the Colombian authorities on certain human rights indicators. In April, US Secretary of State Condoleezza Rice certified that Colombia was making progress on human rights and authorized the release of all 25 per cent of Fiscal Year 2006 certifiable aid. But the US Congress withheld the release of the money to the armed forces, worth some US$55.2 million, because of concerns over extrajudicial executions and the para-political scandal. Despite three rounds of questions and answers, the US Congress did not accept the justification for certifying Colombia's progress on human rights and the money remained on hold at the end of the year.

In December, US President George W. Bush signed into law significant changes in US assistance to Colombia. Military and police assistance under the Foreign Operations funding bill was cut by 31 per cent and social and economic aid increased by 70 per cent. Human rights conditions were extended to 30 per cent of aid and require the Colombian authorities to dismantle "successor armed groups", an acknowledgement by the US government of continued paramilitary activity in Colombia. The total amount of assistance to Colombia was US$44 million less than the amount requested by President Bush for 2008.

Office of the UN High Commissioner for Human Rights

In September the Office of the UN High Commissioner for Human Rights (OHCHR) announced that the Colombian government had agreed to extend the mandate of the OHCHR in Colombia for a further three years.

Regarding the government's compliance with UN human rights recommendations, the OHCHR report on Colombia, published in March, stated that "the picture… was still mixed, particularly in the case of the recommendations on the review of intelligence files, the reduction of impunity, the cutting of links between public servants and members of paramilitary groups, and the improvement of the quality of statistics on human rights and IHL". The report also expressed concerns about the continuing presence of paramilitaries, the increasing reports of extrajudicial executions carried out by the security forces and breaches of IHL by the guerrilla groups, in particular the FARC.

Amnesty International visits/reports

🚌 Amnesty International delegates visited the country in February, June and September.

📄 Killings, arbitrary detentions, and death threats – the reality of trade unionism in Colombia (AMR 23/001/2007)

📄 Colombia: FARC and ELN must release all hostages (AMR 23/019/2007)

📄 Colombia: Latest killing of human rights defender throws controversial paramilitary demobilization process into further doubt (AMR 23/002/2007)

CONGO
(REPUBLIC OF)

REPUBLIC OF CONGO

Head of state :	Denis Sassou-Nguesso
Head of government:	Isidore Mvouba
Death penalty:	abolitionist in practice
Population:	4.2 million
Life expectancy:	54 years
Under-5 mortality (m/f):	113/90 per 1,000
Adult literacy:	84.7 per cent

At least five men arrested in early 2005 continued to be detained without trial. Three asylum-seekers from the Democratic Republic of Congo (DRC) detained in early 2004 remained in military custody without charge or trial. State agents discriminated against members of the minority Pigmy ethnic group. One detainee was shot dead during a mass prison escape in January. Seventeen death sentences were commuted.

Background

The National Resistance Council (Conseil national de résistance, CNR) and the government signed an agreement in April to end hostilities. As part of the agreement, President Denis Sassou-Nguesso appointed CNR leader Frédéric Bitsamou (known as Pasteur Ntoumi) to the post of delegate general in charge of promoting the values of peace and repairing the ravages of war.

In preparation for the June legislative elections, the CNR transformed itself into a political party known as the National Council of Republicans (Conseil national des républicains). When Frédéric Bitsamou and his supporters tried to enter the capital, Brazzaville, in September, government forces opened fire and forced the CNR back into the Pool region.

The ruling Congolese Workers' Party (Parti congolais du travail, PCT) and its allies won an overwhelming victory in the June elections. Civil society organizations and opposition political parties claimed that the elections were largely chaotic and favoured the PCT. When the new National Assembly sat in September, former Prime Minister Bernard Kolelas became its President, as part of the deal in April to ally his party to the PCT.

In October the Republic of Congo was readmitted to the Kimberley Process from which it had been suspended in 2004 for failing to prevent the trafficking of conflict diamonds.

Arbitrary detention

Political detainees

Former army colonel Serge André Mpassi and at least four other former members of the armed forces arrested in early 2005 remained in custody without trial. There was no explanation from the government or the judiciary for their continued detention.

Detention of asylum-seekers

Three former members of the security forces from the DRC continued to be held without charge or trial at the Brazzaville headquarters of the military intelligence service. Germain Ndabamenya Etikilome, Médard Mabwaka Egbonde and Bosch Ndala Umba appeared to be held at the request of the DRC government. The two governments did not respond to public appeals by several local and DRC human rights groups for the release of the three men when DRC President Joseph Kabila visited Brazzaville in September.

Human rights defenders

A senior judicial official claimed in January that human rights defenders Brice Mackosso and Christian Mounzéo were the subject of legal restrictions on their movements following their conviction in December 2006 on charges including breach of trust and forgery. The two men, co-ordinators of civil society groups known as Publish What You Pay, had investigated and publicized allegations of embezzlement of oil revenues by government officials. There was no progress in their appeal against their conviction and sentence, although the restrictions were not enforced. Brice Mackosso and Christian Mounzéo were appointed in September by the government as members of a national body monitoring accountability for revenues from oil and other natural resources in Congo.

Discrimination

Discrimination against members of the minority Pigmy ethnic group continued to be reported.

■ In July state officials housed Pigmy participants in the Panafrican Music Festival in a tent located in a Brazzaville zoo while other participants were given hotel accommodation. The Pigmy participants were subsequently transferred to a school following protests by local human rights defenders.

Prison conditions

One detainee was shot dead by a guard in January when more than 100 prisoners staged a mass escape from Brazzaville central prison. Local human rights organizations stated that overcrowding and government failure to feed prisoners were reasons behind the escape.

Death penalty

President Denis Sassou-Nguesso commuted 17 death sentences to life imprisonment with hard labour in August. It was not clear how many of the sentences had been imposed during 2007.

CÔTE D'IVOIRE

REPUBLIC OF CÔTE D'IVOIRE

Head of state:	Laurent Gbagbo
Head of government:	Guillaume Soro (replaced Charles Konan Banny in March)
Death penalty:	abolitionist for all crimes
Population:	18.8 million
Life expectancy:	47.4 years
Under-5 mortality (m/f):	193/174 per 1,000
Adult literacy:	48.7 per cent

A peace agreement signed in March contributed to the reduction of political tensions in Côte d'Ivoire. The UN Security Council decided that international peacekeeping forces would remain in the country until after presidential elections. Despite the peace agreement, human rights abuses continued to be committed by both sides, particularly against women, and harassment as well as physical assault remained rampant, notably at roadblocks.

Background

In March, President Laurent Gbagbo and Guillaume Soro, Secretary General of the New Forces (Forces Nouvelles), the coalition of armed groups in control of the north since September 2002, signed an agreement in Ouagadougou, capital of Burkina Faso. This aimed at reunifying the country and setting the conditions for presidential elections postponed since 2005. A timetable was set for disarmament and for creating an integrated army. Guillaume Soro was appointed Prime Minister of a new transitional government in March. In September the buffer zone separating government troops and armed elements of the New Forces and controlled by UN and French forces was dismantled and mixed brigades composed of government and New Forces troops began to patrol the area. In September, a process of voter registration was launched and in November the two parties agreed to hold presidential elections by June 2008. They pledged to start the long-awaited disarmament process in December in a step towards forming a new national army.

In October, the UN Security Council decided to renew for a further year the embargo on arms and diamond exports as well as individual sanctions such as travel bans and asset freezes against three political leaders.

Violence against women

Reports of sexual violence against women and girls continued to be received and several alleged perpetrators were released without being brought to trial. This impunity stemmed notably from the fact that the Ivorian Penal Code does not define rape.

■ In July, a 16-year-old girl who worked as a maid in a private house was reportedly raped in Abidjan by the son of her employer. The alleged perpetrator was arrested but released the same day. Despite several requests from the lawyer of the victim, by the end of the year no official investigations were known to have taken place.

■ By the end of the year no measures had been initiated to provide reparation or access to health for the countless women and girls who had been victims of widespread and systematic rape and sexual assault committed by combatant forces or by civilians with close ties to these forces since the beginning of the armed conflict in 2002. This was despite official commitments by the government and the President.

Allegations of sexual abuse by UN peacekeepers

In July, serious allegations emerged of widespread sexual abuse by peacekeepers with the UN Operation in Côte d'Ivoire (UNOCI). The UN sent a mission of inquiry to Ivory Coast but noted that the victims were reluctant to give details of the attacks. In November, a Moroccan mission of inquiry went to Bouaké, the stronghold of the New Forces, but by the end of the year the results of these inquiries had not been made public.

Human rights violations by government forces

The security forces were responsible for arbitrary arrests, torture and extrajudicial executions of detainees, as well as for widespread abuses committed to extort money at checkpoints and during inspections of identity documents.

■ In March, Gombané Bouraima, suspected of theft, died in a police station in Abidjan as a result of torture. Police opened an inquiry but at the end of the year no perpetrators had been identified and brought to trial.

■ In July, Kouassi Kouamé Félix, aged 15, was shot and killed, and five others were wounded, during an attack on a group of taxi drivers in Adjamé, Abidjan, by members of the Command Centre for Security

C

Operations (Centre de commandement des Opérations de Sécurité, CECOS). The attack was reportedly in retaliation after a taxi driver had refused to give money demanded by security officers at a checkpoint. By the end of the year, no inquiry was known to have been opened despite official protests by a taxi drivers' union.

Abuses by the New Forces

Combatants and supporters of the New Forces were responsible for human rights abuses including torture and ill-treatment, arbitrary detention and widespread extortion. A climate of impunity prevailed due to the absence of a functioning judicial system in the north.
■ In August, Koné Drissa, accused of theft, was arrested by members of the Poste de commandement opérationnel (PCO), a branch of the New Forces in Bouaké, and tortured while in detention. He was released a few days later but died soon afterwards as a result of his treatment. The New Forces promised to investigate but by the end of the year none of the alleged perpetrators had been identified.

Amnesty law

In April, President Gbagbo signed a regulation providing for an amnesty for most of the crimes committed in the context of the conflict since 2002. The amnesty did not expressly exclude crimes under international law, including the widespread and systematic acts of sexual violence against women. In July, however, President Gbagbo stressed to an Amnesty International delegation that this amnesty excluded "crimes against human kind" and assured the delegation that "victims [would] have every opportunity to lodge their complaints".

Amnesty International visit/reports

An Amnesty International delegation visited Côte d'Ivoire in July to meet the head of state and organize a workshop with local NGOs on sexual violence against women.

Côte d'Ivoire: Targeting women – the forgotten victims of the conflict (AFR 31/001/2007)

Côte d'Ivoire: Crimes under international law cannot be amnestied (AFR 31/006/2007)

CROATIA

REPUBLIC OF CROATIA
Head of state:	Stjepan Mesić
Head of government:	Ivo Sanader
Death penalty:	abolitionist for all crimes
Population:	4.6 million
Life expectancy:	75.3 years
Under-5 mortality (m/f):	8/7 per 1,000
Adult literacy:	98.1 per cent

The 1991-95 war continued to overshadow human rights in Croatia. Despite some progress in the investigation and prosecution of war crimes, impunity remained widespread for crimes allegedly committed by members of the Croatian Army and police forces. Minorities, including Roma and Croatian Serbs, suffered discrimination, including in economic and social rights. Of at least 300,000 Croatian Serbs displaced by the conflict, approximately 130,000 were officially recorded as having returned home.

Background

Croatia continued to pursue full integration into the European Union (EU). In November, the EU Commission issued its progress report on Croatia which noted that there remained widespread impunity for war crimes committed against Croatian Serbs, as well as a number of obstacles to the sustainable return of Croatian Serbs.

Following parliamentary elections in November, the ruling conservative party Croatian Democratic Union (HDZ) was confirmed as the majority party in the Croatian parliament. The HDZ was closely followed by the centre-left Social Democratic Party. Both parties needed the support of junior coalition parties to form a government. Coalition talks were ongoing at the end of 2007.

In December, the Organization for Security and Co-operation in Europe (OSCE) Permanent Council decided to close the OSCE Mission to Croatia, but to maintain an OSCE office in Zagreb to carry out activities related to war crimes trials and to report on the implementation of the government's "housing care" programmes (see below).

War crimes and crimes against humanity
International prosecutions

The International Criminal Tribunal for the former Yugoslavia (Tribunal) continued to try alleged perpetrators of serious violations of international humanitarian law.

■ In June, Milan Martić, who held various leadership positions in the self-proclaimed Serbian Autonomous District and Republic of Serbian Krajina, was found guilty of various counts of crimes against humanity and war crimes committed against non-Serbs in areas under Croatian Serb control. He was sentenced to 35 years' imprisonment. The Tribunal found that Milan Martić took part in a joint criminal enterprise whose purpose was "the establishment of an ethnically Serb territory through the displacement of the Croat and other non-Serb population".

■ In September, former Yugoslav People's Army officers Mile Mrkšić and Veselin Šljivančanin were sentenced to 20 and five years' imprisonment respectively for their roles in war crimes committed in 1991 in Ovčara, near Vukovar. Mile Mrkšić was found guilty of murder, for having aided and abetted the murder of 194 non-Serbs who had been removed from the Vukovar Hospital, and of the torture and cruel treatment of prisoners of war in Ovčara. Veselin Šljivančanin was found guilty of torture, for having aided and abetted the torture of prisoners of war. A third co-defendant, Miroslav Radić, was acquitted of all charges.

Domestic prosecutions

The Croatian judiciary continued to investigate and prosecute war crimes. However, in the majority of cases criminal proceedings were related to cases where the victims were ethnic Croats. There continued to be widespread impunity for crimes allegedly committed by members of the Croatian Army and Croatian police forces, despite some steps taken to investigate and prosecute war crimes against Croatian Serbs.

■ In June, the trial against Rahim Ademi and Mirko Norac began at the Zagreb County Court, whose case had been transferred by the Tribunal to Croatia in November 2005. The accused, former Croatian Army commanders, were suspected of having committed war crimes against Croatian Serbs during military operations in the so-called "Medak pocket" in 1993. The OSCE Mission to Croatia, which was monitoring proceedings, reported that in September and October 26 prosecution witnesses, including 10 "endangered" witnesses, failed to testify during the trial. The vast majority of these witnesses reside or were believed to reside in Serbia.

■ Proceedings continued against Branimir Glavaš for his alleged involvement in war crimes committed against Croatian Serb civilians in and around Osijek. Branimir Glavaš had formerly been a local leader of the HDZ in the Osijek region and, between 1990 and 1992, was secretary of the Osijek Municipal Secretariat for National Defence. Branimir Glavaš and six other indictees were charged with the unlawful arrest, torture and killing of Croatian Serb civilians in Osijek in 1991. He was also suspected of having failed in 1991 to prevent his subordinates from detaining, ill-treating and killing civilians and of having directly participated in some of the crimes in his capacity as local military leader. Proceedings against Branimir Glavaš were transferred to Zagreb, following requests by the Chief State Prosecutor to reduce pressure on witnesses. The trial before the Zagreb County Court started in October.

Despite significant developments with regard to crimes committed against Croatian Serbs in Osijek, elsewhere in Croatia no meaningful steps were taken to tackle impunity for crimes allegedly committed by members of the Croatian Army and police forces. No progress was made in the investigation of such crimes in Sisak, for example, where according to local organizations more than 100 people, mostly Croatian Serbs, were allegedly murdered in 1991-92 by Croatian forces.

In October, Željko Peratović, a freelance journalist who had reported extensively on war crimes in Croatia, was detained on suspicion of having revealed state secrets on his internet blog, reportedly in connection with information he published on alleged war crimes committed in the Gospić area. He was released on the following day after having been questioned by police.

Right to return

At least 300,000 Croatian Serbs left Croatia during the 1991-95 war, of whom only approximately 130,000 were officially recorded as having returned, a figure widely considered to be an overestimation of the real numbers of those who had returned. A survey commissioned by UNHCR, the UN refugee agency, and published in May estimated that less than half of registered returnees live in Croatia.

Croatian Serbs continued to be victims of discrimination in access to employment and in realising other economic and social rights. Many Croatian Serbs could not return because they had lost their rights to socially owned apartments. Implementation of existing programmes to provide "housing care" to former tenants and occupants remained slow.

Among those who had formerly lived in private properties and who had formally repossessed their homes, some could not return because their homes had been made uninhabitable by looting and devastation.

Violence against women

Croatia was reported as being increasingly a country of destination for female victims of trafficking for the purpose of sexual exploitation. It remained a country of transit for people trafficking. In April, the Delegation of the EU Commission to Croatia and the Office of Human Rights of the Government of Croatia presented an EU-funded project to combat trafficking in human beings. The project aims to improve coordination between law enforcement agencies and co-operation between police, social welfare institutions, non-governmental and international organizations, and to improve protection for victims of trafficking.

In September Croatia ratified the Council of Europe Convention on Action against Trafficking in Human Beings.

Discrimination – Roma

Members of Romani communities in Croatia lacked full access to primary education. Romani children continued to experience discriminatory treatment because of teachers' negative stereotyping and low expectations. Romani children with little or no command of the Croatian language faced extreme difficulties when they started school. The languages spoken by Roma in Croatia were not used in schools, unlike other minority languages. The majority of Romani children remained excluded from pre-school programmes.

In June, a report supported by the Open Society Institute, a non-governmental organization, and the World Bank, presented an assessment of progress in implementing the objectives to which countries taking part in the Decade of Roma Inclusion have

committed. Croatia ranked sixth out of nine countries which have joined the Decade of Roma Inclusion. The report highlighted that the authorities had introduced a range of measures, especially with regard to education, but these remained sporadic and needed to be integrated into more systematic policies.

In May, in the case of Šečić v. Croatia, the European Court of Human Rights found that Croatia had violated provisions prohibiting discrimination and torture or inhuman or degrading treatment or punishment. Šemso Šečić, a Romani man, had been attacked in 1999 by two men who beat him with wooden planks, shouting racial abuse, and had sustained multiple rib fractures. The Croatian authorities failed to promptly, thoroughly and impartially investigate this crime, and the perpetrators have remained unpunished.

Amnesty International visit/report

🚘 Amnesty International delegates visited Croatia in February.

▥ Europe and Central Asia: Summary of Amnesty International's concerns in the region, January-June 2007 (EUR 01/010/2007)

CUBA

REPUBLIC OF CUBA

Head of state and government:	**Raúl Castro Ruz (provisionally replacing Fidel Castro Ruz)**
Death penalty:	**retentionist**
Population:	**11.3 million**
Life expectancy:	**77.7 years**
Under-5 mortality (m/f):	**6/6 per 1,000**
Adult literacy:	**99.8 per cent**

Restrictions on freedom of expression, association and movement remained severe. At least 62 prisoners of conscience remained imprisoned and political dissidents, independent journalists and human rights activists continued to be harassed, intimidated and detained. However, four prisoners of conscience and other political dissidents were released and the government decided to discuss its human rights record with other governments and to ratify human rights treaties. Cubans continued to feel the negative impact of the US embargo.

C

Background

In May, the Cuban government accepted the creation of a Bilateral Consultation Mechanism with the Spanish authorities, which included a formal Human Rights Dialogue. The decision followed a visit by the Spanish Foreign Minister, the first EU foreign minister to visit Havana since the crackdown on dissidents in 2003. This represented the resumption of inter-governmental co-operation, suspended in 2003.

In November, the Special Rapporteur on the Right to Food visited Cuba at the invitation of the Cuban government. The invitation followed the decision by the UN Human Rights Council not to renew the mandate of the human rights Special Representative on Cuba. The Cuban Minister of Foreign Affairs stated that his government had a commitment to co-operate with universal human rights mechanisms "systematically and continuously, as long as Cuba is treated in a non-discriminatory way." On 10 December, he announced that Cuba would soon ratify two key human rights treaties.

Political relations with the USA remained tense. In October President Bush said the USA would maintain its policy of isolating Havana and called for international support.

In November, for the 16th consecutive year, the UN General Assembly passed a resolution calling on the USA to end its embargo on Cuba.

Freedom of expression and association

All print and broadcast media remained under state control.

During 2007, the government refused to renew the visas of a number of foreign correspondents because "their approach to the Cuban situation is not one which the Cuban government finds appropriate."

Justice system
Prisoners of conscience

At the end of the year, 62 prisoners of conscience continued to be held for their non-violent political views or activities. Thirteen others were serving their sentences outside prison because of health concerns. Four prisoners of conscience were conditionally released during 2007.

'Social dangerousness'

The practice of using the criminal justice system to silence political dissidents and critics continued. Many were sentenced for a crime known as "social dangerousness", a pre-emptive measure defined as the "proclivity to commit a crime". Behaviour such as drunkenness, drug addiction and "anti-social behaviour" is criminalized under this legislation. However, it was almost exclusively applied to political dissidents, independent journalists and critics of the government. Those convicted of "dangerousness" face up to four years' imprisonment and can be subjected to "therapeutic treatment", "re-education" or "surveillance by the Revolutionary National Police".

■ José Oscar Sánchez Madan was summarily tried in April and sentenced to four years' imprisonment for "social dangerousness" by the Municipal Court of Union de Reyes. His trial took place four hours after his arrest and no family member was informed of the trial or allowed to participate. José Oscar Sánchez Madan is one of the spokespersons of the dissident Independent Alternative Option Movement (Movimiento Independiente Opción Alternativa).

Arbitrary detention

Harassment of political dissidents, independent journalists and critics for carrying out dissident activities or reporting on the human rights situation in Cuba continued. Some were detained for 24 or 48 hours and then released; others were held for months or even years awaiting trial.

■ Between 21 November and 10 December many political dissidents were arbitrarily detained because of their involvement in peaceful protests. The detentions lasted for short periods of time and were aimed at discouraging demonstrations against the government, particularly on 10 December, International Human Rights Day. At least three people remained detained at the end of the year.

■ On 27 September, 48 people were detained in Havana as they were preparing to attend a demonstration in front of the Ministry of Justice to demand fair treatment for political dissidents. Some were released later that day and others on the following day.

Death penalty

Around 40 people remained on death row. The last known execution took place in April 2003 and death sentences have rarely been imposed in recent years.

Impact of the US embargo

The effects of the US embargo continued to be highly detrimental to the enjoyment of a range of economic,

C

social and cultural rights – such as the right to food, health and sanitation – by Cubans, and especially by the most vulnerable members of the population. Amnesty International believes that the US embargo has also undermined freedom of movement between Cuba and the USA and restricted family reunification.

Amnesty International reports

📄 Cuba: Further information on Fear for safety / Fear of torture / Intimidation / Harassment (AMR 25/001/2007)

📄 Cuba: Amnesty International's human rights concerns (AMR 25/003/2007)

📄 Cuba: Fear for safety/Fear of arbitrary detention – Martha Beatriz Roque Cabello (AMR 25/004/2007)

📄 Cuba: Government should commit to human rights by ending harassment of dissidents (11 December 2007)

CYPRUS

REPUBLIC OF CYPRUS

Head of state and government:	Tassos Papadopoulos
Death penalty:	abolitionist for all crimes
Population:	854,000
Life expectancy:	79 years
Adult literacy:	96.8 per cent

Foreign nationals, including migrants and asylum-seekers, were held in detention for unacceptably long periods and in poor conditions without access to a judicial or other independent review. Some reported being beaten by police upon arrest or by guards once detained. Asylum-seekers reported a number of irregularities in the asylum procedure that could have jeopardized their applications or their families at home. An organization supporting and advising migrants, refugees and asylum-seekers was the target of a racist attack and its chairperson charged in connection with its fundraising activities.

Detention and ill-treatment of foreign nationals

Foreign nationals were held in prolonged administrative detention without the opportunity for appeal before a judicial or similar independent body, in violation of the right not to be arbitrarily deprived of one's liberty. In late September and early October detainees in Block 10 of Nicosia Central Prison, which served as a police detention centre for rejected asylum-seekers who were under deportation orders, protested against the length and conditions of their detention. Several had been held for over 30 months.

Interviewees reported that the conditions in which they were detained were poor and that guards had subjected them to cruel and degrading treatment, including refusing them food and water during the protest. Several alleged that they had been ill-treated by police upon arrest or by guards in detention.

■ The authorities attempted to deport a Sierra Leonean national originally arrested for illegal stay in February 2005. His application for asylum, still pending when his detention began, had been rejected without him being informed or given the opportunity to challenge the decision. At the end of the year he was still in detention.

■ An Iranian national stated that he had been beaten by police upon arrest, then again by guards at the Central Prison whilst on a hunger strike protest in 2006, and a third time during the September-October protests. He stated that following the first beating in August 2005, he had developed a swelling on his head and problems focusing and balancing, and that he had been denied permission for an operation recommended by the doctor who examined him. He also stated that he had previously been detained for nine months in the Lykavitos police station where he was not allowed out into the yard, his cell was overcrowded and there were no adequate hygiene facilities.

By the end of 2007, no response had been received from the Cypriot authorities to Amnesty International's letter expressing concerns.

Human rights defenders

In April the European Network Against Racism reported that the headquarters of its branch in Cyprus, the non-governmental organization Action for Equality, Support and Anti-racism (Kinisi yia Isotita, Styrixi, Antiratsismo – KISA) had been sprayed with swastikas and nationalistic slogans. KISA offers support and legal advice to migrants, refugees and asylum-seekers in Cyprus. Its chairperson faced prosecution in October for the second time in five years on criminal charges relating to the organization's fundraising, in what may have been an attempt to hinder the organization in its work.

Amnesty International visit

🚐 Amnesty International visited Cyprus in October.

C

CZECH REPUBLIC

CZECH REPUBLIC
Head of state: Václav Klaus
Head of government: Mirek Topolánek
Death penalty: abolitionist for all crimes
Population: 10.2 million
Life expectancy: 75.9 years
Under-5 mortality (m/f): 6/5 per 1,000

The Romani minority continued to face discrimination and intolerance. Roma and other marginalized groups were reportedly subjected to police ill-treatment and to racist attacks by individuals. Allegations that the Czech Republic had permitted rendition flights went unanswered.

Discrimination against Roma

Despite anti-discrimination programmes, discrimination against Roma continued, especially in housing, education, healthcare and employment. A poll conducted in April revealed the prevalence of prejudice against Roma, with nine out of 10 respondents indicating they believed that having Romani neighbours would constitute a "problem". In August, the UN Human Rights Committee (HRC) expressed regret that the Czech Republic had failed to adopt an anti-discrimination bill.

Hate speech

In April, Roma rights activists lodged a criminal complaint regarding hate speech against Deputy Prime Minister and Christian Democrat leader Jiří Čunek, mayor of the town of Vsetín, when Romani families were evicted from the municipality in 2006. He was quoted in the tabloid *Blesk* (Lightning) as saying that "in order to be entitled to state subsidies like Roma, other people would need to get a suntan, behave in a disorderly way and light fires in town squares before politicians would regard them as badly off."

In October, the police shelved the criminal complaint. In response several Romani NGOs filed a constitutional complaint against the police. Jiří Čunek resigned in November, following allegations of corruption.

Housing and forced evictions

Ombudsperson Otakar Motejl concluded that the eviction of several Romani families to very isolated parts of the country from the town of Vsetín in 2006 was a "mistake". Thomas Hammarberg, Council of Europe Commissioner for Human Rights, and UN Rapporteur for Housing Rights Miloon Kothari issued a joint statement in October saying that the Czech Republic was in violation of the right to housing, where Roma were concerned. They also criticized local public offices for supporting escalating intolerance of Roma and pointed out that forced evictions of Roma from city centres to isolated areas had become part of public policy. In November, it was announced that a governmental Agency for Removing Social Segregation in Roma Localities would start working in 12 localities in January 2008.

The UN Committee on the Elimination of Racial Discrimination (CERD) expressed concern that Czech law failed to clearly prohibit racial discrimination in the right to housing, and the HRC condemned the persistent evictions and continued existence of Roma "ghettos".

Education

In November, the Grand Chamber of the European Court of Human Rights concluded, in a landmark case, that the Czech Republic had discriminated against Romani children by placing them in special schools for children with learning difficulties solely on the basis of their Romani origin. Following the ruling, the European Commission called on the Czech Republic to take concrete measures on the ground to "bridge segregation" and to end discrimination against Roma children.

Although the HRC and the CERD acknowledged that the Czech Republic had phased out placing Romani children in "special schools" for children with learning difficulties, concerns remained that a disproportionately large number of Romani children were segregated into Roma-only classes in mainstream schools, where they followed different curriculums to the majority of the population. In addition, the curriculums lacked sensitivity to the cultural identity and circumstances of Romani children.

The HRC expressed concern at reports that high numbers of Roma children were being removed from their families and placed in social care institutions.

Police ill-treatment

The CERD and the European Committee for the Prevention of Torture raised concerns about allegations of ill-treatment and excessive use of force by police officers, in particular against Roma and children, including their detention and coercion into confessing minor crimes. In July, the Supreme Court upheld a two-year prison sentence on a former Brno police officer for blackmail and misuse of power by law enforcement officials against a 14-year-old Romani boy. Reports of police misconduct continued, particularly against Roma and other marginalized groups, especially at the time of arrest and detention. The CERD regretted the failure to establish an independent body with authority to investigate complaints of unlawful conduct by the police.

■ In July the Prague City Court of Appeals acquitted Yekta Uzunoglu, a German citizen of Kurdish origin convicted of the blackmail and torture of a foreigner. Yekta Uzunoglu alleged that he had been subjected to torture and ill-treatment when he was arrested by police in 1994. Amnesty International urged the authorities to investigate alleged procedural violations of Yekta Uzunoglu's right to a fair trial.

Forced sterilization

The HRC and the CERD expressed concern that women, most of them Roma, had been subjected to sterilization without their consent. Despite a 1991 ruling to stop such operations, sterilizations without the informed consent of women were carried out as late as 2004.

■ In January the High Court in Olomouc delivered a ground-breaking verdict in the 2001 case of the illegal sterilization of Helena Ferenčíková, requiring the hospital which performed the sterilization to issue a formal apology. However, the High Court did not award Helena Ferenčíková the 1 million Czech *koruna* (approx €35,400) which she had sought as compensation for physical and psychological damage.

Mental health

The HRC concluded in August that mental health care in the country was inhuman and degrading, and called for far-reaching reforms. The Committee expressed concerns about the persistent use of enclosed cage beds in psychiatric institutions. Another concern was the forcible detention of those with mere "signs of mental illness" and inadequate control by courts of the process by which individuals were committed to psychiatric institutions.

Suspected renditions

There were allegations by HRC and other organizations that Czech airports had been used as transit points for rendition flights to countries where detainees were at risk of torture or ill-treatment. The HRC requested an investigation of possible transits through Czech airports. The government denied any knowledge of such incidents.

Ratifications

The Czech Republic remained the only European Union member state not to have ratified the Statute of the International Criminal Court.

Amnesty International visit/reports

🚍 Amnesty International delegates visited the Czech Republic in February.

▥ Europe and Central Asia: Summary of Amnesty International's concerns in the region, July-December 2006 (EUR 01/001/2007)

▥ Czech Republic: Fair trial concerns in the case of Yekta Uzunoglu (EUR 71/001/2007)

▥ Czech Republic: European Court decision on discrimination in education (EUR 71/002/2007)

DEMOCRATIC REPUBLIC OF THE CONGO

DEMOCRATIC REPUBLIC OF THE CONGO

Head of state and government:	Joseph Kabila
Death penalty:	retentionist
Population:	61.2 million
Life expectancy:	45.8 years
Under-5 mortality (m/f):	208/186 per 1,000
Adult literacy:	67.2 per cent

Political and military tensions in the Democratic Republic of the Congo (DRC) resulted in major outbreaks of violence in the capital, Kinshasa, and Bas-Congo province. Unlawful killings, arbitrary arrests and detentions, torture and other cruel, inhuman and degrading treatment by the security forces and by armed groups were common across the country, in many cases directed at perceived

D

political opponents. Rape by security force members and armed group fighters continued at high levels. While security continued to improve in some provinces, a human rights and humanitarian crisis deepened in the two Kivu provinces in the east of the country.

Humanitarian needs remained acute nationwide with more than 1.4 million people displaced by conflict in the country. The delivery of vital social services, including health and education, was hampered by poor governance, a decayed infrastructure and underinvestment.

Background

A new government, formed in February, ended the interim power-sharing administration in place since 2003. Tensions between the government and Jean-Pierre Bemba, the main opposition presidential candidate in 2006, degenerated in late March. Up to 600 people were killed when fighting broke out in Kinshasa between government forces and Jean-Pierre Bemba's armed guard after he refused a government order to disarm. Jean-Pierre Bemba then left the country, and an uneasy co-existence between the government and political opposition developed.

State authority continued to be restored to previously insecure areas of the country. State institutions, though further consolidated, remained weak. A number of armed groups were successfully disarmed and demobilized, notably in Ituri District and Katanga province. However, without the promised assistance to re-enter civilian life, demobilized fighters were a source of local insecurity.

Conflict persisted in the Kivu provinces of eastern DRC. In August, fighting erupted in North-Kivu between the army and forces loyal to Tutsi commander Laurent Nkunda. The fighting, which also involved the Democratic Liberation Forces of Rwanda (FDLR) armed group and mayi-mayi militia, was characterized by grave breaches of international humanitarian law and led to increased tension between the DRC and Rwanda. In November, the two governments agreed a "common approach" to end the threat posed by national and foreign armed groups in the DRC. A government military offensive, supported by the UN peacekeeping force, MONUC, against Laurent Nkunda's forces in December was inconclusive. Plans for a major national conference aimed at bringing peace to the Kivus were announced at the year's end.

Internally displaced people

More than 170,000 people were displaced by the fighting in North-Kivu between August and December, adding to around 200,000 displaced by insecurity there since the end of 2006. Overall, more than 1.4 million people were internally displaced in the DRC, while 322,000 were living as refugees in neighbouring countries.

Police and security forces

The national army, police force, and military and civilian intelligence services routinely operated with little or no regard for Congolese and international law, and committed the majority of the human rights violations reported. An increased number of violations were attributed to the police. Ill-discipline and poor command of these forces, and the widespread impunity they enjoyed, remained a major barrier to improved enjoyment of human rights. A Security Sector Reform programme, aimed at integrating former armed forces and groups into unified state security forces, remained only partly complete. Failure by the government and Laurent Nkunda to respect the national legal framework for army integration was a contributing factor to the violence in North-Kivu.

Civilian protection in the east remained almost wholly dependent on the overstretched MONUC forces. In November, the UN Secretary-General proposed benchmarks that should be met before any reduction of MONUC forces. These included the disarmament and demobilization or repatriation of armed groups in the east and substantial improvements by the DRC security forces in assuring security, protecting civilians and respecting human rights.

Unlawful killings

State security forces as well as Congolese and foreign armed groups committed hundreds of unlawful killings. During military operations, all forces deliberately targeted civilians or failed to take adequate measures to protect civilian populations. During the March fighting in Kinshasa, both government forces and Jean-Pierre Bemba's armed guard used heavy weapons in densely

D

populated residential areas, causing hundreds of civilian deaths.

■ On 31 January /1 February, 95 civilians were killed by the army and police, who used disproportionate force and in some cases extrajudicial executions to quell violent protests in Bas-Congo province. Ten security force members died in the disturbances.

■ Government forces allegedly extrajudicially executed at least 27 suspected supporters of Jean-Pierre Bemba in Kinshasa in late March.

■ In September, 21 bodies were discovered in mass graves in positions vacated by Laurent Nkunda's forces in Rutshuru territory, North-Kivu. Some of the bodies had been bound by their hands and feet.

Torture and other ill-treatment

Acts of torture and ill-treatment were routinely committed by government security services and armed groups, including sustained beatings, stabbings and rapes in custody. Detainees were held incommunicado, sometimes in secret detention sites. In Kinshasa, the Republican Guard (presidential guard) and Special Services police division arbitrarily detained, tortured and ill-treated numerous perceived opponents of the government. Many victims were targeted because they shared Jean-Pierre Bemba's ethnicity or geographical origin in Equateur province. Conditions in most detention centres and prisons remained cruel, inhuman or degrading. Deaths of prisoners from malnutrition or treatable illnesses were regularly reported.

■ Papy Tembe Moroni, a Kinshasa journalist from Equateur province who worked for an opposition television station, spent 132 days in arbitrary detention before being released in April. During his time in police custody, he told Amnesty International, "I was beaten with lengths of wood and clubs as if they were killing a snake".

Sexual violence

High levels of rape and other forms of sexual violence continued across the country, particularly in the east. Soldiers and police, as well as Congolese and foreign armed group members, were among the main perpetrators. An increasing number of rapes by civilians was also reported. Many rapes, notably those committed by armed groups, involved genital mutilation or other extreme brutality. The FDLR armed group and an FDLR splinter group, *Rasta*,

abducted women and girls as sex slaves. Few perpetrators of sexual violence were brought to justice. A 2006 law which strengthened judicial procedures and penalties for crimes of sexual violence was not widely implemented. Rape survivors continued to be stigmatized, suffering social and economic exclusion. Few had access to adequate medical care. The continuing rape crisis is part of a broader pattern of violence and endemic discrimination against women in the DRC.

■ *Mayi-mayi* fighters were allegedly responsible for the mass rape of around 120 women and girls in Lieke Lesole, Opala territory, Orientale province, between 21 July and 3 August. A judicial investigation was in progress at the year's end.

■ On 26/27 May, FDLR or *Rasta* fighters reportedly killed 17 people, including women and children, and abducted and sexually assaulted seven women, in Kanyola, South-Kivu province. The women were later rescued by the army.

Child soldiers

Many hundreds of children remained in the ranks of Congolese and foreign armed groups and some army units. A government programme to identify the children and separate them from the armed forces was largely inoperative by the year's end. Programmes for reintegrating former child soldiers into civilian life remained weak in many areas of the country. Around 5,000 former child soldiers were awaiting reintegration assistance at the end of 2007.

In North-Kivu, Laurent Nkunda's armed group and opposing *mayi-mayi* militia recruited large numbers of children, many of them by force. Nkunda's forces allegedly targeted schools for forced recruitment. Insecurity in North-Kivu undermined NGO programmes aimed at unifying families and reintroducing former child soldiers into the community. Former child soldiers who had been reunited with their families were among those taken by armed groups.

■ In October, more than 160 girls and boys, aged between seven and 18, were sheltered at a stadium in the town of Rutshuru, North-Kivu. They had fled attempts by Laurent Nkunda's forces to forcibly recruit them. Other children were feared captured by armed group fighters or lost in the forest.

Human rights defenders

Human rights defenders continued to suffer attacks and death threats, believed to be perpetrated mainly by government agents. Journalists and lawyers were routinely attacked, arbitrarily arrested or intimidated because of their professional activities.

■ A woman human rights defender was raped by a security official during a work visit to a detention facility in May. In September, the daughters of another woman activist were violently sexually assaulted in their home by soldiers.

■ In June, Serge Maheshe, a journalist for the UN-sponsored Radio Okapi, was murdered in Bukavu in circumstances that were not satisfactorily investigated. After an unfair military trial, four people were sentenced to death in August, including two friends of the victim who were convicted on the basis of the uncorroborated testimony, later retracted, of two men who confessed to the killing. An appeal was pending.

Justice system

The civilian justice system was absent or barely functioning in many areas, and hampered by a lack of independence, resources and personnel. Trials of civilians by military court continued, despite being unconstitutional. Many trials, especially by military courts, were unfair. Death sentences continued to be passed, the vast majority by military courts, but no executions were reported. There were lengthy delays in bringing people to court, although trials themselves were often summary. There were frequent instances of political and military interference in the administration of justice.

■ Théophile Kazadi Mutombo Fofana had been held in unlawful pre-trial detention in Kinshasa's CPRK prison since September 2004. He was illegally extradited from the Republic of Congo in July 2004, on suspicion of involvement in an alleged coup attempt in Kinshasa, and tortured in security service detention. To date, he had not appeared before a court or been allowed to challenge the lawfulness of his detention.

Impunity – international justice

Impunity persisted in the vast majority of cases. There were, however, a growing number of national – predominantly military – investigations and trials for human rights abuses, including a handful for war crimes and crimes against humanity. Prosecutions were undermined by frequent escapes from prisons and detention centres.

■ In October, the government surrendered Germain Katanga, former commander of an Ituri armed group, to the International Criminal Court (ICC). He was indicted by the ICC on charges of crimes against humanity and war crimes allegedly committed in Ituri District in 2003. He was the second Ituri armed group leader to be transferred to the Court, after Thomas Lubanga Dyilo in March 2006. Other men, arrested by the Congolese authorities in early 2005 on charges of crimes against humanity in Ituri, remained in pre-trial detention in Kinshasa's CPRK prison. The military judicial authorities extended their detention several times, in breach of Congolese legal procedure, but made no attempt to bring them to trial.

■ In February, the Bunia (Ituri) military court convicted 13 soldiers of war crimes for killing more than 30 civilians in the village of Bavi in late 2006. The same court convicted six armed group members for the war crime of killing two MONUC military observers in May 2003. The court applied the provisions of the Rome Statute of the ICC in both trials.

■ In June, a military court acquitted all defendants, including military officers and three foreign employees of the multinational company Anvil Mining, of war crimes charges in connection with the 2004 Kilwa massacre in Katanga province. Four of the 12 defendants were convicted of unrelated crimes. There was apparent political interference in the trial. The acquittals were widely condemned as a setback in the struggle against impunity in the DRC.

Amnesty International visits/reports

🚌 Amnesty International delegates visited the country in May and June.

📄 Democratic Republic of Congo: Disarmament, Demobilization and Reintegration (DDR) and Reform of the Army (AFR 62/001/2007)

📄 Democratic Republic of Congo: Torture and killings by state security agents still endemic (AFR 62/012/2007)

📄 Democratic Republic of Congo (DRC): Escalating violence in North-Kivu deepens risk of mass ethnic killings (AFR 62/014/2007)

DENMARK

KINGDOM OF DENMARK

Head of state:	Queen Margrethe II
Head of government:	Anders Fogh Rasmussen
Death penalty:	abolitionist for all crimes
Population:	5.5 million
Life expectancy:	77.9 years
Under-5 mortality (m/f):	6/6 per 1,000

Background

In November, a general election was held, leading to the formation of a new government led by existing Prime Minister Anders Fogh Rasmussen.

In September, Denmark signed the International Convention for the Protection of All Persons from Enforced Disappearance and ratified the Council of Europe Convention on Action against Trafficking in Human Beings.

Torture and other ill-treatment

In April, the UN Committee against Torture (CAT) urged Denmark to make torture a specific offence which could be investigated, prosecuted and punished without time limitations.

By the end of the year there had been no independent investigation of allegations that 31 men captured by Danish Special Forces in Afghanistan in March 2002 and handed over to the US authorities had subsequently been ill-treated while in US custody.

Following the publication of an Amnesty International report on transfers of prisoners to the Afghan authorities from forces, including Danish forces, making up the International Security Assistance Force in Afghanistan, the Minister of Defence announced that Danish troops would in future monitor the treatment of all prisoners transferred from their custody to Afghan custody.

'War on terror'

In a letter to the European Parliament's Temporary Committee investigating the alleged use of European territory and airspace in renditions and secret detention carried out by the US Central Intelligence Agency, the Danish government reported more than 100 flights through Danish airspace, and 45 stopovers in Danish airports, by aeroplanes which

have been credibly alleged to have been involved in rendition flights. The Danish authorities failed to initiate an independent investigation into allegations of Danish involvement in renditions.

Policing

■ In March, the Copenhagen Police closed down the "Ungdomshuset", a centre for alternative culture. In the course of subsequent demonstrations more than 800 people were arrested, amid reports that police officers used excessive force in policing them. Approximately 200 of those arrested were remanded in custody pending trial. Relatives and lawyers reported that some minors were forced to share cells with adult inmates.

Refugees and asylum-seekers

The CAT raised concerns about the long periods that asylum-seekers spent living in asylum centres. According to figures cited by the Council of Europe's Commissioner for Human Rights, an estimated 40 per cent of all asylum-seekers remained in such centres for more than three years.

The Danish government granted visas to around 370 Iraqis, and their immediate families, who had been working for Danish troops in Iraq, allowing them to enter Denmark to seek asylum.

Discrimination
'Starting allowance'

People who had not been permanently resident in Denmark for at least seven of the last eight years were not entitled to claim regular social welfare benefits, but were restricted to the so-called "starting allowance". For people over the age of 25 this amounted to between 45 and 65 per cent of regular social benefits. Newly arrived residents, in particular members of ethnic minorities who experienced more difficulty in finding employment than people born in Denmark, were over-represented among recipients of the "starting allowance".

Requirements for family reunification

For family reunification to take place in Denmark applicants were required to demonstrate ties to Denmark stronger than ties to any other country. In practice it was very difficult for a Danish citizen of foreign origin and his or her spouse to satisfy this requirement, in particular where both the Danish citizen and his or her spouse originated from the same country.

D

The Council of Europe's Commissioner for Human Rights noted that this provision in effect discriminated between citizens who were born as Danish nationals and those who had acquired Danish nationality. He recommended that the government should reduce the length of time (currently 28 years) for which a person has to be resident as a Danish citizen before they can be exempt from these requirements when making an application for a foreign family member to be granted a residence permit.

Amnesty International reports

Denmark: A briefing for the Committee against Torture (EUR 18/001/2007)

Denmark: Authorities must come clean about renditions (EUR 18/003/2007)

DOMINICAN REPUBLIC

DOMINICAN REPUBLIC

Head of state and government:	**Leonel Fernández Reyna**
Death penalty:	**abolitionist for all crimes**
Population:	**9.1 million**
Life expectancy:	**71.5 years**
Under-5 mortality (m/f):	**48/39 per 1,000**
Adult literacy:	**87 per cent**

Haitians and Dominico-Haitians continued to face discrimination. Killings by police in disputed circumstances were reported. Violence against women was widespread. People-trafficking into and out of the country remained a serious concern. Forced evictions left hundreds of families without shelter.

Background

Protests by different sections of the population in favour of stronger government measures to address poverty and the fulfilment of social and economic rights recurred throughout the year. Despite strong economic growth, more than a quarter of the population lived in poverty and the number of undernourished children rose again.

Reforms of the Penal Code, including the decriminalization of abortion, were discussed in Congress but no legislation was passed by the end of the year.

The Dominican authorities reinforced military control of its border with Haiti by deploying a Special Border Security Force. Mass expulsions of irregular migrants were often arbitrary with no right to appeal.

Violence against women

Violence against women was widespread and affected women from all backgrounds. According to official statistics, at least 165 women were killed in domestic disputes by their current or former partner. Prosecutors' offices received more than 6,000 complaints of gender-based violence from across the country in the first six months of the year. There were concerns about under-reporting of cases and inadequate responses from the authorities when women did report abuses.

Discrimination against Haitians and Dominico-Haitians

There were concerns about new measures whereby the children born to undocumented migrants were registered in a Registry for foreigners. This measure was considered discriminatory as it could hamper children of Haitian descent from exercising their right to Dominican nationality. In October, the UN Independent Expert on minority issues and the Special Rapporteur on contemporary forms of racism, racial discrimination, xenophobia and related intolerance visited the country. They noted that discrimination against Haitian migrant workers and Dominico-Haitians was widespread. Racially motivated attacks against Haitian migrant workers were reported throughout the year.

Trafficking in people

There were numerous deaths at sea of people trying to reach Puerto Rico from the Dominican Republic in trafficking operations. Haitian migrant workers continued to be trafficked into the country despite increased surveillance by the border authorities.

■ In November, a military unit of the Special Border Security Force based in Dajabón was replaced after local NGOs exposed their involvement in the ill-treatment of Haitian nationals and reported that they were accepting bribes to allow irregular migrants into the country.

In January, two civilians and two military officers were sentenced to 20 and 10 years' imprisonment respectively for their part in a trafficking ring whose operations led to the deaths by asphyxiation of 25 Haitian migrant workers in January 2006.

Freedom of the press

Intimidation and harassment of media workers and journalists by the authorities and private individuals increased in 2007. Journalists reporting on corruption were attacked.

■ In January, Manuel Vega was threatened with being "burnt alive" after he reported on drug trafficking in Hato Mayor province.

■ In May, the Public Prosecutor's Office of the National District re-opened the case of Narciso Gonazález, a journalist and university teacher who disappeared in May 1994 after reportedly being detained in a military base on the outskirts of Santo Domingo.

Housing rights – forced evictions

Hundreds of families were forcibly evicted from their homes without due process or consultation. In most cases, excessive force was used by police and military officers or private individuals enforcing the eviction resulting in deaths, injuries and destruction of property.

■ In June, police and military officers used pellets and tear gas to evict 75 families from public land in Villa Venecia de Pantojas, Santo Domingo Este. César Ureña, a community leader, was reportedly extrajudicially executed by military officers during the eviction. In December, 45 other families were forcibly evicted from the same community with the use of a forged eviction order. Their homes were destroyed and their belongings were stolen with the alleged complicity of military and police officers overseeing the eviction.

Police and security forces – unlawful killings

Reports of police brutality continued. Between January and May alone, at least 126 people were killed by the police, according to the General Prosecutor's Office. Impunity for police abuses and a complete lack of accountability in the security and justice systems remained the norm.

■ In July, Rafael de Jesús Torres Tavárez was reportedly shot dead by police officers in Navarrete on the night preceding a general strike organized by the Alternative Social Forum.

Amnesty International visit/reports

Amnesty International delegates visited the Dominican Republic in March.

A life in transit – The plight of Haitian migrants and Dominicans of Haitian descent (AMR 27/001/2007)

Dominican Republic: Haitian migrants denied their rights (AMR 27/003/2007)

ECUADOR

REPUBLIC OF ECUADOR

Head of state and government:	**Rafael Vicente Correa Delgado**
Death penalty:	**abolitionist for all crimes**
Population:	**13.6 million**
Life expectancy:	**74.7 years**
Under-5 mortality (m/f):	**29/22 per 1,000**
Adult literacy:	**91 per cent**

The new government initiated constitutional reforms. Environmental activists and community leaders in areas close to extractive industries were threatened and harassed. Several cases of ill-treatment and torture by police were reported.

Background

Rafael Correa was sworn in as President in January and outlined five priority areas of work including reforms in health and education, reducing corruption and reforms of the Constitution.

In May the President set up a truth commission to investigate human rights violations committed under the government of León Febres Cordero (1984-1988). However, the commission had not begun its work by the end of the year. Also in May, Ecuador signed the International Convention for the Protection of All Persons from Enforced Disappearance.

In June, a presidential decree declared the penitentiary system to be in a state of emergency and promised in-depth reforms. The same month, the Constitutional Tribunal declared two articles of the law on military service unconstitutional, thereby making conscientious objection possible.

Hundreds of Colombians fled across the border into Ecuador to escape intense fighting between the security forces and guerrilla forces in the southern

Colombian department of Nariño, and serious human rights violations by army-backed paramilitaries.

Environmental concerns and community activists

In June, a federal court in New York, USA, recognized the jurisdiction of the Ecuadorian justice system in a case being brought against Chevron (formerly Texaco) by Ecuadorians for alleged environmental damage in the Amazonian region between 1964 and 1990. The case was due to reach a conclusion in 2008.

Environmental and community activists were reportedly threatened and harassed in the context of protests against extractive industry projects.

■ Between June and August, community leader Jaime Polivio Pérez Lucero received death threats and activist Mercy Catalina Torres Terán was attacked by an unidentified armed man. They were apparently targeted because of their opposition to a mining project close to their homes in the Intag area of Imbabura Province.

■ In January and March, members of a community in Canton Chillanes, Bolívar Province, were reportedly threatened and harassed by members of the armed forces. They were arrested on charges of sabotage and violence towards the armed forces, but were all released several days later because of insufficient evidence. The arrests were apparently linked to the community's campaign for the right of those affected by a planned hydroelectric dam in the area to be consulted about the project.

■ In November a state of emergency was declared in Orellana Province after demonstrators took over oil wells in the region and cut oil production by around 20 per cent as part of a campaign to demand that the government spend more of the revenue from oil on improving the infrastructure in the province. Around 20 protesters were detained during a military operation to quell the protests in which ill-treatment of detainees was reported.

Police and security forces

Several people were reportedly ill-treated by police in custody. One person died in custody in disputed circumstances. There were continuing concerns about attempts to refer allegations of ill-treatment by police to the police, rather than the civilian, courts.

■ Paúl Alejandro Guañuna Sanguña was detained by two police officers while he was walking home in

Zámbiza, Pichincha Province, in January. The following day the 17-year-old's body was found at the bottom of a ravine. Attempts to refer the case to the police courts resulted in a delay in the start of the judicial process. At the end of the year the trial was continuing in a civilian court.

■ In May, 16-year-old Víctor Javier Tipán Caiza was stopped by police as he was walking home with friends. The others ran away, but Víctor Tipán was caught and taken into custody. His friends later found him at the spot where they had been stopped. He had multiple injuries, including broken teeth and a broken nose. An investigation was apparently opened into this case, but the results were not known at the end of the year.

EGYPT

ARAB REPUBLIC OF EGYPT

Head of state:	Muhammad Hosni Mubarak
Head of government:	Ahmed Nazif
Death penalty:	retentionist
Population:	76.9 million
Life expectancy:	70.7 years
Under-5 mortality (m/f):	38/31 per 1,000
Adult literacy:	71.4 per cent

Constitutional amendments rushed through parliament were the most serious setback for human rights since the state of emergency was reintroduced in 1981. The amendments cemented the sweeping powers of the police and entrenched in permanent law emergency powers that have been used systematically to violate human rights, including prolonged detention without charge, torture and other ill-treatment, restrictions on freedom of speech, association and assembly, and grossly unfair trials before military courts and special emergency courts. Around 18,000 administrative detainees – people held by order of the Interior Ministry – remained in prison in degrading and inhumane conditions. Some had been held for more than a decade, including many whose release had been repeatedly ordered by courts. Egyptian nationals suspected of terrorism, who had been unlawfully transferred to Egypt by other governments, remained in prison. Courts continued to pass death sentences and at least one person was executed.

As the biggest strike wave for decades spread across the country involving public and private sector workers, the authorities closed an independent group defending workers' rights. The strikes, sparked by rising living costs, growing poverty and other grievances, coincided with political protests by the Muslim Brotherhood, the largest opposition force, and secular opposition groups campaigning for democratic reforms. Political activists, journalists and bloggers were jailed for peacefully expressing their views.

Women faced increasing levels of violence, according to reports. The government took further action to end the practice of female genital mutilation (FGM), which was still carried out on most girls.

Legal and constitutional developments
Constitutional amendments
On 19 March parliament amended 34 articles of the Constitution. Draconian changes made to Article 179 cemented the sweeping arrest powers of the police, gave broad authority for state agents to eavesdrop on private communications, authorized the President to bypass ordinary courts and paved the way for new anti-terrorism legislation expected to further erode human rights protection. Other amendments appeared to be politically motivated. One reduced the role of judges in supervising elections and referendums. Another banned the establishment of political parties based on religion – an apparent response to the 2005 electoral success of the Muslim Brotherhood. The amendments were approved a week later in a national referendum boycotted by the main opposition.
Military Justice Code amendments
The Military Justice Code (Law No. 25 of 1966), which established military courts, was amended in April but the changes did not address the fundamental flaws inherent in trying civilians before military courts. It introduced a limited right of appeal by way of cassation before the Supreme Court for Military Appeals, under which the appeal court can review procedural issues during trial but not the factual basis of the charges or evidence leading to conviction. Further, judges of the Supreme Court of Military Appeals are all serving military officers and

the Court's decisions remain subject to ratification by the President or his nominee, who can reduce, alter or suspend the sentence.
Draft anti-terrorism law
The government announced in December that it had completed drafting a bill on counter-terrorism comprising 58 articles and that expert panels would examine it before it was presented to the Council of Ministers and later to parliament.

'War on terror'
An unknown number of Egyptian nationals suspected of terrorism who had been returned forcibly and without any judicial process in previous years by the US and other governments, detained on arrival and tortured by Egyptian security forces, continued to be imprisoned.

■ Muhammed 'Abd al-'Aziz al-Gamal, Sayyid Imam 'Abd al-'Aziz al-Sharif (Abu al-Fadl), 'Isam Shu'aib Muhammed, Khalifa Sayyid Badawi, Uthman al-Samman and Ali Abd al-Rahim, who were unlawfully returned to Egypt from Yemen in February 2002, were still detained without charge or the prospect of a retrial and without access to legal counsel, medical treatment or relatives. All were victims of enforced disappearance after their return to Egypt. In March it was reported that Abu al-Fadl and Muhammed al-Gamal, who were sentenced to death by a military court in 1999, had been transferred from secret detention to Tora Prison, south of Cairo. In July Abu al-Fadl, a founder of the Islamic Jihad organization, publicly renounced political violence in the lead-up to the releases of some 330 Jihad prisoners.

■ Usama Mostafa Hassan Nasr (Abu Omar), who was abducted in Italy and unlawfully transferred to Egypt in 2003, was unexpectedly released without charge in February. At least 16 previous court orders for his release had been ignored. After his return to Egypt his fate and whereabouts had been unknown for 14 months. He was released in April 2004 but rearrested 23 days later because he told relatives he had been tortured while detained. After his release in 2007, he met Amnesty International and described his abduction in Italy and imprisonment in Egypt. He said that he was tortured during the 14 months he was held in General Intelligence and State Security Intelligence (SSI) premises, including with electric shocks to sensitive parts of his body, a form of crucifixion on a metal door and a wooden apparatus, beatings with electric cables and water hoses, and whipping.

Justice system
Military and special courts
A parallel system of emergency justice, involving specially constituted emergency courts and the trial of civilians before military courts, continued. Under this system, safeguards for fair trial, such as equality before the law, prompt access to a lawyer and the ban on using evidence extracted under torture, were routinely violated.

■ The trial of 40 members of the Muslim Brotherhood (seven in their absence) on charges of terrorism and money laundering began in April before a military court although the defendants were civilians. The defendants, who faced charges punishable by death, included Khairat al-Shatir, the Muslim Brotherhood's deputy supreme guide, who was arrested in December 2006 along with 16 other prominent members. All 17 were acquitted of all charges in January by an ordinary criminal court, but were immediately rearrested. In February President Mubarak ordered the 17 cases, and those of 23 other alleged Muslim Brotherhood members, to be transferred to the Supreme Military Court in Heikstep, Cairo. In May a Cairo administrative court ruled that the President's order was invalid, but a few days later the Supreme Administrative Court reversed that decision, after the government appealed. The trial was still continuing at the end of the year but media reporters, national and international observers, including Amnesty International, were barred from its sessions.

Administrative detention
Despite releases of some 530 Islamist detainees in 2007, some 18,000 people continued to be detained without charge or trial on the orders of the Interior Minister under the emergency law. Most were held in conditions that amount to cruel, inhuman or degrading treatment, and hundreds were reportedly ill with tuberculosis, skin diseases and other ailments. Many remained held despite their acquittal by courts and despite repeated orders for their release.

■ Mohamed 'Abd Rahim el Sharkawy, 57, a Pakistan national of Egyptian origin, remained in administrative detention in Liman Tora Prison. He was extradited to Egypt from Pakistan in 1995, held incommunicado for months and allegedly tortured. He was subsequently acquitted by an emergency court. Courts have ordered his release at least 15 times, including in April 2007. His health has suffered because of torture in the 1990s, harsh prison conditions and lack of adequate medical care. In February the prison administration referred him for medical examination, but the request was refused by the SSI.

Torture and other ill-treatment
Torture and other ill-treatment continued to be widespread and systematic, and reportedly led or contributed to at least 20 deaths in 2007. Videos showing torture by police were posted on the internet by Egyptian bloggers.

Commonly cited torture methods included electric shocks, beatings, suspension in painful positions, solitary confinement, rape and threats of death, sexual abuse and attacks on relatives. Allegations of torture were rarely investigated. The few prosecutions of alleged torturers never related to political cases and usually followed incidents where the victim had died.

■ In August Mohamed Mamduh Abdel Rahman, a 13-year-old boy, died in the Nile Delta town of Mansura after alleged police torture. He lost consciousness while being held for six days on suspicion of stealing packets of tea. The authorities transferred him to hospital where he died. He was buried without his family being notified. His brother, detained at the same time, said police burned Mohamed with a heating coil, beat him and gave him electric shocks. He said that when Mohamed had convulsions, a police officer kicked him in the chest. A video of Mohamed in hospital shows what look like burns on his back and testicles. The police said his death was due to natural causes exacerbated by inadequate medical treatment, and that the burns were accidental. The family filed a complaint. In September a government-appointed panel of forensic experts cleared the police of any wrongdoing.

■ In a rare successful prosecution of alleged torturers, two officers from Bulaq Dakrur Police Station in Giza Governorate were sentenced in November to three years' imprisonment for the the unlawful detention, torture and rape of Emad Mohamed Ali Mohamed (Emad al-Kabir), a 21-year-old taxi driver. Emad al-Kabir was arrested in January 2006 after trying to stop an argument between police officers and his cousin. He said officers tied his hands and feet, whipped him and ordered him to call himself degrading names. The officers then removed his trousers and raped him with a stick, recording the torture and circulating it in Emad al-Kabir's neighbourhood in an attempt to break his spirit and intimidate others. The video was posted on the

E

internet in November 2006. Emad al-Kabir was sentenced in January 2007 to three months' imprisonment for "resisting the authorities" and "assaulting a police officer".

Violence against women

Violence against women claimed 247 lives in the first half of the year, according to an Egyptian NGO. In November the Egyptian Centre for Women's Rights (ECWR) said sexual harassment was on the rise and that two women were being raped every hour in Egypt. It also said that of 2,500 women who had reported cases of sexual harassment to ECWR, only 12 per cent had made a complaint to the police. The official National Centre for Social and Criminal Research confirmed that sex crimes were on the rise, but could not provide figures.

Following a hearing in November, the African Commission on Human and Peoples' Rights said it would consider in May 2008 a case filed by 33 human rights organizations against the Egyptian government's failure to prevent and prosecute physical and sexual assaults targeted at women journalists and demonstrators during a protest in May 2005.

Female genital mutilation

UNICEF estimated that three quarters of Muslim and Christian girls aged between 15 and 17 were subjected to FGM and two thirds of girls now aged under three are expected to undergo the practice before they reach the age of 18. According to official Egyptian statistics, 97 per cent of women aged between 15 and 49 have undergone FGM.

FGM was banned for all but "exceptional cases" in 1997, with a maximum penalty of three years in prison. Progress towards the eradication of FGM continued to be made in 2007. In June, following the widely publicized death after FGM of an 11-year-old girl, Bedur Ahmed Shaker, in the Nile village of Maghagha, Menya, the Chief Mufti declared FGM forbidden under Islam. The same month the Health Minister issued a decree banning the medical profession from performing FGM. In September, four doctors and a midwife in the southern province of Menya were reportedly prosecuted for performing FGM and their clinics were closed down. A law to stiffen penalties against anyone performing FGM was reportedly being prepared by the Ministry.

Human rights defenders

Under Egyptian law, the strikes that spread across the country were "illegal" – unauthorized by the state-sponsored General Federation of Trade Unions (GFTU). The authorities responded by increasing repression of trade unionists as well as NGO activists.

■ In March and April the authorities closed three offices of the main independent group defending workers' rights in Egypt – the Centre for Trade Union and Workers' Services (CTUWS) – in Naj' Hammadi, Mahalla al-Kubra and Helwan. The GFTU and the Minister of Manpower had blamed the CTUWS for the strike wave. The authorities continued to refuse applications by the CTUWS to be registered as an association.

■ In September the authorities shut down the Association for Human Rights and Legal Aid (AHRLA). The authorities said the AHRLA had breached Law 84 of 2002, which prohibits organizations receiving foreign funds without the government's permission.

Freedom of expression

Journalists and bloggers faced harassment, prosecution and, in some cases, jail for the peaceful expression of their views or for carrying out their work as journalists.

■ In February, Karim Amer became the first blogger in Egypt to be jailed for the peaceful expression of his political views. His four-year sentence was confirmed on appeal in March. He is a prisoner of conscience. Charges against him included "spreading information disruptive of public order and damaging to the country's reputation", "incitement to hate Islam" and "defaming the President".

■ In September, four newspaper and magazine editors were sentenced to prison terms and a fine for publishing information "likely to disturb public order". All were released on bail pending appeal.

Discrimination – religious minorities

The legal requirement to specify religion on identity papers, and only religions recognized by the state, continued to have serious implications for some minorities. Baha'is, whose faith is not recognized by the state, cannot obtain identity papers without posing as a Muslim, Christian or Jew. Without the papers, they cannot enrol children in school, drive a car, or open a bank account. The lack of identity papers also leaves them vulnerable during police checks. Converts, especially from Islam to Christianity, also faced difficulties changing their papers.

Coptic Christians, who comprise 8-10 per cent of Egypt's population, continued to face discrimination in many walks of life.

E

- In July the Supreme Administrative Court agreed to hear the appeal of Coptic converts to Islam who were seeking to legally revert back to Christianity. The government had tried to get the appeal dismissed.
- In August Mohamed Hegazy, who converted from Islam to Christianity in 2003, began a legal case to have his conversion officially recognized on his identity papers so that his unborn child would be born a Christian. The Interior Ministry rejected Mohamed Hegazy's request to have his conversion registered. Mohamed Hegazy was forced into hiding after receiving death threats following media reports about his case. In November, the case was allowed to proceed and the next session was scheduled for January 2008.

Death penalty

Death sentences continued to be imposed and at least one person was executed. In October the National Council for Human Rights held a round table discussion on the death penalty, but government ministers said abolition was not on the agenda.
- Muhammed Gayiz Sabbah, Usama 'Abd al-Ghani al-Nakhlawi and Yunis Muhammed Abu Gareer staged a hunger strike in late 2006 and early 2007 against death sentences imposed on them in November 2006 after an unfair trial. In May, the African Commission on Human and Peoples' Rights declared the case admissible, after it called on the Egyptian authorities to stay the executions in December 2006. In its session in November, it deferred the case to May 2008 after the government said it would submit additional documents.

Refugees and asylum-seekers

Between 2-3 million migrants, refugees and asylum-seekers, mostly from Sudan, were living in Egypt in 2007, according to UNHCR. Egyptian border police allegedly used excessive force against many migrants, refugees and asylum-seekers who tried to cross into Israel from Egypt, particularly from July onwards. At least four men and two women were shot dead, according to reports. Raids by Egyptian police in the border area in July alone led to the arrest of over 220 mainly Sudanese migrants. In October, the Egyptian authorities reportedly returned to Sudan at least five of the 48 asylum-seekers that were forcibly transferred to them from Israel in August.

A report issued in May by the UN Committee on the Protection of the Rights of All Migrant Workers and Members of Their Families called on the Egyptian government "to initiate training for all officials working in the area of migration, in particular police and border personnel..."

Amnesty International visits/reports

🚌 Amnesty International delegates visited Egypt in February/March and in April and May and met human rights defenders, victims and their relatives and government officials.

📄 Egypt: Systematic abuses in the name of security (MDE 12/001/2007)

📄 Egypt: Proposed constitutional amendments greatest erosion of human rights in 26 years (MDE 12/008/2007)

📄 Egypt: New anti-terror law must not entrench systematic human rights abuses (MDE 12/013/2007)

📄 Egypt: Closing workers advice centre against protecting workers' rights (MDE 12/015/2007)

📄 Egypt: Flawed military trials for Brotherhood leaders – Human rights groups, media barred from observing trial (MDE 12/019/2007)

📄 Egypt: Executions imminent after unfair trials (MDE 12/020/2007)

📄 Justice subverted: trials of civilians before military courts (MDE 12/022/2007)

📄 Egypt: Rights of Individuals intercepted at the border with Israel must be protected (MDE 12/027/2007)

📄 Egypt: Continuing crackdown on Muslim Brotherhood (MDE 12/028/2007)

📄 Egypt: Freedom of expression under attack (MDE 12/031/2007)

📄 Egypt: Sweeping measures against torture needed (MDE 12/034/2007)

E

EL SALVADOR

REPUBLIC OF EL SALVADOR

Head of state and government:	Elías Antonio Saca
Death penalty:	abolitionist for ordinary crimes
Population:	7.1 million
Life expectancy:	71.3 years
Under-5 mortality (m/f):	32/26 per 1,000
Adult literacy:	80.6 per cent

Crime levels remained high and there was widespread concern about public security. The government was criticized for misusing a new anti-terrorism law. Widespread human rights violations committed during the internal armed conflict (1980-1992) remained unpunished.

Background

In October, the Supreme Court found International Labour Organization Convention 87 incompatible with the Constitution. The Convention, which covers freedom of association and protection of the right to organize, was found to be incompatible with a constitutional article which prohibits trade unions in the public sector.

Many communities protested throughout the year against environmental damage caused by mining activities.

Public security

According to reports, 3,476 people were killed during the year. The National Commission for Citizen Security and Social Peace, formed at the request of the President and drawn from different sectors of society, reported a continued increase in homicides. It stated that reported killings of women had increased by 50 per cent since 1999. Several police officers were arrested throughout the year for alleged unlawful killings.

■ On 28 July, five men claiming to be police officers arrived at the home of an alleged gang member, in a town in the eastern part of the San Salvador Department, to arrest him. The five men, whose identification badges and faces were concealed, refused to produce an arrest warrant and told the family to collect the alleged gang member the following day from a nearby police station. His dismembered body was found the following day in three locations. No one had been arrested in connection with the killing by the end of the year.

Impunity

The UN Working Group on Enforced or Involuntary Disappearances criticized the government for failing to resolve some 2,270 cases of enforced disappearance during the period of internal conflict. The Working Group highlighted the role of the 1993 Amnesty Law which allows perpetrators of human rights violations, including enforced disappearance, to evade prosecution.

The National Assembly approved an annual day of remembrance to commemorate the children who were victims of enforced disappearance during the conflict, in accordance with the ruling of the Inter-American Court of Human Rights.

In March, Rufina Amaya, the last remaining survivor of the El Mozote massacre, died of natural causes. According to reports, the El Salvadorian Armed Forces killed 767 people in El Mozote and surrounding areas in an operation carried out in December 1980. To date nobody has been brought to justice for that massacre or others that occurred during the internal armed conflict.

Counter-terrorism – misuse of the anti-terrorism law

The inappropriate and disproportionate use of the 2006 Special Law against Acts of Terrorism was the subject of much criticism both nationally and internationally. Local human rights groups argued that the Special Law was used against political opponents of the government.

■ In July, 13 people were charged with crimes under the Special Law. The 13 individuals, from two separate groups, had been detained after allegedly throwing stones at police officers and blocking roads during a demonstration against government water distribution policies. The 13 were leaders and members of social organizations. All were released on bail, subject to further investigations by the Attorney General's Office, at the end of the year.

EQUATORIAL GUINEA

REPUBLIC OF EQUATORIAL GUINEA

Head of state:	Teodoro Obiang Nguema Mbasogo
Head of government:	Ricardo Mangue Obama Nfube
Death penalty:	retentionist
Population:	0.5 million
Life expectancy:	50.4 years
Adult literacy:	87 per cent

The authorities continued to restrict freedom of expression by holding prisoners of conscience behind bars and by harassing, arresting and briefly detaining political activists. Despite a law forbidding torture, police continued to torture detainees, particularly in the mainland region. Several police

officers were arrested in connection with deaths in custody. At least three people were executed. Scores of families were forcibly evicted from their homes and hundreds more remained at risk of eviction.

Background

In January a wave of fires swept through several Malabo neighbourhoods which were earmarked for demolition, destroying over 100 houses and leaving as many families homeless. Some neighbourhoods were hit by fires several times. One of the fires in the New Building (also known as Campo Yaoundé) neighbourhood occurred two days after the Prime Minister told residents the area was to be demolished in order to build new social housing. The authorities said the fires were accidental, but in mid-January the police said they had arrested 20 people on suspicion of arson. No further information was forthcoming.

In July the UN Working Group on Arbitrary Detention visited the country's prisons and other detention centres. The delegates were able to speak to most prisoners, but were unable to meet four prisoners brought from Benin and Nigeria in 2005 whose imprisonment the authorities denied, despite credible evidence of their being held in Black Beach prison in Malabo.

In August the authorities acknowledged that 60 per cent of the population lived in abject poverty and that only 33 per cent had access to clean water and electricity, despite economic growth over the previous year of 21.5 per cent, one of the fastest in the world.

In October, Parliament approved a bill to reorganize the justice system. One of the agreed measures was the establishment of a Superior Council of the Judiciary to be presided over by the President.

Arbitrary arrests and detention

Fourteen prisoners of conscience, including one held without charge or trial since October 2003, remained in detention.

Security personnel and civilian authorities, as well as members of the ruling Democratic Party of Equatorial Guinea, harassed, arrested or ordered the arrest of, and briefly detained political opponents. Most incidents occurred in the mainland region.

■ In February, Ireneo Sialo Sialo, the Vice-Secretary General of the political party Convergence for Social Democracy (CPDS), was arrested without warrant at his home in the town of Sampaka, Bioko Island. The arrest was apparently at the request of the President of the town council, who accused Ireneo Sialo of publicly insulting him because Ireneo Sialo had questioned his administration during a public meeting. He was forced to carry out heavy work before being released the next day after paying a fine.

■ Secundino Boleko Brown, a businessman resident in Spain since 2000, was arrested in April at Malabo Central Police Station, the day after his arrival in the country, together with the local administrator of his businesses. The administrator was released without charge two weeks later. However, Secundino Boleko remained in detention in the police station without charge or trial until July. He was not told the reason for his arrest, although his lawyer was informally told that the police accused Secundino Boleko of entering the police barracks and drawing a map of the area. Secundino Boleko admitted visiting the barracks where his administrator, a police officer in active service, lived but denied drawing a map, which was never shown to him. The Appeal Court ignored a writ of habeas corpus issued by his lawyer in April.

Torture and other ill-treatment

Despite a November 2006 law prohibiting torture and other ill-treatment, cases of torture continued to be reported. Most incidents occurred in police stations in Bata and other towns on the mainland. At least two people died as a result of torture by police. At least three officers were arrested in connection with these deaths, but were not known to be charged or tried.

■ Salvador Ndong Nguema died in Bata Hospital on 6 October as a result of a beating by a prison guard in Evinayong prison four days earlier. In 2006 he had been convicted of complicity in the killing in December 2005 of a woman by José Nzamyo "Tipú", who was executed on 22 October. On 2 October a soldier on duty at the prison beat him in his cell. Two days later his sister found him there, lying on the floor with a distended abdomen. He died after an operation to repair damage to his intestines, which had been ruptured in several places. The soldier responsible was arrested in November.

■ In February, 16 children aged between five and 16 were briefly arrested and beaten on the soles of their feet by a police officer on the orders of the Vice-Minister of Agriculture and Forestry who suspected they had stolen his watch and clothes while he went for a swim. The children were taken to the local police station in

E

Acurenam, on the mainland , where they were beaten. The officer responsible was not prosecuted.

Unfair trials

Four men "extradited" from Libreville, Gabon, in June 2004 and charged in June 2006 with terrorism and rebellion were tried by a civilian court in Bata in July and convicted of the charges. In November, they were sentenced to prison terms ranging from 10 to 17 years. They were convicted solely on the basis of statements they made under torture, as the prosecution presented no other evidence to sustain the charges. Following their "extradition" from Libreville they had been held incommunicado and handcuffed in Black Beach prison in Malabo for about two years and were tortured on several occasions. They were transferred to the Central Prison (Cárcel Modelo) in Bata in July prior to their trial and were forced to perform unpaid work in the houses of military and civilian authorities.

Death penalty

At least three people were executed during 2007. According to reports, the executions were carried out in a semi-clandestine manner, without the families of the executed being informed, in the Military Academy of Ekuku, in Bata, on the mainland. Salvador Ncogo, who had been arrested in December 2006 for killing a mentally disabled youth, and Benedicto Anvene were executed on 18 May. Details of their trial were not available. According to reports, the two men had been held in chains in Bata Central Prison for several months. José Nzamyo "Tipú" was executed on 22 October. He had been convicted in 2006 of killing his girlfriend in December 2005.

Housing – forced evictions

Forced evictions occurred in Malabo and Bata although on a smaller scale than the previous year. Hundreds of families remained at risk of being forcibly evicted from their homes in both cities. In most cases there was no proper consultation or negotiation and people were not compensated for their losses.

■ One morning in July, a tractor appeared in Ikunde, an area outside Bata, without prior notice and created an open pathway between the river and the road, demolishing the houses and vegetable gardens on its way. About 10 families were left homeless. Reportedly, the path was to facilitate access to a hotel in the village

of Ntobo, some six kilometres away, owned by a relative of the President. There was no prior notification, consultation, compensation or due process and the families were not rehoused.

ERITREA

STATE OF ERITREA

Head of state and government:	Issayas Afewerki
Death penalty:	abolitionist in practice
Population:	4.7 million
Life expectancy:	56.6 years
Under-5 mortality (m/f):	84/78 per 1,000
Adult literacy:	60.5 per cent

Two-thirds of the population remained dependent on international emergency food aid. The government did not allow opposition parties, independent civil society organizations or unregistered faith groups and tolerated no dissent. Thousands of prisoners of conscience were held. There was no recognizable rule of law or justice system, civilian or military. Detainees had no means of legal redress and judges were unable to challenge or question arbitrary detentions or government or military actions violating human rights. Constitutional and legal protections of human rights were not respected or enforced.

Background

Border demarcation following the Eritrea-Ethiopia war of 1998-2000 did not begin and the International Boundary Commission ended its work in November with the dispute unresolved. Eritrea imposed severe restrictions on the UN Mission in Ethiopia and Eritrea (UNMEE), which administered a buffer zone on the Eritrean side of the border. Eritrean government troops moved into the zone and arrested or conscripted several UNMEE Eritrean staff. There were fears of a new outbreak of fighting between the two countries' troops massed along the border, partly because of both countries' involvement in the Somalia conflict. The mandate of the UNMEE was extended by the UN Security Council in December.

Eritrea continued to support Ethiopian armed opposition groups. It supported opposition to

E

Ethiopian troops in Somalia, including the Alliance for the Re-Liberation of Somalia which was formed in Eritrea in mid-2007. Ethiopia supported Eritrean opposition groups formerly based in Sudan.

Freedom of expression

Religious believers

Hundreds of members of minority faiths banned by the government in 2002 were arrested in 2007 and indefinitely detained incommunicado without charge or trial. Many were arrested while worshipping clandestinely in private homes or at weddings or funerals. Their churches were closed down and church properties and welfare projects were seized by the government. Some critics from permitted faiths – the Eritrean Orthodox Church, the Roman Catholic and Lutheran churches, and Islam – were also imprisoned.

■ Patriarch (*Abune*) Antonios, head of the Eritrean Orthodox Church, was transferred to secret security detention in May when a new pro-government Patriarch was appointed contrary to church regulations. He had been under house arrest since January 2006 after criticizing the government's intervention in church affairs and the detention of three Orthodox priests. Aged 79 and in poor health, he was refused medication for diabetes.

At the end of 2007 there were at least 2,000 religious prisoners of conscience, mostly from evangelical churches. They included women and children and some had been held incommunicado for more than three years. Among them were 27 Jehovah's Witnesses, three of whom had been held in Sawa military camp since 1994.

Political prisoners

There were frequent arrests by the security authorities of suspected government critics, and no tolerance of dissent. There was no permitted forum for independent expression of political opinion or political association. The authorities reportedly intercepted telephone and internet communications.

It was difficult to obtain information on people who "disappeared" into secret detention. The security authorities took reprisals against detainees' families if they inquired about an arrest or communicated with international human rights organizations.

■ Eleven former government ministers and Eritrean liberation veterans who had called for democratic reform remained in secret detention. They had not been seen by their families since their arrest in 2001. The government had accused them of treason but never charged them or took them to court. Some, such as General Ogbe Abraha, were reported to have died in detention because of harsh conditions and denial of medical treatment.

Hundreds of other people detained in 2001 also remained in secret detention, along with other people arrested subsequently. The few individuals released were ordered to keep silent about their experience.

■ Aster Yohannes, the wife of Petros Solomon, a detained former government minister, was still detained incommunicado. She was arrested in 2003 when she returned from the USA to see her children.

■ Asylum-seekers forcibly returned by Malta in 2002 and Libya in 2003 were still detained in secret.

Journalists

No independent or private news outlets were allowed. The private press was shut down in 2001.

■ Ten journalists detained in 2001 for allegedly supporting dissident government ministers accused of treason were still held incommunicado and without charge or trial. They were prisoners of conscience. There were unconfirmed reports that Fessayahe Yohannes (known as "Joshua") had earlier died in detention.

Other journalists working for the tightly controlled state media were detained if they seemed to criticize the government. Some of the eight detained in 2007 were reportedly still held at the end of the year, or conscripted into the army.

Military conscription

National military service, in the army or in civilian occupations under military conditions, was indefinite, and was justified by the government because of the military threat from Ethiopia. Military service was compulsory for all citizens aged 18 to 40, with few exemptions allowed. People aged 40 to 50 or who had been demobilized had reserve duties. Women over the age of 27 were informally exempted. There was no exemption for conscientious objection, for example by Jehovah's Witnesses who refused military service although not rejecting development service.

Conscripts performed military duties or construction labour, or worked in the civil service with their salaries reduced to small conscript "pocket money" payments. Some conscripts were sent on foreign military assignments. Two conscripted journalists captured in Somalia in January were illegally transferred to detention in Ethiopia.

The relatives of young people who hid from conscription or fled abroad were detained by police and made to pay large fines if the person did not return. They remained in indefinite detention if they did not or could not pay the fines. This system had no legal basis nor could it be challenged in court.

Children spent their last year of schooling in Sawa military training centre. They then either went into military service or into further education at vocational training colleges, with conscription postponed until graduation. University education was no longer available in the country. Thousands of young people facing conscription and conscripts fled the country to seek asylum.

Torture and other ill-treatment

Torture by means of painful tying, known as "helicopter", continued to be a routine punishment and means of interrogation for religious and political prisoners. Members of evangelical churches were tortured to try to make them abandon their faith. Military offenders were tortured. Many were young people who had tried to flee conscription or who had complained of harsh conditions and the indefinite extension of their national service.

Prison conditions were extremely harsh and constituted cruel, inhuman and degrading treatment. Many prisoners were held in shipping containers, which were overcrowded and unhygienic with no toilet or washing facilities, and varied between extremes of heat and cold. Medical treatment was rarely provided.

Refugees and asylum-seekers

Despite a guideline from the Office of UNHCR, the UN refugee agency, that rejected Eritrean asylum-seekers should not be returned to Eritrea, on account of the serious human rights situation, several were returned by Sudan and detained in late 2007. They included recognized refugees. One asylum-seeker forcibly returned from the United Kingdom was detained. Hundreds of detained Eritrean asylum-seekers in Libya were at risk of forced return. Most Eritrean asylum-seekers were fleeing conscription.

Amnesty International reports

📄 Eritrea: Prominent journalist reported dead in a secret prison (AFR 64/002/2007)

📄 Eritrea: On 6th anniversary of mass detentions of dissidents, human rights violations continue unabated (AFR 64/009/2007)

ESTONIA

REPUBLIC OF ESTONIA

Head of state:	Toomas Hendrik Ilves
Head of government:	Andrus Ansip
Death penalty:	abolitionist for all crimes
Population:	1.3 million
Life expectancy:	71.2 years
Under-5 mortality (m/f):	13/9 per 1,000
Adult literacy:	99.8 per cent

Linguistic minorities continued to experience discrimination, particularly in employment, despite improved access to free Estonian language classes and the government's prioritization of socio-economic integration. Estonia's human rights record came under criticism from both the Council of Europe Commissioner for Human Rights and the UN Committee against Torture (CAT).

Minority rights

The country's linguistic minorities continued to experience discrimination, particularly in employment, affecting some 420,000 people or approximately 30 per cent of the population. In February, the legal status of the Language Inspectorate, a state agency charged with overseeing the implementation of the Language Law, was enhanced. As a result, people fined or reprimanded by the Language Inspectorate found it harder to challenge its practices in court. During the year the government presented its plans for an "Integration in Estonian Society 2008-2013" programme, charged with improving socio-economic integration through enhancing competitiveness and social mobility regardless of ethnicity or language. In June, the government adopted a decree stipulating that prisoners who participated in Estonian language training were to be paid EEK 1,080 (€69) per month.

In his Memorandum to the Estonian government on 11 July, the Council of Europe Commissioner for Human Rights recommended that "increased importance should be given to awareness-raising measures targeting non-citizens about the possibilities of learning the Estonian language and the benefits associated with it". The Commissioner highlighted that the Advisory Committee of the Framework Convention on National Minorities and the European Commission against Racism and Intolerance had expressed concern regarding discriminatory Estonian language proficiency requirements in employment. In several cases the Language Inspectorate imposed disproportionately heavy sanctions on people found not to have sufficient Estonian language skills.

Policing

In April, large-scale demonstrations were held against the removal of a Soviet-era World War II monument from central Tallinn. Most protesters were members of the Russian linguistic minority. There were several reports of peaceful protesters being beaten by police at various locations in Tallinn. There were also reports that peaceful demonstrators were ill-treated and insulted when arrested during the demonstrations.

Commenting on these disturbances, the CAT recommended that Estonia should promptly, thoroughly and impartially investigate all allegations of brutality and excessive use of force by law enforcement personnel and bring the perpetrators to justice.

Detention conditions

In July, the Commissioner for Human Rights of the Council of Europe stated that the deplorable living conditions in prisons amounted to inhuman and degrading treatment. These conditions included detainees being confined to cells 24 hours a day and being allowed to leave the cell only once a week to take a shower, sleeping on a thin mattress on a wooden platform on the floor and having limited access to fresh air and daylight. The Commissioner raised concerns that detainees at Tallinn prison complained that they did not have access to hot water and had to pay for their own toiletries.

The CAT expressed concern in its Concluding Observations on 22 November about prison conditions in Estonia, especially regarding access to adequate HIV medical care for detainees, and recommended that the Estonian authorities improve medical and health services in detention facilities.

Racism

In June, the European Union (EU) sent a formal request to Estonia to implement the EU Racial Equality Directive (2000/43/EC), which Estonia had still failed to do by the end of the year.

Amnesty International report

📖 Europe and Central Asia: Summary of Amnesty International's concerns in the region, January-June 2007 (EUR 01/010/2007)

ETHIOPIA

FEDERAL DEMOCRATIC REPUBLIC OF ETHIOPIA

Head of state:	Girma Wolde-Giorgis
Head of government:	Meles Zenawi
Death penalty:	retentionist
Population:	81.2 million
Life expectancy:	51.8 years
Under-5 mortality (m/f):	164/149 per 1,000
Adult literacy:	35.9 per cent

Nearly a million people in Ethiopia's drought-afflicted Somali Region in the east suffered severe food shortages due to a government blockade on humanitarian supplies and food trade in June. Government forces were responsible for mass arrests, torture, rape and extrajudicial executions in a continuing conflict with an armed group.

Thousands of government opponents were detained without trial. Leaders of the political opposition, journalists and human rights defenders, who were prisoners of conscience, were convicted and jailed after a two-year trial but quickly freed after being granted presidential pardons.

Background

There was an upsurge in the 13-year armed conflict with the Ogaden National Liberation Front (ONLF) in the Somali Region. The conflict with the Oromo Liberation Front (OLF) in the Oromia Region continued. The ONLF and OLF received support from Eritrea, while Ethiopia supported Eritrean opposition groups.

Border demarcation following the Ethiopia-Eritrea war of 1998-2000 did not begin and the International Boundary Commission ended its work in November with the dispute unresolved. Ethiopia refused to implement the Commission's judgment. There were fears of renewed fighting between the two countries' troops massed along the border, partly because of both countries' involvement in the Somalia conflict. The mandate of the UN Mission in Ethiopia and Eritrea (UNMEE), which administered a buffer zone along the border, was extended by the UN Security Council in December.

Ethiopian troops supporting the transitional government in Somalia committed serious violations of international humanitarian law against civilians (see Somalia entry).

E

Prisoners of conscience and other political prisoners

The trial of opposition Coalition for Unity and Democracy (CUD) leaders, journalists and civil society activists, which began in May 2006, continued. The defendants, including elected members of parliament, faced political charges carrying possible death sentences. Demonstrations in connection with disputed elections in May and November 2005 led to violence in which the security forces killed 187 people and demonstrators killed six police officers. The defendants were in effect accused of responsibility for the violence. The security forces were absolved of using excessive force by a parliamentary inquiry commission report in 2006, but the original inquiry leaders fled the country and said their findings had been the opposite.

The prosecution case ended in April, when several defendants were acquitted. The CUD leaders, including Hailu Shawel, Berhanu Nega and Birtukan Mideksa, as well as journalists who were accused of collaborating with them, had refused to present a defence on the grounds that they did not expect a fair trial. CUD leaders were among 38 defendants convicted in June and mostly jailed for life, although the prosecution had demanded death sentences. However, they were all pardoned and freed in July as a result of applying for presidential pardon in negotiations with government representatives. These negotiations took place outside the trial process through mediation by an independent group of Ethiopian "Elders".

Two defendants presented their defence in July: Daniel Bekele, policy director of ActionAid, and Netsanet Demissie, director of the Organization for Social Justice in Ethiopia. The two human rights defenders were denied bail seven times, and their verdict was repeatedly adjourned. They refused to change their pleas to guilty and apply for a pardon. In December they were convicted and sentenced to two years and eight months' imprisonment.

Eight other defendants in this trial and all 33 defendants in a related trial of CUD officials, including MP-elect Kifle Tigeneh, were pressurized to plead guilty and apply for pardon. They too were convicted, then pardoned and freed.

Amnesty International considered that the CUD leaders, journalists and human rights defenders were prisoners of conscience, who were convicted for exercising their right to freedom of expression, assembly and association. Their convictions were based on evidence that did not prove, beyond reasonable doubt, that they committed a crime under Ethiopian law.

Fifty-five people, including CUD members and several Ethiopian Teachers Association (ETA) officials arrested in December 2006, were accused of having links with the armed Ethiopian People's Patriotic Front (EPPF) force in the north-west. They were charged and most were granted bail in late 2007.

Several hundred other CUD members detained in 2005 were still held without trial in prison throughout 2007. Fifteen refugees forcibly returned to Ethiopia by Sudan in August, after two months in prison in Sudan, were detained on arrival in Ethiopia. Five people forcibly returned to Ethiopia by Somaliland in October and suspected of links with the ONLF were detained on arrival; their whereabouts in custody were not known.

Other releases

Some CUD members were reportedly released in a presidential amnesty in September marking the Ethiopian New Year and Millennium. Over 17,000 prisoners were freed, mostly convicted criminals. Prisoners of conscience released earlier included Diribi Demissie and two other officials of the Mecha Tulema Association, an Oromo community welfare association, who had been detained since 2004.

Freedom of expression

Fourteen journalists were charged with political offences in the CUD trial on account of published articles even though these did not advocate violence. Their publications were all shut down. Seven were acquitted in April, including Serkalem Fasil, who was pregnant on arrest in 2005 and later gave birth to a son in custody in hospital. Her publication company, however, was found guilty and fined. The remaining seven were convicted in June, then pardoned.

A new and more restrictive draft Press Law had not been introduced by the end of the year.

Human rights defenders

Human rights defenders and civil society activists were at risk of arrest if they criticized the government too vigorously.

■ Mesfin Woldemariam, founder and former head of the Ethiopian Human Rights Council (EHRCO), was a prisoner of conscience convicted in the CUD trial and released in July. He still had a charge pending of incitement of violence in connection with student demonstrations in 2001.

■ Yalemzawd Bekele, a human rights lawyer working for the European Commission in Addis Ababa, who had previously been detained for several days in October 2006, was charged in July with conspiring to commit an outrage against the Constitution but granted bail pending a trial set for early 2008.

Armed conflict

In the Somali Region, the ONLF attacked an oil installation in Obole village in April, killing soldiers and also 65 Ethiopian and six Chinese civilian workers. The ONLF abducted seven other Chinese workers but released them some days later. In retaliation, the Ethiopian government mounted a blockade on conflict-affected districts in the region, causing severe food shortages.

There were mass arrests, torture, rape and extrajudicial executions of alleged ONLF supporters by government forces. The ONLF assassinated some civilian officials. Civilians were forcibly removed from their homes and conscripted into government militia groups.

A UN fact-finding mission reported on the humanitarian crisis, which the Ethiopian authorities partially alleviated, but killings continued until the end of the year.

Hundreds of people were arrested on political grounds in 2007 in connection with armed conflicts with the OLF and ONLF.

■ Sultan Fowsi Mohamed Ali, a clan elder and government-recognized mediator in conflicts in the Somali Region, was detained in August, reportedly to prevent him giving evidence to a UN fact-finding mission. A prisoner of conscience, he was taken to court but had not been tried by the end of the year.

■ Mulata Aberra, a trader in Harar city, was arrested in November on suspicion of supporting the OLF – his third detention on such grounds. He was reportedly tortured, then remanded in custody by a court for further police investigation.

'War on terror'

In January and February Ethiopian troops in Somalia unlawfully transferred (rendered) at least 85 political prisoners to Ethiopia. Most had been arrested in

Kenya when Kenya closed its border to people fleeing from Somalia after the forces of the Council of Somali Islamic Courts were defeated by Ethiopian troops. Foreign nationals from some 14 western and Middle Eastern countries were released after some months and sent back to the countries they had come from. In May the Ethiopian authorities acknowledged still holding 41 such detainees in military custody and said they would be charged before military courts. By the end of 2007 the authorities had given no details of the individuals detained, their whereabouts, or any charges against them. The detainees included Kenyan citizens of Somali ethnic origin, two Eritrean conscripted journalists captured in Mogadishu, and alleged members of armed Ethiopian opposition groups. (See Kenya entry.)

Torture and other ill-treatment

Some of the CUD members and teachers' association officials arrested in December 2006, were reportedly tortured in the police central investigation bureau in Addis Ababa known as Maikelawi. Detainees unlawfully transferred from Kenya and Somalia were reported to have been tortured or ill-treated in secret military places of detention in Addis Ababa.

Torture including rape by the military was reportedly widespread in the Somali Region after the April ONLF attack. Several defendants in the trial of Kifle Tigeneh and 32 other CUD members claimed in court that they had been tortured, but the judges refused to consider their claims.

Prison conditions for most political prisoners were harsh. Conditions in most parts of Kaliti prison in Addis Ababa, where the CUD trial defendants and several hundred untried OLF suspects were held, were overcrowded and unhygienic.

Trials of former government members

In February, 33 members of the former Dergue military government who had been detained since 1991 and convicted in December 2006 of genocide and mass killings were sentenced to life imprisonment or long prison terms. Trials of other former officials for killings during the "Red Terror" campaign against "anti-revolutionaries" in 1977-79 were almost completed.

E

Death penalty

In July the prosecution appealed for death penalties to be imposed on the jailed Dergue members but the appeal had not been heard by the end of the year.

The same month a man convicted of murdering the former head of security was executed. This was the second execution since 1991. Further death sentences were imposed during 2007. Several dozen prisoners under sentence of death awaited the outcome of appeals or petitions for clemency.

Amnesty International visit/reports

 An Amnesty International representative attended the CUD trial briefly in March. Other representatives were barred in July when they asked for visas to attend the defence presentation.

📄 Ethiopia: Prisoners of conscience and prominent human rights defender convicted (AFR 25/012/2007)

📄 Ethiopia: Political repression must stop (AFR 25/013/2007)

📄 Ethiopia: Call for a Millennium for human rights (AFR 25/022/2007)

FIJI

REPUBLIC OF THE FIJI ISLANDS
Head of state:	Ratu Josefa Iloilovatu Uluivuda
Head of government:	Frank Bainimarama (interim Prime Minister)
Death penalty:	abolitionist for ordinary crimes
Life expectancy:	68.3 years
Adult literacy:	94.4 per cent

Disadvantaged groups continued to be marginalized as a result of high unemployment, widespread poverty and an alarming squatter situation. Unlawful arrests and detentions, violence, and killings by members of the security forces continued. Freedom of expression was severely undermined.

Background

A military coup led by Commodore Frank Bainimarama in December 2006 triggered serious human rights violations in 2007. The judiciary was compromised as the interim government sought to constrain its independence.

Police and security forces
Killings and excessive use of force

■ In January, a man died from a brain haemorrhage within hours of being detained by the military. One soldier was charged for the beating, although others were reported to have taken part.

■ In June, a young man fell into a coma and died, following assaults by soldiers in Nadi. Eight soldiers were later charged with his killing.

■ Another man was killed while being interrogated by police officers in June. The coroner's report concluded that he had died from severe internal injuries. Nine police officers were subsequently charged with his killing.

■ In November, several people accused of planning to assassinate key members of the interim government were detained for more than 48 hours without charge. Some were allegedly brutally beaten by plain clothes soldiers.

Cruel, inhuman and degrading treatment

Prominent political figures including critics of the interim government were arbitrarily arrested, detained and subjected to cruel, inhuman or degrading treatment by members of the army.

■ Between December 2006 and July 2007, hundreds of people were forced to strip naked, run around fields, or touch each other's private parts. Many were also physically assaulted by soldiers and police officers.

Attacks on freedom of expression and movement

A state of emergency imposed between December 2006 and May 2007 severely undermined freedom of expression. Prominent critics of the government, including lawyers and other human rights defenders, were intimidated by the military and banned from travelling without prior notice.

■ In August, a prominent lawyer filed a writ challenging his travel ban. The case was still pending by the end of the year.

That same month, the interim government threatened to arrest bloggers and those responsible for facilitating pro-democracy blog sites. One popular site was closed down. The interim government warned public servants against reading the blogs.

■ A senior civil servant was suspended without pay in August following allegations that he contributed to anti-military blog sites.

After publicly criticizing the interim government, deposed Prime Minister Laisenia Qarase was prevented from travelling by sea or air from his home island to Suva.

Justice system

The Chief Justice was suspended indefinitely after being forced to take leave in January.

The President of the Fiji Court of Appeal challenged the legality of the interim government, prompting the interim Attorney General to call for his resignation in June. In September, six prominent judges of the Fiji Court of Appeal resigned after not being invited to sit on the court.

The integrity and independence of the Fiji Human Rights Commission were called into question after it released a report in January which supported the military takeover.

Violence against women

According to official figures, a total of 127 rape and attempted rape cases were reported in 2007.

Health – HIV and AIDS

People living with HIV or AIDS suffered discrimination and stigmatization.
■ In August, police in a northern town harassed and abused a person living with HIV, "accusing" her of sexual promiscuity.

Housing

A September report showed that 12.5 per cent of the population were living in squatter settlements around urban centres. Appalling living conditions, extreme overcrowding, high inflation and pressure on infrastructure and services meant that the rights of people living in such informal settlements to adequate living conditions, clean water and adequate health services were frequently violated.

FINLAND

REPUBLIC OF FINLAND

Head of state:	Tarja Halonen
Head of government:	Matti Vanhanen
Death penalty:	abolitionist for all crimes
Population:	5.3 million
Life expectancy:	78.9 years
Under-5 mortality (m/f):	5/4 per 1,000

The government failed to take adequate steps to combat violence against women. Asylum-seekers and applicants for residence permits were subjected to unfair procedures. Conscientious objectors to military service continued to be imprisoned.

Violence against women

In May the UN Committee on Economic, Social and Cultural Rights recommended that Finland should consider specific legislation to criminalize domestic violence.

By the end of 2007 the government had not adopted a national action plan to combat violence against women.

Refugees and asylum-seekers

Accelerated asylum-determination procedures continued to deny sufficient time for claims to be considered thoroughly, and for every asylum-seeker to exhaust all avenues of appeal. Some asylum-seekers were expelled while their appeals were still pending.

The strict application of the so-called "Dublin II" regulations led to asylum-seekers being returned to the EU member state in which they first arrived for determination of their claim for asylum, even in circumstances where it was likely they would have been offered some form of subsidiary protection in Finland which might not be available in other EU states.

Asylum-seekers, including children, were detained unnecessarily. In some cases the right of unaccompanied minors to seek family reunification in Finland was not protected.

In some cases, residence permits were denied solely on the basis of information from the security police, which could be withheld from the applicant. The Supreme Administrative Court ruled that Administrative Courts were entitled to consider

F

information from the security police in secret when deciding appeals against refusals of applications for residence permits.

The number of temporary residence permits issued to foreign nationals declined sharply, from 299 in 2006 to only 24 in 2007.

Trafficking

Legislation relating to special residence permits for victims of trafficking continued to require that in most cases such permits should be conditional on co-operation with the authorities in investigating and prosecuting those suspected of trafficking, unless the victim was considered to be particularly vulnerable.

By the end of 2007 Finland had not ratified the Council of Europe Convention on Action against Trafficking in Human Beings.

Prisoners of conscience – conscientious objection

The length of the civilian alternative to military service remained punitive and discriminatory. Conscientious objectors were obliged to perform 395 days of civilian service, 215 days longer than the shortest and most common military service.

In December, Parliament approved changes to legislation which would shorten alternative civilian service to 362 days, and would recognize the right to conscientious objection in times of war or other public emergency. Amnesty International considered that the proposed length of alternative civilian service would remain punitive.

■ Amnesty International considered 12 imprisoned conscientious objectors to be prisoners of conscience. Most were serving sentences of 197 days for refusing to perform alternative civilian service.

FRANCE

FRENCH REPUBLIC

Head of state:	Nicolas Sarkozy (replaced Jacques Chirac in May)
Head of government:	François Fillon (replaced Dominique de Villepin in May)
Death penalty:	abolitionist for all crimes
Population:	60.9 million
Life expectancy:	80.2 years
Under-5 mortality (m/f):	6/5 per 1,000

The rights of asylum-seekers and refugees were violated and undermined. Allegations of police ill-treatment continued. The authorities took steps to ensure that the right to adequate housing was legally enforceable.

Migration, refugees and asylum-seekers

Following the election in May of a new government, responsibility for refugee protection, including the oversight of the government agency that determines the status of refugees (OFPRA), was transferred to the newly created Ministry for Immigration, Integration, National Identity and Co-Development. The move could lead to violations of the rights of asylum-seekers and refugees by blurring the distinction between immigration policy and asylum obligations.

A new law on immigration, integration and asylum entered into force on 21 November. It restricts the right to family reunification and introduces DNA testing to verify family relationships. It was widely criticized on human rights grounds, including by the National Ethics Advisory Committee.

■ On 26 April the European Court of Human Rights found that France had violated the principle of *non-refoulement* and the right to an effective national remedy by ruling to return Asebeha Gebremedhin, an Eritrean asylum-seeker, to Eritrea from the French border in 2005 before his asylum appeal had been heard. The Court noted the obligation under the European Convention on Human Rights (ECHR) to provide a right of appeal with suspensive effect before returning someone to a country where they may be at risk of torture or other serious ill-treatment. The new immigration bill introduces a suspensive right of appeal (ie that prevents the individual from being returned until the appeal decision is made) but includes substantial restrictions, including a 48-hour time limit on lodging an appeal and the possibility for the judge to reject the appeal without interviewing the asylum-seeker in person if the appeal is considered manifestly ill-founded.

■ On 11 May, the UN Committee against Torture (CAT) found that France had violated the Convention against Torture when it expelled an asylum-seeker to Tunisia under an accelerated asylum procedure. Adel Tebourski had been forcibly returned from France to Tunisia in August 2006 after his release from prison. He had made a claim for asylum after he was stripped of his dual French-Tunisian nationality, but his claim was rejected under the accelerated procedure. He was returned to Tunisia before his appeal had been heard and despite a request from the CAT for France to suspend his expulsion while the Committee examined his case.

■ On 3 June Tunisian asylum-seeker Houssine Tarkhani was forcibly returned from France to Tunisia. In May, he had been questioned by a judge in relation to suspected terrorism-related activities, but was never charged with any criminal offence. When he discovered the nature of the suspicions against him, he applied for asylum. His application was rejected under the accelerated procedure. He lodged an appeal with the Refugee Appeals Commission, but was forcibly returned to Tunisia before a decision was made. On arrival in Tunisia, Houssine Tarkhani was detained and, according to reports, taken to the State Security Department in Tunis where he was held incommunicado and tortured before being charged with several broadly defined terrorism offences.

Ill-treatment by police

Allegations of police ill-treatment were made throughout the year. Internal investigatory bodies and criminal courts failed to deal with complaints of human rights violations perpetrated by law enforcement officials with the thoroughness, promptness or impartiality that international law requires.

■ In August, Albertine Sow lodged a complaint with the National Commission on Ethics and Security relating to an incident in August 2006 when she was allegedly ill-treated by police officers while six months pregnant. A criminal complaint by her against the police officers had been closed without investigation by the public prosecutor in November 2006, despite numerous

witness testimonies and medical reports supporting her complaint. Charges against Albertine Sow and her brother Jean-Pierre Yenga Fele for assaulting police officers were still under investigation.

■ In September the investigating judge closed the investigation into the complaint of police ill-treatment submitted by Gwenaël Rihet in January 2005, on the grounds of lack of evidence. Gwenaël Rihet, a journalist, was allegedly assaulted by a police officer on 15 May 2004 while filming a demonstration at the Cannes Film Festival. The incident was recorded on video but the judge refused to view it, stating that she had read a transcript of the video written by the National Police Service Inspectorate. The transcript stated that the video showed no evidence of wrongdoing by the accused police officer. A video containing footage from a town security camera, also believed to have recorded the incident, was lost in the investigating judge's office. Gwenaël Rihet's lawyer submitted an appeal against the closure of the investigation, which was pending at the end of the year.

'War on terror'

On 19 December, five French citizens previously detained in US custody at Guantánamo Bay before being returned to France in 2004 and 2005 were convicted of criminal association in relation to a terrorist enterprise. They were sentenced to a year's imprisonment (taken as time served) plus a suspended sentence of between three and four years. One man was acquitted. The defendants had appeared before the Criminal Court of Paris in July 2006 but the case was suspended when the judge ordered additional information to be provided concerning visits of officers from the French secret services and Ministry of Foreign Affairs to Guantánamo in 2002 and 2004, where they allegedly interviewed the six detainees. Previously classified documents received by the judge reportedly confirmed that the detainees were indeed interviewed by French officers. The defendants' lawyers argued that their clients were appearing in the French court on the basis of testimony extracted from them in Guantánamo, outside any legal jurisdiction and while they were illegally detained, and that, as a result, the French criminal proceedings must be declared void. Four of the men had submitted appeals at the end of the year.

F

Legal developments

A new law was passed on 30 October creating an independent body to inspect places of detention, as required by the UN Optional Protocol to the Convention against Torture. The body can visit all places of detention on French territory, including prisons, migration detention centres, border detention facilities, and secure psychiatric hospital wards. However, the law does not grant the body power to visit places of detention under French jurisdiction that are not on French territory, and allows detention centre authorities to refuse and postpone visits on numerous grounds.

Death penalty

On 2 October France acceded to the Second Optional Protocol to the International Covenant on Civil and Political Rights, aiming at the abolition of the death penalty. On 10 October France ratified Protocol 13 of the ECHR, concerning the abolition of the death penalty in all circumstances.

G

Housing

In February the National Assembly adopted a bill presented by the Minister for Housing and Social Cohesion with the stated aim of creating a legally enforceable right to housing to all legal residents in the country who are unable to access such accommodation, or to remain in it, by their own means. The bill creates "arbitration commissions" that will assess complaints from individuals who allege that their right to adequate housing is not being fulfilled or is threatened. People designated as "priority cases" by these commissions will be entitled to appeal to the administrative court. Irregular migrants are specifically excluded from benefiting from the new provisions.

Amnesty International report

📄 Europe and Central Asia: Summary of Amnesty International's Concerns in the Region; France, January -June 2007 (EUR 01/010/2007)

GAMBIA

REPUBLIC OF THE GAMBIA

Head of state and government:	Yahya Jammeh
Death penalty:	abolitionist in practice
Population:	1.6 million
Life expectancy:	58.8 years
Under-5 mortality (m/f):	117/106 per 1,000
Adult literacy:	42.5 per cent

Human rights defenders, including journalists, remained at risk of arbitrary detention, torture and intimidation by security forces. Amnesty International staff members and a local journalist were briefly detained. People charged with treason were sentenced to long prison terms; others remained in detention without trial. Two people were sentenced to death.

Justice system

Arbitrary detention

■ Two Amnesty International staff members and Yahya Dampha, a local journalist, were detained by police on 6 October. The three were conditionally released on 8 October and their releases were made unconditional on 12 October. Soon after the staff members left the country, Yahya Dampha went into hiding in fear. Soon after, his family reported that members of the National Intelligence Agency (NIA) had come to the house looking for him. Yahya Dampha and his family remained in hiding at the end of the year.

■ Seven perceived opponents of the government – including Chief Manneh, Kanyiba Kanyi, Momodou Lamin Nyassi, Mdongo Mboob, Marcie Jammeh and Haruna Jammeh – remained in incommunicado detention at the end of the year.

Former *Daily Observer* reporter Chief Manneh was sighted in police detention at various locations throughout the country and at the Royal Victoria Teaching Hospital in Banjul, prompting new concerns for his health. The government continued to deny involvement in his arrest or knowledge of his whereabouts. A case before the ECOWAS Community Court of Justice demanding that the government present Chief Manneh was repeatedly ignored by the government, who refused to send representation.

■ Jisacha Kujab Ousman "Rambo" Jatta and Tamba Fofana, both arrested in September 2006 as suspected political opponents, were released in October.

Military and civilian treason trial

Three of the four people charged with treason and tried in a civilian court in connection with an alleged coup attempt in March 2006 were sentenced to 20 years' imprisonment with hard labour in August. The fourth person was acquitted.

Four others – former NIA Director Foday Barry; two NIA officers, Yaya Bajinka, and Baba Saho; and a student – arrested in connection with the same case remained in incommunicado detention at the end of the year. They were charged with conspiracy to commit treason.

Two others – Musa Dibba and former director of the NIA Abdoulie Kujabi – also arrested in 2006, were released. Abdoulie Kujabi was allegedly tortured while in custody and lost an eye as a result. Musa Dibba's passport was seized when he was released.

Ten former members of the military were sentenced to between 10 years and life imprisonment by the Military Court Martial at Yundum Barracks for their role in the alleged coup. Five others were released because of lack of evidence. Claims of torture and ill-treatment while in detention awaiting trial were made by at least one of the accused.

Freedom of expression

An increasing number of journalists went into hiding following intimidation, threats and harassment by the NIA and government officials. Others were arbitrarily detained for varying periods and then released on bail.
■ Mai Fatty, a human rights lawyer who often represented journalists, left the country seeking medical attention after a car accident which he believed to be an assassination attempt.
■ In April, Fatou Jaw Manneh, a US-based Gambian journalist, was arrested at Gambia International Airport and charged with sedition for anti-government comments made in an interview she had given a year earlier. There were significant delays due to confusion about jurisdiction and the trial was continuing at the end of the year.
■ UN Resident Coordinator Dr Fadzai Gwaradzimba was expelled from the country in March after making comments casting doubt on President Jammeh's claim to a gathering of foreign diplomats in February that he was able to cure those infected with HIV.
■ Five employees of the pro-government newspaper *The Daily Observer* – senior editor Sal Jahl, reporter and editor Ousman Darboe, Abdoulie John, Seedy Bojang and

Lamin Dibba – were fired during the year. Two appeared to have been fired in connection with their portrayal of the President's claims about his ability to treat HIV/AIDS.
■ The offices of *The Independent* newspaper remained under police surveillance and were not allowed to open throughout the year.

Death penalty

Two foreign nationals – Tambara Samba, a Senegalese woman, and Sulayman Bah, a Guinean man – were sentenced to death for murder within weeks of each other by the same court. The sentences came in the context of concerns over crimes committed by foreign nationals. An appeal by Tambara Samba was pending at the end of the year.

The Constitution provides for the death penalty, although death sentences are rare and must be signed personally by the President. Although the Constitution requires a review of the death penalty by 2007, no such review took place during the year.

Impunity

No developments were known to have taken place regarding former NIA Director General Daba Marena and four army officers – Ebou Lowe, Alieu Cessay, Alpha Bah and Malafi Corr – who reportedly escaped during a prison transfer in April 2006. There were fears that they had in fact been extrajudicially executed as family members had not seen or heard from them by the end of 2007. No independent investigation had taken place by the end of the year.

The Commonwealth Human Rights Initiative lodged a complaint against the government to the African Commission with respect to the killing of 50 migrants, including 44 Ghanaians, in Gambia in 2005. No suspects had been brought to justice and the alleged perpetrators were thought to be in self-imposed exile at the end of the year.

Amnesty International visit/reports

🚄 Amnesty International delegates visited the Gambia in October.
▨ Gambia: Amnesty International calls for the reopening of *The Independent* and the release of Chief Manneh (AFR 27/001/2007)
▨ Gambia: Amnesty International demands unconditional release of detained staff (AFR 27/003/2007)
▨ Gambia: Amnesty International delegates released unconditionally (AFR 27/004/2007)

G

GEORGIA

GEORGIA

Head of state:	Nino Burdzhanadze
	(replaced Mikheil Saakashvili in November)
Head of government:	Lado Gurgenidze (replaced
	Zurab Noghaideli in November)
Death penalty:	abolitionist for all crimes
Population:	4.4 million
Life expectancy:	70.7 years
Under-5 mortality (m/f):	45/37 per 1,000

There were not enough shelters for women escaping domestic violence, and some measures to protect women from violence were delayed. Police reportedly used excessive force to disperse anti-government demonstrations in November, and throughout the year there were reports of police beating suspects when arresting them. Unfair trials of political opponents of the government were reported.

Background

Mass demonstrations in November called for the resignation of President Mikheil Saakashvili, parliamentary elections, changes to the election rules, and the release of Irakli Batiashvili (see below). On 7 and 8 November police reportedly used excessive force in dispersing demonstrators. The President imposed a state of emergency, restricting the rights to receive and disseminate information, to freedom of assembly, and to strike. On 8 November he announced presidential elections in January 2008 and a referendum on the timing of parliamentary elections. On 25 November he resigned in order to run in the Presidential elections.

International scrutiny

European Committee for the Prevention of Torture

In October the European Committee for the Prevention of Torture published a report which noted progress in preventing ill-treatment of people in police custody but stated that instances of ill-treatment of detainees persisted. It found that conditions in many detention facilities were poor, and in one severely overcrowded facility in Tbilisi, amounted to inhuman and degrading treatment.

UN Human Rights Committee

In October the UN Human Rights Committee expressed concern about torture and other ill-treatment, prison conditions, interference with the independence of the judiciary, domestic violence, reports of forced evictions of internally displaced people and violations of the rights of ethnic minorities. The Committee called on Georgia to draft and implement a comprehensive action plan against torture and other ill-treatment, to investigate allegations and bring perpetrators to justice, and to ensure that victims had access to reparation including compensation. It urged Georgia to investigate women's complaints of violence and bring perpetrators to justice, and to establish sufficient shelters for those escaping domestic violence.

Violence against women

The authorities took some steps to implement the May 2006 Law on Domestic Violence, for example issuing protection and restraint orders, but some key provisions were not implemented swiftly or fully. The number of shelters was insufficient and the government did not provide financial support for shelters run by NGOs. An Action Plan on Measures to Prevent and Combat Domestic Violence (2007-2008) was approved late and appeared to further delay the setting up of shelters.

Police abuses

Although 39 police officers had been sentenced to prison terms for ill-treating detainees since 2004, impunity persisted amid allegations that investigations were often not prompt, thorough or impartial. The authorities failed to introduce identification tags for all police involved in arrests as a safeguard against torture and other ill-treatment.

By the end of 2007 no victim of torture or other ill-treatment had ever received compensation in Georgia. Limited changes in the legislation on compensation did not bring it into line with international standards as it failed to give all victims of abuse an enforceable right to adequate compensation.

The government failed to establish an independent mechanism to prevent torture and other ill-treatment, although, as a party to the Optional Protocol to the Convention against Torture, Georgia was required to do so by July 2007.

G

The investigation into the deaths of Zurab Vazagashvili and Aleksandre Khubulovi, shot by police in May 2006, was allegedly inadequate. The authorities claimed that the men were killed after opening fire at police, but NGO sources alleged that the police had set up an ambush and fired the first shots. In April 2007 the authorities closed the investigation into allegations that police used excessive force for lack of evidence. The lawyers of Zurab Vazagashvili's family alleged that investigators ignored witness statements, pressed witnesses not to testify, destroyed evidence and blocked lawyers defending Zurab Vazagashvili's rights.

Excessive use of force

Police, many of them wearing masks, were said to have used truncheons, rubber bullets, tear gas and water cannons to break up three rallies in Tbilisi on 7 November. Eye-witnesses reported that police beat and kicked demonstrators. Some 500 people reportedly required medical treatment, including 24 police officers.

The Ombudsman, Sozar Subar, reported that on 7 November he witnessed police beating fleeing demonstrators near a church in the centre of Tbilisi. The demonstrators threw stones at the police but stopped at his request. However, another special police unit arrived and beat the demonstrators, and when the Ombudsman remonstrated with police, he himself was kicked and verbally abused. One of his staff members, Daniel Mgeliashvili, was also hit over the head.

Justice system

Some trials of political opponents of the government were reported to be unfair.

NGO sources alleged that the trial of Irakli Batiashvili, who was sentenced to seven years' imprisonment on charges of "complicity" and "conspiracy or uprising to overthrow the constitutional order by force" in May, did not comply with Georgian law and international standards. His lawyers claimed that the authorities had tampered with evidence and that the court did not treat the defence fairly. Tbilisi Appeal Court upheld the verdict in September.

Abkhazia and South Ossetia

The internationally unrecognized territories of Abkhazia and South Ossetia retained the death penalty in law. In January the Parliament of Abkhazia established a moratorium on executions during peacetime. At the end of 2007, there was one prisoner on death row in Abkhazia. South Ossetia continued to have a moratorium on death sentences and executions.

Amnesty International visit/reports

Amnesty International delegates visited Georgia in May.

Georgia: Amnesty International and non-governmental organizations of Georgia urge the government to promptly approve Action Plan on Domestic Violence (EUR 56/006/2007)

Georgia: Briefing to the United Nations Human Rights Committee (EUR 56/008/2007)

Georgia: Authorities must promptly investigate police actions in dispersing demonstrators (EUR 56/011/2007)

GERMANY

FEDERAL REPUBLIC OF GERMANY

Head of state:	Horst Köhler
Head of government:	Angela Merkel
Death penalty:	abolitionist for all crimes
Population:	82.7 million
Life expectancy:	79.1 years
Under-5 mortality (m/f):	5/5 per 1,000

G

Germany failed to address human rights violations committed in the context of the US-led "war on terror", including its involvement in renditions (unlawful transfers of suspects between countries). Additionally, Germany made attempts to obtain diplomatic assurances in deportation cases where individuals may be at risk of serious human rights abuses, in violation of its obligations under international law.

Ill-treatment, including in the context of renditions

In August the Tübingen state prosecutor reopened investigations into allegations that German-born Turkish citizen Murat Kurnaz was tortured and otherwise ill-treated by German Special Forces Command officers while in US custody in Afghanistan in 2002. The reopening of the investigation was prompted by the emergence of three new witnesses. Before his release in 2006, Murat Kurnaz had been detained for four years and nine months in total, mostly in Guantánamo Bay.

■ In late 2007 the parliamentary committee looking into Germany's role in human rights violations committed as a result of its counter-terrorist activities began investigating the case of German national Muhammad Zammar. During the hearings, it emerged that the Federal Criminal Police Office had informed the US authorities of Muhammad Zammar's travel dates for his trip to Morocco in November 2001, from where he was illegally transferred to Syria.

By the end of December 2001 he had been handed over by Moroccan officials to Syria and placed in incommunicado detention, where he was reportedly subjected to torture and ill-treatment.

In November 2002, Muhammad Zammar was interrogated for three days by German intelligence and law enforcement officials whilst in Syrian detention. Upon return to Germany, the officers did not disclose information to the authorities about his whereabouts. He remained in detention at the end of 2007.

■ In September the German government announced that it would not pursue the extradition of 13 US citizens, including at least 10 US Central Intelligence Agency operatives, suspected of illegally detaining a Lebanese-born German national, Khaled el-Masri.

Khaled el-Masri was arrested and unlawfully detained while in Macedonia in December 2003. He was handed over to US agents and secretly flown to Afghanistan as part of the US programme of renditions. Following five months of alleged ill-treatment, he was flown to Albania and released after the US authorities apparently realized they had the wrong man.

Extradition warrants for the 13 US citizens were issued by a Munich prosecutor in January 2007. In April, the Federal Constitutional Court found the prosecutor's decision to tap Khaled el-Masri's lawyer's phone to be illegal.

■ On counter-terrorism, the Council of Europe's Commissioner for Human Rights recommended in July that Germany develop specific guidelines for intelligence services regarding the questioning of detainees abroad; ensure that evidence obtained under inhuman or degrading treatment or torture is not admissible in court; and fully investigate alleged cases of renditions on German territory and adopt effective measures to prevent future unlawful renditions.

Diplomatic assurances

■ On 3 October the European Court of Human Rights indicated to the German government that Hasan Atmaca should not be extradited to Turkey until further notice. On entering Germany in February 2005, Hasan Atmaca was arrested by the German authorities on suspicion of belonging to a criminal organization. The Turkish authorities requested his extradition to Turkey to stand trial on charges of activities in favour of the Kurdistan Workers' Party (PKK).

In May 2006 the German government sought diplomatic assurances from the Turkish authorities that Hasan Atmaca would be detained in a high security prison meeting international standards and that German authorities could visit him. The Turkish authorities pledged that these assurances would be favourably assessed.

The Frankfurt Higher Regional Court had declared his extradition admissible. However, on 31 May 2007 the Darmstadt Administrative Court instructed the German Federal Office for Migration and Refugees to declare Hasan Atmaca a refugee and stated that he could not be deported to Turkey as this might constitute *refoulement* (forcible return to countries where a person may be at risk of serious human rights violations). Under Section 4 of the German Asylum Procedures Act, receiving refugee status does not impede the German authorities from extraditing a person, in contravention of international standards.

In February it was reported that the Federal Ministry of the Interior had sought diplomatic assurances from Algeria not to torture anyone suspected of involvement in terrorist activity, when returned there from Germany.

In July, an Under Secretary of State travelled to Tunisia to request similar assurances from the Tunisian Minister of Interior over two Tunisian nationals suspected of having links to terrorist organizations. The German authorities then issued deportation orders for the two Tunisian nationals who later contested this decision in court. The judicial reviews were still pending at the end of the year.

Migrant and refugee rights

New legislation implementing 11 European Union (EU) directives in the field of asylum failed to provide adequate protection in cases of people fleeing violence. This meant that, for example, asylum-seekers from central and southern Iraq who were not members of a targeted minority often did not receive adequate protection.

■ On 11 July the Council of Europe's Commissioner for Human Rights issued a report on his 2006 visit to Germany. Regarding asylum and immigration, the Commissioner called on Germany to introduce protections for refugees who experience persecution because of outward manifestations of religion or sexual orientation.

■ On 18 April a report was issued on Germany by the European Committee for the Prevention of Torture (CPT). It recommended that, in all German states, "the detention of immigration detainees be governed by specific rules reflecting their particular status" and that "the authorities of Hamburg and Niedersachsen, as well as of all other states in Germany, take the necessary measures to ensure that immigration detainees are accommodated in centres specifically designed for that purpose." The CPT also recommended that the Brandenburg authorities "take steps to ensure the regular presence of a psychologist at Eisenhüttenstadt Detention Centre and develop programmes for the provision of psychosocial care to foreign nationals held there."

Police custody

■ In January the Regional Court of Dessau, overturning an earlier judgment, opened proceedings against two police officers suspected of involvement in the death of Sierra Leonean Oury Jalloh while in police custody. He died in his cell in January 2005.

One police officer was accused of bodily harm with fatal consequences for allegedly switching off the fire alarm several times. Another officer was accused of killing caused by negligence on the grounds that he may have overlooked a lighter during a personal search.

Oury Jalloh had been chained to his bed allegedly because he had resisted arrest. He died of heat shock. Preliminary investigations by the State Attorney concluded that the fire alarm had been switched off during the incident.

GHANA

REPUBLIC OF GHANA

Head of state and government:	John Agyekum Kufuor
Death penalty:	abolitionist in practice
Population:	23 million
Life expectancy:	59.1 years
Under-5 mortality (m/f):	92/88 per 1,000
Adult literacy:	57.9 per cent

The government continued paying reparations to victims of human rights violations under previous governments. The government commuted at least 43 death sentences and granted amnesty to 1,815 prisoners during the year. Although the Domestic Violence Act became law, violence and discrimination against women remained prevalent.

Death penalty

No executions were carried out and no death sentences were handed down. The government was reported to have said that the death penalty has no deterrent effect, but no concrete steps were taken towards abolition during 2007.

In March, 36 death row inmates had their sentences commuted as part of the 50th anniversary of Ghana's independence. In June, President John Kufuor commuted seven death sentences to life imprisonment to commemorate the 47th anniversary of Ghana's republican status. According to the Ghanaian Prisons Service, there were 106 prisoners on death row, including three women and 16 prisoners over the age of 60.

Violence against women

Women continued to be victims of domestic violence and female genital mutilation. The Domestic Violence and Victims Support Units established in the police service remained under-resourced.

The Domestic Violence Act became law, allowing prosecution of marital rape. A plan of action for its implementation was drafted.

Forced evictions

Forced evictions and internal displacement, particularly of marginalized people, remained a threat and continued to occur.

National Reconciliation Commission

The government continued to pay some financial reparations for human rights abuses under former governments, in accordance with the recommendations of the National Reconciliation Commission.

Amnesty International visit

🚌 Amnesty International delegates visited Ghana in December.

GREECE

HELLENIC REPUBLIC

Head of state:	Karolos Papoulias
Head of government:	Constantinos Karamanlis
Death penalty:	abolitionist for all crimes
Population:	11.2 million
Life expectancy:	78.9 years
Under-5 mortality (m/f):	8/7 per 1,000
Adult literacy:	96 per cent

Greece failed to provide asylum to the vast majority who requested it. Migrants suffered ill-treatment, and arbitrary and lengthy detention of asylum-seekers, including children, continued. Allegations of ill-treatment in police custody increased. Victims of such treatment were usually members of marginalized groups. Deaths in custody were reported. Trafficked women and girls remained unidentified as such by the authorities and therefore unable to exercise their rights to protection and assistance. Conscientious objectors were persecuted and conscripts not informed of their right to perform alternative service. Forced evictions were carried out against the Romani community. A new law to tackle domestic violence came into force.

Migration, refugees and asylum-seekers

Violations against migrants, refugees and asylum-seekers continued to be reported at Greece's borders. Protection for refugees remained minimal. In October, the German non-governmental organization Pro-asyl and the Greek Group of Lawyers for the Rights of Refugees and Migrants published a report on the situation of refugees and migrants arriving by sea,
which alleged systematic violations by Greek law enforcement officials in terms of both ill-treatment and denial of access to asylum procedures. Such violations were consistent with reports received by Amnesty International throughout the year. There were frequent reports of individuals attempting to enter Greece by sea, many of whom drowned in the process or were blocked by members of the Coastguard. Those who did manage to reach land were usually returned to their country of origin without legal aid, access to asylum procedures or having their cases individually examined.

Lawyers reported to Amnesty International that in practice asylum-seekers who did access the system could expect their application to be rejected at first instance and the number of individuals granted asylum remained very low. The review mechanism of rejected asylum applications was not independent.

The readmission protocol in existence between Greece and Turkey was used to return Iraqi citizens from Greece to Turkey in spite of the concerns of the UN's refugee agency, UNHCR, that Turkey often returned them to Iraq. Amnesty International considered this breached the prohibition of *refoulement* (the involuntary return of anyone to a country where they would be at risk of serious human rights abuses).

Detention of asylum-seekers, including children, continued. Conditions of detention continued to be reported as unhygienic and overcrowded. In December, a new reception centre was opened on the Aegean island of Samos, replacing the former detention centre where conditions had been notoriously poor.

In November, the long-awaited new asylum law came into force, covering the asylum procedure, the rights to work, education and health care for asylum-seekers, reception centres and vulnerable groups such as unaccompanied minors and survivors of torture.

Ill-treatment by police

Despite judgments from the European Court of Human Rights finding Greece in violation of the European Convention on Human Rights, the number of alleged incidents of ill-treatment by police increased. Reported incidents mainly took place in police custody and appeared to reveal a pattern of discrimination in which the majority of victims came from marginalized groups, particularly migrants and asylum-seekers.

■ On 8 June a Moldovan woman legally residing in Greece was allegedly ill-treated by police officers at the General Police Headquarters of Attica in Athens. The woman said that she had been repeatedly beaten, forced to strip to her underwear and had had clumps of her hair pulled out by police officers, who also threatened to destroy her residence permit.

■ On 16 June video footage appeared on the website *YouTube* showing two young migrants at the Omonia police station in central Athens being beaten by police officers and being forced to insult and slap each other repeatedly. At least five officers were investigated in relation to the incident. Subsequently three further videos appeared online, depicting instances of ill-treatment, including sexual abuse, of detainees in police custody. One police officer, who was involved in two of the videotaped incidents, was remanded in custody pending trial.

Deaths in custody

Public debate about an increase in the number of deaths in prison and police custody reflected serious concerns about the lack of effective monitoring of treatment. At least 10 deaths in custody occurred in the period March-June according to the non-governmental Prisoners' Rights Initiative. In August, *Eleftherotypia* (Free Press) newspaper reported that there had been 30 deaths in custody in the first six months of 2007. Although some of the deaths were drug-related or self-inflicted there were also cases in which the circumstances of death were disputed.

Prison ill-treatment and conditions

Overcrowding, poor standards of hygiene and ill-treatment continued to be reported in prisons and other places of detention. In April, the alleged ill-treatment of an inmate at the Malandrino prison in central Greece sparked protests which subsequently spread to 10 other prisons throughout the country. Prisoners in Malandrino reportedly said that the incident had been "the final straw". Some alleged that their water supply had been cut off for three days, although the authorities denied this. According to media reports, the capacity of Malandrino prison is 280 inmates, while at the time of the incident 460 people were held there.

Trafficking in human beings for sexual exploitation

Greece remained both a transit and a destination country for women and girls trafficked for sexual exploitation. Nevertheless, the number of trafficked women and girls recognized as such by the Greek authorities remained unacceptably low, and resulted in women being unable to exercise their rights to assistance and protection. The few who were identified were able to exercise these rights only on condition that they agreed to co-operate with the authorities in criminal proceedings brought against their suspected traffickers. This failed to recognize women's fear of reprisals and was at variance with the Council of Europe Convention on Action against Trafficking in Human Beings, which Greece failed to ratify and implement. Women were also not receiving the reflection period afforded them in Greek law, the purpose of which was to allow women to make fully considered decisions about the extent of their co-operation with the authorities.

Human rights defenders

Human rights defender and President of the Pakistani Community in Athens, Javed Aslam, faced possible extradition from Greece to Pakistan. Amnesty International was concerned that the Interpol warrant for Javed Aslam's arrest originating in Pakistan may have constituted a tactic of judicial harassment to prevent him from defending the rights of six other Pakistani nationals in Greece who alleged that they had been abducted by agents of the Greek intelligence services in the aftermath of the London bombings of 7 July 2005. In March, the Supreme Court upheld a unanimous decision of the Athens Appeals Court that Javed Aslam should not be extradited to Pakistan. In April, the Supreme Court called for a rehearing of the case to begin on 4 May, apparently after learning from the Greek Ministry of Foreign Affairs that no extradition agreement existed between Greece and Pakistan and that documents had passed unofficially between the Pakistani Embassy in Athens and the Supreme Court. Meanwhile Javed Aslam reported that pressure aimed at silencing him and other members of the Pakistani community in Greece about the alleged abductions continued. The Supreme Court finally rejected the extradition request. In July the investigation into the abductions was reopened.

G

Conscientious objection to military service

In a continuing pattern of harassment of conscientious objectors, a fifth attempt to arrest conscientious objector Dimitris Sotiropoulos, board member of the Association of Greek Conscientious Objectors, was made in May. Dimitris Sotiropoulos has declared his conscientious objection since March 1992 when he was first called up for military service. By the end of the year he had not been apprehended.

While the right to conscientious objection was usually upheld for those objecting on religious grounds, the rate of recognition of conscientious objectors for other convictions remained very low. There were also concerns that conscripts were not being informed of their right to perform an alternative civilian service, a service still punitive in nature and length.

Violations against the Romani community

Violations against the Romani community such as forced evictions continued to be reported by the local human rights organization, the Greek Helsinki Monitor.

■ In July the European Roma Rights Centre (ERRC) expressed concern about the eviction of over 200 Albanian Romani families from their two settlements in Athens. The evictions appear to have taken place as part of a "cleansing" operation in advance of the building of a football stadium. The ERRC was concerned that in none of the cases were even the most rudimentary domestic or international legal standards concerning forced evictions applied. They took place despite the long-term intervention of the Ombudsman, who in October again wrote to the government urging an end to forced evictions.

Violence against women

In January Law 3500/06 on Combating Domestic Violence came into force. However, parts of the law were not fully in line with the duty of the state to protect the rights of women.

Amnesty International visits/reports

🚌 Amnesty International delegates visited Greece in January and June.

📄 Greece: Uphold the rights of women and girls trafficked for sexual exploitation (EUR 25/002/2007)

📄 Greece: Investigation not extradition: Threatened return of human rights defender to Pakistan highlights failures in investigation of alleged abductions (EUR 25/001/2007)

GUATEMALA

REPUBLIC OF GUATEMALA

Head of state and government:	Óscar Berger Perdomo
Death penalty:	retentionist
Population:	13.2 million
Life expectancy:	69.7 years
Under-5 mortality (m/f):	48/36 per 1,000
Adult literacy:	69.1 per cent

For most people the public security situation remained grave as no visible progress was made in improving the quality of investigations and prosecutions of crimes, and police accountability remained virtually negligible. Women continued to experience high levels of violence. The government made little effort to bring to justice former military officers accused of human rights violations, including genocide, committed during the years of internal armed conflict (1960-1996). Human rights defenders continued to face high levels of threats and intimidation. Despite repeated national and international requests to act, the government failed to protect human rights defenders and investigate reports of harassment.

Background

Two rounds of presidential elections were held in September and November. The Guatemalan Human Rights Ombudsman's Office reported an estimated 26 killings of political activists in the context of the elections, which were won by Álvaro Colom Caballeros. He was due to assume the Presidency in January 2008.

In February, three El Salvadorian members of the Central American Parliament (based in Guatemala) and their driver were killed, allegedly by four Guatemalan police officers. Six days after the killings, the four police officers were themselves killed while in custody. The deaths resulted in the resignation of the National Director of Police and the Minister of the Interior in March.

In August, Congress approved the creation of an International Commission Against Impunity in Guatemala. The Commission, organized under the auspices of the UN, will aid national authorities in the investigation and prosecution of members of illegal and armed clandestine groups.

Public security

According to police records, 5,781 people were killed during the year. The Vice-President reported that approximately one per cent of all killings resulted in a conviction. The UN Special Rapporteur on extrajudicial, summary or arbitrary executions issued a report criticizing Guatemala for fostering impunity for killings and noted the involvement of the police and other citizens in killings of those deemed to be socially undesirable. The new National Director of Police resigned in September after it was alleged that police officers, including his bodyguards, had extrajudicially executed five youths, the youngest of whom was 17.

Violence against women

According to police records, 590 women were killed in 2007. The independent National Institute of Forensic Sciences, created in 2006 to improve the quality of forensic investigations, was inaugurated in December.

Land disputes – forced evictions

The Ministry of the Interior reported that there were 49 forced evictions in rural areas. The government failed to implement measures to ensure impartiality in the justice system when dealing with land disputes or to provide adequate shelter for evicted communities. As a result rural and Indigenous communities continued to be displaced and denied access to justice.

There were many protests by rural and Indigenous communities about the environmental impact of mining activities. Various popular referendums were held which sought to formalize opposition to mining activities, using as a framework the International Labour Organization's Convention 169 concerning Indigenous and Tribal Peoples in Independent Countries, which establishes the duty to consult before mining operations are commenced.

Human rights defenders

There were 195 reported attacks against human rights defenders. Those defending economic, social and cultural rights or campaigning on environmental issues continued to face increased risks. Those working on investigating and documenting human rights violations committed during the internal armed conflict were also threatened and intimidated.

■ Environmental activists Carlos Albacete Rosales and Piedad Espinosa Albacete were shot at by three unidentified men as they were in a taxi on their way to Guatemala City in January. They escaped with minor injuries. Both work for the organization Green Tropic (Trópico Verde) which campaigns to protect Mayan nature reserves and they had been active in reporting attempts by cattle ranchers and alleged drug traffickers to take over land inside reserves. No one had been brought to justice for the attack by the end of the year.

Impunity

In December the Constitutional Court ruled that international arrest warrants and extradition requests issued by a Spanish judge in 2006 against former high-ranking military officials, for war crimes and crimes against humanity, would not be implemented. In a widely criticized judgment, the Court failed to recognize the principle of universal jurisdiction for international crimes and seemed to suggest that the crimes concerned were of a political nature. In September General Ríos Montt, former President and part of the group of former high-ranking military officials charged with war crimes and crimes against humanity, was elected to Congress and so gained parliamentary immunity.

A case presented in 2000 against the group in the Guatemalan judicial system made no progress throughout the year. In addition, the government refused to release 25-year-old military documents that allegedly contain evidence that the widespread human rights violations were part of an intentional military strategy during the conflict. The UN Working Group on Enforced or Involuntary Disappearances criticized the government for failing to make any significant progress in determining the fate of approximately 45,000 people who remained "disappeared".

Death penalty

There were no new death sentences passed in 2007; no one was executed. Three people had their death sentences commuted and 19 remained on death row at the end of the year.

Amnesty International reports

▤ Guatemala: Human rights defenders at risk (AMR 34/007/2007)
▤ Persecution and resistance: The experience of human rights

defenders in Guatemala and Honduras (AMR 02/001/2007)

📄 Guatemala: Open Letter from Amnesty International to presidential candidates for the September 2007 elections (AMR 34/020/2007)

GUINEA

REPUBLIC OF GUINEA

Head of state:	President Lansana Conté
Head of government:	Lansana Kouyaté (replaced Eugène Camara in March)
Death penalty:	retentionist
Population:	9.8 million
Life expectancy:	54.8 years
Under-5 mortality (m/f):	145/149 per 1,000
Adult literacy:	29.5 per cent

Security forces used excessive force against demonstrators. Over one hundred demonstrators were killed; many more were injured. Women were raped by military. Arbitrary detention and killings by security forces were reported. Torture and other ill-treatment of protesters and detainees were widespread. Journalists were arbitrarily detained.

Background

Against the background of a serious economic crisis, Guinea's two principal trade unions, supported by the main opposition parties, called a general strike in January. Demonstrations to demand change were organized in main towns, paralysing the entire country.

President Lansana Conté, who took power in 1984 following a coup d'état, attempted to suppress the movement by force. Throughout January, at the beginning of the movement, members of the security forces shot at peaceful demonstrators, killing dozens of people and injuring others. Despite this use of force and the arrest of some civil society leaders and trade unionists, the general strike continued and in late January the trade unions demanded the appointment of a consensus government.

In February, President Conté appointed Eugène Camara as Prime Minister. This provoked widespread protest on the grounds that Eugène Camara was closely linked to the President.

Clashes between the demonstrators and the security forces increased and a state of emergency was declared on 12 February. On 24 February, President Conté asked the National Assembly to extend the state of emergency, but it refused. The general strike was suspended on 27 February. A new government was appointed on 28 March. It contained no members of political parties and was solely composed of people drawn from the civil society.

In May, members of the armed forces took to the streets in the capital, Conakry, and other towns, demonstrating and firing into the air. At least 13 people were killed and others were injured by stray bullets. The soldiers were demanding payment of outstanding wages and the dismissal of certain high-ranking members of the army. The latter demand was successful.

An Independent Commission of Inquiry was established in May "charged with conducting investigations into grave human rights violations and offences committed during the strikes of June 2006 and January and February 2007".

Police and security forces
Killings

More than 135 people, the majority of them unarmed, were killed by members of the security forces during demonstrations calling for the resignation of the President. In several instances, the security forces aimed at the vital organs of demonstrators and shot people in the back as they fled. Some members of the security forces also prevented people helping injured demonstrators.

■ Abdoulaye Diallo was one of several demonstrators shot in the back as they tried to escape when the security forces charged at protesters in January.

■ An 18-year-old student from Kindia was shot in the back during an organized demonstration in February as he tried to go to help someone who had been injured.

Arbitrary detention

Dozens of people, including demonstrators and employees of a private radio station, were arrested for short periods of time by the security forces during the general strike. Some were tortured in custody.

■ In July, Sidibé Keita, a member of an opposition party, was arrested and held for over a month. He was released without charge or trial.

■ In December, Lansana Komara, a member of the executive bureau of the Rally of the Guinean People (Rassemblement du peuple de Guinée, RPG) was held for more than five days at the presidential palace where he was reportedly tortured and hung upside-down from the ceiling. He was later transferred to the military barracks PM III where he remained held without charge at the end of the year.

Torture and other ill-treatment

■ In the Timbo district of Kankan, a teacher aged about 60 was arrested in January in the courtyard of his compound. No reason was given for the arrest, during which he was beaten in front of several people including his children. At the military camp, he was pinned to the ground by four gendarmes while a fifth beat him with his baton.

■ A member of the Union of the Guinean Youth was arrested twice in February. He was beaten with rifle butts and police officers walked on him and kicked him in the chest while he was handcuffed with both arms behind his back. Officers tied both his elbows behind his back, inserted a baton between his arms, pulling on it at regular intervals to increase the pain.

Violence against women

During the period of general strike, a number of women were raped by soldiers or by masked men in military clothes.

Freedom of expression

Freedom of expression came under attack throughout the year. Journalists faced politically motivated and arbitrary detention and imprisonment.

In January, the Minister of Information ordered all private and community radio stations not to broadcast any material on the general strike.

■ In February, the presidential guards arrested two people working for the radio station FM Liberty and looted the broadcasting centre. The soldiers accused the radio station of carrying out interviews which were critical of President Conté.

One of the employees, David Camara, was arrested by members of the security forces who threatened to kill him and stubbed a cigarette out on his neck. He was unconditionally released after two days.

■ In February, two radio stations, Familia FM and Radio Soleil, stopped broadcasting, reportedly after receiving anonymous threats.

In August, a court in Conakry handed down suspended prison sentences to two private newspaper directors in connection with articles alleging corruption by a former government minister.

Death penalty

In April, 23 prisoners held on death row in Conakry civil prison (maison centrale) and Kindia high-security prison, east of Conakry, stated that they had been tortured or ill-treated at the time of arrests and during the first days of detention. Several bore visible marks of beatings or of prolonged restraints with ropes.

In June, the Guinean Minister of Justice and Human Rights, gave assurances that the government was opposed to the death penalty and that people on death row would not be executed.

Amnesty International visit/reports

🚍 Amnesty International delegates visited Guinea in April and held talks with the authorities.

📄 Guinea : The killings must stop immediately (AFR 29/001/2007)

📄 Guinea : Fundamental freedoms must not be jeopardized by the state of siege (AFR 29/002/2007)

📄 Guinea : "Soldiers were shooting everywhere" (AFR 29/003/2007)

📄 Guinea : Security forces still a threat (AFR 29/004/2007)

G

GUINEA-BISSAU

REPUBLIC OF GUINEA-BISSAU

Head of state:	João Bernardo "Nino" Vieira
Head of government:	Martinho Ndafa Cabi (replaced Aristides Gomes in April)
Death penalty:	abolitionist for all crimes
Population:	1.7 million
Life expectancy:	45.8 years
Under-5 mortality (m/f):	206/183 per 1,000
Adult literacy:	44.8 per cent

Dire economic conditions and drug trafficking threatened the country's fragile political stability. Freedom of expression was curtailed and journalists and human rights defenders were persecuted. Children were trafficked out of the country to work as labourers or beggars.

Background

Former navy Commander Mohamed Laminé Sanha was killed in January by unknown assailants. He had been arrested and held without charge or trial several times since 2000. He was last arrested in

August 2006 and accused of plotting to kill the Chief-of-Staff of the Armed Forces. He was released without charge three days later. An inquiry into Commander Sanha's death was reportedly instituted but the outcome was not made public by the year's end. A former Prime Minister who accused President Vieira and senior military officers of involvement in the killing took refuge for three weeks in the office of the United Nations Peace Building Office in Bissau (UNOGBIS) when a warrant was issued for his arrest. He left when the warrant was rescinded.

In March the government resigned after losing a vote of confidence. Over 1,000 people demonstrated against the government in the capital, Bissau, supervised by heavily armed police and military. A new Prime Minister and government were appointed in April.

In March it was estimated that the country needed US$700 million to satisfy basic needs, but donors were reluctant to grant aid because of political instability, which was aggravated by the economic situation.

The country has become a key transit point for drug trafficking from Latin America to Europe, further threatening the country's stability and security. Allegations that members of the armed forces were involved in drug trafficking circulated, particularly after the police arrested four soldiers and two civilians in April with 600kg of cocaine in their car. In October a former Minister of National Security was ordered not to leave the country during an investigation into his involvement in the drug trade.

Freedom of expression

Journalists and human rights defenders faced arrest and threats of violence for alleging that the military authorities were involved in drug trafficking. Some went into hiding or took refuge in the UNOGBIS office, others fled the country.

■ In July, four journalists received threats. Alberto Dabo, a correspondent for Rádio Bombolom and Reuters, went into hiding for a week after receiving anonymous telephone threats. He had published information implicating civil servants and soldiers in the drug trade. In September he was charged with defamation of the Navy Chief-of-Staff, violating state secrets and abusing press freedom. His trial had not started by the end of 2007.

■ Human rights defender Mário Sá Gomes went into hiding in July and subsequently took refuge in the UNOGBIS office after a warrant was issued for his arrest. He had publicly called for the dismissal of the Chief-of-Staff of the Armed Forces in order to solve the drug problem. He left UNOGBIS after three weeks when the Minister of Interior gave assurances for his safety and provided bodyguards. He was questioned by the Procurator General in October but was not charged.

Child trafficking

Children continued to be trafficked out of the country to work in cotton fields in southern Senegal or as beggars in the Senegalese capital. In October and November the police intercepted several vehicles transporting some 200 children aged between five and 12, and arrested at least seven people. The children had been promised an education in Senegal.

HAITI

REPUBLIC OF HAITI

Head of state:	René García Préval
Head of government:	Jacques Édouard Alexis
Death penalty:	abolitionist for all crimes
Population:	8.8 million
Life expectancy:	59.5 years
Under-5 mortality (m/f):	108/93 per 1,000
Adult literacy:	54.8 per cent

While political stability and security improved during most of the year, the human rights situation remained dire with impunity prevailing for most abuses and the bulk of the population unable to exercise basic economic and social rights. Violence against women and the lack of access to justice and support services for survivors, particularly in rural areas, were serious concerns. Journalists continued to be the target of threats and killings. Thousands remained in detention without charge or trial in overcrowded conditions. At least 175,000 children continued to work as domestic workers in conditions equivalent to slave labour and nearly half a million were not in school.

Background

Levels of politically motivated violence remained low, but high rates of unemployment, widespread poverty and drug trafficking resulted in social unrest and violence.

Throughout the year, the UN Stabilization Mission in Haiti (MINUSTAH) conducted robust military operations to dismantle armed gangs operating in major urban centres. More than 800 alleged gang members were arrested. The UN Security Council extended MINUSTAH's mandate until October 2008. Violence reduction programmes started in areas where armed violence was prevalent, but sustained security improvements were hampered by the state's failure to protect and fulfil people's most basic economic and social rights. Disarmament continued at a very slow pace.

Municipal and local mayoral elections held in April completed a three-round process to elect representatives at all levels of government. However, the December elections for the renewal of one-third of the Senate were postponed.

Parliament ratified a treaty to enter Caricom, the Caribbean's single market.

Violence against women and girls

Women and girls continued to face widespread discrimination and violence in all aspects of public and private life, a situation aggravated by the lack of access to justice. Gender-based violence was under-reported, partly due to fear of retaliation and of being ostracized. The scarcity of shelter and other support services also deterred reporting.

Young girls were particularly at risk of sexual violence and harassment. Figures released by NGOs showed that the number of reported rapes increased in comparison to previous years and more than half of the victims were under 17. The justice system failed to provide effective remedies for the survivors of rape and domestic violence. In rural areas, there were reports of judicial authorities pressing rape survivors to accept a financial settlement from the perpetrator instead of treating the case as a criminal offence.

In November, 108 Sri Lankan UN peacekeepers were repatriated to Sri Lanka following allegations of sexual abuse and exploitation of Haitian women and girls.

Justice system

Efforts were made to strengthen the justice system with the adoption of new legislation on the status of magistrates and the Superior Council overseeing their functions, both reinforcing the independence of the judiciary. However, structural and institutional weaknesses, aggravated by corruption and a lack of resources, continued to fuel human rights violations within the justice system.

Prolonged pre-trial detention persistently breached international human rights standards and little effort was made to correct the situation. Only 16 per cent of those detained had been sentenced; only 5 per cent in the case of boys and girls under 18. Others remained imprisoned after completing their sentences.

The President of the Inter-American Commission on Human Rights and Rapporteur on Persons Deprived of Liberty of the OAS noted that some people had been arrested by MINUSTAH personnel without a warrant or been subjected to mass arrests, "without following basic due procedures and without respecting international human rights standards".

Impunity

The government made little progress in investigating cases of past human rights violations.

Freedom of expression – journalists

Journalists were threatened and attacked by individuals suspected of acting on behalf of perpetrators of past human rights abuses or criminals. The killings of at least nine journalists since 2000 remained unsolved.

However, in August, the Independent Commission for Supporting Investigations into the Murders of Journalists (Commission indépendante d'appui aux enquêtes relatives aux assassinats des journalistes, CIAPEAJ) was created. This was a joint initiative by the Haitian President and SOS Journalistes, an NGO working to protect journalists' rights.

■ In March, Radio Nouvelle Génération journalist Robenson Casseus received anonymous telephone death threats after he refused to change his broadcasts to support an opposition political party. He was attacked and beaten, and his house was burned down in an arson attack.

■ In December, two men were found guilty by a criminal tribunal of the murder in 2001 of journalist Brignol Lindor. However, the identities of those

H

responsible for instigating the killing remained unknown at the end of the year.

Human rights defenders

Human rights defenders and activists continued to receive threats from state agents and private individuals. Some cases of kidnapping with clear political connotations were reported.

■ In October, Dérilus Mérilus and Sanièce Petitphat, both members of the Human Rights Committee in Savanette received death threats from relatives of the alleged perpetrator of a rape after they assisted the victim in making a complaint.

■ In August, Lovinsky Pierre-Antoine, the head of the 30 September Foundation, was abducted. His whereabouts remained unknown at the end of the year. He had worked to end impunity for past abuses and to obtain reparation for victims of human rights violations under the military government (1991-1994).

Children's rights

Children's access to education was limited by the impact of poverty, violence and high education fees. UNICEF estimated that nearly 500,000 children were out of school in Haiti.

Corporal punishment in schools was prohibited but its use continued to be reported.

According to data from women's and health organizations, nearly half of all cases of rape and sexual violence reported affected Haitian girls under 17 years of age.

Up to 175,000 children were involved in domestic labour and were for the most part out of school and many were reportedly subjected to abuse and corporal punishment.

The detention of children as young as 10 in prison facilities breached national laws and international standards.

There were several reports of children in orphanages being sexually abused and trafficked.

Amnesty International visits/report

🚌 Amnesty International delegates visited Haiti in March and in September/October.

📄 Haiti: Freedom of expression cannot prevail if there is no justice for murdered journalists (AMR 36/004/2007)

HONDURAS

REPUBLIC OF HONDURAS

Head of state and government:	Manuel Zelaya Rosales
Death penalty:	abolitionist for all crimes
Population:	7.5 million
Life expectancy:	69.4 years
Under-5 mortality (m/f):	48/38 per 1,000
Adult literacy:	80 per cent

Women continued to experience high levels of violence. Human rights defenders, particularly those working on economic, social and cultural rights, were threatened and attacked. Violence against children and young people remained a concern.

Background

In March, the UN Working Group on Enforced or Involuntary Disappearances reported that 125 cases from the early 1980s were still pending clarification. In February Honduras signed the International Convention for the Protection of All Persons from Enforced Disappearance.

Police and security forces – excessive use of force

At least 41 people were reportedly injured by police in Santa Bárbara during anti-mining protests on 17 July. Demonstrators were calling on Congress to pass a new Mining Law which would include stricter provisions on environmental and health protection and ban open cast mining. Police reportedly beat demonstrators and used live ammunition. It was reported that some police officers were also wounded.

Human rights defenders

The absence of government policy on defenders and the lack of effective protection measures left human rights defenders at risk of threats and attacks.

■ In March, Donny Reyes, treasurer of the Rainbow Association (Fundación Arcoiris), a lesbian, gay, bisexual and transgender rights organization, was arbitrarily detained by police officers. At the police station, an officer reportedly told other inmates "look, I'm bringing you a little princess, you know what to do". Donny Reyes told Amnesty International that the other inmates took this as a signal to beat and rape him repeatedly.

- In February, four police officers were detained in connection with the killing of two members of the Environmentalist Movement of Olancho (Movimiento Ambientalista de Olancho) in December 2006. A preliminary hearing took place in December, where charges were presented against the officers, and the trial was due to start in 2008. Members of the Movement reported they had been forced to severely curtail their activities during 2007 because of threats.
- By the end of 2007 no one had been brought to justice for the killing of Dionisio Díaz García, a lawyer working for the Association for a More Just Society (Asociación para una Sociedad Más Justa, ASJ) who was shot dead in December 2006. He had been working on various cases of alleged labour rights abuses by a private security firm. In May 2007, another ASJ lawyer, Félix Antonio Cáceres, received a death threat by text message.

Violence against women

According to official statistics, around 200 women and girls were reported to have been killed in 2007. Continuing high levels of domestic violence were also recorded. Local organizations stated that the lack of investigation into the killings of women and a lack of effective action to tackle domestic violence remained a grave concern.

In April 2007, Special Courts on Domestic Violence began to function in San Pedro Sula and Tegucigalpa.

Killings of children and young people

Official statistics varied, but according to the Public Prosecutor's Office the number of autopsies carried out for murders of children and young people under 19 years of age was approximately 300. In most cases those responsible were not brought to justice.

Amnesty International visit/reports

- Amnesty International delegates visited Honduras in August.
- Honduras: Environmental activists killed in Olancho department (AMR 37/001/2007)
- Persecution and resistance: The experience of human rights defenders in Guatemala and Honduras (AMR 02/001/2007)

HUNGARY

REPUBLIC OF HUNGARY

Head of state:	László Sólyom
Head of government:	Ferenc Gyurcsány
Death penalty:	abolitionist for all crimes
Population:	10 million
Life expectancy:	72.9 years
Under-5 mortality (m/f):	11/9 per 1,000
Adult literacy:	99.4 per cent

Although allegations of ill-treatment and excessive use of force by police continued, the authorities initiated measures aimed at strengthening safeguards against ill-treatment. Widespread prejudice, lack of political will and deficiencies in the criminal justice system presented at times insurmountable obstacles for women in obtaining justice or redress in cases of rape and sexual violence. Roma, particularly Romani women, continued to suffer discrimination in access to housing, health services and education. Rights of asylum-seekers were not fully guaranteed. The police failed to properly protect lesbian, gay, bisexual and transgender (LGBT) people.

Police – excessive use of force and ill-treatment

In February, the Special Commission of Experts on the Demonstrations, Street Riots and Police Measures set up by the Prime Minister issued the report of its investigation into the policing of the demonstrations in Budapest in September-October 2006. Law enforcement officials had reportedly used excessive force during the demonstrations, which were initially peaceful but later turned violent.

The Special Commission called on the authorities to establish a fully resourced independent agency to investigate all allegations of serious human rights violations by law enforcement officers. It urged the authorities to ensure that complaints by individuals concerning alleged human rights violations in the context of the policing of demonstrations and their aftermath were promptly, thoroughly, independently and impartially investigated.

The UN Committee against Torture (CAT) made public in February its observations on Hungary's compliance with the Convention against Torture.

It expressed concern at the length of the initial pre-trial detention phase (up to 72 hours), ongoing pre-trial detention on police premises, and the high risk of ill-treatment to which these provisions exposed detainees. Reports of police ill-treatment and discrimination against people belonging to minority groups and non-citizens were also noted.

The Parliament amended the Police Act in June to create an independent Police Complaints Commission which was due to begin operating in January 2008. In July József Bencze, the National Police Chief, announced the introduction of a 13-point code of ethics covering basic rules of conduct for officers, lawful use of force, discrimination and public trust.

■ Charges relating to an alleged attack on police officers by Ángel Mendoza, a Peruvian citizen, and a 14-year-old friend during the demonstrations of September 2006 were withdrawn in March. They were both detained in Budapest; while Ángel Mendoza and three other detainees were waiting in the reception of the police station, a group of policemen reportedly started to insult and hit them with batons. Ángel Mendoza and his friend were represented by the human rights organization Hungarian Helsinki Committee. The case against the police officers involved in the reported ill-treatment of Ángel Mendoza and the other detainees was still ongoing at the end of the year.

Violence against women
Women victims of rape and other forms of sexual violence faced difficulties in seeking justice and redress. Lack of political will, widespread prejudice and an unsympathetic criminal justice system were among the factors which contributed to a failure to protect the rights of women. Two-thirds of sexual crimes in Hungary are committed by people known to the victim, yet few perpetrators are tried.

The UN Committee on the Elimination of Discrimination against Women (CEDAW) raised concerns about the prevalence of violence against women in Hungary, including domestic violence. It noted that the introduction of restraining orders had not been effective in providing protection to women victims of domestic violence. It also expressed concern about the lack of a specific law on domestic violence against women and reiterated its concern that the definition of rape was based on the use of force, rather than lack of consent.

■ Zsanett E., a 21-year-old woman, was allegedly assaulted by five police officers at the beginning of May in Budapest. While the case was allegedly initially covered up by police, after Zsanett E reportedly identified her alleged attackers, five officers were taken into preliminary custody, but were released a few weeks later. On 20 May, Prime Minister Ferenc Gyurcsány accepted the resignation of the Minister of Justice and Law Enforcement and the chief of the Police Security Service and dismissed the chief of National Police and the Budapest Police chief. In December, the Budapest Prosecutor's Office dropped the investigation into the police officers. Zsanett E.'s lawyer appealed against the decision.

Discrimination – Roma
In May, the UN Committee on Economic, Social and Cultural Rights expressed concern about continuing discrimination faced by Roma. Roma encountered discrimination in the labour market, in housing – inadequate conditions, increasing forced evictions and discriminatory·barriers to accessing social housing – in the denial of access to health services, segregation in hospital facilities and inferior quality of health services provided, and in education, as evidenced by the high number of Romani children segregated in separate schooling.

CEDAW's report, published in August, highlighted the prevalence of violence against Romani women and girls, including harassment and abuse at school, and noted the gaps in Romani women's formal education and the high rates of dropout among Romani girls. The Committee expressed concern about the multiple and intersecting forms of discrimination based on sex, ethnic or cultural background and socio-economic status which Romani women and girls face. It called for a holistic approach to eliminating these forms of discrimination and recommended that the Hungarian government take concrete measures to change stereotypical attitudes towards Romani women.

Detention of asylum-seekers and non-citizens
The CAT expressed concern at the detention policy applied to asylum-seekers and other non-citizens, who often faced detention for up to 12 months in so-called alien policing jails maintained by the Border Guard service. The CAT was also concerned

that the right of non-citizens to claim asylum was not fully guaranteed at the border, and there were reports of unlawful expulsions of asylum-seekers and other non-citizens to third countries by the Border Guard service.

Failure to protect peaceful LGBT demonstrators

Police forces failed to protect participants from attacks by counter-demonstrators during and after the Budapest Pride March on 7 July. Counter-protesters threw eggs, bottles and Molotov cocktails at marchers and several people were injured. The police were present but reportedly took virtually no action. Criminal procedures against eight alleged perpetrators were initiated, and remained pending at the end of the year.

Same-sex partnership bill

In December, the Parliament passed a bill which will allow same-sex couples to register civil partnerships starting from 2009. The law gives the same rights to registered partners as to spouses, except for adoption.

Ratifications

In October Hungary signed the Council of Europe Convention on Action against Trafficking in Human Beings. Hungary also signed the Council of Europe Convention on the Prevention of Terrorism.

Amnesty International visit/reports

🚌 Amnesty International delegates visited Hungary in November.

📄 Europe and Central Asia: Summary of Amnesty International's Concerns in the Region: January-June 2007 (EUR 01/010/2007)

📄 Hungary: Cries unheard – the failure to protect women from rape and sexual violence in the home (EUR 27/002/2007)

📄 Hungary: Health Professional Action – rape and sexual violence in the home (EUR 27/007/2007)

📄 Hungary: Police fail to protect participants of the Budapest Pride March (EUR 27/008/2007)

INDIA

REPUBLIC OF INDIA

Head of state:	Pratibha Patil (replaced APJ Abdul Kalam in July)
Head of government:	Manmohan Singh
Death penalty:	retentionist
Population:	1,135.6 million
Life expectancy:	63.7 years
Under-5 mortality (m/f):	84/88 per 1,000
Adult literacy:	61 per cent

Bomb attacks and armed conflict in various parts of the country left hundreds of people dead. Indo-Pakistan talks as well as initiatives to resolve conflicts in Kashmir and Nagaland made little progress. Rapid strides in some economic sectors fuelled high expectations in urban areas, although moves to acquire land and other resources for business and development projects led to protests in several states. This coincided with an upsurge in activity by armed Maoist groups in some states, raising security and human rights concerns. Marginalized local communities, including *adivasis* (indigenous communities), *dalits* and small farmers, protested against threats to their livelihood, denial of their right to participation in decision-making over development projects, and resettlement and rehabilitation processes. Many types of human rights abuses were reported, including unlawful killings, forced evictions, excessive use of police force, violence against women and harassment of human rights defenders. Institutional mechanisms failed to protect civil and political rights or ensure justice for victims. The failings extended to economic, social and cultural rights, particularly of already marginalized communities.

Background

Hundreds of people were killed in bomb attacks, including 66 passengers on a train to Pakistan in February, 42 in Hyderabad in August and 10 in Uttar Pradesh in November. Concerns over recurrent attacks marked the ongoing Indo-Pakistan talks, which failed to achieve significant progress. Little progress was made in the peace initiatives over Kashmir and Nagaland. In Assam, there were renewed bomb attacks, as well as assaults on migrants from northern states, in January and November.

At least 400 people were killed as police battled Maoists in central and eastern states. Local communities in these states resisted moves to acquire land for business projects and special economic zones. Several states, including West Bengal, Orissa, Jharkhand, Chhattisgarh, Madhya Pradesh, Andhra Pradesh, Karnataka, Tamil Nadu, Pondicherry, Maharashtra and Meghalaya, witnessed protests by local communities whose livelihoods were threatened by fast-tracked irrigation, mining, manufacturing and business projects. Unlawful methods were increasingly used to deal with such protests, and impunity for abuses remained widespread.

High suicide rates by debt-ridden farmers continued in some states, including Maharashtra, despite some relief measures. Inadequate access to health care contributed to a cholera epidemic in *adivasi* communities in south Orissa.

An agreement reached with the USA in 2006 to give India access to strategic nuclear material and equipment for civilian purposes was still not implemented due to domestic political opposition. Arms exports to Myanmar were suspended in November after the suppression of the pro-democracy movement there.

India signed the International Convention for the Protection of All Persons from Enforced Disappearances in February and was re-elected to the UN Human Rights Council. However, India had still not ratified the Convention against Torture and the Convention for the Protection of the Rights of All Migrant Workers and Members of their Families. Requests to visit the country by the UN Special Rapporteurs on torture and on extrajudicial executions remained pending. Invitations were also not issued to the Working Groups on Arbitrary Detention and on Enforced or Involuntary Disappearances.

Economic, social and cultural rights

Around 300 million people – around a quarter of the population – remained in poverty. Concerns grew over protection of the rights of already marginalized communities. Existing constitutional provisions were ignored as resource-rich areas, demarcated as exclusively *adivasi* habitations, were allotted to extractive and other industries. Affected communities were generally excluded from decision-making except in relation to resettlement and rehabilitation following displacement. Authorities continued to be reluctant to disclose crucial information despite legislation on the right to information.

In Nandigram in West Bengal, private militias owing allegiance to the ruling Communist Party of India (Marxist – CPI-M) and armed supporters of local organizations battled for territorial control. The authorities failed to persuade farmers protesting against the decision to relocate an industrial project to the area to lift their blockades. A range of human rights violations followed, including unlawful killings, forced evictions, excessive police force, violence against women, denial of access and information to the media and human rights organizations, harassment of human rights defenders and denial of justice to victims of violations.

■ In January and March, at least 25 people, mostly local residents, were killed in Nandigram, more than 100 were injured and at least 20 women were sexually assaulted by private militias allied to the ruling CPI-M. Earlier, 1,500 people, mostly CPI-M supporters, were displaced from their homes after supporters of local organizations erected blockades during protests against forced displacement.

■ In Orissa, at least 50 people were injured during year-long protests by farmers' organizations against forced displacement because of a steel plant project. An official probe into the killing by police of 12 *adivasi* protesters in Kalinganagar in 2006 remained suspended. After prolonged campaigning by local *adivasis*, in November the Supreme Court ruled against the state government's decision to allow a multinational company to mine in protected forest areas in Niyamagiri.

■ In July, police used excessive force against protesters at Badwani in Madhya Pradesh injuring at least 10 people and detaining 92. The protests were against forced displacement caused by the Narmada dam project.

Violence against *adivasis* and marginalized communities

There was rising violence in Dantewada area in Chattisgarh between armed Maoists and state forces supported by Salwa Judum, a civil militia widely believed to be state sponsored. Civilians, mostly adivasis, were targeted by both sides. Unlawful killings, abductions, torture and mutilation by both sides were reported; instances of sexual assault by state agents and killings after summary trials by the Maoists were reported; an overwhelming majority of these abuses were not fully investigated.

Around 50,000 adivasis continued to be internally displaced from the Dantewada area, a majority of them living in special camps. No serious attempt was made to ensure their voluntary return amid reports that some of their land could be offered for businesses and development projects. At least 10,000 other adivasis were reported to have fled into Andhra Pradesh.

■ On 15 March, at least 55 people, mostly belonging to the Salwa Judum, were killed in an attack by suspected Maoists near Bijapur.

■ On 31 March, 12 adivasis were killed by the state police and the Salwa Judum at Santoshpur.

■ On 14 May, a well-known activist of the People's Union of Civil Liberties, Dr Binayak Sen, was arrested; he was charged under the Chhattisgarh Special Public Security Act 2005 and the amended provisions of the Unlawful Activities (Prevention) Act, 1967. His arrest led to widespread protests by human rights organizations and the medical community.

■ On 10 July, 24 personnel of various security forces and 20 suspected Maoists were killed in attacks and counter-attacks at Konta.

Similar human rights abuses were reported from several other states, including Karnataka, Jharkhand and Andhra Pradesh.

■ On 10 July, five adivasi activists were killed by the Karnataka police at Adyaka in Chikmagalur district.

■ On 20 August, 11 adivasi women were sexually assaulted by the Andhra Pradesh police at Vakpalli in Visakhapatnam district.

■ On 26 October, armed Maoists set off a landmine at Vidyanagar in Nellore district apparently targeting former Andhra Pradesh chief minister N Janardhana Reddy and his wife, N Rajyalakshmi, a minister. Three people in the convoy were killed.

■ On 27 October, armed Maoists fired on a cultural festival at Chikhadia, killing 18 people.

Activists campaigning for land rights or environmental issues relating to marginalized communities faced abuses.

■ In July, Saroj Mohanty, a writer-activist protesting against the threat of displacement of adivasis by the

Utkal Alumina industrial project at Kashipur in Orissa, was detained on charges of dacoity (robbery), trespass and attempted murder.

■ Roma, an activist working among dalits and adivasis in Mirzapur, Uttar Pradesh, was detained under the National Security Act in August.

New legislation guaranteeing adivasis right of access to forest land was largely ignored and communities suffered police violence.

■ In April, police used excessive force against adivasis protesting against threatened forced evictions by the state forest department in Rewa district of Madhya Pradesh. Seven adivasis were injured.

■ In July, seven protesters were killed when police fired into demonstrations for land rights in Khammam district of Andhra Pradesh.

Security and human rights

Demands for new domestic anti-terror legislation continued. The Armed Forces Special Powers Act, 1958, was not repealed despite widespread protests. Uttar Pradesh joined the list of states with legislation for the control of organized criminal activity which provided for arbitrary detention.

Impunity

Impunity remained widespread.

Jammu and Kashmir

State and non-state actors continued to enjoy impunity for torture, deaths in custody, abductions and unlawful killings. A human rights organization reported that in the past 18 years 1,051 people had been victims of enforced disappearance in Baramulla district alone. Human rights organizations challenged official claims that there had been no disappearances until 10 November 2007, saying that 60 people had disappeared since 2006, including nine in 2007. Five people, who had allegedly been detained illegally, were traced. In a few cases criminal action was initiated for human rights violations committed years earlier.

■ In May, the Jammu & Kashmir High Court directed the state police to file murder charges against 11 officials of the Indo-Tibetan Border Police in connection with the disappearance of Ashraf Ahmad Koka, a resident of Gond, in October 2001.

Gujarat

Five years after the violence in which thousands of Muslims were attacked and more than 2,000 killed, justice continued to elude most victims and survivors.

Perpetrators of the violence indicated in the media that members of the ruling Bharatiya Janata Party (BJP) were implicated in the violence, yet no substantive investigation was carried out.

Little action was taken over an official report that more than 5,000 displaced families continued to live in "sub-human" conditions in Gujarat. Several key cases relating to killings and sexual assault of Muslim women were still pending before the Supreme Court.

In May, Gujarat authorities admitted that senior police officials had been involved in the unlawful killing of Sohrabuddin Shaikh and his wife, Kausar Bi, in November 2005. Following this development, relatives of at least three other people killed by the police in previous years sought fresh investigations.

Punjab

A majority of police officers responsible for serious human rights violations during the 1984-94 civil unrest in Punjab continued to evade justice. The findings of a Central Bureau of Investigation probe into allegations of unlawful killings of 2,097 people who were cremated by the police had still not been made fully public, nine years after the investigation was launched. The National Human Rights Commission (NHRC) awarded compensation to the relatives of 1,298 victims of such killings in one district, Amritsar. However, the NHRC was criticized for the slow pace of its investigations, and a commission appointed by the NHRC in 2006 to examine compensation claims was criticized in October by human rights organizations for various failings.

In May, the government ordered an investigation into three unlawful killings by the police in Punjab in 1993-94, after reports that three people, listed as among those killed, surfaced in their native villages.

Karnataka/Tamil Nadu

Eleven years after allegations of unlawful killings, torture, sexual assault and illegal detention of *adivasis* were first levelled against a joint Tamil Nadu-Karnataka force established to catch sandalwood smugglers, the NHRC had failed to initiate charges against any of the 38 officials cited as perpetrators of the abuses. In January, the NHRC ordered interim compensation for 89 of the 140 victims and their relatives who had made the allegations.

Assam

A commission of inquiry into the unlawful killings between 1998 and 2001 of 35 individuals associated with the United Liberation Front of Asom published its findings in November. It concluded that the killings were carried out by surrendered members of the organization at the behest of a former chief minister and the state police. It remained unclear if anyone would be brought to justice.

Death penalty

At least 100 people were sentenced to death although no executions took place. In December, India voted against a UN General Assembly resolution for a moratorium on the death penalty.

Amnesty International visits/reports

🚌 Amnesty International delegates visited India in August and November and met government officials and civil society organizations.

📄 Need for effective investigations and prosecutions as political violence continues in West Bengal (ASA 20/020/2007)

📄 Indian helicopters for Myanmar – making a mockery of embargoes? (ASA 20/014/2007)

📄 A pattern of unlawful killings by the Gujarat police – urgent need for effective investigations (ASA: 20/011/2007)

📄 Five years on – the bitter and uphill struggle for justice in Gujarat (ASA 20/007/2007)

INDONESIA

REPUBLIC OF INDONESIA

Head of state and government:	Susilo Bambang Yudhoyono
Death penalty:	retentionist
Population:	228.1 million
Life expectancy:	69.7 years
Under-5 mortality (m/f):	46/37 per 1,000
Adult literacy:	90.4 per cent

Torture, excessive use of force and unlawful killings by police and security forces were reported. Most perpetrators of gross human rights violations in the past, including in Nanggroe Aceh Darussalam (NAD), Papua, and Timor-Leste, continued to enjoy impunity. The situation in Papua remained tense with increasing targeted attacks and threats against human rights activists and church leaders. The number of possible prisoners of conscience increased sharply with up to 76 people detained for peacefully expressing their political or religious views.

Police and security forces

Human rights violations by police and military personnel included excessive use of force during demonstrations and arrests, fatal shootings and torture.

■ In January, two gay men were reportedly beaten, kicked and verbally abused by neighbours before being arbitrarily detained by police. They were taken to Banda Raya police post, Aceh province, where they suffered further sexual abuse and other forms of torture and ill-treatment. It appears the men were targeted solely because of their sexual orientation.

■ In May, four people, including a pregnant woman, were shot and killed during a clash between marines and villagers over disputed land. A further eight, including a four-year-old child, were injured. In July, the National Human Rights Commission (Komnas HAM) asked the military to allow residents to continue using the disputed land in Pasuruan while awaiting a permanent court ruling, and urged the government and the military to compensate the victims for the losses they and their families have suffered. Thirteen marines were named as suspects in the shootings. By the end of the year, none had been prosecuted and all had resumed their duties.

In November, the Special Rapporteur on torture, Manfred Nowak, visited Indonesia. He concluded that given the lack of legal and institutional safeguards and the prevailing structural impunity, people deprived of their liberty were extremely vulnerable to torture and other ill-treatment.

Freedom of expression

Freedom of expression continued to be severely restricted. There was a sharp increase in attacks and threats against human rights defenders following the visit in June of Hina Jilani, the UN Special Representative of the Secretary General on Human Rights Defenders. The UN Special Representative expressed concerns over the persistent impunity for past violations committed against human rights defenders, and the lack of concrete initiatives by the government to protect defenders including specific protection for defenders working on lesbian, gay, bisexual and transgender (LGBT) rights and HIV/AIDS. She highlighted the continuing harassment and intimidation of defenders by the police, military and other security and intelligence agencies and the restrictions on access to victims and sites of human rights violations, particularly in Papua.

Up to 63 people were arrested and detained for peacefully expressing their views. An additional 13, imprisoned in previous years, remained in jail.

■ In June, at least 21 people were arrested in Ambon, Maluku province, following a visit by the President. According to reports, dancers performing a traditional local dance in front of the President were arrested after they raised the Maluku independence flag. During interrogation they were allegedly beaten and threatened. Most of them were charged with "rebellion" under Articles 106 and 110 of the criminal code that is punishable by a maximum sentence of life imprisonment. They were possible prisoners of conscience.

In July, the Constitutional Court ruled unconstitutional Articles 154 and 155 of the Criminal Code commonly known as the 'hate sowing' offences. The Articles criminalized "public expression of feelings of hostility, hatred or contempt toward the government" and prohibited "the expression of such feelings or views through the public media". These offences had often been used by the government to restrict peaceful criticism and jail political opponents, critics, students and human rights defenders. The ruling was widely welcomed, although it did not apply retroactively. Prisoners of conscience Filep Karma sentenced to 15 years, and Yusak Pakage sentenced to 10 years, remained in jail. Both were convicted partly under these articles in May 2005 for raising the Papuan flag.

Papua

The low-level conflict between the security forces and pro-independence militants in Papua continued. The military repeatedly threatened local community members who supported independence through peaceful means. An army official who had been indicted for crimes against humanity in Timor-Leste, but had yet to face trial, was nominated as military commander in the Papuan capital, Jayapura. Reported human rights violations by security forces included extrajudicial executions, torture and excessive use of force.

■ Albert Rumbekwan, director of the National Human Rights Commission (Komnas HAM) in Papua, received death threats and was kept under surveillance following the visit by the UN Special Representative on Human Rights Defenders.

Death penalty

In April Ayub Bulubili was executed by firing squad for the premeditated murder of a family of six. At least 115 people were known to be under sentence of death at the end of 2007.

In February, a group of Indonesian lawyers filed for a judicial review of the 1997 Narcotics Law before the Constitutional Court. They argued that its provision of death sentences for drug offences contradicted the 1945 Constitution, which guarantees the right to life. Their lawyers represented five people who had been sentenced to death for drug-related offences – Edith Yunita Sianturi, Rani Andriani (Melisa Aprilia), and three Australian citizens, Myuran Sukumaran, Andrew Chan and Scott Anthony Rush. The Constitutional Court rejected the appeal in October.

Impunity

In May, the new Attorney General, Hendarman Supandji, filed for a Supreme Court review of the 2004 murder of human rights activist Munir Said Thalib, for which no one had been held to account.

The Commission of Truth and Friendship (CTF) established jointly by Indonesia and Timor-Leste to document crimes committed in Timor-Leste in 1999 and to promote reconciliation, began its fact-finding work through public and closed hearings in February. In July, the UN Secretary General instructed UN officials not to testify before the CTF unless the terms of reference were revised to comply with international standards, noting that the UN did not endorse or condone amnesties for genocide, crimes against humanity, war crimes or gross violations of human rights, nor should it do anything that might foster amnesties. Concerns were also expressed by national and international observers about the CTF's treatment of victims during hearings and possible biased weighting of the testimonies of military officials, militia members and bureaucrats over those given by victims. The CTF mandate was extended until early 2008.

Discrimination and violence against women

In March, the Human Trafficking Criminal Actions Eradication Draft Bill (anti-trafficking bill) became law. Local NGOs welcomed the inclusion of a definition of sexual exploitation, provisions on the facilitation of trafficking, and immunity for victims. However, they noted insufficient provisions to prevent child trafficking and in particular the need to make this abuse distinct from other provisions related to human trafficking.

Women domestic workers, who are excluded from the national Manpower Act, suffered violations of labour rights as well as physical and psychological abuse, including of a sexual nature, in the workplace. Although the Ministry of Manpower prepared draft legislation on domestic workers in June 2006, no steps were taken to enact the law. Domestic workers therefore remained excluded from legal enforcement of maximum hours of work, a minimum wage and specific protections for female employees covered for other workers in the Manpower Act.

Health

Indonesia has one of the highest rates of maternal mortality in southeast Asia, an estimated 230-310 women die each year for every 100,000 births. In February, the WHO highlighted the main causes, which included female genital mutilation (FGM); marriages at an early age; lack of access to sexual and reproductive health information, education and services; lack of access to professional health services during pregnancy and childbirth; lack of knowledge about sexually transmitted disease, HIV/AIDS and contraceptive services; and the high incidence of unsafe abortions.

In February, a joint study by the Health Ministry and the WHO highlighted the rapid spread of HIV/AIDS among high-risk groups, including drug users, transsexuals and sex workers, particularly in parts of Indonesia with inadequate healthcare services. A government-sponsored survey found that over two per cent of people in Papua were infected with HIV, compared to 0.2 per cent of the general populace in Indonesia. In November, for the first time, a national campaign to promote condom use was launched.

Amnesty International reports

📖 Indonesia: Exploitation and abuse – the plight of women domestic workers (ASA 21/001/2007)
📖 Indonesia (Aceh): Torture of gay men by the Banda Raya police (ASA 21/004/2007)
📖 Indonesia: Briefing to the UN Committee on the elimination of discrimination against women – women and girl domestic workers (ASA 21/007/2007)

📄 Indonesia: Amnesty International deplores death penalty for drug offences (ASA 21/020/2007)

📄 Indonesia: Submission to the UN Universal Periodic Review – First session of UPR Working Group 7-18 April 2008 (ASA 21/021/2007)

IRAN

ISLAMIC REPUBLIC OF IRAN

Head of state:	Leader of the Islamic Republic of Iran: Ayatollah Sayed 'Ali Khamenei
Head of government:	President: Dr Mahmoud Ahmadinejad
Death penalty:	retentionist
Population:	71.2 million
Life expectancy:	70.2 years
Under-5 mortality (m/f):	32/31 per 1,000
Adult literacy:	82.4 per cent

The authorities continued to suppress dissent. Journalists, writers, scholars, and women's rights and community activists were subject to arbitrary arrest, travel bans, closure of their NGOs and harassment. Armed opposition, mainly by Kurdish and Baluchi groups, continued, as did state repression of Iran's minority communities. Discrimination against women remained entrenched in law and practice. Torture and other ill-treatment were widespread in prisons and detention centres. A security clampdown announced in April was marked by a sharp rise in executions; at least 335 people were executed, among them seven child offenders. Sentences of stoning to death, amputation and flogging continued to be passed and carried out.

Background

Iran's uranium enrichment programme continued to be a focus of international tension. Israeli and US authorities refused to rule out the possibility of military action against Iran. In March, the UN Security Council imposed further sanctions. In September, the US government designated Iran's Revolutionary Guards a "terrorist organization" for allegedly supporting insurgents in Iraq and Afghanistan. In December, US intelligence agencies published a report stating that Iran had ended any nuclear weapons programme in 2003. The same month the UN General Assembly condemned the human rights situation in Iran.

Ayatollah Meshkini, Head of the Assembly of Experts that oversees the appointment of the Supreme Leader, died in July. He was replaced by former President Hashemi Rafsanjani.

Increasing numbers of Iranians faced poverty as the economic situation deteriorated. In June rioting followed the introduction of petrol rationing. A three-month strike by workers at the Haft Tapeh Sugar Plant in Khuzestan Province over unpaid wages and benefits was forcibly broken up by security forces in October. Haft Tapeh and other workers and teachers staged large demonstrations, and arrests were made.

Freedom of expression

Vaguely worded laws and harsh practices resulted in widespread repression of peaceful dissent. Demonstrations frequently led to mass arrests and unfair trials. The authorities maintained tight restrictions on internet access. Journalists, academics and webloggers, including some dual nationals, were detained and sentenced to prison or flogging and several publications were closed down. In April, the Minister of Intelligence, Gholam Hossein Eje'i, publicly accused students and the women's movement of being part of an attempt to bring about the "soft overthrow" of the Iranian government.

■ Ali Farahbakhsh, a journalist, was granted an early conditional release in October after 11 months in detention. He was convicted of "espionage" and "receiving money from foreigners" in connection with his attendance at a media conference in Thailand.

Human rights defenders

Independent human rights groups and other NGOs continued to face long delays, often lasting years, in obtaining official registration, leaving them at risk of closure for carrying out illegal activities. Students campaigning for greater respect for human rights faced reprisals, including arbitrary arrest and torture. Individual human rights defenders were persecuted for their work; some were prisoners of conscience.

■ Emaddedin Baghi, Head of the Association for the Defence of Prisoners and a leading campaigner against the death penalty, was detained in October following a summons relating to accusations of "endangering national security". While the family was posting bail, they were told that he now had to serve a suspended sentence imposed in 2003, including for "printing lies".

Another three-year prison term imposed on him in July 2007 for "propaganda in favour of opponents", arising from his work on behalf of Iranian Ahwazi Arabs sentenced to death after unfair trials, was pending appeal. His wife, Fatemeh Kamali Ahmad Sarahi, and daughter, Maryam Baghi, were given three-year suspended prison sentences in October for "meeting and colluding with the aim of disrupting national security" after attending a human rights workshop in Dubai in 2004. In December he suffered a seizure while in custody.

■ Mansour Ossanlu, head of the Union of Workers of the Tehran and Suburbs Bus Company, was detained in July after visiting Europe to gather support for the independent trade union movement in Iran. Following international protests he received medical treatment for an eye injury reportedly sustained during a dispute with prison officials during an earlier detention. In October an appeals court upheld a five-year prison sentence imposed in February.

Discrimination against women

Women continued to face widespread discrimination in law and practice. Thousands were arrested for non-compliance with the obligatory dress code.

Activists working with the Campaign for Equality, which aims to collect a million signatures in Iran calling for an end to legalized discrimination against women, faced harassment and arrest. In August, Nasim Sarabandi and Fatemeh Dehdashti were sentenced to six months' imprisonment, suspended for two years, for "acting against national security through the spread of propaganda against the system". They were the first people to be tried and sentenced for collecting signatures. At the end of the year, four campaign activists remained in detention without charge or trial – Ronak Safarzadeh and Hana Abdi, Kurdish women who were detained in Sanandaj in October and November respectively; and Maryam Hosseinkhah and Jelveh Javaheri, who were detained in Tehran in connection with their work editing the campaign's website. The authorities persistently filtered the website, making access difficult.

Women's rights defender Delaram Ali, who had been arrested in June 2006 following a peaceful demonstration demanding greater respect for women's rights, had her 30-month prison sentence temporarily postponed following local and international campaigning. In March, 33 women activists were arrested outside Tehran's Revolutionary Court during a protest against the trial of five women charged in connection with the June 2006 demonstration. All were released, but some faced trial.

Repression of minorities

Repression continued of Iran's ethnic minorities, who maintained their campaigning for greater recognition of their cultural and political rights.

Arabs

At least eight Iranian Ahwazi Arabs were executed after being convicted in connection with bomb explosions in Khuzestan in 2005. At least 17 other Iranian Arabs were believed to be facing execution after unfair trials related to the bombings. Scores, possibly hundreds, of Ahwazi Arabs were reportedly arrested in April, in advance of the anniversary of riots in 2005 protesting against a letter allegedly written by a presidential adviser, who denied its authenticity, which set out policies for the reduction of the Arab population of Khuzestan.

■ In April, journalist Mohammad Hassan Fallahiya was sentenced to three years in prison with hard labour for writing articles critical of the government and for allegedly contacting opposition groups based outside Iran. He was detained in November 2006 and denied access to a lawyer throughout the judicial process. His family said the Evin Prison authorities refused to allow them to take him medicines required to treat heart and blood disorders, endangering his life.

Azerbaijanis

Hundreds of Iranian Azerbaijani activists were arrested in connection with a peaceful demonstration on International Mother Language Day, 21 February. The demonstrators called for their own language to be used in schools and other education institutions in the areas of north-west Iran where most Iranian Azerbaijanis reside.

■ Prisoner of conscience Saleh Kamrani, a lawyer and human rights defender, was detained in Evin Prison between August and December. In September 2006 he had been sentenced to a year in prison – suspended for five years – for "spreading propaganda against the system". It was unclear whether his arrest was connected to this sentence.

Baluchis

Jondallah, a Baluchi armed group, carried out attacks on Iranian officials, including bombing a bus carrying

Revolutionary Guards in February. It also took hostages, at least one of whom was killed.

■ Nasrollah Shanbeh-zehi was arrested following the bus bombing. Five days later he was publicly executed following a summary trial.

■ Ya'qub Mehrnehad, head of the Voice of Justice Young People's Society, a recognized NGO, was detained in April in Zahedan, initially by the Ministry of Intelligence, following a meeting in the Provincial Office of the Ministry of Culture and Islamic Guidance that the Governor of Zahedan reportedly attended. He remained in Zahedan Prison at the end of the year, without access to a lawyer. He may have been tortured.

■ In May police shot dead Roya Sarani, an 11-year-old Baluchi girl, while she was being driven home from school by her father in Zahedan. The authorities reportedly put pressure on her family to hold a small funeral. No official investigation was believed to have been held into her killing.

Kurds

Members of the Party for a Free Life in Kurdistan (Partiya Jiyana Azadîya Kurdistanê, PJAK) attacked Iranian forces, who shelled parts of northern Iraq where they believed PJAK forces were hiding. Numerous Kurds were arrested, many accused of membership of, or contact with, proscribed groups. Kurdish journalists and human rights defenders were particularly at risk of harassment and detention.

■ Mohammad Sadiq Kabudvand, head of the Human Rights Organization of Kurdistan (HROK) and editor of the banned weekly newspaper *Payam-e Mardom,* was detained in July apparently for "acting against national security", "propaganda against the system" and "co-operating with groups opposed to the system", although he was not formally charged. He complained of poor prison conditions and ill-treatment, including denial of access to the toilet, which was apparently intended to force other leading HROK members to turn themselves in to security officials for questioning.

Religious minorities

Baha'is throughout the country continued to face persecution on account of their religion. At least 13 Baha'is were arrested in at least 10 cities and were subject to harassment and discriminatory practices, such as denial of access to higher education, bank loans and pension payments. Nine Baha'i cemeteries were desecrated.

In August and November, clashes involving Sufis resulted in scores of injuries and, in November,

more than 100 arrests. In September, a couple – a Christian convert who married a Christian woman in an Islamic ceremony – were reportedly flogged in Gohar Dasht in connection with their faith.

Torture and other ill-treatment

Torture and other ill-treatment were common in many prisons and detention centres, facilitated by prolonged pre-charge detention and denial of access to lawyers and family. At least two people died in custody, possibly as a result of torture. Torturers were rarely if ever held to account for their crimes.

■ In May, four students and editors-in-chief of student publications arrested in May at Amir Kabir Polytechnic were tortured, according to their families. The abuse allegedly included 24-hour interrogation sessions, sleep deprivation, beatings with cables and fists, and threats to prisoners and their families. The detainees were arrested in connection with articles deemed by university officials to "insult Islamic sanctities". In July, the families of the detained students sent an open letter to Ayatollah Shahroudi, Head of the Judiciary, describing the alleged torture.

■ Zahra Bani Yaghoub, a medical graduate, died in custody in Hamadan in October. She was arrested for walking in a park with her fiancé and died in detention the next day. The authorities said she had hanged herself. Her family said that she was in good spirits when they spoke to her on the phone half an hour before she was found dead. A report in November indicated that the head of the detention centre had been detained, but was then released on bail and remained in office.

■ In November, a retrial was ordered in the case of the 2003 death in custody of Zahra Kazemi, a Canadian-Iranian photojournalist. She was tortured to death, but the only person prosecuted was acquitted in 2004, a decision upheld in 2005. She had been arrested for taking photographs outside Evin Prison.

Death penalty

The number of executions rose sharply in 2007. Amnesty International received reports that at least 335 people were executed, although the true figure was almost certainly higher. Some people were executed in public, often in multiple hangings. Death sentences were imposed for a wide range of crimes, including drug smuggling, armed robbery, murder, espionage, political violence and sexual offences. A "special" court in eastern Iran established in May 2006 to reduce the time between the crime and the punishment led to a marked rise in the number of Baluchis executed.

Child offenders

At least seven people aged under 18 at the time of the crime were executed and at least 75 other child offenders remained on death row. Following domestic and international protests, the death sentences of at least two child offenders – Sina Paymard and Nazanin Fatehi – were commuted.

■ Makwan Moloudzadeh, an Iranian Kurdish child offender, was executed in December following a grossly flawed trial for three rapes he allegedly committed at the age of 13, eight years earlier. In sentencing him to death, the judge relied on his "knowledge" that the offence had occurred and that Makwan Moloudzadeh had reached puberty at the time of the crime and so could be tried and sentenced as an adult.

Execution by stoning

Ja'far Kiani was stoned to death in Takestan in July, despite an order from the Head of the Judiciary granting a temporary stay of execution. The judge in the case was later said by officials to have been "mistaken". At least nine women, including Ja'far Kiani's co-defendant, and two men remained at risk of stoning. In November, judicial officials said that a new version of the Penal Code had been sent to the Majles for approval and that, if approved, it would provide for the possibility of commuting stoning sentences.

Cruel, inhuman and degrading punishments

Sentences of flogging and amputation continued to be passed and implemented.

■ In November, Soghra Mola'i was flogged 80 times for "illicit relations" after her sentence of death by stoning was overturned following a retrial. She remained in prison to serve a sentence for involvement in the murder of her husband.

At least eight people had their fingers or hand amputated after conviction of theft.

Amnesty International reports

▤ Iran: Human rights abuses against the Baluchi minority (MDE 13/104/2007)
▤ Iran: The last executioner of children (MDE 13/059/2007)

IRAQ

REPUBLIC OF IRAQ

Head of state:	Jalal Talabani
Head of government:	Nuri al-Maliki
Death penalty:	retentionist
Population:	30.3 million
Life expectancy:	57.7 years
Under-5 mortality (m/f):	109/102 per 1,000
Adult literacy:	74.1 per cent

Thousands of civilians, including children, were killed or injured amid continuing sectarian and other violence. All sides involved in the fighting committed gross human rights violations, some of which amounted to war crimes and crimes against humanity. Many civilians died as a result of bomb attacks by groups opposed to the Iraqi government and the US-led Multinational Force (MNF), while others were victims of sectarian killings by Shi'a and Sunni armed groups. Hundreds of people were abducted, tortured and murdered, with their bodies left in the street or found by their families at morgues. The increasingly sectarian nature of the violence caused hundreds of thousands of people to flee their homes, swelling the growing numbers of Iraqi refugees in Syria, Jordan and other states to 2 million and increasing the number of those internally displaced within Iraq to more than 2 million. This added to the growing humanitarian crisis. Iraqi security forces also committed gross human rights violations, including unlawful killings, rape and other torture, and arbitrary arrests and detentions. The MNF killed civilians and held more than 25,000 detainees without charge or trial, including some who had been held for several years. Civilians were also killed by guards employed by private military and security companies who had immunity against prosecution in Iraq until October. The death penalty was used extensively and 33 people were executed, some after grossly unfair trials.

Background

In January, US President George W. Bush announced that 20,000 more US troops would be deployed as part of a military "surge" to improve security, especially in the Baghdad area, and help the Iraqi government to gain greater control. The "surge" was accompanied by economic and political initiatives, including reconstruction and job creation, the holding of provincial elections, and finalizing contentious legislation such as the draft oil law. However, only limited progress was achieved in these areas.

Despite the "surge", violence remained widespread and severe, although it was reported to have decreased towards the end of the year. The government and parliament were hampered by political divisions and a boycott by members of parliament representing political parties opposed to Prime Minister Nuri al-Maliki.

In April, UNHCR convened an international conference in Switzerland in response to the growing humanitarian crisis caused by the exodus of Iraqi refugees and internal displacement within Iraq.

In August, Shi'a religious leader Moqtada al-Sadr announced that the Mahdi Army composed of his followers would cease attacks for up to six months and co-operate with Iraqi security forces.

The same month, the UN Security Council passed resolution 1770 which, among other things, authorizes the UN Assistance Mission for Iraq (UNAMI), at the request of the Iraqi government, to promote political talks among the country's ethnic and religious groups as well as regional negotiations on issues relating to Iraq's border security, energy and humanitarian crisis. The resolution failed adequately to address the grave human rights situation in the country.

In December, UK forces handed over control of Basra province to Iraqi government forces.

Abuses by armed groups

Armed groups, including Islamist and nationalist groups fighting against the US-led forces and the Iraqi government, as well as al-Qa'ida and militias affiliated to Shi'a religious groups, committed gross human rights abuses. Many of the abuses were committed in the course of sectarian violence between Shi'a and Sunni armed groups, who sought to clear mixed neighbourhoods of Sunni and Shi'a respectively, abducting people from their homes or in the streets and murdering them. Often, bodies were dumped bearing evidence of mutilation or torture. Members of other religious and ethnic minorities were also targeted for such abuses, including Yezidis, Christians, Sabeans and Palestinians, as were women, human rights defenders, judges, medical doctors and other professionals.

■ On 18 April at least 140 people were killed by a car bomb detonated at the market in al-Sadriya, a predominantly Shi'a district of Baghdad.

■ On 12 May Dr Adib Ibrahim al-Jalabi, a medical doctor and a leading figure in the Islamic Organization for Human Rights (Mosul), was assassinated by armed men, believed to be from al-Qa'ida, after leaving his clinic in Mosul.

■ On 3 June Chaldean priest, Fr Ragheed Ganni, and three deacons were shot dead by unknown assailants in Mosul.

■ On 7 July some 150 people were killed and more than 265 injured in a suicide car bomb attack at the marketplace in Amerli, a predominantly Shi'a Turkmen village in Salahuddin governorate.

■ In August, Mostafa Ahmad, a taxi driver and Palestinian refugee, was abducted by armed men apparently from the Mahdi Army. Two days later his abductors used his mobile phone to tell his family to collect his body from the morgue; he had been tortured with a drill, his teeth had been ripped out, and he had been shot six times.

■ On 14 August, more than 400 people were killed and at least 300 injured by four suicide bombers who blew up fuel tanks in al-Qahtaniya, al-Jazeera and Tal Uzair, all villages near the Syrian border inhabited mostly by members of the minority Yezidi religious sect. Many children were among the victims.

■ On 28 October Shehab Mohammad al-Hiti, a Sunni and editor of the weekly *Baghdad al-Youm* newspaper, was abducted in al-Jamia, Baghdad. He was later found shot dead.

Killings by Iraqi security forces

Iraqi security forces killed civilians unlawfully. In some cases, investigations were announced but their outcome was not known.

■ On 27 March gunmen wearing police uniforms killed 70 Sunni Arabs in the mixed town of Tal-'Afar near Mosul, apparently in reprisal for a suicide attack by a Sunni insurgent in a Shi'a district of the town. Survivors reportedly said that the gunmen dragged men from their homes, handcuffed and blindfolded them, and then riddled them with bullets. Two days later, the government acknowledged that police had carried out the killings and 13 were reported to have been briefly detained. It was not clear whether any of them were brought to justice.

I

Killings and other violations by the Multinational Force

US forces committed gross human rights violations, including unlawful killings of civilians, arbitrary arrests, destruction of property and violent house searches. A few US and UK soldiers were tried and found guilty of human rights violations in previous years.

■ On 28 September, US forces launched an air raid at night targeting a building in the predominantly Sunni neighbourhood of al-Saha, in south-western Baghdad. At least 10 men, women and children were killed.

■ After heavy clashes on 21 October between US forces and gunmen belonging to the Mahdi Army in al-Sadr City in Baghdad, US forces used helicopters to reportedly target a man suspected of abducting MNF soldiers. During the raid, according to Iraqi police, 13 civilians, including two children, were killed and others injured. A US military official said a committee was reviewing the incident.

■ In August a US soldier was sentenced to 110 years' imprisonment with the possibility of parole for raping and killing 'Abeer Qasim Hamza al-Janabi, a 14-year-old girl, and murdering three of her relatives in Mahmoudiya in March 2006. A military court in Kentucky found the soldier guilty of "rape, conspiracy to commit rape and housebreaking with the intent to commit rape and four counts of felony murder". Two other soldiers, who had earlier admitted raping the girl, received life sentences in February.

Arbitrary arrests and detention

The MNF and Iraqi security forces were holding some 60,000 prisoners as of November, according to the ICRC. Most were detained indefinitely without charge or trial as security internees. In October the MNF Commander of Detainee Operations said the MNF was holding some 25,000 detainees at Camp Bucca in the south, Camp Victory and Camp Cropper near Baghdad International Airport, and other places, including 840 juveniles and 280 foreign nationals, mostly from Arab countries. Shortly before, the MNF began releasing detainees and by December several thousand detainees had been released on condition that they would not pose a security threat and after providing a family guarantee of good conduct.

Torture and other ill-treatment

Reports of torture and other ill-treatment of detainees, including minors, by Iraqi security forces, particularly Interior Ministry forces, were common. Thousands of prisoners were held in hugely overcrowded Iraqi-run prisons, police stations and detention camps, many without access to a lawyer, conditions that facilitate torture. In May, former detainees who had been held at a facility in Baghdad's predominantly Shi'a neighbourhood of al-Kadhimiya told a UN official that they had been subjected to "routine beatings, suspension by limbs for long periods, electric shock treatment to sensitive parts of the body, threats of ill-treatment of close relatives". As in previous years, the government announced investigations into specific allegations of abuses by Iraqi security forces, but failed to make public the outcome, adding to concerns that impunity was widespread.

■ On 4 March British and Iraqi troops found some 30 prisoners, including some who reportedly showed signs of having been tortured, when they stormed the headquarters of a government intelligence agency in Basra.

■ In October, the Prisoners' Association for Justice, an Iraqi human rights NGO, said it had interviewed five children aged between 13 and 17 who had been tortured by Iraqi security forces who suspected them of assisting insurgents and militia.

Death penalty

The death penalty was used extensively, although the Human Rights Minister told the UN Human Rights Council in March that the government was working towards abolition.

At least 199 men and women were sentenced to death and at least 33 prisoners were executed. Most death sentences were passed after unfair trials by the Central Criminal Court of Iraq (CCCI). Defendants complained that confessions extracted under torture were used as evidence against them and that they were not able to choose their own lawyer.

■ In February the Court of Cassation upheld the death sentences for aggravated murder passed against two women. Samar Sa'ad 'Abdullah and Wassan Talib were, respectively, sentenced to death by the Criminal Court of al-Karkh in August 2005, and the CCCI in Baghdad in August 2006.

■ In May, six men – Moazzea Abdul-Khazal, Hussain Jihad Hassan, 'Abdel-Qader Qasim Jameel, Mostafa

Mahmoud Isma'il, Qais Habib Aslem and Islam Mostafa 'Abdel-Sattar – were sentenced to death by the CCCI for the abduction and killing of a man in the Baghdad district of al-Adhamiya. It was not known if they were executed.

Abuses by private military and security guards

Foreign armed guards employed by private military and security firms killed civilians. Security firms were immune from prosecution according to Order 17 issued in 2004 by Paul Bremer, then head of the Coalition Provisional Authority. However, following a major incident in September involving the US-based Blackwater company, the Iraqi government introduced draft legislation that would revoke Order 17.

■ On 16 September, 17 Iraqi civilians were killed and 27 injured when Blackwater security guards opened fire at a busy crossroads in Baghdad's al-Mansour district. The company said that its guards had fired in self-defence but witnesses and the Iraqi government alleged that the guards had fired first. Both the Iraqi authorities and the US State Department announced that they were conducting investigations and in November the US Federal Bureau of Investigation (FBI) concluded that the shooting had been unjustified. The company said that any of its guards guilty of wrongdoing would be held to account. The Iraqi government demanded that Blackwater pay US$8 million in compensation to each of the families of the 17 people killed.

Violence against women

Violence against women increased and many were forced to leave their jobs after receiving death threats or to seek refuge abroad. In Basra, some 42 women were reportedly killed between July and September by Shi'a armed groups vying for control of the area. In most governorates women were increasingly threatened by armed men if they failed to observe a strict dress code. Reportedly, domestic violence and "honour killings" were on the rise and increasing sectarianism put at risk women married to men from another sect.

■ In February, local tribal leaders complained after four Iraqi soldiers reportedly raped a woman belonging to the Turkmen minority after entering her home at Tal-'Afar, near Mosul. A senior Iraqi military official stated that four men had confessed to the rape, but it was not clear whether any action was taken against them.

■ On or around 7 April, Du'a Khalil Aswad, a 17-year-old Yezidi girl, was stoned to death in front of a large crowd in the town of Bashika near Mosul. The victim of an "honour crime", she was killed by a group of eight or nine Yezidi men, including relatives, who accused her of having a relationship with a Sunni Muslim boy. Her death by stoning, lasting for 30 minutes, was recorded on video and posted on the internet. Members of the local security forces were present but failed to intervene.

Refugees and internally displaced people

At least 4.2 million Iraqis were displaced. These included 2.2 million who were displaced within Iraq and some 2 million refugees, mostly in Syria (around 1.4 million) and Jordan (around half a million). In the last months of the year both these neighbouring states, struggling to meet the health, education and other needs of the Iraqi refugees already present, introduced visa requirements that impeded the entry of Iraqis seeking refuge. Within Iraq, most governorates barred entry to Iraqis fleeing sectarian violence elsewhere.

Trials of former officials

The Supreme Iraqi Criminal Tribunal (SICT) continued to try former senior party, army, security and government officials associated with the previous Ba'ath administration headed by Saddam Hussein for gross human rights violations committed during his rule. Several defendants were sentenced to death after grossly unfair trials and three, sentenced in 2006, were executed. Political interference continued to undermine the independence and impartiality of the SICT.

■ In February the SICT Appeals Chamber changed the life sentence previously imposed on former Vice-President Taha Yassin Ramadan to death, and he was executed on 20 March. Two co-defendants, Barzan Ibrahim al-Tikriti and 'Awad Hamad al-Bandar, were hanged on 15 January.

■ The trial of those allegedly responsible for abuses committed during the so-called Anfal campaign of 1988, which caused the deaths of some 180,000 Iraqi Kurds, concluded on 24 June. Three of the six defendants – 'Ali Hassan al-Majid, Sultan Hashim Ahmad al-Ta'i and Hussain Rashid al-Tikri – were sentenced to death for war crimes and crimes against humanity. 'Ali Hassan al-Majid was also convicted of genocide. The SICT Appeals

Chamber confirmed the death sentences on 4 September and the three were expected to be executed within 30 days. However, the US military refused to transfer the three to Iraqi custody because of a legal wrangle between Prime Minister al-Maliki and the Presidential Council.

Northern Iraq

Human rights violations, including arbitrary arrests, torture and executions, were reported in the areas under the control of the Kurdistan Regional Government (KRG) in Northern Iraq. Violence against women was widespread.

■ Mohammad Siyassi Ashkani, a journalist from Sulaimaniya, was arrested in January by Asayish (Security) officials and detained without charge or trial for almost six months. He was held in solitary confinement for the first 55 days before being allowed weekly visits from his family, and was denied access to a lawyer. He was released on 19 July.

■ On 29 May, Heman Mohamed, 'Othman Abdel-Karim, Sherwan Ahmed and Qaraman Rasul were executed in Erbil. They had been convicted in June 2006 of participating in a bomb attack in Erbil a year earlier.

■ Three Turkish men – Metir Demir, Mustafa Egilli and Hasip Yokus – members of the Turkey-based NGO Association for the Rights of Freedom of Thought and Education who had been arrested in June 2006, remained in detention without charge or trial until 12 September, when they were returned to Turkey. One of them told Amnesty International that they had been detained in the Asayish building in Erbil, denied access to lawyers and that two of them had been tortured and held in solitary confinement for six months. Methods of torture included beatings on the body and on the soles of the feet (*falaqa*) and electric shocks.

■ In November, the KRG Human Rights Minister stated that 27 women had been killed in "honour killings" between August and November, but provided no information on any arrests and prosecutions related to these deaths.

Amnesty International reports

- Iraq: A deepening refugee crisis – media briefing (MDE 14/021/2007)
- Iraq: Unjust and unfair – the death penalty in Iraq (MDE 14/014/2007)
- Iraq: The situation of Iraqi refugees in Syria (MDE 14/036/2007)
- Iraq: Millions in flight – the Iraqi refugee crisis (MDE 14/041/2007)
- Iraq: Human rights abuses against Palestinian refugees (MDE 14/030/2007)

IRELAND

IRELAND

Head of state:	Mary McAleese
Head of government:	Bertie Ahern
Death penalty:	abolitionist for all crimes
Population:	4.3 million
Life expectancy:	78.4 years
Under-5 mortality (m/f):	6/6 per 1,000

The system of prison inspections was strengthened, by being made statutory. The Garda Síochána Ombudsman Commission, established to investigate complaints against the police, became operational, and had greater independence than the Complaints Board it replaced. Gaps remained in rights protection in legislation, policy and practice.

Background

A general election in May led to the formation of a new government, led by existing Prime Minister Bertie Ahern, in June. Ireland signed the International Convention on the Rights of Persons with Disabilities and the International Convention for the Protection of All Persons from Enforced Disappearance in March; the Council of Europe Convention on Action Against Trafficking in Human Beings in April; and the Optional Protocol to the UN Convention Against Torture in October.

Conditions in places of detention

In October, the European Committee for the Prevention of Torture (CPT) published its report on its fourth periodic visit to Ireland. During its visit, in October 2006, the CPT heard allegations of ill-treatment in police custody, and observed in some cases injuries consistent with the allegations. The CPT urged that audio-video recording be used for all police interviews, and that lawyers be permitted to be present during police interrogation.

The CPT considered at least three prisons it visited unsafe for both prisoners and prison staff.

■ In April, an independent statutory Commission of Investigation was announced to review the 2006 killing of a prisoner, Gary Douch, by a fellow prisoner in Mountjoy Prison, Dublin.

In May, provisions placing the role of the Inspector of Prisons on a statutory basis came into force. The

Inspector continued to lack the power to investigate or adjudicate on individual prisoner complaints.

Police and security forces

The Garda Síochána Ombudsman Commission (GSOC), established to investigate complaints of ill-treatment by members of the National Police Service (An Garda Síochána), became operational in May. It replaced the Garda Síochána Complaints Board, which had been criticized, including by Amnesty International, as ineffective and lacking independence.

Investigators employed by the GSOC are required to investigate all cases in which it appears that "the conduct of a member of the Garda Síochána may have resulted in the death of, or serious harm to, a person". Other complaints may continue to be investigated by the police themselves.

■ Amongst the cases being investigated by the GSOC is that of Terence Wheelock, who died in 2005 after being found unconscious in a police cell.

Health

In its annual report for 2006, published in March, the Inspectorate of Mental Health Services found "serious deficiencies in community mental health teams", and that "basic staffing" was unavailable in children's mental health services. The report expressed concern at the number of vulnerable patients remaining in long-stay wards, who were living in unacceptable conditions in bleak institutional environments.

Residential facilities for vulnerable groups

In April, the Social Services Inspectorate was placed on a statutory basis, as the Office of the Chief Inspector of Social Services. Its role was expanded beyond residential centres for children in care, to include the inspection and registration of residential services for older people and people with a disability.

By the end of the year not all these functions had come into force, and the system of registration and inspection for these services remained inadequate.

Renditions

In February, a European Parliament resolution urged the Irish government to establish a parliamentary inquiry into the use of Irish territory by the US Central Intelligence Agency (CIA) operated aircraft linked with the practice of extraordinary rendition (illegal transfer of people between states outside of any judicial process).

In December, the Irish Human Rights Commission published a review of Ireland's international obligations regarding extraordinary renditions. It concluded that Ireland was "not complying with its human rights obligations to prevent torture or inhuman or degrading treatment or punishment". It recommended that the authorities should "put in place a reliable and independently verifiable system of inspection [of relevant aircraft]".

Violence against women

In April a new executive agency, the Irish Office for the Prevention of Domestic Violence, was established. Non-governmental organizations working in the area of violence against women were critical of the agency, including because it emphasized awareness-raising over law enforcement.

In October, the Criminal Law (Human Trafficking) Bill was published. If enacted it would create a specific offence of human trafficking.

Discrimination

A National Women's Strategy was published in April, outlining the government's commitments towards achieving women's equality in the period 2007-2016. It lacked measurable targets and timescales for progress towards equality.

In May, the European Commission against Racism and Intolerance published its third report on Ireland, urging the Irish authorities to amend criminal legislation to include sufficiently strong provisions for combating racist acts. It recommended that housing legislation be reviewed and amended where necessary to prevent Travellers being disadvantaged in seeking to access adequate housing.

It also recommended that legislation permitting schools to refuse admission in order to preserve their religious "ethos" should be implemented in a non-discriminatory manner, and that the authorities should promote the establishment of multi-denominational or non-denominational schools.

Arms trade

The Control of Exports Bill 2007 was published in February. It contained proposals welcomed by Amnesty International for controls on the export of goods, technology and technical assistance for military use. Gaps remained, including in the control of overseas licensed production agreements, and in the transit and transhipment of military and security goods. The Bill did not provide for post-export monitoring of delivery and end-use.

Justice system

There was widespread opposition to the Criminal Justice Act 2007, which significantly amended criminal law and procedure, including bail conditions, laws of evidence, and sentencing. It extended the categories of offences in relation to which people may be held in police custody without charge for up to seven days, and the circumstances in which adverse inferences may be drawn from an accused's silence.

ISRAEL AND THE OCCUPIED PALESTINIAN TERRITORIES

STATE OF ISRAEL

Head of state:	**Shimon Peres (replaced Moshe Katzav in June)**
Head of government:	**Ehud Olmert**
Death penalty:	**abolitionist for ordinary crimes**
Population:	**7 million (Israel); 3.9 million (OPT)**
Life expectancy:	**80.3 years (Israel); 72.9 years (OPT)**
Under-5 mortality (m/f):	**6/5 per 1,000 (Israel) 23/18 per 1,000 (OPT)**
Adult literacy:	**97.1 per cent (Israel); 92.4 per cent (OPT)**

The human rights situation in the Israeli Occupied Palestinian Territories (OPT) remained dire. Israeli forces killed more than 370 Palestinians, destroyed more than 100 Palestinian homes and imposed ever more stringent restrictions on the movement of Palestinians. In June, the Israeli government imposed an unprecedented blockade on the Gaza Strip, virtually imprisoning its entire 1.5 million population, subjecting them to collective punishment and causing the gravest humanitarian

crisis to date. Some 40 Palestinians died after being refused passage out of Gaza for urgent medical treatment not available in local hospitals. Most Gazans were left dependent on international aid for survival but UN aid agencies complained that the Israeli blockade made it difficult for them to provide the much needed assistance. In the West Bank, the Israeli authorities continued to expand illegal settlements and build a 700-km fence/wall in violation of international law. Impunity remained the norm for Israeli soldiers and Israeli settlers who committed serious abuses against Palestinians, including unlawful killings, physical assaults and attacks on property. Thousands of Palestinians were arrested, most of whom were released without charge. Those charged with security-related offences often received unfair trials before military courts. Some 9,000 Palestinian adults and children remained in Israeli jails, some of whom had been held without charge or trial for years. Attacks by Palestinian armed groups killed 13 Israelis (see Palestinian Authority entry).

Background

In January, President Moshe Katzav took leave of absence after the Attorney General announced he would be charged with rape. The President resigned in June after striking a plea bargain in which he admitted responsibility for lesser offences, including sexual harassment, indecent assault and harassment of a witness, in exchange for agreement that the rape charges would be dropped and he would be spared prison. One of the plaintiffs petitioned the Supreme Court to set aside the plea bargain, and women's rights organizations called for Moshe Katzav to face trial. The case remained pending. In June, Vice Prime Minister Shimon Peres was elected President.

The Israeli government resumed talks with the Palestinian Authority (PA) and in November the two sides participated in an international meeting in Annapolis, sponsored by the US government, about resuming peace negotiations. However, no concrete measures were announced at the meeting. Prior Israeli undertakings to ease movement restrictions on Palestinians and to remove some Israeli settlement "outposts" had not materialized by the end of the year. In December, the Israeli authorities announced further expansion of Israeli settlements in the OPT, in violation of international law.

Killings of Palestinians

Frequent air strikes and other attacks by Israeli forces killed more than 370 Palestinians, including some 50 children, and injured thousands more. The Israeli authorities maintained their strikes were in response to "Qassam" rocket and mortar attacks by Gaza-based Palestinian armed groups against nearby southern Israeli towns and villages and against Israeli army positions along the perimeter of the Gaza Strip. More than half of the Palestinians killed by Israeli forces were armed militants who were participating in armed confrontations or attacks, or who were extrajudicially executed in air strikes. The rest were unarmed civilians not involved in the hostilities. Some 50 children were among those killed.

■ Five children were killed by Israeli missiles in two separate incidents in Beit Hanoun, northern Gaza, in August. Mahmoud, Sara and Yahia Abu Ghazal, aged eight, nine and 11, were killed on 29 August while grazing their sheep, and Fadi Mansour al-Kafarna and 'Abd al-Qader 'Ashour, aged 11 and 13, were killed and a third child was injured on 21 August while playing in a field.

■ Zaher al-Majdalawi and Ahmad Abu Zubaidah, aged 13 and 14, were killed on 1 June as they were flying kites on the beach in Beit Lahia, northern Gaza.

Killings of Israelis

Seven Israeli civilians and six soldiers were killed by Palestinian armed groups, the lowest annual fatality figure since the outbreak of the intifada in 2000.

■ Shirel Friedman and Oshri Oz were killed in Sderot by "Qassam" rocket attacks on 21 and 27 May.

Justice system

Detentions

Thousands of Palestinians, including scores of children, were detained by Israeli forces in the OPT. The majority of those arrested were later released without charge, but hundreds were accused of security offences. Some 9,000, including more than 300 children and Palestinians arrested in previous years, remained imprisoned at the end of 2007. More than 900 were held in administrative detention without charge or trial, including some held since 2002. Among those detained were dozens of former ministers in the Hamas-led PA government and Hamas parliamentarians and mayors who were seemingly held to exert pressure on Hamas to release

Gilad Shalit, an Israeli soldier captured in 2006 who continued to be held in Gaza by the armed wings of Hamas and the Popular Resistance Committees (PRC).

Almost all the Palestinian detainees continued to be held in jails inside Israel, in violation of international humanitarian law, which bars the removal of detainees to the territory of the occupying power.

In October, following a habeas corpus petition filed by a human rights organization, the Supreme Court ordered the army and the prison administration to explain why the transfers of Palestinian detainees from one place of detention to another were often not recorded. The case remained pending at the end of the year.

Denial of family visits

Israeli authorities frequently denied visiting permits to relatives of Palestinian detainees on unspecified "security" grounds. The prohibition often appeared arbitrary, with the same relatives being allowed to visit on some occasions but not others. Many parents, spouses and children of detainees had not been allowed visits by their relatives for more than four years. In June, the Israeli authorities suspended all family visits for some 900 detainees from the Gaza Strip. The suspension remained in place for the rest of the year. No Israelis serving prison sentences were subjected to such restrictions.

Unfair trials before military courts

Trials of Palestinians before Israeli military courts often did not meet international standards of fairness, and no credible investigations were carried out into allegations of torture and other ill-treatment of detainees.

Prisoner releases

In July, October and December the Israeli authorities released some 770 Palestinian prisoners, mostly members of PA President Mahmoud Abbas' Fatah party. In a deal concluded with Hizbullah in Lebanon in October, the Israeli authorities released a Lebanese man suffering from mental illness who had been captured by Israeli forces in Lebanon and removed to Israel in August 2006, and returned the bodies of two Lebanese Hizbullah fighters in exchange for the body of an Israeli who had drowned and had been washed up on the Lebanese coast years earlier. The Israeli authorities continued to refuse to return to their families the bodies of hundreds of Palestinians killed in attacks and confrontations with Israeli forces in previous years.

Impunity for attacks on Palestinians

Israeli soldiers and other members of the security forces as well as Israeli settlers continued to enjoy impunity for human rights abuses committed against Palestinians, including unlawful killings, torture and other ill-treatment, physical assaults and attacks on their property.

Investigations and prosecutions relating to such abuses were rare and usually limited to cases publicized by human rights organizations and the media. Few investigations were known to have been initiated into such abuses and most were closed for "lack of evidence". In rare cases where soldiers or settlers were convicted of abusing Palestinians they received relatively lenient treatment, while no members of the General Security Service (GSS) were known to have been prosecuted for torturing Palestinians.

Torture and other ill-treatment

Detainees were often held in prolonged incommunicado detention under interrogation and denied access to their lawyers for up to several weeks. There were frequent reports of torture and other ill-treatment during this period. Methods reported included beating, tying in painful positions for prolonged periods, denial of access to toilets and threats to harm the detainees' relatives. In some cases, detainees' parents, wives or siblings were summoned and forced to appear before detainees while dressed in prison uniform to make the detainees believe that they too were being held and ill-treated.

In October, following a petition from a human rights organization, the Supreme Court issued an interim decision ordering the authorities to notify Palestinians held in a detention centre in the West Bank that new regulations allowed them free access to toilets. In March, following a petition from a human rights organization, the Supreme Court ordered the GSS to inform Mohammed Sweiti, a detainee who had been held incommunicado for five weeks, that his wife was not being detained. Mohammed Sweiti had begun a hunger strike and attempted suicide after he was shown his wife and his father dressed in prison uniform and was led to believe that they were being ill-treated.

Blockades and other restrictions

More than 550 Israeli military checkpoints and blockades restricted or prevented the movement of Palestinians between towns and villages in the West Bank. The Israeli authorities continued to expand illegal settlements in the occupied West Bank and to build a 700-km fence/wall, 80 per cent of which runs inside the West Bank. For this purpose, large areas of Palestinian land were seized or rendered inaccessible to Palestinians, depriving them of their source of livelihood and restricting their access to their workplaces, education and health facilities and other necessary services. Palestinians were barred from or had restricted access to more than 300km of roads in the West Bank, which were mostly used by Israeli settlers.

In June the Israeli authorities further strengthened the blockade previously imposed on the Gaza Strip to an unprecedented level. They closed the border with Egypt, the only point of entry/exit for Gaza's inhabitants, and the Karni merchandise crossing. Thousands of Palestinians were left stranded on the Egyptian side of the border for months. Most were allowed to return to Gaza in August but scores remained stranded at the end of the year and thousands of students and workers could not leave Gaza to return to their studies and jobs abroad. Except in some urgent cases, even patients in need of medical care not available in Gaza were prevented from leaving the area and more than 40 died as a result.

The blockade caused a sharp deterioration in the already dire humanitarian situation in Gaza. The few factories that had continued to function despite restrictions imposed in previous years were forced to close because they could not import raw materials or export finished products. Vast amounts of flowers and other agricultural produce were wasted because they could not be exported. There were shortages of meat, dairy products and other basic foodstuffs, and of most other goods, including paper, pencils, clothes, spare parts for hospital equipment and medicine. Extreme poverty, malnutrition and other health problems increased. Eighty per cent of the population was forced to rely on international assistance, but UN aid agencies and humanitarian organizations were also negatively affected by restrictions and the increased operational costs these caused.

Destruction of homes

Israeli forces demolished more than 100 Palestinian homes throughout the West Bank, including in East

Jerusalem, because of lack of building permits – which were systematically denied to Palestinian residents of these areas of the OPT. The demolitions left hundreds of Palestinians homeless.

■ In August, Israeli forces destroyed several homes and animal pens in Humsa, a small village in the Jordan Valley area of the West Bank. The families of Abdallah Hsein Bisharat and Ahmad Abdallah Bani Odeh, totalling some 40 people, most of them children, were made homeless. The army also confiscated the villagers' water tanks and tractor. The villagers had been forced to move from nearby Hadidiya to Humsa after the Israeli army threatened to destroy their homes. The army considers the site a "closed military area" to be used by Israeli forces for shooting practice. In October, the families were again forced to move from Humsa and returned to Hadidiya.

■ In October, more than 200 Palestinians were forced from their homes in Khirbet Qassa, a small village established in the 1950s by Palestinian refugees. The village had been separated from the rest of the West Bank by the fence/wall and for more than a year Israeli forces had harassed the villagers to induce them to move. Their homes were mostly demolished on the grounds that they had been built without licences, which the Israeli authorities refuse to Palestinians in those areas.

Family reunification denied

Foreign nationals, mostly of Palestinian origin married to Palestinian inhabitants of the OPT, were increasingly denied entry to the OPT. Spouses with European and North American nationalities who had previously been able to reside in the OPT by leaving and re-entering Israel every three months in order to renew their visas, were often denied entry to the OPT. After a sustained campaign by those concerned and by human rights organizations, in October the Israeli authorities approved some 3,500 requests for family unification submitted in previous years. However, some 120,000 other outstanding cases were not addressed.

Amnesty International visits/reports

🚌 Amnesty International delegations visited Israel and the OPT in June, July and December.

📄 Israel and the Occupied Palestinian Territories: Enduring Occupation – Palestinians under siege in the West Bank (MDE 15/033/2007)

📄 Israel/Occupied Palestinian Territories: Right to family life denied – foreign spouses of Palestinians barred (MDE 15/018/2007)

📄 Israel/Occupied Palestinian Territories: Update to Comments by Amnesty International on Israel's compliance with its obligations under the

International Convention on the Elimination of all Forms of Racial Discrimination (ICERD) (MDE 15/007/2007)

📄 Occupied Palestinian Territories: Torn apart by factional strife (MDE 21/020/2007)

ITALY

ITALIAN REPUBLIC

Head of state:	Giorgio Napolitano
Head of government:	Romano Prodi
Death penalty:	abolitionist for all crimes
Population:	58.2 million
Life expectancy:	80.3 years
Under-5 mortality (m/f):	6/6 per 1,000
Adult literacy:	98.4 per cent

Several people were handed deportation orders which would have amounted to *refoulement* (forcible return to countries where a person may be at risk of serious human rights violations) if effected, and at least one person was ill-treated in detention following deportation from Italy. Reports of ill-treatment by police officers persisted and the Italian authorities failed to introduce effective police accountability mechanisms. The authorities discriminated against Romani people, and several aspects of Italy's human rights record came under criticism from the UN Committee against Torture (CAT). Italy failed to introduce torture as a crime in its criminal penal code, and still lacked comprehensive asylum legislation.

'War on terror'

The Italian authorities failed to co-operate fully with investigations into human rights violations in the "war on terror" and came under criticism from the European Parliament for their involvement in renditions.

Renditions

■ On 16 February, an Italian judge issued indictments against seven Italian citizens, primarily operatives of the Italian military and security service agency, Servizio per le Informazioni e la Sicurezza Militare (SISMI), in connection with the abduction of Abu Omar. Abu Omar, of Egyptian nationality and resident in Italy, was abducted from a street in Milan in 2003 and sent to

Egypt as part of the US-led programme of renditions. On arrival in Egypt Abu Omar was immediately detained and allegedly subjected to torture; he was released on 11 February 2007 without charge. A Milan court issued extradition requests in July 2006 and in February 2007 it issued indictments against 26 US citizens suspected of being involved in the rendition. By the end of the year the Minister of Justice had failed to forward to the US authorities the extradition requests for 26 US citizens, most of them thought to be agents of the US Central Intelligence Agency (CIA).

In April, the Constitutional Court declared admissible the Italian government's appeal of "conflict of powers". The government claimed that the judiciary had taken on powers it was not constitutionally allowed when collecting some of the evidence in the proceedings against those accused of being responsible for Abu Omar's rendition. On 18 June the trial was suspended pending the outcome of the Constitutional Court's review, and remained suspended at the end of the year.

■ In February, the European Parliament condemned the extraordinary rendition of Italian citizen Abou Elkassim Britel in a resolution on the alleged use of European countries by the CIA for the transportation and illegal detention of prisoners. Abou Elkassim Britel was arrested in Pakistan in March 2002 by the Pakistani police and interrogated by US and Pakistani officials, then subsequently rendered to the Moroccan authorities. The Italian Ministry of Interior reportedly co-operated with foreign secret services concerning the case of Abou Elkassim Britel following his arrest in Pakistan.

Pisanu Law

Italy retained legislation (the so-called Pisanu Law) on urgent measures to combat terrorism which provides for expulsion orders of both regular and irregular migrants without effective protection against forcible return to countries where they may be at risk of serious human rights violations. The Law does not require the person deported to have been convicted of or charged with a crime connected to terrorism. The expulsion can be ordered by the Minister of Interior or, under his/her delegation, by a Prefect (*Prefetto*). The Law does not provide for judicial confirmation or authorization of the expulsion decision and of its implementation. A decision to expel under the Law may be appealed before a judge, but the appeal does not suspend the deportation. In its Concluding Observations on 18 May, the UN Committee Against Torture recommended that Italy comply fully with Article 3 of the Convention against Torture regarding *refoulement*. The Committee expressed particular concern regarding the Pisanu Law.

■ On 4 January, Cherif Foued Ben Fitouri was expelled from Italy to Tunisia under the provisions of the Pisanu Law. According to the expulsion order, he was removed from Italy for being an acquaintance of people involved with Islamic groups allegedly planning terrorist acts. In Tunisia he was held in solitary confinement in the Ministry of Interior. On 16 January, he was transferred to a prison under military jurisdiction. According to reports received by Amnesty International, he was subjected to torture and other forms of ill-treatment whilst in detention in Tunisia. He remained in detention in Tunisia at the end of the year.

■ On 29 May the Italian authorities requested the Tunisian government to provide diplomatic assurances that were Nassim Saadi to be deported from Italy to Tunisia, he would not be subjected to treatment contrary to Article 3 (prohibition of torture and inhuman or degrading treatment) of the European Convention on Human Rights. On 8 August 2006, the Minister of Interior had ordered the deportation of Nassim Saadi to Tunisia. On 14 September 2006, Nassim Saadi launched an appeal to the European Court of Human Rights to suspend his expulsion. The Court issued an interim measure and the expulsion was suspended until further notice.

Police and security forces

Italy continued to lack an effective police accountability mechanism. There were irregularities in legal processes against law enforcement officials accused of human rights violations. One person was shot dead by a law enforcement officer and another died while in police custody under circumstances which at the end of the year were subject to judicial investigations. The first sentences for police ill-treatment during the 2001 G8 summit in Genoa were handed down.

■ On 19 October, the trial against four police officers accused of voluntary manslaughter of Federico Aldrovandi began. Federico Aldrovandi died on 25 September 2005 after being stopped by four police officers in Ferrara. During the pre-trial investigations blood samples taken at the place of Federico Aldrovandi's death disappeared and then re-emerged, and records of phone calls to emergency services the night of his death were tampered with.

■ On 4 April, law enforcement officers reportedly used excessive force to break up a potentially violent clash between AS Roma and Manchester United supporters during a football match at the Stadio Olimpico in Rome. Images and witness statements to Amnesty International showed that between 60 and 100 Italian police officers entered the area of the stadium where Manchester fans were situated and severely beat football supporters with batons. Several victims reported that police officers repeatedly hit them while they were lying on the ground, and on the head or their back from behind. Some of those assaulted had still not recovered from their injuries by the end of the year and some had been told that they would remain partially incapacitated for the rest of their lives.

G8 trials
Trials against law enforcement officials involved in the policing of the G8 summit in Genoa in 2001 continued. It is estimated that over 200,000 people participated in anti-globalization demonstrations on the streets of Genoa in the days immediately preceding and during the summit in 2001.

■ On 17 January, it emerged that key evidence during a hearing in the trial of 29 police officers facing charges of, among others, violence and the fabrication of evidence in relation to the Diaz school building raid, had disappeared. The Genoa *Questura* (police station) stated that they may have been "destroyed by mistake".

■ In May, the first sentence for the G8 events was handed down. The Ministry of Interior was sentenced to pay reparations of €5,000 to Marina Spaccini and €18,000 to Simona Zabetta Coda, who were beaten by police officers in Genoa.

■ In March, the European Court of Human Rights declared admissible the application lodged in the case of Carlo Giuliani, who was fatally shot by a law enforcement official during the G8 summit.

UN Committee against Torture
On 18 May, the CAT published its Concluding Observations on Italy. The CAT recommended that Italy incorporate into domestic law the crime of torture and adopt a definition of torture that covers all the elements contained in Article 1 of the Convention. The CAT further recommended that all law enforcement officers be adequately equipped and trained to employ non-violent means and only resort to the use of force and firearms when strictly necessary and proportionate. The

CAT noted continued allegations of excessive use of force and ill-treatment by law enforcement officials. Regarding accountability for law enforcement officials who engage in disproportionate and unnecessary violence, the CAT recommended that Italy "strengthen its measures to ensure prompt, impartial and effective investigations into all allegations of torture and ill-treatment committed by law enforcement officials."

Migrants and refugees' rights
Italy still lacked a specific and comprehensive asylum law in line with the UN Convention relating to the Status of Refugees.

A governmental draft bill approved on 24 April by the Council of Ministers contained new proposals for detention of migrants. The bill set out guidelines for amendments to the Comprehensive Law on Immigration 286/98 (Testo Unico Immigrazione, known as the Turco-Napolitano law) as modified by Law 189/02 (known as the Bossi-Fini law). These guidelines included rules on unaccompanied minors, detention and deportation. A directive was issued by the Ministry of Interior, requesting that the relevant Prefect allow access to the UNHCR, "humanitarian and international organisations", local NGOs and journalists to centres holding asylum-seekers and irregular migrants.

In its Concluding Observations on 18 May, the CAT stated that Italy should take effective measures to ensure that detention of asylum-seekers and other non-citizens is used only in exceptional circumstances or as a measure of last resort, and then only for the shortest possible time and that Italy should also ensure that courts carry out a more effective judicial review of the detention of these groups.

Discrimination – Roma
On 2 November, an urgent Decree Law came into force which made it possible for the Italian authorities to expel European Union (EU) citizens based on concerns for public security. The Decree Law did not comply with EU Directive 2004/38 /EC and seemed to be directed at Romanian citizens of Romani origin as a reaction to the suspected murder in Rome of an Italian woman by a man described as a Roma from Romania. Within two weeks after the Decree Law came into force 177 persons had been expelled.

In May, the mayors of Rome and Milan signed "Security Pacts" which envisaged the forced eviction of up to 10,000 Romani people. Throughout the year, the Italian authorities engaged in large-scale evictions of Roma communities which contravened international human rights standards. Discriminatory language was used by several leading politicians, including the Prefect of Rome, Carlo Mosca, who reportedly referred to Romanian Roma as beasts ("*bestie*") in early November.

Amnesty International visits/reports

🚌 Amnesty International delegates visited Italy in April and in October.

📋 Europe and Central Asia: Summary of Amnesty International's concerns in the region January-June 2007 (EUR 01/010/2007)

📋 Italy: A briefing to the UN Committee against Torture (EUR 30/003/2007)

JAMAICA

JAMAICA
Head of state: **Queen Elizabeth II, represented by Kenneth Hall**
Head of government: **Bruce Golding (replaced Portia Simpson Miller in September)**
Death penalty: **retentionist**
Population: **2.7 million**
Life expectancy: **72.2 years**
Under-5 mortality (m/f): **21/18 per 1,000**
Adult literacy: **79.9 per cent**

Murder rates and police killings in socially excluded inner-city communities remained at a high level. Police officers were largely unaccountable and rarely brought to justice for human rights violations. Discrimination and violence against women and gay men were widespread.

Background

In September the leader of the Jamaica Labour Party, Bruce Golding, was elected Prime Minister after 18 years of People's National Party government. He pledged to tackle crime and corruption, draft a new charter of fundamental rights and create an independent commission into human rights violations by members of the security forces. At least nine people were killed and many others injured in confrontations between supporters of opposing parties in the run-up to the September elections.

Homicide rates in Jamaica reached another record high; more than 1,500 people were murdered during the year. Firearms were widely available. Victims were mainly young men from marginalized inner-city communities. Perpetrators were usually gang members. At least 20 police officers were killed, many while on duty.

In May, the Jamaican Justice System Reform Task Force launched its preliminary report, with comprehensive reform recommendations. However, no clear plan for their implementation had been devised by the end of the year.

The review of the Jamaica Constabulary Force, initiated by the previous administration, continued. However, there was concern about the lack of consultation with human rights organizations.

Police and security forces

Reports of police brutality increased. According to the Bureau of Special Investigations, 203 people were killed by police between January and September, a significant increase compared with 2006. Victims were mainly from socially excluded inner-city communities. Although the police routinely claimed that these killings occurred during shoot-outs with criminal gangs, eyewitness accounts often alleged that police had extrajudicially executed victims. Corruption and distrust of the police remained the norm.

The pattern of impunity for police abuses and lack of accountability in the security and justice systems continued.

■ Eighteen-year-old Ravin Thomas was wounded by police while visiting his aunt in an inner-city neighbourhood in Kingston in July. Eight soldiers and two police officers chasing a suspect passed next to him and opened fire. Ravin Thomas' injuries when he was put in the police jeep to be taken to hospital were confined to his shoulder and his arm. When his aunt arrived at the hospital, Ravin Thomas was dead. According to the autopsy, he had four gunshot wounds, one in his face and another in his chin. The police recorded the incident as a shoot-out. The case was being investigated by the Police Public Complaints Authority and the Bureau of Special Investigations at the end of the year.

■ Eighteen-year-old André Thomas was shot by police in the arm and leg in Grants Pen in September. He was still conscious when he was put into the police car to be taken to hospital. When his father arrived at the hospital, André Thomas was dead. He had gunshot wounds all over his body, including a fatal shot in the stomach. The father of the victim reported being threatened by local police officers days after the incident. The officers did not reappear or return their vehicle until four days after the shooting. They were charged with attempting to pervert the course of justice and with murder in December. Their trial was scheduled for 2008.

Violence against women and girls

Sexual violence against women and girls was prevalent throughout the country, but the authorities failed to bring those responsible to justice. Rates of HIV infection among women and girls continued to rise and people living with HIV faced discrimination.

A draft bill which would offer greater legal protection to women and children, including making marital rape a criminal offence and increasing punishments for perpetrators of sexual violence, was pending final approval by parliament at the end of the year.

Discrimination

There were several episodes of violence, including mob violence, against people perceived to be gay.

■ On 8 April, a crowd surrounded a church in Mandeville and hurled objects through a window at the back of the church. The attacks were directed at those attending a funeral whom the crowd believed were gay.

Death penalty

No one was executed in 2007; the last execution in Jamaica took place in 1988.

The new government announced there would be a free vote, allowing representatives to vote according to personal conscience, in parliament on the resumption of hangings.

Amnesty International visits/reports

🚌 Amnesty International delegates visited Jamaica in March and in September/October.

📄 Jamaica: Opportunity to include the highest standards of international criminal law into national legislation to stop violence against women (AMR 38/001/2007)

📄 Jamaica: Open letter to the Prime Minister of Jamaica, Mrs Portia Simpson Miller, welcoming improvements to stop violence against women and encouraging new steps forward (AMR 38/002/2007)

📄 Jamaica: Amnesty International condemns homophobic violence (AMR 38/004/2007)

JAPAN

Head of government:	Yasuo Fukuda (replaced Abe Shinzo in September)
Death penalty:	retentionist
Population:	128.3 million
Life expectancy:	82.3 years
Under-5 mortality (m/f):	5/4 per 1,000

Executions continued. Fingerprinting and photographing of all foreigners entering Japan was introduced as an anti-terrorism measure. The Japanese government took no steps to resolve the issue of reparations to victims of Japan's system of sexual slavery during World War II despite increased international pressure.

Background

In July elections to the House of Councillors, the opposition Democratic Party gained a majority. The ruling coalition still has a two-thirds majority in the House of Representatives.

Death penalty

Nine men were executed in 2007. At least 107 prisoners remained on death row.

Under former Minister of Justice, Nagase Jinen, six executions took place in April and August. Under his successor, Minister Kunio Hatoyama, a further three executions took place in December. In September, Minister Hatoyama had publicly announced that he was considering scrapping the provision in the Criminal Procedure Code requiring the signature of the Minister of Justice for executions. The courts finally confirmed sentences in 23 capital cases, the highest annual number since 1962. Executions were typically held in secret, and prisoners were not warned of their execution in advance.

■ One of the three men executed in August, Takezawa Hifumi, had been suffering from mental illness at the time of his arrest following a stroke, which reportedly made him paranoid and aggressive. According to reports of his trial, doctors from both the prosecution and defence diagnosed Takezawa as mentally ill. He was sentenced to death in March 1998.

Lawyers defending death penalty cases were harassed. Some received bullets in envelopes or were denounced by domestic media.

J

In November, Minister Hatoyama met death penalty abolitionist groups, including Amnesty International, and heard their opinions.

Torture and other ill-treatment

In May, the UN Committee against Torture (CAT) examined the Japanese government's initial report, due since July 2000, and raised serious concerns that the daiyo-kangoku (a system of pre-trial detention) does not comply with international standards. It highlighted the lack of an independent system for monitoring police custody and an effective complaints system.

■ In November, the Osaka district court rejected a confession taken during a pre-trial investigation because of the suspicion, based on a digital recording of the interrogation, that it had been forced. This was the first ever acquittal of a suspect at trial due to a digital recording.

Refugees and immigration

A total of 816 applications for refugee status were applied for in 2007 – 500 applicants were from Myanmar. Forty-one people were granted refugee status, among them were 25 Myanmar nationals and three Iranians.

The CAT concluded that the revised Immigration Control and Refugee Recognition Act did not expressly prohibit deportation to countries where there is a risk of torture. There was no independent body to review refugee recognition applications or detention facilities. No independent complaints system existed to review allegations of violence committed by staff members against detained asylum-seekers, and detainees continued to suffer from lack of access to proper healthcare. Asylum-seekers spent an undue length of time in custody between the rejection of the asylum application and deportation. Minors were held in detention for prolonged periods and were at risk of being deported without their parents and without notice.

The fingerprinting and photographing of all foreigners over 16 years old entering Japan, including permanent residents, and fast-track procedures to deport anyone deemed a "possible terrorist" by the Minister of Justice were enforced from October. These measures were combined with a "watch list" with no mechanism to challenge inclusion on the list.

Violence against women

Parliaments around the world adopted resolutions calling for justice for the survivors of Japan's World War II military sexual slavery system. In July, the US House of Representatives passed resolution 121. In November, the Dutch and Canadian parliaments unanimously passed such motions and the European Parliament adopted a resolution on 13 December.

Amnesty International visit/report

🚃 Amnesty International delegates visited Japan in September.

📃 Open letter to the Minister of Justice of Japan, the Hon. Nagase Jinen: Detention of minors seeking asylum in Japan (ASA 22/002/2007)

JORDAN

HASHEMITE KINGDOM OF JORDAN

Head of state:	King Abdullah II bin al-Hussein
Head of government:	Nader al-Dahabi (replaced Ma'arouf Bakhit in November)
Death penalty:	retentionist
Population:	6 million
Life expectancy:	71.9 years
Under-5 mortality (m/f):	23/21 per 1,000
Adult literacy:	91.1 per cent

People arrested on suspicion of involvement in terrorism continued to face unfair trials before the State Security Court (SSC). Defendants were sentenced to prison terms, or death, despite saying they had been tortured. Women continued to suffer from discrimination, domestic violence and "honour" killings.

Background

Following elections in November, that NGOs were not allowed to monitor, a new government was formed headed by Prime Minister Nader al-Dahabi. The 27-member cabinet included four women ministers, three more than the previous cabinet. Jordan hosted some 500,000 Iraqis and almost two million UNRWA-registered Palestinian refugees, most of whom have Jordanian citizenship.

Torture and other ill-treatment

The authorities did not appear to have taken steps to implement most of the recommendations made by the UN Special Rapporteur on torture, following his 5 January report of a 2006 visit. The report concluded that "the practice of torture is widespread… and in some places routine", and urged that criminal investigations be initiated against at least eight identified officials. On 31 January the head of the Foreign Ministry's legal department rejected the report's conclusions as "incorrect and groundless". However, on 1 December the government amended Article 208 of the Penal Code to prohibit torture and adopt an identical definition of torture to that in the UN Convention against Torture. The amendment did not stipulate that penalties for perpetrators of torture should be in line with the Convention.

■ In Swaqa prison on 21 August, following a visit by Human Rights Watch, most of the more than 2,100 detainees were reportedly beaten and had their beards and heads forcibly shaved. One detainee, 'Ala' Abu Utair, died on 22 August, reportedly from injuries caused by beatings. The prison director was dismissed and the authorities set up an investigation into the events but its outcome was not known by the end of the year.

In at least eight cases before the SSC, defendants withdrew "confessions" they had made in pre-trial detention, saying they had been extracted under torture. The SSC was not known to have investigated these allegations adequately.

'War on terror'

At least 20 people suspected of terrorism said they had been tortured in pre-trial detention and coerced into signing "confessions" they later withdrew in court.

On 31 January the head of the Foreign Ministry's legal department denied that the USA operates secret detention centres in Jordan.

On 4 November US authorities transferred three Jordanian inmates from Guantánamo Bay, Cuba, to Jordan. Osama Abu-Kabir, Ahmad Hasan Sulayman, and Ibrahim Zaydan were arrested on arrival, detained for one week and then released. They were denied family or legal visits while held in Jordan, but said they were otherwise well treated.

Prolonged detention without trial

■ 'Isam al-'Utaibi, also known as Sheikh Abu Muhammad al-Maqdisi, remained in solitary confinement in pre-trial detention at the General Intelligence Department (GID) following his arrest on 6 July 2005. The director of the GID stated that he was charged with "conspiracy to commit terrorist acts". He was not allowed a lawyer until 19 April and was then allowed to meet him only once by the end of the year.

■ Samer Helmi al-Barq apparently remained detained without charge since his transfer to Jordan on 26 October 2003. He was arrested in Pakistan on 15 July 2003, detained for two weeks, then handed over to the US authorities and kept for three months in a secret prison outside Pakistan, before being transferred to Jordan.

Violence against women

Seventeen women were reported to have been victims of "honour killings". Perpetrators of such crimes continued to receive reduced sentences.

■ In June the Criminal Court sentenced a man to a reduced six-month sentence for murdering his unmarried sister, because it accepted that he had killed her "in a fit of fury" after she said she was pregnant.

On 10 August the UN Committee on the Elimination of Discrimination against Women recommended that the Jordanian authorities enact a comprehensive gender equality law and modify or repeal discriminatory provisions of the Personal Status Act, Penal Code and Nationality Act. The Committee also recommended amendment of the Penal Code to ensure perpetrators of "honour" crimes and of premeditated "honour" crimes do not benefit from reduced penalties; that article 99 (which halves a perpetrator's sentence when he is excused by the victim's family) is not applicable to "honour" crimes or other cases where the victim is related to the perpetrator; and to ensure a rapist does not escape punishment by marrying his victim.

On 25 November the UN Development Fund for Women reported that in around two-thirds of cases the victim's family drops charges against the perpetrator, making a lighter sentence more likely.

Death penalty

At least five people were sentenced to death following trials before the SSC despite alleging in court that they had been tortured. It was not known whether the SSC took adequate steps to investigate the allegations. Another 12 people were sentenced to death following trials before the criminal court.

In May the Cassation Court directed the SSC to reconsider death sentences it had imposed on nine individuals convicted of planning a chemical attack in Amman. The cases were not completed by the end of the year.

On 29 July King Abdullah commuted the death sentences on seven people allegedly involved in violent events in Ma'an in 2002. The sentences were reduced to terms of 15 years' imprisonment. A number of the defendants said they had been tortured to secure their "confessions".

Freedom of expression

On 21 March the Jordanian parliament passed a new Press and Publication Law while rejecting a clause that would have allowed journalists to be imprisoned for certain publication violations. Journalists could still be imprisoned under other laws including the Penal Code for insulting the king and stirring sectarian strife and sedition.

■ On 9 October the SSC sentenced former MP Ahmad al-'Abbadi to two years' imprisonment for "undermining the prestige and reputation of the state" and "for belonging to an illegal movement", the US-based Jordan National Movement. He had allegedly written a letter to a US Senator citing corruption and human rights abuse in Jordan.

Freedom of assembly and association

The authorities refused permission for a number of peaceful events and proposed a law that would further restrict the activities of NGOs.

■ On 26 October the governor of Amman reportedly denied for the fourth time in two months a request from the New Jordan NGO to host a workshop on civil society monitoring of elections.

■ A draft NGO law proposed by the cabinet on 9 October would ban NGOs from engaging in "political, religious or sectarian" activities and from establishing branches, and increase the scope for governmental influence over the management and financing of NGOs. It had not been enacted by the end of the year.

Refugees

Jordan counts among its population 1.9 million Palestinian refugees, most of whom have Jordanian citizenship. The country has hosted some 500,000 Iraqi refugees over the past few years. During the year an increasing number of Iraqis trying to enter Jordan were turned away. A number of Iraqi asylum-seekers and refugees were arrested in Jordan and forcibly returned to Iraq.

The Jordanian authorities continued to deny entry to some 193 Iranian-Kurdish refugees who now live in appalling conditions in tents in Iraq near the border with Jordan. This contravenes international refugee law.

Migrant workers

■ The authorities failed to protect thousands of migrant workers from abuse. Employees' passports were confiscated, and residency permits were denied, putting them at risk of arrest and deportation. Overtime working was enforced, wages were withheld, some living conditions were inadequate and access to proper medical care was denied. Physical abuse and sexual abuse of employees were reported.

Amnesty International visits/reports

🚗 Amnesty International delegates visited Jordan in March, September and December.

📄 Jordan: Death penalty/torture and ill-treatment (MDE 16/001/2007)

📄 Iraq: Millions in flight: the Iraqi refugee crisis (MDE 14/041/2007)

KAZAKSTAN

REPUBLIC OF KAZAKSTAN

Head of state:	Nursultan Nazarbaev
Head of government:	Karim Massimov (replaced Danial Akhmedov in January)
Death penalty:	retentionist
Population:	14.8 million
Life expectancy:	65.9 years
Under-5 mortality (m/f):	86/60 per 1,000
Adult literacy:	99.5 per cent

Refugees and asylum-seekers from Uzbekistan and China continued to be at risk of abduction and forcible return. Local authorities destroyed the homes of members of a religious minority. The scope of the death penalty was significantly reduced.

K

Background

In May, President Nursultan Nazarbaev signed into law constitutional amendments increasing the powers of parliament. The amendments also impose a two-term limit on future presidents.

The pro-presidential party Nur Otan (Fatherland's Ray of Light) won all the seats in parliamentary elections in August. The OSCE said that the election had not met international standards.

President Nazarbaev dismissed his son-in-law Rakhat Aliev as ambassador to Austria in May and Kazakstani authorities subsequently issued an arrest warrant and an extradition request for him in connection with the beating and abduction of two bank officials in Kazakstan in January. Rakhat Aliev said that the charges were politically motivated. A court in Austria refused to extradite him on the grounds that he would not be guaranteed a fair trial. The trial of Rakhat Aliev began in his absence in November on charges including kidnapping, money laundering, assault and murder.

In September Kazakstan signed the Optional Protocol to the Convention against Torture, allowing unannounced and independent monitoring of all detention facilities.

Refugees and asylum-seekers

The authorities continued to co-operate with Uzbekistan, Russia and China in the name of regional security and the "war on terror" in ways that breached their obligations under international human rights and refugee law. Refugees were not effectively protected and continued to be at risk of *refoulement* or abduction. In August the national security service confirmed that they had detained more than 50 members of banned Islamist parties or groups and returned them to Uzbekistan.

■ Ulugbek Khaidarov, an independent journalist and human rights defender from Uzbekistan, reported that members of the Uzbekistani security services had tried unsuccessfully to abduct him in October in Shimkent, southern Kazakstan. Ulugbek Khaidarov, who had fled to Kazakstan after being released from prison in November 2006, was recognized as a refugee by UNHCR and was awaiting resettlement.

Death penalty

In May the scope of the death penalty was reduced from 10 "exceptionally grave" crimes to the offence of terrorism leading to loss of life. A moratorium on executions remained in force and no death sentences were passed. All 31 prisoners who remained on death row had their sentences commuted to life imprisonment.

Discrimination and house demolitions

In June local authorities authorized the destruction of 12 homes belonging to the Hare Krishna community of Sri Vrindavan Dham in the village of Seleksia outside Almaty. The authorities said that Hare Krishna members had illegally acquired the land on which the community had built or renovated 66 homes when properties were privatized in the 1990s, a charge the Hare Krishna community denied. Only the homes in the village that belonged to members of the Hare Krishna community were destroyed.

Amnesty International reports

📖 Central Asia: Summary of human rights concerns, January 2006-March 2007 (EUR 04/001/2007)
📖 Commonwealth of Independent States: Belarus – the sole executioner (EUR 04/002/2007)

KENYA

K

REPUBLIC OF KENYA

Head of state and government:	Mwai Kibaki
Death penalty:	abolitionist in practice
Population:	36 million
Life expectancy:	52.1 years
Under-5 mortality (m/f):	115/99 per 1,000
Adult literacy:	73.6 per cent

Violence after disputed election results led to hundreds of deaths and thousands of people being displaced. The government closed the border with Somalia, denying refuge to thousands of people fleeing from the Somali conflict. More than 100 people of various nationalities, including Kenyan nationals, were unlawfully transferred to Somalia and Ethiopia as part of the "war on terror". Excessive force and unlawful killings by the police were reported. There were no official investigations. Violence against women and girls, including rape, persisted.

Background

General elections were held on 27 December. On 30 December the Electoral Commission of Kenya announced that President Mwai Kibaki had won the presidential election over opposition candidate Raila Odinga. Raila Odinga's Orange Democratic Movement (ODM) won a large majority of parliamentary seats over Mwai Kibaki's Party of National Unity (PNU) and other parties. Election observers questioned the credibility of the counting and tallying of the presidential vote.

The government of Mwai Kibaki continued to face widespread criticism over its failure to prosecute senior government officials involved in major corruption scandals.

Election violence

There was widespread violence before, during and after the general elections. Following the announcement on 30 December of the disputed results of the presidential vote, hundreds of people were killed, houses and property were burned by groups of armed youths across the country and thousands of people were internally displaced as a result of the violence.

■ On 7 September, Flora Igoki Tera, a parliamentary candidate in Meru district, Central Kenya, was attacked by a gang of three armed men. She was beaten, forced to swallow human faeces and warned to keep out of politics. Police stated that investigations were ongoing but no one had been prosecuted by the end of the year.

■ In December, tens of people were killed, hundreds of homes burnt and over 16,000 people displaced in the Kuresoi area of Molo district after attacks by armed gangs thought to have links with politicians. The area witnessed similar violence in the run-up to the 1992 and 1997 general elections. The violence continued despite the deployment of additional security officers. Although police stated that investigations were under way, there were no reports of prosecutions by the end of the year.

Impunity – human rights violations by police

Allegations of human rights violations by the police persisted, including reports of torture and unlawful killings. The authorities failed to investigate these allegations or ensure police accountability.

On 30 December, police shot and killed dozens of people in different parts of Kenya during protests against alleged fraud in the general elections held three days earlier.

Between June and October, police shot and killed hundreds of individuals in the course of security operations against members of the banned Mungiki group, after the Minister for Internal Security ordered a crackdown on Mungiki members and issued a "shoot-to-kill" order. Mungiki members allegedly killed tens of people, including police officers, in Nairobi and central Kenya, some of whom were beheaded.

Throughout the year, police shot dead criminal suspects in different parts of the country instead of arresting them. Calls by local and international civil society for the government to investigate dozens of such killings were ignored.

Refugees and asylum-seekers

The Kenyan government announced the closure of the Kenya-Somalia border on 3 January, following the resurgence of armed conflict between the Ethiopia-backed Somali Transitional Federal Government and the Council of Somali Islamic Courts (COSIC). The Kenyan government announced that it had closed the border in order to stop the movement of COSIC fighters into Kenya.

The government forcibly returned hundreds of asylum-seekers to Somalia after the border closure. Following the border closure, thousands of people attempting to flee the conflict in Somalia were unable to cross into Kenya, and were highly vulnerable to human rights abuses by parties to the Somali conflict. The border closure also restricted humanitarian access to internally displaced people on the Somali side of the border.

'War on terror'

At least 140 people (nationals of at least 17 different countries, including Kenya) were arrested by Kenyan authorities between December 2006 and February 2007 as they tried to enter Kenya from Somalia. They were detained in several police stations in Nairobi and in Jomo Kenyatta International Airport in Nairobi. Most detainees were held for weeks without charge and some were reportedly tortured or otherwise ill-treated. Some were allegedly beaten by the Kenyan police and forced to undress before being photographed. They were not allowed any contact with their relatives. They were not allowed to claim asylum and were denied access to UNHCR.

In January and February, at least 85 detainees were unlawfully transferred – without recourse to any legal process – to Somalia and then on to Ethiopia, along with other people detained by Ethiopian troops in Somalia. More than 40 were still detained incommunicado and in secret in Ethiopia at the end of 2007. The Kenyan government maintained at the end of the year that no Kenyan citizen was unlawfully transferred.

■ Abdi Mohammed Abdillahi, a Kenyan citizen of Somali heritage whose family is in Kenya, was arrested at Liboi in north-eastern Kenya on the Somalia border in early January after fleeing from Mogadishu. He was detained at Garissa police station and later at various police stations in Nairobi. His family said that in mid-January they visited him at Karen police station in Nairobi and were assured by police that he would be released following interrogation. On 20 January he was transferred by the Kenyan government on a chartered flight to Somalia. He was reportedly held at Mogadishu International Airport in Somalia in late January and in a detention facility in Ethiopia in February. By the end of 2007 he was still believed to be in detention in Ethiopia.

Violence against women

Women and girls continued to face widespread violence. Despite the passage in 2006 of the Sexual Offences Act, media and research reports indicated high levels of rape, child sexual abuse and domestic violence. The risk of violence and sexual abuse was particularly high among girls orphaned by AIDS. Most cases of sexual violence were committed by people known to the victims within the family and community.

Freedom of expression

A revised Media Bill came into effect in November. The new law seeks to monitor and regulate the media through a 13-member Media Council, with authority to grant and withdraw the accreditation of journalists. The original Bill contained a clause forcing editors to disclose their sources if their reports become the subject of court cases, but a national and international outcry forced its removal.

■ On 7 January, a photographer with the *Daily Nation* newspaper was beaten by the President's bodyguards as he attempted to take pictures of the President during a church service in Nairobi.

■ In March, a court ordered Mburu Muchoki, the editor of a tabloid weekly, *The Independent,* to serve a one-year prison sentence after failing to pay a fine of Kshs 500,000 (US$7,000) following a private criminal libel prosecution by the Justice and Constitutional Affairs Minister. The journalist served three months of the one-year sentence and was released under a presidential pardon in June. His appeal against the verdict had not been heard by the time of his release.

■ As political tension mounted following the disputed presidential election results, on 30 December the government banned live broadcasting by the Kenyan media. The statutory Media Council criticized the ban as violating the freedom of the media.

The government continued to target parts of the independent media. In April, just over one year after it raided the Standard Group's office and presses, the government issued written instructions to the state sector to cancel any advertising they were placing with the Standard Group media.

Internally displaced people

More than 100,000 people, approximately 20,000 families, were displaced in Mt. Elgon district near the Kenya-Uganda border following clashes over land. Hundreds of people suffered injuries and about 200 were reportedly killed as a result of gunshot wounds, cuts and burns sustained during attacks.

Forced evictions

By the end of 2007, the government had not fulfilled its 2006 pledge to release national guidelines on evictions, a pledge issued in response to the forced eviction of tens of thousands of residents in forest areas and informal settlements in the past. It also failed to impose a moratorium on enforced evictions until the guidelines were in place.

In October the government reportedly announced that it would resettle and compensate more than 10,500 people who had been evicted from Mau forest in 2006, although the number of people evicted was thought to have been much higher.

Death penalty

Courts continued to impose the death penalty, although no executions were reported.

There was no progress towards the abolition of the death penalty. On 1 August Parliament defeated a motion seeking to abolish the death penalty.

K

Amnesty International visits/reports

🚌 Amnesty International delegates visited Kenya in January, March, May and July.

📄 Kenya: Denied refuge – the effect of the closure of the Kenya/Somalia border on thousands of Somali asylum-seekers and refugees (AFR 32/002/2007)

📄 Kenya: Thousands of Somali refugees and asylum-seekers denied refuge (AFR 32/004/2007)

📄 Kenya: Nowhere to go – forced evictions in Mau forest (AFR 32/006/2007)

📄 Kenya/Ethiopia/Somalia: Horn of Africa – unlawful transfers in the "war on terror" (AFR 25/006/2007)

📄 Kenya: Police operations against Mungiki must comply with Kenya's obligations under international human rights law (AFR 32/008/2007)

📄 Kenya: Renewed appeal for humanitarian access to Somalia (AFR 32/009/2007)

📄 Oral Statements to the 41st Ordinary Session of the African Commission on Human and Peoples' Rights (IOR 63/004/2007)

📄 Kenya: Amnesty International concerned at police killings in election protests (31 December 2007)

KOREA
(DEMOCRATIC PEOPLE'S REPUBLIC OF)

DEMOCRATIC PEOPLE'S REPUBLIC OF KOREA

Head of state:	Kim Jong-il
Head of government:	Kim Yong-il
	(replaced Pak Pong-ju in April)
Death penalty:	retentionist
Population:	22.7 million
Life expectancy:	66.8 years
Under-5 mortality (m/f):	56/49 per 1,000

Systemic violations of human rights continued, including capital punishment, torture and the political and arbitrary use of imprisonment. Dissent of any kind, including leaving the country without permission and unauthorized assembly or association, was severely punished and national and international media were strictly controlled. Access by independent human rights monitors continued to be denied.

Background

In February, the government pledged to shut down and disable the Yongbyon nuclear facility in exchange for economic aid and political concessions.

Severe floods in August affected over 960,000 people, displaced tens of thousands, and at least 450 people were reportedly missing, presumed dead. A food shortfall, already 20 per cent before the floods, was exacerbated by outbreaks of blight and insect infestation. The government relied on international aid, officially asking the World Food Programme to provide immediate food assistance for three months in some counties.

In October, North Korean leader Kim Jong-il met with South Korean President Roh Moo-hyun and the countries' Prime Ministers met in November.

In December, the UN General Assembly approved a resolution expressing very serious concerns about systematic, widespread violations of civil, political, economic, social and cultural rights in North Korea.

Refugees and asylum-seekers

Hundreds of North Koreans were forcibly repatriated from China every month, with approximately 50,000 reportedly still hiding in China, living in constant fear of deportation.

Hundreds of North Koreans continued to be detained in Thailand for several months before being allowed into South Korea where at least 10,000 were granted citizenship. North Koreans faced difficulty in adapting to life in South Korea; over a third were unemployed and many were reported to suffer from Post Traumatic Stress Disorder.

Enforced disappearances

Hundreds of North Koreans forcibly returned from China were unaccounted for. The families of several people who left the country without permission disappeared. They were believed to be victims of enforced disappearance, a form of collective punishment for those associated with someone deemed hostile to the regime ("guilt-by-association"). The North Korean authorities have also abducted nationals of other countries, including South Korea and Japan. The government failed to acknowledge any enforced disappearances.

■ Son Jong-nam was arrested in January 2006 accused of treason, apparently because he visited his brother, Son Jong-hun, in China between May and June 2004. He had been at risk of imminent execution since his arrest. In March 2007, he was transferred to a detention facility in Pyongyang, reportedly in a critical condition following torture by the National Security Agency (NSA). There was no indication that a trial took place, but a sentence was reportedly passed by the NSA.

Denial of access

Despite repeated requests, the government continued to deny access to independent human rights monitors, including the UN Special Rapporteur on the human rights situation in DPRK and the UN Special Rapporteur on the right to food. In December, the UN General Assembly expressed serious concern at the refusal of the DPRK to recognize the mandate of the UN Special Rapporteur on human rights.

UN relief agencies were granted increased access after the August floods. WFP was upholding the long-standing principle of "no access-no food".

Freedom of expression

Opposition of any kind was not tolerated. In April, the Korean Workers' Party reportedly denounced foreign media as aiming to destabilize the regime and ordered the security forces to stop all video cassettes, written material, mobile phones and CDs from entering the country.

The domestic news media continued to be strictly censored and access to international media broadcasts remained severely restricted.

Any unauthorized assembly or association was regarded as a "collective disturbance", liable to punishment. Religious freedom, although guaranteed by the Constitution, was in practice sharply curtailed. People involved in public and private religious activities faced imprisonment, torture and execution.

Death penalty

Executions were by hanging or firing-squad. There were reports of executions of political opponents in political prisons and of people charged with economic crimes.

■ In August it was reported that the president of the export company of the Soonchun Vinalon 1 synthetic fibre factory in South Pyongan Province had been publicly executed. He was charged with selling factory equipment to buy food for starving workers. Subsequently he was also charged with hiding his membership of a grassroots anti-communist civil militia, the *Chi-an-dae* during the Korean War (1950-3).

Prison conditions

Prisoners, particularly political prisoners, reportedly suffered appalling conditions, in a wide range of detention centres and prisons.

North Koreans forcibly returned from China faced torture or ill-treatment and up to three years'

imprisonment. Their punishments depended on their age, gender and experiences. Women and children were generally sentenced to two weeks in a detention centre, although longer sentences of several months in labour camps were also common. People who confessed to meeting South Koreans or missionaries were punished particularly harshly. Summary executions and long sentences of hard labour were enforced. The authorities often released prisoners close to death, who died shortly after release.

KOREA
(REPUBLIC OF)

REPUBLIC OF KOREA

Head of state:	Roh Moo-hyun
Head of government:	Han Duck-soo
	(replaced Han Myeong-sook in March)
Death penalty:	abolitionist in practice
Population:	48.1 million
Life expectancy:	77.9 years
Under-5 mortality (m/f):	5/5 per 1,000

K

In October, the Minister of Justice Chung Soung-jin announced his support for death penalty abolition. However, a National Assembly final vote on a draft abolition bill did not progress.

Migrant workers continued to have limited protection or redress against discrimination and abuse. Many were detained in poor conditions. There was a worrying increase in detentions under the National Security Law, with at least eight prisoners of conscience still imprisoned under it.

Background

Presidential elections dominated political debate. Lee Myung-bak was elected on 19 December, to take office in February 2008.

There were developments in inter-Korean relations with top-level political meetings. Economic co-operation was a focal point of the dialogue, with the first cross-border train journey since 1950.

South Korean troops in Iraq and a Free Trade Agreement with the USA in April attracted heated debate.

Death penalty

There were no executions. Two death row inmates died, one of natural causes, the other committed suicide. Sixty-four prisoners were on death row at the end of the year. South Korea became abolitionist in practice in December, following a decade-long unofficial moratorium on executions.

National Security Law

The 1948 National Security Law (NSL) was not amended or repealed. As of December, there were at least eight detainees charged under vague NSL charges – compared to one in 2006.

■ A freelance journalist, Lee Si-woo, was charged with violating NSL Articles 4, 7 and 8, bailed, but kept under strict surveillance. He was accused of disclosing military secrets after he published information on the US military presence in South Korea. His reportage was based on information obtained legally from the government and military under freedom of information laws and data he collected in 2002 as a leading member of the Korean Campaign to Ban Landmines (KCBL). No legal concerns were raised at the time, and many of the sources used were freely available on the internet.

Freedom of expression

There were widespread strikes protesting irregular employment and the Korea-US Free Trade Agreement. In July, Oh Jung-ryul and Jung Gwang-hoon the Co-Chairs of the Korean Alliance against the Korea-US FTA (KoA) were arrested on charges of carrying out "illegal" and "non/un-permitted" protests. They were released in November. The KoA had reportedly served the requisite notice to the government about holding the protest, and the constitution does not require a permit for rallies.

Conscientious objectors

In December, at least 733 conscientious objectors, mostly Jehovah's Witnesses, were in prison following convictions in 2006 and 2007 for refusing compulsory military service. In October, newspaper sources cited the government's intention to reform military conscription by 2009, offering more, but potentially longer, alternatives to military service.

Migration

In November, there were reportedly 502,082 migrant workers, including at least 230,000 irregular migrant workers. The 2003 Act Concerning the Employment Permit for Migrant Workers failed to provide adequate safeguards against discrimination and abuse. In August, the UN Committee on the Elimination of Racial Discrimination (CERD) expressed concern that migrant workers can only be granted non-renewable, 3-year contracts, face severe restrictions on job mobility, and obstacles in obtaining legal protection and redress against discriminatory treatment and other abuses in the workplace.

Thousands of irregular migrant workers were arrested, detained and immediately deported. Some were detained for months for administrative reasons or whilst attempting to recover unpaid salaries. The Ministry of Justice was reportedly proposing revisions to the Immigration Law dispensing with the need for officials conducting checks on migrant workers to present identification documents or obtain warrants or detention orders prior to arrests.

Poor conditions were reported at migrant detention centres. Ten migrants detained pending deportation were killed and 17 others were injured during a fire at the Yeosu detention facility in February. The relatives of those killed in the fire were given compensation. The other detainees were promptly deported back to the countries of origin, many without any compensation or recourse to unpaid wages.

In July and August, the UN Committee on the Elimination of Discrimination against Women expressed concern about trafficking linked to international marriages. The CERD and the Special Rapporteur on the human rights of migrants noted that foreign women married to Korean nationals were not adequately protected against abuses perpetrated by their husbands or by international marriage agencies.

Arrest and deportation of MTU officials

In December, three senior officials of the Migrant Workers' Trade Union (MTU), President Kajiman Khapung, Vice President Raju Kumar Gurung and General Secretary Abul Basher M Moniruzzaman (Masum) were forcibly returned to their countries of origin without due process. They had been arrested in November whilst planning campaigns against proposed revisions to the Immigration Law. They were reportedly detained for being in an irregular or undocumented situation. At least 20 MTU members had been arrested in such crackdowns since August 2007.

Amnesty International visits/reports

🚍 Amnesty International delegates visited South Korea in May, August/September and October.

📄 Republic of Korea: Briefing to the UN Committee on the Elimination of Discrimination against Women – Women migrant workers' discrimination in employment, July 2007 (ASA 25/005/2007)

📄 Open letter to the President of South Korea, March 2007 (ASA 25/002/2007)

KUWAIT

STATE OF KUWAIT

Head of state:	**al-Shaikh Sabah al-Ahmad al-Jaber al-Sabah**
Head of government:	**al-Shaikh Nasser Mohammad al-Ahmad al-Sabah**
Death penalty:	**retentionist**
Population:	**2.8 million**
Life expectancy:	**77.3 years**
Under-5 mortality (m/f):	**11/11 per 1,000**
Adult literacy:	**93.3 per cent**

Migrant workers, particularly women domestic servants, suffered a wide range of abuses with little hope of redress. Death sentences continued to be imposed and carried out.

Migrant workers

Migrant workers, who make up a large proportion of Kuwait's workforce, continued to suffer a wide range of abuses. Most vulnerable were the many thousands of women employed as domestic servants, mostly nationals of south and south-east Asian countries. They suffered double discrimination, as women and because domestic workers continued to be excluded from the protections afforded to other expatriate workers under the 1964 labour law. Women domestic workers commonly worked excessive hours for little pay and alleged that they were subject to physical and other abuse, including sexual abuse, at the hands of their employers, against which, in practice, they often had no remedy. The minimum wage for foreign domestic workers was reported to be less than half that set for other foreign workers and only a third of the minimum wage paid to Kuwaiti nationals.

A standardized contract for foreign domestic workers introduced in October 2006 led to some improvements, although it appeared to have worsened the situation for domestic workers facing physical or other abuse by their employer by banning them from transferring to a different employer. Under the contract, domestic workers who leave their employer or are dismissed will be deported.

■ In February, some 1,300 Bangladeshi women employed as cleaners by a private company went on strike against non-payment of wages and poor living conditions.

'War on terror'

Two former inmates at the US detention facility in Guantánamo Bay, Cuba, were released in March after being acquitted of terrorism-related charges. Omar Rajab Amin and Abdullah Kamel al-Kandari had been arrested on their return to Kuwait in September 2006. The acquittals were confirmed by the Court of Appeal in May and brought to eight the number of Kuwaitis returned from Guantánamo and acquitted of all charges by Kuwaiti courts.

Four other Kuwaitis continued to be held at Guantánamo.

In June, the Court of Cassation commuted the death sentences of four men – Mohammad Saad, Abdullah Saad, Mohammad Issa and Salah Abdullah – who had been convicted in 2005 on terrorism-related charges, including membership of the Peninsula Lions' Brigade, a group allegedly linked to al-Qa'ida. They and other defendants who had been sentenced with them alleged that they had been tortured during pre-trial interrogation. One reportedly alleged that the State Security Department had "imported" foreign experts to torture them. At the hearing before the Court of Cassation, Mohammad Saad reportedly removed his shirt to expose scars that he said were caused by torture inflicted while he was detained by the State Security Department. No independent investigation into the defendants' torture allegations was known to have been initiated.

Freedom of expression

■ Basher al-Sayegh, editor of the daily *Al-Jarida* newspaper, was arrested in August after a comment criticizing the Emir was posted on a website he hosted, even though he removed the comment within hours. Jassim al-Qames, a journalist who tried to photograph the arrest, was also detained and alleged that he was assaulted by security officials. Both men were released within three days.

K

Death penalty

At least one person, a Pakistan national convicted of drug smuggling, was hanged. At least one person, a Filipina domestic worker convicted of murdering her employer's son, was sentenced to death. The death sentence imposed on another Filipina domestic worker, Marilou Ranario, was commuted to life imprisonment by the Emir in December in response to a direct appeal for clemency by the President of the Philippines. Marilou Ranario was convicted of murdering her Kuwaiti employment sponsor in 2005.

In December, the Court of Appeal confirmed the death sentence imposed on a member of the ruling al-Sabah family, identified only as Talal, after he was convicted of drug smuggling in December 2006.

KYRGYZSTAN

KYRGYZ REPUBLIC

Head of state:	**Kurmanbek Bakiev**
Head of government:	**Igor Chudinov (replaced Almaz Atambaev in December, who replaced Azim Isabekov in March, who replaced Feliks Kulov in January)**
Death penalty:	**abolitionist for ordinary crimes**
Population:	**5.4 million**
Life expectancy:	**65.6 years**
Under-5 mortality (m/f):	**67/56 per 1,000**
Adult literacy:	**98.7 per cent**

Political crises marked the year, with tensions remaining high between the President, government and opposition parties over the Constitution and other issues. Freedom of expression and association were restricted. Torture or other ill-treatment in police detention continued. The Kyrgyzstani authorities sometimes aided Uzbekistani security forces pursuing refugees and asylum-seekers who had fled to Kyrgyzstan in search of safety.

Background

The Constitution remained a source of political conflict, even though a new one had been adopted in 2006. A week-long demonstration in April in the capital Bishkek organized by opposition parties ended in violence when security forces tried to break up a rally. In September the Constitutional Court ruled that the 2003 Constitution should remain in force. This move prompted President Bakiev to hold a referendum in October, in which amendments to the Constitution were approved. The President then dissolved parliament and called new elections, which his party won in December. The election results sparked widespread protests after the opposition Ata Meken (Fatherland) Socialist party was barred from parliament, even though it came second, as a result of changes to the electoral code. Dozens of opposition activists and several human rights activists were briefly detained for taking part in these protests. The OSCE stated that the election failed to meet international standards and criticized a disproportionate use of force by the authorities in dispersing peaceful protests.

Torture and other ill-treatment

Torture or other ill-treatment in detention continued to be widespread and few law enforcement officers were held accountable. Two police officers accused of having tortured a detainee to death in 2006 were acquitted in August by a court in Naryn. The case had reportedly only come to trial because of sustained pressure from human rights defenders.

In August, Aziza Abdirasulova, chairwoman of the Kylym Shamy (Torch of the Century) human rights group, reported that at least 10 cases of torture had come to her attention, including three deaths in custody. While investigating reports that a suspect in pre-trial detention in Naryn died after he was beaten by a police officer in July, she met four young detainees aged 14 and 15 who complained about ill-treatment. They said that police officers had kicked and beaten them, and had placed gas masks on their heads and turned the air supply off to force them to confess to a crime they had not committed.

Freedom of assembly

Increasing restrictions were placed on freedom of assembly and expression, including by limiting the locations where demonstrations could be held in Bishkek. Dozens of protesters were charged with public disorder offences and at least 15 were convicted. Several demonstrations organized by human rights defenders, youth and civil society activists and political opposition parties were dispersed by police and state security officers, and participants were detained.

■ Former Prime Minister Feliks Kulov was detained for questioning by police in April and again in August. He was charged with instigating mass public disorder in relation to

K

the April clashes between opposition supporters and security forces. Two aides of Feliks Kulov were also detained and charged with causing public unrest. They were sentenced to four years in prison in August. They said that the charges were politically motivated.

■ In July police officers dispersed a demonstration by Democracy, an NGO, and confiscated banners and flags. Human rights defender Tursun Islam, who had organized the peaceful rally in defence of human rights, was briefly detained. His son remained in custody for three days.

■ Tolekan Ismailova, chairwoman of the Citizens against Corruption human rights group, was among 11 human rights defenders briefly detained and convicted for taking part in peaceful rallies in Bishkek protesting against the December election results.

Refugees from Uzbekistan

Refugees and asylum-seekers from Uzbekistan continued to be at risk of *refoulement* or abduction by the Uzbekistani security service (SNB) operating sometimes in co-operation with their Kyrgyzstani counterparts. The refugees and asylum-seekers faced incommunicado detention, torture or other ill-treatment as well as long prison terms following unfair trials in Uzbekistan. There were also reports that Kyrgyzstani security officers detained asylum-seekers and sold them to Uzbekistani border guards.

■ In March, four asylum-seekers abducted by SNB officers in 2006 were sentenced to up to 16 years in prison by a court in Namangan, Uzbekistan.

■ Otabek Muminov, an Uzbekistani man who was refused asylum in Kyrgyzstan, was secretly deported in June a month after the authorities received an extradition request from Uzbekistan. The Uzbekistani authorities had accused him of membership of the banned Hizb-ut-Tahrir Islamist party. He was detained in Osh in Kyrgyzstan in 2006 and sentenced to three years' imprisonment in April 2007 for inciting religious hatred and illegally crossing the border. His family had reportedly been given guarantees that he would not be extradited.

Freedom of expression: killing of journalist

■ Alisher Saipov, a 26-year-old independent journalist and editor, was shot dead in Osh in October. A Kyrgyzstani national of Uzbek origin, he was the editor of a new Uzbek-language newspaper *Siyosat* (*Politics*), which covered human rights in Uzbekistan among other issues. Alisher Saipov also worked as a

correspondent for *Voice of America* and contributed to independent websites covering Central Asia. He often covered sensitive subjects and had reportedly received anonymous threats. Parts of the Uzbekistani media had conducted a campaign denouncing his reporting as an attack on the Uzbekistani state.

Death penalty

In May President Bakiev signed several new laws relating to the criminal justice system. One replaced the death penalty with life imprisonment for ordinary crimes, although it was unclear whether this applied to crimes committed in wartime. The cases of the 174 prisoners already sentenced to death were to be reviewed by the Supreme Court within six months. The outcomes of these reviews were still pending at the end of the year.

Amnesty International reports

▤ Central Asia: Summary of human rights concerns, January 2006-March 2007 (EUR 04/001/2007)

▤ Kyrgyzstan: Dismay at murder of independent journalist (EUR 58/002/2007)

▤ Commonwealth of Independent States: Belarus – the sole executioner (EUR 04/002/2007)

L

LAOS

LAO PEOPLE'S DEMOCRATIC REPUBLIC

Head of state:	President Choummaly Sayasone
Head of government:	Bouasone Bouphavanh
Death penalty:	abolitionist in practice
Population:	6.2 million
Life expectancy:	63.2 years
Under-5 mortality (m/f):	129/123 per 1,000
Adult literacy:	68.7 per cent

Ethnic Hmong groups, forced to live in hiding in the jungles, were at risk of attacks by the military. Pressure increased for the forcible return of thousands of Lao Hmong asylum-seekers and refugees in Thailand. Independent monitoring of returnees and the human rights situation in general was not permitted. Freedom of expression and association remained strictly controlled.

Background

A minor government reshuffle took place in July, including a new Minister of Finance, following public calls by the Prime Minister for a crackdown on corruption.

Laos ratified the International Covenant on Economic, Social and Cultural Rights (ICESCR) in February. It has yet to ratify the International Covenant on Civil and Political Rights (ICCPR), which it signed in December 2000.

The death penalty in law remained, although no death sentences were reported throughout the year. The last known executions took place in 1989.

In June, General Vang Pao, the former leader of the CIA-backed "secret army" which fought against Communist Pathet Lao in the 1960s, and 11 others were arrested in the USA and charged with conspiring to buy weaponry and planning the violent overthrow of the Lao government. Following the arrests, there were unconfirmed reports of a crackdown on ethnic Hmong in northern Bokeo province, including killings and mass arrests. In July, five ethnic Hmong in Bokeo were charged with planning to plant bombs at seven strategic locations.

Large-scale projects, including mines and dams, continued to draw criticism for their reported impact on livelihoods and the environment. Environmental groups concluded that although regulatory frameworks on environmental and social standards were satisfactory, their implementation, including public dissemination of impact assessments, was inadequate. Lao government officials announced in September that nine new dams would be constructed over the next eight years.

The International Rivers Network and Norwegian FIVAS criticized the proposed expansion of the Theun-Hinboun hydropower project in central Laos. The groups claimed that 25,000 people had been affected already through the loss of fertile land, declining fish stocks and increased flooding.

Discrimination

Members of the Committee on the Elimination of Racial Discrimination (CERD) held a workshop in Vientiane in April on reporting under the International Convention on the Elimination of All Forms of Racial Discrimination in relation to Laos' 16th and 17th periodic report, due in the first part of 2007. The report had not been submitted by the end of the year.

An unknown number of Hmong people continued to live in destitution, hiding from the authorities, particularly the military, which for decades have carried out attacks, killing and injuring scores of people. The number of reported attacks declined in the second half of the year compared to previous years.

Most frequently, attacks took place against people foraging for food. Reports and photographs from six clandestine visits by foreign journalists in recent years have provided evidence of large numbers of injured and scarred people, including children, living in destitution and hardship. These groups have no access to medical services, and must rely on traditional medicine.

The fate and whereabouts of hundreds of ethnic Hmong who have attempted to come out of the jungle to join mainstream society remained unknown.

Refugees and asylum-seekers

Thousands of Lao Hmong asylum-seekers in Thailand, including over 8,000 in a camp in northern Phetchabun province, lived at risk of being forcibly returned to Laos following negotiations between the two governments. Hundreds were forcibly returned without having had access to any assessment of their protection needs. The fate of the majority of those returned remained unknown.

In September, the two governments further agreed that all Lao Hmong in the Phetchabun camp would be returned to Laos by the end of 2008, without being given access to an independent screening process. Lao authorities insisted that third party monitoring in Laos of returnees would not be allowed.

■In March, Lao authorities publicly claimed to have "found" 21 girls out of a group of 27 Lao Hmong people missing since being forcibly returned from Thailand in December 2005. The 27 had been held in detention since their forcible return. The other six of the group remained unaccounted for. The 21 were not allowed to reunite with their parents in Thailand, but were placed with other family members or unknown clan members inside Laos. At least 12 of the girls subsequently escaped to their families in Thailand. They confirmed their detention and one claimed to have been beaten and raped repeatedly.

During the year the Lao authorities arranged two visits by diplomats and journalists to some Lao Hmong victims of forcible returns. According to observers the individuals who were presented before them had gone through "re-education", but appeared in good health.

Prison conditions

Lack of access by independent human rights monitors prevented an accurate assessment of the number of political prisoners and prison conditions, but reports continued of ill-treatment, lack of food, overcrowding and inadequate medical care.

Several political prisoners sentenced after unfair trials remained imprisoned at Samkhe prison in Vientiane. These included Thao Moua and Pa Fue Khang, ethnic Hmong men, arrested in 2003 after assisting two journalists to visit Hmong in the jungle. Also in Samkhe prison were four prisoners of conscience – Thongpaseuth Keuakoun, Seng-Aloun Phengphanh, Bouavanh Chanhmanivong and Keochay – arrested in October 1999 for attempting to hold a peaceful demonstration.

The fate of Sing Chanthakoummane, detained since 1975 and last reported to be very ill in the remote Prison Camp 7 in Houa Phanh province, was not known.

Health

A study by the World Food Program launched in November showed that half of the children under the age of five in rural Laos suffered from chronic malnutrition. This demonstrated that the high economic growth rate experienced by Laos during the past decade had no discernible impact on lessening child malnutrition.

Amnesty International reports

Lao People's Democratic Republic: Hiding in the jungle, Hmong under threat (ASA 26/003/2007)

Lao People's Democratic Republic: Thao Moua and Pa Fue Khang – Hmong imprisoned after unfair trial (ASA 26/008/2007)

LATVIA

REPUBLIC OF LATVIA

Head of state:	Valdis Zatlers
	(replaced Vaira Vike-Freiberga in July)
Head of government:	Ivars Godmanis
	(replaced Aigars Kalvītis in December)
Death penalty:	abolitionist for ordinary crimes
Population:	2.3 million
Life expectancy:	72 years
Under-5 mortality (m/f):	14/12 per 1,000
Adult literacy:	99.7 per cent

Almost 400,000 people remained stateless in Latvia, while persons belonging to linguistic and sexual minorities suffered discrimination.

Statelessness

Almost 400,000 people continued to live without citizenship. The vast majority were citizens of the former Soviet Union who were living in Latvia at the time of the break-up of the Soviet Union. In order to obtain citizenship, non-citizens must pass a number of tests, for example on the Latvian Constitution, history and language, as well as recite the lyrics of the Latvian national anthem. In May, the UN Committee on Economic, Social and Cultural Rights (the Committee) published its Concluding Observations on Latvia in which it urged Latvia to "ensure that the lack of citizenship of the permanent residents does not hinder equal enjoyment of economic, social and cultural rights, including employment, social security, health services and education".

Linguistic minorities

Almost one-third of Latvia's population belongs to the Russian-speaking minority. The Russian-speaking minority continued to face discrimination in several areas of public life, including employment. In May, the Committee expressed its concern that "the State Language Law which mandates the use of Latvian in all dealings with public institutions, including administrative districts, may be discriminatory in effect against linguistic minorities living in the State party, including the Russian-speaking minority which constitutes a significant proportion of the population. In particular, the Committee is concerned that members of linguistic minorities, especially older

L

persons, may be disadvantaged in their claims to public authorities with regard to their entitlement to public services. This has a negative impact on their enjoyment of economic, social and cultural rights".

The Committee urged Latvia to "ensure that adequate support is provided to members of linguistic minorities, especially older persons, through, inter alia, increased allocation of resources to subsidize language courses, with a view to enhancing opportunities for those wishing to acquire fluency in Latvian". The Committee also recommended that Latvia, in line with Article 10 of the Framework Convention for the Protection of National Minorities to which Latvia is a party, "consider providing translators and interpreters in State and municipal offices, in particular, in regions that have a high concentration of minority language speakers".

The Committee also urged Latvia to enact comprehensive anti-discrimination legislation without further delay.

Rights of lesbian, gay, bisexual and transgender people

On 3 June, a Pride march was held in Riga to celebrate the rights of lesbian, gay, bisexual and transgender people. While participants in similar events in 2005 and 2006 had been subject to physical attacks and did not receive adequate police protection, the 2007 march was adequately protected and no major attacks took place.

Over 400 people, including the Latvian lesbian, gay, bisexual and transgender group Mozaika and dozens of Latvian activists, an Amnesty International delegation of approximately 70 people, several Members of the European Parliament and a Swedish government minister, marched in a park in central Riga. The park was closed off and guarded by hundreds of Latvian law enforcement officials, making it virtually impossible for counter-demonstrators to carry out attacks on participants in the Pride parade.

There was, however, a noticeable presence of a large number of counter-demonstrators at the march. Counter-demonstrators ranged from persons of retirement age to pre-teens; they engaged in loud verbal abuse and made obscene gestures towards the Pride march participants. Two home-made explosives were set off inside the park.

Racism

In January, the first ever prison sentence for racially motivated assault was handed down under Section 78 of Latvia's Criminal Code. The case concerned a man who was attacked in central Riga in the middle of 2006. The second ever prison sentence for a racially motivated crime was announced in May when two teenagers were sentenced for a racially motivated attack which had taken place against a woman of Brazilian origin in December 2006. One of the teenagers was given a prison sentence.

In June, the European Union (EU) sent a formal request to Latvia to implement the EU Racial Equality Directive (2000/43/E), which Latvia had to date failed to do.

LEBANON

LEBANESE REPUBLIC

Head of state:	Emile Lahoud (until November)
Head of government:	Fouad Siniora
Death penalty:	retentionist
Population:	3.7 million
Life expectancy:	71.5 years
Under-5 mortality (m/f):	27/17 per 1,000
Adult literacy:	88.3 per cent

Political violence and instability dominated the year, with more than 40 people killed in bombings and other attacks and hundreds killed in months of fighting between the Lebanese Army and the Fatah al-Islam armed group in and around Nahr al-Bared Palestinian refugee camp. The tension and divisions in the country, still recovering from the devastating war between Israel and Hizbullah in 2006, virtually paralysed parliament and prevented the election of a new President.

Women faced discrimination in law and practice, and the state failed adequately to protect them against violence. Palestinian refugees continued to suffer discrimination and violations of their social and economic rights. Reports of torture and ill-treatment in detention increased. Courts continued to condemn people to death but there were no executions.

Nahr al-Bared

Intense fighting broke out in Nahr al-Bared Palestinian refugee camp on 20 May between Fatah al-Islam, an Islamist armed group that had recently moved into the camp, and Lebanese armed forces. According to reports, 168 Lebanese soldiers, 42 civilians and 220 Fatah al-Islam members were killed before the army gained control of the camp on 2 September.

During the clashes, both sides put civilians at risk. Fatah al-Islam established armed positions in the camp and withdrew to them after attacking an army base. The army carried out heavy and possibly indiscriminate artillery shelling of the camp. The camp was largely destroyed. It appeared that after the army took control there was widespread looting, burning and vandalism of vacated homes and property. In December, the Prime Minister wrote to Amnesty International to say that the army was investigating the reports, noting that one finding was that the army had burned some homes to rid them of a poison spread by Fatah al-Islam.

Most of some 30,000 Palestinian refugees displaced from Nahr al-Bared relocated to Beddaawi refugee camp. They were allowed to return to Nahr al-Bared from October but the majority remained displaced at the end of the year. The camp remained off-limits to the media and local human rights organizations.

■ On 22 May, two civilians were killed and others injured when a UN convoy delivering relief supplies inside the camp was hit by at least one explosive device. The army reportedly denied responsibility. The same day, Naif Selah Selah and a pregnant woman, Maha Abu Radi, were shot dead and other passengers were injured as their bus fleeing the camp approached an army checkpoint. A boy aged 13 or 14 was taken from the bus by armed men, threatened with a knife and given electric shocks to make him "confess" to planning a suicide attack, before being released. There were no known independent investigations into the incidents.

Scores of Palestinians were threatened, humiliated and abused by soldiers, often after being stopped at army checkpoints. Abuses included being stripped, being forced to lie on the road, and being beaten, kicked, hit with rifle butts, insulted and humiliated. In several cases individuals were reportedly whipped, given electric shocks and sexually abused.

Some 200 people were arrested and remained detained on account of their suspected involvement with Fatah al-Islam. Tens of these were reportedly

charged with terrorism offences that can carry the death penalty. There were reports that some detainees were tortured or otherwise ill-treated.

■ On 29 June, three protesters were killed during a peaceful demonstration calling for refugees displaced from Nahr al-Bared to be allowed to return to their homes. Lebanese Army soldiers opened fire on the protesters and then reportedly failed to intervene when Lebanese civilians attacked the demonstrators.

■ On 12 December, General François el-Hajj, the Lebanese Army's chief of operations during the fighting in Nahr al-Bared, and a bodyguard, were killed in a car bomb attack in Ba'abda.

Killings

More than 40 people were killed in bombings and shootings by unknown assailants.

■ Two members of parliament who supported Fouad Siniora's government were assassinated in separate car bomb attacks in Beirut. Walid 'Eido MP and nine others were killed on 13 June, and Antoine Ghanim MP and five others were killed on 19 September.

■ On 24 June, six UN peacekeepers were killed in an explosion targeting their convoy near the southern town of Khiam.

Rafiq al-Hariri assassination

On 30 May the UN Security Council adopted resolution 1757 to establish the Special Tribunal for Lebanon to try those suspected of involvement in the February 2005 killing of former Prime Minister Rafiq al-Hariri and 22 others and, if the court so decides, a number of other possibly related attacks committed since October 2004.

■ Five senior security officials and four other individuals arrested between August and November 2005 in apparent connection with the investigation remained detained without charge.

On 28 November the UN International Independent Investigation Commission submitted its ninth report into the killing and 18 other attacks it is helping to investigate.

Torture and other ill-treatment

There were increased reports of torture and other ill-treatment, particularly of Palestinians, Sunni security suspects and individuals suspected of involvement with Fatah al-Islam. At least two men died in custody, possibly as a result of ill-treatment.

■ Nine men on trial before the Military Court from 21 April alleged that they had been tortured while held incommunicado from March and April 2006 at the Ministry of Defence detention centre in Beirut. Ghassan al-Slaybi said he was given electric shocks, beaten with a stick and forced to participate in the torture of his detained son, Muhammad. Others said that they were subjected to *falaqa* (beating on the soles of the feet) and the *ballanco* (hanging by the wrists tied behind the back). Several of the men said they had signed false confessions under duress. The court reportedly refused their request for a medical examination.

On 20 February the Lebanese authorities and the ICRC signed a protocol giving the ICRC access to "all detainees in all places of detention".

■ On 19 August Fawzi al-Sa'di, a Palestinian suspected of involvement with Fatah al-Islam, died in Roumieh prison, reportedly because he was denied adequate medical care. No investigation was known to have been initiated.

■ In a rare successful prosecution, a private in the Internal Security Forces was sentenced on 8 March by the Beirut Criminal Judge to 15 days' detention for torturing an Egyptian worker in May 2004 at a Beirut police station. He had used the *farruj* (chicken) method, whereby the victim's wrists are tied to the ankles and they are then hung from a bar placed behind the knees.

In February, the UN Working Group on Arbitrary Detention declared the detention of Nehmet Na'im al-Haj, held since November 1998, to be arbitrary and noted that his "confession" was obtained by torture. In May, it declared the detention of Yusef Cha'ban to be arbitrary and noted that he had been convicted largely on the basis of a "confession" allegedly made under torture and denied any right of appeal to a higher judicial authority.

Death penalty

Four men were reportedly sentenced to death on 4 December for murder. At least 40 other prisoners remained on death row, but there were no executions.

Refugees

Several hundred thousand Palestinian refugees, most of whom have lived in Lebanon all their lives, continued to suffer from discriminatory restrictions affecting their economic and social rights, notably their access to employment, healthcare, social security, education and housing. Over half of Palestinian refugees live in decaying and chronically overcrowded camps or in informal gatherings that lack basic infrastructure.

Hundreds of some 50,000 Iraqi refugees were detained for not having valid visas or residence permits. The detainees faced indefinite detention or return to Iraq.

Discrimination and violence against women

Women continued to face widespread discrimination in public and private life. Neither the legal system nor the policies and practices of the state provided adequate protection from violence in the family. Discriminatory practices were permitted under personal status laws, nationality laws, and provisions of the Penal Code relating to violence in the family. Migrant domestic workers continued to receive inadequate protection from workplace exploitation and physical and psychological abuse, including sexual abuse.

At least six female migrant domestic workers reportedly died in suspicious circumstances. It was unclear what investigations were carried out into the deaths or any abuse that might have preceded them.

■ On 25 January it was reported that Bereketi Amadi Kasa, aged 22 from Ethiopia, had fallen to her death while trying to flee her employers' home in al-Zalqaa, north of Beirut.

In August Shi'a cleric Sheikh Muhammad Hussein Fadlallah issued a fatwa against "honour" killings, describing them as a repulsive act banned by Islamic law.

Aftermath of 2006 war

No participants from either side of the 2006 war between Israel and Hizbullah were brought to justice for serious violations of international humanitarian law.

At least seven civilians were killed and 32 civilians were injured in 2007 by hitherto unexploded cluster bomb units fired by Israeli armed forces during the 2006 war. Two other civilians were killed and nine other civilians were injured by other previously unexploded or unidentifiable military ordinance. Five people working with clearance teams were killed and 14 others were injured. The Israeli authorities continued to refuse to furnish the UN with comprehensive cluster bomb strike data.

The fate of two Israeli soldiers seized from northern Israel by Hizbullah militants in July 2006 remained unclear. Hizbullah continued to deny them access to the ICRC.

Impunity

No criminal investigations or prosecutions were initiated into mass human rights abuses that were committed with impunity during and after the 1975-1990 civil war. Abuses included killings of civilians; abductions and enforced disappearances of Palestinians, Lebanese and foreign nationals; and arbitrary detentions by various armed militias and Syrian and Israeli government forces. In 1992 the Lebanese government said that a total of 17,415 people had disappeared during the civil war.

Amnesty International visits/report

Amnesty International delegates visited Lebanon in May/June and in October to research the Nahr al-Bared events and the situation of Palestinian refugees in the country.

Exiled and suffering: Palestinian refugees in Lebanon (MDE 18/010/2007)

LIBERIA

REPUBLIC OF LIBERIA

Head of state and government:	Ellen Johnson-Sirleaf
Death penalty:	abolitionist for all crimes
Population:	3.5 million
Life expectancy:	44.7 years
Under-5 mortality (m/f):	217/200 per 1,000
Adult literacy:	51.9 per cent

The human rights situation improved throughout the year, although challenges remained with regard to the administration of justice. Prisons were overcrowded, with the majority of detainees awaiting trial. No progress was made in the establishment of the Independent Human Rights Commission. The Truth and Reconciliation Commission made little progress in implementing its work. Violence against women remained widespread. There were several incidents of journalists being harassed by the security forces. The trial of former Liberian President

Charles Taylor, indicted for war crimes and crimes against humanity in Sierra Leone, continued in The Hague, Netherlands (see Sierra Leone entry).

Background

The fight against corruption remained a priority for Ellen Johnson-Sirleaf's government. Trials of former members of the National Transitional Government of Liberia charged with theft were ongoing. After a vote of no confidence by members of the House of Representatives, the former Speaker of the House of Representatives, Edwin Snowe, resigned. He was replaced in April by Alex Tyler of the Liberian Action Party.

In July three men, George Koukou, a former speaker of the National Transitional Legislative Assembly, Major General Charles Julu, a former Army Chief of Staff and head of the Anti-Terrorist Unit under Samuel Doe, and Colonel Dorbor were arrested and charged with treason; the trial is ongoing. Sanctions on diamonds and timber were lifted in April and Liberia was admitted to the Kimberley Process verification scheme, an internationally recognized process designed to certify the origin of rough diamonds with the aim to reduce smuggling. Liberian law makers debated a controversial bill aimed at freezing assets of former government officials but the bill was ultimately rejected.

UNHCR-assisted voluntary repatriation was completed in June. Approximately 80,000 Liberians still reside in other countries and some 50,000 refugees, mostly from Côte d'Ivoire, remained in Liberia.

Liberian ex-combatants were alleged to have been involved with the political crisis in Guinea in February. There were also unconfirmed reports of cross border movements of Liberian ex-combatants to Côte d'Ivoire.

In February a donor conference was held and reviewed Liberia's achievements. The USA also cancelled Liberia's US$391 million debt.

In December the mandate of the UN Mission in Liberia (UNMIL) was extended to September 2008.

Violent demonstrations

Delays in payment of state subsistence allowance led to demonstrations by former combatants in at least three cities in Liberia. In January, some 50 members of the Mandingo ethnic group staged a demonstration at the President's mansion demanding action on land disputes in Nimba county. A presidential commission was set up to investigate the situation. Later in the year further violent protests over land erupted in the southeast.

Violent demonstrations involving university students also took place in Gbarnga in mid-April. The protests focused on inadequate facilities on campus. In June protests broke out at the University of Liberia when students demonstrated on behalf of their teachers, who had been on strike for non-payment of their salaries.

In July police investigating theft and violence at Freeport, the main seaport in Monrovia, led to violent clashes in which 50 people were injured. A commission was set up to investigate the incident. Violent protests also took place in Bong Mines, 50 miles from Monrovia. Residents were enraged by what they believed to be police involvement in the death of a five-year-old child. A newly constructed police station was burned down, and the residences of the Liberian National Police and the house of the city mayor were vandalized during the disturbance. In December protests at Firestone rubber plantation and the police response led to five people being injured and plantation facilities were looted.

Security sector reform

Approximately 90,000 former combatants benefited from reintegration programmes, although some 9,000 are still awaiting reintegration opportunities. Some of those who benefited have been participating in army and police training. In July an all-female unit graduated from basic training.

Deficiencies in the judiciary remained a huge challenge. Court officials administered rules and procedures in an inconsistent manner, failed to observe basic human rights standards and engaged in corrupt practices. Although state prosecutors are assigned to every circuit court, the majority of the circuit courts did not have defence counsels. Trial by ordeal – a practice by which the guilt or innocence of the accused is determined by subjecting them to a painful task – remained in wide practice in rural areas. Few improvements were made in the juvenile justice system during the year.

A bill to establish a law reform commission was drafted. The commission will provide an overall review of the laws to ensure that they meet international standards.

Prison conditions remained poor and jailbreaks were frequent. Overcrowding was a problem in Monrovia's central prison, with 780 people detained in a building built to house 470 inmates. The majority of detainees were awaiting trial. UNMIL trained 104 security personnel, with more staff expected to be trained in 2008.

Transitional justice

Little progress was made in setting up an Independent National Commission on Human Rights due to a delay in the appointment of Commissioners.

The work of the Truth and Reconciliation Commission proceeded slowly. In March the Commission's work was suspended due to concerns with transparency. A working group comprising members of the Commission and donors was set up, leading to a number of positive developments including the hiring of key staff. Civil society raised concerns about the lack of progress in the work of the Commission. Public hearings were due to start in January 2008.

Trial of suspected war criminal

The trial of Roy M. Belfast Jr (aka Charles McArthur Emmanuel and Charles "Chuckie" Taylor Jr), the son of Charles Taylor, who was charged with torture, conspiracy to torture, and using a firearm during an act of violent crime while he was serving as the head of the Anti Terrorist Unit, continued.

Women's rights

Despite the passing of a new law on rape in December 2005 providing a clearer definition of rape and more stringent punishments, a high incidence of rape against women and girls continued. There was an increase in the number of rape cases tried in circuit courts and 2007 saw the first successful conviction for rape since the end of the conflict. However, relevant provisions of the 2006 law were not uniformly applied by court officials with the majority of the cases being settled out of court.

Press freedom

In February, following publication by the *Independent* newspaper of photos of a Minister of State of Presidential Affairs in bed with two women, the paper was closed down by the police. In March the Supreme Court of Liberia attempted to lift the ban, however, the Government of Liberia maintained the ban and instructed printing houses not to print the paper; the government lifted the ban in June.

In February journalist Othello Guzean of the government-controlled radio network Liberia Broadcasting System (LBS) was suspended indefinitely by the LBS director after airing an interview with opposition parliamentarian Thomas Fallah of the Congress for Democratic Change party. The LBS director described the airing of the interview as unacceptable and in contravention of the station's editorial policy.

In June, during clashes between students of the University of Liberia and security forces, journalists Daylue Goah of the *New Democrat* and Evan Ballah of the *Public Agenda* newspapers were beaten by security forces. Goah was seriously injured.

In August, Liberia National Police and the Drug Enforcement authority physically attacked and briefly detained the journalist J. Rufus Paul of the *Daily Observer* newspaper. He was arrested for what the police termed "trying to cover a raiding exercise without invitation".

In September the bodyguards of President Ellen Johnson-Sirleaf, from the Special Security Service (SSS), intimidated several local journalists and correspondents of international news organizations, including Jonathan Paylelay of the BBC, Dosso Zoom of Radio France International, and Alphonso Towah of the Reuters News Agency, for what the presidential guards termed a "breach of protocol".

Amnesty International visits

🚌 Amnesty International visited Liberia in February and September.

LIBYA

SOCIALIST PEOPLE'S LIBYAN ARAB JAMAHIRIYA

Head of state:	Mu'ammar al-Gaddafi
Head of government:	al-Baghdadi Ali al-Mahmudi
Death penalty:	retentionist
Population:	6.1 million
Life expectancy:	73.4 years
Under-5 mortality (m/f):	18/18 per 1,000
Adult literacy:	84.2 per cent

After years of diplomatic negotiations, a positive outcome was reached in a high-profile case of political imprisonment, involving six foreign medics sentenced to death after being convicted of infecting hundreds of Libyan children with HIV. Their release paved the way for Libya to conclude arms deals with France and a diplomatic memorandum of understanding with the EU. Some media diversity was permitted, but freedom of expression continued to be severely restricted, exemplified by the absence of independent NGOs and repression of dissident voices. Refugees, asylum-seekers and migrants continued to be ill-treated in detention, but the government failed to address the legacy of past gross human rights violations.

The UN Human Rights Committee commented that "almost all subjects of concern remain unchanged" since it last examined Libya's record on civil and political rights in 1998. It noted some advancement in the status of women, but expressed concern about ongoing discrimination in law and practice.

Freedom of expression

In August the media landscape was broadened when two new private daily newspapers and a private satellite television channel were permitted to open. They were set up by a media corporation reportedly belonging to Saif al-Islam al-Gaddafi, son of Libyan leader Mu'ammar al-Gaddafi. The new dailies published some criticism of the government on economic issues. However, dissident voices addressing more sensitive issues, such as human rights violations or Mu'ammar al-Gaddafi's leadership, were severely repressed.

A new State Security Court was established in August to try individuals accused of offences against state security and unauthorized political activities,

L

raising fears of a new parallel justice system along the lines of the discredited People's Court, abolished in 2005.

■ Fathi el-Jahmi remained in detention at an undisclosed location understood to be a special facility of the Internal Security Agency. A prisoner of conscience, he was arrested in March 2004 after he criticized Mu'ammar al-Gaddafi and called for political reform. His family told Amnesty International that they had not been allowed to visit him since August 2006.

■ Idriss Boufayed and 13 other people were arrested and charged with offences including possession of weapons, incitement to demonstrate and communication with enemy powers. Idriss Boufayed and three of the 13 had issued a communiqué to news websites announcing that they were planning a peaceful demonstration in Tripoli on 17 February to commemorate the anniversary of the killing of at least 12 people during a demonstration in Benghazi in February 2006. Reports indicated that all 14 were held incommunicado for prolonged periods after their arrest and that at least two of them were tortured. Trial proceedings, which began in June, were transferred to the new State Security Court after its creation. Two of the 14 were reportedly not present at any of the court hearings which were held, raising serious concerns about their safety in detention.

'War on terror'

Two Libyan nationals returned from US custody at Guantánamo Bay in December 2006 and September 2007 respectively were detained, apparently without charge or access to a lawyer. In December, the Gaddafi Development Foundation, headed by Saif al-Islam al-Gaddafi, son of Mu'ammar al-Gaddafi, announced that it had visited the two men, was monitoring their treatment and had even purchased a home for the family of one of the detainees. However, neither the Foundation nor the authorities disclosed information regarding the men's exact place of detention or legal status.

No information was available on at least seven Libyan nationals, mainly alleged members of the Libyan Islamic Fighting Group, believed to have been held by US authorities in secret sites before being secretly and illegally transferred to Libya in previous years. Amnesty International received reports that at least five of the seven had been transferred to Libya in 2005 or 2006 and were being held incommunicado.

Death penalty

Nine Libyan citizens were reportedly executed in April, but no details were given. A number of death sentences against foreign nationals convicted of murder were commuted after the victims' relatives agreed to accept monetary compensation.

■ The death sentences against five Bulgarian nurses and a Palestinian doctor convicted of knowingly infecting hundreds of Libyan children with HIV in 1998 were commuted to life imprisonment in July after the victims' families agreed to compensation payments emanating from an international fund. The six medics were forced to sign a document surrendering their right to redress for the torture they said they had suffered in Libya. A week later, the six medics were transferred to Bulgaria under a prisoner exchange agreement between the two countries and pardoned soon after their arrival by Bulgarian President Georgi Parvanov.

Refugees, asylum-seekers and migrants

Allegations that refugees, asylum-seekers and migrants were tortured or otherwise ill-treated on arrest or in detention were persistent. Of particular concern were at least 500 Eritrean nationals who were detained and at risk of forcible return.

■ Some 70 Eritrean men were arrested in July after fleeing to Libya from Eritrea to seek refuge, according to reports. They were taken to a detention facility in the town of Az Zawiyah, where they said they were told to strip naked and were beaten by guards with implements such as metal chains. Some were reportedly beaten on numerous occasions. The detainees said that they had been threatened with deportation by the guards. In September, they were allegedly photographed and made to fill in forms, and were then told by guards that the forms and photographs had been requested by Eritrean embassy officials in Libya to allow them to issue travel documents for their deportation. At the end of the year, however, none of the detainees appeared to have been deported. Many of the Eritrean nationals were believed to have been conscripts, forced into military service in Eritrea for an indefinite period of time.

Discrimination against women

The UN Human Rights Committee reiterated its concern that "inequality between women and men continues to exist in many areas, in law and practice, such as notably inheritance and divorce". It also regretted "that Libyan laws permit the forced detention of some unconvicted women in so-called social rehabilitation facilities" and that the state had "not yet adopted legislation concerning the protection of women against violence, especially domestic violence".

The authorities took the retrogressive step of issuing a decree preventing children of Libyan mothers and foreign fathers from receiving free state education, a right they had previously enjoyed along with children of Libyan men married to either a Libyan or foreign woman. In September, children of Libyan mothers and foreign fathers were reportedly unable to enrol in state schools at the start of the academic year. In October, the authorities announced that the children could study in such institutions on condition that their families agreed to pay fees or were exempted from doing so because of their limited means.

Impunity

Impunity remained a serious concern. Three people, reportedly members of the Revolutionary Guard, were tried and convicted in July of murdering journalist Daif al-Ghazal. He was killed in 2005 in circumstances that indicated he was assassinated because of his writing. However, the rare but positive step of holding the perpetrators to account was marred by the death sentences passed against those convicted and the apparently closed nature of the trial proceedings.

The legacy of gross human rights violations committed in the past remained untackled. The violations, which were committed particularly in the 1970s, 1980s and 1990s, included the enforced disappearance of hundreds of individuals, many of whom were feared to have died in custody while detained on political charges.

No information was made available about the apparently ongoing investigation into events in 1996 at Abu Salim Prison in Tripoli, during which hundreds of prisoners were alleged to have been killed.

Amnesty International visit/reports

🚗 Amnesty International informed the government in May that it wished to visit Libya, but was not granted access by the end of the year.

📃 Libya: Six foreign medics should be released (MDE 19/002/2007)

📃 Libyan Arab Jamahiriya: Briefing to the UN Human Rights Committee (MDE 19/008/2007)

📃 Libyan Arab Jamahiriya: Addendum to briefing to the UN Human Rights Committee (MDE 19/015/2007)

LITHUANIA

REPUBLIC OF LITHUANIA

Head of state:	Valdas Adamkus
Head of government:	Gediminas Kirkilas
Death penalty:	abolitionist for all crimes
Population:	3.4 million
Life expectancy:	72.5 years
Under-5 mortality (m/f):	13/9 per 1,000
Adult literacy:	99.6 per cent

Lesbian, gay, bisexual and transgender (LGBT) peoples' human rights were not respected. Several LGBT events were cancelled in a discriminatory manner and parliament discussed banning information which would put homosexuality in a positive light to minors. Lithuania received a fine from the Union of European Football Associations (UEFA) for a racist banner displayed during a football match between Lithuania and France.

Rights of lesbian, gay, bisexual and transgender people

On 21 May, the mayor of Vilnius, Juozas Imbrasas, refused permission for a European Union (EU) sponsored anti-discrimination truck tour to make its planned stop in the city. The truck tour visited 19 member states as part of a "For Diversity. Against Discrimination" information campaign. The purpose of the truck tour was to raise awareness and distribute information about the European Year of Equal Opportunities for All. The Vilnius City Council also voted unanimously to ban a tolerance campaign rally in support of the human rights of various groups, including LGBT people, which had been due to take place on 25 May, citing "security reasons". The European Commission commented on the bans stating that "the decision by the city authorities shows how much still needs to be done to change behaviour and attitudes towards discriminated groups and to promote awareness of diversity."

The mayor of Vilnius also supported local bus drivers' refusal to drive buses which had advertisements supporting LGBT rights on them. The mayor stated that "with priority for traditional family and seeking to promote the family values, we disapprove [of] the public display of 'homosexual ideas' in the city of Vilnius". The advertisement had

L

been paid for by the Lithuanian Gay League with money granted from the EU.

On 24 October, Vilnius city council refused to grant permission for a public event which would have seen the hoisting of a 30m rainbow flag, a symbol of the LGBT rights movement, in front of approximately 200 LGBT activists in the Town Hall Square.

The Lithuanian parliament was considering legislation that would ban the "propagation of homosexuality" to children. The legislative change regarded an amendment to the existing Law on the Protection of Minors against Detrimental Effect of Public Information. The proposed amendment would put information about homosexuality on par with the portrayal of physical or psychological violence or vandalism; display of a dead or cruelly mutilated body of a person and information that arouses fear or horror, encourages self-mutilation or suicide. The authors of the proposed amendment explained that "the propagation of a non-traditional sexual orientation and exposure to information containing positive coverage of homosexual relations may therefore cause negative consequences for the physical, mental and, first and foremost, moral development of minors".

Racist incidents

On 9 June, the European football governing body UEFA imposed a 15,000 Swiss francs fine on the Lithuanian football federation for fans waving a racist poster during the European qualifier against France on 24 March. Fans had drawn the African continent in outline with the French flag superimposed. Beneath it was written "Welcome to Europe".

MACEDONIA

THE FORMER YUGOSLAV REPUBLIC OF MACEDONIA

Head of state:	Branko Crvenkovski
Head of government:	Nikola Gruevski
Death penalty:	abolitionist for all crimes
Population:	2 million
Life expectancy:	73.8 years
Under-5 mortality (m/f):	17/16 per 1,000
Adult literacy:	96.1 per cent

Impunity continued for war crimes committed in 2001 and in cases of torture and ill-treatment. Little progress was made in the reform of the police and the judiciary. Discrimination against minorities, particularly Roma, continued.

Background

Political disputes between the President and the Prime Minister, the government and ethnic Albanian parties, and amongst ethnic Albanian parties, hampered legislative reform. Albanian politicians accused the government of breaching the Ohrid Agreement, which concluded the 2001 internal conflict and aimed to guarantee the rights of the Albanian community.

No date was set for negotiations on accession to the European Union (EU) due to Macedonia's slow progress in implementing reforms set out in a Stabilization and Association Agreement with the EU. The Council of Europe urged the authorities to speed up reforms on decentralization, the police, the independence of the judiciary and in combating organized crime and corruption.

Impunity for war crimes

The trial of former Minister of the Interior Ljube Boshkovski opened in April at the International Criminal Tribunal for former Yugoslavia (Tribunal). He was indicted in 2005 for violations of the laws and customs of war, including for his failure to investigate, prevent or punish his co-indicted, Johan Tarčulovski, an Escort Inspector in the President's Security Unit, for the deaths of seven ethnic Albanians and the detention and cruel treatment of over 100 others in Ljuboten in August 2001.

There were delays in the adoption of a draft Law on Cooperation with the Tribunal, and disputes between

M

the Ministry of Justice and Macedonia's Public Prosecutor on jurisdiction over four cases due to be returned to Macedonia from the Tribunal by the end of the year. Albanian political parties argued for the application of the law adopted in March 2002, which provided an amnesty for all those involved in the 2001 armed conflict, except those accused of war crimes under the jurisdiction of the Tribunal.

No progress was made in resolving the enforced disappearance during the 2001 internal conflict of three ethnic Albanians, Sultan Memeti, Hajredin Halimi and Ruzdi Veliu.

Torture, other ill-treatment and possible extrajudicial execution

The NGO Macedonian Helsinki Committee for Human Rights (MHC) continued to report on cases of torture and ill-treatment, including during arrest and detention, in which the Ministry of Interior had failed to conduct investigations according to internal procedures, domestic law and international standards. The draft Law on Public Prosecutions failed to include specific time frames for the conduct of investigations.

■ On 15 February, the European Court of Human Rights ruled that the authorities had failed to investigate allegations that Pejrushan Jashar, a Roma from Shtip, had been beaten while in police custody in 1998, in violation of Article 3 of the European Convention on Human Rights. The court ordered Macedonia to pay €3,000 in damages.

Witnesses continued to be examined in a judicial investigation, opened in 2005, into the death in custody of ethnic Albanian Sabri Asani, who had been arrested in 2000 in connection with the killing of three police officers.

Armed opposition groups

The security situation deteriorated: armed opposition groups effectively controlled areas near the border with Kosovo. On 10 September ethnic Albanian police commander Fatmir Halili was killed and two police officers were wounded in Vaksince on the Kosovo border during the course of an attempted arrest; two ethnic Albanians, Skender Halili and Xheladin Hiseni, were killed.

Amnesty International expressed concerns in November at the possible excessive use of force by the Macedonian authorities in operation "Mountain Storm", which aimed to capture members of armed opposition groups, including several men who in August had escaped from Dubrava prison in Kosovo, and who had been hiding in the area close to the border with Kosovo. One escapee, Xhavit Morina, former commander of the armed opposition group Albanian National Army (AKSh), had already been killed by persons unknown near Tetovo on 1 November.

During the operation in Brodec village six people were killed and 13 arrested. Witnesses reported to the MHC that the detained men were beaten, while handcuffed and lying on the ground; five of the men were hospitalized for several days after reportedly resisting arrest. An internal investigation by the Ministry of Interior concluded that "the use of firearms by police officers was appropriate, proportionate, justified and necessary", and that the detainees had been injured while resisting arrest.

'War on terror'

■ In a closed hearing on 18 May, a parliamentary committee considered written statements by the Ministry of Internal Affairs and on behalf of Khaled el-Masri, a German citizen of Lebanese descent. They concluded that the security services had not overstepped their powers in detaining Khaled el-Masri for 23 days in 2003 in a Skopje hotel, before rendering him to the US authorities at Skopje airport, from where he was flown to Afghanistan, and subjected to torture. In June, the Parliamentary Assembly of the Council of Europe concluded that the authorities' account was "utterly untenable".

Discrimination against minorities

In May, the UN Committee on the Elimination of Racial Discrimination (CERD) found Macedonia in breach of its obligations towards the Romani community, including with respect to citizenship, language and access to documentation required to access basic rights. The CERD also expressed concerns about the education of ethnic Albanian children, ethnic Turkish children and Romani children.

The Macedonian authorities failed to uphold the rights of Romani women and girls, who faced double discrimination on the basis of their ethnicity and their gender. Discrimination in education led to few girls completing primary education or attending secondary

M

school; their consequent lack of qualifications and discrimination by employers led to the denial of access to work in the formal economy. Many Romani women were not eligible for health insurance or lacked the necessary documentation; others could not afford the fee for basic medicines. Romani women and girls faced discrimination when they attempted to report domestic violence to the authorities. No comprehensive anti-discrimination legislation was in force. Although in December the authorities reportedly began discussions on such a law, they refused to consider drafts proposed by NGOs.

Refugees from Kosovo

Some 1,860 refugees remained in Macedonia. The majority were predominantly Roma and Ashkalia refugees from Kosovo who had been granted temporary "asylum for humanitarian protection", or those whose applications for asylum had been rejected. The state failed to guarantee refugees access to social and economic rights. Many feared forcible deportation, although in June the authorities agreed to suspend deportations pending the resolution of the status of Kosovo.

Violence against women and girls – child trafficking

Macedonia failed to ratify the Council of Europe's Convention on Action against Trafficking in Human Beings. In February an agreement signed between the Ministry of Interior and the Ministry of Labour and Social Policy established protocols for the protection of trafficked children. The latter Ministry signed an agreement with an NGO providing shelter for an increasing number of internally trafficked people.

Amnesty International visit/reports

🚍 Amnesty International delegates visited Macedonia in December.

📁 Europe and Central Asia: Summary of Amnesty International's concerns in the region, Macedonia: July-December 2006 (EUR 01/001/2007); January-June 2007 (EUR 01/010/2007)

📁 "Little by little we women have learned our rights": The Macedonian government's failure to uphold the rights of Romani women and girls (EUR 65/004/2007)

MALAWI

REPUBLIC OF MALAWI

Head of state and government:	**Bingu wa Mutharika**
Death penalty:	**abolitionist in practice**
Population:	**13.5 million**
Life expectancy:	**46.3 years**
Under-5 mortality (m/f):	**172/162 per 1,000**
Adult literacy:	**64.1 per cent**

Despite a huge maize harvest in 2007, the country remained impoverished. Political squabbles hampered the passage of a budget aimed at development and poverty alleviation. The prevalence of HIV and AIDS remained high, resulting in an increase in the number of households headed by children. Cruel, inhuman or degrading conditions in prisons persisted. The High Court ruled mandatory death sentences unconstitutional.

Background

Tension between the majority opposition United Democratic Front and the Malawi Congress Party and President Wa Mutharika's minority Democratic Progress Party reached its peak in September when Parliament initially refused to consider the 2007/2008 budget supporting development policies. Civic pressure eventually forced Parliament to consider the budget. On 13 September, following the passage of the budget, President Wa Mutharika dissolved Parliament until May 2008.

Vice-President Cassim Chilumpha, arrested on treason charges in April 2006, remained under house arrest throughout 2007. He appeared in court during the first week of December and was released on bail.

Although the law prohibits child labour, children as young as 10 were reported to be working on tobacco farms.

Death penalty

On 27 April the High Court declared mandatory death sentences unconstitutional. The Court found that the death penalty constituted inhuman punishment. There were 23 prisoners on death row. The last execution in Malawi took place in 1992.

Prison conditions

Overcrowding and lack of adequate food and health care in prisons persisted. Some 11,000 prisoners were held in prisons designed to hold 5,000 people. People awaiting trial constituted 17 per cent of the prison population. Approximately 110 deaths of prisoners were recorded in 2007. The Southern African Litigation Centre called on the African Commission on Human and Peoples' Rights to undertake an investigative mission to Malawi.

Health – HIV and AIDS

Fourteen per cent of Malawi's population were living with HIV or AIDS; one million children were believed to have been orphaned by HIV or AIDS-related deaths. While approximately 60,000 people were receiving antiretroviral therapy for free at state hospitals, poverty and the stigma associated with the virus continued to impede access to treatment. AIDS is a priority in the government's growth and development strategy. Some 200,000 people living with HIV or AIDS were receiving food assistance from the World Food Programme.

MALAYSIA

MALAYSIA

Head of state:	**Yang di-Pertuan Agong, Tuanku Mizan Zainal Abidin**
Head of government:	**Abdullah Ahmad Badawi**
Death penalty:	**retentionist**
Population:	**26.2 million**
Life expectancy:	**73.7 years**
Under-5 mortality (m/f):	**12/10 per 1,000**
Adult literacy:	**88.7 per cent**

At least 10 people died in police custody in 2007. Despite continuing reports of such deaths and of excessive use of force against peaceful demonstrations, the Malaysian government failed to implement key recommendations for police reform. Scores of people were detained without trial under various emergency laws. Restrictions on freedom of religion continued. Grievances felt by many among the ethnic Indian Malaysian minority community, including discrimination and economic marginalization, were aggravated by the destruction of reportedly unauthorized Hindu temples. Mandatory death sentences continued to be issued.

Refugees and migrant workers were arbitrarily detained and assaulted during immigration raids.

Police reform

A Bill to establish a Special Complaints Commission (SCC) to monitor and investigate complaints of misconduct by police and other law enforcement officers was introduced. The Bill prompted concerns that the recommendations of a 2005 Royal Commission of Inquiry were not adequately reflected, particularly as regards the proposed SCC's independence and investigative powers. Not only did the Bill grant the Prime Minister broad powers to appoint and dismiss Commissioners, but it also included the Inspector-General of Police as a permanent SCC member. The SCC also did not have the power to oversee police investigation of complaints.

The Criminal Procedure Code was amended to provide increased protection to people under arrest. It required the police to inform detainees arrested without a warrant of the circumstances of their arrest and, in most cases, to allow detainees to contact a family member or a lawyer.

Deaths in custody and excessive use of force

At least 10 people died in custody in 2007 including at least two reported suicides, and police reportedly continued to use excessive force on peaceful demonstrators.

■ On 10 and 25 November, police sprayed peaceful protesters with tear gas and irritant-laced water cannons during two mass demonstrations, the first calling for free and fair elections and the second highlighting the discrimination and other grievances felt by ethnic Indian Malaysians.

Detention without trial

The use or threatened use of the Internal Security Act (ISA) continued to be employed to suppress perceived critics of the government, with a specific threat to bloggers. Following the November demonstrations, the Prime Minister warned that the ISA could be used to prevent "illegal" protests. The ISA allows for detention without trial for up to two years, renewable indefinitely.

■ At least 83 people were detained under the ISA. Most were alleged members of Islamist groups, including Jemaah Islamiah. At least four suspected

M

Jemaah Islamiah members were arrested in 2007, and at least 16 were released during the year, having all been detained for over four years. Many were given restricted residence orders.

■ Others arrested under the ISA included five leaders of the Hindu Rights Action Force, a group campaigning for the rights of ethnic Indian Malaysians, who were sent directly to Kamunting Detention Camp. Five others, arrested for allegedly spreading rumours of racial riots, were subsequently released.

■ In October 2007, Abdul Malek Hussain, an ex-ISA detainee, was awarded damages of 2.5 million ringgit (approximately US$746,000). The judge ruled that he was unlawfully detained in 1998 and that he had been assaulted and tortured in custody.

Suspected criminals continued to be detained under the Emergency Ordinance (EO) (Public Order and Prevention of Crime) and the Dangerous Drugs (Special Preventive Measures) Act (DDA). Under both, suspects could be detained for up to 60 days for investigation after which a two-year detention order, renewable indefinitely, could be applied. Between January and August, 550 people were detained under the DDA. Both the EO and the DDA put suspects at risk of arbitrary detention and torture or other ill-treatment.

Migrant workers, refugees and asylum-seekers

Mass arrests of migrant workers, refugees and asylum-seekers by the People's Volunteer Corps (Rela) continued. According to a government news agency, 24,770 migrants had been detained by Rela as of August 2007. Rela officials continued to be accused of using excessive force and arbitrary detention when conducting raids.

Migrant workers were also subjected to psychological and physical abuse by agencies and employers. They were often denied equal access to benefits and protections guaranteed to Malaysian workers, including maternity provisions, limits on working hours and holidays.

Cruel, inhuman and degrading punishments

Caning continued to be used for many offences, including immigration offences. Irregular migrants (those lacking proper documentation) and refugees were reported to have received canings.

Death penalty

In March, the government passed amendments to the Penal Code introducing mandatory death sentences for acts of terrorism that result in death. Anyone found guilty of providing funds for terrorist acts that result in death would also receive a mandatory death sentence. Death sentences continued to be passed during 2007, with mandatory death sentences for drugs trafficking. The authorities did not disclose details of executions.

Freedom of expression

■ On 13 July, People's Justice party staff member and internet blogger Nathanial Tan was arrested at his office and detained under the Official Secrets Act. He was arrested on suspicion of having access to state secrets, namely official documents relating to corruption allegations, posted on his blog.

Discrimination

Freedom of religion

Restrictions on the right to religious freedom remained. People wishing to convert out of Islam continued to face barriers to having their conversion recognized by the civil courts.

■ In January, Revathi, a Muslim by birth, was detained at the Malacca Syariah High Court while applying to have her religious status recognized as Hindu. She was taken to a religious rehabilitation camp in Selangor and held there for six months. In March, the Islamic authorities removed Revathi's daughter from her husband, and placed her in the custody of Revathi's Muslim mother.

■ A 100-year-old Hindu temple was destroyed in Shah Alam in November, on the eve of the Hindu festival Deepavali. Several people were injured and 14 were arrested as devotees tried to stop the demolition. Other reportedly unauthorized Hindu temples were demolished to make way for development projects in 2007 despite petitions by local Hindu communities.

Rights of transsexuals

■ On 30 July, Ayu, a transsexual, was seriously beaten by officials from the Melaka Islamic Religious Affairs Department (JAIM). They reportedly punched and kicked her, rupturing a pre-existing hernia. A JAIM official stated that Ayu was detained for committing the "offence" of "men dressing as women in a public space", which is punishable by a fine of 1,000 ringgit (US$300), a six-month prison sentence or both under the Melak Syariah Offences Act.

M

MALI

REPUBLIC OF MALI

Head of state:	Amadou Toumani Touré
Head of government:	Modibo Sidibe (replaced Ousmane Issoufi Maiga in October)
Death penalty:	abolitionist in practice
Population:	14.3 million
Life expectancy:	53.1 years
Under-5 mortality (m/f):	209/203 per 1,000
Adult literacy:	24 per cent

People were killed, abducted and injured in the context of unrest in the north of the country. Freedom of expression came under attack; a teacher and five journalists were arrested.

Background

In April, President Amadou Toumani Touré was re-elected for a second five-year term. Voter participation was low at 36.24 per cent. In July, President Touré's ruling coalition, the Alliance for Democracy and Progress (Alliance pour la démocratie et le progrès) won an absolute majority in parliament.

Conflict in Kidal region

In May 2007, unrest broke out again in the Kidal region in the north, despite the peace agreement signed in Algeria in July 2006 between the Touareg armed group, the Democratic Alliance for Change (Alliance démocratique pour le changement) and the government. An armed group, led by Ibrahim Ag Bahanga, launched a series of attacks.

Following an attack by an armed group on a security post in Kidal in May, eight members of the armed group and two members of the Malian armed forces were killed. In August, around 50 soldiers and civilians were abducted by an armed group led by Ibrahim Ag Bahanga. Ten of them were released in September after a military operation led by the Malian army and 16 others in December after mediation by the Algerian authorities.

Freedom of expression under attack

In July, a teacher and five journalists were arrested for causing offence to the head of state. This followed the publication of an article commenting on an assignment set by the teacher, Bassirou Kassim Minta, which concerned the mistress of an imaginary head of state.

Bassirou Kassim Minta was sentenced to two months in prison, banned from teaching and fined following a trial which was held behind closed doors. Seydina Oumar Diarra, a journalist from the *Info Matin* newspaper, was sentenced to 13 days in prison and a fine. *Diarra*'s editor, Sambi Touré, was given an eight-month suspended sentence and a fine. The editors of three other national newspapers, Ibrahima Fall (*Le Républicain*), Alexis Kalambry (*Les Échos*) and Hameye Cissé of the daily *Le Scorpion*, received four-month suspended sentences and a fine.

Death penalty

In September, the government proposed a new law that would provide for the death penalty for those convicted of being the authors of acts connected to terrorism. However, in October, the government adopted a draft bill to abolish the death penalty which was awaiting parliamentary approval at the end of the year.

MALTA

REPUBLIC OF MALTA

Head of state:	Edward Fenech-Adami
Head of government:	Lawrence Gonzi
Death penalty:	abolitionist for all crimes
Population:	0.4 million
Life expectancy:	79.1 years
Under-5 mortality (m/f):	8/8 per 1,000
Adult literacy:	87.9 per cent

The Maltese authorities continued to detain migrants automatically on arrival to the island, contrary to their international obligations. They also failed to adequately protect people stranded at sea. The Council of Europe criticized Malta for its policies regarding detention of migrants.

Refugees, asylum-seekers and migrants
Rescue obligations

The Maltese authorities failed to protect the right to life of people stranded at sea on at least two occasions.

M

■ On 21 May, officers in a Maltese Armed Forces aircraft spotted 53 people in a sinking boat approximately 88 nautical miles south of Malta. According to reports, it took 12 hours for a rescue vessel to reach the boat, by which time it had disappeared. The individuals on the boat, who may have been seeking international protection, reportedly managed to return to Libya where they were detained at the Al Zoura detention centre.

■ On 24 May, a Maltese fishing boat failed to take on board 27 migrants and asylum-seekers whose boat had sunk. The ship-master did allow them to hold onto a tuna cage to prevent them from drowning, and eventually let them on to the vessel. The Maltese authorities failed to rescue them or ensure their safety. They were finally rescued by an Italian vessel.

Detention

Malta continued its policy of automatically detaining migrants and asylum-seekers arriving in Malta, contrary to international laws and standards. At the end of June, approximately 3,000 migrants and asylum-seekers were detained in Malta, more than 1,300 of them in closed detention facilities.

Detention conditions remained poor, including at the Hal Far open migration detention centre, which migrants are allowed to leave, where up to 800 migrants were housed in approximately 25 tents, some of them with holes in them. Those living in the faulty tents were directly exposed to rain, wind and cold temperatures, leading to sleep deprivation and ill health. Those housed at the Hal Far centre included pregnant women. The Maltese authorities said they had no intention of replacing the tents with other structures.

NGO Médecins du Monde (MDM) reported that in August a heavily pregnant Somali woman had given birth in detention. It also said that those detainees who asked for a doctor and found not to be sick, are often punished with solitary confinement. The organization denounced the unhygienic conditions of detention centres.

International scrutiny

On 10 September 2007, the European Committee for the Prevention of Torture (CPT) published its report to the Maltese government on the visit to Malta carried out in June 2005. The CPT noted that Malta still had a policy of systematically detaining all irregular migrants for up to a year and highlighted that unaccompanied minors are still held in detention centres, despite previous recommendations from the CPT to change this practice.

The CPT also said it was concerned that the appeals procedure against asylum decisions took place in private without the person whose case was being considered present. Since the decisions of the Refugees' Appeals Board were not open to appeal, the CPT recommended that it be mandatory to hear from the foreign national him/herself.

The CPT referred to the sanitary facilities at the Safi migration detention facility as "deplorable" and said it was in part overcrowded, with the majority of the centre unheated in winter.

The CPT stated that it had in the past clearly indicated that, at the Floriana Police Lock-Up (a detention facility within a police station), the dormitories for irregular migrants should be used for short stays only. However, at the time of its visit, 120 foreign nationals were nevertheless accommodated there for periods up to several months, in two badly overcrowded dormitories. Because of their general state of dilapidation, limited access to natural light and lack of an outdoor exercise yard, the CPT recommended these two dormitories no longer be used, even in emergencies.

The CPT asked the Maltese authorities to review the role of the armed forces in managing holding centres for irregular migrants. In the CPT's view, these centres should be managed by staff specially recruited and trained for that purpose. It also urged Malta to introduce guidelines regarding the removal of irregular migrants by air, and that these guidelines should be in line with the Council of Europe's Twenty Guidelines on Forced Return.

M

MAURITANIA

ISLAMIC REPUBLIC OF MAURITANIA

Head of state:	**Sidi Ould Cheikh Abdallahi (replaced Colonel Ely Ould Mohamed Vall in April)**
Head of government:	**Zeine Ould Zeidane (replaced Sidi Mohamed Ould Boubacar in April)**
Death penalty:	**abolitionist in practice**
Population:	**3.2 million**
Life expectancy:	**63.2 years**
Under-5 mortality (m/f):	**147/135 per 1,000**
Adult literacy:	**51.2 per cent**

Several possible prisoners of conscience were tried. There were reports of torture in detention. One student was killed when the security forces opened fire on protesters. Slavery became a criminal offence.

Background

Sidi Ould Cheikh Abdallahi won the March presidential election which followed multi-party parliamentary polls in December 2006. This completed a promised handover to civilian rule.

In March, the 24 members of the National Human Rights Commission, set up in May 2006, were appointed.

In April, Mauritania was reintegrated into the African Union, from which it had been suspended after the August 2005 military coup.

In November, the governments of Mauritania and Senegal, together with UNHCR, signed a tripartite agreement in Nouakchott, paving the way for the return of some 24,000 Mauritanian refugees who left the country in the aftermath of the 1989 repression against the black Mauritanian population.

Justice system

Possible prisoners of conscience

Two trials took place of people suspected of belonging to an unauthorized organization and "putting the country at risk of foreign reprisals". Most of those tried were arrested in 2005.

■ In May, the criminal court of Nouakchott tried 21 people accused of forming an unauthorized organization, belonging to a criminal group, and "participating in acts that expose the country to the risk of foreign reprisals". Twenty were acquitted. However, El Khadim Ould Semmane, one of four men who escaped

from Nouakchott Central Prison in April 2006 and were tried in their absence, was convicted of possessing illegal weapons and false documents and sentenced to two years' imprisonment. A number of the suspects had been in preventive detention for over two years and were alleged to have been tortured (see below).

■ In June and July, 14 people accused of belonging to the Algerian Salafist Group for Preaching and Combat (Groupe Salafiste pour la Prédication et le Combat) and of involvement in cross-border attacks in 2005, were tried. Nine were acquitted and five were sentenced to between two and five years' imprisonment. Three men who had faced charges carrying possible death sentences – Tahar Ould Biye, Tiyib Ould Salek and Ely Sheikh Ould Ahmed Vall – received sentences of between five and three years' imprisonment for forgery.

Police and security forces

Torture

Detainees were frequently tortured shortly after arrest and during interrogation.

■ During the two trials (see above), most of the detainees stated that they had been tortured in detention. One of the 21 detainees tried in May said that he had been burned with cigarettes by police to extract confessions. The defence in the first trial maintained that testimonies were inadmissible as statements had been obtained under torture. Their request that those believed to be responsible for the acts of torture be called as witnesses was refused.

Excessive use of force

In November, the security forces fired live bullets at secondary school students protesting at increases in food prices.

■ Eighteen-year-old Cheikhna Ould Taleb Nava was killed when the security forces opened fire on protesters in Kankossa in the south-east.

Counter-terrorism

At least 11 people were arrested in the context of Mauritania's fights against terrorism, some of whom may have been prisoners of conscience.

■ Five Mauritanians and a Moroccan, arrested in March for suspected links to terrorism, were charged in April. They were charged with offences relating to planning attacks, selling arms and financing terrorism. In June, six people, including three Moroccan nationals, were arrested for their suspected involvement with a cell linked to al-Qa'ida. There

M

were concerns that they may have been targeted because of their membership of an Islamic group.

Slavery

In August, slavery was made a criminal offence. Although officially abolished in 1981, evidence indicated the continued existence of the practice. Under the new law, slavery is punishable by up to 10 years in prison and a fine.

MEXICO

UNITED MEXICAN STATES

Head of state and government:	**Felipe Calderón Hinojosa**
Death penalty:	**abolitionist for all crimes**
Population:	**109.6 million**
Life expectancy:	**75.6 years**
Under-5 mortality (m/f):	**22/18 per 1,000**
Adult literacy:	**91.6 per cent**

Human rights violations remained widespread and in some states systematic. The majority of those responsible continued to evade justice. Police used excessive force to disperse demonstrators on several occasions, injuring a number of protesters. Continuing human rights abuses were reported in Oaxaca State. Military personnel performing policing functions killed several people and committed other serious human rights violations. The government also failed to make progress in bringing to justice those responsible for grave human rights violations in previous decades.

Journalists and human rights defenders were killed and threatened. In several states, the authorities reportedly misused the judicial system to subject political and social activists to unfair prosecutions.

Indigenous communities and other disadvantaged groups, such as migrants, continued to face discrimination. Lack of access to basic services and genuine consultation over development projects exacerbated inequalities and led to conflict. Affected communities were often denied effective access to justice.

Despite positive legal reforms, violence against women remained widespread and most survivors were denied effective access to justice.

Background

President Calderón committed his government to combating organized crime, which was allegedly responsible for over 2,500 killings during 2007.

In October the Mexican and US governments announced the Merida Initiative, a regional security cooperation initiative under which the US administration proposed providing US$1.4 billion in security and criminal justice assistance to Mexico and Central America over three years. At the end of 2007 the US Congress continued to deliberate the proposal and its potential impact on human rights and security.

Legal, constitutional and institutional developments

In May the authorities announced the creation of a National Development Plan which included pledges to protect human rights. The government also promised to maintain open access to international human rights mechanisms and tackle the use of torture.

In August the development of a new National Human Rights Programme was announced.

Reforms to the Constitution and the public security and criminal justice systems moved ahead in Congress. These require substantial changes to police and court procedures, including strengthened police and prosecutorial powers to enter homes without judicial authorization and to hold organized crime suspects in a form of pre-charge detention (*arraigo*) for up to 80 days.

National Supreme Court

In February the National Supreme Court ruled that the military had violated the constitutional prohibition on discrimination by dismissing officials on the basis of their HIV positive status.

In December a special inquiry ordered by the Court reported its findings on the case of Lydia Cacho. It concluded that the governor of Puebla State and other senior local officials were responsible for the misuse of the justice system leading to the detention, ill-treatment and unfair prosecution of the journalist for publishing a book on child abuse and pornography networks. Nevertheless, the majority of Supreme Court justices refused to endorse these conclusions.

The results of two other National Supreme Court special inquiries into abuses committed in San Salvador Atenco and Oaxaca State were pending at the end of the year.

M

Reproductive rights

The legislative assembly of the Federal District decriminalized abortions carried out in the first trimester and made abortion services available in Mexico City. The Federal Attorney General's Office and the National Human Rights Commission filed constitutional challenges to these reforms with the Supreme Court which were pending at the end of the year.

Police and security forces – public security

Military personnel

More than 20,000 military personnel were deployed in many states in policing operations to combat drug trafficking gangs. Military personnel were reported to have arbitrarily detained, tortured and unlawfully killed at least five people during these operations.

■ In February, the authorities in Veracruz State concluded that an Indigenous woman, Ernestina Ascencio Rosario, had died from injuries caused by rape, allegedly committed by army personnel carrying out policing operations in the state. However, the National Human Rights Commission concluded that the investigation was flawed and that she had died of natural causes. Despite widespread concern about how the case was dealt with, the inquiry was closed.

■ In May, military officials involved in policing operations arbitrarily detained several people in Michoacán State. Several detainees reported that they had been ill-treated; four teenage girls were allegedly sexually assaulted or raped.

■ In June, soldiers manning a road block in Sinaloa State shot at a car and killed two women and three children. A number of officials were arrested and military investigations were continuing at the end of the year.

Excessive use of force and torture

Police officers were accused of using excessive force and torture.

■ In July in Oaxaca, state and municipal police used tear gas, stones and batons to disperse demonstrators, seriously injuring at least two people. Scores of people were arrested. Emeterio Cruz was photographed in custody in good health, but was then struck repeatedly by police and later taken to hospital in a coma. He was discharged in August with partial paralysis. Five municipal police were detained and charged in connection with the case.

■ In June, state police evicted a group of Indigenous Nahua peasant farmers occupying disputed land in the municipality of Ixhuatlán de Madero, Veracruz State. Police fired repeatedly into the air; one detainee was shot and injured. Those arrested were reportedly beaten and threatened during interrogation to force them to implicate their leader in alleged criminal offences. They were later released on bail, pending prosecution for illegal land occupation.

Impunity

Investigations into allegations of arbitrary detention, torture and other ill-treatment by police officers were frequently inadequate and impunity for human rights violations was widespread.

Reports of human rights violations by military personnel were often dealt with in the military justice system. The National Human Rights Commission found evidence of serious abuses in a number of cases, but failed to recommend that such cases be dealt with by the civilian courts.

■ In October, four soldiers were convicted by a civilian court of the rape of 14 women in July 2006 in the municipality of Castaños, Coahuila State. Other officials implicated in the attack were acquitted or not brought to trial.

Past human rights violations

Human rights violations committed in the 1960s, 1970s and 1980s, which had previously been investigated by the Special Prosecutor's Office, were returned to the Federal Attorney General's Office without any commitment to continue the investigations. The government ignored the concluding report of the Special Prosecutor's Office which acknowledged that the abuses were systematic state crimes. The creation of a fund to compensate victims was announced in October.

■ In July a federal judge found that the massacre of scores of students in Tlatelolco Square in Mexico City in 1968 was genocide but that there was insufficient evidence against former president Luis Echeverría to continue the prosecution. An appeal on this ruling was pending at the end of the year.

Possible enforced disappearances

The Popular Revolutionary Army (Ejército Popular Revolucionario, EPR) accused the authorities of the enforced disappearance of two of its members,

M

Edmundo Reyes Amaya and Gabriel Alberto Cruz Sánchez. The EPR alleged that they had been detained in Oaxaca City on 25 May.

In August the EPR claimed responsibility for several explosions in central Mexico in support of their demand that the authorities acknowledge the detention of the two men. In October, a federal court issued a habeas corpus (amparo) writ requiring the end of their enforced disappearance and for the authorities to ensure their immediate reappearance. The state and federal authorities denied that the two men had been detained or forcibly disappeared and promised to investigate. The whereabouts of Edmundo Reyes Amaya and Gabriel Alberto Cruz Sánchez remained unknown at the end of the year.

Violence against women

In June the National Survey on the Dynamic of Family Relations found that 67 per cent of women over the age of 15 reported experiencing some form of violence in the home, community, workplace or school and nearly one in 10 reported that they had experienced sexual violence.

In February the Federal Law on Women's Access to a Life Free of Violence came into force. Nine states introduced similar legal reforms.

More than 25 women were reported to have been murdered in Ciudad Juárez in 2007. The authorities continued to fail to bring to justice those responsible for many crimes of violence against women in the state in previous years. In other states, such as Mexico State, there were reportedly even higher numbers of women murdered with impunity.

Justice system – arbitrary detention and unfair trials

The criminal justice system continued to be used in some states to prosecute social activists and political opponents. They were subjected to prolonged arbitrary detention and unfair legal proceedings. Despite successful federal injunctions in many cases, state courts frequently failed to correct injustices. No official was held to account for violating fair trial standards.

■ In November, prisoner of conscience, Magdalena García Durán, an Indigenous woman detained during protests in San Salvador Atenco in May 2006, was released on the grounds of insufficient evidence. She was released after a local judge finally complied with a second federal injunction. However, more than 20 other people detained in San Salvador Atenco at the same time were on trial at the end of the year in proceedings characterized by similar unfair procedures.

■ Diego Arcos, a community leader from Nuevo Tila, Chiapas State, was released in December 2007 after spending a year in custody accused of four murders during an attack on the community of Viejo Velasco in November 2006. Despite winning a federal injunction in August, he was only released when the State Minister of Justice reviewed the case and dropped the charges.

■ Ignacio del Valle Medina, Felipe Alvarez Hernández and Héctor Galindo Gochicoa, leaders of a local protest movement in San Salvador Atenco, Mexico State, were each sentenced in May to 67 years in prison after being convicted of kidnapping public officials during local disputes in 2006. There was serious concern about the fairness of the trial and the sentence.

Human rights defenders

Human rights defenders continued to face attack, threats, harassment and unfounded criminal charges in many states, in apparent reprisal for their work.

■ In May, Aldo Zamora, a member of a family of environmental activists campaigning against illegal logging in the municipality of Ocuilán, Mexico State, was shot and killed. His father had filed repeated complaints with the authorities about death threats sent to the family, but no action was taken. Two suspects were arrested in August; two others remained at large at the end of the year.

■ In April, migrants' rights defender Santiago Rafael Cruz was beaten to death in the office of the Farm Labour Organizing Committee (Foro Laboral del Obrero Campesino, FLOC), in Monterrey, Nuevo León State. The state authorities denied the killing was linked to his human rights work, but local human rights organizations expressed concern about the thoroughness of the investigation into his death. One person was charged with the murder and detained pending trial at the end of the year.

■ Human rights defender Aline Castellanos was forced to leave Oaxaca State after an arrest warrant was issued on the basis of fabricated evidence which accused her of involvement in the occupation of a public building.

Freedom of expression – journalists

Journalists, particularly those reporting on drug trafficking and corruption, were repeatedly attacked.

At least six journalists and media workers were murdered and three others were abducted. The majority of official investigations into these crimes and past attacks on journalists made little or no progress.

■ In October, Mateo Cortés Martínez, Flor Vásquez López and Agustín López Nolasco, staff of the newspaper *El Imparcial del Istmo* in Oaxaca, were shot and killed while delivering newspapers. Immediately after the killings, the newspaper's director and two reporters received threats warning them the same would happen to them.

The pattern of attacks on journalists led to increasing self-censorship and undermined freedom of expression.

In April, defamation was decriminalized in federal law, but remained a criminal offence in most state jurisdictions.

Discrimination – marginalized communities

Many marginalized communities continued to have limited access to basic services, despite the government's commitment to increase social spending. This fuelled conflict, inequality and discrimination, particularly affecting many Indigenous communities. The failure to ensure that communities affected by development or investment projects were genuinely informed, consulted and given the opportunity to participate in the formulation of projects, led to increased tensions and disempowerment.

■ Communities opposed to the construction of La Parota hydroelectric dam in Guerrero State won several preliminary legal challenges on the basis that community approval had not been legally obtained. At the end of the year the project remained suspended pending the resolution of several legal actions.

Migrants

There were continued reports of abuses against some of the thousands of irregular migrants crossing the northern and southern borders. Those who provided humanitarian assistance to migrants on their way through Mexico were at risk of being charged with people trafficking.

The government proposed new regulatory procedures on migrant detention centres. The proposal, which would restrict civil society access and increase controls on migrants, was pending executive approval at the end of the year.

Amnesty International visit/reports

🚌 Amnesty International's Secretary General visited Oaxaca City, Mexico City and Guerrero State, met senior government officials and attended Amnesty International's biennial International Council Meeting in Cocoyoc, Morelos State, in August.

📄 Mexico: Laws without justice: Human rights violations and impunity in the public security and criminal justice system (AMR 41/002/2007)

📄 Mexico: Laws without justice – Appeal cases (AMR 41/015/2007)

📄 Mexico: Human rights at risk in La Parota Dam project (AMR 41/029/2007)

📄 Mexico: Oaxaca – Clamour for justice (AMR 41/031/2007)

MOLDOVA

REPUBLIC OF MOLDOVA

Head of state:	Vladimir Voronin
Head of government:	Vasile Tarlev
Death penalty:	abolitionist for all crimes
Population:	4.2 million
Life expectancy:	68.4 years
Under-5 mortality (m/f):	30/26 per 1,000
Adult literacy:	99.1 per cent

The government continued to show willingness to bring the legal system into line with international and European standards, but practice and attitudes still failed to keep pace with these changes. Torture and ill-treatment remained widespread and victims had great difficulty in pursuing their complaints and getting redress. Despite efforts by local and international organizations to publicize the dangers of trafficking, Moldovan men, women and children continued to be trafficked, and prosecutions for trafficking were hampered by inadequate witness protection. The state imposed limitations on freedom of expression.

Torture and other ill-treatment

Torture and other ill-treatment were widespread and systemic. There were inadequate safeguards for detainees who often spent long periods in poor conditions in police detention. Lack of resources for police work and pressure to send as many cases as possible to court encouraged police investigators to extract confessions by force. Investigations into

M

allegations of torture were not carried out effectively and impartially, leading to a climate of impunity. The European Court of Human Rights found in five judgments that Moldova had violated the right to be free from torture and other ill-treatment.

In July, parliament approved amendments to the Law on the Parliamentary Ombudsmen to set up an independent body to monitor places of detention in accordance with Moldova's obligations under the Optional Protocol to the UN Convention against Torture (OPCAT). The amendments proposed setting up a Consultative Committee within the office of the Parliamentary Ombudsmen to include representatives of non-governmental human rights organizations. These amendments, however, failed to guarantee the functional or financial independence and adequate funding of the Consultative Committee as required by OPCAT.

In November, the preliminary report of the European Committee for the Prevention of Torture's (CPT) visit to Moldova in September was published. According to the CPT, about a third of the people interviewed during the visit made credible allegations of torture and other ill-treatment.

■ Viorica Plate told Amnesty International that she was tortured by police from Botanica police station in Chişinău on 19 May. She was arrested at her home in Orhei and accused of stealing US$7,000 from her ex-husband. Three police officers reportedly threw her onto a sofa in her flat, twisted her arms, handcuffed her and then drove her to Botanica police station. She stated that at the police station officers put a gas mask over her head, and beat her on the soles of her feet while closing the air vent on the gas mask causing her to lose consciousness. They then suspended her from a hat stand hung between two chairs and continued to beat her on the soles of her feet. Eventually she managed to take a knife from a desk and cut her wrist, at which point an ambulance was called and she was taken to the hospital. Viorica Plate complained to the Prosecutor General's office and an investigation was opened, but the police officers were not suspended and she reported that in June they threatened to detain her again. Two of the police officers concerned were sentenced at the end of the year to six years' detention and a third police officer was given a suspended sentence.

■ On 23 October the European Court of Human Rights found that Vitalii Colibaba had been ill-treated by police officers in April 2006 and that the state had failed to conduct an effective investigation into the allegations. The Court also found that the state had failed to facilitate access to the European Court because the Prosecutor General wrote to the bar association on 26 June 2006 stating that both Vitalii Colibaba's lawyer and one other lawyer could face criminal prosecution for providing information about torture cases to international organizations. Amnesty International had campaigned on behalf of Vitalii Colibaba and the lawyers, and asked repeatedly for an effective and impartial examination to be carried out into the torture allegations. In June, the Prosecutor General's office informed Amnesty International that Vitalii Colibaba had suffered injuries during his police detention, but that these were not the result of torture or other ill-treatment.

■ On 26 November, eight HIV-positive prisoners detained at remand prison no. 13 in the capital, Chişinău, slit their wrists in protest at the conditions in which they were held. All eight were held in overcrowded conditions in a cell measuring 20 m². Some HIV-positive prisoners also suffered from multi-drug-resistant tuberculosis which put the other prisoners at high risk of contracting the disease. Prison special forces reportedly subdued the protest with rubber batons and several prisoners were injured. Four of the prisoners were subsequently placed together in a punishment cell in the basement, which further damaged their health.

Violence against women

Despite the existence of witness protection programmes, very few victims of trafficking for sexual exploitation were able to benefit from effective witness protection if they agreed to testify. Women were only offered witness protection if the risk of attack by traffickers could be proven and in most cases this required evidence of a previous attack or threat. According to the US State Department *Trafficking in Persons Report* published in June, Moldova failed to address complicity in severe forms of trafficking by government officials.

Freedom of expression

In a resolution passed in October, the Parliamentary Assembly of the Council of Europe called on the Moldovan authorities to "strengthen all the necessary guarantees to ensure the respect of freedom of expression as defined in Article 10 of the European Convention on Human Rights".

M

■ In April, for the third year in a row Chişinău City Hall denied permission to the organization Gender Doc-M to hold a gay pride march. This decision was made despite a Supreme Court ruling in February that a similar refusal in April 2006 had been illegal.

International justice

On 2 October, the Constitutional Court ruled that Moldova could ratify the Rome Statute of the International Criminal Court without requiring a change in the Constitution. Moldova signed the Rome Statute of the International Criminal Court in 2000, but the government then asked the Constitutional Court to decide whether the Rome Statute contradicted the Constitution.

Self-proclaimed Transdniestrian Moldavian Republic (Transdniestria)

In June, local elections were held throughout Moldova. However, Transdniestrian authorities prevented them from taking place in the village of Corjova, one of nine villages that are located geographically in Transdniestria, but are under the control of the central government of Moldova. Valentin Beşleag, who was candidate for mayor in the local elections, was detained at the police station in Dubasari for 15 days and charged with the administrative offence of distributing election materials from abroad. Iurie Cotofan, who tried to cast his vote on 3 June, was allegedly beaten by several Transdniestrian police officers. He was then taken to the Dubasari police station, where he was held until midnight before being released without explanation or charge.

■ The last two remaining members of the "Tiraspol Six", Andrei Ivanţoc and Tudor Petrov-Popa, who were sentenced to prison terms in Transdniestria in 1993 for "terrorist acts", including the murder of two Transdniestrian officials, were released on 2 and 4 June respectively on the expiration of their sentences. They had remained imprisoned in Tiraspol, the capital of Transdniestria, despite a July 2004 judgment by the European Court of Human Rights which found their detention to be arbitrary and in breach of the European Convention on Human Rights. Both men were released and expelled from Transdniestria. Andrei Ivanţoc attempted to return to Transdniestria, but was forced into a car and driven to Chişinău.

Amnesty International visit/reports

🚍 Amnesty International delegates visited Moldova in March, July and October.

📄 Moldova (Self-proclaimed Dnestr Moldavian Republic): Possible prisoner of conscience/ health concern/ legal concern: Valentin Besleag (EUR 59/001/2007)

📄 Moldova: Police torture and ill-treatment: "It's just normal." (EUR 59/002/2007)

📄 Europe and Central Asia: Summary of Amnesty International's concerns in the region, January-June 2007 (EUR 01/010/2007)

MONGOLIA

MONGOLIA

Head of state:	Nambaryn Enkhbayar
Head of government:	Sanjaagiin Bayar
	(replaced Miyegombiin Enkhbold in November)
Death penalty:	retentionist
Population:	2.7 million
Life expectancy:	65.9 years
Under-5 mortality (m/f):	75/71 per 1,000
Adult literacy:	97.8 per cent

The death penalty was carried out in secret. Torture and other ill-treatment appeared to be prevalent in police stations, prisons and detention centres. The state failed to provide adequate protection and assistance for victims of trafficking. Contamination of drinking water by mining companies continued.

Background

The chairperson of the Mongolian People's Revolutionary Party, Sanjaagiin Bayar, was appointed as Prime Minister in November.

An anti-corruption course was introduced at the National Law School and the Management Academy to address endemic corruption.

Despite increasing investments in Mongolia by international mining companies, the government failed to develop legal safeguards for protection against forced evictions, or adequate health, safety and environmental protection. Run-off from mining and exploration activities into rivers contaminated the drinking supply, and harmed the livelihoods of traditional nomadic herders reliant on river water for their livestock.

M

Death penalty

There was a lack of transparency regarding the application of the death penalty. Executions were carried out in secret and no official death sentences or execution statistics were available. Prisoners were reported to be living in appalling conditions and were held on death row for more than 24 months. Authorities failed to notify family members when prisoners on death row were executed.

Health – environmental contamination

Despite passing a law on toxic and hazardous chemicals in 2006, the government failed to monitor the use of toxic chemicals such as mercury and sodium cyanide in mining. Large amounts of these chemicals were reportedly used in more than 20 *soums* (districts) in 9 *aimags* (provinces), polluting the local water supply. According to the National Human Rights Commission, in Khongor *soum* mercury contamination was 100 to 125 times higher than recommended levels and sodium cyanide was 900 times higher than recommended levels.

Violence against women

A dramatic increase in migration contributed to the growing number of women (and girls) trafficked internally and across borders. Women were trafficked for sexual exploitation, forced labour and marriage. There was a lack of protection and assistance for victims of trafficking, and a tendency to prosecute trafficked victims for related offences such as illegal immigration.

Mongolia was not a state party to the Protocol to Prevent, Suppress and Punish Trafficking in Persons, Especially Women and Children, Supplementing the UN Convention against Transnational Organized Crime (Palermo Protocol).

Torture and other ill-treatment

The Mongolian Criminal Code was amended to include a definition of torture and a provision for torture victims to seek compensation. However, there was no recourse to rehabilitation for victims. Torture and other ill-treatment in police stations and pre-trial detention centres remained prevalent. There was a lack of awareness among prosecutors, lawyers and the judiciary of international standards relating to the prohibition of torture.

MONTENEGRO

REPUBLIC OF MONTENEGRO

Head of state:	Filip Vujanović
Head of government:	Željko Šturanović
Death penalty:	abolitionist for all crimes
Life expectancy:	74.1 years
Adult literacy:	96.4 per cent

Montenegro failed to resolve outstanding war crimes and suspected extrajudicial killings, and did not ensure prompt, impartial and effective investigations into allegations of torture or other ill-treatment.

Background

In May, Montenegro joined the Council of Europe. In the same month, the Ministry of Foreign Affairs concluded an agreement – which Amnesty International considered unlawful – with the USA agreeing not to surrender US citizens to the International Criminal Court. In October, Montenegro signed a Stabilization and Association Agreement with the European Union.

A new constitution adopted in October was not fully compatible with the provisions of the European Convention on Human Rights (ECHR), and failed to ensure independence of the judiciary or afford minorities adequate protection against discrimination.

Impunity for war crimes

In June, police assisted in the arrest in Budva of Vlastimir Đorđević, indicted by the International Criminal Tribunal for the former Yugoslavia (Tribunal) for war crimes in Kosovo; he was previously believed to be at large in Russia.

No progress was made in investigations of six former police officers indicted in February 2006 for the enforced disappearance of 83 Bosniak (Bosnian Muslim) civilians in 1992.

■ In related civil proceedings, in 25 out of 38 first instance decisions, Montenegro was found responsible for the enforced disappearances or deaths of the Bosniak civilians, and compensation was awarded to survivors, or to family members for the deaths of their relatives. The state appealed each decision. The court rejected claims that the authorities had violated the relatives' rights under

M

Article 3 of the ECHR in failing to provide information on the fate and whereabouts of the disappeared.

Torture and other ill-treatment

Allegations of torture and ill-treatment continued, including during arrest and detention: the Youth Initiative for Human Rights documented some 23 cases between September and October alone. Victims were often charged with obstruction of police officers, who were rarely charged.

■ In March, the Ministry of the Interior reported on the failure of an internal police investigation into allegations of torture and other ill-treatment of 17 ethnic Albanian men during their arrest and subsequent detention in Podgorica police station in September 2006. In response to a criminal complaint by seven of the men, in June the state prosecutor opened a criminal investigation; by November four police officers were reportedly under investigation.

Trial proceedings against the 17 men, which opened on 14 May at Podgorica District Court, were not conducted in accordance with international standards, including the use in evidence of testimonies which Amnesty International considered had been extracted under duress.

Possible extrajudicial executions and political attacks

An appeal against the acquittal in December 2007 of the only suspect for the murder in May 2004 of Duško Jovanović, editor of daily *Dan,* continued. Investigations continued into the murder in October 2006 of Srdjan Vojičić, driver of novelist Jevrem Brković. Other attacks on journalists critical of the government included:

■ On 1 September, Željko Ivanović, director of Montenegrin daily *Vijesti,* was attacked. Željko Ivanović alleged that the indictment of two men, who according to eye-witnesses were not the perpetrators, was an attempt to cover up a politically motivated attack.

■ On 1 November Tufik Softić, head of the Berane radio station, was hospitalized after being beaten with baseball bats by two unknown assailants. He had previously reported threats to his life. An investigation is ongoing.

The trial of 10 defendants indicted in August 2006 on suspicion of the 2005 murder of former Montenegrin police chief Slavloljub Šćekić opened in January, but had not concluded by the end of 2007.

Human rights defenders

■ After participating in a broadcast on enforced disappearances, journalist Aleksandar Žeković, member of the Council for the Civilian Control of Police, received threatening telephone calls in April. The Supreme Court refused to confirm whether he was under surveillance, citing state security concerns; recordings of calls suggested police involvement.

Minority rights

In June, a survey of participating governments' progress in the Decade of Roma Inclusion ranked Montenegro in ninth (and last) place; denied the right to education, some 87 per cent of the Romani population were estimated to be illiterate.

Refugees

Some 16,155 predominantly Roma refugees from Kosovo, considered to be internally displaced, remained at risk of forcible return; some 1,870 still awaited decisions on displaced person status. A further 8,527 refugees from Bosnia and Herzegovina or Croatia also remained in Montenegro. The Council of Europe, on Montenegro's accession, required the authorities to issue personal documentation to displaced persons and refugees; ensure their access to social, economic, and political rights and prevent those without documentation from becoming stateless.

Trafficking in human beings

The Council of Europe called for increased efforts in the provision of assistance and protection to victims of trafficking, in accordance with the Convention on Action against Trafficking in Human Beings, which Montenegro signed but did not ratify.

Amnesty International report

Europe and Central Asia: Summary of Amnesty International's concerns in the region, July-December 2006 (EUR 01/001/2007); January-June 2007 (EUR 01/010/2007)

M

MOROCCO/ WESTERN SAHARA

KINGDOM OF MOROCCO
Head of state:	King Mohamed VI
Head of government:	Abbas El Fassi
	(replaced Driss Jettou in October)
Death penalty:	abolitionist in practice
Population:	32.4 million
Life expectancy:	70.4 years
Under-5 mortality (m/f):	44/30 per 1,000
Adult literacy:	52.3 per cent

Restrictions on freedom of expression, association and assembly continued, and criticism of the monarchy and other issues considered politically sensitive was penalized by the authorities. Human rights activists, journalists, members of the unauthorized political group Al-Adl wal-Ihsan, and Sahrawi opponents of continuing Moroccan rule in Western Sahara were arrested and prosecuted, and more than 100 Islamists were detained on suspicion of planning or participating in terrorism. Arrests and collective expulsions of migrants continued. Death sentences were passed but the government maintained a de facto moratorium on executions. Violence against women continued, although the authorities launched a campaign to combat it, and men were imprisoned for "homosexual conduct".

Background

In June and August, UN-mediated talks on the Western Sahara were held between the Moroccan government and the Polisario Front, which calls for an independent state in Western Sahara and runs a self-proclaimed government-in-exile in refugee camps in south-western Algeria. Morocco proposed an autonomy plan for the territory it annexed in 1975, while the Polisario Front maintained that a referendum on self-determination should be held, as agreed in previous UN resolutions.

Several suicide attacks resulted in the killing of one police officer and several injuries, and the government raised the terrorist alert level.

Human rights defenders

Several members of the Moroccan Association for Human Rights (Association Marocaine des Droits

Humains, AMDH), all prisoners of conscience, were jailed for "undermining the monarchy", a charge brought after they participated in peaceful demonstrations during which slogans critical of the monarchy were chanted.

Five of them – Thami Khyati, Youssef Reggab, Oussama Ben Messaoud, Ahmed Al Kaateb and Rabii Raïssouni – were arrested in Ksar El Kebir after they joined demonstrations against unemployment on 1 May. They were sentenced to three years' imprisonment and heavy fines. Their prison sentences were increased to four years on appeal. Two other men, Mehdi Berbouchi and Abderrahim Karrad, were arrested in Agadir on the same charge and had their two-year prison sentences confirmed by the appeal court on 26 June.

Ten other members were arrested after participating in a peaceful sit-in on 5 June in the city of Beni Mellal in solidarity with the AMDH members already detained. Mohamed Boughrine, 72, was sentenced to one year's imprisonment, and three others to suspended prison sentences for "undermining the monarchy". Mohamed Boughrine's jail sentence was extended to three years on appeal. The nine others were sentenced to one year in prison and remained at liberty pending appeal to a higher court.

A further three members of AMDH – Azzadin Almanjali, Badr Arafat and Mohamed Kamal Almareini – were arrested along with 44 other people, including children, after demonstrations that turned violent on 23 September in the city of Sefrou. Their trial was postponed until 2008. The defendants denied involvement in violent incidents and said they were arrested arbitrarily. Some alleged that they had been ill-treated by police during arrest and subsequent questioning.

Press freedom restricted

Several journalists were arrested and charged with criminal offences for articles deemed to threaten national security or undermine the monarchy. A new Press Code was drafted by the authorities; it was said to retain offences carrying prison sentences.

■ Mustapha Hormatallah and Abderrahim Ariri, respectively journalist and editor of *Al Watan* newspaper, were arrested on 18 July after publishing an internal security memo on the raised terrorist alert. They were convicted in August of "receiving documents through criminal means". Abderrahim Ariri received a suspended prison sentence. Mustapha

M

Hormatallah was sentenced to eight months' imprisonment, reduced to seven on appeal, but was released on bail in September pending an appeal.

■ On 6 August, Ahmed Benchemsi, editor of the weekly *Nichane* and its sister weekly *Tel Quel*, was charged with "undermining the monarchy" under Article 41 of the Press Code, punishable by up to five years' imprisonment. On 4 August, he had published an editorial commenting on a speech by the King. Copies of *Nichane* were seized. Ahmed Benchemsi remained at liberty awaiting trial scheduled for 2008.

Sahrawi activists

Hundreds of Sahrawi activists suspected of participating in demonstrations against Moroccan rule in 2007 and previous years were arrested, including minors. Dozens alleged torture or ill-treatment during questioning by security forces. Some were tried on charges of violent conduct and others were released after questioning. In May, security forces forcibly dispersed demonstrations by Sahrawi students at university campuses in Moroccan cities calling for independence. Dozens of students were arrested and many were beaten. Sultana Khaya lost an eye, apparently as a result of beatings. Most were released uncharged but around 20 were convicted of violent conduct and sentenced to up to one year in prison. Sahrawi human rights activists continued to be harassed.

■ In March, Brahim Sabbar, Secretary-General of the Sahrawi Association of Victims of Grave Human Rights Violations Committed by the Moroccan State, and his colleague Ahmed Sbai, were sentenced to one year's imprisonment after being convicted of belonging to an unauthorized organization. Their sentence was extended to 18 months on appeal. Politically motivated administrative obstacles had prevented registration of their association. Mohamed Tahlil, head of the association in Boujdour, was sentenced in September to two and a half years in prison for violent conduct. Sadik Boullahi, another member of the association, was held for 48 hours in November and then released.

■ In October, the Collective of Sahrawi Human Rights Defenders had to cancel its founding congress because the local authorities in Laayoune refused to authorize their public meeting. One of the Collective's members, Elwali Amidane, had been sentenced to five years' imprisonment in April for participating in demonstrations against Moroccan rule.

Al-Adl wal-Ihsan activists

Thousands of members of Al-Adl wal-Ihsan, an unauthorized political organization, were reported to have been questioned by police during the year and at least 267 were charged with participating in unauthorized meetings or belonging to an unauthorized association. The trial of the group's spokesperson, Nadia Yassine, who was charged in 2005 with defaming the monarchy, was delayed for a further year.

■ Rachid Gholam, an Al-Adl wal-Ihsan member and religious singer, was convicted of encouraging moral corruption and prostitution in May and sentenced to one month's imprisonment and a fine. He alleged when first brought before a judge that he had been beaten and stripped naked by the police and photographed with a prostitute.

Counter-terrorism

More than 100 suspected Islamist militants were arrested, mostly by police. However, the Directorate for Surveillance of the Territory, a security force accused in previous years of torture and other ill-treatment, allegedly participated in some arrests. Most of the detainees were charged and some were tried on terrorism offences and sentenced to up to 15 years in prison.

Hundreds of Islamist prisoners sentenced after the 2003 Casablanca bombings continued to demand a judicial review of their trials, many of which were tainted with unexamined claims of confessions extracted under torture. Detainees in Sale prison staged hunger strikes to protest against poor prison conditions, including ill-treatment by prison guards and security forces external to the prison, lack of access to medical care, and restrictions on visits by families.

Refugees, asylum-seekers and migrants

Thousands of people suspected of being irregular migrants, among them refugees and asylum-seekers, were arrested and collectively expelled. In most cases, their rights under Moroccan law to appeal against the decision to deport them or to examine the grounds on which the decision was taken were not respected. They were often dumped at the border with Algeria without adequate food and water.

■ On the night of 30/31 July, two Senegalese migrants, Aboubakr Sedjou and Siradjo Kébé, were killed and three others were wounded by police near Laayoune in Western Sahara. They were among more than 30 migrants who, according to the authorities, were

M

attempting to reach the coast to migrate to the Canary Islands and refused to stop when ordered to do so. The authorities declared that an investigation would be opened into the killings, but its outcome was not known.

In March, the national Human Rights Advisory Board published a report on the deaths of migrants at the border with Ceuta and Melilla in 2005. It recommended that the authorities do more to respect their international human rights obligations, but stopped short of recommending an investigation into the deaths.

Discrimination and violence against women

In April, the Nationality Code was amended to allow Moroccan women married to foreign men to pass their nationality to their children.

In November, the authorities reported that 82 per cent of reported ill-treatment of women was due to violence in the home, and launched a campaign to stop violence against women.

Discrimination – imprisoned for 'homosexual conduct'

Six men were sentenced to prison terms of up to 10 months after being convicted of "homosexual conduct". Moroccan law criminalizes same-sex sexual relations between consenting adults in breach of international human rights standards.

Transitional justice

In August, the Human Rights Advisory Board, charged with continuing the work of the Equity and Reconciliation Commission, said that 23,676 people had received compensation for human rights violations committed during the reign of Hassan II. The Commission, established in 2004 to inquire into enforced disappearances, arbitrary detentions and other grave human rights violations committed between 1956 and 1999, completed its work in 2005. No progress was made towards providing victims and survivors with effective access to justice or holding individual perpetrators to account, issues which were excluded from the remit of the Commission.

Polisario camps

The Polisario Front took no steps to address the impunity of those accused of human rights abuses in the camps in the 1970s and 1980s.

Amnesty International reports

▢ Morocco/Western Sahara: Sahrawi activists sentenced to year in prison (MDE 29/004/2007)

▢ Morocco/Western Sahara: Released demonstrators accused of criticizing the monarchy (MDE 29/008/2007)

MOZAMBIQUE

REPUBLIC OF MOZAMBIQUE

Head of state:	Armando Guebuza
Head of government:	Luisa Diogo
Death penalty:	abolitionist for all crimes
Population:	20.5 million
Life expectancy:	42.8 years
Under-5 mortality (m/f):	171/154 per 1,000
Adult literacy:	38.7 per cent

There was an increase in the number of suspected criminals unlawfully killed by the police. The police were also responsible for other human rights violations including arbitrary arrests and detentions and excessive use of force. Floods, which started in December 2006, displaced an estimated 120,000 people by February 2007. The situation was aggravated by Tropical Cyclone Favio, which hit the southern province of Inhambane causing further damage and destruction to homes.

Background

Mozambique ratified the UN Convention on the Rights of Persons with Disabilities in March.

In November the Assembly General granted itself powers to amend the Constitution in order to postpone the first-ever provincial Assembly elections, scheduled for December.

There was a series of explosions in a military arsenal in the capital, Maputo, and one in the city of Beira. More than 100 people were killed, hundreds more injured and hundreds left homeless. The most serious incident was in March when an explosion at the Malhazine military arsenal in Maputo, which had already exploded in February, killed more than 100 people and injured at least 500. Smaller explosions throughout 2007 resulted in further casualties.

M

Extrajudicial executions

There was an increase in the number of suspected criminals unlawfully killed by the police. Few of these cases were investigated and no police officers were prosecuted for human rights violations. In May the Procurator General announced an investigation into the possible existence of "death squads" within the police force who were responsible for these killings. However, to date, the results of the investigation have not been made public. Police officers arrested for human rights violations in 2006 had still not been tried by the end of 2007.

■ In April, three police officers took Sousa Carlos Cossa, Mustafa Assane Momede and Francisco Nhantumbo from a police station in Laulane, Maputo, to a sports field in the neighbourhood of Costa do Sol where they shot them dead. The officers claimed the men were trying to escape. However, autopsy results revealed that the three had been shot in the back of the neck at close range. The officers were suspended from duty, but the police initially refused to arrest them. They were eventually arrested and detained in May, and alleged that they were carrying out superior orders. The investigation into this case was continuing at the end of 2007.

■ Abrantes Afonso Penicela died in hospital in August one day after being kidnapped, beaten, shot and burned by police officers who left him for dead. Before he died he told his family and a police officer that a group of at least five police officers drove in two cars to his home, with one of his friends. His friend's telephone was used to call him and when he came out of the house, the police officers seized him, put him into one of the cars and gave him a toxic injection. They drove him to a secluded area in Xhinavane, some 120km north of Maputo, where they beat him until he lost consciousness. The police officers shot him in the back of the neck and set fire to him, then left, apparently thinking that he was dead. He managed to crawl to a nearby road, where he was found by local people who contacted his family and took him to Xhinavane Hospital. He was then transferred to Maputo Central Hospital. His family reported the case to police at the 5th police station and an officer went to the hospital to hear his testimony. Police officials informed the family that the case was being investigated, but no one had been arrested by the end of 2007.

Arbitrary arrests and detentions

Cases of arbitrary arrests and detentions by the police were reported. The majority were not investigated by the authorities.

■ In March demonstrators in Maputo demanded the resignation of the Minister of National Defence after a second explosion at the Malhazine military arsenal. They argued that he had failed to move the munitions following an earlier explosion in February. Six demonstrators were arrested and detained without charge at the Alto Mãe police station in Maputo. They were released the next morning. Journalist Celso Manguana was arrested at the Alto Mãe police station when he investigated the six arrests. He was detained for two days, then charged with insulting the authorities and transferred to Maputo Civil Prison. Apparently, he had called the police incompetent when they failed to answer his questions. He was released three days after his arrest and the charges against him were dropped.

Amnesty International visit

🚗 Amnesty International delegates visited Mozambique in September.

MYANMAR

UNION OF MYANMAR

Head of state:	Senior General Than Shwe
Head of government:	General Thein Sein (replaced General Soe Win in October)
Death penalty:	abolitionist in practice
Population:	51.5 million
Life expectancy:	60.8 years
Under-5 mortality (m/f):	107/89 per 1,000
Adult literacy:	89.9 per cent

The human rights situation in Myanmar continued to deteriorate, culminating in September when authorities staged a five-day crackdown on widespread protests that had begun six weeks earlier. The peaceful protests voiced both economic and political grievances. More than 100 people were believed to have been killed in the crackdown, and a similar number were the victims of enforced disappearance. Several thousands were detained in deplorable conditions. The government began prosecutions under anti-terrorism legislation against many protestors. International response to the crisis included a tightening of sanctions by Western countries. At least 1,150 additional political prisoners, some arrested decades ago, remained in detention.

M

A military offensive continued in northern Kayin State, with widespread and systematic violations of international human rights and humanitarian law. In western Rakhine State, the government continued negotiations on a large-scale Shwe gas pipeline, preparations for which included forced displacement and forced labour of ethnic communities.

Background

In September, the government completed drafting guidelines for a new Constitution, the second step in their seven-step "Road Map" for moving toward democracy. In December, the government appointed a 54-member commission of military and other officials to draft the Constitution. The National League for Democracy (NLD), the main opposition party, has not participated in this process since the early stages, and legislation criminalizing criticism of the process remained in place.

The government had ceasefires in place with the armies of all but three ethnic groups, but forced displacement, labour, and portering by the military continued in all seven ethnic states.

Following a visit by the Special Advisor to the UN Secretary-General on Myanmar, the Myanmar authorities met with Daw Aung San Suu Kyi toward starting dialogue on national reconciliation, but the NLD party leader remained under house arrest, where she has been for 12 of the past 18 years.

Freedom of expression

Members of the NLD were subjected to harassment and threats all year, forcing many to resign from the party. Campaigners and demonstrators for democracy were arrested. In particular, the 88 Generation Students group (88G), formed in 2005 by former students active in the pro-democracy uprising in 1988, was targeted and threatened by the authorities.

With the economy already in decline, the government raised fuel prices exponentially in August, triggering peaceful protests across the country. When a group of demonstrating monks in Pakokku was attacked by the authorities in September, monks began leading the protests nationwide, primarily in Yangon, Mandalay, Sittwe, Pakokku, and Myitkyina. The authorities violently cracked down on protesters between 25 and 29 September. Monasteries were raided and closed down, property was destroyed and

confiscated and monks were beaten and detained. Other protesters' homes and hiding places were raided, usually at night, and authorities took friends or relatives as hostages to put pressure on wanted persons and to discourage further dissent. The All Burma Monks Alliance (ABMA), a new group formed by the protests' religious leaders, became a main target. The authorities took photographs and recorded the demonstrations, later warning the public that they had these records and used them in their raids. The internet throughout Myanmar was cut during the crackdown, and when a small group demonstrated at the one-month anniversary of the crackdown journalists were targeted and arrested.

Killings and excessive use of force

Two members of the Human Rights Defenders and Promoters group were attacked by more than 50 people on 18 April in Ayeyarwaddy Division, causing their hospitalization with head injuries. Senior members of the village police and the Secretary of the Union Solidarity Development Association (USDA), a state-sponsored social organization, were reportedly present.

Thirty-one people were confirmed killed during the five-day crackdown on protesters in September although the actual number is likely to be over 100. Rubber bullets and live rounds were fired into crowds of peaceful demonstrators by state security personnel or groups supported by them. The total number of people killed or injured by gunfire was not known. Given eye-witness testimony of shots being fired from atop military trucks and from flyover bridges, as well as the profile of the victims, it is likely that the authorities deliberately targeted real or perceived leaders of the demonstrations.

■ Thet Paing Soe and Maung Tun Lynn Kyaw, students at State High School No. 3 in Yangon, were shot and killed on 27 September.

■ Japanese journalist Kenji Nagai was shot and killed at point-blank range on 27 September.

State security personnel and groups supported by them also beat protesters with sticks. Victims included monks as well as men, women and children who were either directly participating in the protests or onlookers. In some cases these beatings were administered indiscriminately, while in other cases the authorities deliberately targeted individuals, chasing them down to beat them.

■ Ko Ko Win, a 22-year-old NLD member, died as a result of injuries sustained when he was beaten near Sule Pagoda in Yangon on 27 September.

Crimes against humanity

In Kayin State, a military offensive by the *tatmadaw* (Myanmar army) continued on a slightly lesser scale but still included widespread and systematic commission of violations of international human rights and humanitarian law on a scale that amounted to crimes against humanity. Destruction of houses and crops, enforced disappearances, forced labour, displacement and killings of Karen villagers were among the abuses.

Political imprisonment

Even before the large-scale demonstrations began in August, the authorities arrested many well-known opponents of the government on political grounds, several of whom had only been released from prison several months earlier.

Once the protests were underway but before the 25-29 September crackdown, more arrests of NLD and 88G activists took place – many of which were clearly a pre-emptive measure before the crackdown.

Mass round-ups occurred during the crackdown itself, and the authorities continued to arrest protesters and supporters throughout the year, making use initially of a three-week curfew in October. Between 3,000 and 4,000 political prisoners were detained, including children and pregnant women, 700 of whom were believed still in detention at year's end. At least 20 were charged and sentenced under anti-terrorism legislation in proceedings which did not meet international fair trial standards. Detainees and defendants were denied the right to legal counsel.

■ Ko Ko Gyi, Min Ko Naing, Min Zeya, Pyone Cho, and Htay Kywe, all 88G leaders, were released from detention without charge the day before the UN Security Council voted on a resolution on Myanmar in January. The first four were detained again on 21 and 22 August for participating in protests, while Htay Kywe – in hiding for about a month – was captured on 13 October.

■ Zargana, a comedian and former prisoner of conscience, was detained at the start of the crackdown on 25 September. He was released on 17 October, only to be detained again for several hours days later.

■ Mie Mie and Thet Thet Aung, women leaders of the 88G, were arrested on 13 and 19 October, respectively. Both had participated in the demonstrations in August but had been forced into hiding. The latter's husband was also detained, as had been her mother and mother-in-law as hostages.

■ U Gambira, head of the ABMA and a leader of the September protests, was arrested on 4 November and reportedly charged with treason. Two of his family members who were previously detained as hostages remained in detention.

■ Su Su Nway, a member of the youth wing of the NLD, released in July 2006 after being detained for reporting forced labour to the International Labour Organization (ILO), was detained on 13 November while putting up anti-government posters.

■ Eight members of the ethnic Kachin Independence Organization (KIO) were arrested on 24 November reportedly on account of the KIO's refusal to publicly renounce a statement by Daw Aung San Suu Kyi regarding national reconciliation talks.

Prisoners of conscience and senior NLD leaders Daw Aung San Suu Kyi, U Tin Oo, Daw May Win Myint and Dr Than Nyein, all held without charge or trial – the latter two since October 1997 – had their detention extended by the maximum term of one year. Senior ethnic leaders, such as U Khun Htun Oo of the Shan National League for Democracy, also remained in detention. Daw Aung San Suu Kyi was permitted to meet three times with the Special Advisor to the UN Secretary-General on Myanmar, but was not released from house arrest.

Enforced disappearances

During and after the September crackdown, there were at least 72 confirmed cases of enforced disappearance.

Prison conditions

Following a deterioration of prison conditions in 2006, standards fell even further during the crackdown when the authorities detained thousands of people during the five-day period. Large-capacity, informal, secret detention centres were opened which failed to meet international standards on the treatment of prisoners. There was inadequate provision of basic necessities such as food, water, blankets, sleeping space, sanitary facilities, and medical treatment. The International Committee of the Red Cross was denied the opportunity to carry out its core mandate activities in prisons throughout the year.

Torture and other ill-treatment

During the crackdown, some detainees, including Zargana, were held in degrading conditions in rooms designed for holding dogs. Torture and other cruel, inhuman and degrading treatment including beatings in custody were reported. One detainee was made to kneel bare-legged for long periods on broken bricks and also made to stand on tiptoe in an uncomfortable position for long periods (known as the bicycle-riding position). Monks held in detention were stripped of their robes and purposely fed in the afternoon when their religion forbids them to eat.

Deaths in custody

An unconfirmed number of prisoners died in detention after the crackdown in September due to their treatment during interrogation.
■ Venerable U Thilavantha, Deputy Abbot of a monastery in Myitkyina, was beaten to death in detention on 26 September, having also been beaten the night before when his monastery was raided.
■ Ko Win Shwe, an NLD member, died in Plate Myot Police Centre near Mandalay on 9 October. Government authorities cremated his body before notifying his family, thereby preventing any confirmation of reports that he died as a result of torture or other ill-treatment.

From 27 to 29 September, a large number of bodies were reportedly burned at the Ye Way municipal crematorium in Yangon during the night. It was reportedly unusual for the crematorium to function at night, and normal employees were instructed to keep away whilst the facility was operated by state security personnel or state supported groups. On at least one night, reports indicate that some of the cremated had shaved heads or signs of serious injury.

International developments

The UN Security Council voted on a resolution criticizing Myanmar on 12 January, which China and Russia vetoed. On 26 February the Government of Myanmar reached a "Supplementary Understanding"

with the International Labour Organization, designed to provide a mechanism to enable victims of forced labour to seek redress without fear of retaliation.

During the crackdown in late September, the Association of Southeast Asian Nations (ASEAN) issued a critical statement on Myanmar, but allowed Myanmar to sign its new Charter in November. The UN Human Rights Council called a Special Session on 2 October and passed a resolution strongly deploring the crackdown on protesters. In November, the UN Special Rapporteur on the Situation of Human Rights in Myanmar visited Myanmar for the first time since 2003. Following this visit, the UN Human Rights Council passed another resolution, based on his report requesting a follow-up mission. The UN Security Council issued a presidential statement in October that strongly deplored the crackdown, while the UN General Assembly strongly condemned the crackdown in a resolution in December.

The Special Advisor to the UN Secretary-General on Myanmar visited Myanmar in October and November. The USA, EU, and other Western nations enacted or tightened sanctions. In December, India reportedly suspended arms sales and transfers to Myanmar.

Amnesty International visits/reports

🚌 Amnesty International delegates visited the Thailand-Myanmar border in October and November.

▥ Myanmar: Amnesty International calls for comprehensive international arms embargo (ASA 16/016/2007)

▥ Myanmar: No return to "normal" (ASA 16/037/2007)

▥ Myanmar: Arrests continue two months on (ASA 16/041/2007)

M

NAMIBIA

REPUBLIC OF NAMIBIA

Head of state and government:	**Hifikepunye Pohamba**
Death penalty:	**abolitionist for all crimes**
Population:	**2.1 million**
Life expectancy:	**51.6 years**
Under-5 mortality (m/f):	**75/68 per 1,000**
Adult literacy:	**85 per cent**

President Sam Nujoma of the ruling South West Africa People's Organization (SWAPO) retired from active politics at the end of 2007; he was Namibia's first President, serving from 1990 to 2005. An attempt to seek the prosecution of former President Sam Nujoma at the International Criminal Court (ICC) caused a political furore about responsibility for past human rights abuses.

International justice – ICC submission

The National Society for Human Rights (NSHR) requested that the ICC investigate human rights abuses carried out in SWAPO camps in exile prior to independence in 1990, and in the north-east of the country in the 1990s. The NSHR cited Sam Nujoma and retired army Lieutenant General Solomon Hawala as responsible for the detention, torture and enforced disappearance of thousands of SWAPO members in Angola in the 1980s. The submission to the ICC also sought the prosecution of former Defence Minister Erkki Nghimtima for the torture of separatist suspects in Caprivi in 1999 and army Colonel Thomas Shuuya for operating an alleged shoot-to-kill policy in the Kavango region in the 1990s. The NSHR's submission was strongly condemned by the ruling party as a threat to the policy of national reconciliation.

The ICC does not have jurisdiction for crimes committed prior to July 2002 and therefore the NSHR's submission would not be admissible.

Caprivi treason trial

There was no end in sight for the Caprivi treason trial, which started in 2004. Most of the 117 people on trial in connection with a separatist uprising in the Caprivi region in 1999 spent their eighth year in detention. The prosecution was not expected to close its case until late 2008.

In a second parallel treason trial, 10 men were convicted of high treason in August 2007. They were sentenced to between 30 and 32 years' imprisonment. Two suspects were acquitted for lack of evidence. Police officers accused of torturing suspects detained in the wake of the uprising had not faced any formal charges or disciplinary action by the end of the year.

Torture and other ill-treatment

Namibia Police Inspector General Sebastian Ndeitunga called on police officers to respect human rights following a series of media reports about assaults against suspects and deaths in custody. The NSHR reported three deaths in police custody and six cases of police torture of suspects during 2007. There were no independent investigations.

Violence against women and girls

The number of reported rapes in Namibia doubled between 1991 and 2005 – rising from 564 cases to 1,184, according to a study by the Legal Assistance Centre. The study found that the conviction rate for rapists was 16 per cent, while one third of rape cases were withdrawn by the complainant before coming to trial. Police statistics indicated that just over one third of rape victims were under the age of 18.

Freedom of expression under attack

The SWAPO Party Congress passed a resolution calling on the government to set up a body to regulate the media because of the "misuse of the media contrary to national reconciliation and the maintenance of peace and stability". During 2007, SWAPO accused the print media of publishing highly critical articles and letters concerning former President Sam Nujoma.

N

NEPAL

NEPAL

Head of state and government:	Girija Prasad Koirala
Death penalty:	abolitionist for all crimes
Population:	28.2 million
Life expectancy:	62.6 years
Under-5 mortality (m/f):	71/75 per 1,000
Adult literacy:	48.6 per cent

Both the government and the Communist Party of Nepal (Maoist) (CPN (M)) largely failed to implement human rights commitments in the Comprehensive Peace Accord (CPA), signed in November 2006. Elections were postponed twice. Measures to address impunity for past violations and abuses were grossly inadequate. Vulnerable groups, including women and minorities, remained at risk of human rights abuses.

Background

The Seven Party Alliance coalition government, which took office after King Gyanendra's reinstatement of the House of Representatives in April 2006, remained in power. On 15 January the House of Representatives ratified an Interim Constitution which established an interim parliament and facilitated Constituent Assembly elections. The Interim Constitution concentrated significant power in the executive and did not address transitional justice and impunity. The UN Security Council established the UN Mission in Nepal (UNMIN) in January to support the peace process and elections.

On 31 March the Seven Party Alliance and the CPN (M) formed an interim government. The CPN (M) left the government in September after disagreements on declaring Nepal a republic and on the voting system to be used in elections. It rejoined the government in late December following a new 23-point agreement. Elections to the Constituent Assembly, scheduled for June and then November 2007, were due to be held by mid-April 2008.

Concerns were raised by a number of parties outside the Seven Party Alliance about being excluded from the political process. Following a proliferation of armed groups and violent uprisings in the southern Terai region, in particular by members of the Madheshi community, the government conceded to some demands from Madheshi and other minority groups. However, few of these commitments were implemented.

Impunity

Inaction by police and public prosecutors

Police and public prosecutors continued to fail in their duty to investigate and prosecute cases of human rights abuse.

■ In the case of Maina Sunuwar, a 15-year-old girl who died after being tortured in Nepal Army custody in 2004, the army failed to cooperate with the police investigation. A DNA sample collected in March from an exhumed body believed to be Maina's, was reportedly only sent for further analysis in November.

Accountability mechanisms

In June appointments to the Constitutional Council were finalized, enabling new appointments to the National Human Rights Commission (NHRC) in August. There had been longstanding vacancies after Commissioners appointed by the King resigned in July 2006, damaging the NHRC's ability to monitor and investigate human rights violations.

The report of a commission to investigate atrocities committed by the government in April 2006 was finally made public in August. The report recommended action against more than 200 people, as well as the prosecution of at least 20 members of the army, police and armed police force. However, little action was taken to implement the recommendations.

Transitional justice mechanisms

The CPA provided for the establishment of a Truth and Reconciliation Commission (TRC) and in July 2007 the Ministry of Peace and Reconstruction invited comments on a draft bill. The UN, several international NGOs, and local NGOs raised concerns about provisions granting amnesty to perpetrators of gross human rights violations.

On 1 June the Supreme Court ordered the government to investigate all allegations of enforced disappearance, introduce a law making enforced disappearances a criminal offence and set up a Commission of Inquiry to investigate disappearances. However, a three-member Commission set up on 26 July to investigate enforced disappearances during the armed conflict did not meet the standards set out in the Supreme Court judgment. The 23-point agreement of late December included provision for a new Act to establish a commission of inquiry into disappearances and to criminalize enforced disappearances. The Interim Parliament passed a bill to amend Civil Code provisions on abduction.

Abuses by armed groups

The youth wing of the CPN (M), the Young Communist League, reportedly committed a number of human rights abuses including abductions and ill-treatment in captivity, assaults and violent disruption of political activities.

According to UNMIN, almost 3,000 under-18s remained within CPN (M) cantonments (military areas where, under the CPA, the CPN (M) had agreed to be quartered). CPN (M) activists reportedly coerced minors who left the cantonments to return.

Members of the CPN (M) were also accused of abductions, torture and killings, including the killing of journalist Birendra Sah following his abduction on 5 October in Bara District, as well as seizing land and property and extorting money.

A number of armed groups committed human rights abuses. Factions of the Janatantrik Terai Mukti Morcha, an armed Madheshi group which split from the CPN (M) in 2004, were allegedly responsible for unlawful killings, kidnappings and bomb attacks. Armed groups carried out bomb attacks including placing devices at the homes of two human rights activists in March, and a series of bomb blasts in Kathmandu in September which killed three people. On 16 September, the killing of a former armed group member, Mohit Khan, triggered violence between different groups in Kapilbastu and Dang districts, reportedly leaving at least 14 dead and thousands displaced.

Violations by police and security forces

There were a number of reports of torture and rape by police and members of the security forces, some of whom were off-duty at the time. Among those raped were women with mental illnesses and girls.

The majority of torture victims received no compensation. National laws to regulate torture fell short of international standards, and were inadequately implemented.

At least 29 civilians were reportedly killed by the police or armed police force, many allegedly as a result of excessive use of force.

Human rights defenders

Human rights defenders across the country reported threats and attacks by security forces personnel, CPN (M) members and others. At least 17 were reportedly threatened with death, rape, kidnapping and beating if they did not stop carrying out their work for WOREC, a local women's rights NGO.

Minority groups

Following pressure from the Nepal Federation of Indigenous Nationalities (NEFIN), the government signed a 20-point agreement on 7 August, including provision for proportional representation of all indigenous groups and castes. However, implementation was slow.

The Madheshi Janadhikar Forum (also known as Madheshi People's Rights Forum (MPRF)), an umbrella political group, organized regular protests to demand autonomy for the Madheshi people in Terai. Some of the demonstrations became violent. On 21 March in Gaur, 27 individuals, most of them linked to the CPN (M), were killed in clashes with MPRF members. The government formed high-level commissions to probe this incident and others during the Terai unrest, but to Amnesty International's knowledge, the commission had not finalized its investigations by the year's end and no one had been held accountable for these killings.

Freedom of expression

According to the Federation of Nepalese Journalists, between May 2006 and 7 November 2007, 619 journalists and media organizations faced intimidation from the government, CPN (M), and other groups. At least two journalists were killed in 2007 and many others were attacked, abducted and threatened with death.

Refugees and internally displaced people

Tens of thousands of people reportedly remained internally displaced as a result of the conflict that ended in 2006 and ongoing violence in the south. There were concerns about the safety of returnees and about property restitution for internally displaced people, mainly due to threats and attacks by CPN (M) activists.

Approximately 106,000 Bhutanese refugees, forcibly expelled from Bhutan in the early 1990s, remained in camps in Nepal. Refugees were reportedly divided about options for voluntary resettlement in third countries, scheduled to begin in 2008, with some fearing that accepting resettlement would end all hopes for repatriation to Bhutan. There were reports of growing frustrations in the camps, prompted by security concerns and uncertainty about durable solutions in Nepal. One refugee was killed and several injured by the Indian Border Security Force on the border with Nepal in May, when thousands of refugees attempted to enter India in an effort to return to Bhutan.

Amnesty International reports

- Nepal: Reconciliation does not mean impunity: A Memorandum on the Truth and Reconciliation Commission Bill (ASA 31/006/2007)
- Nepal at a crossroads – urgent need for delivery on transitional mechanisms for truth, justice, inclusion and security (ASA 31/011/2007)
- Nepal: Amnesty International urges investigation into killings (ASA 31/001/2007)
- Impunity for enforced disappearances in Asia Pacific Region must end (ASA 01/007/2007)

NETHERLANDS

KINGDOM OF THE NETHERLANDS

Head of state:	Queen Beatrix
Head of government:	Jan Peter Balkenende
Death penalty:	abolitionist for all crimes
Population:	16.4 million
Life expectancy:	79.2 years
Under-5 mortality (m/f):	7/6 per 1,000

Local governments failed to tackle discrimination adequately. Around 30,000 foreign nationals became eligible for residence permits under a new scheme.

Discrimination

Fewer than 10 per cent of municipal governments had addressed discrimination and racism at a local level, either through general policies or action plans, according to Amnesty International research published in April. Fewer than 20 per cent of local authorities had developed policies to combat discrimination and racism in specific areas of concern, such as employment or education.

Although most municipalities indicated that they considered discrimination was not a problem in their community, more than half acknowledged that they lacked sufficient information about its occurrence.

Women

In February the UN Committee on the Elimination of Discrimination against Women expressed concerns about the lack of data on violence against women, and the persistence of racism in the Netherlands, particularly against women and girls.

'War on terror'

In February the "Act on expanding the scope for investigating and prosecuting terrorist crimes" came into force. It provided for an increase, to two years, of the maximum period of pre-trial detention for people charged with terrorism offences.

War crimes allegations

In June the Standing Review Committee on the Intelligence and Security Services and an ad hoc Commission of Inquiry delivered separate reports concluding that allegations of torture of detainees by Dutch Military Intelligence personnel in Iraq in 2003 could not be substantiated.

Neither the Committee nor the Commission interviewed the detainees involved.

Migration

The government postponed the introduction of measures that would make it easier to withdraw residence permits from non-nationals convicted of a crime. However, it announced plans to increase the use of exclusion orders against those designated as "undesirable aliens" for violatons of immigration regulations.

In January the European Court of Human Rights ruled that the decision of the Dutch Immigration Service to expel Somali national Abdirizaq Salah Sheekh to a "relatively safe" area within Somalia, would have violated Article 3 of the European Convention on Human Rights, which forbids torture and other inhuman or degrading treatment, had it been put into effect.

In June a so-called "amnesty" (pardonregeling) scheme came into effect. Under the scheme, residence permits were granted to foreign nationals who had applied for asylum before 1 April 2001, under the former Aliens Act, and had been present in the Netherlands since then, even if their applications had previously been rejected. The scheme also applied, in most cases, to their spouses and children. However, it did not extend to those who had been denied refugee status because they were suspected of having committed crimes against humanity or war crimes, nor to their spouses and children. It was estimated that the amnesty would affect 30,000 people.

NICARAGUA

REPUBLIC OF NICARAGUA

Head of state and government:	Daniel Ortega (replaced Enrique Bolaños in January)
Death penalty:	abolitionist for all crimes
Population:	5.7 million
Life expectancy:	71.9 years
Under-5 mortality (m/f):	39/31 per 1,000
Adult literacy:	76.7 per cent

Local organizations continued to call for better enforcement of health and safety standards for workers and protection of freedom of association. Women's organizations continued to challenge a 2006 law prohibiting abortion in all circumstances. Criminalization of gay and lesbian relationships was ended.

Background

Nicaragua signed the Optional Protocol to the UN Convention against Torture in March.

In a speech before the National Assembly in October, President Ortega reportedly stated that Nicaragua would not sign the Rome Statute of the International Criminal Court.

The National Assembly approved a new Criminal Code which omitted an article criminalizing gay and lesbian relationships which had been present in the previous criminal code.

Health – reproductive rights

Approximately 50 appeals challenging as unconstitutional a law which prohibits therapeutic abortions (abortions carried out where the life, physical or psychological integrity of the women would be at risk if the pregnancy proceeded) were before the Supreme Court of Justice at the end of the year. Despite the fact that judgments on the appeals were pending, the National Assembly approved a new criminal code which incorporated the law.

In 2006, the Inter-American Human Rights Commission's Special Rapporteur on the Rights of Women had noted that therapeutic abortion was a necessary service for women and that its prohibition would put women's lives and heath at risk, in addition to presenting difficulties for medical staff.

■ In April, a 24-year-old woman died of complications related to an ectopic pregnancy. A women's health organization that investigated the case believed that a contributing factor to her death was that life-saving treatment (which Health Ministry regulations explicitly require) was delayed by medical staff because of their concerns over the possibility of being prosecuted for carrying out an abortion.

Workers' rights

Local organizations reported that labour rights continued to be poorly enforced. Workers lodged various complaints with the authorities and human rights organizations regarding working conditions, including adverse effects on health, and freedom of association.

NIGER

REPUBLIC OF NIGER

Head of state:	Mamadou Tandja
Head of government:	Seyni Oumarou (replaced Amadou Hama in June)
Death penalty:	abolitionist in practice
Population:	14.9 million
Life expectancy:	55.8 years
Under-5 mortality (m/f):	245/250 per 1,000
Adult literacy:	28.7 per cent

Civilians suspected of supporting a Tuareg-led armed opposition movement were arrested and arbitrarily detained by security forces under an emergency law. At least 16 civilians were reportedly extrajudicially executed by the army and two journalists, both

prisoners of conscience, were arrested for their alleged links with the Tuareg armed movement.

Background

In February, a Tuareg-led armed opposition movement, the Niger People's Movement for Justice (Mouvement des Nigériens pour la justice, MNJ), based in the Agadez region (in the north of the country) staged an uprising to demand better implementation of the peace agreement that put an end to the Tuareg insurrection in 1995. The demands in particular focused on the social and economic provisions of the agreement. MNJ armed groups attacked mining interests in Niger's mineral-rich north, killed more than 40 soldiers and kidnapped dozens of others.

In August, President Mamadou Tandja, declared a three-month state of emergency in Agadez. This gave additional powers to the security forces to arrest and detain suspects beyond the statutory 48-hours *garde à vue*. In November, the state of emergency was extended for a further three months. Despite calls by civil society and political parties to engage in talks with the MNJ, President Mamadou Tandja dismissed the members of this armed movement as "bandits and drug traffickers".

Arbitrary detention, torture and killings

Dozens of civilians were arrested by the security forces in the Agadez region, and some were allegedly tortured. Many were detained after attacks launched by the MNJ. Most were released after several days or weeks of detention without charge or trial, but at least five, including Issoufou Matachi, a former leader of a Tuareg armed opposition group, were transferred to the capital, Niamey, in September. They remained held at the end of the year.

■ In May, three men, aged between 65 and 85, Abtchaw Kunfi, Abbe Kunfi and Kalakoua Immolane, were killed, reportedly by members of the security forces in Tizirzait. The three were thought to have been killed because one of them had a satellite phone which may have raised suspicions of possible links with the MNJ.

■ In December, seven men travelling to Agadez by car were arrested by members of the security forces and killed. Their bodies bore numerous signs of torture, including cigarette burns, as well as bullet wounds to the face and chest.

Freedom of expression under attack

The authorities imposed a blackout on media coverage of the northern unrest. They suspended Radio France International (RFI) for one month and the bimonthly newspaper *Aïr Info* for three months. They also issued formal warnings to several newspapers, including *L'Evénement*, *Libération* and *L'Opinion*.

Two journalists were arrested and charged with having links with the MNJ. Both were prisoners of conscience, detained solely for their peaceful and legitimate activities as journalists.

■ In September, Moussa Kaka, director of the privately owned Radio Saraouniya station and Niger correspondent of RFI, was arrested in Niamey and charged with "complicity in undermining the State's authority", which is punishable by life imprisonment. This charge was apparently based on the fact that Moussa Kaka had telephone contact with MNJ members while working as a journalist. In November, an investigating judge concluded that the tapped conversations on which the charges were based were obtained illegally. The prosecutor lodged an appeal against this decision which was pending at the end of the year.

■ In October, the editor of *Aïr Info*, Ibrahim Manzo Diallo, was arrested in Niamey and transferred to the Agadez region where he was held incommunicado in army custody for three weeks and then charged with associating with criminal elements for his alleged links with the MNJ.

Amnesty International reports

▥ Niger: Emergency legislation infringes non-derogable human rights (AFR 43/001/2007)

▥ Niger: Extrajudicial executions and population displacement in the north of the country, 19 December 2007

NIGERIA

FEDERAL REPUBLIC OF NIGERIA

Head of state and government: **Umaru Musa Yar'Adua** **(replaced Olusegun Obasanjo in April)**
Death penalty: **retentionist**
Population: **137.2 million**
Life expectancy: **46.5 years**
Under-5 mortality (m/f): **193/185 per 1,000**
Adult literacy: **69.1 per cent**

After elections marred by widespread violence and widely criticized by observers, Umaru Musa Yar'Adua was declared winner of presidential elections in April. The security forces continued to commit human rights violations in the oil-rich Niger Delta with impunity, and few among the local population benefited from the region's oil wealth. The police and security forces extrajudicially executed hundreds of people. Religious and ethnic tensions persisted.

Background

The Independent National Electoral Commission (INEC) disqualified Vice-President Atiku Abubakar as presidential candidate, but the Supreme Court ruled shortly before the 21 April election that he could stand. The presidential, governorship, and state and national assembly elections were widely criticized: the ECOWAS observation mission said there were gross irregularities and the EU observation mission said the elections fell short of basic international and regional standards for democratic elections. Nigerian organizations including the Nigerian Bar Association and the Transition Monitoring Group stated that the elections were not credible. In the months following the elections, five governors were removed from office by the Supreme Court.

The new President's agenda focused on development, power and energy, food, security – including in the Delta – wealth, transport, land and education. He expressed his intention to reform the election process. Mike Okiro was appointed as acting Inspector General of Police (IGP), and confirmed in post in November.

In June the UN International Coordinating Committee of National Institutions for the Promotion and Protection of Human Rights refused to renew Nigeria's membership because of the "irregular removal" of the former executive secretary of the National Human Rights Commission (NHRC), Bukhari Bello, who was dismissed four years before the expiry of his contract.

A Freedom of Information Bill was passed by the previous Senate, but was not signed into law by then President Obasanjo. In September, the new President of the Senate stated that the Senate would re-examine the bill.

The first female speaker of the House of Representatives was elected, but she was forced to resign in October after a corruption scandal.

Seven former state Governors were prosecuted for alleged corrupt practices.

Election violence

Widespread political violence linked to the April elections led to the deaths of at least 200 people. Among those killed were candidates running for political office, their supporters, INEC officials and bystanders. The election period also saw attacks on journalists, intimidation and harassment of voters, and widespread destruction of property. There was also political violence around the local government elections in November and December.

Politicians used armed gangs in their electoral campaigns to attack their opponents and their supporters. The government failed to take effective action to deal with the violence or to address the role of politicians in fomenting it.

President Yar'Adua reportedly ordered the acting IGP to reopen the investigation into several unsolved political killings from previous years, including those of Chief Bola Ige, Marshall Harry, Chief Funsho Williams, Chief Barnabas Igwe and his wife, and Godwin Agbroko.

Death penalty

In December Amnesty International and Nigerian NGOs uncovered evidence of at least seven executions by hanging carried out in 2006 in Kaduna, Jos and Enugu prisons, although on 15 November 2007, a Nigerian government representative at the UN had stated "we have not carried out any capital punishment in recent years in Nigeria". After Amnesty International revealed its findings, a Kano state official confirmed to the BBC that the executions had taken place. Nigeria has not officially reported any executions since 2002.

At the end of 2007, 784 inmates were on death row, more than 200 of whom had been there for over 10 years. In 2007 at least 20 death sentences were handed down.

In May, the Presidential Commission on Reform of the Administration of Justice reiterated the conclusion of the National Study Group on the Death Penalty in 2004 and called for an official moratorium on executions until the Nigerian criminal justice system could ensure fair trials in death penalty cases.

The Minister of Information announced on 17 May that Nigeria had granted an amnesty to all prisoners over 70 and to those 60 or older who had been on death row for 10 years or more. According to the minister, they were to be released before the inauguration of the new President on 29 May. However, the government did not make public whether this had happened, and no reports of releases were received.

On 1 October, on the 47th anniversary of Nigeria's independence, four state governors announced pardons and commutation of sentences for 57 death-row prisoners.

The Niger Delta

The security forces continued to commit frequent human rights violations in the Niger Delta. Violations included extrajudicial executions, torture and destruction of homes. Militants kidnapped dozens of oil workers and their relatives, including children, and attacked many oil installations.

In the run-up to the April 2007 elections, violence in the Delta increased as politicians used armed gangs to attack their opponents. After the elections, the violence, rather than decreasing, increased yet further.

In August, rival gangs clashed in the streets of Port Harcourt, killing at least 30 people and injuring many more, including bystanders. More died when the Joint Military Taskforce (JTF) intervened using helicopters and machine-guns – at least 32 gang members, members of the security forces and bystanders were killed. Following the clashes, a curfew was imposed. Many people with no connection to the gangs were reportedly arrested, although the commander of the JTF denied this. The violence continued and intensified towards the end of the year. By the end of 2007 the JTF was still deployed in the city and the curfew was still in place.

No action was known to have been taken to bring to justice members of the security forces suspected of being responsible for grave human rights violations in previous years. Reports of two judicial commissions of inquiry were not made public. The commissions examined events in February 2005 – a raid by members of the JTF in Odioma, in which at least 17 people were killed, and a protest at the Escravosoil terminal, when soldiers fired on protesters.

People living in the Niger Delta lacked drinking water and electricity, and had few functioning schools or health care centres.

Extrajudicial executions

Members of the police and security forces extrajudicially executed hundreds of people. These included killings by police during routine road checks or for refusing to pay a bribe, shootings of suspected armed robbers on arrest, and extrajudicial executions of detainees in police stations. The military were also frequently involved in extrajudicial executions, especially in the Niger Delta. On 27 March, the UN Special Rapporteur on extrajudicial, summary or arbitrary executions stated at the Human Rights Council that Nigeria must end extrajudicial executions by police.

The acting IGP stated that in the first 100 days he was in office, 1,628 armed robbers were arrested and 785 were killed by the police. NGOs alleged that the number of killings was higher. Despite the alarming number of such killings, the government took very little action to address the problem. On the contrary, the police were encouraged to shoot armed robbers. On 23 October, the Commissioner of Police of the Federal Capital Territory, for example, ordered his men to shoot on sight armed robbers caught in the act of committing a crime.

Torture and other ill-treatment

The culture of impunity for torture and ill-treatment by the police continued. The UN Special Rapporteur on torture concluded in March that torture and ill-treatment were widespread in police custody, and particularly systemic in criminal investigation departments.

Violence against women

In January, the Federal Minister of Women's Affairs expressed the government's intention to promote

N

gender equality as well as the welfare and rights of Nigerian women and children. However, violence against women remained pervasive, including domestic violence, rape and other sexual violence by state officials and private individuals. The underlying factors included the entrenched culture of impunity for human rights violations committed by the police and security forces, and the authorities' consistent failure to exercise due diligence in preventing and addressing sexual violence by both state and non-state actors.

In May a bill to implement the UN Convention on the Elimination of All Forms of Discrimination against Women failed to pass in the National Assembly. Nigeria ratified the Convention in 1985.

The Domestic Violence and Other Related Matters Bill was passed by the Lagos House of Assembly. At federal level, a bill addressing domestic violence failed to become law.

The Nigeria Law Reforms Commission proposed in August that rape should carry a 15-year jail term.

Justice system
Despite several announcements by the government that it would reform prisons, no action was evident.

Of a prison population estimated by the government at 45,000, approximately 25,000 were awaiting trial, many for over five years.

On 10 January, the chairman of the Presidential Committee on Prisons Reform and Rehabilitation made public that N7.8 billion (approximately US$ 6.7million) had been reserved for the first phase of a prison reform program. However, no action to implement the program was reported during the year.

In May the Presidential Committee published a list of 552 inmates recommended for release. They included detainees who had spent over 10 years awaiting trial or whose case files had been lost; inmates with life-threatening diseases; inmates older than 60; and inmates who had spent more than 10 years on death row. The federal government did not follow this recommendation, but announced the release of all inmates older than 70. However, no such releases were reported.

Long delays in the justice system, appalling conditions and severe overcrowding contributed to growing despair and frustration amongst inmates. There were riots in at least three prisons – Kuje, Kano

central and Agodi – in which at least 20 inmates died and many were injured.

Freedom of expression
Human rights defenders and journalists critical of the government continued to face intimidation and harassment. Many were arrested by the State Security Service (SSS) and released after interview.

■ A US citizen and director of a Nigerian-based NGO, a Nigerian staff member and two German journalists were arrested by the SSS in September on suspicion of spying. They were later released without charge.

■ In September a journalist was beaten unconscious when he covered a prison riot in Ibadan.

■ The SSS arrested several journalists in October who had criticized the governors of Borno and Akwa Ibom states.

Forced evictions
Several incidents of forced evictions were reported as well as frequent threats of forced evictions. In July President Yar'Adua ordered that the arbitrary demolition of houses must be stopped and that due process should be followed. The Federal Capital Territory (FCT) however, continued demolishing houses in Abuja. By the end of 2007, there were more than 450 cases pending in the FCT courts objecting to demolitions.

Following the violence between armed gangs in Port Harcourt, the governor decided in August to demolish homes in the waterfront area of the city and replace them with 6,000 new housing units. This plan was suspended in October when the governor was removed.

Discrimination – LGBT rights
A draft bill to punish with a five-year prison term anyone involved in a same-sex marriage, or who aided or abetted such a marriage, was discussed by the National Assembly in February. First introduced in 2006, it was not passed by the National Assembly before the change of government. A similar bill was discussed by the previous Lagos state House of Assembly; the bill did not pass.

■ In April, five women went into hiding in Kano after they were accused by the Hisbah, the Islamic police, of holding a lesbian marriage ceremony in a theatre. The women denied that they had married each other and emphasized that the ceremony was to raise money. Following this incident, the Hisbah demolished several theatres in the city.

■ In August, 18 men were arrested in Bauchi state and charged with belonging to an unlawful society, committing indecent acts and criminal conspiracy.

Amnesty International visits/reports

🚌 Amnesty International delegates visited Nigeria in January, March and July.

📄 Nigeria: Joint statement on ending political violence and human rights abuses as April elections approach (AFR 44/002/2007)

📄 Nigeria: Impunity for political violence in the run-up to the April 2007 elections (AFR 44/004/2007)

📄 Nigeria elections: Attack impunity not human rights! (AFR 44/010/2007)

📄 Nigeria: Are human rights on the political agenda? (AFR 44/013/2007)

📄 Nigeria: Amnesty International delegates say prison conditions 'appalling' (AFR 44/019/2007)

📄 Nigeria: Violence in Port Harcourt escalates (AFR 44/020/2007)

📄 Nigeria: 47th Independence Day – A new opportunity to abolish the death penalty (AFR 44/021/2007)

📄 Nigeria: Local government elections – No lessons learned (AFR 44/027/2007)

📄 Nigeria: Stop executions – Adopt a moratorium, joint public statement by Nigerian NGOs and Amnesty International – 17 December 2007 (AFR 44/030/2007)

PAKISTAN

ISLAMIC REPUBLIC OF PAKISTAN

Head of state:	Pervez Musharraf
Head of government:	Muhammadmian Soomro (caretaker, replaced Shaukat Aziz in November)
Death penalty:	retentionist
Population:	164.6 million
Life expectancy:	64.6 years
Under-5 mortality (m/f):	95/106 per 1,000
Adult literacy:	49.9 per cent

Thousands of lawyers, journalists, human rights activists and political workers were arbitrarily detained. The independence of the judiciary was curbed. Some victims of enforced disappearance reappeared but hundreds remained missing. "Honour" killings and resort to *jirgas* (informal tribal councils) continued. Violence against women continued with impunity. Some 310 people were sentenced to death and at least 135 executed. Members of pro-Taleban and other Islamist groups took hostages, unlawfully killed civilians, and committed acts of violence against women and girls.

Background

Two phases of confrontation between the government and the judiciary dominated the political process. In March, Chief Justice Iftikhar Chaudhry was suspended for alleged misconduct but reinstated by the Supreme Court in July. On 3 November, General Pervez Musharraf declared an emergency, suspended the Constitution and replaced it with the Provisional Constitutional Order (PCO).

After Supreme Court judges sworn in under the PCO confirmed Pervez Musharraf's eligibility as President, he resigned his army office on 28 November and was sworn in as civilian President.

On 15 November a caretaker government was installed in preparation for elections due in January 2008. The emergency was lifted on 15 December and an amended Constitution restored.

Former Prime Ministers Benazir Bhutto and Nawaz Sharif returned from exile to contest elections. In December, Benazir Bhutto was killed during an attack by a suicide bomber following which there was widespread violence. Elections were postponed to February 2008.

In tribal areas bordering Afghanistan and in Swat (North West Frontier Province), Islamist armed groups and local Taleban forces consolidated their control during the year. Military attacks on suspected armed Islamist armed groups (referred to as "militants" by the government) or Taleban targets involved indiscriminate killing of civilians.

Legal and constitutional developments

The PCO suspended fundamental constitutional rights, including safeguards relating to arrest and detention, as well as rights to security of the person, freedom of expression, assembly and association.

In November, judges of the higher judiciary were required to take a new oath of office under the PCO. Twelve of 17 Supreme Court judges, including the Chief Justice, and around 40 judges of the provincial high courts were either not invited to take the oath or refused to do so. The Supreme Court judges who took the PCO oath then validated the PCO and the emergency.

On 10 November, President Musharraf amended the Army Act to allow the court-martial of civilians suspected of treason, sedition and undefined "statements conducive to public mischief" committed since January 2003.

On 21 November, President Musharraf promulgated a constitutional amendment that bars judicial scrutiny of the emergency, the PCO and any actions taken during the emergency.

Hundreds of cases before the Supreme Court and the four provincial High Courts were delayed as lawyers boycotted courts presided over by judges sworn in under the PCO.

Arbitrary arrests and detention

During the period of emergency rule, the right to freedom of assembly was curbed by rigorous enforcement of Section 144 of the Code of Criminal Procedure, which prohibits the gathering of more than four people in public without police authorization. Most of the detainees were held without reference to any law; others for breach of Section 144 and for threatening the maintenance of public order. Some were held in administrative detention under the Maintenance of Public Order Ordinance (MPO). A number of protesters were charged with terrorism offences or sedition.

Between March and July, hundreds of lawyers and political activists supporting the Chief Justice were detained. Elderly party workers were dragged from their homes in the night and activists were detained in prisons far from their homes. In the run-up to the expected return of former Prime Minister Nawaz Sharif in September, hundreds of party workers were arrested.

Following the declaration of an emergency, several of the dismissed judges, including the Chief Justice, were placed under de facto house arrest and denied access to family and friends, without reference to any law. Thousands of lawyers and other human rights defenders were detained, including some 55 human rights activists who had gathered at the office of the NGO Human Rights Commission of Pakistan (HRCP) in Lahore on 4 November. HRCP chairperson and UN Special Rapporteur for freedom of religion, Asma Jahangir, was detained in her home under a 90-day MPO detention order that was lifted on 16 November. A 90-day detention order issued against Hina Jilani,

UN Special Representative of the Secretary General on Human Rights Defenders, was not enforced after she returned to the country.

■ On 5 November, Baloch nationalist leader Hasil Bizenjo; Ayub Qureshi, provincial chief of the Baloch National Party; Yusuf Mastikhan, Vice President of the National Workers Party; trade unionist leaders Liaquat Sahi; and Farid Awan were arrested in Karachi on charges of sedition and rioting, after making speeches against the imposition of the emergency. They were released on bail on 22 November, but charges remained pending.

Torture and other ill-treatment

Many of those arbitrarily arrested were reportedly tortured or otherwise ill-treated, including by sleep deprivation and denial of urgently needed medical treatment. Torture and other ill-treatment were routinely used against criminal suspects.

■ Mohammad Shahid Rind was arrested on 28 July and reportedly tortured by police who allegedly mistook him for the brother of a wanted criminal. Sindh High Court ordered his release and medical treatment, and instituted an inquiry into his arrest and torture. He was still in detention at the end of the year.

Enforced disappearance

The Supreme Court heard petitions of more than 400 people subjected to enforced disappearance in the context of the government's "war on terror" and other national security campaigns. Almost 100 of the disappeared were subsequently located. Some of those who reappeared had been detained on apparently false charges.

On 5 October, then Chief Justice Iftikhar Choudhry asserted that there was "irrefutable proof" that the missing people were in the custody of secret agencies and that those responsible would be prosecuted. He ordered all those still unaccounted for to be brought before the Court. Hearings continued until 2 November, when the Court adjourned proceedings until 13 November. However, following the imposition of emergency on 3 November and the dismissal of several Supreme Court judges, no further disappearance hearings were held.

The fate and whereabouts of hundreds of people remained unclear and they were feared to be at risk of torture and other ill-treatment.

P

■ Saud Memon, who allegedly owned the shed where abducted US journalist Daniel Pearl was murdered in 2002, was found near his Karachi home on 28 April 2007. He had lost his memory, was unable to speak and weighed only 36kg. He died on 18 May in hospital. He was believed to have been arrested by US Federal Bureau of Investigation (FBI) agents in South Africa in March 2003. It remained unclear where and in whose custody he was subsequently held.

Unlawful transfers of victims of enforced disappearance to countries where they could be at risk of torture and other ill-treatment continued.

■ Osman Alihan, an ethnic Uighur from the Xinjiang Uighur Autonomous Region (XUAR) of China, was held at an unknown place of detention after arrest in Rawalpindi on 4 July. He was wanted by the Chinese authorities for alleged membership of the banned East Turkistan Islamic Movement. He was unlawfully handed over to China at the end of July. His fate remained unknown. Another Uighur, Ismail Semed, was executed in the XUAR on 8 February 2007 for "attempting to split the motherland" and other offences. He had been forcibly returned to China from Pakistan in 2003 (see China entry).

Excessive use of force

During several waves of protests, security forces used unnecessary or excessive force against peaceful demonstrators.

■ On 29 September, over 80 lawyers and political workers protesting in Islamabad against forthcoming presidential elections were injured, some seriously, when police officers, many in plain clothes, beat them with batons. On 1 October, the Supreme Court held the Islamabad Police Chief responsible for ordering disproportionate force and ordered his immediate suspension. On 23 October, the Supreme Court ruled that the deployment of police officers in plain clothes was illegal.

After failing to arrest and seek to prosecute clerics and students of the Red Mosque in Islamabad who abducted, beat and threatened people whom they considered in breach of Islamic norms, security forces in July first laid siege to, then stormed the mosque. At least 100 people were estimated to have been killed. Among the dead were unarmed women and children possibly used as human shields by those barricaded in the mosque. The clerics and students were earlier told by President Musharraf that they would be killed if they did not surrender.

Police were complicit in violent attacks allegedly carried out by political allies of the government, particularly during a lawyers' campaign against the Chief Justice's suspension in March. On 12 May, at least 40 people holding a welcoming rally for the Chief Justice in Karachi were killed in such attacks. Police reportedly failed to protect demonstrators, including lawyers, and to prevent the violence.

In the tribal areas and in Swat, the army said they had killed hundreds of "militants", but local people said that many of the victims were women and children. The military carried out several aerial bombardments of villages, reportedly resulting in the deaths of many unarmed civilians. Few attempts were made to arrest and try alleged "militants".

■ On 7 October, fighter jets bombed supposed "militant hideouts" in North Waziristan, killing some 250 people, reportedly including civilians. Thousands of villagers reportedly fled the area.

Freedom of expression curtailed

Many journalists covering protest rallies were beaten, threatened and detained. After the imposition of emergency rule, independent television and radio news channels were closed. New laws arbitrarily restricting print and electronic media were issued in November. Independent Pakistani television channels were prohibited from broadcasting within Pakistan unless they signed a Code of Conduct restricting criticism of the government.

Abuses by armed groups
Hostage-taking and killings

Members of Islamist armed groups were responsible for hostage-taking, killing of captives and other unlawful killings. After the Red Mosque siege, suicide attacks against government and army installations increased, leading to some 400 deaths. In July alone, 194 people, including many civilians, were killed in 13 suicide attacks.

Members of Islamist groups carried out execution-style killings of dozens of people deemed to have contravened Islamic law or to have co-operated with the government, in some cases after hearings before Islamic councils (*shura*).

In August, a pro-Taleban group in South Waziristan released a video that appeared to show a teenage boy beheading a captured member of a pro-government paramilitary force. The video also raised concerns that the group was using children to carry out grave human rights abuses.

Violence against girls and women

Girls and women were increasingly targeted for abuses in the areas along the border with Afghanistan under Taleban control.

■ In Bannu, North West Frontier Province, the bodies of two women were found in September. A note attached to one woman's body said that she had been killed to punish her for immoral activities.

Discrimination against religious minorities

The authorities failed to protect religious minorities.

■ In September, two Ahmadi doctors were killed in Karachi allegedly on account of their minority faith. No one was arrested.

Prosecutions under blasphemy laws continued and many people were sentenced to death.

■ Younus Masih, a Christian, was sentenced to death for blasphemy by a court in Lahore on 30 May in a trial that was reportedly unfair. He was falsely accused of making derogatory remarks against the prophet of Islam at a religious service in 2005. He was a prisoner of conscience.

Violence against women

Custodial violence, including rape, continued. The state failed to prevent and prosecute violence in the home and community, including mutilation, rape and "honour" killings. The NGO Aurat Foundation said that in the first 10 months of 2007 in Sindh alone, 183 women and 104 men were murdered for supposedly harming family "honour". Despite a ban on *jirgas* by the Sindh High Court in 2004, official support continued. In November, caretaker Minister for Information Nisar Memon stated that *jirgas* were a reality and should be "brought into the mainstream".

The higher judiciary on several occasions ordered the prosecution of people responsible for *swara*, the handing over of a girl or woman for marriage to opponents to settle a dispute. The practice was made punishable with up to 10 years' imprisonment by a 2005 law, but continued to be widespread.

Children's rights ignored

The number of juvenile courts remained inadequate. Children continued to be tried and detained along with adults. Children were detained under the collective responsibility clause of the Frontier Crimes Regulation in the tribal areas for offences committed by others, a clear violation of the prohibition in international law of collective punishment.

Death penalty

Some 307 people were reportedly sentenced to death, mostly for murder. At least 135 people were executed, including at least one child offender.

■ Muhammad Mansha was executed in Sahiwal in November. He had been sentenced to death in March 2001 for a murder committed when he was around 15 years old.

Cruel, inhuman and degrading punishments

The Hudood ordinances continued to provide for flogging and amputation, but no such punishments were carried out in 2007. In June, the Federal Shariat Court set aside a sentence of amputation of the right hand and left foot imposed in January 2006 on Afghan national Ajab Khan for robbery. The Court ruled that mandatory punishments such as amputation cannot be imposed under Islamic law unless the reliability of witnesses was ascertained.

Amnesty International visit/reports

🚌 An Amnesty International delegation visited Pakistan in December.

📄 Pakistan: Fatal erosion of human rights safeguards under emergency (ASA 33/040/2007)

📄 Pakistan: Amnesty International's call to political parties to commit themselves to uphold a 12-point plan on human rights (ASA 33/052/2007)

P

PALESTINIAN AUTHORITY

President:	**Mahmoud Abbas**
Prime Minister:	**Salam Fayyad (replaced Isma'il Haniyeh in June)**
Death penalty:	**retentionist**
Population:	**3.9 million**
Life expectancy:	**72.9 years**
Under-5 mortality (m/f):	**23/18 per 1,000**
Adult literacy:	**92.4 per cent**

Inter-factional political violence between Palestinians escalated dramatically in the first half of 2007 and led to different factions governing the West Bank and Gaza Strip in the second half of the year. Clashes between security forces and armed groups loyal to the Fatah party of Palestinian Authority (PA) President Mahmoud Abbas and to the Islamic Resistance Movement (Hamas) of Prime Minister Isma'il Haniyeh caused hundreds of deaths. In June, after Hamas forcibly seized control of the Gaza Strip, President Abbas dismissed Prime Minister Haniyeh's government, declared a state of emergency and established an emergency government which excluded Hamas members. Both factions committed grave human rights abuses, including arbitrary detention and torture.

Air strikes and other attacks by Israeli forces killed hundreds of Palestinians and destroyed more than 100 Palestinian homes and properties. Economic and social problems caused by decades of Israeli occupation, military attacks, stifling blockades and punitive economic measures in the Occupied Palestinian Territories (OPT) grew more severe. The Israeli blockade on the Gaza Strip was tightened to an unprecedented level, trapping its entire 1.5 million population and forcing most Gazans into poverty and dependency on international aid that sometimes could not reach them (see Israel-OPT entry).

Palestinian armed groups killed 13 Israelis, seven of whom were civilians; Israeli forces killed some 370 Palestinians, almost half of them civilians and including some 50 children.

Background

Armed clashes between Palestinian factions and the deepening economic crisis both intensified in the first half of the year, particularly in the Gaza Strip, where Israeli and international economic sanctions had been imposed following the Hamas victory in the PA elections in 2006. The deteriorating economic conditions for Palestinians were exacerbated by the Israeli authorities' further tightening of their blockade on the Occupied Palestinian Territories (OPT) and frequent Israeli military attacks on, and destruction of, Palestinian civil infrastructure.

In March 2007 Fatah and Hamas leaders agreed to end the in-fighting and formed a unity government led by Prime Minister Haniyeh. Armed clashes soon resumed, however, and intensified. On 14 June Hamas forces and their militias seized control of all Fatah-controlled PA security installations and government buildings in the Gaza Strip. The same day, President Abbas dismissed the unity government and established an emergency government based in the West Bank. He appointed Salam Fayyad as Prime Minister. Hamas refused to recognize the emergency government and set up a Hamas de facto administration which governed the Gaza Strip for the rest of the year. The EU, the USA and other international donors tightened sanctions on the Hamas de facto administration in Gaza and resumed direct financial aid to the PA emergency government in the West Bank. The Israeli government returned part of the previously confiscated tax revenue to the PA emergency government and simultaneously reinforced its blockade of the Gaza Strip. Among other measures, it refused to allow medical supplies to enter Gaza or patients in need of urgent medical treatment to leave. Some 40 patients died as a result.

In November the Israeli government and the PA President and emergency government participated in a US-sponsored international meeting in Annapolis, USA, from which Hamas was excluded. The meeting was aimed at resuming peace negotiations but no tangible progress was evident by the end of 2007. Contrary to their pre-meeting undertakings, the Israeli authorities did not lift their movement restrictions on Palestinians in the OPT and continued to expand Israeli settlements in the West Bank.

Throughout the year the main Palestinian armed groups – Islamic Jihad, Popular Resistance Committees (PRC), al-Aqsa Martyrs' Brigades

P

(Fatah's armed wing) and the 'Izz al-Din al-Qassam Brigades (Hamas' armed wing) – frequently fired homemade "qassam" rockets from the Gaza Strip into southern Israel, killing two Israeli civilians and injuring several others.

Hamas' takeover in the Gaza Strip

In June, after Hamas forces and militias seized control of PA security installations and institutions, President Abbas ordered all PA security forces and judicial institutions in the Gaza Strip to suspend operation. The Hamas de facto administration filled the resulting legal and institutional vacuum by setting up security and judicial bodies. These lacked appropriately trained personnel, accountability mechanisms and human rights safeguards.

Some 40,000 members of the PA security forces and civil servants were dismissed by the PA emergency government because they were suspected of working for institutions controlled by Hamas in the Gaza Strip. Tens of thousands of others, who had not been paid in full for more than a year, received their salaries from the West Bank-based PA emergency government on condition that they did not continue to work in the Gaza Strip.

Hamas forces frequently harassed former members of the security forces and other officials loyal to the PA emergency government. On 16 August Hamas forces briefly detained the PA Attorney General and ordered him not to undertake any activities. On 4 September the Hamas administration announced the establishment of an alternative Supreme Justice Council to appoint judges to the Justice Department in the Gaza Strip – a move which contradicted the principle of the independence of the judiciary and breached Palestinian laws.

The Fatah-Hamas divisions exacerbated the huge obstacles faced by the inhabitants of Gaza when seeking justice or redress from the PA's malfunctioning judicial and security institutions.

In June, after Hamas' forcible takeover in Gaza, Fatah gunmen carried out retaliatory attacks against known or suspected Hamas supporters in the West Bank, abducting and assaulting several people and burning down dozens of properties. They did so with impunity, often in the presence of PA security forces who failed to intervene and uphold the law.

Killings, lawlessness and impunity
January-June

The climate of lawlessness and impunity evident in previous years intensified in the first half of 2007 as inter-factional fighting escalated between Fatah and Hamas militants in the Gaza Strip.

Some 300 Palestinians were killed in the inter-factional fighting. Most were members of rival security forces and militias but dozens were unarmed civilian bystanders. Gunmen carried out attacks and gun battles in densely populated residential areas, including in and around hospitals, in reckless disregard for the lives of residents and passers-by.

Members of PA security forces and armed groups affiliated to Fatah and Hamas carried out unlawful killings and abductions of rivals with impunity. In June Hamas gunmen hunted down members of the PA security forces and Fatah's militia, the al-Aqsa Brigades, killing some and shooting others in the legs. Fatah gunmen also carried out similar attacks against Hamas members, although on a lesser scale.

■ Mohammed Swerki, a cook with the Presidential Guard, was thrown to his death from a building in Gaza City on 10 June, after he and a colleague were captured by Hamas gunmen when they went to the wrong building to deliver food. Fatah gunmen retaliated by abducting suspected Hamas sympathizer Husam Abu Qinas when he was returning home from work and throwing him to his death from another building.

■ A peaceful march calling for an end to the Fatah-Hamas clashes, organized by left-wing parties and others on 13 June in Gaza, was fired on. Three protestors were killed: Taghreed Salah al-'Alia , Shadi Tayseer al-'Ijla and Mohammad Mahmoud Adas.

June-December

Lawlessness, unlawful killings and abductions in the Gaza Strip decreased significantly after Hamas seized control in June. However, Hamas forces and militias frequently attacked Fatah activists and other critics and demonstrators, as well as journalists who covered such attacks. Meanwhile, members of Hamas forces were at times targeted in bomb attacks which Hamas blamed on Fatah activists.

■ On 12 November at least six demonstrators were killed and dozens were injured when Hamas forces fired on protesters at a mass rally organized by Fatah activists to commemorate the third anniversary of the death of Yasser Arafat, former PA President and Fatah chairman.

P

In the West Bank, PA forces attacked demonstrators on several occasions.

■ On 27 November in Hebron, one protester was shot dead at a demonstration against the Israeli-PA meeting in Annapolis.

The PA emergency government, under intense pressure from Western donors, took some steps to curb the lawlessness which had become rife in previous years, notably frequent abductions, assaults and other attacks by the al-Aqsa Brigades. In October the PA security forces implemented a set of measures devised by US security envoy General Keith Dayton to improve security in Nablus, an al-Aqsa Brigades stronghold. This led to a significant decrease, though not a total cessation, of attacks by such groups, but the PA failed to bring to justice al-Aqsa Brigades militants responsible for killings, abductions and other attacks.

Arbitrary detention, torture and other ill-treatment

Gaza

After mid-June, Hamas forces and militias detained some 1,500 people in a politically motivated detention campaign. Hundreds of people, mostly Fatah supporters, were arbitrarily detained for participating in non-violent demonstrations. Most were released within 48 hours but were required as a condition of release to sign pledges not to participate in further protests or other opposition. In many cases Hamas forces also demanded that detainees pay "fines". Those detained were mostly held in former PA security installations and other locations which were not authorized to be used as detention facilities under Palestinian law.

Many detainees alleged that they were tortured or otherwise ill-treated by being beaten, tied in painful positions (*shabeh*) and threatened. Some said they were told that they would be shot in the legs. At least two detainees – Walid Abu Dalfa and Fadhel Dahmash – died in detention apparently as a result of torture or other ill-treatment.

■ Tariq Mohammed Asfour, a former policeman, was detained by Hamas forces and militias in late June. He was beaten for six hours with metal wires, sticks and a shovel, and had nails driven into his shins with a hammer.

■ Wa'el Ghalban, a Fatah activist, was severely beaten on the feet and other parts of the body by Hamas forces when he was detained overnight in November.

West Bank

After mid-June, PA security forces launched a crackdown on Hamas supporters throughout the West Bank and arrested some 1,500 people. Most were released within a few days without charge and often on condition that they denounced Hamas and pledged not to support it. Scores of others were detained for several weeks or months but then released uncharged.

From September on, however, Israeli forces frequently arrested those released from detention by the PA. Most detentions by the PA were carried out by security forces, notably Preventive Security, that were not authorized by Palestinian law to detain suspects, and detainees were also held in unauthorized places of detention. Families were rarely notified of detainees' arrests or whereabouts and in some cases security forces moved detainees from one place to another to prevent them appearing before a judge or to avoid complying with judges' orders to release them. Detainees were often not brought before a judge within the time required under Palestinian law.

Reports of torture and other ill-treatment, rare at first, became more common from August, with detainees reporting that they had been tied in deliberately painful positions (*shabeh*). Most victims, however, were reluctant to complain for fear that they would be rearrested by PA forces or detained by Israeli forces.

■ Ahmad Doleh was arrested by PA forces in Nablus in early July and detained for five months without charge or trial in various places. Within days of his release from PA detention in early December he was arrested by Israeli forces.

■ Hussein al-Sheikh, a lawyer from the Bethlehem area, was detained by PA forces for 13 days in September and then released without charge, but arrested by Israeli forces a week later and placed in administrative detention without charge or trial.

Impunity

Neither the PA in the West Bank nor Hamas in the Gaza Strip took any credible measures to ensure accountability for members of their security forces and militias, who continued to enjoy impunity for human rights abuses they committed, including unlawful killings, hostage-taking, arson and other attacks on people and property.

Abuses by armed groups

Palestinian armed groups carried out indiscriminate attacks on Israeli civilians. Thirteen Israelis, including seven civilians, were killed in such attacks, the lowest annual fatality figure since the outbreak of the intifada in 2000.

Palestinian armed groups frequently launched home-made "qassam" rockets from the Gaza Strip towards the nearby Israeli town of Sderot and surrounding areas, killing two Israelis and injuring several others.

■ Shirel Friedman and Oshri Oz were killed in Sderot by "qassam" rocket attacks on 21 and 27 May.

Suicide bombings and shooting attacks almost ceased in 2007. One suicide attack was carried out by an Islamic Jihad group in Eilat on 29 January.

■ Emile Ameliach, Israel Zamalloa and Michael Ben Sa'don were killed in a suicide bomb attack on a bakery in Eilat on 29 January.

In the first half of the year Palestinian armed groups continued to abduct members of rival groups and foreign nationals. Several Palestinian hostages were killed (see above), though most were released unharmed.

■ In March the Army of Islam, a small and previously little known group, abducted British journalist Alan Johnston in Gaza City and held him for 114 days, threatening to kill or harm him on several occasions. He was released in early July following pressure from Hamas.

■ In June Hamas and the PRC released an audio recording of Gilad Shalit, the Israeli soldier they captured in June 2006, but continued to refuse him access to the International Committee of the Red Cross (ICRC) or any communication with his family.

Violence against women

More than 10 women were killed in alleged "honour killings" and scores of others were killed or injured in attacks by Israeli forces or in inter-factional fighting between rival Palestinian groups.

■ Nisreen Mohammad Abu Bureik and In'am Jaber Daifallah were killed in July and August respectively in Gaza. According to their families, they were both killed by male relatives in so-called "honour" crimes.

Women's lives were made even more difficult by the deteriorating humanitarian conditions, and the Israeli blockades on the OPT further restricted their access to health and other crucial services. At least

three women gave birth at Israeli military checkpoints after they were prevented from passing through to reach nearby hospitals.

Amnesty International visits/reports

Amnesty International delegates visited Gaza and the West Bank in June-July and in December.

Occupied Palestinian Territories: Torn apart by factional strife (MDE 21/020/2007)

Palestinian Authority: New government must end impunity for lawlessness (MDE 21/002/2007)

Palestinian Authority: New unity government must put civilian protection above politics (MDE 21/001/2007)

PAPUA NEW GUINEA

PAPUA NEW GUINEA

Head of state:	Queen Elizabeth II, represented by Paulias Matane
Head of government:	Michael Somare
Death penalty:	abolitionist in practice
Population:	6.1 million
Life expectancy:	56.9 years
Under-5 mortality (m/f):	82/93 per 1,000
Adult literacy:	57.3 per cent

High levels of violent crime plagued the country. Public faith in the law-enforcement system did not improve. Violence against women and children remained endemic. Civil society responses to these problems became increasingly prominent.

Background

Parliamentary elections were marred by attacks against electoral officials and police, as well as fatal clashes between supporters of rival candidates. The National Alliance Party (NAP) returned the highest number of candidates and formed a coalition government with 12 other political parties and independent MPs.

Long-running tribal conflicts worsened in many parts of the country, with Enga and Western Highlands among the worst affected.

P

While a year-long state of emergency in the Southern Highlands was lifted in August, security concerns remained high in Bougainville with weapons disposal a pressing issue for the Autonomous Government.

Proliferation of illegal small arms

High levels of violent crime, fuelled by the unchecked proliferation of illegal firearms, showed no signs of abating, deepening the sense of fear and insecurity in the population.

A broad-based civil society advocacy initiative known as the Coalition to Stop Guns Violence was formed in response to government inaction over implementing the 2005 National Gun Committee's recommendations to combat the proliferation and use of illegal firearms.

Police and security forces

The police appeared to have neither the ability nor the will to guarantee security. Investigations into crimes were not routine; arrests of perpetrators of violations were rare. Many victims of crime were denied justice as cases collapsed under a lack of police evidence or incompetent prosecution.

In an attempt to raise public confidence in the police, an agreement was signed in June between the police force and the Ombudsman Commission to form a Police Complaints Ombudsman. The Defence Force and the Correctional Services were in line to set up similar accountability mechanisms.

Violence against women

Gender-based violence, including sexual violence, was endemic in the home and in the community. In the context of the elections, women were traded for guns while gang rapes were reported among warring tribes.

Despite almost daily condemnations of abuses against women in the press, including a string of vehement statements by key government leaders and law enforcement officials, few incidents were investigated. Alleged perpetrators, including policemen and others in powerful positions, escaped justice and little concrete action to fight impunity materialised.

In August, the Supreme Court turned down an appeal by a re-elected MP against a 12-year sentence for rape. The Electoral Commission had earlier been criticized for effectively condoning rape by accepting the convicted MP's nomination.

Women human rights defenders were increasingly active and organized in their advocacy. In a high-profile silent protest action on 9 October, more than 100 black-clad women activists with white ribbons, together with the Minister for Community Development and the only female MP, Dame Carol Kidu, petitioned the parliament to address violence against women.

Violence against women was seen as a key reason behind the HIV/AIDS epidemic, which, in turn, is fuelling more abuses against women, as HIV/AIDS deaths were sometimes believed to be the result of sorcery. Alleged witches were tortured and killed by mobs who believed they were responsible for deaths.

PARAGUAY

REPUBLIC OF PARAGUAY

Head of state and government:	**Nicanor Duarte Frutos**
Death penalty:	**abolitionist for all crimes**
Population:	**6.4 million**
Life expectancy:	**71.3 years**
Under-5 mortality (m/f):	**46/36 per 1,000**
Adult literacy:	**93.5 per cent**

Indigenous communities held protests against the extreme levels of poverty they continued to experience and the government's failure to address their needs. Members of armed civilian patrols and the police were accused of ill-treating peasants during evictions. There were reports of harassment of journalists. A bill regarding maternal health was rejected by the Senate.

Background

In October the Supreme Court of Justice quashed the 10-year prison sentence of army commander and then presidential candidate General Lino Oviedo. He had been sentenced in 1998 for an attempted coup in 1996 against the then President Juan Carlos Wasmosy. The ruling restored Lino Oviedo's rights to vote and to stand for public office.

Discrimination – Indigenous rights

Throughout the year Indigenous communities, including the Enxet, Mbyá, Aché and Tobas communities, protested outside government offices in the capital, Asunción. They called for free access to land, guaranteed to Indigenous communities in law. They were also protesting at the lack of educational programmes and extreme poverty in their communities.

Among the concerns expressed by the UN Committee on Economic, Social and Cultural Rights in November were the increasing numbers of forced evictions of peasant families and Indigenous communities. It established that "nearly 45 per cent of Indigenous communities have no legal titles to their ancestral lands". It recommended, among other things, that steps be taken by the state to reduce the level of poverty and to increase efforts to demarcate Indigenous land and ancestral territories.

Arbitrary detentions and ill-treatment

Peasant leaders complained before the Congressional Permanent Commission that police and armed civilian patrols operating in the Department of Itapúa were responsible for arbitrary detention and ill-treatment.
■ In April, members of the police and armed civilians entered the community of Paraguái Pyahu, in San Pedro Department, and beat and arrested five peasants. They were allegedly charged with environmental crimes and the illegal cultivation of marijuana. The following day, three detainees were released by the local prosecutor who apologized for the incident; one was subsequently released and one remained in detention at the end of the year.

Maternal health

In November the Chamber of Senators rejected a bill on maternal, sexual and reproductive health. This bill aimed to promote government policies to reduce maternal mortality and provide better health care to women during pregnancy and childbirth.

Freedom of expression – journalists

The Executive Committee of the Paraguayan Union of Journalists protested against a wave of repression and harassment against journalists and accused the authorities of attempting to intimidate and silence critics.
■ In June, Vladimir Jara and Victor Benitez, journalists for Radio Chaco Boreal, reported receiving death threats and having their phones illegally tapped after reporting on alleged corruption within Paraguay's National Anti-Drug Secretariat. The journalists asked the district attorney to investigate the incidents. It was not known if any such investigation had been initiated by the end of the year.
■ In August 2007, Maria Bartola Fernández, coordinator of Radio Tekoporã, in Puerto Presidente Franco, Alto Paraná Department, reported receiving death threats from members of the regional government which she believed were linked to her criticism of the authorities for failing to provide basic services. An investigation was initiated after she made a statement before the National Congress and the Human Rights Department of the Senate.

PERU

REPUBLIC OF PERU

Head of state and government:	Alan Garcia Peréz
Death penalty:	abolitionist for ordinary crimes
Population:	28.8 million
Life expectancy:	70.7 years
Under-5 mortality (m/f):	50/41 per 1,000
Adult literacy:	87.9 per cent

Important steps were taken to bring to justice those responsible for human rights violations during the years of armed conflict (1980-2000). Environmentalists and community leaders campaigning against mining projects continued to be at risk of harassment and attack. Women living in poor marginalized communities continued to face discrimination in accessing maternal health services.

Background

A bill on international co-operation which would have placed NGOs under closer state scrutiny was ruled unconstitutional.

In January Congress rejected a bill to modify the use of the death penalty in terrorism-related cases. Two other bills on the death penalty remained pending before Congress at the end of the year.

P

Teachers, health professionals and miners went on a series of strikes throughout the year to protest against government economic and labour policies.

In August, a set of legislative decrees to combat organized crime was issued. There were concerns that the decrees could be used to criminalize legitimate social protest.

Small groups of members of the armed opposition group Shining Path (Sendero Luminoso) continued to operate in some areas. Peasant farmers in Ayacucho Department continued to be falsely charged with terrorism-related offences for alleged involvement in attacks carried out by Shining Path.

Impunity – justice for past violations

Former President Alberto Fujimori was extradited to Peru from Chile in September. He faced charges including the killing of 15 people in 1991 and the enforced disappearance and killing of nine students and a professor in 1992. His trial was continuing at the end of the year.

An effective programme for protecting those who survived human rights abuses during the 20-year armed conflict, their relatives as well as witnesses and lawyers had not been implemented by the end of the year.

Progress on the implementation of the recommendations of the Truth and Reconciliation Commission remained limited. In August, the Human Rights Ombudswoman highlighted that only one new case had been opened during the first six months of the year and that 28 out of the 47 cases filed before the Public Ministry by the Commission remained pending.

The National Council for Reparations, established in 2006 to oversee reparations to victims of human rights abuses documented by the Commission, began its work. By the end of the year it had registered cases in more than 800 communities.

In November, the Supreme Court of Justice ruled that those responsible for the crime of enforced disappearance include not only those who carry out the killing and hide the body, but also those in the chain of command. In its ruling the Supreme Court confirmed the sentences of two military officers for the 1991 enforced disappearance of four people in Ayacucho Department.

■ The Inter-American Court of Human Rights ruled in July that the state was responsible for the killing of Saúl Cantoral Huamaní and Consuelo Trinidad García Santa Cruz in February 1989 by members of the military.

Prison conditions

Challapalca Prison, which is situated over 4,600m above sea level, reopened in October. Twenty-four prisoners were immediately transferred there. The prison had been closed in 2005 following national and international pressure, including recommendations by the Inter-American Commission on Human Rights, that it be closed because its inaccessibility seriously limits prisoners' rights to maintain contact with the outside world, including with relatives, lawyers and doctors.

Health – maternal health in rural areas

In April, the government stated that it was taking steps to ensure that women would no longer be fined for failing to attend antenatal appointments and that certificates of live birth issued by health centres would not be withheld from those who gave birth at home.

A report issued by the Ombudswoman's Office in May highlighted the continuing economic and geographic barriers faced by women in rural areas in accessing health care, the lack of accessible information on health services and the absence of culturally appropriate health provision.

In February the UN Committee on the Elimination of Discrimination against Women recommended that Peru ensure all women were provided with identity documents, including birth certificates, and in particular that it ensure women from rural, Indigenous and minority communities had full access to justice, education and health services.

Human rights defenders – mining projects

■ Human rights defender Javier Rodolfo Jahncke Benavente received death threats in March, apparently because of his work in Piura Province with the Muqui network which works to ensure that communities have access to information about projected mining activities and to a transparent and fair consultation process before any such activities are carried out.

■ In August the Inter-American Commission on Human Rights requested that protective measures, including medical diagnoses and treatment, be provided to 65 people from the town of La Oroya, Yauli Province, in the region of Junín, following decades of mining.

Amnesty International visit

An Amnesty International delegate visited Peru in November to research issues surrounding the trial of former President Alberto Fujimori.

PHILIPPINES

REPUBLIC OF THE PHILIPPINES

Head of state and government:	**Gloria Macapagal Arroyo**
Death penalty:	**abolitionist for all crimes**
Population:	**85.9 million**
Life expectancy:	**71 years**
Under-5 mortality (m/f):	**33/22 per 1,000**
Adult literacy:	**92.6 per cent**

Life for activists and many others was coloured by fear of extrajudicial executions and enforced disappearance, although fewer killings were reported than in 2006. The link between the military and political killings was further established by international and national institutions. There was much opposition to enhanced powers under an anti-terrorism law given to the armed forces and police. Negotiations progressed between the government and Muslim separatists, but talks with the communist National Democratic Front (NDF) remained stalled.

Political killings and enforced disappearances

Amid conflicting reports, at least 33 people were allegedly victims of political killings, a slight decrease over the previous year, and several people disappeared.

■ Siche Bustamante Gandinao, a member of Bayan Muna (People First), a leftist political party, and Misamis Oriental Farmers Association was killed on 10 March. She had testified before the UN Special Rapporteur on extrajudicial, summary or arbitrary executions about the murder of her father-in-law, Dalmacio Gandinao, also a member of Bayan Muna. Like her father-in-law, Siche Gandinao campaigned against human rights violations committed by soldiers against residents of their village suspected of being rebels or rebel supporters.

■ Nilo Arado and Luisa Posa-Dominado were abducted in April after being stopped in their truck by men in army fatigues. Their companion, Jose Garachico, was shot and wounded and left on the road while the other two were driven off in the truck. The burned out truck was found the next day with no sign of Nilo Arado and Luisa Posa-Dominado. Three hearings to consider habeas corpus writs were held in which military officers were named but failed to appear.

In February the Commission of Inquiry headed by former Supreme Court Justice José Melo published its report on political killings. It concluded that circumstantial evidence linked a group of military personnel to the killings. The Commission stated that further evidence, particularly the testimony of witnesses and the co-operation of activist groups, was needed to secure criminal convictions, while finding that under the principle of command responsibility, some senior military officers may be held responsible for their failure to prevent, punish or condemn the killings.

Public concern about political killings and disappearances mounted in 2007. The Supreme Court convened a summit with government and civil society actors in July. Recommendations included amendments to the law on habeas corpus to allow courts to give families or petitioners access to suspected places of detention. In September, the Supreme Court issued The Rule on the Writ of Amparo, which allows courts to order temporary protection, inspection or production of documents or witnesses where an individual's life, liberty or security have been violated or are under theat. The Writ of Amparo was subsequently used by human rights groups in cases of enforced disappearance. On 26 December, the Court of Appeals issued a decision that recognized the involvement of General Jovito Palparan and other military personnel in the abduction and disappearance of Raymond and Reynaldo Manalo in 2006.

A report issued in November by the UN Special Rapporteur on extrajudicial, summary or arbitrary executions criticized government institutions, particularly the military, for continued extrajudicial killings. The Rapporteur underlined the main causes as the failure of the judicial system to address impunity and the military counter-insurgency strategies that increasingly target civil society groups as fronts for communist insurgents. Recommendations included ensuring the accountability of military officials, reforming

P

the witness protection programme, ensuring the respect of human rights in the peace process, enabling effective congressional oversight of the security sector, and calling on the Supreme Court to take all available measures to ensure the effective prosecution of cases.

Few prosecutions were brought against those responsible for political killings and disappearances. In a rare case, two soldiers were charged with murder in May following the killing in 2006 of Isaias Sta. Rosa, a pastor, in Daraga, Albay province. Shortly after, however, the charges were dropped due to lack of evidence.

Arbitrary arrests and detentions

Arrests and harassment of politicians and activists continued. Following a mission to the Philippines by the Inter-Parliamentary Union in April to investigate politically motivated arrests, criminal cases against six opposition members of parliament, including Satur Ocampo and Crispin Beltran, were dismissed.

■ Satur Ocampo, Congress Representative and co-founder of Bayan Muna, was detained for 19 days on charges of murder in connection with left-wing activities during the rule of former President Marcos. He was released on bail on 3 April.

■ Crispin Beltran, Congress Representative for the Anakpawis (Toiling Masses) party, was released in April. He had been detained in February 2006 and faced fabricated charges of rebellion.

Legal developments

The Human Security Act, passed in July, allows for suspects to be detained without warrant or charge for up to 72 hours, and for surveillance and seizure of assets. The government said the law was introduced in response to the ongoing conflict with armed groups in the south, primarily the Muslim separatist group Abu Sayaff which had kidnapped and killed civilians.

Widespread opposition to the legislation included a petition by former senators, members of the House of Representatives, the Integrated Bar of the Philippines and others. There were fears that the Act could be used to stifle legitimate political dissent.

Armed groups

Talks between the government and the separatist Moro Islamic Liberation Front resumed after many delays but with limited progress due to continuing disagreement on the definition of ancestral domain land within autonomous Muslim regions in the south of the country. Negotiations also continued on sharing wealth from the mineral deposits, forests and farmlands in the region.

The arrest in August of Jose Maria Sison, the founder and former leader of the Communist Party of the Philippines (CPP) living in exile in the Netherlands, threatened permanently to stall peace talks between the government and the NDF. Jose Maria Sison was charged with ordering the murder in the Philippines of two former members of the CPP's military wing, the New People's Army, in 2003 and 2004. He was released in September after a Dutch judge found that there was insufficient evidence against him.

Amnesty International reports

Philippines: All parties must act on political killings ahead of elections (ASA 35/001/2007)

Philippines: Possible enforced disappearance/fear for safety (ASA 35/003/2007)

Philippines: Investigate claims and protect Manalo brothers (ASA 35/004/2007)

POLAND

REPUBLIC OF POLAND

Head of state:	Lech Kaczyński
Head of government:	Donald Tusk (replaced Jarosław Kaczyńzki in November)
Death penalty:	abolitionist for all crimes
Population:	38.5 million
Life expectancy:	75.2 years
Under-5 mortality (m/f):	10/9 per 1,000
Adult literacy:	99.8 per cent

Poland denied allegations that it had permitted secret US detention centres on its soil and rebuffed several requests to reopen an investigation into the issue. Lesbian, gay, bisexual and transgender (LGBT) people continued to be subjected to discrimination and intolerance. There were concerns about conditions of detention of asylum-seekers and the rights available for people with "tolerated stay" status.

Background

Early parliamentary elections were held in October after Parliament (*Sejm*) voted to dissolve itself on 7 September following the governing coalition's loss of its majority after the withdrawal of one of its junior parties. The turnout was the highest since the first post-Communist elections in 1991. A former opposition party, Civic Platform, won the elections and formed a new government in November. The previous administration's policy of opposing the incorporation of the EU Charter of Fundamental Rights into Polish law was continued by the new government.

'War on terror'

Poland's alleged involvement in the USA's programme of secret detentions and renditions flights continued to be of concern. In February, the European Parliament's Temporary Committee on allegations of illegal activity in Europe by the US Central Intelligence Agency (CIA) concluded that Poland failed to properly investigate claims that the US had secret detention facilities in their territory. It concluded that investigations had not been conducted independently, and that statements by the government to the Committee's delegation were contradictory and compromised.

In April, the UN Committee against Torture (CAT) urged Poland to disclose details of its parliamentary investigation into the presence of secret CIA detention centres in the country. In its concluding observations in July, CAT expressed its concern at the persistent allegations of Poland's involvement in extraordinary renditions. When asked about this issue, the then Prime Minister Jarosław Kaczyński said the government regarded the allegations as a "closed issue".

In June, the Rapporteur on secret detentions for the Parliamentary Assembly of the Council of Europe (PACE), Dick Marty, issued a second report revealing new evidence that US "high-value detainees" were held in CIA secret detention centres in Poland and Romania between 2002 and 2005. A 2001 secret agreement among NATO members provided the basic framework for this and other illegal CIA activities in Europe, the report alleged.

In June, PACE commented that "it is now established with a high degree of probability that secret detention centres operated by the CIA, forming part of the High Value Detainee program, existed for some years in Poland and Romania". PACE called for democratic oversight of military intelligence services and foreign intelligence services operating in both countries. It also called for transparent investigations and urged compensation for victims of unlawful transfers and detention. Poland denied involvement with secret detention centres.

In response, the EU Justice, Freedom and Security Commissioner, Franco Frattini, wrote to the government in July to highlight its obligations under the European Convention on Human Rights to establish whether the allegations were true. He had warned in 2005 that member states could face penalties – including suspension of EU voting rights – if they were found to have taken part in the secret CIA prison system. By the end of the year, Poland had not responded.

In September, the European Committee for the Prevention of Torture denounced the use of secret detention and renditions in the fight against terrorism.

Discrimination – sexual orientation

Discriminatory attitudes against LGBT people persisted. Openly homophobic language continued to be used by highly placed politicians, including President Kaczyński and the then Deputy Prime Minister and Minister of Education, Roman Giertych.

There were also concerns about proposals announced by the government in March which sought to "prohibit the promotion of homosexuality and other deviance" in Polish schools, and to "punish whoever promotes homosexuality or any other deviance of a sexual nature in educational establishments". Failure to comply could lead to dismissal, fine or imprisonment.

Although following the dissolution of Parliament these measures were never put into practice, European institutions raised concerns that such measures would be a violation of Poland's international obligations, the Polish Constitution and the commitments undertaken when the country joined the EU in 2004. They would institutionalize discrimination in Poland's school system and criminalize anyone who promoted equality.

The European Commissioner for Employment, Social Affairs and Equal Opportunities, Vladimir Špidla, stated that the European Commission would use all the powers and instruments at its disposal to

P

combat homophobia. Meanwhile, the European Parliament expressed anger and concern at growing intolerance towards LGBT people across Europe. Polish authorities were singled out and called on "to publicly condemn and take measures against declarations by public leaders inciting discrimination and hatred based on sexual orientation".

In June, the Council of Europe's Human Rights Commissioner expressed strong concerns about a number of aspects of the Polish government's approach to LGBT people. The Commissioner found "the portrayal and depiction of homosexuality... offensive, out of tune with principles on equality, diversity and respect for the human rights of all". The Commissioner also expressed his concerns about proposed measures to penalize the alleged promotion of homosexuality in schools. The Commissioner deplored "any instances of hate speech towards homosexuals" and called on the Polish authorities to take a similar stance.

Freedom of expression

In September, the European Court of Human Rights dismissed an appeal by Poland against its original ruling in May in favour of LGBT rights activists from Poland. The activists had successfully challenged a ban on the LGBT Equality Parade in Warsaw in June 2005 by the then Mayor of Warsaw and current President, Lech Kaczyński. The Court upheld its original and unanimous decision that the ban was illegal and discriminatory.

Refugees and asylum-seekers

People with "tolerated stay" status, many of them Chechens from the Russian Federation, continued to be excluded from integration programmes available only to recognized refugees.

There were allegations that asylum-seekers in some detention centres received inadequate medical assistance. The CAT raised concerns also about conditions in transit zones and deportation detention centres where foreign nationals awaiting deportation were held.

■ Despite requests, the authorities failed to answer questions about the death of a Chechen national from the Russian Federation, Isa Abubakarow, in October 2006, allegedly after being denied adequate medical care. He had been sent to the refugee detention centre of Lesznowola after being returned to Poland from Belgium in June 2006. The Polish Ombudsperson filed a complaint about reception conditions and lack of medical care in the Lesznowola centre with the Regional Prosecutor of Grójec which was still pending at the end of 2007.

Death penalty

Although in September the government opposed proposals by the Council of Europe for the inauguration of a European Day Against the Death Penalty, in December the new government announced its support for the initiative.

Discrimination against women

In February, the UN Committee on the Elimination of Discrimination against Women expressed its concerns about the repeated rejection by Parliament of a comprehensive law on gender equality. The Committee also expressed concerns about the abolition of the Government Plenipotentiary for Equal Status of Women and Men in 2005. The new government declined to re-establish the post, despite appeals by NGOs.

Amnesty International visit/reports

🚍 Amnesty International delegates visited Poland in May.

▥ Europe and Central Asia: Summary of Amnesty Internationals' concerns in the region: January-June 2007 (EUR 01/010/2007)

▥ Poland: School bill would violate students' and teachers' rights and reinforce homophobia (EUR 37/001/2007)

▥ Poland and Romania: Take responsibility for secret detention sites (EUR 37/003/2007)

▥ Poland: Submission to the UN Universal Periodic Review: first session of the HRC UPR Working Group 7-18 April 2008 (EUR 37/005/2007)

PORTUGAL

PORTUGUESE REPUBLIC
Head of state: **Aníbal António Cavaco Silva**
Head of government: **José Sócrates Carvalho Pinto de Sousa**
Death penalty: **abolitionist for all crimes**
Population: **10.6 million**
Life expectancy: **77.7 years**
Under-5 mortality (m/f): **7/7 per 1,000**
Adult literacy: **93.8 per cent**

Allegations of ill-treatment by police and subsequent effective impunity continued. Violence against women persisted. The Office of Public Prosecutions opened a judicial investigation into suspected CIA rendition flights believed to have stopped over in Portugal.

Ill-treatment

Allegations of ill-treatment by police and subsequent impunity continued in 2007.

■ On 29 May the Criminal Court in Lisbon acquitted all seven defendants in a criminal case brought against prison officers accused of assaulting Albino Libânio in Lisbon Prison in 2003. The Prison Service Inspectorate of the General Directorate of Prison Services had investigated the incident and concluded that Albino Libânio had indeed been assaulted by prison officers as he alleged. The court recognized the injuries suffered by Albino Libânio, but acquitted the defendants on the grounds of lack of evidence proving their responsibility. Albino Libânio lodged an appeal with the Court of Appeal on the basis that the court had failed to conduct basic investigations that would have provided the information necessary to secure a conviction. The appeal was pending at the end of the year.

Migration

A new immigration law, which entered into force on 4 July, introduced certain legal rights for migrants awaiting decision on their expulsion from or admission into Portuguese territory, with particular emphasis on the rights of unaccompanied minors. The law also specifies that facilitating illegal migration in a manner that endangers the life of the migrant or constitutes inhuman or degrading treatment can be punished by two to eight years' imprisonment. Victims of trafficking are no longer classified as illegal immigrants.

Violence against women

The third National Plan Against Domestic Violence entered into force in June. One of its key provisions is guaranteed free access to health care for victims of domestic violence. In July the government stated that 39 women had been killed by their husbands or partners during 2006.

'War on terror'

On 25 January the Minister for Foreign Affairs stated that the government's investigations into alleged CIA flight stopovers in Portugal during illegal transfers of suspects between countries (renditions) had been closed, stating that there was no evidence to support the continuation of the inquiry. However, on 5 February the Office of Public Prosecutions announced that it was opening a criminal investigation into possible torture and other ill-treatment related to suspected CIA rendition flights, on the basis of information provided to it by a Portuguese Member of the European Parliament and a journalist. No further information was publicly available at the end of the year.

Amnesty International report

📄 Europe and Central Asia: Summary of Amnesty International's concerns in the region, January-June 2007 (EUR 01/010/2007).

PUERTO RICO

COMMONWEALTH OF PUERTO RICO
Head of state: **George W Bush**
Head of government: **Aníbal Aceveda-Vilá**
Death penalty: **abolitionist for all crimes**
Population: **4 million**
Under-5 mortality (m/f): **12/10 per 1,000**

There were continuing concerns about the excessive use of force by Federal Bureau of Investigation (FBI) agents and police brutality.

Police and security forces

An inquiry by the Office of Inspector General (OIG) into the killing of independence activist Filiberto Ojeda Ríos by the FBI in September 2005 raised a number

P

of concerns. The inquiry had cleared the FBI of wrongdoing. However, Amnesty International remained concerned that the discharge by police of more than 100 rounds of ammunition into a building which may have housed unarmed individuals appeared inconsistent with international standards on the use of deadly force. It also questioned the level of perceived threat from within the house, given as the basis for the FBI delaying entry after Filiberto Ojeda Ríos was shot and fatally wounded; and whether he posed an immediate threat to life when he was shot. Amnesty International called for a review of FBI standards on the use of deadly force and asked what measures the US government had taken to address the OIG's criticisms of aspects of the planning and execution of the operation. No response from the US government had been received by the end of the year.

Amnesty International received no response to its request for information about whether an investigation had been carried out into allegations that members of the FBI had used pepper spray and unjustified force against a group of journalists in February 2006.

There were complaints of police brutality during a crackdown on drugs crime in Villa Cañona, a neighbourhood in the town of Loíza. Residents complained that officers from the Puerto Rico Police Department conducted indiscriminate strip searches of black youths, subjecting them to racial abuse and, in some cases, physical assault.

In December, an external inquiry was appointed to investigate reports of police ill-treatment of unarmed demonstrators protesting against a luxury coastal housing development. Demonstrators blocking lorry access to the site at Paseo Caribe were allegedly punched or dragged across the ground, with a number sustaining injuries.

Amnesty International reports

📄 Puerto Rico: Amnesty International concerned at reports of police violence against unarmed demonstrators (AMR 47/001/2007)

📄 USA/Puerto Rico: Amnesty International's concerns regarding the FBI shooting of Filiberto Ojeda Ríos (AMR 51/198/2007)

QATAR

STATE OF QATAR
Head of state:	Shaikh Hamad bin Khalifa al-Thani
Head of government:	Shaikh Hamad bin Jassim bin Jabr al-Thani (replaced Shaikh Abdullah bin Khalifa al-Thani in April)
Death penalty:	retentionist
Population:	0.9 million
Life expectancy:	75 years
Under-5 mortality (m/f):	13/11 per 1,000
Adult literacy:	89 per cent

The authorities restored the nationality of some 2,000 people, but hundreds were believed to be still deprived of their nationality. Political prisoners remained in jail without charge or after unfair trials. Migrant workers were exploited and, if they protested, deported. Courts continued to pass sentences of death and flogging, although no one was executed.

Background

Qatar was elected to the UN Human Rights Council in May after the government promised to implement recommendations of human rights treaty bodies.

Nationality rights

The authorities restored Qatari nationality to some 2,000 people, including many al-Ghufran members of al-Murra tribe. However, some alleged that their birth records had been amended to indicate erroneously that they were born outside Qatar, rendering them ineligible to vote. Other cases of arbitrary deprivation of nationality remained unresolved and several new cases were reported.

■ Maher Ibrahim Mohamed Hanoon, a Qatari national of Palestinian origin, his former wife, Abeer Tameem Mohamed al-Adnani, and their two children, Tameem, 14, and Raneem, 10, reportedly had their Qatari nationality arbitrarily withdrawn by the Interior Ministry in July, leaving them at risk of deportation.

■ 'Abdul Hameed Hussain al-Mohammed, together with his six children and two brothers, were reportedly stripped of their Qatari nationality and ordered to be deported in October 2002. They were dismissed from their jobs, lost their employment rights and were denied publicly provided housing assistance which they had previously received as Qatari nationals. This action was taken against them after 'Abdul Hameed Hussain al-Mohammed and his two brothers were sentenced to prison terms in December 2001 following a dispute with another individual.

'War on terror'

At least two foreign nationals continued to be held at the state security prison in Doha: Mussa Ayad, an Egyptian national held since March 2006, who was reportedly held in solitary confinement without charge; and Ali Hassan Sairaka, a Syrian national held since 2005 and sentenced to five years in prison in 2007.

■ Fahad al-Mansouri, arrested in November 2005 and sentenced to 10 years' imprisonment for "belonging to a secret organization", was released in early September 2007.

Violence against women

The authorities failed adequately to address discrimination and violence against women.

■ In January, the Appeal Court reduced to a one-year suspended sentence the three-year prison sentence imposed on a Jordanian man convicted of murdering his 16-year-old sister. The Court held that he had not intended to kill his sister, whom he suspected of having an illicit relationship.

Migrant workers

Foreign migrant workers, who make up a large proportion of Qatar's workforce, complained that they were exploited, including by non-payment of wages. They continued to have inadequate protection under the law.

■ In May, hundreds of Nepalese workers staged protests to demand an increase in and monthly payment of their salaries and benefits. They were reportedly arrested and ill-treated before being deported to Nepal.

Cruel, inhuman and degrading punishments

Sentences of flogging continued to be imposed.

■ In January, a court in Doha sentenced an Egyptian national to 40 lashes for drinking alcohol.

Death penalty

One person was sentenced to death and at least 22 people were on death row, but no executions were reported.

■ In April, an unnamed Qatari man convicted of having sexual relations with his 14-year-old daughter was sentenced to death.

Amnesty International visit

🚌 Amnesty International's Secretary General visited Qatar in May.

ROMANIA

ROMANIA

Head of state:	Traian Băsescu
Head of government:	Călin Popescu-Tăriceanu
Death penalty:	abolitionist for all crimes
Population:	21.5 million
Life expectancy:	71.9 years
Under-5 mortality (m/f):	23/17 per 1,000
Adult literacy:	97.3 per cent

Romania denied allegations that it had permitted secret US detention centres on its soil and rebuffed several requests to reopen an investigation into the issue. Romani people continued to face intolerance and discrimination, as did lesbian, gay, bisexual and transgender (LGBT) people. Law enforcement officials were allegedly responsible for unlawful killings. Concern remained about the care and treatment of patients in mental health institutions.

Background

Political instability in Romania in 2007 was widely attributed to rivalry between Prime Minister Călin Popescu-Tăriceanu and President Traian Băsescu. In April President Băsescu was suspended by Parliament, but in a referendum on impeachment in May a majority of the electorate voted for his retention.

On 1 January, Romania became a member state of the EU. In its progress report in June, the European Commission urged Romania to implement a more transparent and efficient judicial process and warned that Romania must take tougher action to fight corruption.

R

'War on terror'

Romania's alleged involvement in the USA's programme of secret detentions and renditions continued to be of concern.

In February, the European Parliament concluded that Romania and Poland had failed to properly investigate claims that the USA operated secret detention facilities in their territory. It criticized Romania's inquiry into the issue as superficial, and expressed concern about the lack of control by the authorities over US activities in Romanian military bases.

In June, the Rapporteur on secret detentions for the Parliamentary Assembly of the Council of Europe (PACE), Dick Marty, issued a second report revealing new evidence that US "high-value detainees" were held in secret US Central Intelligence Agency (CIA) detention centres in Poland and Romania between 2002 and 2005. A 2001 secret agreement among NATO members provided the basic framework for this and other illegal activities by the CIA in Europe, the report alleged.

In June, PACE commented that "it is now established with a high degree of probability that secret detention centres operated by the CIA, forming part of the High Value Detainee program, existed for some years in Poland and Romania". PACE called for democratic oversight of military intelligence services and foreign intelligence services operating in both countries. It also called for transparent investigations and urged compensation for victims of unlawful transfers and detention. Romania denied involvement with secret detention centres and subsequently the Romanian delegation announced its withdrawal from PACE.

In response, the EU Justice, Freedom and Security Commissioner, Franco Frattini, wrote to the government in July to highlight its obligations under the European Convention on Human Rights to establish whether the allegations were true. He had warned in 2005 that member states could face penalties – including suspension of EU voting rights – if they were found to have taken part in the secret CIA prison system.

In November, Romania replied, denying allegations that secret CIA prisons had operated on its soil, and reiterated that a committee of inquiry set up by the government had already concluded that the allegations were unfounded.

In September, the European Committee for the Prevention of Torture denounced the use of secret detention and renditions in the fight against terrorism.

Discrimination – Roma

Minorities, and in particular Roma, continued to confront serious discrimination, including in employment, housing, health and education.

UNICEF reported in March that up to 70 per cent of Roma households had no direct water supply and that the segregation of Romani children into inferior schools and "Roma-only" classes also continued to be a concern.

Hate speech and intolerance by the media and some public authorities continued. In May, President Traian Băsescu reportedly called a journalist a "dirty gypsy", but later apologized. The National Council for Combating Discrimination called for the President to explain himself.

There were tensions with Italy over Italy's declared intention to expel Roma with Romanian nationality. In November, the Minister of Foreign Affairs Adrian Cioroianu said in a televised debate that he had considered "buying a piece of land in the Egyptian desert to send there all the people who tarnish the country's image". Adrian Cioroianu later apologized publicly but refused to resign. The Prime Minister "deplored" his Minister's comments but took no further action. Several human rights organizations subsequently issued open letters demanding Adrian Cioroianu's resignation, and a Roma NGO, Romani-CRISS, filed a complaint with the National Council for Combating Discrimination (Consiliul Naţional pentru Combaterea Discriminării, CNCD).

Discrimination – sexual orientation

LGBT people continued to face widespread discrimination and hostility.

At June's Bucharest GayFest parade, around 500 LGBT rights activists marched through the capital to demonstrate against discrimination and to call for the legalization of same-sex marriages. The march was opposed by the Orthodox Church and some politicians. Romanian riot police detained dozens of counter-demonstrators who tried to break up the march. Police fired tear gas to hold the counter-demonstrators at bay after some threw stones and attempted to break through protective cordons.

R

Police and security forces

In July, the UN Interim Administration Mission in Kosovo (UNMIK) reported that it was unable to identify which members of the Romanian Formed Police Unit stationed in Kosovo had been responsible for the deaths of two men during a demonstration in February in Pristina. (See Serbia/Kosovo entry.) In part, they could not identify the officers because they had been repatriated to Romania. The Romanian authorities did not acknowledge any personal responsibility among the officers, but a criminal investigation was opened under a military prosecutor in Bucharest.

■ In July, the European Court of Human Rights issued its judgment in the case of Belmondo Cobzaru, a Romani man beaten in custody by police officers in Mangalia in 1997. The Court ruled that Romania was in breach of the prohibition of inhuman and degrading treatment, the right to an effective remedy, and the prohibition of discrimination.

Mental health care

Concerns remained for people committed to psychiatric institutions, in particular children. In April, the Centre for Legal Resources (Centrul de Resurse Juridice, CRJ), an NGO, and UNICEF released a report citing cases of alleged violations of the human rights of children and young people with mental disabilities, including malnutrition; lack of adequate clothing, medication or treatment; lack of trained staff; abusive application of patient restraint measures; and isolation from the rest of the community.

The report also highlighted cases of children who were allegedly confined to psychiatric hospitals without a specific treatment or diagnosis. It further accused local authorities of committing orphans to psychiatric institutions, in the absence of any alternative care.

Following a visit to the Rehabilitation and Recovery Centre in Bolintinul din Vale, the CRJ reported in June that conditions were virtually unchanged since its previous visit in 2003. Almost all 107 residents were poorly dressed or lacked any clothing at all, there were no rehabilitation activities, and patients were undernourished. Living conditions were inadequate with no privacy for the patients and extremely poor hygiene, resulting in the alleged spread of parasites and infections among patients.

In October, the CRJ filed a complaint with the Prosecutor's Office of the Supreme Court against its decision to close the investigation into deaths at the Poiana Mare psychiatric hospital, where 17 patients died in 2004 due to malnutrition or hypothermia.

Amnesty International reports

📄 Europe and Central Asia: Summary of Amnesty International's concerns in the region: January-June 2007 (EUR 01/010/2007)

📄 Poland and Romania: Take responsibility for secret detention sites (EUR 37/003/2007)

RUSSIAN FEDERATION

RUSSIAN FEDERATION

Head of state:	Vladimir Putin
Head of government:	Viktor Zubkov
	(replaced Mikhail Fradkov in September)
Death penalty:	abolitionist in practice
Population:	141.9 million
Life expectancy:	65 years
Under-5 mortality (m/f):	24/18 per 1,000
Adult literacy:	99.4 per cent

The Russian authorities were increasingly intolerant of dissent or criticism, branding it 'unpatriotic'. A crackdown on civil and political rights was evident throughout the year and in particular during the run-up to the State Duma (parliament) elections in December. Given the strict state control of TV and other media, demonstrations were the flashpoint during the year for political protests, with police detaining demonstrators, journalists, and human rights activists, some of whom were beaten. Activists and political opponents of the government were also subjected to administrative detention.

The number of racist attacks that came to the attention of the media rose; at least 61 people were killed across the country. Although authorities recognized the problem and there was an increase in the number of prosecutions for racially motivated crimes, these measures failed to stem the tide of violence.

R

The European Court of Human Rights ruled that Russia was responsible for enforced disappearances, torture and extrajudicial executions in 15 judgments relating to the second Chechen conflict which began in 1999. There were fewer reported cases of disappearances in the Chechen Republic than in previous years; however, serious human rights violations were frequent and individuals were reluctant to report abuses, fearing reprisals. Ingushetia saw an increase in serious violations, including enforced disappearances and extrajudicial executions.

NGOs were weighed down by burdensome reporting requirements imposed by changes to legislation. Torture was used by police against detainees, including to extract "confessions"; violence against inmates in prisons was also reported.

Background

Pervasive corruption undermined the rule of law and people's trust in the legal system. A new structure, the Investigation Committee, was established within the office of the Prosecutor General, and was charged with responsibility for criminal investigations. It was unclear at the end of the year what impact these changes would have on the work of the Prosecutor's office.

New laws regulating immigration were brought in designed to simplify immigration procedures and the obtaining of work permits, but at the same time increasing the penalties for employing irregular migrants. The January 2007 law against foreign workers in Russian retail markets, presented by President Putin as a way of protecting "native Russians", was perceived by some as legitimizing xenophobia.

The ruling United Russia party won a clear majority in State Duma elections in December; President Putin headed the party's electoral list. An observation mission of parliamentarians from the Organization for Security and Co-operation in Europe (OSCE) and the Council of Europe pronounced the elections "not fair".

The North Caucasus remained a violent and unstable region. The security situation in Ingushetia deteriorated with armed groups launching numerous attacks, often fatal, against members of law enforcement agencies. Unidentified gunmen committed numerous attacks against non-Ingush civilians, including ethnic Russians. In Chechnya sporadic fighting continued, with incursions by armed groups into the capital Grozny and other areas. Ramzan Kadyrov was appointed President of Chechnya in March, following the resignation of Alu Alkhanov.

Human rights defenders

Government representatives and state-controlled media repeatedly accused human rights defenders and members of the opposition movement of working for foreign interests and being "anti-Russian". Human rights defenders and civil society activists were subjected to harassment and intimidation. Criminal charges, such as for using unlicensed computer software or for inciting hatred, were taken out selectively against human rights defenders and independent journalists.

■ Oleg Orlov, head of the human rights centre Memorial, and three journalists from a Russian TV station, who had all planned to monitor a demonstration against serious abuses by law enforcement officials in Ingushetia, were abducted on 24 November from a hotel in Ingushetia by armed masked men. They stated that they were beaten and threatened with being shot before being left in a field.

In April Russian NGOs were obliged for the first time to submit information about their activities under the new law on NGOs to the Federal Registration Service (FRS). In the following months, many human rights defenders were subjected to repeated reviews of their activities, were forced to re-register their NGOs in lengthy bureaucratic procedures and to challenge allegations against their NGOs in court.

■ Citizen's Watch, a human rights organization in St Petersburg focusing on such issues as police reform and combating racism, used non-Russian donor funding for their publications. The FRS considered that printing the names of donors on their publications constituted advertising for the donors, for which the NGO would have had to pay tax. In July the FRS demanded copies of all the NGO's outgoing communications since 2004. Citizen's Watch disputed the right of the FRS to receive such information.

In August, new amendments to the law on combating "extremist activities" came into force. They added a new motivation of hatred against a specific group to the list of possible "extremist" motivations: the list now includes hatred against not only a specific race, religion, or ethnicity but also political, ideological and social groups. The law allows for acts of minor hooliganism to be more severely punished if committed on grounds of hatred against a specific

R

group. Human rights defenders were concerned that the law may be used to clamp down on dissent.

■ On 27 January, the Supreme Court upheld the conviction of human rights defender Stanislav Dmitrievskii, who had received a conditional sentence in 2006 for inciting ethnic enmity after publishing articles by Chechen separatist leaders. In November a court in Nizhnii Novgorod imposed stricter conditions on him.

■ Nine people reportedly were charged in relation to the October 2006 murder of human rights journalist Anna Politkovskaya.

Freedom of expression

In the months prior to the State Duma elections, the authorities became more restrictive of public expressions of dissent. Scores of people, including journalists and monitors, were briefly detained prior to, during and following demonstrations and many were convicted of violations of the Administrative Code in trials which did not always meet international standards of fair trial.

■ In November opposition leader Garry Kasparov was sentenced to five days' administrative detention after he had participated in a "dissenters' march" in Moscow a week before the Duma elections. Amnesty International considered him a prisoner of conscience and called for his immediate release.

Police used excessive force on a number of occasions in order to break up demonstrations organized by opposition parties and anti-government activists. Following a demonstration in St Petersburg on 15 April, several people had to undergo hospital treatment.

The authorities used various methods to prevent journalists, well-known political activists and human rights activists from attending and monitoring demonstrations. In May, Moscow mayor Yuri Luzhkov banned a gay rights march in Moscow. Gay rights activists, including several members of the European Parliament, were briefly detained when they attempted to hand over a petition to Yuri Luzhkov, urging him to respect the right to freedom of expression and protesting against his decision to ban a gay rights march from taking place in Moscow.

Armed conflict in the North Caucasus

Federal and local law enforcement agencies operating in the region responded in an arbitrary and unlawful fashion to violent attacks by armed groups. Serious human rights violations, including enforced disappearances and abductions, arbitrary detention, torture including in unofficial places of detention, and extrajudicial executions, were reported in the Republics of Chechnya, Ingushetia, Dagestan and North Ossetia. People were convicted of crimes in cases where forced "confessions" formed part of the evidence against them. People mounted demonstrations in Ingushetia and Dagestan against disappearances and other arbitrary actions by law enforcement agencies. A rally against disappearances was banned in Chechnya's capital, Grozny, in October. Human rights abuses, including abductions, were reportedly committed by armed groups against civilians in the region.

In Ingushetia, in at least six cases where men were shot dead by law enforcement officers, witnesses claimed that the men had been summarily executed; the authorities stated that they had put up armed resistance. Relatives of a six-year-old boy, shot dead by law enforcement during a raid on the family home in November, claimed he had been killed deliberately. Detainees were tortured and ill-treated in order to extract "confessions" or information. At least three people subjected to enforced disappearance or abduction during the year remained missing at the end of the year.

■ Ibragim Gazdiev was seized by armed men in camouflage in August in Karabulak, Ingushetia, and subsequently disappeared. The armed men were allegedly law enforcement officials from the Federal Security Service (FSB). The authorities officially denied that Ibragim Gazdiev had been detained. He has not been seen or heard from since.

In Chechnya the number of reported enforced disappearances and abductions decreased, compared with previous years, although cases continued to be reported. Torture and ill-treatment by Chechen law enforcement officials was reported, including in illegal and secret places of detention. During his visit to Chechnya in March, the Commissioner for Human Rights of the CoE stated that he had "the impression that torture and ill-treatment are widespread" and added that perpetrators of torture had a feeling of "utter impunity". The European Committee for the Prevention of Torture (CPT) issued its third public statement on Chechnya in March, naming six police detention facilities where detainees were at a high risk of torture.

R

In Kabardino-Balkaria a trial began in October against 59 suspects accused of an armed attack on Nalchik in October 2005 in which over 100 people died. Many of the detainees, including former Guantánamo detainee Rasul Kudaev, alleged they were tortured into giving confessions.

Impunity

Victims of human rights violations and their relatives were frequently afraid to submit official complaints. In some cases the victim or their lawyer was directly threatened not to pursue a complaint. Human rights groups in the region publicizing the violations and offering assistance to victims came under pressure from the authorities. Some individuals were reportedly reluctant to lodge applications at the European Court of Human Rights, because of reprisals against applicants before them.

■ 76-year-old Sumaia Abzueva was allegedly beaten up on the way to the market in Argun on 9 January by a group of young men. She had been seeking an investigation into the killing of her son in 2005. She said she had been threatened more than once by the men who had detained and taken her son away from the family home, and who were suspected to be members of Chechen security forces.

When investigations concerning human rights violations were opened they were often ineffectual, and suspended for failure to identify any suspect. The CPT highlighted gross inadequacies in many of the investigations opened into allegations of torture. There was no single comprehensive list of disappeared persons, no work to collect DNA from relatives of the disappeared, no work to exhume the mass graves, and no fully functioning forensic laboratory carrying out autopsies. Very few cases reached trial.

■ In June, a military court in Rostov-on-Don convicted four members of a special Russian military intelligence unit for killing six unarmed civilians from Dai village, Chechnya, in January 2002. They were sentenced to imprisonment in strict-regime prison colonies for terms of nine to 14 years. This was the third hearing into the case. Three of the four were sentenced in their absence, having failed to appear. The Supreme Court of the Russian Federation upheld the convictions.

European Court of Human Rights rulings

In 15 judgments the European Court ruled Russia responsible for enforced disappearances, torture and extrajudicial executions relating to the second Chechen conflict. The Court sharply criticized the ineffectual investigations.

■ Peace activist Zura Bitieva was tortured in 2000 in an unofficial detention centre at Chernokozovo, and killed in 2003, along with three members of her family. She had filed a case with the Court relating to her torture. The Court ruled that her detention in Chernokozovo had been in "total disregard of the requirement of lawfulness"; that her and her relatives' killing could be attributed to the State; and that there had been no effective, prompt and thorough investigation into the killings.

Internally displaced people

Many thousands of people remained internally displaced in the North Caucasus as a result of the second Chechen conflict. At least seven temporary · accommodation centres were closed in Grozny. Some individuals were reportedly forced to leave without a guaranteed safe and sustainable return to their homes, without adequate alternative housing being offered, and without due process being followed. Reportedly some individuals were forced to sign statements that they left voluntarily.

Over 18,000 people displaced by the Chechen conflict were estimated to be living in Ingushetia and Dagestan at the end of 2007, some of them living in extremely poor conditions in temporary camps. Thousands of others remained displaced in Ingushetia from the Prigorodnii district, a territory disputed with North Ossetia.

Forcible return

Individuals who were detained under deportation or extradition proceedings, were denied access to a meaningful asylum procedure and were vulnerable to arbitrary actions by law enforcement agencies. Amnesty International was aware of at least three cases of forcible return to countries (in these cases Uzbekistan and China), where they faced a high risk of serious human rights violations including torture, in violation of the principle of non-refoulement. In one case, an individual was returned over 24 hours after the European Court of Human Rights had issued an order to stay the deportation. In May, the head of a detention centre for foreigners in Moscow was convicted of exceeding official authority for his participation in the October 2006 deportation of Uzbekistani national Rustam Muminov, in violation of Russian and international law.

R

Torture and other ill-treatment

There were many reports of torture and ill-treatment during investigations by law enforcement officials and in places of detention. Police and investigators allegedly beat detainees, placed plastic bags or gas masks over their heads, used electroshocks and threatened them with further forms of torture and ill-treatment if they refused to admit their "guilt" and to sign a "confession".

During the year a number of police officers were found guilty of crimes relating to torture and ill-treatment during investigations and interrogations.

■ In July, Valerii Dontsov, an elderly disabled man from Kstovo in the region of Nizhnii Novgorod, was reportedly beaten and ill-treated by police in order to make him confess to the murder of his son. After being subjected to ill-treatment by the police, he had to undergo hospital treatment.

Riots in several prison colonies were reported. Prisoners were protesting against ill-treatment and violations of their rights, such as denials of family visits and receipt of food parcels, and the frequent use of punishment cells for minor violations of prison rules. Similar reports were received from prison colonies in Krasnodar, Sverdlovsk and Kaluga Regions. The media reported that three prisoners died as a result of the suppression of a riot in Sverdlovsk Region.

In January President Putin spoke in favour of ratifying the Optional Protocol to the UN Convention against Torture. Proposals to allow for public monitoring of places of detention were under discussion; however, by the end of the year no effective system of unannounced inspections was in place.

Fair trial concerns

In April, the Parliamentary Assembly of the Council of Europe called on the Russian authorities to "use all available legal means" to release Igor Sutiagin, Valentin Danilov and Mikhail Trepashkin. The parliamentarians expressed concern about the authorities' failure to meet international fair trial standards and about alleged inadequate medical treatment.

■ Igor Sutiagin, sentenced in 2004 to 15 years' imprisonment for espionage, spent three months in a punishment cell, for reportedly being in possession of a mobile phone in the prison colony.

■ Lawyer and former security service officer Mikhail Trepashkin was sentenced in 2004 for revealing state secrets and unlawful possession of ammunition. He was transferred in March from an open prison colony to a stricter regime for allegedly violating prison rules, but his lawyers and human rights defenders believed this to be a punishment for his complaints against the prison authorities. On 30 November Mikhail Trepashkin was released.

■ New charges were filed against imprisoned former YUKOS oil company head Mikhail Khodorkovskii and his associate Platon Lebedev in February, alleging their involvement in money laundering and embezzlement. The Office of the Prosecutor General failed to respect court decisions concerning the criminal proceedings and the men's legal team was harassed.

Violence against women

Violence against women in the family was widespread. Government support for crisis centres and hotlines was totally inadequate. No measures under Russian law specifically addressed violence against women in the family.

Racism

Violent racist attacks occurred with alarming regularity, mostly concentrated in big cities such as Moscow, St Petersburg and Nizhnii Novgorod, where the majority of foreigners and ethnic minorities lived. While exact figures for numbers of attacks and racist incidents were hard to verify, the non-governmental SOVA Information and Analytical Centre reported that at least 61 people were killed and at least 369 were injured in racially motivated attacks, an increase on 2006. Anti-Semitic attacks and desecration of Jewish cemeteries were also reported. The real level of such violence remained hidden due to chronic under-reporting.

Despite increased efforts by authorities to recognize the issue of racism, and some indications that legal provisions against racially motivated crimes were being used more effectively, there were few convictions for racist attacks and victims stated that their attempts to report racist attacks to the police were futile.

Amnesty International visits/reports

🚗 Amnesty International delegates visited Russia in July and December. An October visit to Chechnya was postponed at the request of authorities.

R

📄 Russian Federation: What justice for Chechnya's disappeared?
(EUR 46/015/2007)

📄 Russian Federation: Update briefing: What progress has been made since May 2006 to tackle violent racism? (EUR 46/047/2007)

📄 Russian Federation: New trial of Mikhail Khodorkovskii and Platon Lebedev must meet international fair trial standards
(EUR 46/052/2007)

📄 Russian Federation: Human rights defenders at risk in the North Caucasus (EUR 46/053/2007)

RWANDA

REPUBLIC OF RWANDA

Head of state:	Paul Kagame
Head of government:	Bernard Makuza
Death penalty:	abolitionist for all crimes
Population:	9.4 million
Life expectancy:	45.2 years
Under-5 mortality (m/f):	204/178 per 1,000
Adult literacy:	64.9 per cent

Rwanda abolished the death penalty in 2007. Freedom of expression, association and movement continued to be restricted. The security services were implicated in human rights violations, including the use of excessive force and torture. Fair trial standards continued to be flouted, particularly in the community-based gacaca tribunals, whose powers to try genocide suspects were extended during the year. Tensions persisted between and within Rwanda's main ethnic groups.

Excessive use of force, torture and other ill-treatment

The security services, and in particular the police and Local Defence Forces (LDF), reportedly used unlawful and excessive force when arresting suspects. The LDF are an armed civilian force working alongside the national police.

■ In May, it was reported that François Rukeba, who had recently been extradited from Uganda to Rwanda, had been tortured. According to reports, he was severely beaten during the first days of his detention by the Rwandan security forces.

In November, it was reported that the government would shortly submit the issue of ratification of the UN Convention against Torture to Parliament.

Freedom of expression
Press freedom

In 2007, Rwanda was ranked 181 out of 195 countries in terms of respect for press freedom by the USA-based organization, Freedom House.

Harassment, threats, intimidation and violent attacks against journalists, in particular those working for non-state media, continued. The authorities failed to protect and uphold the rights of these journalists.

■ On 9 February, Jean Bosco Gasasira, the editor of Umuvigizi newspaper, was assaulted with iron bars by three unidentified men in the capital, Kigali. Jean Bosco Gasasira was rushed to hospital where he remained in intensive care for several days. He had published several articles in Umuvigizi newspaper that were critical of the Rwandan Patriotic Front (RPF), the ruling political party. One article alleged nepotism within the RPF.

■ Also on 9 February, the government-controlled radio station, Radio Rwanda, reportedly broadcast remarks by the Director of Radio Rwanda and the President of the High Press Council threatening the independent newspaper Umuco. Accusing the newspaper of fomenting ethnic hatred, they compared it to the defunct newspaper Kangura, which incited hatred of Tutsi people before and during the 1994 genocide. Following this radio broadcast, Bonaventure Bizumureymi, the editor of Umuco, received telephone calls threatening him.

The press is still viewed by some with fear since it played such an instrumental role in whipping up the genocide in 1994. In 2007, the government continued to accuse journalists critical of the authorities of inciting ethnic hatred in order to silence them.

■ In September, four government ministers, including the Ministers of Interior and of Communication, and two members of the security forces threatened independent journalists during a programme broadcast by Radio Rwanda and Télévision rwandaise (TVR) if they carried on criticizing the government. The Interior Minister allegedly said that the police should arrest any journalist who published a leaked official document and that the journalist should remain in detention until he revealed the source of the leak. In addition, these journalists were branded as "enemies" of the country. Journalists working for the newspaper *Umuseso* were particularly targeted.

The government increasingly used criminal laws and sanctions to stifle free expression of opinion. Two draft laws, one related to the Press Law and one to the Criminal Code, which were being considered by Parliament at the end of 2007, contained provisions which would unduly restrict freedom of expression.

Human rights defenders

The work of human rights defenders was under intense scrutiny by the authorities.

■ In February, Congolese law professor Idesbald Byabuze Katabaruka was arrested and charged with "threatening state security" and "discrimination and sectarianism". He was in Kigali to teach a university law course. The public prosecutor issued the charges in relation to several public documents which Idesbald Byabuze Katabaruka had allegedly written or co-authored. They included an article, *Alerte Rwanda* (*Rwanda Warning*), which was highly critical of the RPF. About one month later, after international pressure, the charges against him were dropped and he was released from Kigali Central Prison.

Death penalty

In July, Rwanda abolished the death penalty, the first country in the Great Lakes region to do so. The retention of the death penalty constituted one of the main obstacles preventing the transfer of detainees held by the International Criminal Tribunal for Rwanda (ICTR), and indicted genocide suspects living abroad, to Rwanda's national jurisdiction.

Gacaca trials

Trials continued under the gacaca system - a community-based system of tribunals established in 2002 to try people suspected of crimes during the 1994 genocide.

In March, a new gacaca law was enacted which substantially changed the previous 2004 law. Under the new law, the jurisdiction of gacaca tribunals was extended so that they could try categories of people, such as "notorious killers", who previously came under the jurisdiction of the national courts. The gacaca tribunals were also empowered to hand down life sentences. In addition, the number of judges

(*Inyangamugayo*) required to sit on a gacaca tribunal was reduced from nine to seven in order to increase the number of sessions. Although the government's stated intention was to close down the gacaca courts as soon as possible, in early December the Secretary General of the gacaca jurisdictions announced that the gacaca tribunals would be extended into 2008.

While the provisions of the 2007 law speeded up the gacaca trials, this was at the expense of the fairness and quality of the rulings. There were regular reports that fair trial guarantees were not being applied in the gacaca process, leading to miscarriages of justice.

■ François-Xavier Byuma, a prominent human rights defender, was sentenced to 19 years' imprisonment in May for participating in weapons training during the 1994 genocide, after an unfair trial by the gacaca community court in Bilyogo, Kigali. The judge who presided over the trial had been under investigation by François-Xavier Byuma's NGO, Turengere Abana (Rwandan Association for the Protection and Promotion of the Child, l'Association Rwandaise pour la Protection et la Promotion de l'Enfant) for the alleged rape of a 17-year-old girl. The judge's conflict of interest denied François-Xavier Byuma his right to a fair trial before an independent and impartial tribunal.

Poorly qualified, ill-trained and corrupt gacaca judges in certain districts fuelled widespread distrust of the gacaca system.

In December, the League for Human Rights in the Great Lakes Region (LDGL) reported that seven judges of the gacaca court of the Kibirizi sector, South Province, had been arrested in November for tampering with evidence.

Rwandans continued to flee the gacaca system to neighbouring countries. Some were afraid that the tribunals would expose their involvement in the genocide. Others fled out of fear of false accusations.

■ Teachers and other staff from the University of Butare reportedly fled the country out of fear of being wrongly accused of involvement in the genocide.

Rwandan sources also reported throughout the year that gacaca judges and witnesses (for the prosecution and the defence alike) had been threatened and in some cases killed.

Detention without trial

In October, during a parliamentary session, Rwandan senators raised concerns about illegal detentions.

R

Several thousand detainees remained incarcerated on a long-term basis without trial.

■ Dominique Makeli, a former journalist for Radio Rwanda, remained in detention without trial after almost 13 years. The charges against him repeatedly changed. The authorities' latest accusation was that he had incited genocide in a programme for Radio Rwanda in 1994.

■ Two Catholic nuns, Sisters Bénédicte Mukanyangezi and Bernadette Mukarusine, were finally tried in July 2007 after more than 12 years in detention without trial. The gacaca court that took up their cases released them for lack of evidence.

■ Tatiana Mukakibibi, a former presenter and producer with Radio Rwanda, was acquitted of genocide charges by a gacaca court in the southern district of Ruhango on 6 November after 11 years in detention without trial.

Prison conditions

In early 2007, the government announced the provisional release of 8,000 detainees, many of whom had reportedly confessed to participation in the genocide. This was the third wave of mass releases since 2003 in an attempt to address prison overcrowding. Despite these releases, the prisons remain overcrowded. By July, there were 97,000 prison inmates. This figure dropped to 70,000 in September following an official instruction which allowed some detainees to carry out work of benefit to local communities, known as TIG (work of general interest), in camps outside the prisons.

Prison conditions remained extremely harsh and amounted to cruel, inhuman or degrading treatment.

Political prisoners

In April, Pasteur Bizimungu was transferred from prison to house arrest. Pasteur Bizimungu and Charles Ntakirutinka had been sentenced in 2005 to 15 and 10 years' imprisonment respectively on charges of inciting civil disobedience, associating with criminal elements and embezzlement of state funds. Both men had, prior to their arrest, launched a new political party, the Democratic Party for Renewal (Parti Démocratique de Renouveau, PDR-Ubuyanja). Many human rights observers considered that their prosecution was an attempt to eliminate political opposition.

Charles Ntakiruntinka remained in Kigali's Central Prison.

Investigations of genocide and war crimes

In October, the Rwandan commission of inquiry to investigate the role of the French military in the genocide presented its report to President Kagame.

The Spanish judicial authorities continued to investigate the murder of Spanish nationals and other crimes committed between 1990 and 2002 in Rwanda and the Democratic Republic of the Congo. The investigation focused on the alleged direct involvement of 69 members of the RPF, some of whom were high-ranking figures in the military.

Foreign governments, such as those of the UK, France, Canada and the Netherlands initiated judicial proceedings against alleged Rwandan genocide suspects residing, sometimes under false identities, in their countries.

International Criminal Tribunal for Rwanda

Trials of prominent genocide suspects continued before the ICTR, which held 61 detainees at the end of 2007. Twenty-eight trials, involving multiple and single defendants, were ongoing. Eighteen suspects indicted by the ICTR were still at large.

Since opening in 1996, the ICTR has rendered 32 definitive judgments. The ICTR was mandated by the UN Security Council to complete all trials by the end of 2008. In accordance with its completion strategy, the prosecutor proposed the transfer of three cases to European jurisdictions and five to Rwandan jurisdiction. Since its inception, the ICTR has tried only members and supporters of the government in place in April 1994. It did not fully implement its mandate by investigating all war crimes and crimes against humanity committed in 1994, notably those committed by the RPF.

Enforced disappearances

■ Augustin Cyiza, a prominent member of civil society, and Léonard Hitimana, a member of the Transitional National Assembly, were reportedly victims of enforced disappearance in 2003. Since then, officials have denied knowledge of their whereabouts, and have carried out no rigorous investigations into their disappearances.

Amnesty International reports

▤ Rwanda: Freedom of expression under attack (AFR 47/002/2007)
▤ Rwanda: Give Dominique Makeli a trial or let him go (postcard) (AFR 47/006/2007)

📖 Rwanda: Fear for safety/Legal concern: François Xavier Byuma (AFR 47/007/2007)

📖 Rwanda: Abolition of the death penalty (AFR 47/010/2007)

📖 Rwanda: Suspects must not be transferred to Rwandan courts for trial until it is demonstrated that trials will comply with international standards of justice (AFR 47/013/2007)

📖 Rwanda: Genocide suspects must not be transferred until fair trial conditions met (AFR 47/014/2007)

SAUDI ARABIA

KINGDOM OF SAUDI ARABIA

Head of state and government:	King Abdullah Bin 'Abdul 'Aziz Al-Saud
Death penalty:	retentionist
Population:	25.8 million
Life expectancy:	72.2 years
Under-5 mortality (m/f):	25/17 per 1,000
Adult literacy:	82.9 per cent

The human rights situation remained dire although legal reforms were announced and there was continuing public debate about women's rights. Hundreds of people suspected of terrorism were arrested and detained in virtual secrecy, and thousands of people arrested in previous years remained in prison. Those arrested included prisoners of conscience, among them peaceful advocates of political reform. Women continued to suffer severe discrimination in law and practice. Torture and other ill-treatment of detainees were common and prisoners were sentenced to flogging and amputation. At least 158 people were executed, including a child offender.

Background

There were sporadic acts of violence by security forces and armed men apparently opposed to the government. The violence resulted in the death or injury of civilians, suspected political opponents and, in rare cases, members of security forces, but few details were available.

In February, an attack by an armed group killed four French nationals who were with a group of tourists in the Western Desert. In April, the government announced that the main suspect had been killed when security forces stormed his home in the holy city of Madina.

Legal developments

In October, the government introduced two laws to restructure the courts and amend the rules governing the judicial profession, and allocated US$1.8 billion to implement the changes. It remained to be seen how this positive move would impact on the three key problems: the secrecy and lack of transparency of the criminal justice system; the lack of adherence to international fair trial standards, such as the rights to legal representation and to appeal; and the lack of independence of the judiciary. These deficiencies remained clearly evident throughout the year and contributed to human rights violations. For example, the judiciary remained silent or was complicit in violations committed in the context of countering terrorism, and it continued to apply discriminatory legislation and issue discriminatory judgments in cases involving women.

Counter-terrorism

Hundreds of suspected supporters of religious opposition groups, officially termed "misguided groups", were detained and thousands arrested in previous years continued to be held without trial and denied basic prisoners' rights.

Those detained during 2007 included terrorism suspects forcibly returned by the authorities of other states, including the USA and Yemen. However, most arrests were made in Saudi Arabia. In some cases, armed security forces killed alleged militants in unclear circumstances during alleged attempts to arrest them. The authorities said that 172 people suspected of planning violent attacks were arrested in April and a further 208 in November in different parts of the country, but did not disclose further details and it was unclear precisely how many suspects were arrested and where they were being held. It was also unclear how many suspects detained in previous years remained in prison, although they were believed to number several thousand. In July, the Interior Ministry said it had detained 9,000 security suspects between 2003 and 2007, of whom 3,106 remained in detention. Most were reportedly subject to a "reform" programme conducted by religious and psychological experts. In November, the government announced the

S

release of 1,500 detainees who had apparently completed the programme.

■ In May, detainees were shown on television confessing to membership of "misguided groups" and describing plans to bomb oil installations and other targets. The government said it would try them on the basis of their confessions. They included Nimr Sahaj al-Baqmi and Abdullah al-Migrin, whose confessions were reportedly ratified by judges. It was unclear whether the two detainees had been allowed access to lawyers, despite the likelihood that they would be charged with offences punishable by death. The fate of all the detainees remained shrouded in secrecy.

'War on terror'

One Saudi Arabian national, Yasser Talal al-Zahrani, died in US custody in Guantánamo Bay, Cuba. At least 77 others were released by the US authorities and returned to Saudi Arabia, where they were immediately arrested but allowed family visits. Some were subsequently released; others remained in detention apparently undergoing the government's "reform" programme for security detainees.

Prisoners of conscience

Over 100 people arrested on account of their religious affiliation or sexual orientation were or appeared to be prisoners of conscience. They included foreign workers belonging to al-Ahmadiyya, who consider it a sect of Islam, members of the Shi'a community, Sunni reformists and peaceful dissidents. They also included women who staged protests in July outside al-Mabahith al-'Amma (General Intelligence Department) prison in Buraida, north of Riyadh. The women were calling for the trial or release of male relatives who had been detained for years without trial and without access to lawyers or the courts to challenge the legality of the detentions. Most of these detainees were released after short periods, but those who were foreign nationals, such as the Ahmadis, were dismissed from their jobs and deported without being allowed to challenge the legality of the action taken against them.

However, at least 12 prisoners of conscience were still held without trial or access to lawyers at the end of the year. They included Dr Abdul Rahman al-Shumayri and nine others, all university professors, writers or lawyers, who had been arrested in February after they issued a petition calling for political reform.

They were held at al-Mabahith al-'Amma prison in Jeddah. They were held incommunicado for nearly six months before being allowed family visits. At least two were reportedly held in solitary confinement.

In an unusual move, prisoner of conscience Dr Abdullah al-Hamid was released on bail after being detained briefly in connection with the women's protest and then tried before an ordinary criminal court in a partly public hearing. He and his brother, who was tried with him on charges arising from the women's protest, were convicted and sentenced to six and four months' imprisonment respectively and required to give an undertaking not to incite further protests. They lodged an appeal but the hearing was not concluded by the end of the year.

Hundreds of former prisoners of conscience, human rights activists, and advocates of peaceful political change remained banned from travel abroad. They included Matrouk al-Falih, a university professor, and one of the reformists imprisoned from March 2004 to August 2005 who was told by the Interior Ministry that he would not be allowed to travel abroad until March 2009. Others were said to have had their bans renewed after they expired.

Discrimination and violence against women

Two cases highlighted the severe nature and extent of legal and other discrimination against women in Saudi Arabia and provoked debate within the country and internationally.

■ The brother of a woman known as Fatima, a mother of two, invoked his legal authority as her male guardian to have a court rule that she be divorced from her husband against her and her husband's will. The brother contended that the husband's tribe was of lower status and that he had failed to disclose this when seeking permission to marry Fatima. Despite the couple's opposition, the court ruled them divorced on the basis of the tribal rule of parity of status between families and tribes as a condition of the validity of their marriage. Fearing that she could be at risk from her relatives, Fatima chose to live in prison rather than go to her brother's home and was subsequently moved to a woman's shelter with her two children. She was unable to meet her former husband as this would mean committing a *khilwa* offence (a meeting between a male and female who are not members of the same immediate family), which could put them both at risk of prosecution and punishment by flogging and imprisonment.

■ A 20-year-old woman, known as the "al-Qatif girl" to protect her identity, was gang-raped by seven men in 2006 in al-Qatif city. When the case came to court, she and a male companion who had been with her before the rape were each sentenced to 90 lashes for committing a *khilwa* offence. The rapists were sentenced to prison terms ranging from one to five years in addition to flogging. All the sentences were then increased on appeal. The rape victim and her male companion were sentenced to six-month prison terms and 200 lashes, while the rapists' sentences were increased to prison terms ranging from two to nine years in addition to flogging. The rape victim's lawyer declared publicly that his client, as the victim of the crime, should not have been punished. In response, the Justice Ministry stated that by committing *khilwa* the young woman was partly responsible for her own rape and began disciplinary action against the lawyer, accusing him of breaching the law and disclosing the case to the media. In December, the King pardoned the rape victim and the case against her and the male companion was reportedly withdrawn. The disciplinary action against her lawyer was also stopped and he was allowed to resume his work.

In September, women's rights activists petitioned the King to allow women to drive vehicles, as permitted in all other countries. There were also calls for Saudi Arabian women to be allowed to compete in international sporting events along with their male counterparts.

Discrimination fuelled violence against women, with foreign domestic workers particularly at risk of abuses such as beatings, rape and even murder, and non-payment of wages. There was concern that discriminatory laws relating to marriage caused women to be trapped in violent and abusive relationships from which they had no legal recourse.

The government submitted its first report to the Committee on the Elimination of Discrimination against Women (CEDAW) and was scheduled to appear before the committee in January 2008.

Torture and other ill-treatment

Torture and other ill-treatment were widespread and generally committed with impunity. Security forces were alleged to use various methods, including beatings with sticks, punching, suspending detainees by their wrists, sleep deprivation and insults. A video clip released in April showed images of prisoners being tortured in al-Hair Prison, Riyadh. The government said it would investigate the incident and the prison authorities later said that one soldier had been disciplined for the torture and suspended for a month and another had been suspended for 20 days for failing to intervene and stop the assaults on prisoners. It was not known whether any independent investigation was carried out or whether the perpetrators had been brought to justice.

At least six cases alleging torture and deaths in custody were brought against the religious police, the Committee for the Promotion of Virtue and Prevention of Vice (CPVPV), in various courts, but in all of those completed the accused CPVPV officials were exonerated. There was, however, increased media coverage of these cases.

Cruel, inhuman and degrading punishments

Judicial corporal punishments were routinely ordered by courts. Flogging sentences were frequently handed down as a main or additional punishment for most criminal offences and carried out almost daily. The highest number of lashes imposed in cases recorded by Amnesty International was 7,000 – against two men convicted of sodomy in October by a court in al-Baha. Children were among those sentenced to floggings.

At least three people had their right hand amputated at the wrist after being convicted of theft.

Death penalty

At least 158 people, 82 Saudi Arabians and 76 foreign nationals, were executed. They included three women and at least one child offender, Dhahian Rakan al-Sibai', who was 15 at the time of the alleged murder for which he was condemned. He was executed in July in Taif. Those executed were convicted of murder, rape, drug offences, witchcraft, apostasy and other charges, but virtually no information was available about their trials or any appeal, or whether the defendants had received legal representation. Most of the executions were carried out in public.

Several hundred people were believed to remain on death row. Among them were child offenders, including Rizana Nafeek, a Sri Lankan domestic

S

worker, who was sentenced to death for a murder in 2005 when she was 17.

Amnesty International visit

🚃 Amnesty International again asked to visit Saudi Arabia to discuss human rights, but the government had still not agreed dates for such a visit by the end of 2007.

SENEGAL

REPUBLIC OF SENEGAL

Head of state:	Abdoulaye Wade
Head of government:	Cheikh Hadjibou Soumaré (replaced Macky Sall in June)
Death penalty:	abolitionist for all crimes
Population:	12.2 million
Life expectancy:	62.3 years
Under-5 mortality (m/f):	124/118 per 1,000
Adult literacy:	39.3 per cent

Hundreds of civilians fled to neighbouring countries to escape sporadic fighting in the southern Casamance region. Torture and ill-treatment continued to be used in detention centres and at least one detainee died as a result. Supporters of opposition parties, human rights defenders and journalists continued to be harassed and some were detained in an attempt to stifle freedom of expression. Despite formal commitments by the authorities, no real progress was made in the long-awaited trial of former Chadian President Hissène Habré.

Background

In March, President Abdoulaye Wade was re-elected in the first round of elections. There were accusations of fraud by his political opponents and clashes between supporters of rival candidates. In June, President's Wade ruling coalition won legislative elections marked by a low turnout and a boycott by most opposition parties.

Sporadic fighting in Casamance

Three years after the December 2004 general peace accord, no progress had been made in the peace process in southern Casamance where sporadic fighting resumed. In January, armed elements of the Democratic Forces of Casamance Movement (Mouvement des forces démocratiques de Casamance, MFDC) launched attacks along the border with Guinea-Bissau against Senegalese soldiers in a protest against mine clearance operations which the MFDC perceived as a pretext to attack their bases.

The long-standing internal divisions between different factions of the MFDC were exacerbated by the death in January of the MFDC's historic leader, Father Augustin Diamacoune Senghor. In March, violent clashes resumed between two rival factions of the MFDC, resulting in the flight of hundreds of civilians to neighbouring Gambia. Despite appeals from members of the government and some MFDC officials, talks to implement the peace accord had not resumed at the end of the year.

Torture and death in detention

Torture and ill-treatment of criminal suspects in police stations continued to be reported. At least one detainee died in detention.

■ In April, Dominique Lopy, aged 23, was arrested in Kolda, some 600km south-east of Dakar, by police officers who suspected him of stealing a television. His family saw him with visible marks of beatings when he was brought back to his home for a house search. He died in detention the following day. Following protests, the authorities agreed to conduct an autopsy, but by the end of the year no results had been made public.

Freedom of expression under attack

Supporters of opposition parties, human rights defenders and several journalists were arrested and harassed in an attempt to stifle freedom of expression and criticism of the President.

■ In January, a banned peaceful demonstration organized by opposition parties was broken up and some political leaders were beaten and briefly detained.

■ In July, Alioune Tine, Secretary General of the African Assembly for the Defense of Human Rights (Rencontre Africaine pour la Défense des Droits de l'Homme, RADDHO) was briefly detained after weapons were found at the organization's headquarters. These arms appeared in fact to be decommissioned weapons handed over by the Senegalese army to be burned in the context of an international campaign against the proliferation of arms. Alioune Tine was released without charge.

International justice – Hissène Habré

In July 2006, the AU had called on Senegal to try Hissène Habré, living in exile in Senegal, for torture and other crimes committed during his rule (1982-1990). However, by the end of 2007 an investigating judge had not been appointed, despite the Senegalese government's announcement that it would allow the Dakar Assise Court to organize a possible trial of Hissène Habré and, to this end, to receive financial and logistical support from foreign countries, such as Switzerland and France.

In November, experts of the UN Committee against Torture said that the case was progressing too slowly. The Committee urged the Senegalese authorities to speed up the implementation of the Committee's May 2006 decision, which called upon Senegal to start criminal proceedings against Hissène Habré. Senegal promised the Committee that it would open an investigation in the coming months, while continuing to stress that it needed international funding and support for the trial. In the same month the AU decided that the case was moving too slowly and appointed former Benin minister Robert Dossou as its special representative to speed up proceedings.

Amnesty International report

📋 Senegal: Commentary on implementing legislation for the Rome Statute (AFR 49/002/2007)

SERBIA

REPUBLIC OF SERBIA

Head of state:	Boris Tadić
Head of government:	Vojislav Koštunica
Death penalty:	abolitionist for all crimes
Life expectancy:	73.6 years
Adult literacy:	96.4 per cent

The year was dominated by the failure of the Serbian government and ethnic Albanian authorities to agree on the future status of Kosovo. Continuing uncertainty about the final status of Kosovo heightened security concerns amongst minority communities and fears of further human rights violations. Impunity for war crimes, including enforced disappearances, persisted. Discrimination against minority communities continued.

Background

Following elections in January, Serbia remained without a government until May, when Prime Minister Vojislav Koštunica of the Democratic Party of Serbia and President Boris Tadić of the Democratic Party formed a coalition government. The right-wing Serbian Radical Party (SRS) remained the largest opposition party.

In May, Serbia assumed the Chair of the Committee of Ministers of the Council of Europe. Negotiations with the European Union (EU) on Serbia's Stabilization and Association Agreement (SAA) resumed in June, after suspension following Serbia's failure to cooperate with the International Criminal Tribunal for the former Yugoslavia (Tribunal). The SAA was initialled on 7 November.

Elections in Kosovo in November were won by the Democratic Party of Kosovo, led by Hashim Thaçi, former political leader of the Kosovo Liberation Army (KLA).

S

Final status of Kosovo

Kosovo remained part of Serbia, administered under UN Security Council (UNSC) Resolution 1244/99 by the UN Interim Administration Mission in Kosovo (UNMIK). After the failure of the parties to agree on the future status of Kosovo, the UN Secretary General's Special Envoy for the Future Status

Process for Kosovo presented to the UNSC in March a "Comprehensive Proposal for the Final Status of Kosovo (Ahtisaari Plan)", advocating "supervised independence".

The Ahtisaari Plan proposed jurisdiction by Kosovo over legislative, executive and judicial functions, a European Security and Defence Policy mission responsible for international judiciary, prosecutors and police force, and an International Civilian Representative charged with implementation of the settlement. The plan provided for the protection of Serbian cultural and religious heritage; the right to return of refugees; and the protection of minority communities in majority-Serb municipalities.

Serbia considered the plan violated Serbia's sovereignty and territorial integrity. Russia threatened to veto proposed UNSC resolutions. In July the UN Secretary General charged a Troika of the EU, Russia and the US to continue talks, but no agreement was reached by December. The EU and US persuaded the prime minister designate to delay a unilateral declaration of independence.

Serbia

War crimes – international prosecutions

The Chief Prosecutor to the Tribunal expressed serious concerns at the lack of cooperation by Serbia, including the failure to surrender Bosnian Serb general Ratko Mladić. Serbian authorities cooperated in the arrests of indicted suspects Vlastimir Đorđević in Montenegro and Zdravko Tolimir in Bosnia and Herzegovina (BiH).

Proceedings opened in March against Ramush Haradinaj, former KLA leader and former Prime Minister of Kosovo, indicted with others for crimes against humanity and violations of the law or customs of war. Police in Kosovo failed to protect prosecution witnesses; by November three witnesses who refused to testify had been indicted for contempt of court.

Proceedings continued against six senior Serbian political, police and military officials jointly indicted for crimes against humanity and violations of the laws and customs of war in Kosovo. They include former Serbian president Milan Milutinović, former police colonel general Sreten Lukić, former deputy prime minister of the Federal Republic of Yugoslavia Nikola Šainović, former General Chief of Staff of the Yugoslav Army Dragoljub Ojdanić and former Yugoslav Army colonel generals Nebojša Pavković and Vladimir

Lazarević. In September the trial concluded of three Yugoslav People's Army officers (the "Vukovar Three", see Croatia, International prosecutions).

In September, the Appeals Chamber upheld the conviction in 2005 of Haradin Bala, sentenced to 13 years' imprisonment for the murder of at least 22 Serbs and Albanians, their illegal imprisonment, torture and inhuman treatment. The acquittal of two other former KLA members was upheld.

The trial of Vojislav Šešelj, leader of the SRS, charged with the persecution and forcible deportation of non-Serbs in both Croatia and BiH, recommenced in November.

On 26 February, the International Court of Justice (ICJ) ruled that Serbia had not committed genocide at Srebrenica, but had breached the Genocide Convention by failing to prevent genocide at Srebrenica and to punish those responsible; the ICJ called on Serbia to transfer Ratko Mladić, indicted for genocide and complicity in genocide, to the Tribunal.

War crimes – domestic prosecutions

Between 32 and 35 cases of war crimes were reportedly under investigation by the War Crimes Chamber of the Belgrade District Court, although few prosecutions were completed. Assistance to victim-witnesses in most cases was provided by the Humanitarian Law Centre (HLC), an NGO.

■ On 11 April, four former members of the paramilitary unit known as the Scorpions were convicted of war crimes for the killing in 1995 of six Bosniak (Bosnian Muslim) civilians from Srebrenica at Godinjske bare, near Trnovo in BiH, and sentenced to between five and 20 years' imprisonment. The prosecutor appealed against the acquittal of one defendant and the five-year sentence of one of the convicted men.

■ The retrial began in March of 14 low-ranking soldiers charged with the murder of Croatian prisoners of war and civilians at Ovčara farm in 1991 (the "Vukovar Three"; see Croatia, International prosecutions); the HLC had criticized as unfounded the Supreme Court's decision in 2006 to overturn the conviction and order a retrial. The trial continued of eight former police officers indicted in 2006 for the murder of 48 ethnic Albanian civilians in Suva Reka in Kosovo in March 1999.

Enforced disappearances

Seven years after investigations opened, indictments had still not been issued in connection with the transfer in refrigerated trucks to Serbia in 1999 of the bodies of at least 900 ethnic Albanians.

Proceedings continued against serving police officers indicted for the murder of the three Albanian-American Bytiçi brothers in Kosovo in July 1999; the trial was reportedly marred by interruptions and abuse from police "observers".

Political killings

In February, Milorad "Legija" Luković-Ulemek and Radomir Marković were convicted in a retrial which confirmed their sentencing to 15 and eight years' imprisonment respectively for the 1999 assassination attempt on former foreign minister Vuk Drasković. In December, the Supreme Court overturned the first instance rulings for a third time. In May "Legija" and Žveždan Jovanović were convicted and sentenced to 40 years' imprisonment for their roles in the murder of former prime minister Zoran Đinđić, along with 10 others, who were sentenced to between eight and 37 years' imprisonment.

Discrimination against minorities

Cases of ethnically and religiously motivated attacks continued, including against Albanians, Croats, Bosniaks, Hungarians, Roma, Ruthenians and Vlachs, ranging from attacks with explosive devices, hate-speech and verbal abuse by fans at football matches. Perpetrators were seldom brought to justice.

■ Života Milanović, a member of the Hindu religious community in Jagodina, who had been assaulted five times since 2001, was in June stabbed in the stomach, arms and legs. In November the NGO Youth Initiative for Human Rights applied on his behalf to the European Court of Human Rights in respect of Serbia's failure to protect the right to life, provide an efficient legal remedy and ensure freedom from torture and discrimination.

In June, the UN Committee on the Elimination of Discrimination against Women (CEDAW) urged Serbia to address inadequate health-care services and provide equal access to education for marginalized groups of women and girls, in particular Roma. UNICEF, the UN children's agency, reported that over 80 per cent of Romani children experienced "unacceptable deprivation and multidimensional discrimination". In December, the mayor of Topola reportedly stated that the Roma community in the town should be enclosed behind barbed wire.

Inter-ethnic violence

Political disputes and violent clashes continued in the Sandžak region. Incidents included shootings between rival faith communities in Novi Pazar. At least 13 men believed to be of the Wahhabi faith were arrested and indicted in September for conspiring against Serbia's security and constitutional order. One suspect, Ismail Prentic, was killed in a police raid in the village of Donja Trnava near Novi Pazar; two men were arrested in December.

■ Amnesty International was concerned at the detention of Bekto Memić, aged 68 and in poor health, arrested in March in connection with the search for his son, Nedžad Memić. Bekto Memić was released then re-arrested in April at a health clinic in Novi Pazar. Family members reported that he was ill-treated en route to the hospital wing of Belgrade central prison, where he has been held since.

■ In April, Ižet Fijuljanin was convicted and sentenced for the attempted murder of three members of the Wahhabi faith in November 2006 after they had allegedly tried to take over a Novi Pazar mosque.

Human rights defenders

In June NGOs called on the Parliament to apply the UN Declaration on Human Rights Defenders. They emphasized the risks, including physical violence, malicious prosecutions and public stigmatization, to which women defenders in Serbia were exposed.

■ In July Maja Stojanović, convicted in November 2005 for displaying posters calling for the arrest of Ratko Mladić, was required to serve 10 days' imprisonment following her refusal to pay a fine imposed by the court, but instead her fine was paid by NGOs. Amnesty International considered her a potential prisoner of conscience.

Violence against women

In their consideration of Serbia's report on implementation of the UN Women's Convention, the CEDAW expressed concern at the prevalence of domestic violence and the apparent reduction in penalties. They recommended the adoption of a national action plan on gender equality and the adoption of a law to consolidate existing provisions within the Criminal Code. CEDAW also urged Serbia to adopt a draft National Plan against Human Trafficking.

Kosovo

Impunity for the international community

UNMIK failed to implement measures ensuring access to redress and reparations for violations of rights by members of the international community. In February, the former international Ombudsperson in Kosovo was appointed chair of the Human Rights Advisory Panel

(HRAP), which had been introduced into law in March 2006 to provide remedies for acts and omissions by UNMIK; the HRAP did not convene until November.

■ In May, the Grand Chamber of the European Court of Human Rights ruled inadmissible two complaints against member states of the NATO-led Kosovo Force (KFOR), considering that acts and omissions by UNMIK and KFOR could not be attributed to those states, as they did not take place on their territory, nor through any decision taken by their authorities. Agim Behrami had sought redress after his 12-year-old son Gadaf was killed in March 2000 by an unexploded cluster bomb, which a contingent of KFOR led by France had failed to detonate or mark; his younger son Bekim was severely injured.

There were allegations of political interference in the process of appointing a new Ombudsperson by the Kosovo Assembly, which failed to adhere to procedures set down in law, including that candidates failed to meet the criteria for the post. In October after domestic and international NGOs, including Amnesty International, expressed concern the appointment was postponed.

Unlawful killings

■ Mon Balaj and Arben Xheladini were killed and Zenel Zeneli was seriously injured on 10 February during a demonstration called by the NGO Self-Determination (Vetëvendosje!), against the Ahtisaari Plan. An investigation by the UNMIK Department of Justice concluded that the men had been killed by members of the Romanian Formed Police Unit, deployed to the largely non-violent demonstration, and that the deaths of Mon Balaj and Arben Xheladini were caused by "improper deployment of rubber bullets by at least one and perhaps two Romanian gunners".

In March, the Romanian authorities had withdrawn from Kosovo 11 police officers reportedly in possession of information crucial to the investigation; the Romanian authorities subsequently reported they had found insufficient evidence to open a criminal investigation. The HRAP announced in December that they would consider an application by the families of Mon Balaj and Arben Xheladini.

Fair trial standards

■ There were concerns that the trial of Albin Kurti, leader of the NGO Vetëvendosje! in connection with the organization of and participation in the demonstration of 10 February, was not conducted in accordance with law applicable in Kosovo or international standards for fair trial. The prosecution appeared to be politicized and proceedings before a panel of international judges demonstrated a lack of judicial independence. Albin Kurti remained under house arrest at the end of the year.

Impunity for war crimes, including enforced disappearances and abductions

A lack of prompt and effective investigations, the absence of witness protection, a backlog of appeal cases and a declining number of international judiciary and prosecutors to consider cases of war crimes, including enforced disappearances, contributed to continuing impunity for these crimes.

Impunity remained in over 3,000 cases of enforced disappearances and abductions. Relatives of the missing complained at being repeatedly interviewed when new UNMIK police contingents took over cases; prosecutors complained that witnesses refused to come forward.

Some 1,998 persons remained unaccounted for, including Albanians, Serbs and members of other minorities. Exhumations of 73 bodies or part-bodies were conducted by the Office of Missing Persons and Forensics. Some 455 exhumed bodies remained unidentified.

Minority rights

Members of minority communities were excluded from talks on the future status of Kosovo. Anti-discrimination legislation in force was not used. Fear of inter-ethnic attacks restricted the freedom of movement of Serbs and Roma.

Buses carrying Serb passengers were stoned by Albanian youths; grenades or other explosive devices were thrown at buses or houses. Orthodox churches continued to be looted or vandalized, including in an attack with a rocket-propelled grenade on the Orthodox monastery in Dečan/Deçani. A roadside grenade attack was perpetrated on a minibus carrying Albanians through the predominantly Serbian north in July.

Perpetrators of inter-ethnic attacks were infrequently brought to justice. Some 600 to 700 cases remained unresolved from the inter-ethnic violence of March 2004.

■ Esmin Hamza and a minor, 'AK', were convicted in June 2007 at Prizren District Court of inciting national, racial and religious hatred and participating in a joint criminal enterprise during March 2004, and sentenced respectively to four years' imprisonment and two years in a correctional facility.

Progress was made in a few long-standing cases. In March, Jeton Kiqina was convicted and sentenced to 16 years' imprisonment for the murder or attempted murder in August 2001 of five members of the family of Hamit Hajra, an ethnic Albanian police officer who had worked for the Serbian authorities. In October an ethnic Albanian was arrested on suspicion of involvement in the murder of 14 Serb men in Staro Gračko in July 1999. In October proceedings opened against Florim Ejupi, indicted for the bombing of the Niš Express bus near Podujevo/ë in February 2001, in which 12 Serbs were killed and 22 severely injured.

The right to return – minorities

Some EU and Council of Europe member states planned to forcibly return to Kosovo persons from minority communities, before conditions for their return in safety and security were established.

Roma who had lived in lead-contaminated camps were among 280 individuals who returned to new accommodation in the Roma neighbourhood of south Mitrovica/ë; others remained displaced, including in Leposavić in northern Kosovo, where Romani families continued to live without access to basic amenities and under threat of eviction. Serbs displaced in March 2004 were unable to return to their homes; there was little government coordination of return and reintegration agreements, although some municipal authorities assisted voluntary return.

Violence against women

Trafficking into forced prostitution continued, the majority of women being internally trafficked or trafficked from Albania. The authorities failed to implement an administrative directive providing assistance and support to trafficked persons.

The judiciary failed to implement legislation on domestic violence relating to protection orders, which were not issued within the time specified by law, and which failed to protect women from violence.

Amnesty International visit/reports

🚌 Amnesty International delegates visited Kosovo in November-December.

📄 Kosovo (Serbia): No Forcible Return of Minority Communities to Kosovo (EUR 70/004/2007)

📄 Europe and Central Asia: Summary of Amnesty International's concerns in the region, Serbia (including Kosovo): July-December 2006 (EUR 01/001/2007); January-June 2007 (EUR 01/010/2007)

SIERRA LEONE

REPUBLIC OF SIERRA LEONE

Head of state and government:	Ernest Bai Koroma
	(replaced Ahmad Tejan Kabbah in November)
Death penalty:	retentionist
Population:	5.8 million
Life expectancy:	41.8 years
Under-5 mortality (m/f):	291/265 per 1,000
Adult literacy:	34.8 per cent

The overall security situation was generally stable, with a few instances of violence linked to the elections in the middle of the year. There was some progress in implementing the recommendations of the Truth and Reconciliation Commission. Three laws were passed that improve the protection of women's rights.

Background

The second elections since the conflict ended in 2002 were held on 11 August. In a run-off election in September, Ernest Koroma of the All People's Congress (APC) won 54.6 per cent of the final vote. The inauguration took place on 15 November in Freetown. Vice-President Solomon Berewa of the governing Sierra Leone People's Party (SLPP) winning 45.4 per cent.

The trial of former Liberian President Charles Taylor was delayed but was due to start in early 2008. Two of the three trials before the Special Court were in appeal after convictions and sentencing; the third was ongoing. Three people on trial for treason were released.

During the year the UN Peacebuilding Fund pledged US$35 million and the UN Peacebuilding Commission made significant progress and agreed on five priorities. The mandate of the peace-building entity the UN Integrated Office in Sierra Leone (UNIOSIL) was renewed for another year.

Sierra Leone remained one of the poorest countries in the world, with extremely low life expectancy and high illiteracy rates.

Special Court for Sierra Leone

In July, three Armed Forces Revolutionary Council (AFRC) members – Alex Tamba Brima, Brima Bazzy Kamara and Santigie Borbor Kanu – were each found

S

guilty on 11 charges of war crimes and crimes against humanity, including committing acts of terrorism, murder, rape and enslavement and conscripting children under the age of 15 into armed groups. They were each acquitted on three other charges, including sexual slavery and forced marriage. Alex Brima and Santigie Kanu were sentenced to 50 years each, and Brima Kamara to 45 years. The case was on appeal at the end of the year.

In February, Civil Defence Forces (CDF) member Chief Hinga Norman, who had been indicted before the Special Court on eight counts of war crimes and crimes against humanity, died from complications following surgery in Senegal.

In August, CDF members Moinina Fofana and Allieu Kondewa were found guilty of four counts of war crimes, crimes against humanity and serious violations of international humanitarian law. In October, the Special Court Trial Chamber sentenced Moinina Fofana and Allieu Kondewa to six and eight years respectively. The court justified the relatively low sentences on the ground that their murders of civilians, many of whom were women and children hacked to death with machetes, were committed in a "palpably just and defendable cause", to restore democracy.

Postponements of the trial of Charles Taylor in The Hague occurred throughout 2007. The trial was expected to start again in early 2008. Initial delays were due to the lack of adequate time that the defence had to prepare for the case.

The defence cases for the Revolutionary United Front (RUF) accused – Issa Sesay, Morris Kallon and Augustine Gbao – opened in May 2007 and were expected to last until April 2008.

Release of political opponents

On 1 November, Omrie Golley, former spokesman of the RUF, Mohamed Alpha Bah and David Kai-Tongi were released after being on trial for over a year for treason. The Attorney General had declared that there was no case against them.

Press freedom

In January, the Attorney General sought the extradition of Ahmed Komeh, Bai Bureh Komeh and Aminata Komeh, children of Fatmata Hassan, ruling SLPP Member of Parliament. The three had fled to the UK following the death of Harry Yansaneh,

editor of the independent newspaper *For Di People*, in 2005.

■ Philip Neville, publisher and editor of privately-owned *Standard Times*, was twice charged with "seditious libel", once in February and again in June. The second incident was linked to the publication of an article on government conduct. Bail was set at 200 million leones (US$68,135) – an amount considered unreasonably high.

Intimidation around elections took place on several occasions. On 29 June, Hon Ansu Kaikai of the ruling SLPP allegedly threatened to shut down Radio Wanjei in Pujehun and have its station manager arrested if he allowed members of the People's Movement for Democratic Change (PMDC) living outside the country to use the radio to inform its members about the August polls.

Policing and justice system

Public order policing during the election period was largely successful. Violent incidents were few and police were reported to have conducted themselves within international standards on policing and human rights.

There remained a serious lack of trained judges, magistrates, defence lawyers and prosecutors. This resulted in long delays of trials, and extended periods of pre-trial detention – in some cases of up to six years.

Detention facilities in Sierra Leone did not meet international standards. A UN report found that the country's prisons were vastly overcrowded — Pademba Road Prison, designed to house 350, housed over 1,000 inmates. The report found that prison inmates had been awaiting trial for up to two years, and 90 per cent of the detainees interviewed did not have legal representation.

Women's rights

In June, parliament passed a child rights bill. However, the bill was passed only after provisions criminalizing female genital mutilation (FGM) were dropped. Approximately 94 per cent of the female population undergo FGM.

Parliament passed bills on domestic violence, intestate succession and the registration of customary marriage and divorce in June. These were seen as a victory in the strengthening of women's rights in rural areas. Nonetheless, women continued to face

S

widespread discrimination and violence, compounded by a lack of access to justice.

A gender protection task force was established. Led by the non-governmental organization International Rescue Committee, it included representatives of civil society and government.

Transitional justice
National Human Rights Commission
The Human Rights Commission of Sierra Leone (HRCSL) established in December 2006 set up office and carried out training and an awareness-raising tour of the country.
Truth and Reconciliation Commission
A conference initiated by the HRCSL and attended by representatives of civil society, UN agencies and the government, discussed the implementation of recommendations made by the Truth and Reconciliation Commission (TRC) on 13 and 14 November. Government participation in the conference signalled a reinvigorated commitment to ensure the TRC recommendations were carried out comprehensively.
Reparations
The National Commission for Social Action was mandated by the Vice President's office to implement the Reparations Programme. The Task Force on Reparations presented a report to the government on setting up the Special Fund for War Victims and the Reparations Programme.

A mass rally calling for reparations was held in Makeni by Amnesty International members. The Vice President publically committed to ensuring justice and full reparations for the tens of thousands of Sierra Leonean women victims of sexual violence.

Death penalty
Despite efforts by civil society to achieve abolition of the death penalty, a key recommendation of the TRC, 18 people, remained under sentence of death. Eleven people including Sierra Leone Army (SLA) and retired SLA members and others, had been charged with treason. During the year one died and two were released, and at the end of the year seven were waiting for judgments on their appeals, and one appealed and the death sentence was reconfirmed. A further 10 were convicted of murder.

Amnesty International visits/report
🚗 Amnesty International delegates visited in March, June and November.
📄 Sierra Leone: Getting reparations rights for survivors of sexual violence (AFR 51/002/2006)

SINGAPORE

REPUBLIC OF SINGAPORE

Head of state:	S R Nathan
Head of government:	Lee Hsien Loong
Death penalty:	retentionist
Population:	4.4 million
Life expectancy:	79.4 years
Under-5 mortality (m/f):	4/4 per 1,000
Adult literacy:	92.5 per cent

Criticism of the government grew despite restrictions on freedom of expression and assembly. Suspected Islamic militants continued to be held without charge or trial under the Internal Security Act amid concerns that some were at risk of torture or other ill-treatment during questioning. Death sentences were imposed and at least two people were executed. Criminal offenders were sentenced to caning.

Background
Critics pointed to a persistent misuse of laws by the ruling People's Action Party (PAP) and a perceived bias within the judicial system, reiterating the continuing influence of Minister Mentor Lee Kuan Yew in maintaining the country's restrictive human rights climate. The authorities rejected a proposal to de-criminalize homosexuality. Concerns emerged about a reported increase in the gap between rich and poor. Singapore chaired the Association of Southeast Asian Nations (ASEAN), during a year in which the regional body adopted a charter including human rights commitments.

Freedom of expression and assembly
Criminal charges, civil defamation suits and other restrictive measures were variously brought against government critics and human right defenders, foreign news media, peaceful demonstrators and conscientious objectors.

The revised Penal Code broadened the scope of the offence of unlawful assembly.

■ Falun Gong practitioners were fined or jailed for holding peaceful public demonstrations against the Chinese government.

■ Dr Chee Soon Juan, leader of the opposition Singapore Democratic Party (SDP), was imprisoned for two weeks for attempting, as a bankrupt, to leave the

S

country without permission. He had been bankrupted in 2006 following a series of civil defamation suits filed by PAP leaders. He faced numerous other charges, including speaking in public without a permit and selling books on the street without permission.

■ The *Far Eastern Economic Review* was banned and faced a defamation suit for a 2006 article in which it interviewed Chee Soon Juan. The *Financial Times*, rather than contest a defamation suit, apologized to Prime Minister Lee Hsien Loong and the Minister Mentor for an article that linked them with alleged nepotism. Reporters without Borders ranked Singapore 141 out of 169 countries in its press freedom index.

■ A visiting delegation of European and Asian parliamentarians were refused a permit to speak at a SDP forum on the development of democracy internationally.

Justice – detention without trial

At least 37 suspected Islamic militants reportedly remained detained without charge or trial under the Internal Security Act at the end of the year. At least six arrests, some reportedly after "rendition" from abroad, and at least eight releases were reported during the year. Concerns about the risk of ill-treatment or torture continued, despite government assurances that such prisoners were protected by law.

Death penalty

Singapore opposed a UN vote for a worldwide moratorium on the death penalty. Death penalty legislation was reportedly expanded to cover terrorist-linked kidnapping cases.

Trials continued to fall short of international human rights standards due to mandatory death sentences and presumptions of guilt for a number of capital offences. At least two death sentences were handed down after convictions for drugs trafficking and murder. Two convicted drugs traffickers, both foreign nationals, were executed.

Cruel, inhuman and degrading punishments

Criminal offenders were sentenced to caning.

■ Despite his allegedly low IQ, Emmanuel Munisamy was sentenced to 24 strokes for armed robbery and assaulting a policeman. The sentence was overturned on appeal.

SLOVAKIA

SLOVAK REPUBLIC

Head of state:	Ivan Gašparovič
Head of government:	Robert Fico
Death penalty:	abolitionist for all crimes
Population:	5.4 million
Life expectancy:	74.2 years
Under-5 mortality (m/f):	9/9 per 1,000

The Romani minority faced discrimination in access to education, housing, health care and other services, as well as persistent prejudice and hostility. Authorities failed to respond adequately to attacks on foreigners and members of minorities. Failed asylum-seekers were granted increased protection against forcible return, but the acceptance of "diplomatic assurances" against torture and other ill-treatment continued to be a cause of concern.

Discrimination against Roma

Many Roma continued to be caught in a cycle of marginalization and poverty. In November, the European Commission called on Slovakia to take concrete measures on the ground to "bridge segregation" and to end discrimination against Romani children in education. Several Slovak Members of the European Parliament also urged their government to deal with segregation of Roma in housing and schooling, which they referred to as a "time bomb".

Education

Huge numbers of Romani children were still being placed unnecessarily in special schools and classes for children with mental disabilities and learning difficulties, where they followed a reduced curriculum which gave little possibility for reintegrating into mainstream schools or advancing to secondary education. Others were segregated in Roma-only mainstream schools across the country. Poor housing conditions, physical and cultural isolation, poverty and lack of transport continued to hinder Romani children's ability to attend school.

The persistent segregation of Romani children in the education system violated their right to an education free from discrimination, and their future employment prospects remained blighted by the failure of the government to provide them with adequate education.

Housing – forced evictions

Many Roma experienced very poor living conditions, lacking access to plumbing, gas, water and sanitation facilities and connection to the electricity grid. Romani settlements are very often physically segregated from the main town or village, with little public transport; when it exists, many Romani families cannot afford the bus fare.

Roma continued to suffer forced evictions. In January, the NGOs Milan Šimečka Foundation and the Centre on Housing Rights and Evictions along with the European Roma Rights Centre released a report on what they described as a wave of forced evictions experienced by Roma in Slovakia.

■ In September, reportedly more than 200 Roma were forcibly evicted from their houses in Nové Zámky, moved to neighbouring villages and allocated inadequate housing. The Plenipotentiary for Romani communities of the Slovak government, Anina Botošová, criticized the increasing policy of evictions by several municipalities and said that those acts were "illegal".

Forced sterilization of women

In January, the Constitutional Court demanded the reopening of an inquiry into the forced sterilization of three Romani women. In a landmark decision, the Constitutional Court asked the Košice Regional Court to compensate the three women, who were subjected to forced sterilizations between 1999 and 2002. The women were to be awarded damages of 50,000 Slovak koruna (approximately €1,420). Previously, the authorities had refused to admit that any forced sterilisations took place in the country's hospitals, only recognizing that there were "procedural shortcomings".

Attacks against foreigners and minorities

Minorities and foreigners continued to be subjected to racist attacks. NGOs expressed fears that these attacks were on the rise.

■ In March, a man from Nigeria was assaulted in Bratislava. According to the NGO People Against Racism (PAR), the attackers allegedly shouted: "What are you doing here, negro! This is not Africa!" and knocked him to the ground. PAR reported that when police arrived and the man pointed out his attackers, the police officers told him: "Shut up, you're not in Africa!"

■ In May, Hedviga Malinová lodged a complaint with the Constitutional Court after the police halted a criminal prosecution opened in relation to an alleged ethnically motivated attack on her by two men in Nitra in August 2006.

A police investigation in October 2006 had concluded that Hedviga Malinová fabricated her account, and in May criminal proceedings were opened against her for alleged perjury. In July, Police Chief Ján Packa admitted that Hedviga Malinová had been assaulted but "not as she described". In September, Prosecutor General Dobroslav Trnka admitted that some evidence from the investigation was lost in "procedural errors by the police and the prosecutor's office".

Hedviga Malinová filed a complaint with the European Court of Human Rights in November, claiming that she has been subjected to inhumane and humiliating treatment by the Slovak authorities.

■ In November, three men reportedly attacked and shouted Nazi slogans at a 16-year-old half-Cuban girl and told her to "get out of Slovakia". The girl suffered head and spinal injuries. Two attackers were detained and charged with causing bodily harm and advocating incitement to hatred.

Refugees and asylum-seekers

In January, rejected asylum-seekers were given increased protection against forcible return to countries where they may be in danger of serious human rights violations. However, the UN refugee agency, UNHCR, remained concerned at the low number of successful asylum applications in Slovakia. The government's Migration Office reported that between January and September 2007, Slovakia granted refugee status to only eight people out of 2,259 applicants.

'War on terror'

The government failed to reject the use of so-called "diplomatic assurances" from states not to torture people subject to an extradition procedure.

■ In November, the Bratislava regional court ruled that the extradition of Mustapha Labsi, an Algerian national, was admissible. Accused of terrorist activities in France and the UK, Mustapha Labsi had been held in custody in Slovakia since May on the basis of an extradition request by Algeria. The Slovak Prosecutor's Office told the court and media that it had assurances from the

Algerian authorities that Mustapha Labsi would not face torture or the death sentence. In September, the Migration Office of Slovakia refused Mustapha Labsi's request for asylum and for subsidiary protection.

Amnesty International urged the authorities on several occasions not to extradite Mustapha Labsi, where he would be at risk of serious human rights violations, including incommunicado detention at a secret location, torture or other ill-treatment. Amnesty International urged the Minister of Justice not to accept any diplomatic assurances from Algeria. By the end of the year, no substantive response from the Slovak authorities had been received.

Police – allegations of ill-treatment

■ In November, Balli Marzec, a journalist and Polish citizen of Kazakh descent, was arrested for protesting in front of the Presidential Palace during a visit by the Kazakh President. Although her demonstration was reportedly lawful, a police officer asked her to stop disrupting "the public peace". She refused, and was taken to a police car by two police officers. She told Amnesty International that she was punched in the stomach and hit on the head by one of the police officers. A medical examination performed during her detention, the results of which she was not given access to, showed minor injuries. Balli Marzec was released from police custody shortly before midnight, accompanied by the Polish consul. Once in Poland, she underwent a second medical examination and was operated on to stop severe internal bleeding allegedly caused to the assault. In December, Minister of Interior, Robert Kaliňák, announced that the head of the Bratislava police involved would be fired.

Amnesty International visits/reports

🚌 Amnesty International delegates visited Slovakia in January, March and November.

📄 Europe and Central Asia: Summary of Amnesty International's concerns in the region: January-June 2007 (EUR 01/010/2007)

📄 Slovak Republic: Still separate, still unequal: Violations of the right to education of Romani children in Slovakia (EUR 72/001/2007)

📄 Slovakia: Romani children denied equal education free from discrimination (EUR 72/009/2007)

📄 Slovak Republic: Open letter regarding the Slovak chairmanship of the Committee of Ministers at the Council of Europe (EUR 72/010/2007)

📄 Slovakia: Extradition to Algeria would put Mustapha Labsi at risk of torture or other ill-treatment (EUR 72/011/2007)

SLOVENIA

REPUBLIC OF SLOVENIA

Head of state:	Danilo Türk
	(replaced Janez Drnovšek in December)
Head of government:	Janez Janša
Death penalty:	abolitionist for all crimes
Population:	2 million
Life expectancy:	77.4 years
Under-5 mortality (m/f):	7/7 per 1,000
Adult literacy:	99.7 per cent

There was continued concern about the status of thousands of people who were removed from the registry of permanent residents in 1992 (known as the "erased"). Members of Romani communities faced discrimination, including in access to education.

The 'erased'

The Slovenian authorities failed to restore the status of permanent residents of a group of people known as the "erased" or to ensure that they have full access to economic and social rights. Moreover, those affected by the "erasure" continued to be denied access to full reparation, including compensation.

The "erased" included at least 18,305 individuals unlawfully removed from the Slovenian registry of permanent residents in 1992. They were mainly people from other former Yugoslav republics, many of them Roma, who had been living in Slovenia and had not acquired Slovenian citizenship after Slovenia became independent. While some were forcibly expelled, many lost their jobs and/or could no longer be legally employed. They had no, or limited, access to comprehensive healthcare after 1992, in some cases with serious consequences for their health. Of those "erased" in 1992, thousands remained without Slovenian citizenship or a permanent residence permit.

In October the government presented to parliament a draft constitutional law, which was intended to resolve the status of the "erased". Amnesty International called for the withdrawal of the draft law which, as it was presented to parliament, continued to violate the human rights of the "erased" and further aggravated their disadvantaged position. The draft law maintained discriminatory treatment of the "erased",

S

provided new legal grounds for more discriminatory actions by the authorities, including the possibility of revising decisions on individual cases where permanent residency had been restored, and failed to retroactively restore the status of permanent residents of all the "erased". The draft also disclaimed responsibility by state bodies for the "erasure" and explicitly excluded the possibility of compensation for the human rights violations suffered by the "erased".

Discrimination against Roma

The authorities failed to fully integrate Romani children in education and tolerated in certain primary schools the creation of special groups for Romani children, where in some cases a reduced curriculum was taught.

The so-called "Bršljin model", used at the Bršljin elementary school in the city of Novo Mesto, provided tuition in separate groups for pupils who needed help in certain subjects. Teachers in Bršljin admitted that such groups were composed mostly, and sometimes exclusively, of Roma. The Slovenian authorities claimed that such a model did not result in the segregation of Romani children and that pupils were only temporarily placed in separate groups. Amnesty International was informed that the model was still being developed. Further details had not been received by the end of the year.

Amnesty International reports

📄 Slovenia: Amnesty International condemns forcible return of 'erased' person to Germany (EUR 68/002/2007)

📄 Slovenia: Draft Constitutional Law perpetuates discriminatory treatment suffered by the 'erased' (EUR 68/003/2007)

📄 Europe and Central Asia: Summary of Amnesty International's concerns in the region: January-June 2007 (EUR 01/010/2007)

SOMALIA

SOMALI REPUBLIC
Head of state of Transitional Federal Government: **Abdullahi Yusuf Ahmed**
Head of government of Transitional Federal Government: **Nur Hassan Hussein (replaced Ali Mohamed Gedi in November)**
Head of Somaliland Republic: **Dahir Riyaale Kahin**
Death penalty: retentionist
Population: 8.8 million
Life expectancy: 47.1 years
Under-5 mortality (m/f): 192/182 per 1,000

The humanitarian crisis continued to worsen during 2007. Somalia had no effective central government or justice system. Repeated outbreaks of armed conflict led to thousands more civilian deaths and more than a million people displaced by the end of 2007. Several thousand people were detained by militias and police outside any recognizable legal process. Human rights defenders and journalists were in danger.

In the north-west, the self-declared Republic of Somaliland, whose independence is not recognized by international bodies, enjoyed relative stability.

Background

Violence escalated following the defeat, in late December 2006, of the forces of the Council of Somali Islamic Courts (COSIC), which had controlled Mogadishu for some months, by Ethiopian forces supporting the Transitional Federal Government (TFG). An insurgency in Mogadishu was met by Ethiopian-led counter-insurgency operations in March and April, and there was further fierce fighting in the last three months of 2007. Over 6,000 were killed in the conflict, and hundreds of thousands were displaced, including 600,000 from Mogadishu. Thousands of other people fled to other countries. The Kenyan border, however, remained officially closed throughout 2007 to people fleeing conflict in south-western and central Somalia.

TFG leaders moved to the capital Mogadishu in early 2007 but most government ministers and the Transitional Federal Parliament remained in Baidoa town, 80 km to the west. The TFG did not succeed in establishing peace or governance in Mogadishu. A National Reconciliation Conference was held in

S

Mogadishu between August and October but was boycotted by TFG opponents and former Islamic Courts leaders. Some of these opponents formed the Alliance for the Re-Liberation of Somalia (ARS) in Eritrea in September and declared support for the insurgents, particularly opposing the Ethiopian military presence in Somalia.

In January the UN mandated an AU peace-support force (AMISOM). Uganda provided 1,600 troops, less than one-fifth of the projected 8,000 force, joined by a smaller Burundian contingent in December. It had little impact on human rights. The AU and UN had envisaged a UN peace-keeping operation replacing AMISOM and Ethiopian troops, but in November the UN Security Council rejected a UN peace-keeping operation because of the severity of the conflict. The UN arms embargo was widely flouted.

Implementation of the agreed five-year transition from state collapse to an elected democratic government expected in 2009 was delayed. A new government was being formed by the new Prime Minister in December after the former Prime Minister was dismissed by the President.

Somaliland

The Somaliland Republic, which declared itself a separate state in 1991, continued to seek international recognition. In October there was a brief resumption of conflict near Las Anod town in an area claimed by both Somaliland and Puntland (a semi-autonomous regional state in north-eastern Somalia). Several people were killed in fighting between local clan militias which escalated into confrontation between both authorities. Tens of thousands of people were displaced by the fighting.

Armed conflict

The conflict in Mogadishu between insurgents and the TFG, supported by Ethiopian troops, was marked by numerous violations of international humanitarian law. These included indiscriminate and disproportionate attacks on civilian neighbourhoods in response to insurgent attacks.

In January US airships attacked remnants of the COSIC forces in the south-west who had fled from Mogadishu. Dozens of civilians were reportedly killed by the US attack, as well as COSIC fighters.

In March and April Ethiopian forces killed hundreds of civilians in Mogadishu in attacks on civilian areas. Ethiopian forces were also accused of extrajudicial executions of civilians and rape during counter-insurgency operations from October, after the failed National Reconciliation Conference.

Justice and rule of law

The Transitional Federal Parliament approved a three-month state of emergency in January, which was not renewed. It established a new National Security Agency.

The UN provided support to revive the system of justice and policing in Mogadishu and also other less conflict-afflicted areas, but generally there was still no recognizable rule of law or system of courts. Arbitrary detention of TFG opponents and suspected insurgents was frequent throughout 2007, particularly during counter-insurgency operations. Several thousand people were detained by TFG militias and police without any fair or recognizable legal process. In July the TFG declared a general amnesty for insurgents but arrests resumed in new military operations from October. Most detainees were released within weeks, often on payment of bribes. Many were held in Mogadishu central prison in overcrowded, unhygienic cells. Others were held in unauthorized places of detention, with their whereabouts unknown to their families.

■ Ahmed Diriye Ali, a Hawiye clan council leader, was arrested in Mogadishu in November and held in secret detention without charge or trial on political grounds. His relatives were not allowed to send him medication for diabetes and high blood pressure.

■ Raha Janaqow, head of Saacid women's organization in Mogadishu was detained for some days in April in a secret prison.

■ Idris Osman, director of the UN World Food Programme in Mogadishu, was arrested by TFG security forces in October and held incommunicado for several days without charge or explanation.

Freedom of expression
Human rights defenders

Human rights defenders were at high risk from all sides.

■ Isse Abdi Isse, founder-director of Kisima, a human rights organization in Kismayu, was murdered in Mogadishu in March.

■ The President of the Supreme Court, Yusuf Ali Harun, was detained in Baidoa in October after

S

declaring the President's dismissal of Prime Minister Ali Mohamed Gedi unconstitutional. The TFG authorities subsequently charged him with corruption, including misuse of UN funds, which he denied.

■ In Somaliland, three leaders of the new Qaran opposition party were jailed in August for three years nine months for seditious assembly and banned from political activities for five years. The trial was unfair and their defence lawyers were convicted of contempt of court, fined and barred from practising for a year. Mohamed Abdi Gabose, Mohamed Hashi Elmi and Jamal Aideed Ibrahim were prisoners of conscience. They were pardoned by the President and freed in December but the political ban remained in force.

Journalists

Dozens of journalists were detained for short periods, and several media agencies were shut down briefly. Eight journalists were murdered during 2007. Some killings were politically motivated and no one was brought to justice for any of them. In late 2007, the violence against the media in Mogadishu reached levels not seen since 1991. In December the Transitional Federal Parliament passed a media law which included restrictions on journalists and private media agencies.

■ Bashir Nur Gedi, manager of Shabelle Media Network in Mogadishu, was killed at his home by unidentified gunmen in October.

■ Yusuf Abdi Gabobe, chief editor of the *Somaliland Times* and *Haatuf* newspapers in Somaliland, was arrested in January for criticizing corruption. He was sentenced to two years' imprisonment after an unfair trial. He was freed in March by a presidential pardon.

Over 50 journalists from Mogadishu fled to neighbouring countries. In December the Somaliland government ordered 24 journalists who had fled there from Mogadishu to leave the country but after appeals did not implement the order.

Violence against women

There were numerous reports of rape during the conflict in Mogadishu by Ethiopian troops, TFG militiamen and armed bandits. Internally displaced women in camps and others fleeing Mogadishu in public vehicles were also raped, particularly women from minority communities.

Women's organizations continued to campaign against female genital mutilation and domestic violence. In the Transitional Federal Parliament,

women were still denied their full representation set by the Transitional Federal Charter in 2004.

Refugees and internally displaced people

The Kenyan government's closure of its border with Somalia in January violated international refugee law and hindered humanitarian access to south-western Somalia. Thousands of asylum-seekers fleeing conflict in Mogadishu and the south-west were turned back at the border in January. (See Kenya entry.)

The number of internally displaced people (IDPs) fluctuated as the intensity of the conflict varied in Mogadishu, the south-western port of Kismayu and other parts of the country.

By the end of the year, the total number of internally displaced people was estimated at over a million, about 400,000 of whom (mainly members of minorities) had been living in IDP camps for several years. Conditions for the displaced were dire. Many lacked water, sanitation and medical assistance, and violence including rape and looting by former militia members was widespread. International humanitarian agencies could not reach many of the displaced, and several staff of local partner NGOs were killed and relief supplies looted. TFG officials frequently obstructed the delivery of humanitarian aid. Some officials accused humanitarian agencies of "feeding terrorists".

Over 1,400 displaced Somalis and Ethiopian nationals died at sea in trafficking operations from Puntland to Yemen.

'War on terror'

At least 140 people fleeing Somalia in January who managed to enter Kenya were detained by the Kenyan authorities. At least 85 of these detainees, who were detained incommunicado without charge or trial on suspicion of links with COSIC, were unlawfully transferred (rendered) to Somalia in January. They were detained in Mogadishu or Baidoa and then transferred onwards to Ethiopia, along with other people detained by Ethiopian troops in Somalia on similar grounds. Some were released but 41 acknowledged by Ethiopia were still detained incommunicado and in secret at the end of 2007.

Death penalty

Death sentences were imposed by courts in all areas. Some sentences were commuted to *diya*

S

(compensation payments to victims' families), but there were also several executions.

■ A former TFG militia member was publicly executed by shooting in Mogadishu in July after a swift and unfair trial for homicide.

In Somaliland, death sentences imposed in 2004 on seven men allegedly linked to al-Qa'ida who were convicted of killing three international aid workers were commuted on appeal by the Supreme Court. Three people were executed in 2007.

Amnesty International visit/reports

🚌 Amnesty International representatives visited Somaliland in December.

📄 Kenya/Ethiopia/Somalia – Horn of Africa unlawful transfers in the 'war on terror' (AFR 25/006/2007)

📄 Somalia: Amnesty International denounces abuses in escalating Mogadishu conflict and killing of human rights defender (AFR 52/006/2007)

📄 Somalia: Protection of civilians must be a priority (AFR 52/009/2007)

📄 Somalia: Journalists suffering worst time since 1991 state collapse (AFR 52/016/2007)

SOUTH AFRICA

REPUBLIC OF SOUTH AFRICA

Head of state and government:	**Thabo Mbeki**
Death penalty:	**abolitionist for all crimes**
Population:	**47.7 million**
Life expectancy:	**50.8 years**
Under-5 mortality (m/f):	**77/70 per 1,000**
Adult literacy:	**82.4 per cent**

In a context of widespread poverty and unemployment, police responded to a number of public protests with excessive force and arbitrary arrests. Torture of criminal suspects in police custody and poor prison conditions continued to be reported. The failure of the authorities to respect the principle of *non-refoulement* was criticized by the UN. Violence against women, including rape, was prevalent and barriers to access to protection and justice persisted. A new strategic plan on HIV/AIDS was adopted, but less than half of those needing antiretroviral treatment had access to it.

Background

Growing criticism within the ruling African National Congress (ANC) of government economic policies and President Mbeki's leadership style culminated in the election in December of Jacob Zuma as ANC president. His supporters gained all senior ANC positions. Political tensions grew when, days after, Jacob Zuma was indicted in the Pietermaritzburg High Court on 16 charges of fraud and other offences. The trial was due to start in 2008.

In September, President Mbeki suspended the National Director of Public Prosecutions (NDPP), Vusi Pikoli, who was investigating alleged corrupt activities by the National Commissioner of the South African Police Service, Jackie Selebi. The suspension, shortly after the NDPP had obtained a court warrant for the arrest of Jackie Selebi was widely criticized, including by the Law Society of South Africa. The Police Commissioner remained under investigation at the end of the year.

More than 43 per cent of South Africans were living below a poverty line of R3,000 (US$440) per year and unemployment was at least 25 per cent. Over 11 million people were receiving state-provided social assistance grants. While delivery of essential services to communities was improving, access to adequate housing remained a serious challenge and a cause of social conflict as well as human rights litigation in the courts.

High levels of violent crime continued to cause widespread public concern, with increased pressure on government and police for effective responses. Government bodies and civil society made progress in developing a service charter for victims of crime.

In July, a parliamentary committee recommended the establishment of an umbrella human rights body incorporating the South African Human Rights Commission (SAHRC) and other bodies, including the Commission on Gender Equality, to improve their effectiveness, reduce costs and promote the indivisibility of human rights.

Refugees, asylum-seekers and migrants

The rights of non-nationals held in police and immigration detention continued to be abused and asylum-seekers faced barriers in accessing asylum determination procedures.

The UN Special Rapporteur on human rights and counter-terrorism expressed concern at the administrative detention for 30 days or more of immigrants without mandatory judicial review, and at the failure of the authorities to respect the principle of *non-refoulement*.

In February, the Pretoria High Court dismissed an application to declare unlawful the handing over of a Pakistani national, Khalid Mehmood Rashid, to Pakistan in November 2005 without proper safeguards. The court also refused to order the government to investigate his subsequent 18-month disappearance. In October 2007, the court refused a second application for leave to appeal against its February ruling. A further application for leave to appeal was lodged before the Supreme Court of Appeal.

In a case involving a Libyan asylum-seeker, the Pretoria High Court in September declared unlawful the decisions of asylum determination bodies to deny refugee status to Ibrahim Ali Abubakar Tantoush, and declared him a refugee entitled to asylum.

Use of excessive force by police

Police responded to a number of public protests over socio-economic grievances with excessive force and arbitrary arrests.

■ In September, unarmed demonstrators in the Durban area protested at the lack of adequate housing. The rally organizers, the Shackdwellers Association, had complied with the requirements of the Gatherings Act. Participants were peacefully waiting to present a petition when the police dispersed them without warning, using water cannon, stun grenades, baton charges and rubber bullets. They pursued fleeing marchers, beating them indiscriminately. Fourteen activists were arrested, including one of the organizers, Mnikelo Ndabankulu, who had gone to the police station to check on the welfare of others. They were charged with public violence. Court proceedings were postponed in November until 2008. Some of those arrested suffered injuries from beatings and rubber bullets, including Mariet Nkikine, who was shot five times in the back at close range.

In Limpopo province, villagers denied access to their lands, subjected to the effects of mine blasting and facing large-scale relocations protested against Anglo-Platinum and other mining companies.

■ In January, 15 protesters, mainly women from Ga-Puka village who were trying to stop the mining company from fencing off their fields, were punched, pushed and kicked by police officers. One physically disabled woman said that she was beaten by police and had pepper spray sprayed into her eyes at close range, although she was already in their custody. The protesters were all subsequently released uncharged.

■ In May, in Maandagshoek, police arrested 18 protesters, including a pregnant woman and a woman with a breastfeeding baby, and detained them unlawfully for 12 days. They were released on bail after being charged with public violence. Earlier, in March, the regional magistrate's court dismissed charges against other residents of Maandagshoek whose demonstration in June 2006 had been dispersed by police using excessive force.

Torture and other ill-treatment

Torture and other ill-treatment by police as part of criminal investigations continued to be reported. Corroborated cases included the use of police dogs to attack shackled crime suspects, suffocation torture, hitting with gun butts, and kicking and beating of suspects all over the body. The assaults took place in a variety of locations including in or near the suspects' homes. In some cases injured detainees were denied urgently needed medical care.

■ Z. S. was attacked by police dogs while handcuffed and held prone on the ground by police in September. His wounds turned septic before he received any medical care while detained at a Durban area police station.

The police oversight body, the Independent Complaints Directorate (ICD), reported that between April 2006 and March 2007, it received 23 complaints of torture and 530 complaints of assault with intent to cause grievous bodily harm. In the same 12-month period it received 279 new reports of deaths in custody and 419 deaths as a result of police action, including 141 suspects fatally shot during arrest. Nearly 50 per cent of these 698 deaths occurred in two provinces, Gauteng and KwaZulu Natal.

Prison conditions

In September, warders and security officers at Durban Medium B prison allegedly assaulted unarmed prisoners who refused to vacate their cells, using guard dogs, electric shock shields and batons. Human rights monitors reported four weeks later that some prisoners still had visible injuries, but were unable to obtain timely agreement for them to be examined by an independent forensic doctor.

S

Criminal proceedings against prison officers from Ncome prison in KwaZulu Natal province were postponed for further investigation into the assault on some 50 prisoners in 2003. The Jali Commission of Inquiry in 2006 had recommended criminal charges and criticized prison authorities for inaction.

The oversight body, the Judicial Inspectorate of Prisons, conducted a national inspection of 235 prisons and concluded that overcrowding, lack of rehabilitation programmes and staffing shortages were "systemic" problems, and that the state of health care provision was "in crisis".

Impunity

In July, relatives of victims of apartheid-era human rights violations, the Khulumani Support Group and two other NGOs launched proceedings in the Pretoria High Court to declare invalid amendments in 2005 to the National Prosecution Policy which would have the effect of allowing impunity for perpetrators who had not cooperated with the Truth and Reconciliation Commission or had been refused amnesty by it. Proceedings were continuing at the end of 2007.

In August, the Pretoria High Court imposed suspended sentences on former apartheid-era Minister of Law and Order, Adriaan Vlok, and four others after accepting a plea bargain. They had expressed "remorse" for the attempted murder of an anti-apartheid leader, Frank Chikane, in 1989 and agreed to cooperate in other investigations. All five accused had pleaded guilty to the attempted murder charge.

In October, the Ministry of Justice and Constitutional Development issued a statement reiterating the government's opposition to a lawsuit brought in the USA by victims of human rights violations. The group are seeking damages from 50 US, European and Canadian corporations for alleged complicity in abuses during the apartheid era. The statement was made in response to the decision of the New York Circuit Court of Appeal to reverse the decision of a lower court to dismiss the suit. The Minister stated that the responsibility for rehabilitation and redress lay with the South African government and not foreign courts.

Violence against women

High levels of sexual and other forms of violence against women continued to be reported.

According to police statistics, reported incidents of rape had decreased by 4.2 per cent over the previous six years. However, between April 2006 and March 2007, 52,617 rapes were reported. There were also 9,327 reported cases of "indecent assault" – including anal rape and other types of sexual assault which did not then fall within the definition of rape. In December new crime statistics for the period April to September 2007 included 22,887 reported rapes.

Police officials reported to Parliament that between July 2006 and June 2007, police recorded 88,784 incidents of "domestic violence" in terms of the 1998 Domestic Violence Act (DVA). The Department of Justice reported that over 63,000 protection orders were issued by the courts between April 2006 and March 2007. However, the ICD reported in November that of 245 police stations audited in 2006, only 23 per cent were compliant with their obligations under the DVA, ranging from none in Mpumalanga and Limpopo provinces to all of those audited in the Western Cape.

Women experiencing violence and service-providing organizations told Amnesty International that while some police facilitated women's access to protection orders, others referred complainants back to their families, or failed to seize dangerous weapons, or refused to take any steps unless the complainant laid criminal charges first.

The effectiveness of the police response to cases of gender-based violence reportedly deteriorated as a consequence of the disbandment of the Family Violence, Child Protection and Sexual Offences specialized units and the relocation of staff to local police stations. The Department of Justice suspended further development of specialized sexual offences courts despite their higher conviction rates in rape trials.

In December, President Mbeki signed into law the Criminal Law (Sexual Offences and Related Matters) Amendment Act, ending a nearly 10-year legislative reform process. The Act defines rape in gender-neutral terms, applicable to all forms of "sexual penetration" without consent. It obliges the authorities to develop a national policy framework and national instructions to ensure training and coordination in implementation of its provisions. However, the Act's protective measures and services for complainants and witnesses are more limited than originally sought by advocacy organizations. Provisions allowing for compulsory HIV testing of arrested suspects were criticized with respect to the interests of the complainant and the rights of the accused.

Health – people living with HIV

An estimated 5.5 million people were living with HIV. In May a new National Strategic Plan on HIV/AIDS for 2007 to 2011 (NSP) was adopted by Cabinet, following six months of consultations involving government departments, civil society organizations and healthcare providers. The NSP aimed to expand access to treatment, care and support to 80 per cent of people living with HIV and to tackle systemic barriers to prevention, treatment and care. President Mbeki's dismissal in August of the Deputy Minister of Health, Nozizwe Madlala-Routledge, who had played a key role in the development of the NSP, raised concern that the government was not fully committed to the plan.

According to government figures released in May, a total of 303,788 patients were on antiretroviral treatment (ART) programmes in the public health sector. However, organizations monitoring health rights expressed concern that this represented less than half of those needing ART. In rural areas, access to health services and women's ability to adhere to treatment were impeded by physical inaccessibility of health services, costs of transport, shortage of health personnel, delays in the "accreditation" of facilities to provide ART, lack of daily access to adequate food and socio-economic inequalities.

In May, the SAHRC held public hearings on the right to access healthcare services, as a result of receiving complaints and observing poor service delivery in many provinces. It had not published its findings by the end of the year.

Amnesty International visits/reports

🚗 Amnesty International delegates visited South Africa in March and May.

📄 Pakistan/South Africa: Khalid Mehmood Rashid appears after 18 months of secret detention (AFR 53/003/2007)

📄 South Africa: Submission to the UN Universal Periodic Review First Session of the UPR Working Group 7-11 April 2008 (AFR 53/005/2007)

SPAIN

KINGDOM OF SPAIN
Head of state: King Juan Carlos I de Borbón
Head of government: José Luis Rodríguez Zapatero
Death penalty: abolitionist for all crimes
Population: 43.6 million
Life expectancy: 80.5 years
Under-5 mortality (m/f): 6/5 per 1,000

Reports of human rights violations by law enforcement officers and subsequent impunity continued to be widespread. Asylum-seekers and migrants were denied access to Spanish territory and processed in extra-territorial centres in conditions that did not comply with international standards. Unaccompanied minors were expelled without adequate guarantees for their safety. Victims of domestic violence continued to face obstacles in obtaining protection, justice and reparation, with migrant women facing additional difficulties in accessing essential resources. The armed Basque group Euskadi Ta Askatasuna (ETA) declared its "permanent ceasefire" over in June and resumed bomb attacks.

Police and security forces
Torture and other ill-treatment
Reports of torture and other ill-treatment by law enforcement officers continued to be widespread. Law enforcement bodies and judicial authorities failed to investigate such cases in line with international standards, leading to effective impunity.

■ During investigations into the case of 22 people arrested in January 2006 on terrorism-related charges, several detainees told the investigating judge that they had been tortured and otherwise ill-treated by Civil Guard agents while held incommunicado. No criminal investigation into these claims was known to have been made by the end of the year.

■ Three Civil Guard officers were convicted on 27 April of offences relating to the death in custody of Juan Martínez Galdeano at the Roquetas de Mar police station on 24 July 2005. The commanding officer, José Manuel Rivas, was convicted of minor assault and degrading treatment. He was sentenced to 15 months' imprisonment, three years' disqualification from office and a fine. Two other officers were convicted of injury

S

and abuse of authority, and fined. Five officers were acquitted. The prosecution and the defence both lodged appeals.

■ On 19 July a Ghanaian man, Courage Washington, was seriously injured in a shooting incident at Madrid's Barajas airport. Two police officers dressed in civilian clothes approached Courage Washington and asked for his identity papers. It was alleged that Courage Washington, who suffers from mental health difficulties, took a toy gun from his pocket and the police officers shot him four times. According to witnesses, some shots were fired after Courage Washington had fallen to the ground. A criminal investigation was subsequently launched against Courage Washington for assault on a public agent. His lawyer lodged a complaint against the police.

Tasers
Several law enforcement agencies announced their acquisition of electro-shock taser weapons, and they were already in use by local police forces in at least three of the Autonomous Communities. The National Police and Civil Guard do not use them. There was insufficient regulation and control regarding the possession and use of such weapons by law enforcement officers.

Migration

Abuses during deportation
In July the Interior Ministry announced a new draft protocol for the National Police and Civil Guard on the safe repatriation of detainees, including irregular migrants. However, it did not adequately reflect relevant European human rights standards or the recommendations of international organizations relating to the use of force and immobilization techniques by law enforcement officers during expulsions. The protocol included "reinforced tape", "immobilizing belts and clothes" and "protective helmets" on the list of materials approved for use in expulsions, which may violate the international prohibition of cruel, inhuman or degrading treatment and risk causing asphyxia or other serious physical harm to the person being forcibly deported.

■ On 9 June Nigerian citizen Osamuyia Akpitaye died during an attempt to forcibly deport him. According to witnesses, the two law enforcement officers accompanying him on the flight from Madrid to Lagos tied his feet and hands and gagged his mouth, allegedly with adhesive tape, to counteract his resistance to being deported. Osamuyia Akpitaye died shortly after take-off. An autopsy determined the cause of death as asphyxiation.

Extra-territorial procedures
Many rescue operations were conducted by the Spanish authorities to save migrants and asylum-seekers in danger as they attempted to reach Europe by sea. However, the rights of many were violated in interception and extra-territorial processing procedures. The conditions of detention and rights of access to asylum procedures of those detained in extra-territorial processing centres did not comply with international standards.

■ On 30 January, the Spanish sea rescue service intercepted *Marine I*, which had 369 people aboard. The passengers, believed to be from Asia and Sub-Saharan Africa, were travelling to the Canary Islands. The Spanish rescue service assisted the boat to a position 12 miles off the coast of Mauritania. The boat remained stranded there for almost two weeks until the Mauritanian and Spanish authorities agreed on 12 February to allow the boat to land in Mauritania. Part of the agreement allowed the Spanish authorities to manage the welfare and processing of the migrants and asylum-seekers in Mauritania. The Spanish authorities agreed to process the asylum claims of 10 Sri Lankans on board, who were transferred to the Canary Islands along with 25 others. However, despite a positive report from UNHCR, the UN refugee agency, the asylum claims were not admitted into the Spanish asylum procedure and all 10 individuals were deported on 25 March. In April it was reported that of the 369 people aboard *Marine I*, 35 were returned to Guinea, 161 to India and 115 to Pakistan. Twenty-three reportedly remained in a hangar in Mauritania under the effective control of Spanish authorities in conditions of detention that did not comply with Spanish law. On 18 May, 17 of them were transferred to a detention centre under Mauritanian jurisdiction, and in June they were returned to Pakistan. The remaining six were transferred to Melilla (Spain) to receive psychological treatment as a result of their experience in detention.

■ In March a boat, *Happy Day*, carrying 260 irregular migrants from Senegal to the Canary Islands, was intercepted by an Italian vessel operating as part of the EU border agency, Frontex, under Spanish guidance. Following disputes between Spain, Senegal and Guinea (believed to be the boat's original departure point), the 260 people spent a week on the boat anchored at

S

Kamsar in Guinea as the Guinean authorities refused to allow them to disembark. Amnesty International was unable to trace what happened to the migrants after this point.

Unaccompanied minors

Family reunification of unaccompanied minors failed to guarantee that the best interests of the child were adequately taken into account. Unaccompanied minors were expelled to Morocco without adequate guarantees for their safety.

Law on Aliens

In November the Constitutional Court ruled unconstitutional provisions in the 2000 Law on Aliens that restrict migrants' rights of association, access to basic education and free legal assistance.

Violence against women

Women continued to face obstacles in obtaining protection, justice and reparation two years after the law against gender-based violence was introduced. Key provisions of the law were still being developed or were being implemented too slowly. However, some positive measures were introduced, such as a protocol for health workers dealing with victims of domestic violence. The number of women killed by their partner or former partner reached 71 in 2007. Of these, 48 were foreign nationals. Migrant women remained particularly vulnerable to violence as they continued to suffer discrimination in law and practice when trying to access justice and essential resources such as financial assistance, psychological treatment and access to shelters.

On 22 March legislation was approved extending refugee status to women fleeing gender-based persecution.

Armed groups

Following the end of its "permanent ceasefire", ETA resumed attacks in Spain. The ceasefire, effectively broken on 30 December 2006 by a bomb attack on Madrid's Barajas airport which killed two people, was officially declared over on 5 June 2007. On 24 August a car bomb exploded outside the Civil Guard station in Durango in the Basque Country, causing damage to property but no casualties. On 9 October the bodyguard of a Basque councillor was injured in a further bomb attack. On 1 December, two unarmed Spanish Civil Guard officers were shot and killed by suspected ETA members in Capbreton, France. A

man and a woman were arrested and charged with murder; a third suspect escaped.

Counter-terrorism

On 4 October, 22 people believed to be involved in the directorship of the Basque political party Batasuna, banned in 2003 under the Law on Political Parties, were arrested at a meeting on the grounds of membership of a terrorist organization.

On 19 December the National Criminal Court issued its sentence in relation to the so-called Macroproceso 18/98 trial, in which 47 people were convicted of membership of, or various degrees of collaboration with, ETA as a result of their work with various Basque nationalist organizations. The sentence stated that the organizations constituted a part of ETA and/or received instructions from it. Appeals against the sentence were pending at the end of the year. Several of those convicted had publicly stated their opposition to ETA and the use of violence for political ends.

'War on terror'

Allegations about the involvement of Spanish police in interrogations of detainees at the US detention centre at Guantánamo Bay between 2002 and 2005 came to light in early 2007. Responding to inquiries by Amnesty International, the Interior Ministry confirmed that two visits by Spanish police to Guantánamo Bay had taken place, in July 2002 and February 2004.

On 19 December, three former UK residents detained at Guantánamo Bay were released and returned to the UK. Two of the men, Jamil El Banna and Omar Deghayes, appeared in court on 20 December in a preliminary hearing in connection with an extradition request issued by Spain on terrorism-related charges. The men opposed the request. A decision was pending at the end of the year.

At least 50 CIA-operated flights travelling to or from Guantánamo Bay stopped over in Spanish territory between 2002 and 2007, according to media reports citing information from the Spanish Airport and Air Navigation Institution. The last known was in February 2007. In some cases, planes landed at military bases also used by US forces. The information was passed to the judge investigating suspected CIA flights via Spain that were involved in renditions – illegal transfers of suspects between countries. It was alleged that the government had knowledge of these

S

flights, but did not mention them to the Spanish parliament despite its request for all available information on this topic in April 2006, or to investigators from the Council of Europe and European Parliament.

The trial began in February of 28 people accused of involvement in the 11 March 2004 attacks on commuter trains in Madrid. In October the national criminal court convicted 21 of them and acquitted seven. Three men were sentenced to 42,000 years' imprisonment.

Impunity

In November parliament passed a law concerning the victims of Francoism and the 1936-39 civil war. Despite some positive features, the law fell short of international standards on the rights to a remedy and reparations for the victims of gross human rights violations.

Amnesty International visits/reports

🚌 Amnesty International delegates visited Spain in February, March, June and November.

📄 Spain: Adding insult to injury – the effective impunity of police officers in cases of torture and other ill treatment (EUR 41/006/007)

📄 Europe and Central Asia: Summary of Amnesty International's concerns in the region, January-June 2007 (EUR 01/010/2007)

SRI LANKA

DEMOCRATIC SOCIALIST REPUBLIC OF SRI LANKA
Head of state: Mahinda Rajapaksa
Head of government: Ratnasiri Wickremanayake
Death penalty: abolitionist in practice
Population: 21.1 million
Life expectancy: 71.6 years

2007 was characterized by impunity for violations of international human rights and humanitarian law. Soaring human rights abuses included hundreds of enforced disappearances, unlawful killings of humanitarian workers, arbitrary arrests and torture. Lack of protection for civilians was a key concern as heavy fighting resumed between government forces and the Liberation Tigers of Tamil Eelam (LTTE).

Background

In January, the military took control of Vakarai in the east after weeks of heavy fighting. Tens of thousands of civilians fled the area. In March, an LTTE air strike hit a military base next to the main airport. Also in March, heavy fighting in Batticaloa District resulted in a surge in displacement. People displaced by fighting in the area reached almost 160,000 by late March, doubling the previous month's figures. In July, the government claimed it had successfully "liberated" the east from the LTTE.

Civilians in the north and east faced immense hardship with a significant number being killed in indiscriminate raids. Lack of transport links to Jaffna Peninsula affected food supplies to over 500,000 people there. The only access road into the area remained closed and civilians needed a military permit to enter and exit.

In June, the security forces drove several hundred Tamils from Colombo. Further forcible evictions were stopped by a Supreme Court order.

In October, the UN Special Rapporteur on torture concluded that torture was widespread throughout Sri Lanka. The UNHCHR criticized the government for failing to properly record, investigate and prosecute cases of abductions, disappearances and killings.

In November, the political head of the LTTE, S.P. Thamilchelvan, was killed in a Sri Lankan air force strike. On 28 November, two bombings in the capital, Colombo, killed 18 and wounded more than 30 people. The military blamed the LTTE.

Calls by rights groups for the creation of a local wing of the Office of the High Commissioner for Human Rights to address the security of civilians in Sri Lanka were repeatedly rejected by the government.

In December, the USA suspended military aid to Sri Lanka due to human rights concerns.

Enforced disappearances

Several hundred cases of enforced disappearances were reported in the first six months of 2007. Jaffna Peninsula was particularly affected with 21 cases of enforced disappearances reported in the first three weeks of August alone. Enforced disappearances in the north and east appeared to be part of a systematic counter-insurgency strategy devised by the government. There were also a number of abductions and suspected enforced disappearances reported from Colombo.

The Human Rights Council's Working Group on Enforced or Involuntary Disappearances expressed concern about the high number of such cases in Sri Lanka.

Internally displaced people

The number of people displaced as a result of conflict since April 2006 totalled more than 200,000 in 2007. In addition, many people remained displaced on a long-term basis. In the north-west town of Puttalam, for example, Muslim families from the north spent their 17th year in displacement. The physical security of the internally displaced was frequently compromised. On several occasions, the government forced them to return to their homes in conditions of insecurity and in contravention of international standards.

Child soldiers

The recruitment of child soldiers by the LTTE and the Tamil armed group known as the Karuna faction continued in the north and east. In May 2007, the UN Security Council Working Group on Children and Armed Conflict threatened action against the LTTE if it continued to recruit children. The UN Special Representative for Children and Armed Conflict identified the LTTE as "a repeat offender who has been on the Secretary General's list of violators for four years".

■ On 18 June, the LTTE released 135 child soldiers and pledged to rid its ranks of all children by the end of the year. According to UNICEF, recruitment of child soldiers by the LTTE declined in 2007.

■ In April, UNICEF said that among the 285 children recruited by the Karuna group there were 195 outstanding cases.

Arrests and arbitrary detentions

The Sri Lankan police conducted mass arrests of more than 1,000 Tamils, allegedly in response to the suicide bombings carried out in Colombo on 28 November. The arrests were made on arbitrary and discriminatory grounds using sweeping powers granted by emergency regulations. According to reports, "Tamils were bundled in bus loads and taken for interrogation". More than 400 of those arrested, including 50 women, were taken to the Boosa Camp near Galle in the south, a facility reputed to be overcrowded, and lacking proper sanitation facilities and adequate drinking water.

Freedom of expression

The number of attacks on journalists, particularly those considered part of the Tamil media, escalated.

■ On 29 April, Selvaraja Rajivaram, a young *Uthayan* journalist, was shot dead near the newspaper's office in Jaffna.

■ On 2 August, Sahathevan Deluxshan, 22, a part-time journalist, was shot dead by unidentified men in Jaffna town.

The authorities failed to effectively investigate or prosecute those responsible for such unlawful killings. Journalists from all communities were arrested in connection with articles critical of the government.

■ On 16 August, the personal security provided by the government to the defense columnist Iqbal Athas was removed. Iqbal Athas had been given police protection after being repeatedly threatened by members of the security forces angered by his coverage of arms deals.

Impunity

A proposed Commission of Inquiry (CoI) failed to gain the confidence of all parties to the conflict. Serious concerns were raised regarding witness protection.

The National Human Rights Commission (NHRC) lost credibility due to the political appointment of Commissioners.

■ In December, the International Co-ordinating Committee of National Human Rights Institutions downgraded the NHRC's accreditation. To function properly, the NHRC must be independently appointed and fully resourced.

As human rights abuses in the context of the conflict increased, a climate of impunity persisted. The government promised a prompt investigation into the unlawful killing of two volunteers from the Sri Lanka Red Cross in June, but the investigation was stalled. Throughout 2007, the Sri Lankan police were criticized for their inaction and failure to identify perpetrators of violent crimes.

S

Amnesty International reports

Sri Lanka: Urgent need for effective protection of civilians as conflict intensifies, Media Briefing (ASA 37/009/2007)

Sri Lanka: Amnesty International calls on the United Nations Human Rights Council to address violations (ASA 37/019/2007)

SUDAN

REPUBLIC OF SUDAN

Head of state and government:	**Omar Hassan al-Bashir**
Death penalty:	**retentionist**
Population:	**37.8 million**
Life expectancy:	**57.4 years**
Under-5 mortality (m/f):	**113/100 per 1,000**
Adult literacy:	**60.9 per cent**

The Sudan People's Liberation Movement (SPLM) withdrew from the government from October to 27 December, citing failure to implement the 2005 Comprehensive Peace Agreement (CPA) that had ended the decades-long conflict between north and south Sudan.

Conflict and insecurity persisted in Darfur, as arms and armed groups continued to proliferate. Some 280,000 people were newly displaced. The UN Security Council voted unanimously in July for a 26,000-strong peacekeeping force to be sent to Darfur. The force took over from the African Union Mission in Sudan (AMIS), which was unable to stop continued killings and rapes in Darfur, on 31 December. Peace negotiations between the government and armed groups had stalled by the end of the year.

The security services used lethal force against peaceful demonstrators, including people protesting against the construction of the Kajbar Dam in northern Sudan. The security services continued to detain suspected opponents incommunicado for long periods. Torture and ill-treatment of Darfuris and other marginalized groups were systematic. At least 23 people were sentenced to death and seven were executed. Freedom of expression was restricted and journalists were detained as prisoners of conscience. In southern Sudan arbitrary detention continued.

Armed groups also carried out human rights abuses, including deliberate killing of captives and other unlawful killings, unlawful detention of opponents and hostage-taking.

Background

In October the SPLM suspended its participation in the Government of National Unity (GNU) under President Omar Hassan al-Bashir, complaining of the failure of the ruling National Congress Party (NCP)

ministers to implement provisions of the CPA and the sidelining of First Vice President Salva Kiir Mayardit. An official SPLM statement cited issues including: obstruction of democratic transformation; delays in the national reconciliation process; non-implementation of the Abyei protocol (Abyei is an oil-rich area given special status under the CPA); delays in demarcating the north-south borders; and lack of transparency in the distribution of oil revenues. The SPLM ministers rejoined the GNU on 27 December but disagreements over the protocol on Abyei were not resolved by the end of the year.

The Peace Agreement signed with armed groups from eastern Sudan in 2006 remained in place and opposition leaders from the east entered the GNU. Some prominent figures claimed that easterners close to the NCP received a disproportionate number of government posts.

The harmonization of domestic legislation with the provisions of the CPA faced many delays. Among bills not passed in 2007 were the National Security Service Act, the National Police Act, the Armed Forces Act and the Elections Act. In addition, draft bills were not presented on the National Human Rights Commission, Electoral Commission and Land Commission.

International scrutiny of Darfur

The Secretary-General of the UN reported monthly to the Security Council on the situation in Darfur. There were also regular reports from the Special Rapporteur on the situation of human rights in Sudan. The UN Mission in Sudan (UNMIS), set up under the CPA, had more than 10,000 troops in the south and in Abyei, Blue Nile and the Nuba Mountains. UNMIS had 70 human rights monitors throughout Sudan, including 33 in Darfur. UNMIS issued periodic reports on particular human rights incidents but ceased to issue regular human rights updates.

A five-member high-level mission mandated by the December 2006 Special Session on Darfur of the UN Human Rights Council (HRC) was not granted visas by Sudan. The mission visited Chad and other areas and reported in March to the Human Rights Council.

In March the HRC convened a group of experts to pursue previous recommendations made by UN human rights bodies on Darfur. The Sudanese government-appointed Human Rights Advisory Council responded to these recommendations but according to the report presented to the HRC in

November, few of the recommendations were implemented. The HRC voted to end the mandate of the group of experts but maintained the mandate of the Special Rapporteur on the situation of human rights in Sudan.

In December the HRC urged Sudan to implement all outstanding recommendations identified by the group of experts on Darfur, extended, for one year, the mandate of the UN Special Rapporteur on the situation of human rights in Sudan and requested her to pursue the implementation of these recommendations.

A Panel of Experts set up under Security Council Resolution 1591 in 2005 to monitor the arms embargo reported that all sides breached the embargo and named further individuals guilty of breaching the embargo.

In July the Security Council passed Resolution 1769 setting up the African Union-United Nations Hybrid Operation in Darfur (UNAMID), a hybrid AU and UN peacekeeping force of more than 26,000, including more than 6,000 UN police. The government of Sudan obstructed swift deployment of the force by failing to approve the list of contributing countries, which included a number of non-African countries. At the same time UN member states did not contribute vital equipment such as helicopters. UNAMID took over from AMIS on 31 December, but with only some 9,000 personnel, including 6,880 troops and 1,540 police officers.

In February, the Prosecutor of the International Criminal Court (ICC) presented evidence of war crimes and crimes against humanity in Darfur to the ICC Pre-Trial Chamber against Ahmad Muhammad Harun, former Minister of State for the Interior then Minister of State for Humanitarian Affairs, and Janjawid militia leader Ali Mohammad Ali Abdel-Rahman (Ali Kushayb). In April the ICC Pre-Trial Chamber issued arrest warrants for the two men. The government of Sudan said it would refuse to hand them over. In December the UN Security Council failed to agree a Presidential Statement supporting the ICC Prosecutor's condemnation of Sudan's failure to cooperate with the ICC.

Darfur

All major parties to the conflict committed violations of international human rights and humanitarian law including unlawful killings, arbitrary detention, attacks on humanitarian personnel and equipment, torture and ill-treatment, and hostage-taking.

Armed groups continued to proliferate, mostly breakaway factions of the Sudan Liberation Army (SLA) and the Justice and Equality Movement (JEM). There were said to be more than 30 armed groups by the end of 2007, including armed groups representing Arabs. Armed groups were increasingly divided along ethnic lines.

Janjawid militias attacked civilians with support, including air support, from the Sudan Armed Forces. Some Janjawid militia were reported however to have become opposed to the government. The Sudan Air Forces (SAF) bombed civilians and non-military targets using Antonov bombers and helicopters. Some SAF aircraft were painted white to resemble UN aircraft. Armed groups fought against the government and against each other. The proliferation of arms encouraged minor clashes to escalate into major conflicts and there were frequent conflicts between ethnic groups, including between different Arab groups incorporated in government paramilitary forces. Ethnic conflicts and attacks by armed groups spread to neighbouring Kordofan.

AMIS was short of personnel, means of transport and heavy weapons.

The timelines of the 2006 Darfur Peace Agreement, which was signed by the government and the Sudan Liberation Army/Minni Minawi and rejected by most armed groups in Darfur, were not respected.

Conferences were organized by the UN/AU in Arusha, Tanzania, in August and by the SPLA in Juba, southern Sudan, in October-December to try to unify groups and ensure a common negotiating position. Some armed groups did unite. A number of attempts were made by regional actors and the UN and AU to revive the peace process. In October a new peace conference was held under UN/AU auspices in Sirte, Libya, but the most prominent armed groups refused to attend.

As a result of attacks, particularly by government and paramilitary groups, some 280,000 people were displaced bringing the number of displaced in Darfur to more than 2,387,000.

Large parts of Darfur were unsafe for travel. All parties to the conflict, including government paramilitary forces, set up checkpoints where they extorted money or detained travellers.

S

- In April government Antonov aircraft and helicopters bombed the village of Umm Rai in North Darfur in an indiscriminate attack, hitting a school and killing two people.
- Between January and August, northern Rizeiqat men, mostly wearing Border Intelligence or Popular Defence Force uniforms, attacked members of the Tarjum ethnic group, many of them also members of government paramilitary forces. Altogether some 500 people were killed in several attacks.
- In August more than 50 Janjawid abducted 17 men travelling from the town of Nyala to internally displaced people (IDP) camps. They detained their captives tied to trees. After more than 70 days they were released after paying 110,000,000 Sudanese pounds (US$55,000).
- In September, two armed opposition groups, reportedly offshoots of JEM and of SLA/Unity, attacked and looted the AMIS base in Haskanita in north Darfur. They killed 10 AMIS peacekeepers and looted arms. Following this, the Sudanese army occupied the town and burned it to the ground.

Violence against women

Rape continued to be widespread, especially of displaced women and girls collecting firewood outside their camps. Sometimes women were beaten, or attacked but managed to escape. They rarely reported what happened to the police. Men continued to leave the task of collecting firewood to women because the men feared being killed if they ventured outside the camps.

- Several internally displaced women, including teenage girls, were raped as they went outside IDP camps in Zalingei to collect firewood in the second half of 2007. In August a woman was raped who was already eight months pregnant.

Female genital mutilation continued to be systematically practised in northern Sudan.

Arbitrary detentions, torture and other ill-treatment

The national intelligence and security service (NISS), military intelligence and police continued to commit human rights violations, including arbitrary arrests, torture and ill-treatment, and use of excessive force. Political detainees, criminal suspects, Darfuris and others from marginalized areas, and students in Khartoum were routinely subjected to torture and ill-treatment. Floggings continued to be imposed for a variety of public order offences including unlawful sexual intercourse and trading in alcohol. Demonstrations were frequently repressed using excessive force.

- At least 30 people were arrested in June and July in connection with protests against the Kajbar Dam. During a peaceful march in June the police killed four demonstrators and wounded 11 others. Among those arrested was a group who came to investigate the killings, including Mohammed Jalal Ahmad Hashim, a lecturer at Khartoum University; members of the committee against the Kajbar Dam, including spokesperson Osman Ibrahim; and journalists. Detainees, including journalists, were held incommunicado for up to 10 weeks and required to sign a statement promising in future not to comment on the dam.
- Mubarak al-Fadel al-Mahdi, President of the Umma Party Reform and Renewal (UPRR), was arrested with at least 40 people, including many former army officers, in July and accused of smuggling arms and planning a coup. Soon after, an order was issued forbidding discussion of the case in the press. On 1 August Ali Mahmoud Hassanain, aged 73, a human rights lawyer and Deputy Chairman of the Democratic Unionist Party (DUP), was arrested. Many of this group of detainees were tortured in incommunicado detention which lasted up to six weeks, apparently to force them to confess to an alleged plot. Reported methods of torture included beatings, prolonged sitting or standing, and suspension with wrists and ankles tied behind the back (the *tayyara*, aeroplane). In November Mubarak al-Fadel al-Mahdi and Ali Mahmoud Hassanain, a diabetic, went on hunger strike in protest at illegalities and delays in the pre-trial process. On 4 December the state released Mubarak al-Fadel al-Mahdi without charge and on 31 December all other detainees received a Presidential pardon.
- In August police and NISS surrounded Kalma camp near Nyala in Darfur and arrested about 35 displaced people, after two police had reportedly been killed. Most detainees were beaten during arrest and afterwards at Nyala Wasat police station where they were held in prolonged incommunicado detention. They were released in October without being charged or tried.
- More than 100 people, including students, participated in a demonstration in September on the

S

occasion of the "Global Day for Darfur". Eight students were arrested after the demonstrations and held for two days. They were reportedly blindfolded and tortured by the NISS. On the third day they were transferred to the police and the torture ceased.

Unfair trials and the death penalty

At least 23 people were known to have been sentenced to death and seven people executed by hanging during 2007. The true figures were believed to be much higher. Death sentences continued to be frequently passed after unfair trials in which confessions extracted under torture were used as evidence. On several occasions defendants were sentenced to death after trials where they had no defence lawyer.

Death sentences continued to be passed on women for adultery but no such sentence was known to have been carried out. In Darfur, Special Courts and Special Criminal Courts continued to conduct unfair trials. The Special Criminal Court on the Events in Darfur did not hear any cases during the year.

In South Sudan death sentences were passed on many people who had been tried without defence counsel. However, no one was known to have been judicially executed during 2007.

■ Sadia Idriss Fadul and Amouna Abdallah Daldoum, both originally from Darfur, were sentenced in February and March respectively to be stoned to death for adultery by the Criminal Court in Managil Province, Gazira State. It was believed that the sentence was commuted.

■ In November, 10 people originally from Darfur, including al-Tayeb Abdel Aziz, aged 16, and Idris Mohammed al-Sanousi, aged 71, were sentenced to death by the Khartoum Criminal Court for the murder of a newspaper editor, Mohammed Taha. All 10 retracted confessions which they said were extracted under torture. The Court refused defence lawyers' requests to order medical examinations.

■ Two members of military intelligence, Bakhit Mohammed Bakhit and Abdel Malik Abdallah, were executed by hanging in May in Shalla Prison, al-Fasher, Darfur. They had been tried before the Special Criminal Court on the Events in Darfur in August 2005 and sentenced to death for murder after the death of Adam Idris Mohammed as a result of torture in custody. The head of military intelligence was acquitted.

Freedom of expression

Restrictions on freedom of expression and association continued. Provisions of the 2004 Press Act were used to censor newspapers and limit freedom of expression. The government imposed gagging orders including arbitrary prohibitions on reporting criminal cases relating to the Darfur conflict; on investigations into killings of civilians in demonstrations against the Kajbar Dam; and relating to the case of Mubarak al-Fadel al-Mahdi.

■ In November, two journalists from al-Sudani newspaper were detained for 12 days after refusing to pay a fine of 10,000 Sudanese pounds (US$5,000). They had been convicted of defamation for writing an article criticizing the NISS for detaining four other journalists. They were prisoners of conscience.

Southern Sudan

In Southern Sudan, an autonomous region according to the CPA, several CPA Commissions were established by Presidential decree, including the Southern Sudan Commission on Human Rights. In November an Army Bill was passed by the South Sudan Legislative Assembly. Draft bills on the Civil Service, Population and Census, and Disarmament Demobilization and Reintegration (DDR) were due to be presented.

Clashes between different militias continued, often resulting in killings of civilians or abductions. People continued to be arbitrarily detained, sometimes as hostages for other family members. Partly because of a shortage of lawyers, many people were convicted without defence lawyers. A number of death sentences were passed but no judicial executions were known to have been carried out.

■ Mapet Daniel Dut was sentenced to death for murder in October by the Court of Justice in Rumbek. He reportedly had no defence lawyer. He later escaped from prison and police detained his brother and father in his place. Two sisters, who brought them food, were also detained, but released after a few days. Mapet Daniel Dut was not recaptured and his father remained in detention at the end of the year.

Amnesty International reports

⬚ Sudan: Time is running out: Protect the people of Darfur (AFR 54/016/2007)

⬚ Sudan: Arms continuing to fuel serious human rights violations in Darfur (AFR 54/019/2007)

S

▤ Sudan: Arrest Now! Darfur, the Sudan: Ahmad Harun and Ali Kushayb
(AFR 54/027/2007)

▤ Darfur: When will they protect us? (AFR 54/043/2007)

▤ Sudan: Obstruction and Delay (AFR 54/006/2007)

SWAZILAND

KINGDOM OF SWAZILAND

Head of state:	King Mswati III
Head of government:	Absalom Themba Dlamini
Death penalty:	abolitionist in practice
Population:	1 million
Life expectancy:	40.9 years
Under-5 mortality (m/f):	144/126 per 1,000
Adult literacy:	79.6 per cent

More than two-thirds of Swaziland's population lived in poverty, and more than a quarter were infected with HIV. Only 28 per cent of those needing antiretroviral treatment were receiving it. Funding enabled more orphans and other vulnerable children to have access to education. Access to justice improved with new judicial appointments. Reports of sexual violence continued to increase and legal reforms affecting women's rights were delayed. Police continued to use excessive force against criminal suspects and against peaceful demonstrators.

Legal and constitutional developments

The independence of the judiciary and the ability of High Court judges to hear cases, in particular those involving constitutional law issues, were affected by delays in judicial appointments and the continued use of temporary contracts. The High Court was reduced to just one permanent judge by February. In March the Law Society of Swaziland welcomed signs of improvement when the King confirmed the appointment on permanent contracts of two judges to the High Court and one to the Industrial Court. In June retired Malawian judge Richard Banda was sworn in as Chief Justice, on a temporary basis.

In November the High Court dismissed an application brought in 2006 by the National Constitutional Assembly, trade union officials and others challenging the validity of the Constitution. The hearing had been delayed by the shortage of judges. A High Court ruling on the legality of registering political parties under the Constitution was still pending at the end of the year. Attempts by members of the police and correctional services to form trade unions were opposed by the authorities. The High Court had not ruled by the end of 2007 on an application by Khanyakweze Mhlanga and the Swaziland Police Union for an order confirming the constitutionality of their union's registration.

Commonwealth experts visited Swaziland to assist the review and reform of laws not in compliance with the Constitution and international standards. They also assisted in furthering the process towards the establishment of a human rights commission, required under the Constitution.

Legislation intended to give effect to the gender equality provisions of the 2006 Constitution, such as the draft Sexual Offences and Domestic Violence Bill and draft Marriage Bill, had still not been enacted by the end of the year.

Human rights violations by law enforcement officials

Police continued to use excessive force against criminal suspects and against peaceful demonstrators including members of trade unions and political organizations. Police who committed human rights violations were not brought to justice.

■ On 11 August, police from the Serious Crimes Unit shot dead Ntokozo Ngozo, who had told a journalist a week earlier that the police intended to kill him. According to witnesses, police called for him to come out of a house in the Makhosini area and he emerged naked to the waist with his hands in the air. He was shot in the thigh, abdomen and back at close range. Police delayed taking him to hospital. The initial police statement that he had been shot running away was inconsistent with the medical evidence. Witnesses complained that they had been assaulted by police, including Nsizwa Mhlanga, who was arrested and held until 16 August without being brought before a court. He was eventually released on bail pending possible charges. No inquiry into the shooting of Ntokozo Ngozo had been announced by the end of the year.

■ In April police forcibly dispersed supporters of the opposition People's United Democratic Movement (PUDEMO) involved in a demonstration at Swaziland's border posts on the anniversary of the 1973 decree which had banned political parties. Protesters who refused to disperse were bundled into vehicles and removed, including George Hleta, who was grabbed by five armed police officers, one of whom throttled him before he was pushed into a police van. Six arrested PUDEMO members were charged with sedition, apparently on account of the wording on their banners, and held for 12 days. Five had the charges dropped and were released after paying an admission-of-guilt fine for "jaywalking". However, Sicelo Vilane was held for a further three weeks before being released on bail. He had not been brought to trial on the sedition charge by the end of 2007. At the time of his arrest he was still receiving medical treatment for injuries and health problems resulting from being assaulted in police custody in 2006.

In September the Prime Minister received the report of the one-person commission of inquiry established after the High Court in March 2006 ordered the government to investigate allegations of torture made by 16 defendants charged with treason. The government had not published the inquiry's findings by the end of the year.

Violations of the right to fair trial

By the end of the year, 16 defendants charged in 2006 with treason and other offences had still not been brought to trial. The state's appeal on a technicality against the March 2006 High Court ruling granting the defendants conditional bail had still not been heard. The accused remained under restrictive bail conditions.

Health – people living with HIV/AIDS

More than one in four adults aged 15-49 (26 per cent) were infected with HIV, according to information released in June by the Central Statistical Office, citing findings of a Demographic and Health Survey (DHS) conducted between July 2006 and February 2007. Forty-nine per cent of women between the ages of 25 and 29 were found to be infected, while the highest infection rate for men, 45 per cent, occurred between the ages of 35 and 39.

In October a report published by the National Emergency Response Council on HIV/AIDS (NERCHA) with a South African partner found that among the nearly quarter of a million people living with HIV, only 28 per cent of those clinically needing antiretroviral treatment (ART) were receiving it.

Approximately 40 per cent of Swaziland's population required food aid, with an increase since 2006 in the number of individuals not eating for an entire day. At least 69 per cent of the population were living in poverty. Poverty and limited access to adequate daily food continued to impede the ability of people living with HIV and AIDS to access health services and adhere to treatment.

Advocacy and humanitarian organizations continued to lobby government and donors for resources to be directed at addressing the crisis. Members of Parliament and the Swaziland National Network of People Living with HIV and AIDS urged the government in November to provide monthly grants to improve access to treatment and care.

Children's rights

The DHS report found that 35 per cent of children were either orphaned or classified as "vulnerable" because their parents or carers were sick or dying and they lacked secure access to health care, education, food, clothing, psychosocial care or shelter. Some were classified as vulnerable because they were at risk of sexual or physical abuse.

The Swaziland National Association of Teachers sought an order in the High Court in 2006 to compel the government to pay schools to give orphans and other vulnerable children access to education. Although the case was not heard, in November the government reported to Parliament that, with NERCHA's support, it had paid funds to 187 schools towards educating orphaned and vulnerable children.

Violence against women

The number of reported incidents of rape and other forms of gender-based violence continued to rise. The Commissioner of Police reported in January that cases had increased by 15 per cent in 2006 compared with the preceding year. At the end of the year Superintendent Leckinah Magagula, head of the Domestic Violence, Sexual Offences and Child Abuse unit, reported that the unit had recorded 707 cases of child rape and 463 cases of rapes of adult women in 2006 and 2007. The service-providing organization, the Swaziland Action Group Against Abuse (SWAGAA), reported in April that it had received 2,414 cases of abuse in

S

the preceding year, including incidents of emotional, financial, physical and sexual abuse.

In September UNICEF published preliminary findings of a study of violence against girls and young women aged between 13 and 24. One in three surveyed had experienced some form of sexual violence before the age of 18. In addition, one in six girls between 13 and 17 and one in four women between 18 and 24 had experienced sexual violence in the preceding year.

In April UN agencies and the NGO Gender Consortium, with the Ministry of Justice and Constitutional Affairs, launched a year-long campaign against gender-based violence.

There were continuing improvements in the police response to crimes of sexual violence through the work of the specialist Domestic Violence, Sexual Offences and Child Abuse unit in co-operation with SWAGAA. However, access to justice for survivors was still hampered by lack of training for medical practitioners, the failure to reform forensic medical documentation systems and delays in the reform of the legal framework and procedures in rape trials.

Death penalty

Swaziland abstained in the December UN General Assembly vote on a resolution calling for a global moratorium on executions.

Although the 2006 Constitution permits the use of capital punishment, no executions have been carried out since July 1983. No new death sentences were imposed in 2007.

SWEDEN

KINGDOM OF SWEDEN

Head of state:	King Carl XVI Gustaf
Head of government:	Fredrik Reinfeldt
Death penalty:	abolitionist for all crimes
Population:	9.1 million
Life expectancy:	80.5 years
Under-5 mortality (m/f):	4/4 per 1,000

The new government reversed a decision by the previous administration which had led to multiple human rights violations against two people summarily expelled to Egypt. Asylum-seekers continued to face a risk of being returned to Eritrea, despite recommendations from international bodies that all such returns should be stopped.

'War on terror'

In March, the new Swedish government, elected in October 2006, formally reversed an order made by the previous administration to expel Mohammed El Zari to Egypt. In May it did the same with regard to the order made to expel Ahmed Agiza to Egypt.

Two UN human rights bodies, the Committee against Torture and the Human Rights Committee, have now found that the Swedish authorities were responsible for multiple human rights violations suffered by these two men following their summary expulsion from Sweden to Egypt in 2001.

In May, it was reported that the Swedish Migration Board had rejected Mohammed El Zari's application for a residence permit. According to reports this decision was reached on the basis of advice from the Swedish Security Police (Säpo), on the grounds that Mohammed El Zari would pose a threat to Swedish national security if permitted to return there.

The final decision in such cases is taken by the government. No such final decision on the application of Mohammed El Zari had been taken by the end of the year.

In October, it was reported that the Migration Board had also rejected an application for a residence permit made by Ahmed Agiza. The reason given for this decision was that Ahmed Agiza would be unable to make use of a residence permit for the foreseeable future, since he remained in prison in Egypt. Again, no final decision on his application had been reached by the end of the year.

By the end of the year no decision had been made public as to the applications for reparation in the form of financial compensation which the two men have made.

Refugees and asylum-seekers

The Swedish authorities continued to refuse applications made by Eritrean asylum-seekers, therefore exposing them to a risk of being returned to Eritrea, despite recommendations to all states by the UNHCR, the UN refugee agency, to halt all forcible returns to Eritrea.

SWITZERLAND

SWISS CONFEDERATION

Head of state and government:	**Micheline Calmy-Rey**
Death penalty:	**abolitionist for all crimes**
Population:	**7.3 million**
Life expectancy:	**81.3 years**
Under-5 mortality (m/f):	**6/5 per 1,000**

The UN Special Rapporteur on contemporary forms of racism criticized the lack of effective action by the government against growing racism and xenophobia. Federal elections were held on 21 October; election posters used by the Swiss People's Party were widely considered racist and drew strong criticism. Allegations of ill-treatment, excessive use of force, and racism by law enforcement officers continued. New cases of impunity were reported.

Racism and xenophobia

In January, the UN Special Rapporteur on contemporary forms of racism, racial discrimination, xenophobia and related intolerance published a report on his visit to Switzerland in 2006. He concluded that the lack of relevant comprehensive national legislation and the lack of a coherent national policy to address racism and xenophobia posed a major obstacle to the effectiveness of the

fight against racism. The report recommended that the Swiss authorities prepare a comprehensive political strategy to combat racism and xenophobia and highlighted the need for the government to oppose and condemn all racist and xenophobic political platforms. It also recommended that the Swiss authorities establish an independent mechanism to investigate allegations of racism and xenophobia.

The Swiss People's Party provoked controversy with its federal election campaign, which was widely considered to promote racist and discriminatory ideas. On 21 October the election result increased the Swiss People's Party's representation in parliament. The UN Special Rapporteur on contemporary forms of racism and the Special Rapporteur on the human rights of migrants sent a joint letter to the Swiss government asking for an official explanation for the Swiss People's Party campaign posters, which showed white sheep kicking a black sheep off the Swiss flag. In its response, the Federal Council stated that it would not tolerate any form of racism but highlighted the importance of freedom of expression, particularly in the context of political debate, and stated that it was up to the courts to determine if the clause of the Penal Code against racism (the "anti-racism norm") had been infringed.

Police and security forces

Human rights violations allegedly committed by law enforcement officers and their subsequent impunity continued to be reported. Insufficient training on multiculturalism and the lack of a system of independent and impartial mechanisms to investigate allegations of human rights violations were criticized. In response, some cantons and towns took measures to improve training and issue new protocols concerning police interventions.

Migrants, refugees and asylum-seekers

Following the entry into force of new asylum legislation adopted in 2006, a Swiss non-governmental organization, the Swiss Refugee Council, announced that many asylum-seekers were denied access to the asylum procedure on the grounds that they lacked identity documents. Non-governmental organizations working with asylum-seekers reported that under the new legislation, rejected asylum-seekers – including families – who were having their application

S

reconsidered had been told to leave their homes and live in a special residence while they awaited the decision on their case.

On 17 December the National Council (one of the houses of parliament) approved a decision to authorize the use of electro-shock (taser) weapons and police dogs during the forcible expulsion of foreign nationals. The decision was condemned by human rights organizations. Parliament will take a final decision on the text in 2008.

Violence against women

On 1 June a new law came into force granting greater protection to victims of domestic violence. However, migrant victims of domestic violence continued to be at risk of losing their residence rights if they cease cohabiting with a violent partner. Victims of human trafficking can be given a temporary residence permit for the duration of any criminal procedure in which they testify, but lose the right to remain when the procedure ends.

SYRIA

SYRIAN ARAB REPUBLIC

Head of state:	Bashar al-Assad
Head of government:	Muhammad Naji al-'Otri
Death penalty:	retentionist
Population:	20 million
Life expectancy:	73.6 years
Under-5 mortality (m/f):	20/16 per 1,000
Adult literacy:	80.8 per cent

The state of emergency, in force since 1963, continued to give security forces sweeping powers of arrest and detention. Freedom of expression and association were severely restricted. Hundreds of people were arrested and hundreds of others remained imprisoned for political reasons, including prisoners of conscience and others sentenced after unfair trials. Human rights defenders were harassed and persecuted. Women and members of the Kurdish minority faced discrimination in law and practice. Torture and other ill-treatment were committed with impunity. Public executions resumed.

Background

Syria hosted up to 1.4 million Iraqi refugees, including many who entered during 2007, as well as some 500,000 Palestinian refugees who are long-term residents. Tens of thousands of Syrians remained internally displaced due to Israel's continuing occupation of the Golan.

In February, Syria ratified the Arab Charter on Human Rights.

On 6 September Israeli Air Force planes bombed a building in north-eastern Syria. Israeli media reports suggested that the target was a nuclear facility; President Bashar al-Assad said it was an unused military building. The head of the International Atomic Energy Agency criticized Israel for "taking the law into its own hands" and said the Israeli authorities had provided no evidence that the target was a secret nuclear facility.

The ninth report by the UN Independent Investigation Commission on the 2005 assassination of former Lebanese Prime Minister Rafiq al-Hariri, issued in November, said "more precise preliminary conclusions" had been reached and reaffirmed Syria's co-operation with the Commission.

Arbitrary arrests and detentions
Political prisoners

Some 1,500 people were reportedly arrested for political reasons, including prisoners of conscience. Hundreds of others arrested in previous years remained in prison. The majority of more than 170 people sentenced in 2007 after grossly unfair trials before the Supreme State Security Court (SSSC), Criminal Court or Military Court were alleged to be Islamists.

■ On 11 March, the SSSC convicted 24 men from the Qatana area, near Damascus, of being part of a "group established with the aim of changing the economic or social status of the state" and "weakening nationalist sentiments", apparently solely on the basis of "confessions" which the men alleged were obtained under torture. The SSSC sentenced them to between four and 12 years in prison. Arrested between May and November 2004, the men had been held incommunicado for over a year at the Palestine Branch of Military Intelligence, Damascus, notorious for torture and other ill-treatment. The SSSC failed to investigate the men's torture allegations.

S

- On 10 May, the Criminal Court convicted Kamal al-Labwani of "scheming with a foreign country, or communicating with one to incite it to initiate aggression against Syria" and sentenced him to 12 years' imprisonment. The charge related to his 2005 visit to Europe and the USA where he met human rights organizations and government officials and called for peaceful democratic reform in Syria. Kamal al-Labwani previously spent three years in prison for his involvement in the peaceful pro-reform movement of 2000-2001 known as the "Damascus Spring".
- On 13 May, the Criminal Court convicted Michel Kilo and Mahmoud 'Issa of "weakening nationalist sentiments" and sentenced them to three years' imprisonment. They were among 10 people arrested in May 2006 in relation to the Beirut-Damascus Declaration, a petition signed by 300 Syrian and Lebanese nationals calling for the normalization of relations between the two countries.
- Of some 40 people arrested for attending a meeting on 1 December of the unauthorized umbrella grouping, the National Council of the Damascus Declaration for Democratic National Change, seven remained detained incommunicado at the end of the year.

UN Working Group on Arbitrary Detention

It was announced in February that the UN Working Group on Arbitrary Detention had declared in May 2006 that the detention of Riad Drar al-Hamood was arbitrary because of the non-observance of fair trial standards and because he was convicted for exercising his right to free expression. Riad Drar al-Hamood was convicted by the SSSC in April 2006 of belonging to a "secret organization", "publishing false news" and "inciting sectarian strife", and sentenced to five years' imprisonment. The charges related to a speech he gave at the funeral of Kurdish Islamic scholar Sheikh Muhammad Ma'shuq al-Khiznawi, who had been abducted and killed.

In June 2007, the Working Group stated that Ayman Ardenli, held for three years in Syria without charge, had been detained arbitrarily as the detention could not be justified "on any legal basis", and that Muhammad Zammar, held for nearly five years without charge before being sentenced by the SSSC on 11 February to 12 years' imprisonment, was being detained arbitrarily because of non-observance of fair trial standards (see below).

Freedom of expression

Freedom of expression remained strictly controlled.
- On 17 June, the SSSC convicted Maher Isber Ibrahim, Tareq al-Ghorani, Hussam 'Ali Mulhim, Diab Siriyeh, 'Omar 'Ali al-'Abdullah, 'Allam Fakhour and Ayham Saqr of "taking action or making a written statement or speech which could endanger the State or harm its relationship with a foreign country, or expose it to the risk of hostile action" for their involvement in developing a youth discussion group and for publishing pro-democracy articles on the internet. Maher Isber Ibrahim and Tareq al-Ghorani were also convicted of "broadcasting of false news" and sentenced to seven years' imprisonment while the other five received five-year prison terms. All were arrested by Air Force Intelligence officials in early 2006 and reportedly detained incommunicado until November 2006. The men repudiated "confessions" they had made in pre-trial detention, alleging that they were obtained under torture and duress. However, the SSSC failed to investigate their allegations and accepted the "confessions" as evidence against them.
- Fa'eq al-Mir, a leader of the People's Democratic Party, was convicted by the Criminal Court on 31 December of "spreading false information harmful to the nation". This apparently related to a telephone call he made to a Lebanese politician to express condolences over the assassination of a Lebanese government minister. He was sentenced to 18 months' imprisonment.
- Kareem 'Arabji was arrested on 7 June by Military Intelligence officers in Damascus, allegedly for moderating the internet youth forum www.akhawia.net. He was still held incommunicado at the end of the year.

Torture and other ill-treatment

Detainees continued to be tortured and otherwise ill-treated; five reportedly died, possibly as a result. The authorities took no action to investigate torture allegations.
- 'Aref Dalilah, aged 64, remained in solitary confinement in a small cell in 'Adra prison, serving a 10-year sentence for his involvement in the "Damascus Spring". He suffers from diabetes, high blood pressure and the effects of a stroke, but was denied access to adequate medical care.
- The body of 'Abd al-Mo'ez Salem was reportedly returned to his family in Areeha on 4 July and buried in the presence of Military Intelligence agents who did not

S

allow the body to be seen or prepared for burial. He had apparently been held incommunicado for up to two years, including at the Palestine Branch.

■ 'Aref Hannoush, 16, was among up to nine youths allegedly tortured and otherwise ill-treated while detained in Damascus in August. They said they were confined in cramped and degrading conditions, denied sleep or access to a toilet, and beaten, including by the *dulab* (being forced into a car tyre and beaten).

'War on terror'

■ Muhammad Zammar, arrested in Morocco and forcibly transferred to Syria in December 2001 apparently under the US-led renditions programme, was convicted in February after an unfair trial on four charges, including membership of the outlawed Syrian Muslim Brotherhood organization. No evidence of such membership was presented during the trial and the Muslim Brotherhood denied that Muhammad Zammar had ever been a member or had any active links with it or any of its members.

Violence and discrimination against women

The Minister of Social Affairs and Labour was reported in January to have declared the Syrian Women's Association illegal. It had been functioning since 1948. In February, the Minister ordered the dissolution of another women's rights group, the Social Initiative Organization, and in September refused to license five NGOs, including the Organization to Support Women and Victims of Domestic Violence.

In February, Syrian Grand Mufti Sheikh Ahmed Badreddin Hassoun said that "honour" crimes were wrong, that proving an act of adultery requires four witnesses, and that he had asked the Minister of Justice to set up a committee to amend the law on "honour" crimes.

In June, the UN Committee on the Elimination of Discrimination against Women recommended that the Syrian authorities take steps to improve the status of women. The Committee called for: the repeal or amendment of discriminatory laws, including relevant provisions of the Personal Status Act, Penal Code and Nationality Act; the criminalization of marital rape; perpetrators of "honour" crimes not to be exonerated or to benefit from any reduction in penalty; the establishment of shelters and other services for women who are victims of violence; and women's rights and other human rights NGOs to be allowed to function independently of the government.

Discrimination against the Kurdish minority

Syrian Kurds continued to suffer from identity-based discrimination, including restrictions on the use of the Kurdish language and culture. Tens of thousands of Syrian Kurds remained effectively stateless and therefore denied equal access to social and economic rights.

■ Kurdish artist Salah 'Amr Sheerzad was detained and ill-treated at a security branch in Aleppo after participating in a music concert, according to reports in March.

■ Eight Kurds were arrested on 5 April and detained for 10 days at a Political Security branch in Damascus, according to reports. They appear to have been arrested for wearing wristbands showing the colours of the Kurdish flag.

Human rights defenders

Several unauthorized human rights organizations remained active even though their members were at risk of arrest, harassment and being prevented from travelling abroad.

■ On 24 April the Criminal Court convicted Anwar al-Bunni, a lawyer and head of the Syrian Centre for Legal Studies and Research, of "spreading false information harmful to the nation" and sentenced him to five years' imprisonment. This related to a statement he made in April 2006 about the death in custody of Muhammad Shaher Haysa, apparently as a result of ill-treatment possibly amounting to torture. Anwar al-Bunni, a prisoner of conscience, was beaten severely by prison guards on 25 January.

■ On 1 November, the authorities prevented human rights lawyers Muhannad al-Hasani, Khalil Ma'atouq, Mustafa Osso, Radif Mustafa and Hasan Masho from travelling to Egypt to attend a workshop organized by the International Federation for Human Rights and the Cairo Institute for Human Rights Studies.

Death penalty

The death penalty remained in force for a wide range of offences. At least seven people were executed, reportedly in public. They had been condemned to death following grossly unfair trials

S

before the Field Military Court in which defendants have no legal representation and to which there is no right of appeal.

■ Five prisoners – Radwan 'Abd al-Qadr Hassan Muhammad, Kheiro Khalif al-Fares, 'Abd al-Hai Faisal 'Abd al-Hai, Saleh Youssef Mahmoud and Hassan Ahmed Khallouf – were hanged in public in Aleppo on 25 October. The latter two were no more than 18 years old at the time of their execution and so may have been child offenders. According to Syrian state media, those executed had committed "various murders, and armed robberies and had terrorized innocent citizens".

Enforced disappearances

The fate of some 17,000 people, mostly Islamists who were victims of enforced disappearance after they were detained in the late 1970s and early 1980s, and hundreds of Lebanese and Palestinians who were detained in Syria or abducted from Lebanon by Syrian forces or Lebanese and Palestinian militias, remained unknown.

Amnesty International visit/report

🚍 Amnesty International visited Syria in June to look into the situation of Iraqi refugees and to gather information about human rights abuses in Iraq.

▤ Iraqi refugees in Syria (MDE 14/036/2007)

TAIWAN

TAIWAN
Head of state: **Chen Shui-bian**
Head of government: **Chang Chun-hsiung**
(replaced Su Tseng-chang in May)
Death penalty: **retentionist**

Aside from some legislative changes, the authorities failed to introduce significant human rights reforms.

Background

In July, the authorities released around 10,000 prisoners under a clemency bill for those convicted of minor offences who had already served half of their terms.

Public events were organized to commemorate the 60th anniversary of the "228 incident" – the brutal military suppression of public protests in February 1947 which resulted in thousands of deaths and injuries.

Death penalty

No executions were carried out during 2007. Five people were sentenced to death, joining around 70-100 prisoners on death row.

In response to campaigning, the President emphasized the need for a gradual approach to abolition in order to forge a national consensus. The Ministry of Justice produced a research report analysing measures necessary for abolition, but this was not made public.

■ Chong De-shu, whose execution order was signed at the end of 2006, remained under sentence of death. Chang Pao-hui tried to commit suicide at Hualien prison in March by swallowing 13 batteries, apparently because he was unable to bear the stress of waiting for his execution.

■ In June, the Taiwan High Court once again sentenced Liu Bing-lang, Su Chien-ho and Chuang Lin-hsun – known as the "Hsichih Trio" – to death overturning its 2003 not guilty verdict. The decision followed their 11th retrial in connection with murder charges originally imposed in 1991. In November, the Supreme Court rejected the verdict and returned the case to the High Court for another retrial. The case was based almost entirely on their confessions which were allegedly extracted through torture by the police.

T

Freedom of expression

Human rights activists continued to campaign for reforms to the Assembly and Parade Law. The law requires police permission to hold a public demonstration and is used to suppress protests about student fees, environmental concerns and other issues.

■ Several protesters were detained and harassed by police for protesting against the eviction of around 300 elderly residents of the Lo-sheng Leprosy Sanitorium in Taipei. The Government plans to demolish the facility to make way for a public transport system.

Violence against women

In March, the legislature passed several amendments to the Domestic Violence Prevention Law and expanded the scope of the law to include cohabiting same-sex and unmarried couples. Women reportedly continued to be trafficked into Taiwan, often to work as sex workers.

Amnesty International report

📄 Taiwan: Miscarriage of justice – "Hsichih Trio" re-sentenced to death, 16 July 2007 (ASA 38/001/2007)

TAJIKISTAN

REPUBLIC OF TAJIKISTAN

Head of state:	Imomali Rakhmon
Head of government:	Okil Okilov
Death penalty:	retentionist
Population:	6.7 million
Life expectancy:	66.3 years
Under-5 mortality (m/f):	116/103 per 1,000
Adult literacy:	99.5 per cent

Further restrictions were imposed on freedom of religion. Dozens of suspected members of banned Islamist groups were detained and allegedly tortured or otherwise ill-treated. Some were convicted after grossly unfair trials.

Background

A presidential amnesty marked the 10th anniversary of the 1997 peace agreement that ended the five-year civil war. The amnesty covered former opposition combatants, but excluded those convicted of terrorism or murder. The UN Tajikistan Office of Peacebuilding ended its seven-year mission in July.

The Supreme Court banned 10 organizations as terrorist, including the Islamic Party of Turkestan, also known as the Islamic Movement of Uzbekistan (IMU); and Tojikistoni Ozod (Free Tajikistan), an Uzbekistan-based political party that the authorities considered a threat to Tajikistan's national security.

In March President Imomali Rakhmonov removed the Russian suffix from his surname, changing it to Rakhmon. He recommended that all newborn children be registered with Tajik surnames.

Freedom of religion

Freedom of religion was under attack. Unregistered mosques were closed down or demolished in the capital, Dushanbe. Urban redevelopment plans in Dushanbe reportedly threatened the city's synagogue and several churches. A proposed new law on religion included stringent registration requirements that would make it very difficult for religious minorities to apply or reapply for legal status. The draft law also proposed to limit the number of registered places of worship and to ban missionary activity. Pending the adoption of the new

T

law, the government did not accept new applications for legal status.

■ In October the government revoked the legal status of the Jehovah's Witnesses and banned all their activities. The Jehovah's Witnesses were first registered in 1994. Officials told representatives that the decision was based on Jehovah's Witnesses' refusal to perform military service and their proselytizing activities. Two Protestant groups were also suspended for three months. All three organizations appealed against the decisions.

Abuses against alleged Islamists

Dozens of members and suspected members of banned Islamist groups, including the IMU, were detained on national security grounds and allegedly tortured or otherwise ill-treated in detention. At least 20 alleged IMU members were sentenced to long prison terms after trials that fell far short of international standards of fairness, including the public branding of defendants as guilty before trial.

'War on terror'

In August, two men who had been transferred to Tajikistan in March after six years in US custody at Guantánamo Bay were sentenced to 17 years in prison by a court in Dushanbe. They were convicted of illegally crossing the border into Afghanistan in 2001 and fighting with the IMU against US and Allied forces.

Earlier in March, a court in southern Tajikistan sentenced another former Guantánamo detainee to 23 years in prison for his part in a bomb attack in Tajikistan in 2000. He had reportedly been captured by US forces in Afghanistan.

Amnesty International report

📖 Central Asia: Summary of human rights concerns, January 2006–March 2007 (EUR 04/001/2007)

TANZANIA

UNITED REPUBLIC OF TANZANIA

Head of state:	Jakaya Kikwete
Head of government:	Edward Lowassa
Head of Zanzibar government:	Amani Abeid Karume
Death penalty:	abolitionist in practice
Population:	39.7 million
Life expectancy:	51
Under-5 mortality (m/f):	169/153 per 1,000
Adult literacy:	69.4 per cent

High levels of violence against women persisted. Thousands of refugees and migrants from neighbouring countries were forcibly returned to their countries. Prison conditions remained harsh. Talks on legal and electoral reform in semi-autonomous Zanzibar between the ruling party, Chama Cha Mapinduzi (CCM), and the opposition Civic United Front (CUF), which were due to end in August, continued.

Violence against women

Violence against women, including domestic violence, remained widespread. Female genital mutilation continued to be illegally practised, especially in rural areas. Reports indicated that in parts of the country, between 18 and 100 per cent of girls were subjected to female genital mutilation. No prosecutions were reported.

Migrants' rights

The government continued the forcible return of refugees from Rwanda, Burundi and the Democratic Republic of the Congo that began in May 2006. In early 2007 thousands of individuals deemed to be "illegal immigrants" were forcibly returned to these countries. Many of those returned had been registered as refugees or were in the process of seeking refugee status and some had lived in Tanzania for 15 years or more. Many complained of harassment, beatings and looting of property by the law enforcement officials carrying out the process of repatriation.

Prison conditions

Prison conditions remained harsh, with new reports of severe overcrowding in most prisons. In March and September, pre-trial detainees in prisons in

T

Dar es Salaam, Arusha and Dodoma protested against delays in their court hearings and against harsh prison conditions.

Impunity

The authorities failed to investigate allegations of human rights violations, including unlawful killings by the police.

■ On 5 September, police in Moshi shot at close range and killed 14 people. Police alleged that the 14 were armed and were preparing to raid a bank. By the end of 2007 there had been no investigations by the authorities into these killings.

Freedom of expression

In February the government published a draft Media Services Bill 2007 to regulate the media. It proposed setting up a registration mechanism for both individual journalists and media outlets, and a statutory Media Standards Board responsible for regulating the print media. The bill was criticized on the grounds that it imposed restrictions on the work of journalists, allowed for political interference in the broadcast media, and required every publisher and broadcaster to deposit a cash bond. Critics argued that the system was open to abuse and could be used to suppress criticism in the media. By the end of 2007 the bill had not been passed by parliament.

Death penalty

All death sentences in mainland Tanzania were commuted to life imprisonment in 2006. However, the death penalty remained part of the penal law and there were no efforts by the government to abolish it during the year.

THAILAND

KINGDOM OF THAILAND

Head of state:	King Bhumibol Adulyadej
Head of government:	General Surayud Chulanont
Death penalty:	retentionist
Population:	65.3 million
Life expectancy:	69.6 years
Under-5 mortality (m/f):	26/16 per 1,000
Adult literacy :	92.6 per cent

Violence in the south continued unabated. Both security forces and armed groups were responsible for abuses of human rights and international humanitarian law. Civilians suffered disproportionately, and human rights defenders and others were victims of enforced disappearances. A new law gave police and security forces immunity from prosecution for human rights abuses.

Martial law remained in effect in 31 provinces, while the Emergency Decree remained in effect in the south. Freedom of expression and assembly were curtailed. The government tightened restrictions on refugees and asylum-seekers, especially in relation to Burmese asylum seekers and those in detention, and forcibly returned several groups of Lao Hmong asylum-seekers.

Background

A new Constitution was approved in August and national elections took place on 23 December. The political process was dominated by fighting between the Council for National Security (CNS) and allies of deposed Prime Minister Thaksin Shinawatra. The People Power Party, aligned with Thaksin Shinawatra, received the highest number of votes. Due to alleged irregularities, however, it was not clear whether they would be allowed to form a government.

Armed groups

Civil unrest increased in the four predominantly Muslim southern provinces of Narathiwat, Pattani, Yala, and Songkhla, bringing the total number of deaths to more than 2,700 since January 2004. Near daily attacks by armed groups occurred, usually against police and security forces. As militarization escalated in the south, the Prime Minister increased the use of civilian militias. The majority of the victims were Muslim civilians, although Buddhist civilians were increasingly targeted by armed groups. The closure in June of more than 300 schools in Narathiwat Province alone was indicative of the extent of the violence.

Arbitrary detention

Starting in June more than 600 people were arrested in the southern provinces, many without warrants; most were held beyond the maximum 37-day period permitted by law and sent to "voluntary" training camps. A court freed nearly 400 in October, accepting that their participation was not truly voluntary. However, they were not permitted to return to the three southern provinces from which they were taken.

Human rights defenders

Human rights defenders remained under threat, with three killed in November alone. Members and affiliates of the Working Group on Justice for Peace, chaired by Angkhana Neelapaijit, widow of Muslim lawyer Somchai Neelapaijit (disappeared and killed in 2004), were at particular risk.

Enforced disappearances

At least 26 people have disappeared since 2001. Few of these cases have come before a court, and none has been conclusively solved. In March, 24 southern Muslims sought asylum in Malaysia citing enforced disappearances as a reason.

Justice system and impunity

All five officers implicated in the enforced disappearance of Somchai Neelapaijit, including the only one convicted in 2006, were allowed to return to work. No disciplinary action was taken against them. A court ruled in April that Somchai Neelapaijit's widow could not sue the Police Chief for redress.

The Ministry of Justice established a committee to prosecute human rights violations under Prime Minister Thaksin Shinawatra's government, focussing on extrajudicial executions during the 2003 war on drugs. However, little progress was made.

In May a court found three military personnel responsible for the deaths of 32 people at the April 2004 Krue Se mosque attack, in which more than 100 people were killed during clashes with security forces. None was prosecuted and one was subsequently appointed to the Internal Security Operations Command (ISOC) in charge of combating violence in the south.

Police interfered with an inquest into the Tak Bai incident of October 2004 in which 85 people died, most from suffocation while being detained in military trucks. Although the police admitted misconduct, no officers were disciplined. Compensation was paid to victims on condition that a legal case against the authorities was dropped.

The ISOC law was passed on 20 December, conferring immunity from prosecution for human rights abuses on nearly all authorities who act "in good faith".

Freedom of expression

In April a television station regarded as pro-Thaksin had its licence revoked by the CNS. Three Bangkok radio stations were shut down in May after airing the deposed Prime Minister's call for a swift return to democracy. A Computer Related Offences Act was passed in May that allowed for wide-ranging action against computer use. Websites deemed anti-coup or pro-Thaksin were closed down. Access to YouTube was blocked from April to August because of a video deemed critical of the monarchy.

Three members of the White Dove anti-coup group were detained by police in Chiang Mai during demonstrations in May.

■ The Constitutional Court ordered the disbanding of Thaksin's Thai Rak Thai party and the suspension of 111 of its members from all political activities for five years, on the grounds of electoral fraud in 2006. In June, the government lifted a general nationwide ban on political activities.

■ In July, six leaders of the Democratic Alliance Against Dictatorship group were detained during an anti-coup rally that turned violent. They were only released on condition that they cease further political activity.

Refugees and asylum-seekers

In January the Prime Minister named "illegal border crossings by migrant workers and human traffickers" as the second of six threats facing Thailand, and announced that the government would begin regulating "illegal hilltribe aliens, such as the Hmong".

In the same month international pressure led the authorities to halt the deportation of 143 recognized Lao refugees, most of whom were children, and the Prime Minister asserted that they would be allowed to resettle in third countries.

T

At least 179 Lao Hmong refugees were forcibly returned to Laos during the year, in contravention of Thailand's international obligations. A bilateral border agreement was signed with Laos which envisaged the return of 8,000 Lao Hmong in 2008. No adequate process was set up to identify those needing international protection. Thousands of refugees from Myanmar were turned back at the border.

■ Aye Oo, a young refugee man, was shot to death on 15 December by Thai security officers in Ban Mae Nai Soi refugee camp when a large number of refugees demonstrated against continued abuses by the officers. The Camp Commander was moved to an inactive post.

Torture and other ill-treatment

In March a number of Thai security officers in Ban Mae Nai Soi refugee camp in Mae Hong Son Province severely beat a naturalized Karenni man. He was living in the camp with his refugee parents. He remained in a coma for nine days. Neither the officers nor the Camp Commander were disciplined. At least 10 cases of torture by the authorities were reported in the south.

Legal developments

The ISOC law empowered the Prime Minister to send individuals suspected of involvement in the violence in the south to six-month "voluntary training programmes" rather than face criminal charges. It also empowered him to take command of state agencies and to suppress groups and individuals deemed "threatening". The law also restricted freedom of assembly and movement, freedom from arbitrary detention and unreasonable searches, and the right to privacy and fair trial procedures.

In August, Thailand signed the Statute of the International Criminal Court, and in October signed the UN Convention against Torture.

Death penalty

The death penalty remained in effect with about 1,000 people on death row, including many for drug-related offences. No one was executed.

TIMOR-LESTE

DEMOCRATIC REPUBLIC OF TIMOR-LESTE

Head of state:	José Manuel Ramos-Horta (replaced Kay Rala Xanana Gusmão)
Head of government:	Kay Rala Xanana Gusmão (replaced Estanislau da Silva in August who replaced José Manuel Ramos-Horta in May)
Death penalty:	abolitionist for all crimes
Population:	1.1 million
Life expectancy:	59.7 years
Under-5 mortality (m/f):	118/110 per 1,000
Adult literacy:	50.1 per cent

Although Presidential and Parliamentary elections were relatively fair and peaceful, sporadic violent protests and incidents erupted throughout the year. The police and judiciary remained weak institutions. The numbers of internally displaced people continued at high levels. Investigations and prosecutions of those responsible for the human rights violations in 2006 progressed, although impunity continued for violations committed under Indonesian occupation.

Background

Timor's first Presidential elections since independence were held in April. They were described as relatively free and fair by observers. Parliamentary elections which followed in June left an unclear majority. The newly elected President, José Ramos-Horta, announced in August that former President Xanana Gusmão would be appointed Prime Minister.

In February, the UN Integrated Mission in Timor-Leste (UNMIT), whose mandate included the fostering of stability and supporting national elections, had its mission extended until early 2008.

Following the violent unrest of April/May 2006, which killed an estimated 38 people and displaced some 150,000 others, low level violence continued throughout 2007. In August, following the appointment of the new government, violent incidents erupted throughout the country leading to deaths and destruction of property.

Police and security forces

The programme to rebuild the national police force, including rigorous screening of all existing personnel,

T

continued. By August, 1,200 police officers out of 3,000 had been given provisional certification.

Reports continued of human rights violations committed by police and military personnel, including cruel, inhuman and degrading treatment, arbitrary arrests, excessive use of force and fatal shootings.

Allegations of excessive use of force and cruel and degrading treatment by UNMIT police officers and international security forces were also reported.

Internally displaced people

Around 100,000 people remained internally displaced throughout the country as a result of the 2006 or 2007 events. They were in urgent need of adequate food and shelter as well as water and sanitation facilities.

Justice system – 2006 unrest

Investigations into criminal acts perpetrated by both military and police officers during the 2006 events made some progress and prosecutions were initiated. The law on truth and clemency measures adopted in June by Parliament was declared unconstitutional by the court of appeal in August. If promulgated, there were concerns that it could have undermined investigations and prosecutions of the 2006 events.

Former Prime Minister Mari Alkatiri was cleared of suspected involvement in illegal activities in relation to the arming of civilian militia during the 2006 events.

Impunity

UNMIT re-established the Serious Crimes Investigation Team to complete investigations into outstanding cases from the events surrounding the independence referendum of 1999 when serious human rights violations were committed. However the prosecution branch was not reinstated. Both the Timorese and Indonesian governments resisted further initiatives to bring to justice all perpetrators of the 1999 crimes.

The Commission of Truth and Friendship (CTF), established jointly by Indonesia and Timor-Leste to document crimes committed in Timor-Leste in 1999 and to promote reconciliation, began its investigations via public and closed hearing. In July, the UN Secretary-General instructed UN officials not to testify because the CTF could recommend amnesty for serious crimes. National and international observers expressed concerns about the CTF's treatment of

victims during hearings, and possible biased weighting of the testimonies of military officials, militia members and bureaucrats over victims' testimonies.

TOGO

TOGOLESE REPUBLIC

Head of state:	Faure Gnassingbé
Head of government:	Komlan Mally (replaced Yawovi Agboyibo in December)
Death penalty:	abolitionist in practice
Population:	6.3 million
Life expectancy:	57.8 years
Under-5 mortality (m/f):	136/119 per 1,000
Adult literacy:	53.2 per cent

Despite some reforms, freedom of expression continued to be curtailed. Regular reports were received that pre-trial detainees were tortured and ill-treated. No steps were taken to address cases of former victims who lodged complaints for past human rights abuses.

Background

Legislative elections held in October were declared free and fair by international observers, including ECOWAS. The Constitutional Court announced that the Rally of the Togolese People (Rassemblement du peuple togolais, RPT) had won the majority of seats. The opposition party, the Union of Forces for Change (Union des forces pour le changement, UFC), which took part in the legislative elections for the first time since the beginning of the democratic process in 1990, challenged the results.

In February, Parliament passed a law on the status of the Togolese armed forces. The law aimed to guarantee that the army operate within the law and that its role in the country be non-political but did not address the accountability of security forces accused of human rights violations. In April, the governments of Ghana and Togo signed a tripartite agreement with the UN refugee agency, UNHCR, on the voluntary repatriation of Togolese refugees who had lived in Ghana since 1992.

T

Visit of the Special Rapporteur on torture

In April, the UN Special Rapporteur on torture visited the country. While noting that the government had taken some positive steps in the recent past, he expressed concern that many people were detained without clear legal basis for prolonged periods in appalling conditions. He also noted that many detainees held by the police and the gendarmerie had been beaten by cord and wooden sticks in order to extract confessions.

Freedom of expression

The High Authority for Audiovisual and Communication (Haute autorité de l'audio visuelle) continued to exert pressure on independent media and journalists.

■ In January, Radio Victoire, a private FM radio, was suspended for 15 days for alleged unprofessional conduct. It appeared that this decision was taken after the radio management refused to ban a journalist who criticized the brother of the Head of State who was the former president of the Togolese Confederation of football.

■ In March, the authorities banned private radio Nana FM journalist Daniel Lawson-Drackey, after he criticized a government minister on air.

Impunity

A collective of more than 100 victims of human rights abuses committed during the 2005 presidential elections filed several complaints throughout the year. Despite the fact that the Togolese authorities publicly committed themselves to put an end to impunity, no progress was known to have been made in the examination of these complaints.

TRINIDAD AND TOBAGO

REPUBLIC OF TRINIDAD AND TOBAGO

Head of state:	George Maxwell Richards
Head of government:	Patrick Manning
Death penalty:	retentionist
Population:	1.3 million
Life expectancy:	69.2 years
Under-5 mortality (m/f):	20/16 per 1,000
Adult literacy:	98.4 per cent

There were further reports of abuses by the police. Impunity continued in cases of alleged killings by police. Death sentences continued to be imposed, but there were no executions.

Background

In November, the ruling People's National Movement was re-elected. Predicted widespread political violence at election time did not materialize.

Despite receiving an official communication requesting access to Trinidad and Tobago, the authorities did not invite the UN Special Rapporteur on extrajudicial, summary or arbitrary executions to visit the country.

There were a reported 388 homicides during the year, a record high.

Police and security forces

A Parliamentary Joint Select Committee issued a report in July which was highly critical of the police service. The report highlighted the persistent failure by police officers to appear in court as complainants or witnesses, leading to many cases being dismissed. The report noted a disturbingly high number of disciplinary charges against officers and the need to combat the increased levels of indiscipline within the police service. The report also spoke of a "serious lack of accountability from top to bottom" in the force.

Killings

Several people were killed by the police. In most cases the police claimed that the victims had been killed in a "shoot-out". These claims were disputed by witnesses. Those responsible for such killings were rarely brought to justice; only 6 per cent of cases of killings by the police had gone to trial since 1999.

■ On 17 August, four men and a woman were killed by police in the town of Wallerfield. The four men were travelling in the same car when they were shot. Wendy Courtney, a mother of five, was reportedly hit by a stray bullet in her bedroom. The police officers claimed that the men opened fire when they stopped the car to search it. A police investigation was reportedly continuing at the end of the year.

■ Sheldon Des Vignes was shot dead by police on 9 November after he reportedly came to the aid of his cousin who was being questioned by police officers in Laventille. The police reportedly claimed that a man who accompanied Sheldon Des Vignes had shot at them forcing them to return fire. A police officer was charged with his murder at the end of December.

Justice system

The Justice Protection Programme to protect witnesses was widely criticized, with many witnesses reportedly declining to give evidence at the last moment because of threats.

■ A 17-year-old state witness, Ishmael Sobers, was fatally shot in the head by armed men near his house in the St James neighbourhood of the capital Port-of-Spain in September. He had been due to testify against two men charged with a murder committed in September 2005.

Death penalty

Several people were sentenced to death during the year. In May, the Prime Minister stated publicly that he wanted hangings resumed in Trinidad and Tobago as he believed "capital punishment is an essential element in crime fighting". In November, Trinidad and Tobago voted against the UN resolution calling for a global moratorium on the death penalty.

TUNISIA

REPUBLIC OF TUNISIA

Head of state:	Zine El 'Abidine Ben 'Ali
Head of government:	Mohamed Ghannouchi
Death penalty:	abolitionist in practice
Population:	10.3 million
Life expectancy:	73.5 years
Under-5 mortality (m/f):	23/20 per 1,000
Adult literacy:	74.3 per cent

Tunisia's good economic performance and positive legal reforms enhanced its international reputation. This masked, however, a darker reality in which legal safeguards were often violated, political suspects were tortured with impunity, and human rights defenders were harassed. Freedom of expression and association remained severely restricted. Many people were sentenced to lengthy prison terms following unfair trials on terrorism-related charges, including before military courts, and hundreds of others sentenced after unfair trials in previous years remained in prison, some for over a decade. They included possible prisoners of conscience.

Legal and institutional developments

In July, a decree amended the composition of the Higher Committee for Human Rights and Fundamental Freedoms, the body in charge of receiving complaints about human rights violations. The amendment increased representation but did not include independent human rights organizations.

'War on terror'

Abdellah al-Hajji and Lotfi Lagha, two of 12 Tunisians held by the US authorities in Guantánamo Bay, were returned to Tunisia in June. They were arrested on arrival and detained at the State Security Department of the Interior Ministry, where they alleged they were ill-treated and forced to sign statements. Abdellah al-Hajji complained that he was deprived of sleep, slapped in the face and threatened that his wife and daughters would be raped. In October, Lotfi Lagha was convicted of associating with a terrorist organization operating abroad and sentenced to three years' imprisonment. Abdellah al-Hajji was retried before a military court in Tunis after he challenged a 10-year prison sentence imposed when he was tried

T

in his absence in 1995. In November, he was convicted of "belonging in times of peace to a terrorist organization operating abroad" and sentenced to seven years' imprisonment.

Nine Tunisians were returned by the Egyptian authorities in January and March and reportedly detained for up to several weeks for interrogation. Most were released but at least two, Ayman Hkiri and Adam Boukadida, remained in detention awaiting trial. The nine had all been detained with other foreign and Egyptian students in Egypt in November 2006 and reportedly tortured while being interrogated about an alleged plot to recruit people in Egypt to fight against the US-led coalition in Iraq.

Justice system

Trials of people facing terrorism-related charges, some of which were held before military courts, were frequently unfair and generally resulted in defendants being sentenced to long prison terms. Those accused included people arrested in Tunisia as well as Tunisians forcibly returned by the authorities of other states, including France, Italy and the USA, despite concerns that they would be at risk of torture. Often, convictions rested exclusively on "confessions" made in pre-trial detention that defendants retracted in court, alleging that they had been obtained by torture. Examining judges and courts routinely failed to investigate such allegations.

At least 16 civilians were reported to have been convicted and sentenced to prison terms of up to 11 years after trial before the military court in Tunis. Most were convicted of having links to terrorist organizations operating outside the country. Such trials failed to satisfy international fair trial standards; defendants' right of appeal was restricted.

■ In November, 30 men stood trial before the Tunis Court of First Instance in what was known as the "Soliman Case". They were charged with an array of offences, including conspiracy to overthrow the government, use of firearms and belonging to a terrorist organization. All were arrested in December 2006 and January 2007 in connection with an armed clash between security forces and alleged members of the Soldiers of Assad Ibn al-Fourat armed group. They were detained well beyond the legal six-day limit of garde à vue (pre-arraignment police custody), and alleged that they were tortured or otherwise ill-treated. Their lawyers asked both the examining judge and the trial court to order medical examinations for evidence of torture, but their requests were denied. On 30 December, the court sentenced two of the defendants to death, eight to life imprisonment and the rest to prison terms ranging from five to 30 years.

Releases of political prisoners

In all, some 179 political prisoners were released, of whom around 15 had reportedly been held in pre-trial detention as suspected members of the Salafist Group, an armed group allegedly linked to al-Qa'ida. Most of the others had been imprisoned since the early 1990s for membership of the banned Islamist organization, Ennahda (Renaissance).

Torture and other ill-treatment

Torture and other ill-treatment by the security forces, notably in the State Security Department, continued. Detainees held incommunicado were especially at risk. The security forces frequently breached the six-day garde à vue limit and held detainees incommunicado for up to several weeks. During such detention, many alleged that they were tortured including by beatings, suspension in contorted positions, electric shocks, sleep deprivation, rape and threats to rape female relatives. In virtually all cases, the authorities failed to carry out investigations or bring alleged perpetrators to justice.

■ Mohamed Amine Jaziri, one of the co-defendants in the Soliman Case (see above), was arrested on 24 December 2006 in Sidi Bouzid, south of Tunis, and detained in secret first at the city's police station and then at the State Security Department in Tunis until 22 January. His relatives made repeated inquiries but the authorities denied holding him prior to his release. He alleged that while detained incommunicado he was beaten all over his body, given electric shocks, suspended from the ceiling for several hours, doused with cold water, deprived of sleep and had a dirty hood placed over his head during interrogation. In December, he was sentenced to 30 years' imprisonment.

Prison conditions

Many political prisoners reportedly suffered discrimination and harsh treatment. Some went on hunger strike to protest against ill-treatment by prison guards, denial of medical care, interruption of family visits and harsh conditions, including prolonged solitary confinement.

■ Ousama Abbadi, Ramzi el Aifi, Oualid Layouni and Mahdi Ben Elhaj Ali were allegedly punched, tied up and kicked by prison guards at Mornaguia Prison in October. Ousama Abbadi sustained a serious eye injury and a deep, open leg wound and was in a wheelchair, unable to stand, when seen by his lawyer. Other inmates at Mornaguia Prison were reportedly stripped naked by guards and dragged along a corridor in front of prison cells. No investigation was known to have taken place, despite complaints by the prisoners' lawyers.

Freedom of expression

The authorities severely restricted freedom of expression. Hundreds of political prisoners continued to serve sentences imposed on account of their alleged involvement in peaceful opposition to the government.

Press freedom

Editors and journalists pursued their professional activities in a climate of intimidation and fear. Foreign publications were censored and journalists who criticized the government faced smear campaigns or criminal prosecutions for libel. Journalists were prevented, including by force, from attending and reporting on events organized by independent human rights organizations or at which the government would be criticized.

■ In December, a court in Sakiet Ezzit (Sfax) sentenced freelance journalist Slim Boukhdir to one year's imprisonment after an unfair trial. He was charged with "insulting a public officer during the performance of his duties", "breaching public morality" and "refusing to show his identity card". He was arrested on 26 November while on his way from Sfax to Tunis following a summons to collect his passport. Earlier in the year he had reported receiving death threats following an interview he gave to al-Hiwar (Dialogue), a UK-based TV channel, in which he criticized members of President Ben 'Ali's family. The week before these threats he was assaulted by police officers in plain clothes.

The authorities continued to block a number of websites that carried political and other criticism of the government on the grounds of "security" or their "harmful" content. The websites of reputable national and international human rights organizations and newspapers were among those affected.

Religious freedom

Expression of religious belief was restricted. Women were harassed for wearing the *hijab* (Islamic headscarf). Some were made to remove their *hijab* before being allowed into schools, universities or workplaces, while others were forced to remove them in the street. In May, women wearing the *hijab* were prevented from attending the Tunis International Book Fair. A number of women reported that they were taken to police stations and forced to sign a written commitment that they would stop wearing the *hijab*; some of those who refused were assaulted by police officers.

Human rights defenders

The authorities severely impeded the activities of human rights organizations. Telephone lines and internet connections were frequently disrupted or diverted to hamper their communication with others in Tunisia and abroad. Individual human rights defenders were harassed and intimidated. Security forces kept human rights defenders and their families under constant close surveillance and in some cases physically assaulted them.

■ Raouf Ayadi, a lawyer and human rights defender, was assaulted by a police officer in April as he was about to enter a courtroom to represent a defendant facing terrorism-related charges. In June, Raouf Ayadi's car was vandalized. In November, he was insulted, thrown to the floor and dragged by police officers seeking to prevent him from visiting a human rights activist and a journalist who were on hunger strike to protest against the authorities' refusal to issue them with passports. No action was taken by the authorities against those responsible for the assaults on Raouf Ayadi.

■ Lawyer and human rights defender Mohammed Abbou was released in July after having served 28 months of a three-and-a-half-year prison sentence imposed in April 2005 after an unfair trial. Following his conditional release, he was prevented from leaving the country to travel abroad on at least three occasions.

Death penalty

Three death sentences were handed down, reportedly bringing the number of prisoners on death row to more than 100, but there were no executions.

In March, the Minister of Justice and Human Rights said that the government was not in favour of

T

abolition. In June, a national Coalition against the Death Penalty was formed by Tunisian human rights organizations, including Amnesty International Tunisia. In November, the Tunisian government representative did not vote to oppose a UN resolution calling for a worldwide moratorium on executions.

Amnesty International visits/report

🚗 Amnesty International delegates visited Tunisia in June/July and November/December and met human rights defenders, victims and their relatives, government officials and representatives of EU governments.

📄 Tunisia: human rights briefing for 20th anniversary of President Ben Ali's rule (MDE 30/010/2007)

TURKEY

REPUBLIC OF TURKEY

Head of state:	**Abdullah Gül (replaced Ahmet Necdet Sezer in August)**
Head of government:	**Recep Tayyip Erdoğan**
Death penalty:	**abolitionist for all crimes**
Population:	**75.2 million**
Life expectancy:	**71.4 years**
Under-5 mortality (m/f):	**47/37 per 1,000**
Adult literacy:	**87.4 per cent**

In the wake of increased political uncertainty and army interventions, nationalist sentiment and violence increased. Freedom of expression continued to be restricted. Allegations of torture and other ill-treatment and the use of excessive force by law enforcement officials persisted. Prosecutions for violations of human rights were ineffective and insufficient, and fair trial concerns persisted. The rights of refugees and asylum-seekers were violated. There was little progress in providing shelters for victims of domestic violence.

Background

An atmosphere of intolerance prevailed following the shooting in January of Turkish-Armenian journalist Hrant Dink. From May onwards a marked escalation in armed clashes between the Turkish armed forces and the Kurdistan Workers' Party (PKK) led to human rights abuses. The military declared temporary security zones in three districts bordering Iraq in June and a further three districts in December.

The inability of parliament to elect a new president resulted in early parliamentary elections in July. The government was re-elected and in August parliament elected Abdullah Gül as President. In September, the government appointed a commission to draft major constitutional amendments. In November, the Constitutional Court began proceedings to ban the pro-Kurdish Democratic Society Party (DTP).

Bomb attacks by unknown individuals or groups on civilian targets killed and injured dozens of people. In May and October, bombs exploded in İzmir, killing two people and injuring many others. In May, a bomb in the Ulus district of Ankara killed nine people and injured more than 100. In September, an attack on a minibus in the province of Şırnak caused multiple casualties.

In December, Turkish armed forces launched military interventions in the predominantly Kurdish northern Iraq, targeting PKK bases.

Freedom of expression

The peaceful expression of opinion continued to be restricted in law and practice. Lawyers, journalists, human rights defenders and others were harassed, threatened, unjustly prosecuted and physically attacked. An increased number of cases were brought under Article 301 of the Penal Code, which criminalizes "denigration of Turkishness", despite national and international opposition to the Article.

■ On 19 January, journalist and human rights defender Hrant Dink was shot dead. He had previously been prosecuted under Article 301. The suspected gunman allegedly stated that he shot Hrant Dink because he "denigrated Turkishness". An estimated 100,000 people attended Hrant Dink's funeral in an unprecedented display of solidarity. While a police investigation into the murder resulted in a number of suspects being brought to trial, the full culpability of the security services was not examined. In October, Hrant Dink's son, Arat Dink, and Sarkis Seropyan, respectively assistant editor and owner of the Turkish-Armenian weekly *Agos*, were convicted under Article 301 and each received a one-year suspended sentence.

■ In April, two Turkish nationals and a German citizen who all worked for a Christian publishing house in Malatya were killed. The three reportedly had their

T

hands and feet bound together and their throats cut. The trial of people charged in connection with the murders began in November.

Article 216 of the Penal Code, which criminalizes "inciting enmity or hatred among the population", was applied in an arbitrary and overly restrictive manner.

■ In November, lawyer Eren Keskin received a one-year prison sentence for her use of the word "Kurdistan". The sentence was later commuted to a fine of 3,300 liras (approximately US$2,800).

Prosecutions were also brought under Article 7(2) of the anti-terrorism law that criminalizes "making propaganda for a terrorist organization or for its aims".

■ In November, Gülcihan Şimşek, a DTP member and mayor of the city of Van, received a one-year prison sentence for referring to PKK leader Abdullah Öcalan as "Mr".

Human rights defenders

Human rights defenders were prosecuted for their peaceful activities.

■ In January, the bank accounts of Amnesty International Turkey were frozen on the demand of Istanbul Governor's office on the grounds of alleged "illegal fundraising" and in May an administrative fine was imposed on the organization's chairperson for the same offence. Amnesty International Turkey appealed, but both issues remained unresolved at the end of the year.

■ In June, three people associated with the Human Rights Association (İHD) were each sentenced to two years and eight months in prison for criticizing the "return to life" prison operation by state authorities in 2000.

■ Serpil Köksal, Murat Dünsen and İbrahim Kizartıcı were prosecuted for taking part in a campaign against compulsory military service. They were acquitted in December.

■ Istanbul Governor's office applied to the courts for the closure of the lesbian, gay, bisexual and transgender people's organization Lambda Istanbul on the grounds that the name and objectives of the group were against "law and morals".

Impunity

Investigations into human rights violations perpetrated by law enforcement officials remained flawed and there were insufficient prosecutions. Official human rights mechanisms remained ineffective. In June,

parliament amended the Law on the Powers and Duties of the Police, giving police further powers to use lethal force by allowing them to shoot escaping suspects if they ignore a warning to stop.

■ In April, all four police officers tried for killing Ahmet Kaymaz and his 12-year-old son Uğur outside their home were acquitted. The officers said that the deaths were the result of an armed clash, but forensic reports showed that both victims had been shot at close range several times.

■ The conviction was overturned of two military police officers and an informer found guilty of the 2005 bombing of a bookshop in the south-east town of Şemdinli in which one person was killed and others were injured. The retrial was heard by a military court. At the first hearing in December, the two military police officers were released to resume their duties.

■ In November, 10 police officers were found not guilty of the torture of two women in Istanbul police custody in 2002. The two women, "Y" and "C", reportedly suffered torture including beatings, being stripped naked and then sprayed with cold water from a high pressure hose, and attempted rape. The verdicts followed a new medical report requested by the defendants that did not show "definite evidence that the crime of torture had been committed".

Unfair trials

Fair trial concerns persisted, especially for those prosecuted under anti-terrorism laws. In protracted trials, statements allegedly extracted under torture were used as evidence.

■ In June, Mehmet Desde was imprisoned after being convicted with seven others of supporting or membership of an "illegal organization" because of links to the Bolshevik Party (North Kurdistan/Turkey). The Bolshevik Party has not used or advocated violence and the connection between it and those convicted was not proven. The conviction of Mehmet Desde was based largely on statements allegedly extracted under torture.

■ Selahattin Ökten spent the whole of 2007 in pre-trial detention after his arrest on suspicion of taking part in PKK activities. The charge was based on a single witness statement that was allegedly extracted under torture and was subsequently retracted.

Killings in disputed circumstances

Fatal shootings by the security forces continued to be reported, with failure to obey a warning to stop usually given as justification. However, incidents often involved a disproportionate use of force by security forces and some killings may have been extrajudicial executions. In a number of instances, investigations were compromised when evidence was lost by law enforcement officials.

■ In August, Nigerian asylum-seeker Festus Okey died after being shot in police custody in Istanbul. A crucial piece of evidence, the shirt he wore on the day of the shooting, was apparently lost by the police. A police officer was charged with intentional killing.

■ In September, Bülent Karataş was shot dead by military police in the Hozat province of Tunceli. According to Rıza Çiçek, who was also seriously injured in the incident, military police forced the pair to remove their clothes before shots were fired. An investigation was being conducted in secret.

Torture and other ill-treatment

Allegations of torture and other ill-treatment continued, especially outside official places of detention.

■ In June, Mustafa Kükçe died after being detained in several different police stations in Istanbul. Relatives who identified his body said that it was apparent that he had been tortured before his death. No case was brought against police officers.

■ Lawyer Muammer Öz was allegedly beaten by police officers while drinking tea with family members in the Moda district of Istanbul. An official medical report failed to show that his nose had been broken in the attack. Muammer Öz told Amnesty International that police beat him with batons and their fists and told him that they would never be punished. Two police officers were prosecuted and were awaiting trial.

Members of the security forces continued to use excessive force when policing demonstrations.

■ In some of the Labour Day demonstrations on 1 May in various parts of the country, police used batons and tear gas against peaceful demonstrators. More than 800 people were detained in Istanbul alone, although the total number of arrests was not known.

Prison conditions

Harsh and arbitrary punishments continued to be reported in "F-type" prisons. A circular published in January granting greater rights to prisoners to associate with one another remained largely unimplemented. Some prisoners were held in solitary confinement and small-group isolation. Widespread protests called for an end to the solitary confinement of PKK leader Abdullah Öcalan, and for an investigation into his treatment.

In May, the European Committee for the Prevention of Torture (CPT) visited the prison island of Imralı where Abdullah Öcalan remained imprisoned to examine the conditions of his detention and his state of health. The CPT findings had not been made public by the end of the year.

Conscientious objectors

Conscientious objection to military service was not recognized and no civilian alternative was available.

■ Persistent conscientious objector Osman Murat Ülke was again summoned to serve the remainder of his prison sentence for failing to perform military service. In seeking to punish him, Turkey remained in defiance of the 2006 judgment of the European Court of Human Rights in the *Ülke* case, which required Turkey to implement legislation to prevent the continuous prosecution of conscientious objectors.

Refugees and asylum-seekers

Refugees continued to be denied access to a fair and effective national asylum system. The Turkish authorities forcibly returned recognized refugees and asylum-seekers to countries where they were at risk of serious human rights violations, in violation of international law.

■ In October, Ayoub Parniyani, recognized as a refugee by UNHCR, his wife Aysha Khaeirzade and their son Komas Parniyani, all Iranian nationals, were forcibly returned to northern Iraq. The action followed the forcible return to Iraq in July of 135 Iraqis who were denied the right to seek asylum.

Violence against women

Laws and regulations to protect women victims of domestic violence were inadequately implemented. The number of shelters remained far below the amount stipulated under the 2004 Law on Municipalities, which required a shelter in all settlements with a population of more than 50,000. A telephone hotline for victims of domestic violence ordered by the Prime Minister in July 2006 had not been set up by the end of the year.

🚌 Amnesty International delegates visited Turkey in May, July and September.

📄 Turkey: Three dead in attack on freedom of expression and religion (EUR 44/006/2007)

📄 Turkey: The entrenched culture of impunity must end (EUR 44/008/2007)

📄 Turkey: Justice for Hrant Dink (EUR 44/012/2007)

TURKMENISTAN

TURKMENISTAN

Head of state and government:	Kurbanguly Berdymukhammedov
Death penalty:	abolitionist for all crimes
Population:	5 million
Life expectancy:	62.6 years
Under-5 mortality (m/f):	104/85 per 1,000
Adult literacy:	98.8 per cent

While President Kurbanguly Berdymukhammedov reversed some of his predecessor's most severely criticized decisions, reforms were very limited. There was no fundamental improvement in human rights, although, as in previous years, some prisoners were released after intervention by the international community. Dozens of people imprisoned following unfair trials remained behind bars, many held incommunicado. Politically motivated harassment, detention and imprisonment were reported. The authorities continued to deny that any human rights violations took place in the country.

Background

Kurbanguly Berdymukhammedov was elected President in February; he had been acting President since President Saparmurad Niyazov's death in December 2006. All six presidential candidates were members of the Democratic Party of Turkmenistan, the only registered party.

President Berdymukhammedov restored cuts in the length of school and university education imposed by his predecessor and reinstated pension payments abolished in 2006. Several internet cafes opened across the country, but were too expensive for most

people. Several websites critical of the authorities remained blocked and the authorities closely monitored internet use. Internal travel restrictions were largely abolished but the system of registration inherited from Soviet times (widely referred to by the Russian word *propiska*) continued to make it virtually impossible for citizens to live and find employment in parts of the country other than where they were registered.

In August the President established the Interdepartmental Commission of Human Rights. It was tasked with preparing reports to UN treaty bodies (several of which were long overdue) and drafting a National Human Rights Programme. The authorities invited the UN Special Rapporteur on freedom of religion or belief to visit Turkmenistan. Other UN special procedures received no favourable responses to similar requests.

Continuing his predecessor's approach, President Berdymukhammedov addressed fundamental problems such as corruption and nepotism in government agencies mainly through personnel changes rather than fundamental reforms.

Politically motivated repression

There were reports of harassment, detention and imprisonment of dissidents, independent journalists, civil society activists and members of religious minorities. The authorities prevented civil society activists from communicating with international delegations visiting Turkmenistan. Dissidents, religious believers and their relatives were frequently prevented from leaving the country.

■ Ovezgeldy Ataev, who was dismissed from his post as Speaker of Parliament shortly after the late President died, was sentenced to four or five years' imprisonment in February. There were allegations that he was targeted as part of a power struggle following the late President's death. According to the Constitution, the Speaker of Parliament was the constitutionally designated successor to the President.

■ Vyacheslav Kalataevsky, a Baptist leader in the Caspian port city of Turkmenbashi, was sentenced to three years' imprisonment in May for crossing the border illegally in 2001. The charge was reportedly brought to punish him for his religious activities. He was pardoned in October but subsequently denied a residence permit in Turkmenistan. Vyacheslav Kalataevsky was born in the Turkmen Soviet Socialist

T

Republic but obtained Ukrainian citizenship while in Ukraine when the Soviet Union broke up. He had to leave Turkmenistan in December, leaving behind his parents, wife and children.

Prisoner releases

Some prisoners whose cases had been raised by the international community were released or had their suspended sentences cancelled in pardons in August and October. They included: environmental activist Andrei Zatoka; former Mufti Nasrullah ibn Ibadullah; conscientious objectors Nuryagdy Gairov, Suleiman Udaev and Aleksandr Zuev; and former director of the Government Association *Turkmenatlary* (Turkmen Horses) Geldy Kyarizov.

Prisoners held incommunicado

Dozens of prisoners continued to be denied all access to families, lawyers and independent bodies including the International Committee of the Red Cross. Labelled as "enemies of the people" by the authorities, they were sentenced following unfair trials in connection with an alleged assassination attempt on the late President in 2002. Many were allegedly tortured following their arrests. According to non-governmental sources, most were held in Ovadan-depe prison, known for its particularly harsh conditions. According to an unconfirmed report, since 2002 at least eight prisoners had died as a result of torture, other ill-treatment, harsh prison conditions and lack of appropriate medical treatment. Relatives of several prisoners reportedly asked the new government for permission to send parcels and letters at least once a year, and asked for the names of those who had died in prison. They received no written reply but government officials reportedly told them that their requests were denied.

Conscientious objectors

At least six Jehovah's Witnesses stood trial for refusing to serve in the army on conscientious grounds. The courts handed down sentences ranging from 18 months' suspended to 18 months' imprisonment. On appeal the courts commuted the prison sentences to suspended sentences. Three of the men were pardoned in October. However, two others, Bayram Ashirgeldiev and Begench Shakhmuradov, whose sentences had been suspended, had restrictions imposed on their movements and the authorities refused to issue them with a document necessary to find employment.

■ Begench Shakhmuradov was called up for military service in May and in September received a suspended two-year prison sentence from a court in Ashgabat for "evasion of call-up to military service". He had already served a prison term on the same charge in 2005. While in detention he reportedly contracted tuberculosis.

Institutional developments

On 19 February President Berdymukhammedov established the State Commission to review citizens' complaints regarding the activities of law enforcement agencies. He became its chairman. There was a lack of transparency in establishing the Commission, in publishing its rules and procedures, and in reporting on its work. In some cases the Commission passed on complaints to the government agency which was the subject of the complaint. Complainants received replies stating that the complaints were unfounded, but giving no further information.

■ Ruslan Tukhbatullin complained to the Commission about being dismissed from the army in 2005. He was allegedly dismissed to put pressure on his brother, Farid Tukhbatullin, director of the NGO Turkmenistan Initiative for Human Rights, who has lived in exile since 2003. Ruslan Tukhbatullin received a reply from the Ministry of Defence, the agency that had dismissed him, stating that the dismissal had not been a violation of his rights.

Amnesty International reports

Turkmenistan: Victims need justice now! A compilation of cases (EUR 61/004/2007)

Europe and Central Asia: Summary of Amnesty International's concerns in the region, January-June 2007 (EUR 01/010/2007)

UGANDA

REPUBLIC OF UGANDA

Head of state and government:	**Yoweri Kaguta Museveni**
Death penalty:	**retentionist**
Population:	**30.9 million**
Life expectancy:	**49.7 years**
Under-5 mortality (m/f):	**135/121 per 1,000**
Adult literacy:	**66.8 per cent**

Peace talks continued between the government and the armed group, the Lord's Resistance Army (LRA), aimed at ending the 20-year conflict in northern Uganda. The talks reportedly focused on withdrawal of the International Criminal Court's arrest warrants for four senior LRA leaders. A ceasefire agreed in 2006 was extended. The independence of the judiciary was threatened and attacks on freedom of expression and press freedom continued. Violence against women and girls remained widespread. Reports of torture by state security agents persisted.

Trial of Kizza Besigye

The trial of opposition leader Dr Kizza Besigye and six others accused of treason remained pending in the High Court in Kampala. On 1 March, the six co-accused still detained were released on bail by order of a court, but government security personnel invaded the court premises and rearrested them. The defendants, one defence lawyer and a journalist were reported to have been ill-treated by the security personnel. The defence lawyer subsequently required medical treatment. The armed raid on the court provoked national and international outcry. Following the raid, the judiciary suspended its work and lawyers went on strike. The President issued a public apology to the judiciary and promised an investigation into the incident. By the end of the year, the process and results of this investigation had not been made public.

After their re-arrest the six defendants were charged in two upcountry courts with new charges of murder. All six were later granted bail on the murder charges. By the end of 2007, three of the defendants remained in detention after failing to meet the bail conditions and three others had been released.

Armed conflict

Peace talks between the government and the LRA continued in southern Sudan. Both parties agreed to extend the cessation of hostilities in April, and in May both signed a document entitled Comprehensive Solutions to the Northern Uganda Conflict. On 29 June, the parties signed an agreement on "reconciliation and accountability", an agreement purportedly establishing a framework to address crimes committed during the conflict in northern Uganda. Negotiations reportedly focused on bringing about the withdrawal of the International Criminal Court's (ICC) arrest warrants for four senior LRA leaders – Joseph Kony, Vincent Otti, Okot Odhiambo and Dominic Ongwen – by setting up alternative national processes. In 2005, the ICC charged the men with crimes against humanity and war crimes. Rumours persisted that Vincent Otti, one of the LRA leaders charged with crimes against humanity and war crimes, had been killed by the LRA in October following an alleged disagreement with Joseph Kony.

By the end of 2007, both parties had reportedly engaged in consultations with victims of the conflict, as stipulated in the agreement. The outcome of this consultation exercise had not yet been made public. Speculation over the future of the peace process continued but the government stated that the peace process was still on course.

Freedom of expression

Attacks on freedom of expression and press freedom continued. Some journalists faced criminal charges because of their work.

■ In October, a private radio station, Life FM, in south-west Uganda went off air for several days following an attack by unknown armed assailants who poured acid on the station's transmitters. The attack was thought to be linked to the airing of a radio programme critical of the delivery of public services by the local government. No one was apparently prosecuted for this crime.

■ In October, three journalists working for *The Monitor* newspaper were charged with sedition in relation to a story alleging that soldiers were secretly trained as policemen in order to try and bring the police force under military control.

■ In November, two journalists from *The Monitor* newspaper were charged with criminal libel over a story alleging that the Inspector General of Government had been taken back onto the government payroll after retirement, in breach of the public service regulations.

U

Accountability

The government started investigations into corruption allegations regarding the mismanagement of the Global Fund against HIV/AIDS, Tuberculosis and Malaria in Uganda. Following these investigations, a former Health Minister and his two former deputies were referred to the police for further investigations. In May, the former minister, his two former deputies and one government official were charged with embezzlement and abuse of office.

Refugees and asylum-seekers

In July, the government of Uganda signed a Tripartite Agreement with the government of Rwanda and UNHCR, in preparation for the repatriation of Rwandese asylum-seekers and refugees living in Uganda. On 3 October, about 3,000 refugees and asylum-seekers were returned to Rwanda from Uganda. Ugandan government officials stated that this process was voluntary and that UNHCR was informed of the process. The Rwandan Minister for Local Government reportedly stated that the 3,000 people did not have refugee status and were not seeking asylum in Uganda. However, many individuals complained that they were forcibly returned and were not given the opportunity to seek asylum in a fair and effective process. They claimed that they feared for their lives and security in their country of origin. At the end of the year there were also fears that Burundian refugees and asylum-seekers would be forcibly returned.

Internally displaced people

As of May 2007, an estimated 1.6 million people remained displaced in camps throughout northern Uganda. In the Acholi sub-region, the area most affected by the conflict in northern Uganda, UNHCR estimated in September that nearly 63 per cent of the 1.1 million internally displaced people (IDPs) in 2005 were still living in their original IDP camps. As of May, the UNHCR estimated that just over 7,000 people had returned permanently to their places of origin in the Acholi sub-region.

Torture and other ill-treatment

Reports of torture and other ill-treatment committed by the police force and state security services persisted. In particular, the Rapid Response Unit (RRU), formerly the Violent Crimes Crack Unit (VCCU), was criticized by organizations including the Uganda Human Rights Commission for numerous incidents of torture and other ill-treatment, and for prolonged and arbitrary detention of suspects. By the end of the year, there was no government response to calls for investigations into these allegations of torture and other ill-treatment.

■ In August, members of the RRU arrested 41 individuals, including Ugandans and foreign nationals, in an operation ahead of the Commonwealth Heads of Government Meeting held in Kampala in November. During the arrest, police officers beat some of the detainees with batons and rifles butts, breaking one person's arm. The 41 were held in incommunicado detention for five days, with 23 individuals held together in a 3m x 3m cell.

■ On 29 October, police in Apac district arrested and detained about 30 people and allegedly tortured at least 22 of them while questioning them over an alleged theft of cattle. Up to 20 police officers took turns to beat the detainees using sticks while questioning them. Four of the men suffered serious injury during the beating, one of whom was beaten until his trousers were torn and soaked with blood.

■ In November, Hassan Nkalubo, a resident of Mbale district, was allegedly detained and tortured by the RRU based in Mbale. He was accused of illegal possession of an AK 47 rifle, and was critically ill as a result of his treatment.

Violence against women

An official government study published in August confirmed a high prevalence of violence against women, including rape and domestic violence, throughout the country. In northern Uganda, despite the cessation of hostilities in 2006, women and girls continued to face violence by government soldiers, LRA rebels who returned to their communities, law enforcement officials and members of their families and communities. The weak and ineffective justice system left female victims of sexual and gender-based violence traumatized and without any recourse to justice, legal, medical and psychological support.

Discrimination – lesbian, gay, bisexual and transgender people

Abuses against lesbian, gay, bisexual and transgender (LGBT) people continued. Homosexuality remained a criminal offence. Following a high-profile media campaign by local LGBT organizations in August, government officials, the media, church groups and other groups, including teachers, condemned LGBT people and called for them to be arrested.

■ In September, *The Red Pepper* newspaper published a list of people it asserted were gay and lesbian and published their workplaces and home addresses. Some of the individuals on the list subsequently complained of harassment and discrimination.

Death penalty

Civilian courts continued to impose the death penalty for capital offences. No executions following convictions by a civilian court have been carried out since 1999. In September the Prisons Services reported that at least 520 inmates were on death row in Uganda. Military courts continued to hand down death sentences and order executions of soldiers in the Uganda Peoples' Defence Forces (UPDF). The exact number of soldiers put to death under military law remained unclear.

■ On 20 September, a UPDF soldier, Corporal Geoffrey Apamuko, was sentenced to death by hanging for murder.

In October, the government's Internal Affairs Minister, Dr Ruhukana Rugunda, ruled out the imposition of the death penalty for LRA leaders if they were tried in Ugandan courts for crimes committed during the conflict in northern Uganda.

Amnesty International visits/reports

🚍 Amnesty International delegates visited northern Uganda and Kampala in May and August.

📄 Uganda: Doubly Traumatised – The lack of access to justice by female victims of sexual and gender-based violence in northern Uganda (AFR 59/005/2007)

📄 Uganda: Justice system fails victims of sexual violence (AFR 59/011/2007)

📄 Uganda: Detainees tortured during incommunicado detention (AFR 59/006/2007)

📄 Uganda: Proposed national framework to address impunity does not remove government's obligation to arrest and surrender LRA leaders to the International Criminal Court (AFR 59/002/2007)

UKRAINE

UKRAINE

Head of state:	Viktor Yushchenko
Head of government:	Yulia Tymoshenko
	(replaced Viktor Yanukovych in December)
Death penalty:	abolitionist for all crimes
Population:	45.5 million
Life expectancy:	67.7 years
Under-5 mortality (m/f):	19/14 per 1,000
Adult literacy:	99.4 per cent

Perpetrators of torture or other ill-treatment enjoyed impunity. Refugees and asylum-seekers continued to be at risk of enforced return, and foreigners and members of ethnic minorities were subject to racist attacks and harassment. Measures taken to combat people trafficking and domestic violence were inadequate.

Background

A political crisis escalated in May as a result of a power struggle between the President, Viktor Yushchenko, and the Prime Minister, Viktor Yanukovych. On 2 April, Viktor Yushchenko issued a decree dissolving parliament and calling for early parliamentary elections. Parliament contested the legality of the decree and it was referred to the Constitutional Court. After a power struggle during which both sides fought over control of key government offices, a decision was reached to hold parliamentary elections in May, which were subsequently postponed to 30 September.

The elections strengthened the position of the coalition of parties led by Viktor Yushchenko and Yulia Tymoshenko, the original leaders of the so-called "orange revolution", when mass public protests in 2004 and 2005 against electoral fraud in the presidential elections led to a re-vote and victory for Viktor Yushchenko.

Torture and other ill-treatment

Torture and other ill-treatment in police detention continued to be widely reported. In May, the UN Committee against Torture (CAT) considered Ukraine's fifth periodic report on the implementation of the Convention against Torture. The CAT expressed concern about the impunity

U

enjoyed by law enforcement officers for acts of torture; the failure of the Prosecutor General's Office to conduct prompt, impartial and effective investigations into complaints of torture; and the use of confessions as principal evidence for prosecutions.

In June, the European Committee for the Prevention of Torture (CPT) published the report of its visit to Ukraine in October 2005. The CPT found that there had been a "slight reduction as regards the scale of the phenomenon of ill-treatment", but that persons detained by the police still ran a "significant risk" of being subjected to ill-treatment, and even torture, particularly during interrogation. The CPT drew attention to the misuse of the Administrative Code to bring people into police custody for questioning about criminal offences, the fact that judges often failed to react to allegations of ill-treatment, and that forensic reports in cases of allegations of ill-treatment could only be provided with authorization from the police.

■ Edvard Furman was reportedly tortured at the offices of the Ukrainian State Security Services (SBU) in Dnipropetrovsk. He was arrested on 11 April and police investigators allegedly beat him, pressed their fingers into his eye sockets and applied electric shocks to his testicles to try and force him to confess to having shot and killed three people in a jeep in Dnipropetrovsk in March. Several other people were also detained in connection with the same crime. Edvard Furman's family was allegedly not informed of his arrest, and did not discover his whereabouts until 24 April. Police investigators reportedly forced him to renounce his lawyer and to accept a lawyer appointed by them. However, in October Edvard Furman was granted the right to see the lawyer he initially appointed. Reportedly, no medical examinations were carried out despite the fact that Edvard Furman complained to a judge that he had been subjected to torture and ill-treatment. The Prosecutor General's Office refused to open an investigation into the allegations.

Refugees and asylum-seekers

In a position paper published in October, the UNHCR, the refugee agency, advised states against returning third country asylum-seekers to Ukraine because of the risk that such people would be refused readmission; may not have access to a fair and efficient refugee status determination procedure or be treated in accordance with international refugee standards; or may face the risk of being returned to countries where they could face serious human rights violations. In its consideration of Ukraine's fifth periodic report, the CAT expressed concern that people were being returned by Ukraine to states where they would be in danger of being subjected to torture. Refugees and asylum-seekers were exposed to xenophobia.

■ Lema Susarov, a Chechen refugee, was arrested on 16 June by officers of the SBU following an extradition request from Russia. On 27 July the Prosecutor General's Office ordered his extradition. Lema Susarov's lawyer unsuccessfully appealed against the decision to detain him. An appeal against the extradition order was pending at the Kyiv Administrative Court. Lema Susarov registered as an asylum-seeker with the Kyiv City Migration Service on 8 August, because he feared being subjected to torture and other severe human rights violations if he returned to Russia.

Racism

In November, the UN Committee on Economic, Social and Cultural Rights considered Ukraine's fifth periodic report on its implementation of the International Covenant on Economic, Social and Cultural Rights. The Committee expressed concern about "reports of police abuse and denial of effective protection against acts of discrimination and violence against ethnic and religious minorities especially Roma, Crimean Tatars, Asian and African asylum-seekers as well as Muslims and Jews".

Asylum-seekers and foreigners living in Ukraine often suffered racist attacks by members of the public and were subjected to racist treatment at the hands of the police, including disproportionately frequent document checks. Two Bangladeshis, a Georgian, a Korean and an Iraqi asylum-seeker died in the course of the year as a result of violent attacks. There were no statistics for the number of racist crimes, and most racist attacks were classified by the police as hooliganism. In meetings with Amnesty International in September, representatives of the Ministry of Internal Affairs and the SBU denied the existence of racism in Ukraine.

■ One refugee from the Democratic Republic of the Congo told Amnesty International that she had frequently been subjected to racist abuse from members of the public and racist treatment by the police. In June, she was approached by a policeman in a drunken state outside her apartment block. He asked to see her documents, queried her registration, and invited her to a café. When she refused, he asked for sex, and tried to force her to go with him. She was bruised and scratched in the ensuing struggle. When she tried to report the incident to the local police station no one would take her statement and the same policeman who had assaulted her offered to accompany her home. She reported the incident at a different police station, and a criminal investigation was started. At the trial, the policeman denied the allegations and was acquitted. In a previous incident when police officers had detained her to check her documents they reportedly forced her to undress, calling other officers "to come and see what a monkey's body looks like".

■ The trial against three people accused of the murder of a Nigerian, Kunuon Mievi Godi, in Kyiv in October 2006 was ongoing at the end of the year. One is charged with murder and the other two with "violation of citizens' equality based on their race".

Violence against women

In February, the Ukrainian parliament held the first discussion of a new draft law "On amendments to some legislative acts of Ukraine (concerning improving the legislation of Ukraine to counteract violence in the family)", and recommended further changes. The proposed amendments to the Law on the Prevention of Violence in the Family and other relevant articles of the Administrative Code were broadly in line with the recommendations made by Amnesty International in 2006, but did not ensure adequate short-term and long-term alternative housing for victims of domestic violence. By the end of the year the amended legislation had not been approved.

In March, the Cabinet of Ministers adopted the National Anti-Trafficking in Persons Programme covering the period up to 2010. According to an anti-trafficking NGO, the Programme did not include sufficient indicators to measure its effectiveness and was not given enough funding. The US State Department's *Trafficking in Persons Report,* published in June, highlighted the "failure of Ukraine to provide evidence of increasing efforts to combat trafficking in persons over the last year, particularly in the area of punishing convicted traffickers". The report stated

that many traffickers received probation rather than prison sentences; government officials were involved in trafficking; and victims were not given sufficient protection and rehabilitation services, including witness protection.

Impunity

The trial against three police officers charged with murdering the investigative journalist, Georgiy Gongadze, in September 2000 continued. On 16 February, President Yushchenko awarded former Prosecutor General, Mykhailo Potebenko, the Order of Prince Yaroslav the Wise for his contribution to the building of a law-abiding state. Mykhailo Potebenko was Prosecutor General at the time of Georgiy Gongadze's murder. In its 2005 decision, the European Court of Human Rights found that the Prosecutor General's Office had ignored repeated requests for assistance from Georgiy Gongadze in the weeks before his death, when he reported being followed by state law enforcement officials, and termed its response "blatantly negligent". Following the recovery of Georgiy Gongadze's decapitated body, the European Court stated, "The State authorities were more preoccupied with proving the lack of involvement of high-level State officials in the case than discovering the truth about the circumstances of [his] disappearance and death."

Amnesty International visit/reports

🚍 An Amnesty International delegate visited Ukraine in September.

🗐 Briefing for the Committee against Torture on Ukraine (EUR 50/001/2007)

🗐 Europe and Central Asia: Summary of concerns in the region, January–June 2007 (EUR 01/010/2007)

U

UNITED ARAB EMIRATES

UNITED ARAB EMIRATES
Head of state:	Shaikh Khalifa bin Zayed Al-Nahyan
Head of government:	Shaikh Mohammed bin Rashid Al Maktoum
Death penalty:	retentionist
Population:	4.8 million
Life expectancy:	78.3 years
Under-5 mortality (m/f):	9/8 per 1,000
Adult literacy:	88.7 per cent

Two men were detained incommunicado for long periods during which they alleged they were tortured; one was later sentenced to a prison term after an unfair trial. Scores of teachers suspected of Islamist views were transferred to other state jobs. Courts sentenced journalists and internet owners and writers to prison terms on defamation charges. At least one sentence of flogging and two death sentences were passed.

Incommunicado detention and torture

In February, 'Abdullah Sultan al-Subaihat was arrested by Amn al-Dawla (State Security) officers in the Emirate of 'Ajman. He remained held incommunicado at an undisclosed location until June when he appeared before the Federal Supreme Court in Abu Dhabi on charges of "obtaining secret information on state security". The court, whose verdicts cannot be appealed, sentenced him to three years' imprisonment in September. During the trial, whose sessions were held in secret, 'Abdullah Sultan al-Subaihat alleged that he had been tortured while detained by Amn al-Dawla by being beaten with a hosepipe, deprived of sleep, forced to hold a chair above his head for prolonged periods and threatened with sexual assault. The court failed to order any investigation into these allegations. 'Abdullah Sultan al-Subaihat had previously been detained with two others in August 2005; all three were held incommunicado and for undisclosed reasons until October 2005, when they were released uncharged.

Pakistan national Rashed Mahmood was detained in the Emirate of 'Ajman in June and held incommunicado for more than three months. He was released without charge in September and expelled to Pakistan. He was reported to have been severely beaten during the first two weeks of detention.

A Sudanese national who was arrested and detained for two days without explanation after he arrived in the UAE in September subsequently went missing, raising fears that he was the victim of an enforced disappearance. Al-Sadiq Sediq Adam Abdalla was still missing at the end of the year.

Freedom of expression

A court in Ras al-Khaimah sentenced Mohammed Rashed al-Shehhi, the owner of an internet website (majan.net), to one-year's imprisonment and a fine in August for defaming a local official. The court ordered the website to be closed. In September, Mohammed Rashed al-Shehhi received a five-month prison sentence and a fine in a second defamation case involving another local official. He was released on bail at the end of September and in November his two prison sentences, totalling 17 months, were overturned by an appeal court after the officials who he was alleged to have defamed withdrew their complaints. In November, Mohammed Rashed al-Shehhi received a one-year suspended prison sentence after he was convicted in a third defamation case.

In September, after two journalists working for the *Khaleej Times* were sentenced to two-month prison terms for defamation, Shaikh Mohammed bin Rashid Al-Maktoum, Vice-President, Prime Minister and Ruler of Dubai, decreed that no journalist should receive a prison sentence for press-related offences. He also urged for the enactment of a new press and publications law.

In November, in an administrative measure widely seen as punitive, the UAE authorities moved more than 80 teachers to other state jobs apparently because they were suspected of holding Islamist views.

Cruel, inhuman and degrading punishment

A court in al-'Ain convicted an unnamed teenage girl to 60 lashes for having "illicit sex" with a man when she was 14. The sentence was upheld on appeal in June. It was not known if the sentence was carried out.

U

Migrant workers

A draft labour law intended to streamline employment practices was issued in February. It provided for the punishment of striking workers, but not for the right to organize, bargain collectively or strike. The draft excluded domestic workers, who do not formally have the right to a weekly day of rest, limits on hours of work, paid holidays or forms of compensation, as well as farmers, public sector workers and private security staff.

In August and October, hundreds of construction workers went on strike in Dubai to protest against low salaries and poor housing conditions, including a lack of safe water supplies. By the end of the year, their demands had not been met.

International human rights bodies

The government failed to respond to UN human rights bodies in respect to requests for access and on individual cases raised in 2006. Citing concerns about trafficking for the purposes of forced labour, in May the Special Rapporteur on the trafficking in persons reiterated a previously unmet request to visit the UAE. In March the Special Rapporteur on the human rights of migrants expressed "his interest in receiving a reply" on cases of abuses against migrant workers in previous years. The Special Rapporteur on extrajudicial, summary or arbitrary executions reported in March that the UAE government had not responded to concerns from 2006 on death penalty safeguards.

UN Special Rapporteurs, including those responsible for human rights defenders, violence against women, the independence of judges and lawyers, and freedom of expression, all reported that the government failed to reply to concerns raised by their offices.

Death penalty

At least two people were sentenced to death for murder. In November the UAE government voted not to oppose a UN resolution calling for a worldwide moratorium on executions.

UNITED KINGDOM

**UNITED KINGDOM
OF GREAT BRITAIN AND NORTHERN IRELAND**

Head of state:	Queen Elizabeth II
Head of government:	Gordon Brown (replaced Tony Blair in June)
Death penalty:	abolitionist for all crimes
Population:	60 million
Life expectancy:	79 years
Under-5 mortality (m/f):	6/6 per 1,000

The UK continued to attempt to return individuals to states where they would face a real risk of grave human rights violations on the strength of unenforceable "diplomatic assurances". Secrecy in the implementation of counter-terrorism measures led to unfair judicial proceedings. There were continued failures of accountability for past violations, including in relation to alleged state collusion in killings in Northern Ireland. The government sought to limit the extraterritorial application of human rights protection, in particular in relation to the acts of its armed forces in Iraq. Women who were subject to immigration control and had experienced violence in the UK, including domestic violence and trafficking, were unable to access the support they needed. Rejected asylum-seekers continued to be forced into destitution.

'War on terror'
Control orders

As of December there were 14 "control orders" in force, under powers in the Prevention of Terrorism Act 2005 (PTA).

■ In October the UK's highest court, the Appellate Committee of the House of Lords (the Law Lords), ruled on four test cases concerning the system of control orders. The Law Lords confirmed, among other things, that the 18-hour curfew which the Home Secretary had attempted to impose on one group of individuals amounted to a deprivation of liberty beyond what the law allowed. The Law Lords ordered the High Court to reconsider the fairness of the hearing which two individuals received when challenging the control orders served on them. The substance of the allegations against these two men had been withheld from them and from their lawyers of choice.

U

- In January an individual was convicted of a breach of control order obligations, the first conviction for an offence under the PTA, and was sentenced to five months' imprisonment.

Deportations with assurances

The UK authorities continued to seek to deport people whom they asserted posed a threat to the UK's national security, despite substantial grounds for believing that the people concerned would face a real risk of grave human rights violations if returned to their countries of origin. The authorities continued to maintain that diplomatic assurances received from the countries to which they were seeking to deport these individuals were sufficient to protect them from that risk, despite those assurances being unenforceable in any court. Proceedings by which these deportations could be challenged, in the Special Immigration Appeals Commission (SIAC), were unfair, in particular because of their reliance on secret material undisclosed to the appellants or to their lawyers of choice.

During the year eight individuals whom the UK had sought to deport to Algeria on grounds of national security waived their right to continue to appeal against their deportation, and were returned.

- In January, two Algerian men – Reda Dendani, referred to in legal proceedings as Q, and another man referred to in legal proceedings as H – were deported from the UK to Algeria. Before deportation, both men had reportedly been given verbal assurances by the Algerian authorities that they were not wanted in Algeria. Both were arrested and detained following their return, and charged with "participation in a terrorist network operating abroad". According to reports, both H and Reda Dendani were convicted in November, and sentenced to three and eight years' imprisonment respectively.
- In May, Moloud Sihali, an Algerian, won his appeal against deportation on national security grounds. The SIAC ruled that he was not a threat to national security.
- In July, the Court of Appeal ruled on the appeals of three Algerians against the decisions of the SIAC upholding the orders for their deportation on national security grounds. The three were Mustapha Taleb, referred to in legal proceedings as Y; a man referred to as U; and another referred to as BB. The Court of Appeal ruled that the SIAC should reconsider all three cases. In the cases of BB and U the Court of Appeal reached this conclusion on grounds that were not disclosed to the individuals, their lawyers of choice or

the public. In November the SIAC reaffirmed its earlier decision that all three could safely and lawfully be returned to Algeria.

- In February, the SIAC dismissed the appeal of Omar Mahmoud Mohammed Othman, also known as Abu Qatada, against his deportation on national security grounds to Jordan. The SIAC concluded that the Memorandum of Understanding (MoU) which the UK concluded with Jordan in 2005 would ensure his safety in Jordan. At the end of the year an appeal against this decision was pending.
- In April, the SIAC blocked the attempt to deport two Libyan nationals – referred to in legal proceedings as DD and AS – to their country of origin on national security grounds. The SIAC concluded that, notwithstanding the assurances given in an MoU between the UK and Libya, there was a real risk that upon return to Libya DD and AS would be tried in proceedings that would amount to a "complete" denial of a fair trial, and would be sentenced to death.

Guantánamo detainees with UK links

In April, Bisher Al Rawi, a former UK resident, was returned to the UK after more than four years in US military custody at Guantánamo Bay.

In August the UK authorities wrote to their US counterparts to request the release from Guantánamo Bay and return to the UK of former UK residents Jamil El Banna, Omar Deghayes, Shaker Aamer, Binyam Mohammed and Abdennour Sameur. No request was made on behalf of a sixth former resident, Ahmed Belbacha, an Algerian who had reportedly been cleared for release and would face a real risk of secret detention, which would put him at risk of torture or other ill-treatment, if returned to Algeria.

In December, Jamil El Banna, Omar Deghayes and Abdennour Sameur were returned to the UK. All three were detained on arrival. Abdennour Sameur was released without charge. Jamil El Banna and Omar Deghayes were released on bail, pending a full hearing of a request for their extradition to Spain to stand trial there.

At the end of the year Binyam Mohammed, Shaker Aamer and Ahmed Belbacha remained in Guantánamo Bay.

Renditions

In July the Intelligence and Security Committee (ISC) published a report on the UK's alleged involvement in the US-led programme of renditions. The report made

U

limited criticisms of the UK authorities, including of the failure to keep "proper searchable records" of requests to conduct rendition operations through UK airspace, but concluded that there was "no evidence" that the UK had been complicit in "extraordinary renditions" as the ISC defined that term.

The ISC reports directly to the Prime Minister, who decides whether to place its reports before Parliament. Amnesty International considered it insufficiently independent of the executive to conduct the necessary independent and impartial investigation into allegations of UK involvement in renditions.

Reports continued to emerge suggesting that UK territory, including the island of Diego Garcia, may have been used by aeroplanes involved in rendition flights. The UK authorities told Amnesty International that the UK "does not routinely keep records of flights in and out of Diego Garcia", but that they were "satisfied with [the] assurance" given by the US that they "do not use Diego Garcia for any rendition operations".

UK armed forces in Iraq

The government continued to seek to limit the application of its human rights obligations outside UK territory, in particular in relation to the acts of its armed forces in Iraq.

■ In March, the court martial of seven UK military personnel concluded. They were charged in relation to the torture and death in September 2003 of Baha Mousa, and the treatment of a number of other Iraqi civilians arrested and detained at a UK military base in Basra at around the same time as him. One defendant pleaded guilty to a charge of inhumane treatment, a war crime. He was acquitted of the other charges against him. Six others were acquitted of all charges.

The judge noted that hooding detainees, keeping them in stress positions and depriving them of sleep had become "standard operating procedure" within the battalion responsible for detaining the men.

■ In June, the Law Lords ruled on six cases brought under the name *Al Skeini*, concerning the deaths of six Iraqi civilians. Five of the six were shot and fatally wounded, in disputed circumstances, in the course of operations carried out by UK armed forces; the sixth was Baha Mousa.

The Law Lords ruled that the first five individuals were not within the UK's jurisdiction at the time of their deaths, and that the UK's obligations under the European Convention on Human Rights (ECHR) were therefore not applicable to them. They ruled that Baha Mousa had come within the UK's jurisdiction, albeit only from the moment of his arrival at the UK-run detention facility, rather than the time of his arrest. The Law Lords directed that Baha Mousa's case should return to a lower court, for it to determine whether there had been a violation of the rights to life and to freedom from torture. By the end of the year these judicial proceedings had not resumed.

■ In December the Law Lords ruled on a challenge to the detention without charge or trial for more than three years of Hilal Al-Jedda, one of approximately 75 "security internees" held by UK forces in Iraq. They ruled that Hilal Al-Jedda was within the UK's jurisdiction, since his detention was legally attributable to the UK, not (as the UK had argued) to the UN. However they held that UN Security Council Resolution 1546 effectively allowed the UK to intern people in Iraq, notwithstanding that to do so would otherwise have been incompatible with the UK's obligations under the ECHR.

Police shootings and deaths in custody

■ In November a jury convicted the Office of the Commissioner of the Metropolitan Police of an offence under health and safety legislation in relation to the policing operation which led to the fatal shooting of Jean Charles de Menezes in July 2005.

Following the verdict, the Independent Police Complaints Commission (IPCC) published its report into the shooting. The IPCC reiterated concern at the attempt made by the police to prevent the IPCC from carrying out from the outset the investigation into the shooting.

In December a hearing opened to consider whether the coroner's inquest into the death, which had been adjourned pending completion of the criminal prosecution, should resume. The IPCC announced that four police officers involved in the operation would face no disciplinary charges.

Updates

■ In June, the Court of Appeal upheld the 2004 verdict of an inquest jury that police officers who fatally shot Derek Bennett in 2001 had acted lawfully.

■ In August, the IPCC announced that none of the

U

eight Metropolitan Police officers involved in the events leading to the death in custody of Roger Sylvester in January 1999 would face disciplinary action.

Northern Ireland

In May, direct rule came to an end with the restoration of the devolved Northern Ireland Assembly, suspended since 2002.

Collusion and political killings

In January, the Office of the Police Ombudsman for Northern Ireland published a report of an investigation which found evidence of collusion between the police and loyalist paramilitaries as recently as 2003.

In June, the Committee of Ministers of the Council of Europe adopted its second interim resolution concerning the UK's compliance with a number of judgments of the European Court of Human Rights. The cases in question were brought by the families of individuals who had allegedly been killed by, or with the collusion of, UK security forces in Northern Ireland. The Court had held in each case that the UK had failed to instigate adequate investigations into these killings. The Committee of Ministers regretted that "in none of the cases [has] an effective investigation… been completed".

■ In June, the Northern Ireland Court of Appeal reversed a December 2006 High Court decision, which had ruled unlawful the decision to hold the inquiry into allegations of state collusion in the killing of Billy Wright under the Inquiries Act 2005. The inquiry proceeded under the Inquiries Act.

In October the inquiry panel announced its intention to produce an interim report early in 2008 on the co-operation given to the inquiry by the Police Service of Northern Ireland (PSNI), in particular in relation to significant gaps in the material provided to the inquiry by the PSNI.

■ By the end of the year the government had still not established an inquiry into allegations of state collusion in the 1989 killing of Patrick Finucane.

■ In December, the verdict was delivered in a criminal prosecution relating to the 1998 Omagh bombing, among other incidents. The only defendant was acquitted of all charges against him. The judge was critical of the prosecution case, in particular the use made of DNA evidence. He accused two police employees of "deliberate and calculated deception", and referred the case to the Police Ombudsman for Northern Ireland.

Refugees and asylum-seekers

In October, the UK Borders Act was passed. The Act failed to end the forced destitution of rejected asylum-seekers caused by existing legislation.

The UK government continued to enforce the return of rejected Iraqi asylum-seekers to northern Iraq.

Ongoing legal action prevented the UK government from removing rejected asylum-seekers to Zimbabwe.

In November, the Law Lords overturned a Court of Appeal ruling that it was "unduly harsh" to send refused asylum-seekers from Darfur back to the Sudanese capital Khartoum.

Violence against women

Women who were subject to immigration control and had experienced violence in the UK, including domestic violence and trafficking, found it almost impossible to access the housing benefit or income support they needed, as a result of the "no recourse to public funds" rule. This provides that certain categories of immigrants who have leave to enter and remain in the UK for a limited period only have no right (subject to limited exceptions) to access such benefits.

Trafficking in human beings

In March the UK signed the Council of Europe Convention on Action against Trafficking in Human Beings, but had not ratified it by the end of the year.

In December, it was reported that four women who had been trafficked to the UK for sexual exploitation were to be awarded financial compensation by the Criminal Injuries Compensation Authority, a decision which could lead to other victims of trafficking becoming eligible for compensation.

NGOs were concerned at the lack of appropriate government-funded accommodation for victims of trafficking.

Amnesty International visit/reports

🚗 Amnesty International delegates observed judicial hearings in the UK, including some under counter-terrorism legislation.

📄 United Kingdom: Deportations to Algeria at all costs (EUR 45/001/2007)

📄 Europe and Central Asia: Summary of Amnesty International's concerns in the region, January–June 2007 (EUR 01/010/2007).

U

UNITED STATES OF AMERICA

UNITED STATES OF AMERICA
Head of state and government:	George W. Bush
Death penalty:	retentionist
Population:	303.9 million
Life expectancy:	77.9 years
Under-5 mortality (m/f):	8/8 per 1,000

The US authorities continued to hold hundreds of foreign nationals at the US Naval Base in Guantánamo Bay, Cuba, although more than 100 were transferred out of the facility during the year. Detainees in Guantánamo were held indefinitely, the vast majority of them without charge, and effectively without recourse to the US courts to challenge the legality of their detention. Most detainees in Guantánamo were held in isolation in maximum security facilities, heightening concerns for their physical and mental health. The Central Intelligence Agency (CIA) programme of secret detention and interrogation was re-authorized by President Bush in July. In December, the Director of the CIA revealed that the agency had destroyed videotapes of detainee interrogations.

Soldiers refusing to serve in Iraq on grounds of conscience were imprisoned. Prisoners continued to experience ill-treatment at the hands of police officers and prison guards. Dozens of people died after police used tasers (electro-shock weapons) against them. There were serious failings in state, local and federal measures to address sexual violence against Native American women. Discrimination remained a concern in a variety of areas, including policing practices, the operation of the criminal justice system and housing rights. There were 42 executions during the year. In late September, the decision of the Supreme Court to review the constitutionality of lethal injections led to a de facto moratorium on executions by this method. In December, New Jersey became the first US state in more than four decades to legislate to abolish the death penalty.

'War on terror'

For the sixth year running, the US authorities continued to hold foreign nationals they had designated "enemy combatants" in indefinite military detention without charge at Guantánamo Bay. At the end of 2007, there were approximately 275 detainees held in Guantánamo. During the year, more than 100 detainees were transferred to their home countries for release or continued detention. Four detainees, described by the Pentagon as "dangerous terror suspects", were transferred to Guantánamo. One person described by the Pentagon as a "high-level member of al-Qa'ida" was transferred to the base from CIA custody.

Fourteen men described by the US authorities as "high value" detainees and transferred to Guantánamo in September 2006 for the stated purpose of standing trial had yet to be charged by the end of 2007. The men had spent up to four and half years in secret CIA custody prior to the transfer and their cases had been used by the administration to obtain the Military Commissions Act of 2006 (MCA). On 9 August, the Pentagon announced that all 14 had been affirmed as "enemy combatants" by the Combatant Status Review Tribunals (CSRTs), panels of military officers able to rely on secret and coerced information in making their decisions. The CSRTs for the 14 men were held behind closed doors on the grounds that the detainees had classified information about the CIA secret detention programme, including interrogation techniques, conditions of detention and the location of CIA detention facilities. Allegations made by some of the men of torture in CIA custody were censored from the CSRT transcripts. By the end of 2007, only one of the 14 had had access to legal counsel for the narrow judicial review of the CSRT decisions provided for in the Detainee Treatment Act (2005). No such review of any of the Guantánamo detentions had been conducted by the end of the year.

On 20 February, the Court of Appeals for the District of Columbia Circuit ruled that provisions of the MCA stripping the courts of the jurisdiction to consider habeas corpus petitions applied to all detainees held in Guantánamo "without exception". On 2 April, the Supreme Court dismissed an appeal against this ruling. However, on 29 June, the Supreme Court took the historically unusual step of vacating its 2 April order and agreeing to hear the case after lawyers for detainees filed new information about the inadequacy of the CSRT scheme. The new information was provided by a

U

military officer who had been involved in CSRT reviews. The Court's ruling was pending at the end of 2007.

■ Ali al-Marri, a Qatari national resident in the USA who was designated an "enemy combatant" in June 2003 by President Bush, remained in indefinite military detention on the US mainland at the end of the year. In June, a three-judge panel of the Court of Appeals for the Fourth Circuit ruled that the MCA did not apply to Ali al-Marri's case and ruled that his military detention "must cease". However, the government successfully sought a rehearing in front of the full Fourth Circuit court; a ruling was pending at the end of the year. Military commission proceedings resumed at Guantánamo.

■ In March, Australian national David Hicks became the first – and by the end of the year, only – Guantánamo detainee to be convicted by the USA. He pleaded guilty under the MCA to one charge of "providing material support for terrorism". A panel of military officers recommended seven years in prison, but six years and three months of the sentence was suspended under the terms of a pre-trial agreement. David Hicks was transferred out of Guantánamo in May to serve the remainder of his nine-month sentence in Australia. He was released from Yatala prison in Adelaide on 29 December.

Three other Guantánamo detainees were facing charges at the end of the year, including two who were under 18 years old when they were taken into custody.

Conditions of detention in Guantánamo and their impact on the health of detainees already distressed by the indefinite nature of their detention continued to cause serious concern. One detainee, a Saudi Arabian national, was reported to have committed suicide on 30 May. By mid-January, 165 detainees had been transferred to Camp 6 where they were confined in individual steel cells with no external windows for at least 22 hours a day. Contrary to international standards, the cells have no access to natural light or air, and are lit 24 hours a day by fluorescent lighting. Around 100 other detainees were held in Camp 5, where detainees have been confined for up to 24 hours a day in small cells with some access to natural light, although with no view to the outside. Some 20 more detainees were believed to be held in Camp Echo, where detainees are held for between 23 and 24 hours a day in windowless cells with no natural light.

On 20 July, President Bush issued an executive order that the programme of secret detention and interrogation operated by the CIA would comply with Article 3 common to the four Geneva Conventions of 1949. Amnesty International wrote to President Bush emphasizing that if the CIA programme received detainees as it had before, he would have re-authorized the international crime of enforced disappearance. No reply had been received by the end of the year.

One detainee, 'Abd al-Hadi al-Iraqi, was reported to have been transferred from CIA custody to Guantánamo during the year. The Pentagon announced the transfer on 27 April, but gave no details about when he was detained or where he had been held before the transfer. In June, Amnesty International and five other human rights organizations published a list of more than 36 individuals believed to have been detained in the CIA programme whose fate and whereabouts remained unknown.

In December, the Director of the CIA revealed that in 2005 the agency had destroyed videotapes of interrogations conducted in 2002 of detainees held in secret custody. It was reported that the tapes depicted hundreds of hours of interrogations of Abu Zubaydah and 'Abd al-Rahim al-Nashiri, two of the "high-value" detainees transferred to Guantánamo in September 2006. Both alleged at their CSRTs in 2007 that they had been tortured in CIA custody. Abu Zubaydah was among those reported to have been subjected to "waterboarding" (simulated drowning).

Hundreds of people remained in US custody in Afghanistan and Iraq. There were also concerns about killings in Iraq by private US contractors (see Afghanistan and Iraq entries).

Torture and other ill-treatment

There were reports of ill-treatment in jails and police custody on the US mainland, often involving cruel use of restraints or electro-shock weapons.

Sixty-nine people died after being shocked with tasers, bringing to nearly 300 the number of such deaths since 2001. Many of those who died were subjected to multiple shocks or had health problems which could have made them more susceptible to the adverse effects of tasers. Although such deaths are commonly attributed to factors such as drug intoxication, medical examiners have concluded that

U

taser shocks caused or contributed to a number of deaths. The vast majority of those who died were unarmed and did not pose a serious threat when they were electro-shocked. Many police departments continued to authorize the use of tasers in a wide range of situations, including against unarmed resisters or people who refused to comply with police commands. Amnesty International presented its concerns to a Justice Department inquiry into taser deaths and reiterated its call on the US authorities to suspend the use of tasers and other stun weapons, pending the results of a rigorous, independent inquiry, or to limit their use to situations where officers would otherwise be justified in using deadly force.

Thousands of prisoners continued to be confined in long-term isolation, in high-security units where conditions sometimes amounted to cruel, inhuman or degrading treatment.

■ Herman Wallace and Albert Woodfox, both inmates of the Louisiana State Penitentiary in Angola, remained in extended isolation. For more than 30 years, they had been confined alone to small cells for 23 hours a day with only three hours of outdoor exercise a week. Both men were reportedly suffering from serious health problems as a result of their conditions. A lawsuit claiming the prisoners' treatment was unconstitutional remained pending at the end of the year.

The two men had originally been placed in "lockdown" after being accused of involvement in the killing of a guard during a prison riot in 1972, charges they have always denied. Amnesty International remained concerned that their long-term isolation was based, at least in part, on their past political activism in prison, including membership of the Black Panther Party (a black radical organization).

Prisoners of conscience

Army Specialist Mark Lee Wilkerson served three and a half months in jail after being sentenced to seven months' imprisonment for refusing to serve in Iraq on conscientious grounds. Another conscientious objector to the Iraq war, US Army Medic Agustín Aguayo, was sentenced to eight months' imprisonment on similar grounds. He was released after one month as time spent in custody awaiting trial was taken into consideration. Several other soldiers refusing to serve in Iraq because of their opposition to the war faced possible prosecution at the end of the year.

Justice system

Jose Padilla, a US citizen previously held for more than three years without charge or trial in US military custody as an "enemy combatant", was convicted in a federal civilian court in August of conspiracy to provide material support for terrorism. His sentencing was pending at the end of the year. The court dismissed his lawyers' claims that torture and other ill-treatment in military custody had left him unfit to stand trial. The government declined to introduce information obtained during his military detention, which may have been open to challenge on the grounds that it was coerced. Amnesty International remained concerned about the lack of accountability for his three years of unlawful treatment, and the damage done to his right to be presumed innocent by the government repeatedly and publicly branding him a "dangerous terrorist".

Gary Tyler, an African American, remained in prison in Louisana for the murder of a white schoolboy during a racially charged incident in 1974. During his 33 years in prison, Gary Tyler, who was 16 at the time of the killing, has consistently maintained his innocence. He was convicted by an all-white jury following a trial which was seriously flawed. Appeals to the outgoing state governor to grant him a pardon were unsuccessful.

In August an oral hearing took place in the case of five Cuban nationals convicted in Miami in June 2001 of conspiring to act as agents of the Republic of Cuba and other charges (USA v Gerardo Hernandez et al). Grounds for the appeal included insufficient evidence and alleged improper statements by the prosecution during the trial. The appeal court's decision was pending at the end of 2007. The US government continued to refuse to grant the wives of two of the prisoners visas to visit them in prison.

Discrimination

Continuing concerns about discrimination in the USA included racial disparities in police stops and searches and other areas of the criminal justice system, and the treatment of non-US nationals held in the context of the "war on terror" (see above).

■ Mychal Bell was tried in July – on charges of attempted second-degree murder – in an adult court, despite being a minor at the time of the alleged offence. The case raised concerns about disparities in the treatment of black and white teenagers. He

U

was one of six black high school students in Jena, Louisiana, who were charged with assaulting a white student in December 2006 during a period of racial tension triggered when white students hung three nooses from a tree in the high school grounds. The black students were originally charged with attempted second-degree murder, which could have put them in prison for decades. Charges against the defendants were later reduced and Mychal Bell was transferred to a juvenile court, following civil rights demonstrations.

Death penalty

A total of 42 prisoners were put to death in the USA during the year, bringing to 1,099 the total number of executions carried out since the US Supreme Court lifted a moratorium on the death penalty in 1976. This represented the lowest annual judicial death toll in the USA since 1994 and was in part due to the halt in executions that followed the Supreme Court's announcement on 25 September that it would consider a challenge to the three-chemical lethal injection process used in Kentucky, and in most other states that use this method.

In June, the Supreme Court blocked the execution of Scott Panetti, a Texas death row inmate suffering from severe delusions. The ruling found that the US Court of Appeals for the Fifth Circuit had employed a "flawed" and "too restrictive" interpretation of the Supreme Court's 1986 ruling affirming that the execution of an insane prisoner is unconstitutional. The ruling had the potential to provide additional protection for condemned prisoners suffering from serious mental illness.

South Dakota carried out its first execution since April 1947. Elijah Page was executed for a murder committed in 2000 when he was 18 years old and emerging from a childhood of deprivation and abuse. He had given up his appeals. His execution meant that 34 states and the federal government had conducted at least one execution since 1976.

On 2 January, the New Jersey Death Penalty Study Commission – set up by the state legislature in 2006 to study all aspects of capital punishment in New Jersey – released its final report in which it recommended abolition of the death penalty. In December New Jersey became the first US state since 1965 to legislate to abolish the death penalty when the legislature passed, and the governor signed, legislation replacing capital punishment with life imprisonment without the possibility of parole.

New York effectively became the 13th abolitionist state in the USA in October when its highest court refused to make an exception to its 2004 ruling finding the state's death penalty statute unconstitutional. The challenge to that ruling had been brought by the state in the case of the last person left on New York's death row.

More than 120 people have been released from death rows in the USA since 1975 on the grounds of innocence.

■ Curtis Edward McCarty, who had spent 21 years in prison, 16 of them on Oklahoma's death row, was released in May after a federal judge ordered that the charges against him be dismissed. DNA evidence helped to exonerate him, and the judge ruled that the case against him had been tainted by the questionable testimony of a discredited former police chemist.

■ In December, Michael McCormick was acquitted at his retrial for a murder for which he had spent 16 years on death row in Tennessee.

■ In December, prosecutors dismissed all charges against Johnathan Hoffman in the crime for which he had served nearly a decade on death row in North Carolina.

■ Joseph Nichols was executed in Texas on 7 March for the murder of Claude Shaffer in 1980. His co-defendant, Willie Williams, who had been tried first, had pleaded guilty and been executed in 1995. At the trial of Joseph Nichols, the state argued that regardless of the fact that Willie Williams fired the fatal shot, Joseph Nichols was guilty under Texas' "law of parties", under which the distinction between principal actor and accomplice in a crime is abolished and each may be held equally culpable. The jury was unable to reach a sentencing verdict and Joseph Nichols was retried. This time the prosecution argued that Joseph Nichols had fired the fatal shot and the jury voted for a death sentence.

■ Philip Workman was executed in Tennessee on 9 May despite compelling evidence that a key state witness lied at the trial and that the police officer he was convicted of killing may have been accidentally shot by a fellow officer. Philip Workman had been on death row for 25 years.

■ On 16 July, less than 24 hours before he was due to be put to death, Georgia death row inmate Troy Davis received a stay of execution from the state Board of Pardons and Paroles. He had been on death row for more than 15 years for the murder of a police officer. There was no physical evidence against him and the weapon used in the crime was never found. The case against him consisted entirely of witness testimony, most of which had subsequently been recanted. On 3 August, the Georgia Supreme Court granted an extraordinary appeal and agreed to hear his case for a new trial. A decision was pending at the end of 2007.

Violence against women

Native American and Alaska Native American women continued to suffer disproportionately high levels of rape and sexual violence, but faced barriers accessing justice. This was due to the complex maze of tribal, state and federal jurisdictions, which allowed perpetrators to escape justice; underfunding by the government of key services; and failure at state and federal level to pursue cases. Recommendations by Congress for increased funding to tackle some of these concerns were pending government approval at the end of the year.

Housing rights – Hurricane Katrina

Thousands of evacuees from Gulf Coast areas affected by Hurricane Katrina in 2005 remained displaced with little prospect of returning to their homes. Many continued to live in precarious situations in temporary accommodation throughout the USA, without work or access to their former support networks.

Civil rights and community groups expressed concern about proposals to demolish a large proportion of the public housing units in New Orleans even though they suffered only minor flood damage and could reportedly be repaired and rehabilitated. It was feared that the absence of affordable housing had created a demographic shift in which poor, largely African American, communities were unable to return to their homes.

Amnesty International reports

📄 USA: New Jersey Death Penalty Study Commission recommends abolition (AMR 51/003/2007)

📄 USA: The experiment that failed – A reflection on 30 years of executions (AMR 51/011/2007)

📄 USA: "Where is the justice for me?" – The case of Troy Davis, facing execution in Georgia (AMR 51/023/2007)

📄 Maze of injustice: The failure to protect Indigenous women from sexual violence in the USA (AMR 51/035/2007)

📄 USA: Justice delayed *and* justice denied? Trials under the Military Commissions Act (AMR 51/044/2007)

📄 USA: Cruel and inhuman: Conditions of isolation for detainees at Guantánamo Bay (AMR 51/051/2007)

📄 USA: An "uncomfortable truth": Two Texas governors – more than 300 executions (AMR 51/076/2007)

📄 USA: Prisoner-assisted homicide – more "volunteer" executions loom (AMR 51/087/2007)

📄 USA: Off the record – US responsibility for enforced disappearances in the "war on terror" (AMR 51/093/2007)

📄 USA: Supreme Court tightens standard on "competence" for execution (AMR 51/114/2007)

📄 USA: Law and executive disorder – President gives green light to secret detention program (AMR 51/135/2007)

📄 USA: Amnesty International's concerns about Taser use: Statement to the US Justice Department inquiry into deaths in custody (AMR 51/151/2007)

📄 USA: No substitute for *habeas corpus* – Six years without judicial review in Guantánamo (AMR 51/163/2007)

📄 USA: Slippery slopes and the politics of torture (AMR 51/177/2007)

📄 USA: Amnesty International's briefing to the Committee on the Elimination of Racial Discrimination (AMR 51/178/2007)

📄 USA: A tool of injustice: Salim Hamdan again before a military commission (AMR 51/189/2007)

📄 USA: Destruction of CIA interrogation tapes may conceal government crimes (AMR 51/194/2007)

📄 USA: Breaking a lethal habit – A look back at the death penalty in 2007 (AMR 51/197/2007)

📄 USA: Unlawful detentions must end, not be transferred (AMR 51/200/2007)

U

URUGUAY

EASTERN REPUBLIC OF URUGUAY
Head of State and government: **Tabaré Vázquez Rosas**
Death penalty: **abolitionist for all crimes**
Population: **3.5 million**
Life expectancy: **75.9 years**
Under-5 mortality (m/f):   **16/12 per 1,000**
Adult literacy: **96.8 per cent**

The authorities failed to provide redress to relatives of the victims of human rights abuses during the military government (1973-1985). People continued to be imprisoned for years pending sentencing. A national plan to promote women's rights was introduced.

Impunity – justice for past abuses

The Expiry Law of 1986, which grants members of the security forces immunity from prosecution for crimes committed during the military government (1973-1985), remained in force.

Draft legislation which would provide reparations to relatives of victims of human rights violations during the military government was before Congress at the end of the year.

A request for the extradition of former Colonel Juan Manuel Cordero from Brazil for his involvement in human rights violations during the military government, including the murder of Zelmar Michelini and Héctor Gutíerrez Ruiz remained pending at the end of the year.

In July the Humanities Faculty Anthropology team from the University of the Republic began excavations in the Tablada military compound, searching for the remains of detainees who were the victims of enforced disappearance during the military period.

In September new exhumations began on military premises in search of the remains of Elena Quinteros, a member of the opposition Party for People's Victory, who was kidnapped from the Venezuelan Embassy in June 1976 by members of the security forces.

In June the Executive excluded 17 cases previously covered by the Expiry Law, including at least five transfers of detainees from Argentina to Uruguay between February and August 1978. In September it also excluded the kidnapping of Nelson Santana and Gustavo Inzaurralde in Paraguay in 1977. The decision paved the way for judicial investigations into these cases. A total of 47 cases of victims of human rights violations have been excluded from the Expiry Law by the current administration.

In September the appeals court confirmed the trial and detention of former President Juan Maria Bordaberry (1971-1976) as co-author of 10 homicides. In December, former President General Gregorio Alvarez (1981-1985) was arrested and charged as co-author of the enforced disappearances of more than 30 people.

Violence against women

Domestic violence resulted in the deaths of at least 17 women between November 2006 and October 2007, according to a report published in November 2007 by the National Observatory on Violence and Crime of the Ministry of Interior.

In June the National Women's Institute published the First National Plan of Equality on Opportunities and Rights to address discrimination against women.

Health – reproductive rights

In November the Senate passed a bill on reproductive rights which decriminalized abortions carried out within the first 12 weeks of pregnancy in certain circumstances. Under existing legislation abortion is punishable by up to nine months imprisonment for the women and two years' imprisonment for the person carrying out the abortion. The bill was awaiting approval by the Chamber of Deputies at the end of the year.

Justice system

In a report published in May, the Inter-American Commission on Human Rights recommended that all necessary steps be taken to release Jorge, José and Dante Peirano, held under preventive detention since 2002, while their trial continued. The three men had been released by the end of the year.

According to the Minister of Interior, more than 60 per cent of inmates in Uruguayan prisons had not been sentenced.

Children

In July the UN Committee on the Rights of the Child expressed its regret at the authorities' failure to institute a national plan of action on children's rights and at the lack of an independent institution to which complaints of violations of children's rights could be referred. It expressed concern about discrimination against children of Afro-descent and about the large numbers of children in detention, some of whom had been tortured or subjected to degrading treatment by law enforcement officials.

UZBEKISTAN

REPUBLIC OF UZBEKISTAN

Head of state:	Islam Karimov
Head of government:	Shavkat Mirzioiev
Death penalty:	retentionist
Population:	27.4 million
Life expectancy:	66.8 years
Under-5 mortality (m/f):	72/60 per 1,000
Adult literacy:	99.4 per cent

Despite the government's professed commitment to improving the rights of its citizens, there was no real progress on human rights. The authorities continued to refuse to allow an independent, international investigation into the mass killings in Andizhan in 2005. Freedom of expression and assembly continued to deteriorate and pressure on human rights defenders, activists, and independent journalists showed no sign of abating. Widespread torture or other ill-treatment of detainees and prisoners continued to be reported. Corruption in law enforcement and the judiciary contributed to a climate of impunity. Several thousand people convicted of involvement with banned Islamic organizations and movements continued to serve long prison terms in conditions which amounted to cruel, inhuman and degrading treatment. The authorities continued to actively seek the extradition of members or suspected members of banned Islamist parties or Islamic movements. The authorities refused to impose a moratorium on executions, despite a presidential decree introducing the abolition of the death penalty from January 2008.

Background

The socioeconomic situation deteriorated, increasing already significant poverty levels; the UN estimated that just under 30 per cent of the population were living below the poverty line. Although officially unemployment stood at 3 per cent, the World Bank and other economic observers believed the figure to be closer to 40 per cent. Hundreds of thousands left the country to seek employment in Kazakstan and the Russian Federation, often working as irregular migrants on building sites or in markets. Many faced harsh working and living conditions, including low pay, beatings, discrimination and no access to protection, health or housing. Some observers signalled poverty and its perceived discriminatory nature as driving factors behind the growth of banned Islamic movements or Islamist parties such as Hizb-ut-Tahrir.

Pressure on international media and NGOs continued. In July the authorities refused to extend the visa and work permit of the country director of Human Rights Watch. Criminal prosecutions for tax evasion were brought against three local correspondents for the German international radio and television station *Deutsche Welle* who had been critical in their reporting. Faced with a possible prison sentence, one of the correspondents fled the country.

In the run-up to the December presidential elections access to independent information became increasingly difficult with independent or opposition-affiliated websites virtually blocked. President Islam Karimov won the elections and a third term in office with nearly 90 per cent of the vote despite the constitution limiting presidents to two terms in office.

International scrutiny

Two years after the killing of hundreds of people in Andizhan, when security forces fired on mainly peaceful demonstrators, the authorities continued to refuse to hold an independent, international investigation into these events. They agreed, however, to hold a second round of expert talks with representatives of the European Union (EU) in the capital, Tashkent, in April.

In May, the first formal EU-Uzbekistan Human Rights Dialogue was held in Tashkent in advance of the EU's General Affairs and External Relations Council (GAERC) session. GAERC remained seriously concerned about the human rights situation in Uzbekistan and linked the lifting of sanctions to Uzbekistan's implementation of international human rights standards. GAERC decided to extend sanctions aimed at Uzbekistan; a visa ban imposed on 12

U

Uzbekistani officials in November 2005 was extended for six months for eight of the officials, and an ongoing arms embargo was left unchanged. The Uzbekistani Ministry of Foreign Affairs responded to GAERC in a public statement calling the EU decision "unfounded and biased" and an "instrument of systematic pressure on Uzbekistan dressed up in human rights rhetoric". In a reversal of its May position and despite opposition from some member states, GAERC voted in October to suspend the visa ban on the remaining eight officials for six months. In the same month GAERC called for the release of all jailed human rights defenders but failed to mention specifically the need for an independent international investigation into the Andizhan killings.

In March, the UN Human Rights Council (HRC) voted to accept the recommendations of its Working Group on Situations to discontinue consideration of Uzbekistan under the HRC's confidential 1503 Procedure. This meant that the mandate of the UN Independent Expert on Uzbekistan appointed under the confidential 1503 Procedure was also terminated and that Uzbekistan's human rights record would no longer be under special scrutiny by the HRC.

In November, the UN Committee against Torture (CAT) published its concluding observations and recommendations following CAT's examination of Uzbekistan's third periodic report. CAT welcomed the introduction of habeas corpus and urged Uzbekistan to "apply a zero-tolerance approach to the continuing problem of torture, and to the practice of impunity".

Human rights defenders

The situation for human rights defenders and independent journalists continued to deteriorate and the authorities further restricted their freedom of speech, assembly and movement in the run-up to the December presidential elections. In early 2007, two human rights defenders and an opposition political activist were sentenced to long terms of imprisonment on what appeared to be politically-motivated charges. All three cases were linked either directly or indirectly to the 2005 Andizhan events.

At least 14 human rights defenders continued to serve long prison terms in cruel, inhuman and degrading conditions having been convicted after unfair trials. Several were reportedly tortured or otherwise ill-treated in detention. Those human rights activists and journalists not forced into exile and not

in detention were routinely monitored by law enforcement officers; human rights defenders were called in for questioning to their local police stations, placed under house arrest or otherwise prevented from attending meetings with foreign diplomats or delegations or from taking part in peaceful demonstrations.

Human rights defenders and journalists continued to report being threatened by members of the security services for carrying out legitimate activities. Several reported being assaulted and beaten and detained by law enforcement officers or people they suspected working for the security services. Relatives spoke of being threatened and harassed by security forces; some were detained in order to put pressure on human rights defenders. A disturbing trend emerged during the year with the authorities coercing defendants to renege on their NGO affiliations in return for suspended sentences.

■ In December, Ikhtior Khamroev, the 22-year-old son of Bakhtior Khamroev, the head of the Dzhizzakh section of the Human Rights Society of Uzbekistan, was released from the prison punishment cell to which he had been confined for 10 days. He told his father that he had been beaten and locked in a punishment cell, and that he had cut himself in the abdomen in protest at his ill-treatment. Ikhtior Khamroev was serving a three-year prison sentence handed down in September 2006 following an unfair trial. He was believed to have been detained because of the human rights activities of his father. He may have been beaten to punish his father for anti-government statements made at an international conference on human rights defenders in Dublin, Ireland in November.

■ In January, Rasul Tadzhibaev was granted a second visit with his sister, the jailed human rights defender Mutabar Tadzhibaeva held in Tashkent Women's Prison. She had been sentenced to eight years in prison on economic and political charges in March 2006 and her appeal against the verdict was turned down in May 2006. Mutabar Tadzhibaeva claimed she had not been permitted to meet with her lawyer and continued to be put in solitary confinement for alleged infringements of prison rules. In letters smuggled out of prison, Mutabar Tadzhibaeva described cruel, inhuman and degrading conditions of detention and punishments suffered by herself and other inmates. Members of her family continued to be harassed by the authorities. In March, Rasul Tadzhibaev was detained in order to prevent him from attending a demonstration in Tashkent calling for the release of detained female activists. He was also evicted from his apartment and was threatened with expulsion from Tashkent.

■ In May, Umida Niazova, a human rights activist and independent journalist, was sentenced to seven years' imprisonment by a district court in Tashkent on charges of illegally crossing the border, smuggling and distributing material causing public disorder after a two-day trial which fell far short of international standards. On 8 May Umida Niazova was released from the court-room after an appeal court changed her sentence to a three-year suspended one. She pleaded guilty to all three charges during the appeal hearing and accused international organizations of having misled her. Umida Niazova had worked for Human Rights Watch as a translator at the time of the Andizhan mass killings in 2005 and was in their employ at the time of her arrest. She had previously worked for other international NGOs.

■ Gulbahor Turaeva, a 40-year-old pathologist and human rights activist from Andizhan who had spoken out to foreign media and questioned the official version of the 2005 Andizhan events, was detained in January at the border on her way back from Kyrgyzstan, reportedly carrying around 120 publications in her bags, including books by the exiled leader of the banned secular opposition Erk party. Charged with attempting to overthrow the constitutional order and distributing subversive materials, she was sentenced to six years in prison in April. She was also charged with defamation. Following a second trial in May she was found guilty and fined. In June, her prison term was commuted on appeal to a six-year suspended sentence and she was released from detention. Gulbahor Turaeva pleaded guilty to all charges at the appeal hearing and denounced her work as a human rights defender as well as the activities of other human rights activists.

Torture and other ill-treatment

Persistent allegations of widespread torture or other ill-treatment of detainees and prisoners by law enforcement personnel continued. These reports stemmed not only from men and women suspected of membership of banned Islamic groups or of having committed terrorist offences but from all layers of civil society, including human rights

activists, journalists and former – often high-profile - members of the government and security forces.

The failure by the relevant authorities to properly investigate such allegations remained a serious concern. Very few law enforcement officers were brought to trial and held accountable for the human rights violations they committed and yet thousands of people – in pre-trial detention or convicted – routinely alleged that they had been tortured or otherwise ill-treated in custody in order to extract a confession. In January, the Deputy Minister of Internal Affairs informed Amnesty International that six or seven police officers had been convicted on torture-related offences in 2005 and 2006. Amnesty International welcomed the fact that prosecutions of people responsible for torture and ill-treatment had taken place. However, the numbers of convictions were alarmingly low considering that during the year an estimated 6,000 prisoners remained in detention after being convicted on politically-motivated charges in reportedly unfair trials. Many of these prisoners were reportedly tortured or otherwise ill-treated in detention and in November the UN CAT in examining Uzbekistan's compliance with the Convention against Torture found that torture or other cruel, inhuman or degrading treatment or punishment were routine.

Forcible return of terrorism suspects

The Uzbekistani authorities continued to actively seek the extradition of members or suspected members of banned Islamist parties or Islamic movements, such as Hizb-ut-Tahrir, from neighbouring countries as well as the Russian Federation and Ukraine. Most of those forcibly returned to Uzbekistan were held in incommunicado detention, increasing their risk of being tortured or otherwise ill-treated. Refugees who had fled after the Andizhan events and who voluntarily returned to Uzbekistan alleged that their movements were restricted. Some returnees were reportedly arrested on return to Uzbekistan. It was not possible to obtain any information on the whereabouts of those detained.

Authorities in the Russian Federation ignored decisions by the European Court of Human Rights to halt deportations of Uzbekistani asylum-seekers pending examinations of their applications to the court. Russian officials also confirmed that officers of the Uzbekistani security forces had been operating on the territory of the Russian Federation.

U

In October 2006, Rustam Muminov, a citizen of Uzbekistan, was extradited from the Russian Federation to Uzbekistan despite a request by the European Court of Human Rights to the Russian Federation for interim measures to halt the deportation. In March 2007, human rights groups learned that Rustam Muminov had been sentenced to five-and-a-half years' imprisonment after being held in incommunicado detention for three months following extradition.

■ In December, Russian human rights organizations received official confirmation that officers of the Uzbekistani security forces had detained asylum-seeker Mukhammadsalikh Abutov in the Russian Federation in July. An interstate warrant for his arrest was only issued after his detention and reportedly backdated by the Uzbekistani authorities. Mukhammadsalikh Abutov was still in detention in the Russian Federation at the end of the year.

Death penalty

A new law adopted by the Senate in June amended the criminal, criminal procedural and criminal executive codes by replacing the death penalty with life or long-term imprisonment. The law was scheduled to come into effect from 1 January 2008, marking the formal abolition of the death penalty in Uzbekistan. The authorities failed to introduce moratoria on executions and death sentences pending full abolition.

Some local NGOs claimed there were hundreds of prisoners under sentence of death held in conditions which amounted to cruel, inhuman and degrading treatment. According to the NGO Mothers Against the Death Penalty and Torture, 20 of at least 38 prisoners on death row in Tashkent prison (six of whom were sentenced to death in the first half of 2007), were reported to be infected with tuberculosis (TB) and were not receiving adequate medical treatment. There was no clarity as to how individual cases would be reviewed in light of the scheduled abolition of the death penalty, or about ongoing detention arrangements.

■ Iskandar Khudaiberganov, held on death row in Tashkent prison since November 2002, was diagnosed with TB in 2004 but has never received adequate medical treatment. His family were able to provide him with some anti-TB drugs, but it was feared that he risked developing drug-resistant strains of the disease.

Amnesty International reports

▤ Central Asia: Summary of human rights concerns, January 2006-March 2007 (EUR 04/001/2007)

▤ Crackdown on human rights defenders: Secret trials and torture in the 'information age, (EUR 62/002/2007)

▤ Uzbekistan: The government should ensure the concrete and effective implementation of the recommendations of the UN Committee against Torture as a matter of priority, (EUR 62/00X/2007)

▤ Iskandar Khudaiberganov: ongoing health concerns, (EUR 62/006/2007)

VENEZUELA

BOLIVARIAN REPUBLIC OF VENEZUELA

Head of state and government:	Hugo Chávez Frías
Death penalty:	abolitionist for all crimes
Population:	27.7 million
Life expectancy:	73.2 years
Under-5 mortality (m/f):	28/24 per 1,000
Adult literacy:	93 per cent

Thousands of government and anti-government supporters took to the streets on several occasions. A number of demonstrations ended in violent clashes between different groups of protesters and between protesters and the police. A new law on the right of women to live without fear of violence gave hope to thousands of women who experience violence in the home, community or workplace.

Background

President Hugo Chávez Frías took office for a third term in January and Congress granted him powers to pass legislation by decree for 18 months on a wide range of issues including public security and institutional reform. In December, Venezuelans rejected controversial constitutional changes in a referendum. Concerns had been expressed, including by the UN Special Rapporteur on freedom of opinion and expression, the Special Representative of the Secretary-General on Human Rights Defenders and the Special Rapporteur on the independence of judges and lawyers, that some of the constitutional changes proposed would have curtailed fundamental human rights.

V

Violence against women

A new law on the right of women to live free from violence came into force in March. Although women victims of violence are guaranteed greater protection under the new legislation, a fully resourced plan of action to implement the law had not yet been developed by the end of the year.

Political violence

The authorities did not take effective action to stop an escalation of violence in the context of demonstrations by supporters and opponents of government policies. There were reports of violent clashes between civilians, and between civilians and police officers throughout the year which resulted in scores of injuries and at least two deaths.

Scores of demonstrators, mainly students, including several who were under 18 were injured or arrested in the context of protests over the authorities' decision not to renew the licence of Radio Caracas Televisión (RCTV) in May. Several police officers were also injured in the clashes.

Confrontations between both law enforcement officials and demonstrators, and between demonstrators and armed civilians, also took place in the context of tensions over the proposed constitutional reforms.

Human rights defenders

Human rights defenders continued to face intimidation and attack.

■ José Luis Urbano, human rights defender and president of the Organization for the Defence of the Right to Education (Pro-Defensa del Derecho a la Educación) was shot and wounded in February, in his home town of Barcelona, in the northern state of Anzoátegui. The attack appeared to have been linked to his public criticism of the quality of education available to poor children in the state and his allegations of corruption. José Luis Urbano received protection until April. However, by the end of the year no one had been brought to justice for the attack.

Police and security services

According to the Attorney General, between 2000 and 2007 more than 6,000 complaints were filed at his office for alleged extrajudicial executions by the police. Of the 2,000 officers reportedly involved, less than 400 had been provisionally detained by the end of the year.

None of the recommendations made by the National Commission for Police Reform had been implemented by the end of the year. Among the recommendations of the Commission were measures to improve the accountability of the police, training on human rights and the use of force, the regulation and control of arms used by the security forces, and legislation to integrate the different police bodies.

Arms control

The use of firearms in killings and other violent crimes remained high, including in prisons. The Scientific, Penal and Criminal Investigations Unit, which carries out criminal investigations under the supervision of the Attorney General's Office, registered 9,568 homicides from January to September 2007, 852 more than during the same period in 2006. Despite the fact that firearms were involved in most of these killings, no steps were taken to implement the recommendations of the National Plan to Control Arms which came into force in 2006.

Amnesty International visit

🚍 An Amnesty International delegation visited Venezuela in July to research violations against women.

VIET NAM

SOCIALIST REPUBLIC OF VIET NAM

Head of state:	Nguyen Minh Triet
Head of government:	Nguyen Tan Dung
Death penalty:	retentionist
Population:	86.4 million
Life expectancy:	73.7 years
Under-5 mortality (m/f):	36/27 per 1,000
Adult literacy:	90.3 per cent

Freedom of expression and association continued to be tightly controlled. Political activists and dissidents were arrested and detained; some were sentenced to lengthy prison terms under national security legislation after unfair trials. At least 83 people were sentenced to death, including 14 women. Statistics on executions remained classified a "state secret", although discussion on the

effectiveness of the death penalty continued. Scores of ethnic minority Montagnards in the Central Highlands and members of the Khmer Krom community in southern An Giang province fled to Cambodia seeking asylum from persecution.

Background

In August a new government was formed following National Assembly elections. The President and Prime Minister remained in their posts.

In March Decree CP-31 on administrative detention was abolished. It had often been used to detain peaceful religious and political dissidents under house arrest without bringing them before a court. However, other administrative detention provisions remained in place.

In June hundreds of poor farmers from at least 10 provinces demonstrated outside the National Assembly building in Ho Chi Minh City in protest over corruption and arbitrary land confiscation. They were joined by Thich Quang Do, the deputy leader of the outlawed Unified Buddhist Church of Vietnam (UBCV), who had been subjected to administrative detention for many years, and other UBCV members. The demonstrations lasted for almost a month, until they were broken up in July by security officials.

Freedom of expression and association

Prior to the first ever visit of a Vietnamese President to the USA in June, two prisoners of conscience were released. internet dissident Nguyen Vu Binh had served over four years of a seven-year sentence on charges of "spying". He was released from prison but remained under three years' house arrest. Le Quoc Quan, a lawyer and pro-democracy activist, had been arrested on 8 March after returning home from a year-long fellowship in the USA. In May, Phan Van Ban, a long-term political prisoner, was released and allowed to join his family in the USA. He had been sentenced to life imprisonment in 1985 for distribution of anti-government leaflets.

Following the hosting of the APEC summit in November 2006 and the conclusion of major international trade agreements, a crackdown on peaceful dissent and freedom of expression and association intensified. At least 35 people, among them lawyers, trade unionists, religious leaders and internet dissidents, were arrested between November 2006 and the end of 2007, an increased number over previous years. Most had connections to Bloc 8406, a

movement calling for peaceful political change and respect for human rights. Nineteen among the 35 were known to have been tried and sentenced under vaguely worded and repressive national security legislation used to criminalize peaceful political dissent.

■ On 30 March Father Nguyen Van Ly, a former prisoner of conscience, was sentenced to eight years' imprisonment for "conducting propaganda against the Socialist Republic of Viet Nam" under Article 88 of the Penal Code. He was manhandled by guards as he tried to challenge the court. Two co-defendants were sentenced to six and five years' imprisonment, and two women were given suspended prison terms. Father Ly was a founding member of Bloc 8406 and the Viet Nam Progression Party (VNPP) in September 2006 and had spent 15 years in prison for peacefully criticizing the government.

■ Two human rights lawyers, Nguyen Van Dai and Le Thi Cong Nhan, were sentenced to five and four years' imprisonment respectively in May, reduced by one year each on appeal. Nguyen Van Dai was among the founding members of Bloc 8406. Le Thi Cong Nhan is a spokesperson for the VNPP. Both had held human rights workshops and documented human rights violations. At the appeal hearing in November their lawyers argued that Article 88 of the Penal Code, under which they had been charged, was unconstitutional and did not conform to international conventions that Viet Nam has signed, and should be reviewed.

■ Truong Quoc Huy remained detained without trial since August 2006. He was charged under Article 258 of the Penal Code with "abusing democratic freedoms to infringe upon the interests of the State, the legitimate rights and interests of organizations and/or citizens". He was accused, among other things, of joining an internet forum and disseminating anti-government flyers.

■ In November six people were arrested in Ho Chi Minh City, where they had been meeting to discuss peaceful democratic change. The police claimed to have found "subversive" leaflets and stickers, and official media stated that they were being investigated under Article 84 (Terrorism) of the Penal Code. The six comprised two Vietnamese nationals; Nguyen Thi Thanh Van, a French citizen and a journalist and activist; two US citizens and a Thai national, all of Vietnamese origin. Nguyen Thi Thanh Van and one US citizen were released and deported in December.

Discrimination

Reports continued of harassment of ethnic minority Montagnards in the Central Highlands, including forced denunciation of their religion, short-term detentions and ill-treatment. More than 200 sought asylum in neighbouring Cambodia. In a reported incident in June, one Montagnard was arrested and tortured in detention for two days. He had previously described human rights violations against Montagnards to a UNHCR official who had interviewed him in the presence of Vietnamese security officials. On his release he fled to Cambodia. At least 250 Montagnards were still serving long prison terms in connection with protests in 2001 and 2004 over land ownership and religious freedom.

A number of people from the Khmer Krom community fled to Cambodia seeking asylum. They alleged persecution, including the forced disrobing of Buddhist monks. On 1 August the Vietnamese authorities reported that they had arrested Tim Sakorn, a Buddhist monk, who had previously been living in Cambodia. He was sentenced to one year's imprisonment on 9 November under national security legislation and is a prisoner of conscience. (See Cambodia entry.)

Death penalty

At least 83 people, including 14 women, were sentenced to death for drug trafficking offences, some after unfair trials. The true number is believed to be much higher.

■ Pham Thi Tuyet Lan was sentenced to death in February for alleged involvement in a land fraud. However, the appeals court overturned the verdict as it emerged that she had been charged with the wrong offence and defence lawyers had been excluded from the investigation. A reinvestigation was ordered.

At least 15 death sentences were upheld by the Supreme People's Court. They included a UK citizen of Vietnamese origin who was reported to be suffering from mental health problems.

Amnesty International reports

- Viet Nam: Internet activist priest imprisoned (ASA 41/003/2007)
- Viet Nam: Silence critics must be released (ASA 41/004/2007)
- Viet Nam: Crackdown on activists must end (ASA 41/005/2007)
- Viet Nam: Lead a union, go to prison (ASA 41/011/2007)

YEMEN

REPUBLIC OF YEMEN

Head of state:	'Ali Abdullah Saleh
Head of government:	Ali Mohammed Megawar (replaced 'Abdul Qader Bajammal in April)
Death penalty:	retentionist
Population:	22.3 million
Life expectancy:	61.5 years
Under-5 mortality (m/f):	83/75 per 1,000
Adult literacy:	54.1 per cent

Routine violations of civil and political rights impacted negatively on economic and social aspects of people's lives. The violations were exacerbated by renewed armed clashes in the north and protests in the south. Torture and other ill-treatment remained common. Sentences of death and flogging were imposed and carried out. Human rights activists remained firm in the face of these challenges.

Background

Renewed clashes broke out in January between security forces and armed followers of the late Hussain Badr al-Din al-Huthi, a prominent Zaidi – a Shi'a Muslim community in the Sa'da Governorate. The clashes continued intermittently throughout the year despite a ceasefire mediated by the Qatari government. Security forces carried out mass arrests, civilians were reportedly killed by government forces and some 30,000 people were internally displaced as a result of the violence. The government denied journalists and almost all independent observers access to the area and maintained a high degree of censorship, so few details emerged during the first six months of the clashes.

In July, seven Spanish tourists and two Yemeni drivers accompanying them were killed in Ma'rab in an attack by a suicide bomber. The government blamed the attack on al-Qa'ida.

In August, scores of retired soldiers from the army of the former People's Democratic Republic of Yemen (PDRY) and their supporters were arrested after they staged peaceful protests in Aden and other southern cities over their inferior pensions and terms and conditions of work compared to soldiers from the north. All were released uncharged by November and the government agreed to consider their grievances. The PDRY and the Yemen Arab Republic unified in 1990.

Y

Killings by security forces

There were unconfirmed reports of extrajudicial executions by security forces in the context of the violence in Sa'da. People alleged to be armed members of al-Qa'ida were also killed in unclear circumstances while reportedly resisting arrest.

■ On 10 September, security forces shot dead Walid Salih 'Ubadi and another person during a peaceful demonstration in al-Dali' in support of the retired soldiers. Eight other demonstrators were wounded. The incident was reportedly under investigation, but the outcome was not known.

■ In October, security forces killed four protesters at a peaceful demonstration in Radfan and wounded 15 others. It was not known if any investigation was carried out.

Political prisoners

Hundreds of people were arrested as suspected followers of Hussain Badr al-Din al-Huthi or members or supporters of al-Qa'ida following the upsurge in violence in Sa'da and the July attack on Spanish tourists. Others were arrested in connection with the retired soldiers' protests, but all were subsequently released. Most of those arrested in connection with al-Qa'ida and the Sa'da clashes remained held without charge or trial, mainly in Sa'da, Hajja, Dhamar, Ibb, Sana'a and Hudaida.

■ Muhammad Abdel Karim al-Huthi and at least four other members of the al-Huthi family, and Abdul Qadir al-Mahdi, remained in the Political Security prison in Sana'a. Muhammad Abdel Karim al-Huthi was arrested on 28 January. Abdul Qadir al-Mahdi was arrested on 19 February and held incommunicado for two months before his family was permitted to visit him. His salary was suspended, causing his wife and children hardship.

Among the political prisoners were people arrested in previous years.

■ Walid al-Kayma' remained held without charge at the Political Security prison in Sana'a since his arrest in 2004 or 2005. Like others held there, he was allowed family visits but was denied access to a lawyer and did not know whether he would be charged and tried or released.

'War on terror'

Five prisoners returned to Yemen after being held by the US authorities at Guantánamo Bay, Cuba, and detained on arrival, were released without charge during the year. They included Sadiq Muhammad Isma'il and Fawaz Nu'man Hamoud. Five others detained on arrival in December 2006 were released in March without charge, but another, Tawfiq al-Marwa'i, was released after he was tried and convicted of forging a passport.

Unfair trials

At least 109 people tried before the Specialized Criminal Court (SCC) and two tried before ordinary criminal courts did not receive fair trials. At least 73 of them appeared before the SCC in seven separate cases on charges that included planning attacks on oil installations and the US embassy, seeking to smuggle weapons to Somalia, and forging papers for volunteer fighters to travel to Iraq. In the six cases that were concluded, at least 53 people were convicted and sentenced to up to 15 years in prison and five were acquitted.

In the other case, known as the Sana'a Cell 2 case, 15 defendants faced charges including murder, planning to poison Sana'a's drinking water and other violent crimes in connection with the events in Sa'da. One defendant, journalist Abdel Karim al-Khaiywani, was charged in connection with his media reporting of the violence in Sa'da, and was therefore a prisoner of conscience.

As in previous cases, lawyers and human rights activists criticized the SCC for failing to conform to international fair trial standards, including by denying defendants and their lawyers full access to their case files and so limiting their ability to prepare their defence. Lawyers defending the accused in the Sana'a Cell 2 case appealed to the Constitutional Court to declare the SCC unconstitutional, but no ruling was announced by the end of the year.

In July, Ta'iz Appeal Court ordered the release of four men shortly before they were due to complete one-year sentences imposed by an ordinary court for challenging the integrity of local and national elections held in September 2006. In a separate case also related to the 2006 elections, at least 36 people were tried before an ordinary court in Sana'a in connection with a dispute in Hajja in which an official was killed; six people were sentenced to death and others received prison terms of up to 15 years. There were concerns about the fairness of both trials.

Y

Freedom of expression

In June, the Information Ministry announced that a new press law would be introduced, raising concern that this would further restrict press freedom. The law would prohibit publication of information deemed harmful to national stability and further hamper media reporting of politically sensitive issues, such as the violence in Sa'da. Vague concepts such as national security and national stability had routinely been invoked as justification for restriction of press freedom and punishment of journalists. The law had not been introduced by the end of the year.

Journalists were harassed. The authorities blocked websites carrying political and other critical commentary and prohibited the use of some phone messaging services.

■ Journalists Abdel Karim al-Khaiwani and Ahmad 'Umar Ben Farid were abducted in August in Sana'a and Aden respectively by unidentified assailants believed to be connected to the security authorities. The two men were beaten and dumped in deserted areas. Abdel Karim al-Khaiwani was believed to have been targeted because of his reporting about events in Sa'da, and Ahmad 'Umar Ben Farid because of his writing about the protests in the south.

■ In July, a regular weekly gathering of supporters of the NGO Women Journalists Without Restrictions who were demanding that they be allowed to publish a magazine, was violently disrupted, apparently by security officials. A number of people were injured.

Discrimination and violence against women

Women continued to face discrimination and violence at the hands of both state and non-state actors, including rape and other sexual violence, and trafficking. Such abuses were particularly severe in rural areas, where 80 per cent of women live, girls generally have less access to education than boys, and women are particularly vulnerable to economic hardship.

In a shadow report to Yemen's sixth report to CEDAW, a collective of women's and human rights organizations criticized laws that continue to discriminate against women and called for government action to protect women's rights, including the criminalization of domestic violence.

■ Anissa al-Shu'aybi brought a court case against officers at the Criminal Investigation department in Sana'a alleging that she was raped and otherwise tortured by them in previous years. Her testimony of torture and other ill-treatment of women in the prison was widely publicized. The case was not concluded by the end of the year.

■ Samra al-Hilali, a 15-year-old girl, said she was tortured by police in Ibb before being tried and acquitted in August on murder charges.

Torture and other ill-treatment

Torture and other ill-treatment in police custody were common. Many detainees held by Political Security and National Security, two security police agencies, were reportedly tortured, including with beatings with fists, sticks and rifle butts; scalding with hot water; tight handcuffs; prolonged blindfolding; denial of water and access to a toilet; and death threats.

■ In April, Shayef al-Haymi said he had been tortured so badly during 40 days of incommunicado detention by National Security officials that his limbs became paralysed and his body was covered with scars. The case was investigated by the prosecuting authorities, and the authorities released him and paid a sum of money to his family. However, no one was brought to justice and, after he made his ordeal public, the authorities said that his injuries were self-inflicted and rearrested him.

Cruel, inhuman and degrading punishments

Courts across the country imposed sentences of flogging almost daily for alcohol and sexual offences. The floggings were carried out immediately in public without appeal.

Death penalty

At least 15 people were executed, including one child offender, although Yemeni law prohibits the execution of child offenders. Another child offender, Hafez Ibrahim, had his death sentence annulled, but others were among several hundred prisoners who remained on death row.

■ Adil Muhammad Saif al-Mu'ammari was executed in February despite international appeals and medical evidence that he was below the age of 18 at the time of the murder for which he was sentenced to death.

■ Radfan Razaz, another possible child offender, remained at risk of imminent execution. He was initially sentenced to imprisonment because of his age, but the appeal court changed his sentence to death.

Z

At least 90 prisoners were held on death row at Ta'iz Prison. In one particularly disturbing incident in September, two prisoners – Sharaf al-Yusfi and 'Issam Tahla – were reportedly killed by prison guards after they survived initial attempts to execute them. The attempted executions had left them both seriously injured.

Amnesty International visits

🚌 Amnesty International delegates visited Yemen in January and September.

ZAMBIA

REPUBLIC OF ZAMBIA

Head of state and government:	Levy Mwanawasa
Death penalty:	abolitionist in practice
Population:	12.1 million
Life expectancy:	40.5 years
Under-5 mortality (m/f):	169/153 per 1,000
Adult literacy:	68 per cent

Freedom of expression, assembly and movement were restricted, especially in the context of continuing controversy over constitutional reforms. A bill which threatened to restrict the activities of NGOs was put before Parliament.

Background

President Levy Mwanawasa further delayed the constitutional review process, which was rescheduled for completion in 2011. The controversial National Constitution Conference Act was passed in August. Concerns were raised that the Act was not consistent with the recommendations of the Constitution Review Commission (CRC), which had called for the Constitution to be repealed and replaced.

The trial of former President Frederick Chiluba on charges of corruption was repeatedly postponed because of his poor health. However, in May, in a case brought by the Zambian government against Frederick Chiluba and 19 of his associates, the High Court of Justice of England and Wales ruled that

Frederick Chiluba "actively participated" in large-scale money laundering in which two UK law firms were also complicit.

Freedom of expression and assembly

There were further reports of government officials threatening journalists critical of the government. Civil society organizations supporting the recommendations of the CRC found their freedom of assembly restricted.

■ On 19 July, police in Lusaka prevented Q-FM, a private radio station, from covering live a demonstration outside Parliament organized by the OASIS forum, a coalition of civil society and church groups, and the Collaborative Group on the Constitution. Though the conveners of the demonstration had informed the police in advance, police claimed that the demonstration was illegal.

■ In November, the government temporarily withdrew the passport of opposition leader Michael Sata after he returned from the USA where, in an address to students, he was allegedly critical of Chinese investments in Zambia. The Minister of Home Affairs, Ronnie Shikapwasha, accused him of obtaining the passport without following procedure.

Legal developments

In July the government introduced the NGO Bill in Parliament. Among other provisions, the Bill seeks to empower the Interior Minister to form a board comprised of eight government representatives and two representatives from civil society. The Board would have the power to reject applications for registration of an NGO if its proposed activities do not fit with an undefined "national development plan" for Zambia. Without proper safeguards, there were fears that some of the provisions of the Bill could be used by the government to curtail the work of civil society organizations and restrict their independence. In August, following pressure from civil society, the Minister of Justice deferred parliamentary debate on the Bill to allow for further consultation.

Death penalty

There were no executions in 2007. President Levy Mwanawasa commuted 97 death sentences to life imprisonment in August 2007. The commutation was without prejudice to the right of the prisoners to appeal for further clemency.

Z

ZIMBABWE

REPUBLIC OF ZIMBABWE

Head of state and government:	Robert Mugabe
Death penalty:	abolitionist in practice
Population:	13.2 million
Life expectancy:	40.9 years
Under-5 mortality (m/f):	120/106 per 1,000
Adult literacy:	89.4 per cent

The human rights situation in Zimbabwe continued to deteriorate in 2007 with an increase in organized violence and torture, and restrictions on the rights to freedom of association, assembly and expression. Hundreds of human rights defenders and members of the main opposition party, the Movement for Democratic Change (MDC), were arrested for participating in peaceful gatherings. Scores were tortured while in police custody. The economy continued to decline. About four million people required food aid due to the declining economy, erratic rains and shortage of agricultural inputs such as maize seed and fertilizer. Victims of the 2005 mass forced evictions continued to live in deplorable conditions, and the government failed to remedy their situation.

Background

In March the Southern Africa Development Community (SADC) held an extraordinary summit in Tanzania and appointed President Thabo Mbeki of South Africa to facilitate dialogue between the government of Zimbabwe and the MDC. The dialogue started at a very slow pace and missed several deadlines. Amnesty International and local human rights organizations were concerned about the mediation process' silence on human rights violations. The SADC mediation process did not have a clear strategy for civil participation. While the talks were ongoing, the police in Zimbabwe continued to target MDC members and human rights defenders. Following agreements reached during the talks, in October the Constitutional Amendment (No.18) Act was passed, aiming to synchronize presidential, parliamentary and local government elections and to create a human rights commission. In December Parliament passed a number of other Bills in line with agreements reached during the talks, including the Public Order and Security Amendment Bill and the Electoral Laws Amendment Bill.

The economy continued to decline, severely eroding household incomes and capacity to access food, health care and education. The World Food Programme estimated that about four million Zimbabweans were in need of food aid. Annual inflation was running at over 7,900 per cent at the end of September, but the Central Statistical Office failed to release the October, November and December figures. In June the government introduced price controls, ostensibly to arrest spiralling food prices. This policy resulted in panic buying and by the beginning of July most goods including maize meal, the staple diet, could not be found in shops. During the enforcement of the price controls the police arrested more than 7,000 business people for flouting price control regulations. There were reports of corrupt conduct by price enforcement agents, including hoarding by state security agents.

Freedom of assembly and association

Throughout the year police imposed severe restrictions on the rights to freedom of association and assembly of human rights defenders, students, trade unionists and members of the MDC. Police used excessive force to break up peaceful demonstrations. Detainees in police custody were tortured, in particular by being beaten severely, and ill-treated. Repeatedly, detainees were denied access to lawyers, food and medical care.

On 21 February police in Harare announced a three-month ban on demonstrations in parts of the city. This ban appears to have breached Section 27 of the Public Order and Security Act (POSA), which only allows police to impose a one-month ban.

While police used excessive force to break up demonstrations or meetings organized by the MDC and civil society organizations, there were no reports of police stopping any meeting or demonstration organized by the ruling Zimbabwe African National Union – Patriotic Front (ZANU-PF) party or its partner organizations, including the Zimbabwe National Liberation War Veterans Association.

■ On 18 February, police in Harare stopped the MDC from holding a rally at the Zimbabwe grounds in Highfield, a low-income suburb in Harare. The MDC faction led by Morgan Tsvangirai had called a rally to launch its presidential campaign for the 2008 elections. Despite a High Court order obtained by the MDC on 17 February barring police from blocking the rally, police mounted checkpoints to stop people reaching the venue. At least 50 people were injured, five of them seriously, when police beat participants at random. Police first assaulted the MDC supporters with baton sticks and later used dogs, tear gas and water canons to disperse them. Injuries were also reported among the police. Police were also reported to have gone door to door beating suspected MDC supporters. On 19 February police arrested several MDC leaders in Highfield.

■ On 11 March at least 50 activists were arrested in Highfield after attempting to attend a prayer meeting organized by the Save Zimbabwe Campaign, a coalition of political parties, civil society organizations and churches. The meeting was in protest at the police's three-month ban on demonstrations in parts of Harare. Those arrested included MDC faction leaders Morgan Tsvangirai and Arthur Mutambara; National Constitutional Assembly (NCA) chairperson Lovemore Madhuku; and senior MDC members Sekai Holland and Grace Kwinjeh. They were taken to Machipisa police station where police kicked them and beat them with baton sticks. The beatings continued at various police stations where the detainees were later transferred. Several activists suffered serious injuries including fractures and deep skin lacerations. They were denied access to lawyers and only Lovemore Madhuku and Morgan Tsvangirai were allowed access to medical care. Police defied a High Court order to present the detainees at the High Court on 13 March. Police also failed to present the detainees before a magistrate by midday on the same day. Police at Harare Central police station refused permission for some of the seriously injured to be transported by ambulance to court, turning ambulances away. The detainees spent at least four hours at Rotten Row magistrate court without anyone attending to them. Police only allowed the detainees to be taken to hospital after the intervention of officers from the Attorney General's office. At midnight on 13 March the detainees were taken back to court and released into the custody of their lawyers.

■ On 25 July, at least 200 NCA activists were arrested by police in Harare after participating in a peaceful march. They were taken from the NCA offices to Harare Central police station where they were severely assaulted by police and unidentified people in plain clothes. Among those assaulted were two elderly women aged 68 and 72 who were singled out for

beating by police and accused of "inciting young people to demonstrate against the government". Six babies were also taken into custody with their mothers. The mothers were singled out and beaten in front of their children. The beatings lasted for about six hours and the activists were released at midnight without charge. The activists were reportedly made to sing revolutionary songs denouncing Morgan Tsvangirai. At least 32 of the activists were later hospitalized and 14 had fractured limbs as a result of the beatings. Among the injured was a 19-month-old baby who had been beaten by police with a baton stick.

Women human rights defenders

Members of the women's activist organization Women of Zimbabwe Arise (WOZA) were arrested throughout the year after engaging in peaceful protest. WOZA leaders Jenni Williams and Magodonga Mahlangu were arrested several times and were threatened by police officials. Some of the threats amounted to death threats.

■ On 6 June, seven WOZA members were arrested in Bulawayo after participating in a peaceful protest. In solidarity with the seven detainees Jenni Williams and Magodonga Mahlangu turned themselves in and were also detained. Jenni Williams and Magodonga Mahlangu were charged under the Criminal Codification Act and released on bail on 9 June. WOZA members were also reportedly arrested in other parts of Zimbabwe including Mutare, Masvingo and Filabusi.

■ On 1 October about 200 WOZA members were arrested in Bulawayo after taking part in a peaceful march protesting against piece-meal constitutional amendments. They were released without charge.

■ On 15 October, 58 WOZA activists peacefully protesting outside parliament in Harare were arrested and detained for nine hours at Harare Central police station. They were released without charge.

■ On 6 November police in Harare arrested 98 WOZA members peacefully marching to protest against violence and demanding the repeal of repressive laws such as POSA. The activists were arrested outside parliament by riot police. They were taken to Harare Central police station and released seven hours later without charge.

Extrajudicial executions

On 11 March police in Highfield shot and killed NCA activist Gift Tandare who was taking part in a protest prayer meeting organized by the Save Zimbabwe Campaign. No independent investigation was conducted following this incident. Police alleged that Gift Tandare was part of a group which failed to take heed of a police warning to disperse. Police later fired live bullets at mourners during Gift Tandare's funeral wake, injuring two mourners. State security agents reportedly took his body from a local funeral parlour and forced his relatives to bury it in Mt Darwin at his rural home.

Torture and other ill-treatment

Reports of people being tortured in police custody persisted throughout the year. Many torture victims had been arrested after engaging in peaceful protest or were MDC members accused by police of involvement in alleged terrorism attacks and bombings.

■ On and around 28 March police rounded up dozens of MDC workers, activists and senior officials throughout the country; accusing them of terrorist activities and petrol bombings. Most of the detainees were allegedly tortured while in police custody. Thirty-two of those arrested were later charged and detained for between two and four months. Philip Katsande, the MDC's Harare province secretary for policy and research, was among those arrested. He was shot during arrest as he hid above the ceiling. Police also allegedly assaulted his wife and children during the arrest. He was later taken by police to Parirenyatwa hospital. Paul Madzore, MDC Member of Parliament for Glen View, was arrested by police from his home on 28 March. Police arrested other occupants at his home including children. He was tortured by police at Harare Central police station. Charges against 30 of the detainees were later dropped because of insufficient evidence.

■ In June, six men, including a retired army officer, appeared in court accused of plotting a coup. Albert Mugove Mutapo, ex-soldier Nyasha Zivuka, Oncemore Mudzuradhona, Emmanuel Marara, Patson Mupfure and Shingirai Matemachani were reportedly tortured. Their trial was continuing at the end of the year.

Abductions and assaults

MDC members were abducted and assaulted by people suspected of being state security agents.

■ On 18 March Nelson Chamisa, MDC Member of Parliament for Kuwadzana, was attacked with iron bars outside Harare International Airport by people believed to be state security personnel. He was on his way to Brussels to attend an EU-ACP joint parliamentary meeting. By the end of 2007, no one had been arrested for this assault.

■ In March Last Maengahama, an MDC official, was abducted by suspected state security agents at Borrowdale shopping centre in Harare after attending Gift Tandare's memorial service. Last Maengahama was bundled into a truck and assaulted before being dumped in Mutorashanga, some 100km from Harare.

■ On 18 May Cleopas Shiri, the MDC chairperson for Gweru Urban district, was abducted by four men in a green Mazda 323 car on his way home from work. He was blindfolded and taken to a building where he was tortured, including by having electric rods attached to his toes. After he passed out, his abductors dumped him in the bush. Cleopas Shiri later regained consciousness, managed to reach the road and got a lift to Bulawayo, where he was hospitalized for a month. When he returned to Gweru he found that his house was under surveillance. The surveillance only stopped after he had complained to the police district commanding officer.

■ On 22 November, at least 22 NCA members were rounded up by unidentified people and bundled into two minibuses in Harare's central business district area. They were reportedly taken to ZANU-PF's Harare provincial offices along Fourth Street where they were beaten on the soles of their feet with sticks and iron bars and ordered to maintain stress positions, including simulating sitting on a chair, for long periods and to roll on the ground. They were later ordered to mop the floor of the room and a toilet with bare hands. After the captors allegedly called the police, the victims were taken to Harare Central police station where police charged them with "obstruction of justice" under the Criminal (Codification and Reform) Act and they were fined. None of the perpetrators was arrested. Ten of the victims required hospital treatment.

Rule of law

In October magistrates and prosecutors went on strike demanding a 900 per cent pay rise. Many judicial officers' salaries were below the poverty line, which compromised the justice system.

On 6 November Attorney-General Sobusa Gula-Ndebele was arrested on suspicion of "conduct contrary or inconsistent with duties of a public officer". The arrest followed a reported meeting in

September with former National Merchant Bank deputy managing director James Andrew Kufakunesu Mushore, who was wanted by police for foreign currency offences. The Attorney-General was charged with contravening Section 174 (1) of the Criminal Law (Codification and Reform) Act, cautioned and released. In December President Mugabe suspended the Attorney General and announced the setting up of a three-member tribunal to look into allegations that he had abused his office.

Amnesty International visits/reports

Amnesty International delegates visited Zimbabwe in February/March, August, October/November and November/December.

Open letter from Amnesty International's Secretary General Irene Khan to President Robert Mugabe (AFR 46/006/2007)

Zimbabwe: End harassment, torture and intimidation of opposition activists (AFR 46/007/2007)

Call for Africa leaders to speak out against brutality in Zimbabwe (AFR 46/011/2007)

Zimbabwe: Human rights in crisis – Shadow report to the African Commission on Human and Peoples' Rights (AFR 46/016/2007)

Zimbabwe: Between a rock and hard place – women human rights defenders at risk (AFR 46/017/2007)

Zimbabwe: Women at the forefront of challenging government policy face increasing repression (AFR 46/023/2007)

Z

Police officers detain an opposition
supporter on 31 December 2007 during
riots at the Kibera slum in Nairobi, Kenya.
There was widespread violence before,
during and after the general elections.

AMNESTY INTERNATIONAL REPORT 2008
PART THREE: SELECTED HUMAN RIGHTS TREATIES

This container is home to one of the Romani families at the settlement at Letanovce, Slovakia, February 2007. Many Roma in the country lack access to basic services and live under the threat of forced eviction.

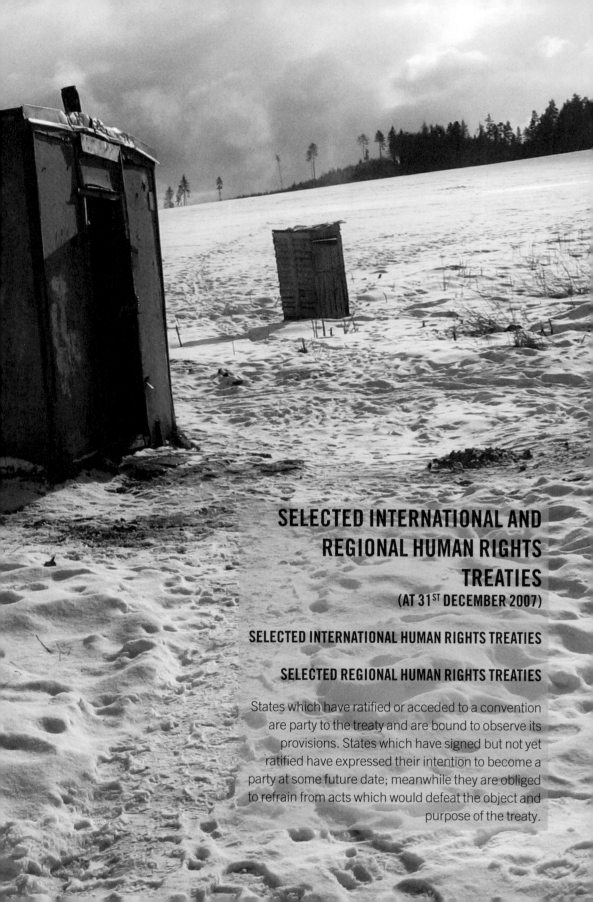

SELECTED INTERNATIONAL AND REGIONAL HUMAN RIGHTS TREATIES
(AT 31ST DECEMBER 2007)

SELECTED INTERNATIONAL HUMAN RIGHTS TREATIES

SELECTED REGIONAL HUMAN RIGHTS TREATIES

States which have ratified or acceded to a convention are party to the treaty and are bound to observe its provisions. States which have signed but not yet ratified have expressed their intention to become a party at some future date; meanwhile they are obliged to refrain from acts which would defeat the object and purpose of the treaty.

	International Covenant on Civil and Political Rights (ICCPR)	(first) Optional Protocol to the ICCPR	Second Optional Protocol to the ICCPR, aiming at the abolition of the death penalty	International Covenant on Economic, Social and Cultural Rights	Convention on the Elimination of All Forms of Discrimination against Women (CEDAW)	Optional Protocol to CEDAW	Convention on the Rights of the Child (CRC)	Optional Protocol to the CRC on the involvement of chidren in armed conflict	International Convention on the Elimination of All Forms of Racial Discrimination	Convention against Torture and Other Cruel, Inhuman or Degrading Treatment or Punishment
Afghanistan	●			●	●		●	●	●	●28
Albania	●	◐	◐	●	●	●	●		●	●
Algeria	●	●		●	●		●		●	●22
Andorra	●	●	●		●	●	●	●	●	●22
Angola	●	●		●	●	◐	●	◐		
Antigua and Barbuda					●	●			●	●
Argentina	●	●	○	●	●	◐	●	●	●	●22
Armenia	●	●		●	●	●	●	●	●	●
Australia	●	●	●	●	●		●	●	●	●22
Austria	●	●	●	●	●	●	●	●	●	●22
Azerbaijan	●	●		●	●	●	●	●	●	●22
Bahamas					●		●		●	
Bahrain	●			◐	●		●		●	●
Bangladesh	●			●	●	●10	●	●	●	●
Barbados	●	●		●	●		●		●	
Belarus	●	●		●	●	●	●	●	●	●
Belgium	●	●	●	●	●	●	●		●	●22
Belize	●			○	●	●10	●	●	●	●
Benin	●	●		●	●	○	●	●	●	●
Bhutan					●		●	○	○	
Bolivia	●	●		●	●	●	●	●	●	●22
Bosnia and Herzegovina	●	●	●	●	●	●	●	●	●	●22
Botswana	●				●	◐	●	●	●	●
Brazil	●			●	●	●	●	●	●	●22
Brunei Darussalam					●		●			
Bulgaria	●	●	●	●	●	●	●	●	●	●22
Burkina Faso	●	●		●	●	●	●	◐	●	●
Burundi	●			●	●	○	●	○	●	●22

Optional Protocol to the Convention against Torture	Convention relating to the Status of Refugees (1951)	Protocol relating to the Status of Refugees (1967)	Convention relating to the Status of Stateless Persons (1954)	Convention on the Reduction of Statelessness (1961)	International Convention on the Protection of the Rights of All Migrant Workers and Members of their Families	Rome Statute of the International Criminal Court	
	●	●				●	Afghanistan
●	●	●	●	●	◐	●	Albania
	●	●	●		●	○	Algeria
						●	Andorra
	●	●				○	Angola
	●	●	●			●	Antigua and Barbuda
●	●	●	●		◐	●	Argentina
●	●	●	●	●		○	Armenia
	●	●	●	●		●	Australia
○	●	●		●		●	Austria
○	●	●	●	●	●		Azerbaijan
	●	●				○	Bahamas
						○	Bahrain
					○	○	Bangladesh
			●			●	Barbados
	●	●					Belarus
○	●	●	●			●	Belgium
	●	●	●		●	●	Belize
●	●	●			○	●	Benin
							Bhutan
●	●	●	●	●	●	●	Bolivia
	●	●	●	●	●	●	Bosnia and Herzegovina
	●	●	●			●	Botswana
◐	●	●	●	◐		●	Brazil
							Brunei Darussalam
	●	●				●	Bulgaria
○	●	●			●	●	Burkina Faso
	●	●				●	Burundi

● state is a party

◐ state became party in 2007

○ signed but not yet ratified

◔ signed in 2007, but not yet ratified

10 Declaration under Article 10 not recognizing the competence of the CEDAW Committee to undertake confidential inquiries into allegations of grave or systematic violations

22 Declaration under Article 22 recognizing the competence of the Committee against Torture (CAT) to consider individual complaints

28 Reservation under Article 28 not recognizing the competence of the CAT to undertake confidential inquiries into allegations of systematic torture if warranted

12 Declaration under Article 12(3) accepting the jurisdiction of the International Criminal Court (ICC) for crimes in its territory

124 Declaration under Article 124 not accepting the jurisdiction of the ICC over war crimes for seven years after ratification

* Signed the Rome Statute but have since formally declared their intention not to ratify

** Acceded in 1962 but in 1965 denounced the Convention; denunciation took effect on 2 April 1966

	International Covenant on Civil and Political Rights (ICCPR)	(first) Optional Protocol to the ICCPR	Second Optional Protocol to the ICCPR, aiming at the abolition of the death penalty	International Covenant on Economic, Social and Cultural Rights	Convention on the Elimination of All Forms of Discrimination against Women (CEDAW)	Optional Protocol to CEDAW	Convention on the Rights of the Child (CRC)	Optional Protocol to the CRC on the involvement of children in armed conflict	International Convention on the Elimination of All Forms of Racial Discrimination	Convention against Torture and Other Cruel, Inhuman or Degrading Treatment or Punishment
Cambodia	●	○		●	●	○	●	●	●	●
Cameroon	●	●		●	●		●	○	●	●22
Canada	●	●	●	●	●	●	●	●	●	●22
Cape Verde	●	●	●	●	●		●	●	●	●
Central African Republic	●	●		●	●		●		●	
Chad	●	●		●	●		●	●	●	●
Chile	●	●	○	●	●	○	●	●	●	●22
China	○			●	●		●	○	●	●28
Colombia	●	●	●	●	●	◐10	●	●	●	●
Comoros					●		●		●	○
Congo (Republic of)	●	●		●	●		●		●	●
Cook Islands					●		●			
Costa Rica	●	●	●	●	●	●	●	●	●	●22
Côte d'Ivoire	●	●		●	●		●		●	●
Croatia	●	●	●	●	●	●	●	●	●	●22
Cuba					●	○	●	◐	●	●28
Cyprus	●	●	●	●	●		●	●	●	●22
Czech Republic	●	●	●	●	●	●	●	●	●	●22
Democratic Republic of the Congo	●	●		●	●		●	●	●	●
Denmark	●	●	●	●	●	●	●	●	●	●22
Djibouti	●	●		●	●		●	○	○	●
Dominica	●			●	●		●	●		
Dominican Republic	●	●		●	●	●	●	○	●	○
Ecuador	●	●	●	●	●	●	●	●	●	●22
Egypt	●			●	●		●	◐	●	●
El Salvador	●	●		●	●	○	●	●	●	●
Equatorial Guinea	●	●		●	●		●		●	●28
Eritrea	●			●	●		●	●	●	

Optional Protocol to the Convention against Torture	Convention relating to the Status of Refugees (1951)	Protocol relating to the Status of Refugees (1967)	Convention relating to the Status of Stateless Persons (1954)	Convention on the Reduction of Statelessness (1961)	International Convention on the Protection of the Rights of All Migrant Workers and Members of their Families	Rome Statute of the International Criminal Court	
●	●	●			○	●	Cambodia
	●	●				○	Cameroon
	●	●		●		●	Canada
	●				●	○	Cape Verde
	●	●				●	Central African Republic
	●	●	●	●		●	Chad
○	●	●			●	○	Chile
	●	●					China
	●	●	○		●	●124	Colombia
					○	●	Comoros
	●	●				●	Congo (Republic of)
							Cook Islands
●	●	●	●	●		●	Costa Rica
	●	●				○12	Côte d'Ivoire
●	●	●	●			●	Croatia
							Cuba
○	●	●				●	Cyprus
●	●	●	●	●		○	Czech Republic
	●	●				●	Democratic Republic of the Congo
●	●	●	●	●		●	Denmark
	●	●				●	Djibouti
	●	●				●	Dominica
	●	●		○		●	Dominican Republic
○	●	●	●		●	●	Ecuador
	●	●			●	○	Egypt
	●	●	○		●		El Salvador
	●	●					Equatorial Guinea
						○	Eritrea

● state is a party

● state became party in 2007

○ signed but not yet ratified

○ signed in 2007, but not yet ratified

10 Declaration under Article 10 not recognizing the competence of the CEDAW Committee to undertake confidential inquiries into allegations of grave or systematic violations

22 Declaration under Article 22 recognizing the competence of the Committee against Torture (CAT) to consider individual complaints

28 Reservation under Article 28 not recognizing the competence of the CAT to undertake confidential inquiries into allegations of systematic torture if warranted

12 Declaration under Article 12(3) accepting the jurisdiction of the International Criminal Court (ICC) for crimes in its territory

124 Declaration under Article 124 not accepting the jurisdiction of the ICC over war crimes for seven years after ratification

* Signed the Rome Statute but have since formally declared their intention not to ratify

** Acceded in 1962 but in 1965 denounced the Convention; denunciation took effect on 2 April 1966

	International Covenant on Civil and Political Rights (ICCPR)	(first) Optional Protocol to the ICCPR	Second Optional Protocol to the ICCPR, aiming at the abolition of the death penalty	International Covenant on Economic, Social and Cultural Rights	Convention on the Elimination of All Forms of Discrimination against Women (CEDAW)	Optional Protocol to CEDAW	Convention on the Rights of the Child (CRC)	Optional Protocol to the CRC on the involvement of chidren in armed conflict	International Convention on the Elimination of All Forms of Racial Discrimination	Convention against Torture and Other Cruel, Inhuman or Degrading Treatment or Punishment
Estonia	●	●	●	●	●		●	○	●	●
Ethiopia	●			●	●		●		●	●
Fiji					●		●	○	●	
Finland	●	●	●	●	●	●	●	●	●	●[22]
France	●	●	●	●	●	●	●	●	●	●[22]
Gabon	●			●	●	●	●	○	●	●
Gambia	●	●		●	●		●	○	●	○
Georgia	●	●	●	●	●	●	●		●	●[22]
Germany	●	●	●	●	●	●	●	●	●	●[22]
Ghana	●	●		●	●	○	●	○	●	●[22]
Greece	●	●	●	●	●	●	●	●	●	●[22]
Grenada	●			●	●		●		○	
Guatemala	●	●		●	●	●	●	●	●	●[22]
Guinea	●	●		●	●		●		●	●
Guinea-Bissau	○	○	○	●	●	○	●	○	○	○
Guyana	●	●		●	●		●		●	●
Haiti	●				●		●	○	●	
Holy See							●	●	●	●
Honduras	●	●	○	●	●		●	●	●	●
Hungary	●	●	●	●	●	●	●	○	●	●[22]
Iceland	●	●	●	●	●	●	●	●	●	●[22]
India	●			●	●		●	●	●	○
Indonesia	●			●	●	○	●	○	●	●[22]
Iran	●			●			●		●	
Iraq	●			●	●		●		●	
Ireland	●	●	●	●	●	●	●	●	●	●[22]
Israel	●			●	●		●	●	●	●[22]
Italy	●	●	●	●	●	●	●	●	●	●[22]

Optional Protocol to the Convention against Torture	Convention relating to the Status of Refugees (1951)	Protocol relating to the Status of Refugees (1967)	Convention relating to the Status of Stateless Persons (1954)	Convention on the Reduction of Statelessness (1961)	International Convention on the Protection of the Rights of All Migrant Workers and Members of their Families	Rome Statute of the International Criminal Court	
●	●	●				●	Estonia
	●	●					Ethiopia
	●	●	●			●	Fiji
○	●	●	●			●	Finland
○	●	●	●	○		●124	France
○	●	●			○	●	Gabon
	●	●				●	Gambia
●	●	●				●	Georgia
○	●	●	●	●		●	Germany
○	●	●			●	●	Ghana
	●	●	●			●	Greece
							Grenada
○	●	●	●	●	●		Guatemala
○	●	●	●		●	●	Guinea
	●	●			○	○	Guinea-Bissau
					○	●	Guyana
	●	●				○	Haiti
	●	●	○				Holy See
●	●	●	○		●	●	Honduras
	●	●	●			●	Hungary
○	●	●				●	Iceland
							India
					○		Indonesia
	●	●				○	Iran
							Iraq
○	●	●	●	●		●	Ireland
	●	●	●	○		○*	Israel
○	●	●	●			●	Italy

SELECTED TREATIES
INTERNATIONAL

● state is a party
● state became party in 2007
○ signed but not yet ratified
○ signed in 2007, but not yet ratified

10 Declaration under Article 10 not recognizing the competence of the CEDAW Committee to undertake confidential inquiries into allegations of grave or systematic violations

22 Declaration under Article 22 recognizing the competence of the Committee against Torture (CAT) to consider individual complaints

28 Reservation under Article 28 not recognizing the competence of the CAT to undertake confidential inquiries into allegations of systematic torture if warranted

12 Declaration under Article 12(3) accepting the jurisdiction of the International Criminal Court (ICC) for crimes in its territory

124 Declaration under Article 124 not accepting the jurisdiction of the ICC over war crimes for seven years after ratification

* Signed the Rome Statute but have since formally declared their intention not to ratify

** Acceded in 1962 but in 1965 denounced the Convention; denunciation took effect on 2 April 1966

	International Covenant on Civil and Political Rights (ICCPR)	(first) Optional Protocol to the ICCPR	Second Optional Protocol to the ICCPR, aiming at the abolition of the death penalty	International Covenant on Economic, Social and Cultural Rights	Convention on the Elimination of All Forms of Discrimination against Women (CEDAW)	Optional Protocol to CEDAW	Convention on the Rights of the Child (CRC)	Optional Protocol to the CRC on the involvement of chidren in armed conflict	International Convention on the Elimination of All Forms of Racial Discrimination	Convention against Torture and Other Cruel, Inhuman or Degrading Treatment or Punishment
Jamaica	●			●	●		●	●	●	
Japan	●			●	●		●	●	●	●
Jordan	●			●	●		●	◐	●	●
Kazakhstan	●	○		●	●	●	●	●	●	●
Kenya	●			●	●		●	●	●	●
Kiribati					●		●			
Korea (Democratic People's Republic of)	●			●	●		●			
Korea (Republic of)	●	●		●	●	●	●	●	●	●22
Kuwait	●			●	●		●		●	●28
Kyrgyzstan	●	●		●	●	●	●	●	●	●
Laos	○			◐	●		●	●	●	
Latvia	●	●		●	●		●	●	●	●
Lebanon	●			●	●		●	○	●	●
Lesotho	●	●		●	●	●	●	●	●	●
Liberia	●	○	●	●	●	○	●	○	●	●
Libya	●	●		●	●	●	●	●	●	●
Liechtenstein	●	●	●	●	●	●	●	●	●	●22
Lithuania	●	●	●	●	●	●	●	●	●	●
Luxembourg	●	●	●	●	●	●	●	●	●	●22
Macedonia	●	●	●	●	●	●	●	●	●	●
Madagascar	●	●		●	●	○	●	●	●	●
Malawi	●	●		●	●	○	●	○	●	●
Malaysia					●		●			
Maldives	●	●		●	●	●	●	●	●	●
Mali	●	●		●	●	●	●	●	●	●
Malta	●	●	●	●	●		●	●	●	●22
Marshall Islands					●		●			
Mauritania	●			●	●		●		●	●22

Optional Protocol to the Convention against Torture	Convention relating to the Status of Refugees (1951)	Protocol relating to the Status of Refugees (1967)	Convention relating to the Status of Stateless Persons (1954)	Convention on the Reduction of Statelessness (1961)	International Convention on the Protection of the Rights of All Migrant Workers and Members of their Families	Rome Statute of the International Criminal Court	
	●	●				○	Jamaica
	●	●				●	Japan
						●	Jordan
○	●	●				●	Kazakstan
	●	●				●	Kenya
			●	●			Kiribati
							Korea (Democratic People's Republic of)
	●	●	●			●	Korea (Republic of)
						○	Kuwait
	●	●			●	○	Kyrgyzstan
							Laos
	●	●	●	●		●	Latvia
							Lebanon
	●	●	●	●	●	●	Lesotho
●	●	●	●	●	○	●	Liberia
			●	●	●		Libya
●	●	●	○			●	Liechtenstein
	●	●	●			●	Lithuania
○	●	●	●			●	Luxembourg
○	●	●	●			●	Macedonia
○	●		**			○	Madagascar
	●	●				●	Malawi
							Malaysia
●							Maldives
●	●	●			●	●	Mali
●	●	●				●	Malta
						●	Marshall Islands
	●	●			●		Mauritania

- ● state is a party
- ● state became party in 2007
- ○ signed but not yet ratified
- ○ signed in 2007, but not yet ratified

10 Declaration under Article 10 not recognizing the competence of the CEDAW Committee to undertake confidential inquiries into allegations of grave or systematic violations

22 Declaration under Article 22 recognizing the competence of the Committee against Torture (CAT) to consider individual complaints

28 Reservation under Article 28 not recognizing the competence of the CAT to undertake confidential inquiries into allegations of systematic torture if warranted

12 Declaration under Article 12(3) accepting the jurisdiction of the International Criminal Court (ICC) for crimes in its territory

124 Declaration under Article 124 not accepting the jurisdiction of the ICC over war crimes for seven years after ratification

* Signed the Rome Statute but have since formally declared their intention not to ratify

** Acceded in 1962 but in 1965 denounced the Convention; denunciation took effect on 2 April 1966

	International Covenant on Civil and Political Rights (ICCPR)	(first) Optional Protocol to the ICCPR	Second Optional Protocol to the ICCPR, aiming at the abolition of the death penalty	International Covenant on Economic, Social and Cultural Rights	Convention on the Elimination of All Forms of Discrimination against Women (CEDAW)	Optional Protocol to CEDAW	Convention on the Rights of the Child (CRC)	Optional Protocol to the CRC on the involvement of chidren in armed conflict	International Convention on the Elimination of All Forms of Racial Discrimination	Convention against Torture and Other Cruel, Inhuman or Degrading Treatment or Punishment
Mauritius	●	●		●	●	○	●	○	●	●
Mexico	●	●	◐	●	●	●	●	●	●	●[22]
Micronesia					●		●	○		
Moldova	●	○	●	●	●	●	●	●	●	●
Monaco	●		●	●	●		●	●	●	●[22]
Mongolia	●	●		●	●	●	●	●	●	●
Montenegro	●	●	●	●	●	●	●	◐	●	●[22]
Morocco	●			●	●		●	●	●	●
Mozambique	●		●		●		●	●	●	●
Myanmar					●		●			
Namibia	●	●	●	●	●	●	●	●	●	●
Nauru	○	○					●	○	○	○
Nepal	●	●	●	●	●	◐	●	◐	●	●
Netherlands	●	●	●	●	●	●	●	○	●	●[22]
New Zealand	●	●	●	●	●	●	●	●	●	●[22]
Nicaragua	●	●	○	●	●		●	●	●	●
Niger	●	●		●	●	●	●		●	●
Nigeria	●			●	●	●	●	○	●	●
Niue							●			
Norway	●	●	●	●	●	●	●	●	●	●[22]
Oman					●		●	●	●	
Pakistan				○	●		●	○	●	
Palau							●			
Panama	●	●	●	●	●	●	●	●	●	●
Papua New Guinea					●		●		●	
Paraguay	●	●	●	●	●	●	●	●	●	●[22]
Peru	●	●		●	●	●	●	●	●	●[22]
Philippines	●	●	○	●	●	●	●	●	●	●

SELECTED TREATIES INTERNATIONAL

Optional Protocol to the Convention against Torture	Convention relating to the Status of Refugees (1951)	Protocol relating to the Status of Refugees (1967)	Convention relating to the Status of Stateless Persons (1954)	Convention on the Reduction of Statelessness (1961)	International Convention on the Protection of the Rights of All Migrant Workers and Members of their Families	Rome Statute of the International Criminal Court	
●						●	Mauritius
●	●	●	●		●	●	Mexico
							Micronesia
●	●	●				○	Moldova
	●					○	Monaco
						●	Mongolia
●	●	●	●		○	●	Montenegro
	●	●			●	○	Morocco
	●	●				○	Mozambique
							Myanmar
	●	●				●	Namibia
						●	Nauru
							Nepal
○	●	●	●	●		●	Netherlands
◐	●	●		●		●	New Zealand
○	●	●			●		Nicaragua
	●	●		●		●	Niger
	●	●				●	Nigeria
							Niue
○	●	●	●	●		●	Norway
						○	Oman
							Pakistan
							Palau
	●	●				●	Panama
	●	●					Papua New Guinea
●	●	●			○	●	Paraguay
●	●	●			●	●	Peru
	●	●	○		●	○	Philippines

● state is a party
● state became party in 2007
○ signed but not yet ratified
○ signed in 2007, but not yet ratified

10 Declaration under Article 10 not recognizing the competence of the CEDAW Committee to undertake confidential inquiries into allegations of grave or systematic violations

22 Declaration under Article 22 recognizing the competence of the Committee against Torture (CAT) to consider individual complaints

28 Reservation under Article 28 not recognizing the competence of the CAT to undertake confidential inquiries into allegations of systematic torture if warranted

12 Declaration under Article 12(3) accepting the jurisdiction of the International Criminal Court (ICC) for crimes in its territory

124 Declaration under Article 124 not accepting the jurisdiction of the ICC over war crimes for seven years after ratification

* Signed the Rome Statute but have since formally declared their intention not to ratify

** Acceded in 1962 but in 1965 denounced the Convention; denunciation took effect on 2 April 1966

	International Covenant on Civil and Political Rights (ICCPR)	(first) Optional Protocol to the ICCPR	Second Optional Protocol to the ICCPR, aiming at the abolition of the death penalty	International Covenant on Economic, Social and Cultural Rights	Convention on the Elimination of All Forms of Discrimination against Women (CEDAW)	Optional Protocol to CEDAW	Convention on the Rights of the Child (CRC)	Optional Protocol to the CRC on the involvement of children in armed conflict	International Convention on the Elimination of All Forms of Racial Discrimination	Convention against Torture and Other Cruel, Inhuman or Degrading Treatment or Punishment
Poland	●	●	○	●	●	●	●	●	●	[28]●[22]
Portugal	●	●	●	●	●	●	●	●	●	●[22]
Qatar							●	●	●	●
Romania	●	●	●	●	●	●	●	●	●	●
Russian Federation	●	●		●	●	●	●	○	●	●[22]
Rwanda	●			●	●		●	●	●	
Saint Kitts and Nevis					●	●	●		●	
Saint Lucia					●		●		●	
Saint Vincent and the Grenadines	●	●		●	●		●		●	●
Samoa					●		●			
San Marino	●	●	●	●	●	●	●	○	●	●
Sao Tome and Principe	○	○	○	○	●	○	●		○	○
Saudi Arabia					●		●		●	●[28]
Senegal	●	●		●	●	●	●	●	●	●[22]
Serbia	●	●	●	●	●	●	●	●	●	●[22]
Seychelles	●	●	●	●	●	○	●	○	●	●[22]
Sierra Leone	●	●		●	●	○	●	●	●	●
Singapore					●		●	○		
Slovakia	●	●	●	●	●	●	●	●	●	●[22]
Slovenia	●	●	●	●	●	●	●	●	●	●[22]
Solomon Islands				●	●	●	●		●	
Somalia	●	●		●			○	○	●	●
South Africa	●	●	●	○	●	●	●	○	●	●[22]
Spain	●	●	●	●	●	●	●	●	●	●[22]
Sri Lanka	●	●		●	●		●	●	●	●
Sudan	●			●			●	●	●	○
Suriname	●	●		●	●		●	○	●	
Swaziland	●			●	●		●		●	●

Optional Protocol to the Convention against Torture	Convention relating to the Status of Refugees (1951)	Protocol relating to the Status of Refugees (1967)	Convention relating to the Status of Stateless Persons (1954)	Convention on the Reduction of Statelessness (1961)	International Convention on the Protection of the Rights of All Migrant Workers and Members of their Families	Rome Statute of the International Criminal Court	Country
●	●	●				●	Poland
○	●	●				●	Portugal
							Qatar
○	●	●	●	●		●	Romania
	●	●				○	Russian Federation
	●	●	●	●			Rwanda
	●					●	Saint Kitts and Nevis
						○	Saint Lucia
	●	●	●				Saint Vincent and the Grenadines
	●	●				●	Samoa
						●	San Marino
	●	●			○	○	Sao Tome and Principe
							Saudi Arabia
●	●	●	●	●	●	●	Senegal
●	●	●	●		○	●	Serbia
	●	●			●	○	Seychelles
○	●	●			○	●	Sierra Leone
							Singapore
	●	●	●	●		●	Slovakia
◐	●	●	●			●	Slovenia
	●	●				○	Solomon Islands
	●	●					Somalia
○	●	●				●	South Africa
●	●	●	●			●	Spain
					●		Sri Lanka
	●	●				○	Sudan
	●	●					Suriname
	●	●	●	●			Swaziland

● state is a party
◐ state became party in 2007
○ signed but not yet ratified
○ signed in 2007, but not yet ratified

10 Declaration under Article 10 not recognizing the competence of the CEDAW Committee to undertake confidential inquiries into allegations of grave or systematic violations

22 Declaration under Article 22 recognizing the competence of the Committee against Torture (CAT) to consider individual complaints

28 Reservation under Article 28 not recognizing the competence of the CAT to undertake confidential inquiries into allegations of systematic torture if warranted

12 Declaration under Article 12(3) accepting the jurisdiction of the International Criminal Court (ICC) for crimes in its territory

124 Declaration under Article 124 not accepting the jurisdiction of the ICC over war crimes for seven years after ratification

* Signed the Rome Statute but have since formally declared their intention not to ratify

** Acceded in 1962 but in 1965 denounced the Convention; denunciation took effect on 2 April 1966

	International Covenant on Civil and Political Rights (ICCPR)	(first) Optional Protocol to the ICCPR	Second Optional Protocol to the ICCPR, aiming at the abolition of the death penalty	International Covenant on Economic, Social and Cultural Rights	Convention on the Elimination of All Forms of Discrimination against Women (CEDAW)	Optional Protocol to CEDAW	Convention on the Rights of the Child (CRC)	Optional Protocol to the CRC on the involvement of chidren in armed conflict	International Convention on the Elimination of All Forms of Racial Discrimination	Convention against Torture and Other Cruel, Inhuman or Degrading Treatment or Punishment
Sweden	●	●	●	●	●	●	●	●	●	●22
Switzerland	●		●	●	●	○	●	●	●	●22
Syria	●			●	●		●	●	●	●28
Tajikistan	●	●		●	●	○	●	●	●	●
Tanzania	●			●	●	●	●	●	●	
Thailand	●			●	●	●	●	●	●	◐
Timor-Leste	●		●	●	●	●	●	●	●	●
Togo	●	●		●	●		●	●	●	●22
Tonga							●		●	
Trinidad and Tobago	●			●	●		●		●	
Tunisia	●			●	●		●	●	●	●22
Turkey	●			●	●	●	●	●	●	●22
Turkmenistan	●	●	●	●	●		●		●	●
Tuvalu					●		●			
Uganda	●	●		●	●		●	●	●	●
Ukraine	●	●	◐	●	●	●	●	●	●	●22
United Arab Emirates					●		●		●	
United Kingdom	●		●	●	●	●	●	●	●	●
United States of America	●			○	○		○	●	●	●
Uruguay	●	●	●	●	●	●	●	●	●	●22
Uzbekistan	●	●		●	●		●		●	●
Vanuatu					●	◐	●	◐		
Venezuela	●	●	●	●	●	●	●	●	●	●22
Viet Nam	●			●	●		●	●	●	
Yemen	●			●	●		●	◐	●	●
Zambia	●	●		●	●		●		●	●
Zimbabwe	●			●	●		●		●	

354

SELECTED TREATIES INTERNATIONAL

Optional Protocol to the Convention against Torture	Convention relating to the Status of Refugees (1951)	Protocol relating to the Status of Refugees (1967)	Convention relating to the Status of Stateless Persons (1954)	Convention on the Reduction of Statelessness (1961)	International Convention on the Protection of the Rights of All Migrant Workers and Members of their Families	Rome Statute of the International Criminal Court	Country
●	●	●	●	●		●	Sweden
○	●	●	●			●	Switzerland
					●	○	Syria
	●	●			●	●	Tajikistan
	●	●				●	Tanzania
						○	Thailand
○	●	●			●	●	Timor-Leste
○	●	●				○	Togo
							Tonga
	●	●	●			●	Trinidad and Tobago
	●	●	●	●			Tunisia
○	●	●			●		Turkey
	●	●					Turkmenistan
	●	●					Tuvalu
	●	●	●		●	●	Uganda
●	●	●				○	Ukraine
						○	United Arab Emirates
●	●	●	●	●		●	United Kingdom
		●				○*	United States of America
●	●	●	●	●	●	●	Uruguay
						○	Uzbekistan
							Vanuatu
		●				●	Venezuela
							Viet Nam
	●	●				○	Yemen
	●	●	●			●	Zambia
	●	●	●			○	Zimbabwe

Legend

- ● state is a party
- ● state became party in 2007
- ○ signed but not yet ratified
- ○ signed in 2007, but not yet ratified

10 Declaration under Article 10 not recognizing the competence of the CEDAW Committee to undertake confidential inquiries into allegations of grave or systematic violations

22 Declaration under Article 22 recognizing the competence of the Committee against Torture (CAT) to consider individual complaints

28 Reservation under Article 28 not recognizing the competence of the CAT to undertake confidential inquiries into allegations of systematic torture if warranted

12 Declaration under Article 12(3) accepting the jurisdiction of the International Criminal Court (ICC) for crimes in its territory

124 Declaration under Article 124 not accepting the jurisdiction of the ICC over war crimes for seven years after ratification

* Signed the Rome Statute but have since formally declared their intention not to ratify

** Acceded in 1962 but in 1965 denounced the Convention; denunciation took effect on 2 April 1966

	African Charter on Human and Peoples' Rights (1981)	Protocol to the African Charter on the Establishment of an African Court on Human and Peoples' Rights (1998)	African Charter on the Rights and Welfare of the Child (1990)	Convention Governing the Specific Aspects of Refugee Problems in Africa (1969)	Protocol to the African Charter on Human and Peoples' Rights on the Rights of Women in Africa (2003)
Algeria	●	●	●	●	○
Angola	●	○	●	●	○
Benin	●	○	●	●	●
Botswana	●	○	●	●	
Burkina Faso	●	●	●	●	●
Burundi	●	●	●	●	○
Cameroon	●	○	●	●	○
Cape Verde	●		●	●	●
Central African Republic	●	○	○	●	
Chad	●	○	●	●	○
Comoros	●	●	●	●	●
Congo (Republic of)	●	○	●	●	○
Côte d'Ivoire	●	●	◐	●	○
Democratic Republic of the Congo	●	○		●	○
Djibouti	●	○	○	○	●
Egypt	●	○	●	●	
Equatorial Guinea	●	○	●	●	○
Eritrea	●		●		
Ethiopia	●	○	●	●	○
Gabon	●	●	◐	●	○
Gambia	●	●	●	●	●
Ghana	●	●	●	●	○
Guinea	●	○	●	●	○
Guinea-Bissau	●	○	○	●	○
Kenya	●	●	●	●	○
Lesotho	●	●	●	●	●
Liberia	●	○	○	●	○
Libya	●	●	●	●	●
Madagascar	●	○	●	○	○

	African Charter on Human and Peoples' Rights (1981)	Protocol to the African Charter on the Establishment of an African Court on Human and Peoples' Rights (1998)	African Charter on the Rights and Welfare of the Child (1990)	Convention Governing the Specific Aspects of Refugee Problems in Africa (1969)	Protocol to the African Charter on Human and Peoples' Rights on the Rights of Women in Africa (2003)
Malawi	●	○	●	●	●
Mali	●	●	●	●	●
Mauritania	●	●	●	●	●
Mauritius	●	●	●	○	○
Mozambique	●	●	●	●	●
Namibia	●	○	●	●	●
Niger	●	●	●	●	○
Nigeria	●	●	●	●	●
Rwanda	●	●	●	●	●
Sahrawi Arab Democratic Republic	●		○		○
Sao Tome and Principe	●				
Senegal	●	●	●	●	●
Seychelles	●	○	●	●	●
Sierra Leone	●	○	●	●	○
Somalia	●	○	○	○	○
South Africa	●	●	●	●	●
Sudan	●	○		●	
Swaziland	●	○	○	●	○
Tanzania	●	●	●	●	● (became party 2007)
Togo	●	●	●	●	●
Tunisia	●	● (became party 2007)	○	●	
Uganda	●	●	●	●	○
Zambia	●	○	○	●	●
Zimbabwe	●	○	●	●	○

● state is a party
● state became party in 2007
○ signed but not yet ratified
○ signed in 2007, but not yet ratified

This chart lists countries that were members of the African Union at the end of 2007.

	American Convention on Human Rights (1969)	Protocol to the American Convention on Human Rights to Abolish the Death Penalty (1990)	Additional Protocol to the American Convention on Human Rights in the Area of Economic, Social and Cultural Rights	Inter-American Convention to Prevent and Punish Torture (1985)	Inter-American Convention on Forced Disappearance of Persons (1994)	Inter-American Convention on the Prevention, Punishment and Eradication of Violence Against Women (1994)	Inter-American Convention on the Elimination of All Forms of Discrimination against Persons with Disabilities (1999)
Antigua and Barbuda						●	
Argentina	●[62]	○	●	●	●	●	●
Bahamas						●	
Barbados	●[62]					●	
Belize						●	
Bolivia	●[62]		●	●	●	●	●
Brazil	●[62]	●	●	●	○	●	●
Canada							
Chile	●[62]	○	○	●	○	●	●
Colombia	●[62]		●	●	●	●	●
Costa Rica	●[62]	●	●	●	●	●	●
Cuba*							
Dominica	●					●	○
Dominican Republic	●[62]		○	●		●	●
Ecuador	●[62]	●	●	●	●	●	●
El Salvador	●[62]		●	●		●	●
Grenada	●						
Guatemala	●[62]		●	●	●	●	●
Guyana						●	
Haiti	●[62]		○	○		●	○
Honduras	●[62]			○	●		
Jamaica	●					●	○
Mexico	●[62]	●	●	●	●	●	●
Nicaragua	●[62]	●	○	○	○	●	●
Panama	●[62]	●	●	●	●	●	●

	American Convention on Human Rights (1969)	Protocol to the American Convention on Human Rights to Abolish the Death Penalty (1990)	Additional Protocol to the American Convention on Human Rights in the Area of Economic, Social and Cultural Rights	Inter-American Convention to Prevent and Punish Torture (1985)	Inter-American Convention on Forced Disappearance of Persons (1994)	Inter-American Convention on the Prevention, Punishment and Eradication of Violence Against Women (1994)	Inter-American Convention on the Elimination of All Forms of Discrimination against Persons with Disabilities (1999)
Paraguay	●62	●	●	●	●	●	●
Peru	●62		●	●	●	●	●
Saint Kitts and Nevis						●	
Saint Lucia						●	
Saint Vincent and the Grenadines						●	
Suriname	●62		●	●		●	
Trinidad and Tobago						●	
United States of America	○						
Uruguay	●62	●	●	●	●	●	●
Venezuela	●62	●	○	●	●	●	●

● state is a party
● state became party in 2007
○ signed but not yet ratified
○ signed in 2007, but not yet ratified

This chart lists countries that were members of the Organization of American States at the end of 2007.

62 Countries making a Declaration under Article 62 recognize as binding the jurisdiction of the Inter-American Court of Human Rights (on all matters relating to the interpretation or application of the American Convention)

* In 1962 the VIII Meeting of Consultation of Ministers of Foreign Affairs decided to exclude Cuba from participating in the Inter-American system.

	European Convention for the Protection of Human Rights and Fundamental Freedoms (ECHR) (1950)	Protocol No. 6 to the ECHR concerning the abolition of the death penalty in times of peace (1983)	Protocol No. 12 to the ECHR concerning the general prohibition of discrimination (2000)	Protocol No. 13 to the ECHR concerning the abolition of the death penalty in all circumstances (2002)	Framework Convention on the Protection of National Minorities (1995)
Albania	●	●	●	●	●
Andorra	●	●	○	●	
Armenia	●	●	●	○	●
Austria	●	●	○	●	●
Azerbaijan	●	●	○		●
Belgium	●	●	○	●	○
Bosnia and Herzegovina	●	●	●	●	●
Bulgaria	●	●		●	●
Croatia	●	●	●	●	●
Cyprus	●	●	●	●	●
Czech Republic	●	●	○	●	●
Denmark	●	●		●	●
Estonia	●	●	○	●	●
Finland	●	●	●	●	●
France	●	●		●	
Georgia	●	●	●	●	●
Germany	●	●	○	●	●
Greece	●	●	○	●	○
Hungary	●	●	○	●	●
Iceland	●	●	○	●	○
Ireland	●	●	○	●	●
Italy	●	●	○	○	●
Latvia	●	●	○	○	●
Liechtenstein	●	●	○	●	●
Lithuania	●	●		●	●

	European Convention for the Protection of Human Rights and Fundamental Freedoms (ECHR) (1950)	Protocol No. 6 to the ECHR concerning the abolition of the death penalty in times of peace (1983)	Protocol No. 12 to the ECHR concerning the general prohibition of discrimination (2000)	Protocol No. 13 to the ECHR concerning the abolition of the death penalty in all circumstances (2002)	Framework Convention on the Protection of National Minorities (1995)
Luxembourg	●	●	●	●	○
Macedonia	●	●	●	●	●
Malta	●	●		●	●
Moldova	●	●	○	●	●
Monaco	●	●		●	
Montenegro	●	●	●	●	●
Netherlands	●	●	●	●	●
Norway	●	●	○	●	●
Poland	●	●		○	●
Portugal	●	●	○	●	●
Romania	●	●	●	●	●
Russian Federation	●	○	○		●
San Marino	●	●	●	●	●
Serbia	●	●	●	●	●
Slovakia	●	●	○	●	●
Slovenia	●	●	○	●	●
Spain	●	●	○	○	●
Sweden	●	●		●	●
Switzerland	●	●		●	●
Turkey	●	●	○	●	
Ukraine	●	●	●	●	●
United Kingdom	●	●		●	●

● state is a party
● state became party in 2007
○ signed but not yet ratified
○ signed in 2007, but not yet ratified

This chart lists countries that were members of the Council of Europe at the end of 2007.

Abu Abdullah, right, in the debris of his
shop in the Sadriyah outdoor market,
Baghdad. Two of his sons were killed in a
suicide bombing on 4 February 2007,
along with at least 130 other people.

AMNESTY INTERNATIONAL REPORT 2008
PART FOUR

A police officer aims his gun at a woman as people protest beside a body after a shootout between police and suspected drug traffickers at the Complexo do Alemão favela in Rio de Janeiro, Brazil, 13 February 2007.

AMNESTY INTERNATIONAL
SECTIONS

Algeria ❖ Amnesty International,
10, rue Mouloud ZADI (face au 113 rue
Didouche Mourad), Alger Centre,
16004 Alger
email: amnestyalgeria@hotmail.com
www.amnestyalgeria.org

Argentina ❖ Amnistía Internacional,
Av. Rivadavia 2206 - P4A,
C1032ACO Ciudad de Buenos Aires
email: administracion@amnesty.org.ar
www.amnesty.org.ar

Australia ❖ Amnesty International,
Locked Bag 23, Broadway NSW 2007
email: servicecentre@amnesty.org.au
www.amnesty.org.au

Austria ❖ Amnesty International,
Moeringgasse 10,
A-1150 Vienna
email: info@amnesty.at
www.amnesty.at

Belgium ❖
Amnesty International **(Flemish-speaking)**,
Kerkstraat 156, 2060 Antwerpen
email: amnesty@aivl.be
www.aivl.be
Amnesty International **(francophone)**,
Rue Berckmans 9, 1060 Bruxelles
email: aibf@aibf.be
www.aibf.be

Benin ❖ Amnesty International,
Carré 865, Immeuble François Gomez,
Quartier Aidjedo (après le Centre d'Accueil
en venant de la BIBE),
Cotonou
email: aibenin@leland.bj

Bermuda ❖ Amnesty International,
PO Box HM 2136, Hamilton HM JX
email: aibda@ibl.bm

Canada ❖
Amnesty International **(English-speaking)**,
312 Laurier Avenue East, Ottawa,
Ontario, K1N 1H9
email: info@amnesty.ca
www.amnesty.ca
Amnistie Internationale **(francophone)**,
6250 boulevard Monk, Montréal,
Québec, H4E 3H7
email: info@amnistie.ca
www.amnistie.ca

Chile ❖ Amnistía Internacional,
Oficina Nacional, Huelén 164 - Piso 2,
750-0617 Providencia, Santiago
email: info@amnistia.cl
www.amnistia.cl

Côte d'Ivoire ❖ Amnesty International,
04 BP 895, Abidjan 04
email: aicotedivoire@yahoo.fr

Denmark ❖ Amnesty International,
Gammeltorv 8, 5, DK - 1457 Copenhagen K.
email: amnesty@amnesty.dk
www.amnesty.dk

Faroe Islands ❖ Amnesty International,
Hoydalsvegur 6, FO-100 Tórshavn
email: amnesty@amnesty.fo
www.amnesty.fo

Finland ❖ Amnesty International,
Ruoholahdenkatu 24, D 00180 Helsinki
email: amnesty@amnesty.fi
www.amnesty.fi

France ❖ Amnesty International,
76 Boulevard de la Villette, 75940 Paris, Cédex 19
email: info@amnesty.fr
www.amnesty.fr

Germany ❖ Amnesty International,
Heerstrasse 178, 53111 Bonn
email: info@amnesty.de
www.amnesty.de

Greece ❖ Amnesty International,
Sina 30, 106 72 Athens
email: info@amnesty.org.gr
www.amnesty.org.gr

Hong Kong ❖ Amnesty International,
Unit D, 3/F, Best-O-Best Commercial Centre,
32-36 Ferry Street, Kowloon
email: admin-hk@amnesty.org.hk
www.amnesty.org.hk

Iceland ❖ Amnesty International,
Hafnarstræti 15, 101 Reykjavík
email: amnesty@amnesty.is
www.amnesty.is

Ireland ❖ Amnesty International,
1st Floor, Ballast House,
18-21 Westmoreland St, Dublin 2
email: info@amnesty.ie
www.amnesty.ie

Israel ❖ Amnesty International,
PO Box 14179, Tel Aviv 61141
email: amnesty@netvision.net.il
www.amnesty.org.il

Italy ❖ Amnesty International,
Via Giovanni Battista De Rossi, 10,
00161 Roma
email: info@amnesty.it
www.amnesty.it

Japan ❖ Amnesty International,
4F Kyodo Bldg., 2-2 Kandanishiki-cho, Chiyoda-ku,
Tokyo 101-0054
email: info@amnesty.or.jp
www.amnesty.or.jp

Korea (Republic of) ❖ Amnesty International,
Gwanghwamun PO Box 2045, Chongno-gu,
Seoul, 110-620
email: info@amnesty.or.kr
www.amnesty.or.kr

Luxembourg ❖ Amnesty International,
Boîte Postale 1914, 1019 Luxembourg
email: info@amnesty.lu
www.amnesty.lu

Mauritius ❖ Amnesty International,
BP 69, Rose-Hill
email: amnestymtius@intnet.mu

Mexico ❖ Amnistía Internacional,
Insurgentes sur 327 Oficina C,
Col. Hipódromo Condesa, CP 6100, Mexico DF
email: informacion@amnistia.org.mx
www.amnistia.org.mx

Morocco ❖ Amnesty International,
281 avenue Mohamed V, Apt. 23, Escalier A,
Rabat
email: amorocco@sections.amnesty.org

Nepal ❖ Amnesty International,
PO Box 135, Amnesty Marga, Basantanagar,
Balaju, Kathmandu
email: info@amnestynepal.org
www.amnestynepal.org

Netherlands ❖ Amnesty International,
Keizersgracht 177, 1016 DR Amsterdam
email: amnesty@amnesty.nl
www.amnesty.nl

New Zealand ❖ Amnesty International,
PO Box 5300, Wellesley Street, Auckland
email: info@amnesty.org.nz
www.amnesty.org.nz

Norway ❖ Amnesty International,
Tordenskiolds gate 6B, 0106 Oslo
email: info@amnesty.no
www.amnesty.no

Peru ❖ Amnistía Internacional,
Enrique Palacios 735-A, Miraflores, Lima
email: admin-pe@amnesty.org
www.amnistia.org.pe

Philippines ❖ Amnesty International,
17-B, Kasing-kasing Street, Corner K-8th,
Kamias, Quezon City 1101
email: section@amnesty.org.ph
www.amnesty.org.ph

Poland ❖ Amnesty International,
ul. Piêkna 66a, lokal 2, I pietro, 00-672,
Warszawa
email: amnesty@amnesty.org.pl
www.amnesty.org.pl

Portugal ❖ Amnistia Internacional,
Av. Infante Santo, 42, 2°, 1350 - 179 Lisboa
email: aiportugal@amnistia-internacional.pt
www.amnistia-internacional.pt

Puerto Rico ❖ Amnistía Internacional,
Calle Robles 54, Oficina 11, Río Piedras, 00925
email: amnistiapr@amnestypr.org
www.amnistiapr.org

Senegal ❖ Amnesty International,
35a Boulevard du Général de Gaulle, BP 35269,
Dakar Colobane
email: asenegal@sections.amnesty.org
www.amnesty.sn

Sierra Leone ❖ Amnesty International,
PMB 1021, 16 Pademba Road, Freetown
email: aislf@sierratel.sl

Slovenia ❖ Amnesty International,
Beethovnova 7, 1000 Ljubljana
email: amnesty@amnesty.si
www.amnesty.si

Spain ❖ Amnistía Internacional,
Fernando VI, 8, 1° izda, 28004 Madrid
email: info@es.amnesty.org
www.es.amnesty.org

Sweden ❖ Amnesty International,
PO Box 4719, S-11692 Stockholm
email: info@amnesty.se
w.ww.amnesty.se

Switzerland ❖ Amnesty International,
PO Box, 3001 Berne
email: info@amnesty.ch
www.amnesty.ch

Taiwan ❖ Amnesty International,
3F., No. 14, Lane 165, Sec. 1,
Sinsheng S. Rd, Da-an District,
Taipei City 10656
email: amnesty.taiwan@gmail.com
www.aitaiwan.org.tw

Togo ❖ Amnesty International,
2322 Avenue du RPT, Quartier Casablanca,
BP 20013, Lomé
email: aitogo@cafe.tg

Tunisia ❖ Amnesty International,
67 Rue Oum Kalthoum, 3ème étage, Escalier B,
1000 Tunis
email: admin-tn@amnesty.org

United Kingdom ❖ Amnesty International,
The Human Rights Action Centre,
17-25 New Inn Yard, London EC2A 3EA
email: sct@amnesty.org.uk
www.amnesty.org.uk

United States of America ❖
Amnesty International,
5 Penn Plaza, 16th floor, New York,
NY 10001
email: admin-us@aiusa.org
www.amnestyusa.org

Uruguay ❖ Amnistía Internacional,
Wilson Ferreira Aldunate 1220, CP 11100,
Montevideo
email: oficina@amnistia.org.uy
www.amnistia.org.uy

Venezuela ❖ Amnistía Internacional,
Edificio Ateneo de Caracas, piso 6,
Plaza Morelos Los Caobos,
Caracas 1010A
email: admin-ve@amnesty.org
www.amnistia.org.ve

Moldova ❖ Amnesty International,
PO Box 209, MD-2012 Chişinău
email: info@amnesty.md
www.amnesty.md

Mongolia ❖ Amnesty International,
PO Box 180, Ulaanbaatar 210648
email: aimncc@magicnet.mn
www.amnesty.mn

Paraguay ❖ Amnistía Internacional,
Tte. Zotti No. 352 casi Emilio Hassler,
Barrio Villa Morra, Asunción
email: ai-info@py.amnesty.org
www.py.amnesty.org

Turkey ❖ Amnesty International,
Müeyyitzade Mh. Galipdede Cd.
No. 149 Kat:1, D:4, Beyoğlu,
Istanbul
email: posta@amnesty.org.tr
www.amnesty.org.tr

Ukraine ❖ Amnesty International,
vul. Kravchenko, 17, kv.108, Kiev
email: info@amnesty.org.ua
www.amnesty.org.ua

AMNESTY INTERNATIONAL
STRUCTURES

Burkina Faso ❖ Amnesty International,
303 Rue 9.08, 08 BP 11344,
Ouagadougou 08
email: aiburkina@fasonet.bf

Czech Republic ❖ Amnesty International,
Provaznická 3, 110 00, Prague 1
email: amnesty@amnesty.cz
www.amnesty.cz

Hungary ❖ Amnesty International,
Rózsa u. 44, II/4, 1064 Budapest
email: info@amnesty.hu
www.amnesty.hu

Malaysia ❖ Amnesty International,
E6, 3rd floor, Bangunan Khas,
Jalan 8/1E, 46050 Petaling Jaya, Selangor
email: amnesty@tm.net.my
www.aimalaysia.org

AMNESTY INTERNATIONAL
PRE-STRUCTURES

Bolivia ❖ Amnistía Internacional,
Calle Tal Tal No. 582, Esquina
Presbitero Medina (zona Sopocachi),
La Paz
email:direccioneejecutiva_aibolivia@bo.amnesty.org
www.bo.amnesty.org

Mali ❖ Amnesty International,
Badala Sema 1, Immeuble MUTEC
(Ex Jiguissèmè), Rue 84, porte 14, BP E 3885,
Badalabougou, Bamako
email: amnesty.mali@ikatelnet.net

Slovakia ❖ Amnesty International,
Karpatska 11, 811 05 Bratislava
email: amnesty@amnesty.sk
www.amnesty.sk

Thailand ❖ Amnesty International,
641/8 Vara Place, Ladprao Road, Soi 5,
Ladyao, Chatuchak, Bangkok 10900
email: info@amnesty.or.th
www.amnesty.or.th

AMNESTY INTERNATIONAL
SPECIAL PROJECTS

There are Amnesty International Special Projects in the following countries:

Brazil, Croatia, Ecuador, Ghana, India, Kenya, South Africa, Zimbabwe.

AMNESTY INTERNATIONAL
GROUPS

There are also Amnesty International groups in:

Angola, Aruba, Bahamas, Bahrain, Barbados, Belarus, Botswana, Cameroon, Cape Verde, Chad, Colombia, Curaçao, Dominican Republic, Egypt, Estonia, Gambia, Guyana, Jamaica, Jordan, Kuwait, Kyrgyzstan, Lebanon, Liberia, Malta, Mozambique, Palestinian Authority, Pakistan, Russian Federation, Trinidad and Tobago, Uganda, Yemen, Zambia.

More information and contact details on both Amnesty International groups and Amnesty International Special Projects can be found online at www.amnesty.org.

AMNESTY INTERNATIONAL
OFFICES

International Secretariat (IS)
Amnesty International,
Peter Benenson House,
1 Easton Street,
London WC1X 0DW,
United Kingdom
email: amnestyis@amnesty.org
www.amnesty.org

ARABAI (Arabic translation unit)
c/o International Secretariat,
Peter Benenson House, 1 Easton Street,
London WC1X 0DW,
United Kingdom
email: arabai@amnesty.org
www.amnesty-arabic.org

Éditions Francophones d'Amnesty International (EFAI)
17 Rue du Pont-aux-Choux, 75003 Paris,
France
email: ai-efai@amnesty.org
www.efai.org

Editorial de Amnistía Internacional (EDAI)
Calle Valderribas 13, 28007 Madrid,
Spain
email: mlleo@amnesty.org
www.edai.org

European Union (EU) Office
Amnesty International,
Rue d'Arlon 37-41, B-1000 Brussels,
Belgium
email: amnesty-eu@aieu.be
www.amnesty-eu.org

IS Beirut – Middle East and North Africa Regional Office
Amnesty International,
PO Box 13-5696, Chouran Beirut 1102 - 2060,
Lebanon
email: mena@amnesty.org

IS Dakar – Development Field Office
Amnesty International,
SICAP Sacré Coeur Pyrotechnie,
Extension No. 25, BP 47582, Dakar,
Senegal
email: Kolaniya@amnesty.org

IS Geneva – UN Representative Office
Amnesty International,
22 Rue du Cendrier, 4ème étage, CH-1201 Geneva,
Switzerland
email: gvunpost@amnesty.org

IS Hong Kong – Asia Pacific Regional Office
Amnesty International,
16/F Siu On Centre, 188 Lockhart Rd, Wanchai,
Hong Kong
email: admin-ap@amnesty.org

IS Kampala – Africa Regional Office
Amnesty International,
Plot 20A Kawalya Kaggwa Close, PO Box 23966, Kampala,
Uganda
email: ai-aro@amnesty.org

IS Moscow – Russia Resource Centre
Amnesty International,
PO Box 212, Moscow 119019,
Russian Federation
email: msk@amnesty.org
www.amnesty.org.ru

IS New York – UN Representative Office
Amnesty International,
777 UN Plaza, 6th Floor, New York, NY 10017,
USA

IS Paris – Research Office
Amnesty International,
76 Boulevard de la Villette, 75940 Paris, Cédex 19,
France
email: pro@amnesty.org

I WANT
TO HELP

WHETHER IN A HIGH-PROFILE CONFLICT OR A FORGOTTEN CORNER OF THE GLOBE, **AMNESTY INTERNATIONAL** CAMPAIGNS FOR JUSTICE AND FREEDOM FOR ALL AND SEEKS TO GALVANIZE PUBLIC SUPPORT TO BUILD A BETTER WORLD

WHAT CAN YOU DO?

Activists around the world have shown that it is possible to resist the dangerous forces that are undermining human rights. Be part of this movement. Combat those who peddle fear and hate.

- Join Amnesty International and become part of a worldwide movement campaigning for an end to human rights violations. Help us make a difference.

- Make a donation to support Amnesty International's work.

Together we can make our voices heard.

I am interested in receiving further information on becoming a member of Amnesty International

name

address

country

email

I wish to make a donation to Amnesty International (donations will be taken in UK£, US$ or euros)

amount

please debit my: Visa ☐ Mastercard ☐

number ☐☐☐☐☐ ☐☐☐☐☐ ☐☐☐☐☐ ☐☐☐☐

expiry date

signature

Please return this form to the Amnesty International office in your country.
(See pages 368-371 for further details of Amnesty International offices worldwide.)
If there is not an Amnesty International office in your country, please return this form to the International Secretariat in London:
Peter Benenson House, 1 Easton Street, London WC1X 0DW, United Kingdom

www.amnesty.org

AMNESTY INTERNATIONAL PRODUCES A WIDE RANGE OF MATERIALS, INCLUDING CAMPAIGNING AND COUNTRY REPORTS, FOCUS SHEETS, LEGAL BRIEFINGS AND POLICY PAPERS.

The nine titles on these pages are just a small sample of our recently published work. For more information on these, visit

www.amnesty.org

To order copies, contact the Amnesty International office in your country (addresses on pages 368-371). If there is no office in your country, contact the Marketing and Supply team at the International Secretariat:

Amnesty International
International Secretariat
Peter Benenson House
1 Easton Street
London WC1X 0DW
United Kingdom
00 44 20 7413 5814/ 5507
orderpubs@amnesty.org

Enduring occupation: Palestinians under siege in the West Bank
(MDE 15/033/2007)

More than two million Palestinians in the West Bank are hemmed in by a web of Israeli military checkpoints and blockades, and a winding 700-kilometre fence/wall encircling villages and neighbourhoods around East Jerusalem. This report shows how such stringent restrictions are disproportionate, discriminatory and violate the right to freedom of movement.

Format: A4, 48 pages
Price: £5.50
Languages available: Arabic, English, French, Spanish

Safe schools: Every girl's right
(ACT 77/001/2008)

Every day, girls face being assaulted on their way to school or inside school premises. Some are threatened by other students, offered higher marks by teachers in exchange for sexual favours, even raped in the staff room. Every girl has a right to education in a safe environment. In this illustrated book, which draws on examples from around the world, we demand that states take immediate action to make schools safe for girls.

ISBN: 978-0-86210-434-4
Format: cropped A4, 72 pages
Price: £8.50
Languages available: Arabic, English, French, Spanish

USA: Close Guantánamo – symbol of injustice
(AMR 51/001/2007)

Hundreds of men of different nationalities have been transported to the USA's offshore prison camp at Guantánamo Bay, Cuba. The first detainees arrived in January 2002. Six years on, hundreds are still there. Many have been tortured or ill-treated. All, in Amnesty International's opinion, are unlawfully detained.

ISBN: 978-0-86210-420-7
Format: A4, 16 pages
Price: £4.00
Languages available: Arabic (PDF only), English, French, Spanish

Iran: The last executioner of children

(MDE 13/059/2007)

Iran is the world's last official executioner of children. This report draws attention to this grave and long-standing violation of human rights. It supports the valiant efforts by activists in Iran to stop child executions and end the use of the death penalty for child offenders.

Format: A4, 41 pages
Price: £3.50
Languages available: English, Persian, Spanish

Afghanistan: Detainees transferred to torture: ISAF complicity?

(ASA 11/011/2007)

Hundreds of Afghans have been detained by the International Security Assistance Force (ISAF) – comprising military personnel from 37 countries – during the ongoing conflict in Afghanistan. This report documents the failure of ISAF states to uphold basic principles of international humanitarian and human rights law in transferring detainees to Afghan authorities.

Format: A4, 41 pages
Languages available: Arabic, Dari, English, French, Pashtu, Spanish
Available online only.

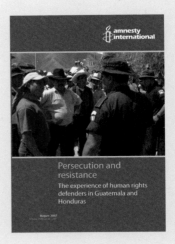

Persecution and resistance: Human rights defenders in Guatemala and Honduras

(AMR 02/001/2007)

Human rights defenders in Honduras and Guatemala risk serious human rights violations, including killings, attacks, threats and intimidation, while trying to carry out their work.

Format: A4, 30 pages
Price: £5.50
Languages available: English, French, Spanish

Still separate, still unequal: Violations of the right to education of Romani children in Slovakia
(EUR 72/001/2007)

Romani children in Slovakia continue to be segregated and, in practice, provided an inferior education. But as this report shows, the underlying causes of violations of Romani children's right to education have not been effectively or consistently tackled.

Format: A4, 52 pages
Price: £8.50
Languages available: English, Slovak

Poems from Guantánamo – The detainees speak
(Arabic edition)

A collection of poems written "behind the wire" by detainees held in the US military detention centre in Guantánamo Bay, Cuba. Now translated by Amnesty International into Arabic, the book includes an introduction by the editor, explaining the extraordinary process he went through to secure the release of these poems by the US authorities. The original English hardback edition is published by University of Iowa Press, edited by Marc Falkoff.

ISBN: 978-9953-71-292-5
Format: A5, 72 pages Price: £6.00
Publisher: Al-Farabi Printing and Publishing House

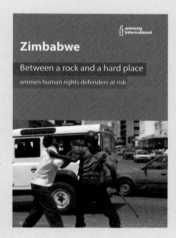

Zimbabwe: Between a rock and a hard place
(AFR 46/020/2007)

Hundreds of Zimbabwean women activists are confronting the government in response to grave violations of economic and social rights. They demand respect for their own human rights and those of their communities. Being both a woman and a human rights defender compounds the violations faced by these activists.

Format: A4, 40 pages
Price: £2.30
Languages available: English

INDEX OF SELECTED TOPICS*

A

abductions
(see also: armed groups)
Afghanistan 46; Central African Republic 88-9; Chad 91; Palestinian Authority 233-4; Russian Federation 249; Serbia 262-3; Zimbabwe 335
HOSTAGE-TAKING
Colombia 99-100; Pakistan 229-30

anti-terrorism
(see also: counter terror, "war on terror")
Canada 83; Chile 90; Egypt 115, 116; El Salvador 118-20, Japan 171; Myanmar 213-4; Philippines 236; Turkey 300-1

arbitrary arrests and detentions
(see also: detention)
Bahrain 62; Bangladesh 64; Burundi 80; Cambodia 83-84; Cuba 107; Equatorial Guinea 123; Gambia 134; Guinea 144-5; Iraq 162; Mexico 206; Mozambique 215; Niger 224; Pakistan 229; Palestinian Authority 234; Paraguay 237; Philippines 240; Sri Lanka 279; Sudan 282-3; Syria 288-9; Thailand 295

armed groups
(see also: abductions, armed conflict, killings)
Afghanistan 46-7; Burundi 80-1; Central African Republic 87-8; Chad 90; Colombia 97-8; Democratic Republic of the Congo 111-2; Ethiopia 127-9; Guinea 144; Iraq 161; Kenya 178; Lebanon 189; Macedonia 197; Nepal 221; Nigeria 226; Pakistan 230-1; Palestinian Authority 232-3, 235; Papua New Guinea 236; Philippines 240; Russian Federation 248-50; Somalia 270-1; Spain 277; Sudan 280-82; Thailand 294-5

armed conflict
(see also: armed groups, child soldiers, violence against women)
Middle East and North Africa overview 35-6; Afghanistan 46; Colombia 97, 99-100; Côte d'Ivoire 103; Ethiopia 129; Iraq 161; Israel/OPT 167; Kenya 178; Lebanon 189; Mali 201; Pakistan 228, 230-1; Palestinian Authority 232-3, 235; Russian Federation 249-50; Senegal 258; Somalia 270; Sri Lanka 279; Sudan 280-1; Uganda 307

arms trade
Austria 58; Belgium 68; Ireland 165-6; Venezuela 327

asylum-seekers
(see also: refugees)
Africa overview 8-9; Europe and Central Asia overview 28; Australia 57; Austria 57-8; Bahamas 61; Belgium 67-8; Bulgaria 78-9; Cambodia 84; Canada 87; China 96; Congo (Republic of) 102; Denmark 114; Egypt 121; Eritrea 126; Finland 131-2; France 132-3; Greece 140; Hungary 150-1; Italy 171; Japan 174; Kazakstan 177; Kenya 178; Korea (Democratic People's Republic of) 180; Kyrgyzstan 185; Laos 186-7; Libya 194; Malaysia 200; Malta 201-2; Morocco/Western Sahara 213-4; Poland 242; Slovakia 267; South Africa 272-3; Spain 276; Sweden 287; Switzerland 287-8; Thailand 295-6; Turkey 304; Uganda 308; Ukraine 310; United Kingdom 316

C

children's rights
(see also: child soldiers, discrimination, violence against women)
Africa overview 5-6; Chad 90; Haiti 146-7; Honduras 148; Iraq 162; Jamaica 172; Macedonia 197; Namibia 219; Pakistan 230-1; Spain 276; Swaziland 285; Uruguay 322
DEATH PENALTY
Iran 160; Saudi Arabia 257
TRAFFICKING
Albania 48; Guinea-Bissau 146; Macedonia 197

child soldiers
(see also: armed conflict, children's rights)
Chad 90; Democratic Republic of the Congo 112; Sri Lanka 278

conscientious objection
(see also: freedom of expression, prisoners of conscience)
Finland 132; Greece 142; Turkey 304; Turkmenistan 305-6

counter-terror
(see also: anti-terrorism, "war on terror", renditions)
Algeria 50; Bahrain 62; El Salvador 122; Germany 137; Mauritania 203; Morocco/Western Sahara 213; Saudi Arabia 255; Spain 277; United Kingdom 313-4

cruel, inhuman and degrading punishments
(see also: torture and other ill-treatment, Death penalty)
Middle East and North Africa overview 37; Fiji 130; Iran 159; Malaysia 199-200; Pakistan 231; Qatar 244-5; Saudi Arabia 257; Singapore 265; United Arab Emirates 312; Yemen 331

D

death penalty
(see also: cruel, inhuman and degrading punishments)
Africa overview 8-9; Americas overview 13-4; Asia-Pacific overview 21-2; Europe and Central Asia overview 29; Middle East and North Africa overview 38-9; Afghanistan 46; Albania 48; Algeria 52; Bahamas 61; Bahrain 62; Bangladesh 64; Belarus 66; Bosnia and Herzegovina 72; Burundi 79; Canada 86; China 93, 95; Congo (Republic of) 102; Cuba 107; Egypt 120; Equatorial Guinea 123; Ethiopia 129; France 133; Gambia 135; Georgia 136; Ghana 139; Guatemala 143; Guinea 145; India 154; Indonesia 155; Iran 159-160; Iraq 160, 162; Jamaica 172; Japan 173; Jordan 175; Kazakstan 176; Kenya 179; Korea (Democratic People's Republic of) 180; Korea (Republic of) 181; Kuwait 183; Kyrgyzstan 185; Laos 185; Lebanon 189; Libya 194; Malawi 198; Malaysia 200; Mali 201; Mongolia 209; Nigeria 225; Pakistan 231; Peru 237; Poland 242; Qatar 245; Rwanda 251, 252; Saudi Arabia 257; Sierra Leone 264; Singapore 265; Somalia 271; Sudan 282; Swaziland 285; Syria 290; Taiwan 291; Tanzania 293; Thailand 295; Trinidad and Tobago 298; Tunisia 301; Uganda 308; United Arab Emirates 312; United States of America 316, 319; Uzbekistan 322, 325; Vietnam 328; Yemen 331; Zambia 332
CHILDREN
Iran 160; Saudi Arabia 257

deaths in custody
Angola 53; Armenia 56; Austria 58; Bangladesh 63; Germany 138; Greece 140; Kyrgyzstan 184; Malaysia 199; Myanmar 217; Saudi Arabia 257; Senegal 258; Syria 290; United Kingdom 315

detention
(see also: arbitrary arrests and detentions, police and security forces, torture and other ill-treatment, cruel inhuman and degrading punishment)
Middle East and North Africa overview 37; Algeria 50; Angola 53; Bahrain 62; Bangladesh 63; Burundi 79-80, 81; Cameroon 84; China 93; Congo (Republic of) 101; Cuba 103; Cyprus 107-8; Egypt 118-19; Equatorial Guinea 122-3; Eritrea 124-5; Estonia 126; Gambia 134; Greece 140; Guinea 144; Hungary 150; Iran 159; Iraq 161; Ireland 164; Israel/OPT 166-7; Italy 171; Japan 173; Jordan 175; Kyrgyzstan 184; Lebanon 189; Libya 193-4; Malaysia 199; Malta 201; Mexico 205-6; Mozambique 214; Myanmar 216-7; Niger 223; Pakistan 228; Palestinian Authority 233-4; Paraguay 236; Philippines 239; Poland 240-1; Romania 245-6; Rwanda 253; Senegal 258; Sierra Leone 264; Singapore 265; Somalia 269; Sri Lanka 278; Sudan 281; Syria 288-9; Thailand 294; United Arab Emirates 311-2

disappearances
(see enforced disappearances)

discrimination

(see also: children's rights, Indigenous Peoples, violence against women)

Algeria 51; Australia 56; Belarus 66; Bosnia and Herzegovina 72; Bulgaria 77; Chile 92; Congo (Republic of) 102; Croatia 105-6; Czech Republic 108-9; Denmark 114; Dominican Republic 115; Egypt 120; Estonia 126, 127; Hungary 150; India 152-3; Iran 158; Italy 171; Korea (Republic of) 182; Malaysia 200; Mexico 206; Pakistan 230; Paraguay 236; Romania 246; Serbia 260, 263; Slovakia 266, 267; Slovenia 268; Syria 290; Viet Nam 329

LESBIAN, GAY, BISEXUAL AND TRANSGENDER PEOPLE

Europe and Central Asia overview 29; Cameroon 84; China 96; Hungary 150; Indonesia 155; Jamaica 172; Latvia 188; Lithuania 195-6; Malaysia 200; Moldova 209; Morocco/Western Sahara 213; Nigeria 227; Poland 241; Romania 246; Russian Federation 249; Uganda 308

RACISM

Europe and Central Asia overview 31-2; Belgium 67; Estonia 127; Kazakstan 177; Laos 185-6; Latvia 188; Lithuania 196; Macedonia 197; Netherlands 221-2; Puerto Rico 244; Russian Federation 251; Slovakia 266; Switzerland 287; Ukraine 310-1; United States of America 319

ROMA

Bosnia and Herzegovina 72-3; Bulgaria 78; Croatia 106; Czech Republic 109; Greece 142; Hungary 150; Italy 171-2; Montenegro 21; Romania 246; Serbia 261; Slovakia 266-7; Slovenia 269

WOMEN

China 94; Indonesia 155-6; Iran 157-8; Ireland 165; Lebanon 190; Libya 194; Morocco/Western Sahara 213; Netherlands 222; Poland 242; Saudi Arabia 256; Syria 289-90; Yemen 331

E

economic social and cultural rights

(see also: housing, forced evictions, discrimination, maternal health, land rights)

Africa overview 4; Americas overview 17-8; Asia-Pacific overview 20-1; Europe and Central Asia overview 27; Middle East and North Africa overview 33-34; Angola 52-3; Argentina 55; Azerbaijan 58-9; Cambodia 83; Czech Republic 108-9; Dominican Republic 115; Ecuador 116; Equatorial Guinea 123-4; Ghana 139; Guatemala 142; India 151-2; Indonesia 154; Kazakstan 177; Kenya 179; Nigeria 226; Peru 237; Slovakia 265; South Africa 271

enforced disappearances

Algeria 50-1; Bosnia and Herzegovina 71; Chad 91; Korea (Democratic People's Republic of) 180; Macedonia 196; Mexico 205; Montenegro 210; Myanmar 217; Pakistan 229; Philippines 238-9; Russian Federation 249; Rwanda 254; Serbia 260, 262; Sri Lanka 278; Syria 290; Thailand 294

excessive use of force

Azerbaijan 59; Bahamas 61; Benin 69; Fiji 130; Georgia 137; Honduras 148; Hungary 149-50; Italy 171; Malaysia 199; Mauritania 203; Mexico 205; Myanmar 216; Pakistan 230; Rwanda 252; South Africa 273; Turkey 304

extrajudicial executions

(see also: killings)

Brazil 74; Colombia 97, 100-1; Macedonia 196; Montenegro 210; Mozambique 214; Nigeria 226; Philippines 238; Russian Federation 247; Venezuela 326; Zimbabwe 334

F

forced evictions

(see also: economic, social and cultural rights, housing)

Angola 52-3; Cambodia 83; Czech Republic 108-9; Dominican Republic 115; Equatorial Guinea 123-4; Ghana 139; Guatemala 142; Kenya 179; Nigeria 227; Slovakia 266

freedom of expression

(see also: conscientious objection, prisoners of conscience, political prisoners, human rights defenders)

Africa overview 9-10; Asia-Pacific overview 21-2; Europe and Central Asia overview 31-2; Middle East and North Africa overview 38; Afghanistan 46-7; Algeria 51; Angola 53-4; Armenia 55; Azerbaijan 58-9; Bahrain 61; Bangladesh 64; Belarus 65; Bolivia 69; Burundi 81-2; Cameroon 85; Central African Republic 89; Chad 91; China 94; Cuba 106; Dominican Republic 115; Egypt 120; Eritrea 124; Ethiopia 128; Fiji 130; Gambia 134-5; Guinea 144; Guinea-Bissau 145; Haiti 147; Indonesia 154-5; Iran 157; Jordan 175; Kenya 178-9; Korea (Democratic People's Republic of) 180; Korea (Republic of) 181; Kuwait 183; Kyrgyzstan 184-5; Liberia 192; Libya 193; Malaysia 200; Mali 200-1; Mexico 206; Moldova 208; Myanmar 215-16; Namibia 219; Nepal 221; Niger 224; Nigeria 227; Pakistan 230; Paraguay 236-7; Poland 241; Russian Federation 248; Rwanda 252; Senegal 258; Sierra Leone 263-4; Singapore 265; Somalia 270; Sri Lanka 279; Sudan 283; Syria 289; Taiwan 291; Tanzania 293; Thailand 295; Togo 297; Tunisia 300; Turkey 302; Turkmenistan 305; Uganda 307; United Arab Emirates 312; Viet Nam 327; Yemen 330; Zambia 332

CONSCIENTIOUS OBJECTORS

Finland 131; Greece 141; Turkey 304; Turkmenistan 305-6

FREEDOM OF ASSEMBLY

Jordan 175; Kyrgyzstan 184; Singapore 265; Zambia 331; Zimbabwe 333-4

FREEDOM OF ASSOCIATION

Belarus 65-6; Cuba 106; Jordan 175; Viet Nam 327-8; Zimbabwe 333-4

FREEDOM OF RELIGION

China 94; Egypt 120; Eritrea 124; Iran 158-9; Malaysia 200; Tajikistan 292; Tunisia 301

H

health

(see also: economic, social and cultural rights, HIV/AIDS, maternal health)

Indonesia 156; Ireland 164; Laos 186; Mongolia 209; Nicaragua 222; Paraguay 236; Peru 238; Romania 246; Uruguay 322

MENTAL HEALTH CARE

Bulgaria 78-9; Czech Republic 109; Romania 246-7

HIV/AIDS

(see also: economic, social and cultural rights, health)

Africa overview 4; Americas overview 18; Asia-Pacific overview 24; Brazil 75; Burundi 81; Estonia 126; Fiji 130; Gambia 135; Indonesia 155, 156; Jamaica 173; Libya 194; Malawi 199; Mexico 204; Moldova 208; Papua New Guinea 236; South Africa 272-4; Swaziland 284-5; Uganda 307

housing

(see also: economic, social and cultural rights, forced evictions, land rights)

Albania 49; Angola 52; Czech Republic 108-9; Dominican Republic 115; Equatorial Guinea 123-4; Fiji 130; France 133; Slovakia 267; United States of America 321

human rights defenders

(see also: freedom of expression, prisoners of conscience)

Africa overview 9-10; Americas overview 12; Asia-Pacific overview 22-3, Europe and Central Asia overview 31-2; Middle East and North Africa overview 40; Angola 53-4; 25; Azerbaijan 59-60; Bahrain 62; Bangladesh 64; Brazil 77; Cambodia 83-4; China 94; Colombia 100-1; Congo (Republic of the) 102; Cyprus 108; Democratic Republic of the Congo 113; Egypt 120; Ethiopia 128-9; Greece 141; Guatemala 143; Guinea-Bissau 146; Haiti 148; Honduras 148-9; Iran 157-8; Mexico 206; Montenegro 211; Morocco/Western Sahara 212; Nepal 221; Nigeria 227; Peru 238; Russian Federation 248-9; Rwanda 253; Serbia 261; Somalia 270-1; Syria 290; Thailand 295; Tunisia 301; Turkey 303; Uzbekistan 324-5; Venezuela 327; Zimbabwe 334

I

impunity
Africa overview 5-6; Americas overview 15-6; Europe and Central Asia overview 29; Afghanistan 45-6; Algeria 50-1; Argentina 54-5; Armenia 56; Brazil 77; Chile 92-3; Colombia 98-9; Democratic Republic of the Congo 113; El Salvador 122; Gambia 135; Guatemala 143; Haiti 147-8; India 153-4; Indonesia 156; Israel/OPT 168; Kenya 178; Lebanon 191; Libya 195; Mexico 205; Montenegro 210-1; Nepal 220-1; Palestinian Authority 233-4; Peru 238; Russian Federation 250; Serbia 261-2; South Africa 274; Spain 278; Sri Lanka 279; Tanzania 294; Thailand 295; Timor-Leste 297; Togo 298; Turkey 303; Ukraine 311; Uruguay 322

Indigenous Peoples
(see also: discrimination)
Argentina 55; Australia 56-7; Brazil 76-7; Canada 86; Chile 93; Colombia 100; Nepal 221; Paraguay 237

internally displaced people
Azerbaijan 60; Bosnia and Herzegovina 72; Central African Republic 89; Chad 92; Democratic Republic of the Congo 111; Iraq 163; Kenya 179; Nepal 221; Russian Federation 250; Somalia 271; Sri Lanka 279; Timor-Leste 297; Uganda 308

international justice
Bosnia and Herzegovina 70; Democratic Republic of the Congo 113; Moldova 209; Namibia 219; Russian Federation 251; Rwanda 254; Senegal 259; Sierra Leone 263-4; Somalia 270; United Arab Emirates 313; Zimbabwe 335-6
WAR CRIMES
Bosnia and Herzegovina 70-1; Croatia 105; Liberia 192; Macedonia 196-7; Montenegro 210; Rwanda 253-4; Serbia 260

J

justice system
(see also: unfair trials, detention)
Americas overview 15-6; Afghanistan 45; Bangladesh 65; Burundi 81; Cambodia 83; China 94; Cuba 107; Democratic Republic of the Congo 113; Egypt 119; Fiji 131; France 134; Gambia 134; Georgia 137; Haiti 147; Ireland 166; Israel/OPT 167; Liberia 192; Malaysia 199; Mauritania 203; Mexico 206; Nepal 220-1; Nigeria 227; Pakistan 228-9; Philippines 240; Saudi Arabia 255; Sierra Leone 263-4, 265; Somalia 270; Swaziland 284-5; Thailand 295; Timor-Leste 297; Trinidad and Tobago 299; Tunisia 300; United States of America 319; Uruguay 322; Zambia 332; Zimbabwe 335-6

K

killings
(see also: armed conflict, extrajudicial executions, police and security forces)
Afghanistan 46-7; Cambodia 83; Honduras 149; Lebanon 189; Myanmar 216-7; Pakistan 230-1; Trinidad and Tobago 298-9; Turkey 304
UNLAWFUL KILLINGS
Central African Republic 87-8; Chad 90; Democratic Republic of the Congo 111-2;
POLITICAL KILLINGS
Algeria 50; Serbia 261

L

land rights
(see also: economic, social and cultural rights, housing)
Argentina 55; Brazil 76-7; Guatemala 143; Indonesia 155; Kazakstan 177

M

maternal health
(see also: economic, social and cultural rights, health, violence against women)
Indonesia 156; Mexico 205; Nicaragua 223; Paraguay 236-7; Peru 237-8; Uruguay 322

migrants rights
(see also: refugees and asylum-seekers)
Africa overview 8-9; Europe and Central Asia overview 28; Middle East and North Africa overview 39-40; Algeria 51; Bahamas 61; Belgium 67-8; France 132-3; Germany 138-9; Greece 140; Italy 171; Korea (Republic of) 182; Libya 194; Malta 201-2; Mexico 207; Morocco/Western Sahara 213-4; Netherlands 222-3; Portugal 242; South Africa 272-3; Spain 276-7; Switzerland 287-8; Tanzania 293
MIGRANT WORKERS
Jordan 176; Korea (Republic of) 182; Kuwait 183; Malaysia 200; Qatar 245; United Arab Emirates 313

P

police and security forces
(see also: deaths in custody, detention, excessive use of force)
Angola 53; Argentina 55; Brazil 74-5; Georgia 136-7; Kenya 178; Malaysia 199; Papua New Guinea 234; Sierra Leone 264; Switzerland 287; Timor-Leste 296-7; Trinidad and Tobago 298
KILLINGS
Cameroon 85-6; Canada 87; Central African Republic 88; Colombia 97; Dominican Republic 116; El Salvador 122; Fiji 130; Guinea 144; Iraq 161, 162; Jamaica 172; Myanmar 216-7; Niger 224; Puerto Rico 243-4; Turkey 304; United Kingdom 315-6; Yemen 330
TORTURE AND OTHER ILL-TREATMENT
Albania 49; Austria 58; Azerbaijan 59; Bangladesh 63-4; Bosnia and Herzegovina 72; Brazil 75; Burundi 80; Czech Republic 109-10; Democratic Republic of the Congo 111; Ecuador 116-17; Egypt 119-20; Equatorial Guinea 123-4; Estonia 127; Ethiopia 129; Fiji 130; France 133; Greece 140-1; Georgia 136-7; Hungary 149-50; Ireland 165; Iraq 162, 163; Israel/OPT 168; Japan 174; Jordan 175; Kyrgyzstan 184; Macedonia 197; Mauritania 203; Mexico 205; Moldova 207-8; Montenegro 211; Namibia 218; Nepal 221; Niger 224; Nigeria 226; Pakistan 229; Paraguay 237; Portugal 243; Russian Federation 251; Rwanda 252; Saudi Arabia 257; Senegal 258; Slovakia 268; South Africa 273; Spain 275-6; Sudan 282-3; Syria 289; Thailand 296; Tunisia 300; Turkey 304; Uganda 308; Ukraine 309-10; United States of America 318-9; Uzbekistan 325; Yemen 331; Zimbabwe 335

political prisoners
(see also: freedom of expression, prisoners of conscience)
Eritrea 125-6; Ethiopia 128-9; Korea (Democratic People's Republic of) 181; Laos 187; Rwanda 254; Syria 288-9; Tunisia 300; Yemen 330
POLITICAL PERSECUTION
Algeria 50; Congo (Republic of) 102; Montenegro 211; Myanmar 217; Philippines 239-40; Turkmenistan 305-6

prison conditions
Albania 48-9; Angola 53; Argentina 55; Benin 69; Brazil 75; Burundi 81-2; Cameroon 85-6; Congo (Republic of) 102; Eritrea 125; Greece 141; Iran 159; Ireland 164-5; Korea (Democratic People's Republic of) 181; Laos 187; Malawi 198-9; Myanmar 217-8; Nigeria 227; Peru 238; Rwanda 254; South Africa 273-4; Tanzania 293-4; Tunisia 300-1; Turkey 304
PRISONERS HELD INCOMMUNICADO
Turkmenistan 306; United Arab Emirates 312-3